Rick Steves'®

SCANDINAVIA

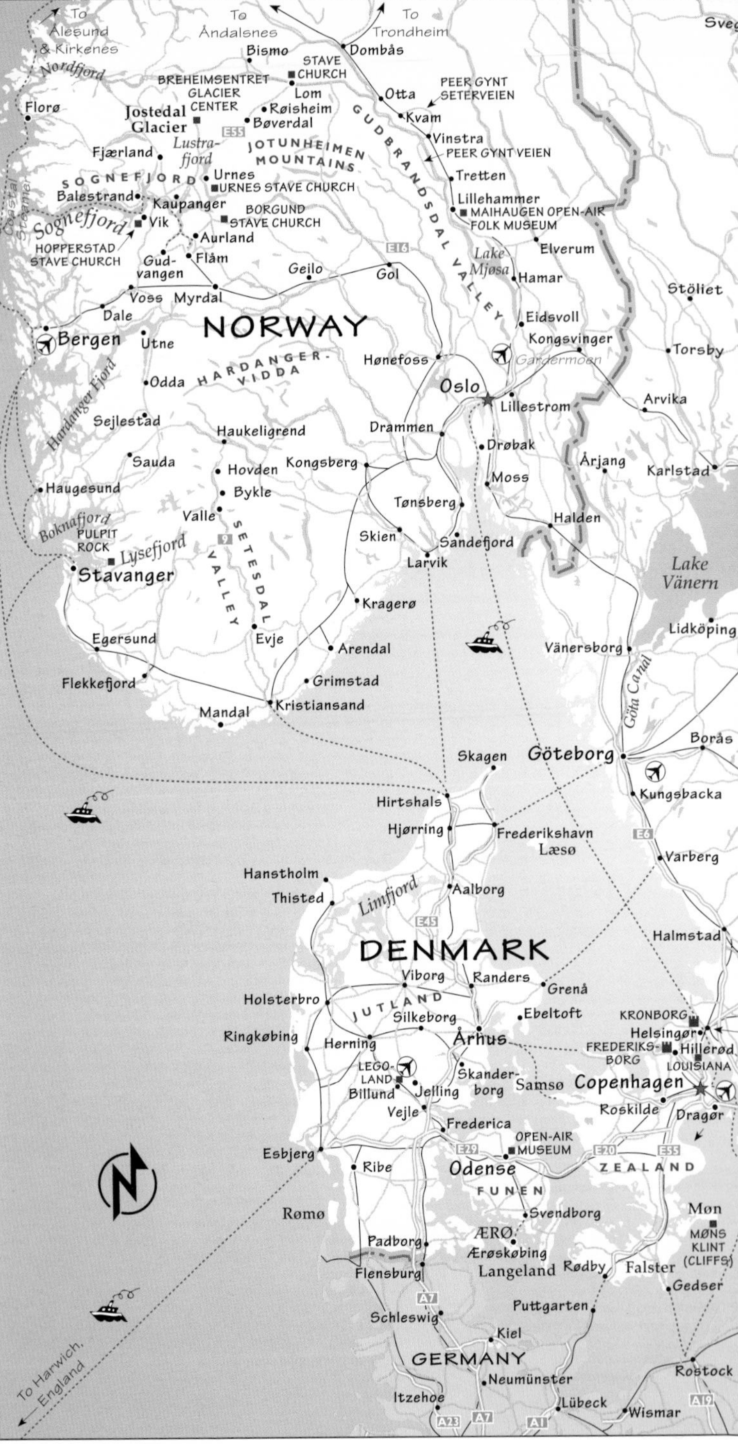
To Ålesund & Kirkenes
To Åndalsnes
To Trondheim
Nordfjord
Florø
Jostedal Glacier
BREHEIMSENTRET GLACIER CENTER
Bismo
STAVE CHURCH
Lom
Røisheim
Bøverdal
Dombås
Otta
Kvam
PEER GYNT SETERVEIEN
Vinstra
PEER GYNT VEIEN
Tretten
Lillehammer
MAIHAUGEN OPEN-AIR FOLK MUSEUM
GUDBRANDSDAL VALLEY
JOTUNHEIMEN MOUNTAINS
Fjærland
Lustrafjord
SOGNEFJORD
Urnes
URNES STAVE CHURCH
Balestrand
Kaupanger
BORGUND STAVE CHURCH
Sognefjord
Vik
HOPPERSTAD STAVE CHURCH
Aurland
Flåm
Gudvangen
Coastal Steamer
Voss
Myrdal
Dale
Geilo
Gol
Elverum
Lake Mjøsa
Hamar
Eidsvoll
Stöliet
NORWAY
Bergen
Utne
Kongsvinger
Torsby
Gardermoen
Hønefoss
Oslo
Lillestrom
Arvika
HARDANGERVIDDA
Hardanger Fjord
Odda
Sejlestad
Haukeligrend
Drammen
Drøbak
Sauda
Hovden
Kongsberg
Moss
Årjang
Karlstad
Haugesund
Bykle
Tønsberg
Boknafjord
Valle
Halden
PULPIT ROCK
Lysefjord
Skien
Sandefjord
Stavanger
SETESDAL VALLEY
Larvik
Lake Vänern
Kragerø
Egersund
Evje
Arendal
Vänersborg
Lidköping
Flekkefjord
Grimstad
Göta Canal
Mandal
Kristiansand
Skagen
Göteborg
Borås
Hirtshals
Kungsbacka
Hjørring
Frederikshavn
Læsø
Varberg
Hanstholm
Thisted
Limfjord
Aalborg
Halmstad
DENMARK
Viborg
Randers
Grenå
Holsterbro
JUTLAND
Silkeborg
Ebeltoft
KRONBORG
Helsingør
Ringkøbing
Herning
Århus
FREDERIKSBORG
Hillerød
LOUISIANA
LEGOLAND
Billund
Jelling
Skanderborg
Samsø
Copenhagen
Vejle
Roskilde
Dragør
Frederica
Esbjerg
Ribe
OPEN-AIR MUSEUM
Odense
ZEALAND
FUNEN
Rømø
Svendborg
Møn
MØNS KLINT (CLIFFS)
Padborg
ÆRØ
Ærøskøbing
Langeland
Rødby
Falster
Flensburg
Gedser
Puttgarten
Schleswig
Kiel
To Harwich, England
GERMANY
Rostock
Neumünster
Itzehoe
Lübeck
Wismar
Sveg
E55
E16
E6
E45
E29
E20
E55
A7
A23
A7
A1
A19
9

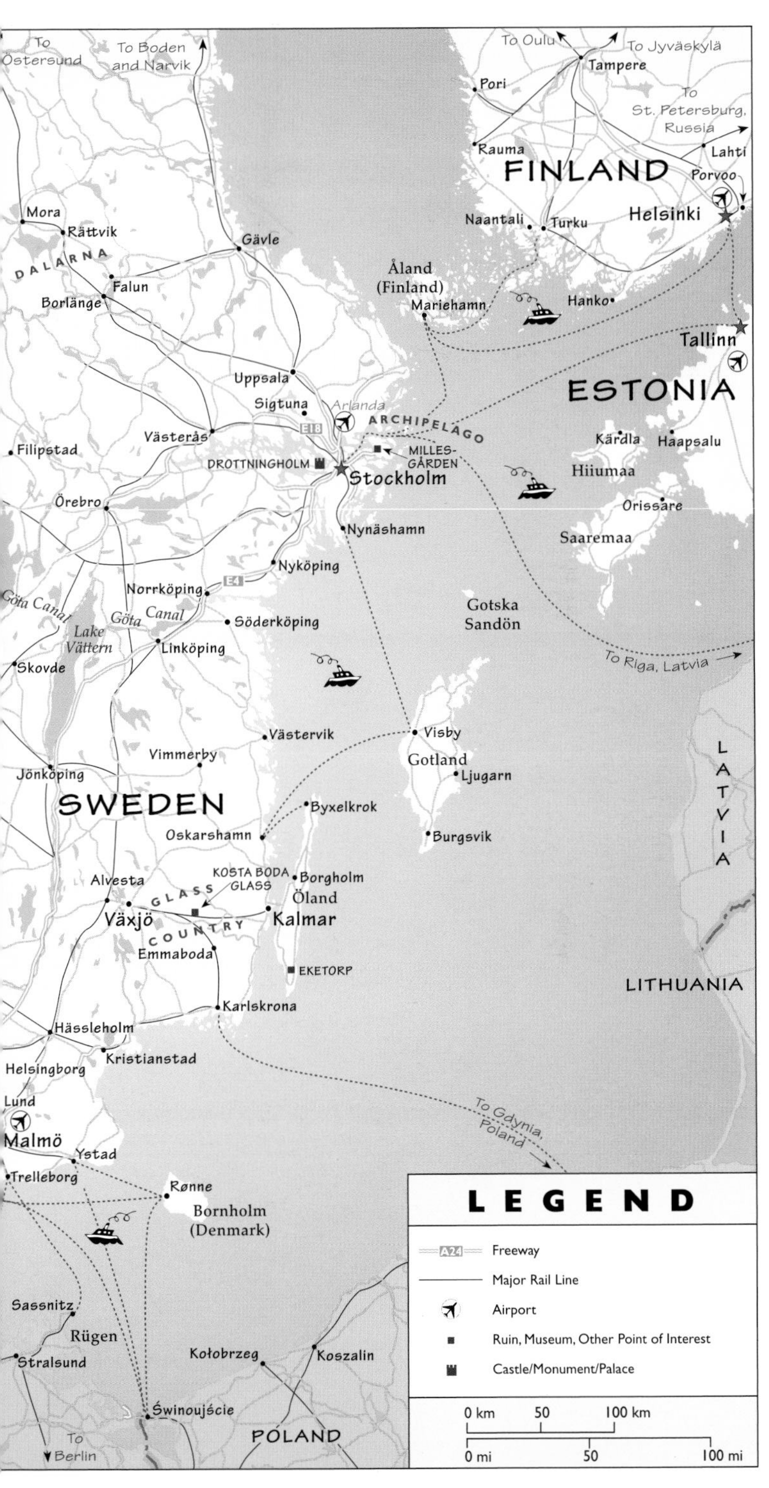

To Östersund
To Boden and Narvik
To Oulu
To Jyväskylä
Tampere
Pori
To St. Petersburg, Russia
Rauma
Lahti
FINLAND
Porvoo
Helsinki
Naantali
Turku
Mora
Rättvik
DALARNA
Gävle
Falun
Borlänge
Åland (Finland)
Mariehamn
Hanko
Tallinn
ESTONIA
Uppsala
Sigtuna
Arlanda
ARCHIPELAGO
E18
Västerås
Filipstad
DROTTNINGHOLM
MILLES-GÅRDEN
Stockholm
Kärdla
Haapsalu
Hiiumaa
Örebro
Orissare
Nynäshamn
Saaremaa
Nyköping
E4
Norrköping
Göta Canal
Göta Canal
Gotska Sandön
Söderköping
Lake Vättern
Linköping
Skovde
To Riga, Latvia
Västervik
Visby
Vimmerby
Gotland
Jönköping
Ljugarn
LATVIA
SWEDEN
Byxelkrok
Oskarshamn
Burgsvik
KOSTA BODA GLASS
Alvesta
Borgholm
GLASS COUNTRY
Öland
Växjö
Kalmar
Emmaboda
EKETORP
LITHUANIA
Karlskrona
Hässleholm
Kristianstad
Helsingborg
Lund
To Gdynia, Poland
Malmö
Ystad
Trelleborg
Rønne
Bornholm (Denmark)
LEGEND
A24 Freeway
Major Rail Line
Airport
Ruin, Museum, Other Point of Interest
Castle/Monument/Palace
Sassnitz
Rügen
Stralsund
Kołobrzeg
Koszalin
Świnoujście
To Berlin
POLAND
0 km 50 100 km
0 mi 50 100 mi

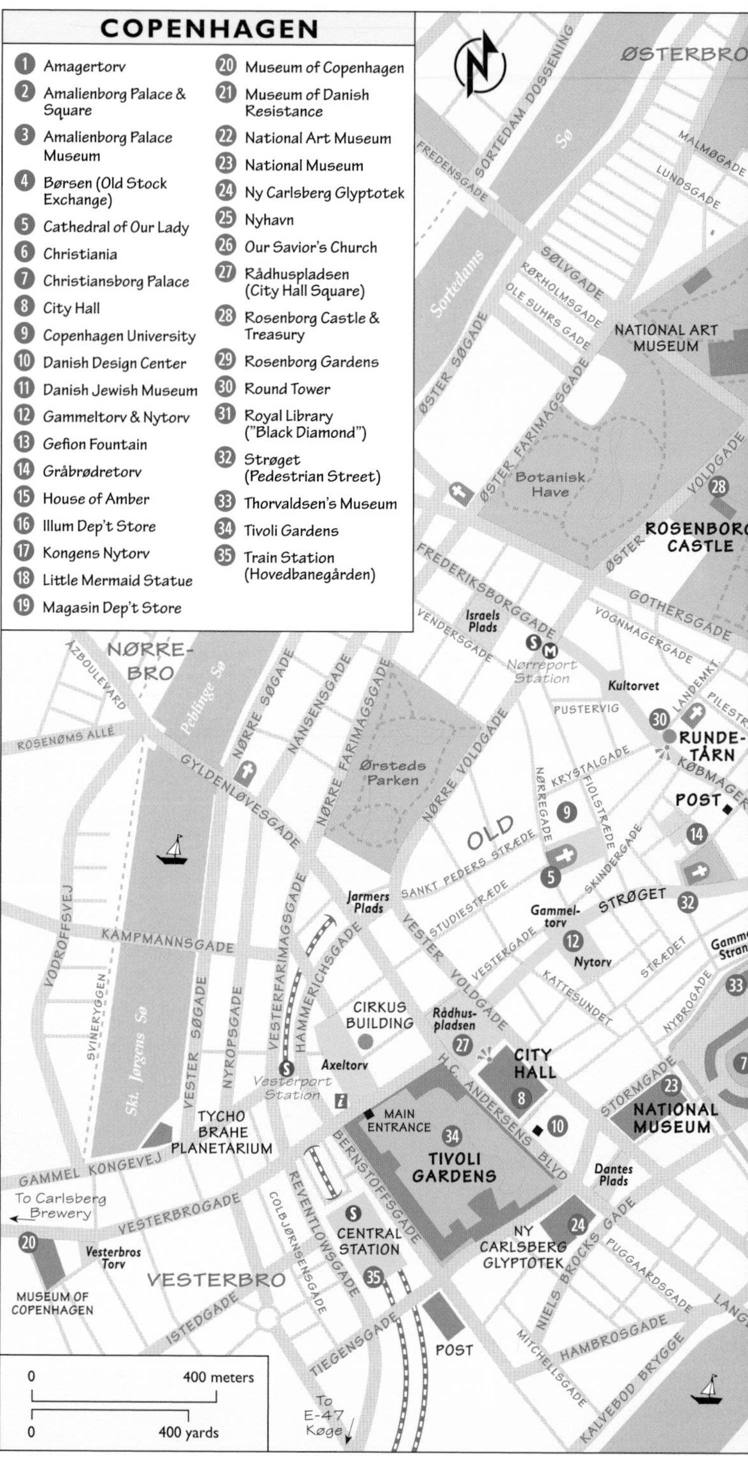

COPENHAGEN
1 Amagertorv
2 Amalienborg Palace & Square
3 Amalienborg Palace Museum
4 Børsen (Old Stock Exchange)
5 Cathedral of Our Lady
6 Christiania
7 Christiansborg Palace
8 City Hall
9 Copenhagen University
10 Danish Design Center
11 Danish Jewish Museum
12 Gammeltorv & Nytorv
13 Gefion Fountain
14 Gråbrødretorv
15 House of Amber
16 Illum Dep't Store
17 Kongens Nytorv
18 Little Mermaid Statue
19 Magasin Dep't Store
20 Museum of Copenhagen
21 Museum of Danish Resistance
22 National Art Museum
23 National Museum
24 Ny Carlsberg Glyptotek
25 Nyhavn
26 Our Savior's Church
27 Rådhuspladsen (City Hall Square)
28 Rosenborg Castle & Treasury
29 Rosenborg Gardens
30 Round Tower
31 Royal Library ("Black Diamond")
32 Strøget (Pedestrian Street)
33 Thorvaldsen's Museum
34 Tivoli Gardens
35 Train Station (Hovedbanegården)
ØSTERBRO
NATIONAL ART MUSEUM
Botanisk Have
ROSENBORG CASTLE
Israels Plads
Nørreport Station
Kultorvet
RUNDETÅRN
POST
NØRRE-BRO
Ørsteds Parken
OLD
Jarmers Plads
Gammeltorv
Nytorv
STRØGET
CIRKUS BUILDING
Rådhuspladsen
CITY HALL
Axeltorv
Vesterport Station
MAIN ENTRANCE
TYCHO BRAHE PLANETARIUM
TIVOLI GARDENS
NATIONAL MUSEUM
Dantes Plads
To Carlsberg Brewery
CENTRAL STATION
NY CARLSBERG GLYPTOTEK
Vesterbros Torv
VESTERBRO
MUSEUM OF COPENHAGEN
POST
To E-47 Køge
0 400 meters
0 400 yards

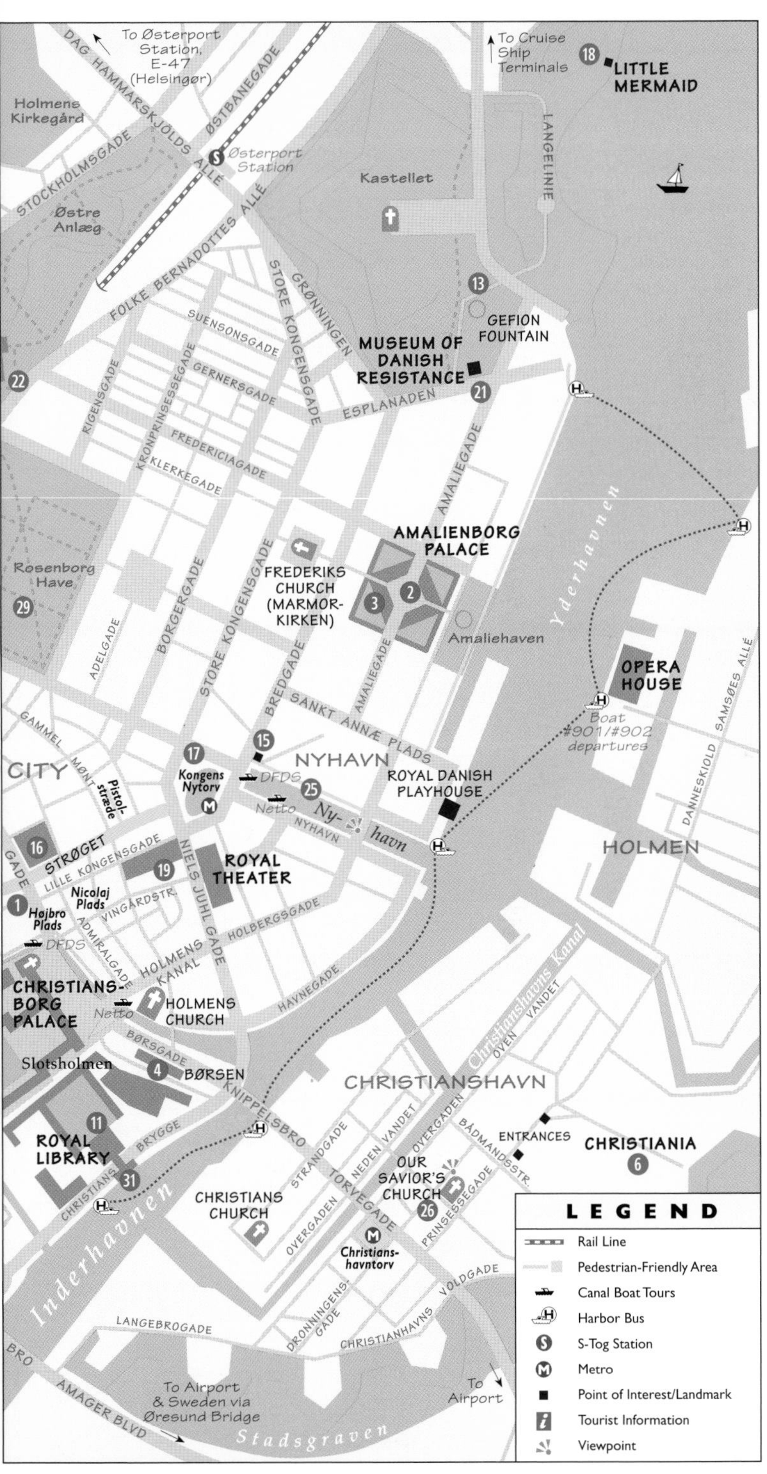

To Østerport Station, E-47 (Helsingør)
To Cruise Ship Terminals
LITTLE MERMAID
18
DAG HAMMARSKJÖLDS ALLÉ
ØSTBANEGADE
Holmens Kirkegård
Østerport Station
Kastellet
LANGELINIE
STOCKHOLMSGADE
Østre Anlæg
FOLKE BERNADOTTES ALLÉ
STORE KONGENSGADE
GRØNNINGEN
13
GEFION FOUNTAIN
SUENSONSGADE
MUSEUM OF DANISH RESISTANCE
21
GERNERSGADE
22
RIGENSGADE
KRONPRINSESSEGADE
ESPLANADEN
FREDERICIAGADE
KLERKEGADE
AMALIEGADE
AMALIENBORG PALACE
FREDERIKS CHURCH (MARMORKIRKEN)
3
2
Rosenborg Have
29
BORGERGADE
Amaliehaven
Yderhavnen
ADELGADE
BREDGADE
OPERA HOUSE
SANKT ANNÆ PLADS
Boat #901/#902 departures
SAMSØES ALLÉ
GAMMEL MØNT
15
17
NYHAVN
CITY
Pistolstræde
Kongens Nytorv
DFDS
25
ROYAL DANISH PLAYHOUSE
DANNESKIOLD
Netto
Nyhavn
16
STRØGET
NIELS JUHL GADE
ROYAL THEATER
HOLMEN
GADE
LILLE KONGENSGADE
19
Nicolaj Plads
1
Højbro Plads
VINGÅRDSTR.
ADMIRALGADE
HOLBERGSGADE
DFDS
HOLMENS KANAL
CHRISTIANSBORG PALACE
HOLMENS CHURCH
Netto
HAVNEGADE
Christianshavns Kanal
OVEN VANDET
BØRSGADE
Slotsholmen
4
BØRSEN
CHRISTIANSHAVN
KNIPPELSBRO
11
ROYAL LIBRARY
BRYGGE
STRANDGADE
NEDEN VANDET
OVERGADEN
BÅDMANDSSTR.
ENTRANCES
CHRISTIANIA
6
31
CHRISTIANS
OUR SAVIOR'S CHURCH
TORVEGADE
CHRISTIANS CHURCH
26
PRINSESSEGADE
OVERGADEN
Christianshavntorv
Inderhavnen
VOLDGADE
DRONNINGENSGADE
CHRISTIANHAVNS
LANGEBROGADE
CHRISTIANSHAVNS
BRO
AMAGER BLVD
To Airport & Sweden via Øresund Bridge
To Airport
Stadsgraven
LEGEND
Rail Line
Pedestrian-Friendly Area
Canal Boat Tours
Harbor Bus
S-Tog Station
Metro
Point of Interest/Landmark
Tourist Information
Viewpoint

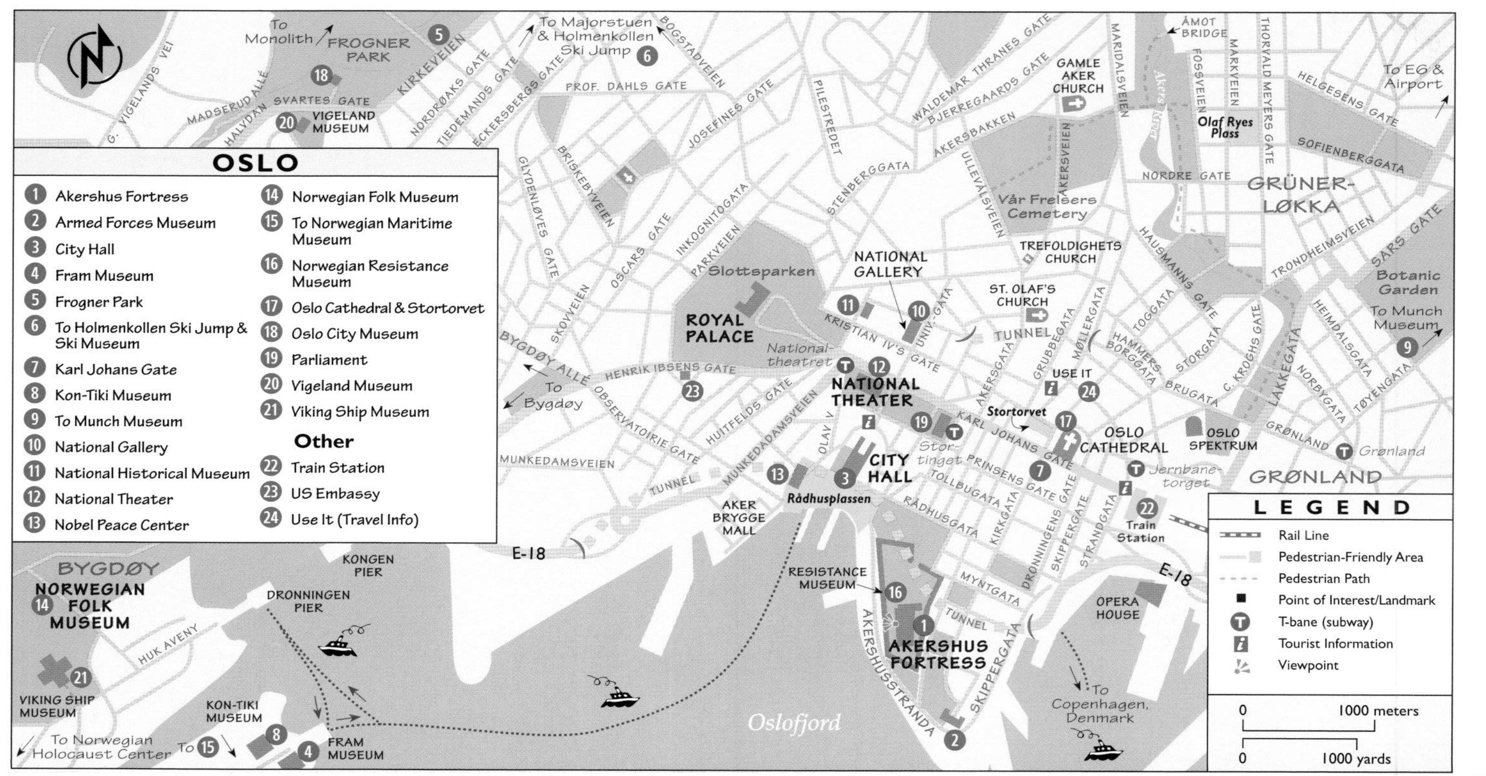
OSLO
1 Akershus Fortress
2 Armed Forces Museum
3 City Hall
4 Fram Museum
5 Frogner Park
6 To Holmenkollen Ski Jump & Ski Museum
7 Karl Johans Gate
8 Kon-Tiki Museum
9 To Munch Museum
10 National Gallery
11 National Historical Museum
12 National Theater
13 Nobel Peace Center
14 Norwegian Folk Museum
15 To Norwegian Maritime Museum
16 Norwegian Resistance Museum
17 Oslo Cathedral & Stortorvet
18 Oslo City Museum
19 Parliament
20 Vigeland Museum
21 Viking Ship Museum
Other
22 Train Station
23 US Embassy
24 Use It (Travel Info)
LEGEND
Rail Line
Pedestrian-Friendly Area
Pedestrian Path
Point of Interest/Landmark
T-bane (subway)
Tourist Information
Viewpoint
0 1000 meters
0 1000 yards
To Monolith
FROGNER PARK
VIGELAND MUSEUM
To Majorstuen & Holmenkollen Ski Jump
To E6 & Airport
ÅMOT BRIDGE
Akers River
Olaf Ryes Plass
GRÜNER-LØKKA
GAMLE AKER CHURCH
Vår Frelsers Cemetery
TREFOLDIGHETS CHURCH
ST. OLAF'S CHURCH
Botanic Garden
To Munch Museum
NATIONAL GALLERY
ROYAL PALACE
Slottsparken
National-theatret
NATIONAL THEATER
USE IT
Stortorvet
OSLO CATHEDRAL
OSLO SPEKTRUM
Grønland
GRØNLAND
Jernbane-torget
Train Station
CITY HALL
Stor-tinget
Rådhusplassen
AKER BRYGGE MALL
RESISTANCE MUSEUM
AKERSHUS FORTRESS
OPERA HOUSE
To Copenhagen, Denmark
Oslofjord
To Bygdøy
E-18
TUNNEL
KONGEN PIER
DRONNINGEN PIER
BYGDØY
NORWEGIAN FOLK MUSEUM
VIKING SHIP MUSEUM
KON-TIKI MUSEUM
FRAM MUSEUM
To Norwegian Holocaust Center
To 15
G. VIGELANDS VEI
MADSERUD ALLÉ
HALVDAN SVARTES GATE
KIRKEVEIEN
NORDRØAKS GATE
TIEDEMANDS GATE
ECKERSBERGS GATE
BOGSTADVEIEN
PROF. DAHLS GATE
JOSEFINES GATE
PILESTREDET
WALDEMAR THRANES GATE
BJERREGAARDS GATE
AKERSBAKKEN
MARIDALSVEIEN
FOSSVEIEN
MARKVEIEN
THORVALD MEYERS GATE
HELGESENS GATE
SOFIENBERGGATA
NORDRE GATE
GLYDENLØVES GATE
BRISKEBYVEIEN
STENBERGGATA
ULLEVÅLSVEIEN
AKERSVEIEN
INKOGNITOGATA
PARKVEIEN
OSCARS GATE
SKOVVEIEN
BYGDØY ALLÉ
HENRIK IBSENS GATE
KRISTIAN IV'S GATE
UNIV.-GATA
AKERSGATA
GRUBBEGATA
MØLLERGATA
HAUSMANNS GATE
TOGGATA
HAMMERS-BORGGATA
STORGATA
BRUGATA
C. KROGHS GATE
LAKKEGATA
TRONDHEIMSVEIEN
SARS GATE
HEIMDALSGATA
NORBYGATA
TØYENGATA
GRØNLAND
OBSERVATORIE GATE
HUITFELDS GATE
MUNKEDAMSVEIEN
OLAV V
KARL JOHANS GATE
PRINSENS GATE
TOLLBUGATA
RÅDHUSGATA
KIRKGATA
DRONNINGENS GATE
SKIPPERGATE
STRANDGATA
MYNTGATA
AKERSHUSSTRANDA
SKIPPERGATA
HUK AVENY

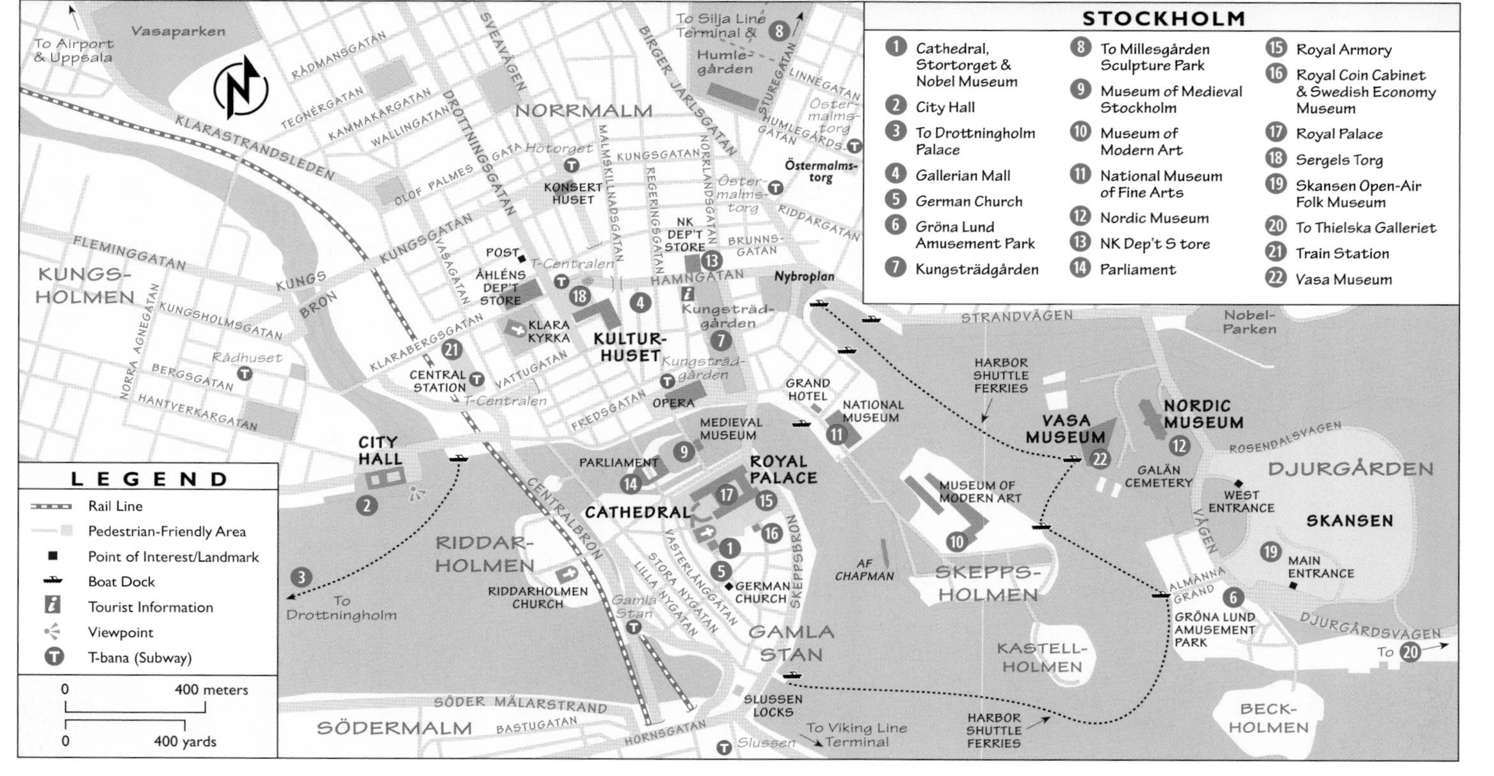
STOCKHOLM
1 Cathedral, Stortorget & Nobel Museum
2 City Hall
3 To Drottningholm Palace
4 Gallerian Mall
5 German Church
6 Gröna Lund Amusement Park
7 Kungsträdgården
8 To Millesgården Sculpture Park
9 Museum of Medieval Stockholm
10 Museum of Modern Art
11 National Museum of Fine Arts
12 Nordic Museum
13 NK Dep't S tore
14 Parliament
15 Royal Armory
16 Royal Coin Cabinet & Swedish Economy Museum
17 Royal Palace
18 Sergels Torg
19 Skansen Open-Air Folk Museum
20 To Thielska Galleriet
21 Train Station
22 Vasa Museum
LEGEND
Rail Line
Pedestrian-Friendly Area
Point of Interest/Landmark
Boat Dock
Tourist Information
Viewpoint
T-bana (Subway)
0 400 meters
0 400 yards
To Airport & Uppsala
Vasaparken
To Silja Line Terminal &
Humlegården
NORRMALM
KUNGSHOLMEN
RIDDARHOLMEN
GAMLA STAN
SÖDERMALM
SKEPPSHOLMEN
KASTELLHOLMEN
BECKHOLMEN
DJURGÅRDEN
SKANSEN
CITY HALL
CATHEDRAL
ROYAL PALACE
KULTURHUSET
VASA MUSEUM
NORDIC MUSEUM
Nybroplan
Östermalmstorg
Nobel-Parken
STRANDVÄGEN
HARBOR SHUTTLE FERRIES
To Drottningholm
To Viking Line Terminal
SLUSSEN LOCKS
GRÖNA LUND AMUSEMENT PARK
MAIN ENTRANCE
WEST ENTRANCE
GALÄN CEMETERY
MUSEUM OF MODERN ART
AF CHAPMAN
GRAND HOTEL
NATIONAL MUSEUM
MEDIEVAL MUSEUM
PARLIAMENT
OPERA
CENTRAL STATION
KLARA KYRKA
ÅHLÉNS DEP'T STORE
POST
KONSERT HUSET
NK DEP'T STORE
GERMAN CHURCH
RIDDARHOLMEN CHURCH
To 20

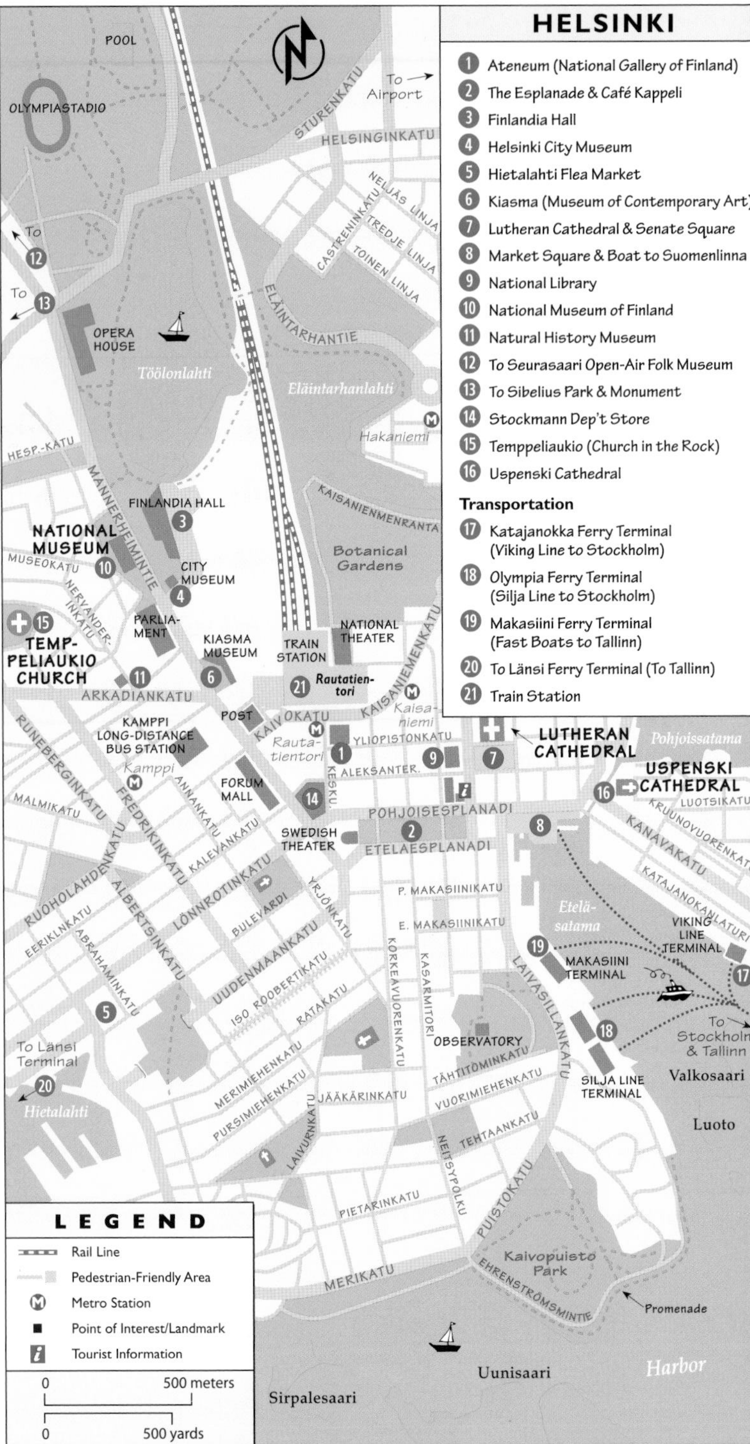
HELSINKI
1 Ateneum (National Gallery of Finland)
2 The Esplanade & Café Kappeli
3 Finlandia Hall
4 Helsinki City Museum
5 Hietalahti Flea Market
6 Kiasma (Museum of Contemporary Art)
7 Lutheran Cathedral & Senate Square
8 Market Square & Boat to Suomenlinna
9 National Library
10 National Museum of Finland
11 Natural History Museum
12 To Seurasaari Open-Air Folk Museum
13 To Sibelius Park & Monument
14 Stockmann Dep't Store
15 Temppeliaukio (Church in the Rock)
16 Uspenski Cathedral
Transportation
17 Katajanokka Ferry Terminal (Viking Line to Stockholm)
18 Olympia Ferry Terminal (Silja Line to Stockholm)
19 Makasiini Ferry Terminal (Fast Boats to Tallinn)
20 To Länsi Ferry Terminal (To Tallinn)
21 Train Station
POOL
OLYMPIASTADIO
To Airport
STURENKATU
HELSINGINKATU
NELJÄS LINJA
TREDJE LINJA
TOINEN LINJA
CASTRENINKATU
ELÄINTARHANTIE
OPERA HOUSE
Töölonlahti
Eläintarhanlahti
Hakaniemi
HESP.-KATU
MANNERHEIMINTIE
FINLANDIA HALL
NATIONAL MUSEUM
MUSEOKATU
NERVANDER-INKATU
CITY MUSEUM
KAISANIEMENRANTA
Botanical Gardens
PARLIA-MENT
TEMP-PELIAUKIO CHURCH
KIASMA MUSEUM
TRAIN STATION
NATIONAL THEATER
Rautatien-tori
KAISANIEMENKATU
Kaisa-niemi
ARKADIANKATU
KAMPPI LONG-DISTANCE BUS STATION
Kamppi
POST
KAIVOKATU
Rauta-tientori
YLIOPISTONKATU
LUTHERAN CATHEDRAL
Pohjoissatama
USPENSKI CATHEDRAL
LUOTSIKATU
RUNEBERGINKATU
MALMIKATU
FREDRIKINKATU
ANNANKATU
FORUM MALL
KESKU.
ALEKSANTER.
POHJOISESPLANADI
SWEDISH THEATER
ETELAESPLANADI
KRUUNOVUORENKATU
KANAVAKATU
KATAJANOKANLATURI
RUOHOLAHDENKATU
KALEVANKATU
LÖNNROTINKATU
YRJÖNKATU
P. MAKASIINIKATU
E. MAKASIINIKATU
Etelä-satama
VIKING LINE TERMINAL
ALBERTSINKATU
EERIKINKATU
ABRAHAMINKATU
BULEVARDI
UUDENMAANKATU
ISO ROOBERTINKATU
RATAKATU
KORKEAVUORENKATU
KASARMITORI
MAKASIINI TERMINAL
LAIVASILLANKATU
To Stockholm & Tallinn
To Länsi Terminal
OBSERVATORY
TÄHTITORNINKATU
Valkosaari
MERIMIEHENKATU
JÄÄKÄRINKATU
VUORIMIEHENKATU
SILJA LINE TERMINAL
Hietalahti
PURSIMIEHENKATU
LAIVURINKATU
TEHTAANKATU
Luoto
NEITSYTPOLKU
PUISTOKATU
PIETARINKATU
LEGEND
Rail Line
Pedestrian-Friendly Area
Metro Station
Point of Interest/Landmark
Tourist Information
0 500 meters
0 500 yards
MERIKATU
Kaivopuisto Park
EHRENSTRÖMSMINTIE
Promenade
Uunisaari
Harbor
Sirpalesaari

Rick Steves'®

SCANDINAVIA

AVALON TRAVEL

CONTENTS

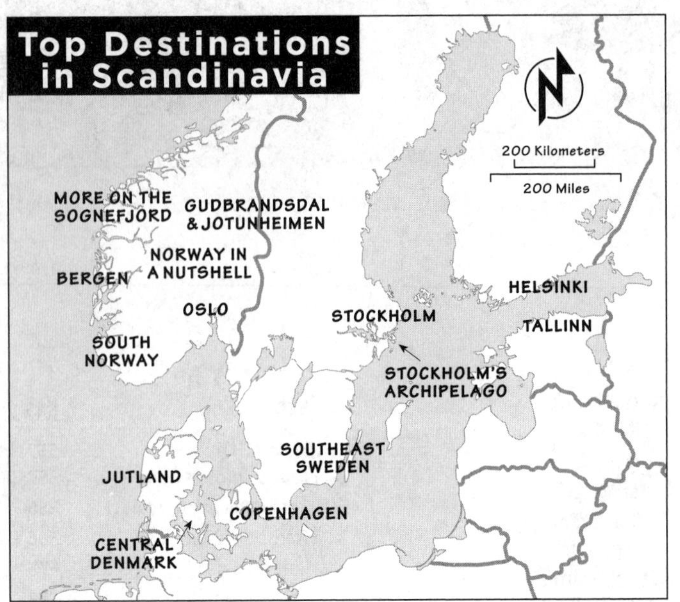
Top Destinations in Scandinavia
200 Kilometers
200 Miles
MORE ON THE SOGNEFJORD
GUDBRANDSDAL & JOTUNHEIMEN
NORWAY IN A NUTSHELL
BERGEN
OSLO
SOUTH NORWAY
STOCKHOLM
HELSINKI
TALLINN
STOCKHOLM'S ARCHIPELAGO
SOUTHEAST SWEDEN
JUTLAND
COPENHAGEN
CENTRAL DENMARK

INTRODUCTION

Scandinavia—known for its stunning natural beauty, fun-loving cities, trend-setting design, progressive politics, high latitudes, and even higher taxes—is one of Europe's most enjoyable and most interesting corners. A visit here connects you with immigrant roots, modern European values, and the great outdoors like nowhere else. You'll gasp at breathtaking fjords, glide on a cruise ship among picturesque islands, and marvel at the efficiency and livability of its big cities. Yes, Scandinavia is expensive. But, delightfully, the best time to visit—summer—is also the best time to get great deals on the fancier hotels.

This book breaks Scandinavia into its top big-city, small-town, and rural attractions. It gives you all the information and opinions necessary to wring the maximum value out of your limited time and money. If you plan a month or less in Scandinavia, this book has all the information you'll need.

Experiencing the culture, people, and natural wonders of Scandinavia economically and hassle-free has been my goal throughout three decades of traveling, guiding tours, and travel writing. With this book, I pass on to you the lessons I've learned.

This book is balanced to include a comfortable mix of exciting capital cities and cozy small towns. It covers the predictable biggies and mixes in a healthy dose of Back Door intimacy. Along with seeing Tivoli Gardens, Hans Christian Andersen's house, and *The Little Mermaid,* you'll take a bike tour of a sleepy, remote Danish isle, dock at a time-passed fjord village, and wander among eerie, prehistoric monoliths in Sweden. And for an exciting Baltic side trip, I've added my vote for the most interesting city in that corner of Europe—Tallinn, Estonia.

To save time, maximize diversity, and avoid tourist burn-out, I've been very selective. I don't suggest you cruise both the

Budget Tips

While Scandinavia is expensive, the transportation passes, groceries, alternative accommodations, and admissions are affordable (about what you'd pay in England or Italy). Being aware of your budget options will save you money.

It's fun to take advantage of midsummer hotel discounts, but keep in mind that these discounts are generally offered only by the more expensive hotels. You'll save much more by staying in private homes or, cheaper still, in hostels (many hostels have double rooms and great breakfasts).

The breakfasts offered at your lodgings are all-you-can-eat, and so hearty that you'll need only a sandwich for lunch. If you'd prefer more of a meal, the good news is that restaurant lunch specials can be under $15. At most restaurants, tap water is served free (except in Denmark), as are seconds on potatoes. So, even if a restaurant's entrées cost $25, one entrée can easily make a complete dinner. Beer is expensive, and wine is even more so (quench your thirst in Denmark, where alcohol isn't quite as pricey as it is farther north). With a broad array of affordable dishes, convenience stores rescue those shell-shocked by restaurant prices. You're never too far from a picnic-friendly park.

A Eurail Scandinavia pass can make train travel one of your smaller expenses; bus travel is even cheaper—and sometimes faster. At sights, ask about discounted admission costs, as many aren't posted (see page 13).

The great scenery is free. When things are pricey, remind yourself you're not getting less for your travel dollar. Up here there simply aren't any lousy or cheap alternatives to classy, cozy, sleek Scandinavia. Electronic sensors flush youth-hostel toilets.

This book will help you save a shipload of money and days of headaches. Read it carefully. Many of the skills and tricks that are effective in Copenhagen work in Oslo and Stockholm as well.

Geirangerfjord and Sognefjord. Cruise just the better of the two: Sognefjord.

The best is, of course, only my opinion. But after spending a third of my adult life exploring and researching Europe, I've developed a sixth sense for what travelers enjoy. Just thinking about the places featured in this book makes me want to belly up to a *smörgåsbord*.

About This Book

Rick Steves' Scandinavia is your smiling Swede, your Nordic navigator, and a tour guide in your pocket. The book is organized by destination, each one a mini-vacation on its own—filled with

Map Legend

Symbol	Meaning	Symbol	Meaning	Symbol	Meaning
	Viewpoint		Airport		Pedestrian Zone
	Entry Point	T	Taxi Stand		Funicular
i	Tourist Info	M	Metro Stop		Railway
WC	Restroom	T	Tram Stop		Tram Line
	Castle	B	Bus Stop		Stairs
	Church		Boat Stop		Trail
	Mosque	P	Parking		Tunnel

Use this legend to help you navigate the maps in this book.

exciting sights, strollable neighborhoods, homey and affordable places to stay, and memorable places to eat.

This book is updated regularly, but things change. For the latest, visit www.ricksteves.com/update, and for reports and experiences—good and bad—from fellow travelers, check www.ricksteves.com/feedback.

In the following chapters, you'll find these sections:

Planning Your Time suggests a schedule with thoughts on how best to use your limited time.

Orientation includes specifics on public transportation, helpful hints, local tour options, easy-to-read maps, and tourist information (abbreviated **TI** in this book).

Self-Guided Walks take you through interesting neighborhoods, with a personal tour guide in hand.

Sights, described in detail, are rated:

▲▲▲—Don't miss.
▲▲—Try hard to see.
▲—Worthwhile if you can make it.
No rating—Worth knowing about.

Sleeping describes my favorite hotels, from good-value deals to cushy splurges.

Eating serves up a range of options, from inexpensive takeout joints to fancy restaurants.

Connections outlines your options for reaching nearby destinations by bus, train, plane, and boat. In car-friendly regions, I've also included route tips for drivers.

Country Introductions give you an overview of each country's culture, customs, money, history, current events, cuisine, language, and other useful practicalities.

The **Scandinavian History** chapter introduces you to some key people and events in these nations' complicated pasts, making your sightseeing that much more meaningful.

The **appendix** is a traveler's tool kit, with telephone tips, useful phone numbers, transportation basics (on trains, buses, boats, car rentals, driving, and flying), recommended books and films, a festival list, climate chart, handy packing checklist, and a hotel reservation form.

Browse through this book and choose your favorite sights. Then have a great trip! Traveling like a temporary local and taking advantage of the information here, you'll get the absolute most out of every mile, minute, and krone. I'm happy you'll be visiting places I know and love, and meeting some of my favorite Scandinavian people.

Planning

This section will help you get started on planning your trip—with advice on trip costs, when to go, and what you should know before you take off.

Travel Smart

Your trip to Scandinavia is like a complex play—easier to follow and really appreciate on a second viewing. While no one does the same trip twice to gain that advantage, reading this book's chapters on your intended destinations before your trip accomplishes much the same thing.

Design an itinerary that enables you to visit sights at the best possible times. Note holidays, festivals, and days when sights are closed. Sundays have the same pros and cons as they do for travelers in the US (special events, limited hours, banks and many shops closed, limited public transportation, no rush hour). Saturdays are virtually weekdays, with earlier closing hours and no rush hour. Many museums in Scandinavia are closed on Mondays.

Be sure to mix intense and relaxed periods in your itinerary. To maximize rootedness, minimize one-night stands (and, where possible, opt for three-night stands). It's worth a long drive (or train ride) after dinner to be settled in a town for two nights. Hotels are also more likely to give a good price to someone staying more than one night. Every trip—and every traveler—needs at least a few slack days (for picnics, laundry, people-watching, and so on). Pace yourself. Assume you will return.

Reread this book as you travel, and visit local TIs. Upon arrival in a new town, lay the groundwork for a smooth departure; write down (or print out from an online source) the schedule for the train, bus, or boat you'll take when you depart. Drivers can study the best route to their next destination.

While traveling, take advantage of the Internet and phones to make your trip run smoothly. By going online at Internet cafés or your hotel, and using the phone (buy a phone card or carry a

Scandinavia's Best Three-Week Trip by Train

Day	Plan	Sleep in
1	Arrive in Copenhagen	Copenhagen
2	Copenhagen	Copenhagen
3	Copenhagen	Copenhagen
4	Roskilde, Odense, Ærø	Ærøskøbing
5	Ærø	Ærøskøbing
6	Ærø to Kalmar	Kalmar
7	Kalmar	Kalmar
8	Kalmar, early train to Stockholm	Stockholm
9	Stockholm	Stockholm
10	Stockholm, night boat to Helsinki	boat
11	Helsinki	Helsinki
12	Helsinki, jet boat to Tallinn	Tallinn
13	Tallinn, night boat to Stockholm	boat
14	Stockholm, afternoon train to Oslo	Oslo
15	Oslo	Oslo
16	Oslo	Oslo
17	Train to Aurland	Aurland
18	Aurland to Bergen via fjord cruise	Bergen
19	Bergen	Bergen
20	Free day: more fjords, Århus, resting, or whatever	
21	Trip over	

If you want to see Legoland (near Billund) and the "bog man" (in Århus), visit these from Odense (closer) or Copenhagen. You could save lots of time by flying from Tallinn to Oslo.

mobile phone), you can get tourist information, learn the latest on sights (special events, tour schedules, etc.), book tickets and tours, make reservations, reconfirm hotels, research transportation connections, and keep in touch with loved ones.

Connect with the culture. Enjoy the hospitality of the Scandinavian people. Slow down and be open to unexpected experiences. Ask questions—most locals are eager to point you in their idea of the right direction. Keep a notepad in your pocket for organizing your thoughts. Wear your money belt, and learn the local currency and how to estimate prices in dollars. Those who expect to travel smart, do.

Trip Costs

Five components make up the cost of your trip: airfare, surface transportation, room and board, sightseeing and entertainment,

Scandinavia's Best Three-Week Trip by Car

Day	Plan	Sleep in
1	Arrive in Copenhagen	Copenhagen
2	Copenhagen	Copenhagen
3	Copenhagen	Copenhagen
4	Sights near Copenhagen, into Sweden	Växjö
5	Växjö, Glass Country, Kalmar	Kalmar
6	Kalmar to Stockholm	Stockholm
7	Stockholm	Stockholm
8	Stockholm	Boat to Helsinki
9	Helsinki	Boat to Stockholm
10	Uppsala to Oslo	Oslo
11	Oslo	Oslo
12	Oslo	Oslo
13	Lillehammer, Gudbrandsdal Valley	Jotunheimen area
14	Jotunheimen Country	Lustrafjord area or Aurland
15	Sognefjord, Norway in a Nutshell	Bergen
16	Bergen	Bergen
17	Long drive south, Setesdal Valley	Kristiansand
18	Jutland, Århus, Legoland	Århus/Billund
19	Jutland to Ærø	Ærøskøbing
20	Ærø	Ærøskøbing
21	Odense, Roskilde	Copenhagen

Flying "open jaw" into Copenhagen and home from Bergen (with a likely transfer in Copenhagen) can be wonderfully efficient; if you opt for this, you can see Jutland and Ærø sights near Copenhagen at the beginning of your trip. Otherwise, it's about 20 hours by train from Bergen to Copenhagen (transfer in Oslo).

and shopping and miscellany.

Airfare: A basic round-trip US-to-Copenhagen flight costs $750–1,300, depending on where you fly from and when (cheaper in winter). Always consider saving time and money in Europe by flying "open jaw"—into one city and out of another—for example, into Copenhagen and out of Bergen.

Surface Transportation: For the three-week whirlwind trip described above, allow $650 per person for public transportation. This pays for a second-class Eurail Scandinavia pass (4-country, 10 days in 2 months; also covers 50 percent of the boat fare between Stockholm and Helsinki) and the extra boat rides that aren't covered by the pass (such as Helsinki–Tallinn and Tallinn–Stockholm).

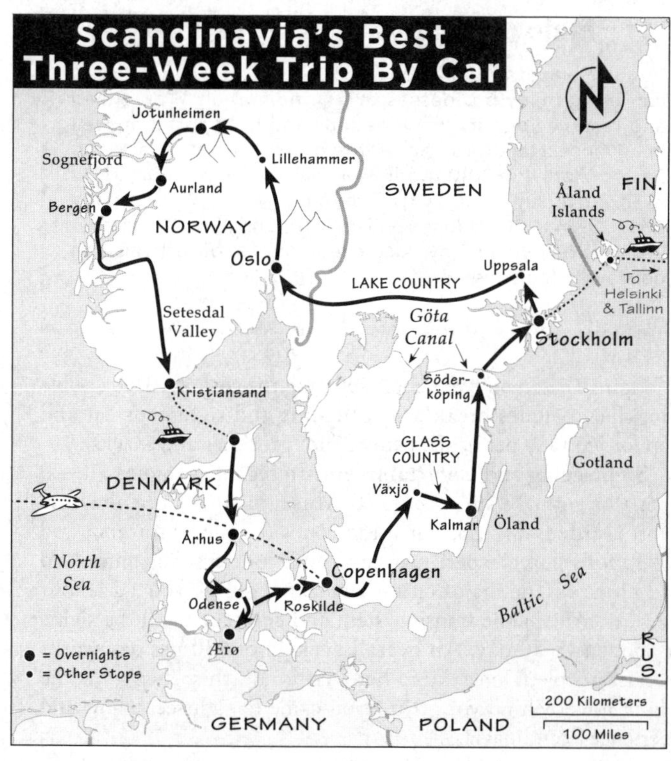

By car, figure about $1,000 per person: $900 per person (based on two people sharing a car and related expenses) for a three-week car rental, tolls, gas, and insurance; add a minimum of about $180 per person for the round-trip boat fare between Stockholm and Helsinki. Ferrying to and from Tallinn will add another $100. Long-term car rental is usually cheapest if arranged from the US (see "Car Rental," page 569). Consider flying. Hopping on a plane to zip from Tallinn (Estonia) to Copenhagen (Denmark) in an hour can be an excellent time-saver.

Room and Board: You can thrive in Scandinavia on an average of $115 a day per person for room and board. A $115-a-day budget allows an average of $15 for lunch, $25 for dinner, and $75

Major Holidays and Weekends

Popular places are even busier on weekends, and holidays can bring many businesses to a grinding halt. Plan ahead and reserve your accommodations and transportation well in advance. Mark these dates in red on your travel calendar: Easter (April 4 in 2010, April 24 in 2011), Ascension Day (May 13 in 2010, June 2 in 2011), Whitsunday and Whitmonday (May 23–24 in 2010, June 12–13 in 2011), Christmas, December 26, and New Year's Day. Also check the list of festivals and holidays in the appendix.

for lodging (based on two people splitting the cost of a $150 double room that includes breakfast). Students and tightwads eat and sleep for $55 ($30 per hostel bed, $25 for groceries and snacks).

Sightseeing and Entertainment: In big cities, figure $10–20 per major sight (Oslo's *Kon-Tiki* Museum-$10, Copenhagen's Tivoli Gardens-$17), $5 for minor ones (climbing towers), and $25–30 for splurge experiences (e.g., folk concerts, bus tours, and fjord cruises). The major cities have cards giving you a 24-hour free run of the public transit system and entrance to all the sights for about $45–50/day. An overall average of $30 per day works for most people. Don't skimp here. After all, this category is the driving force behind your trip—you came to sightsee, enjoy, and experience Scandinavia.

Shopping and Miscellany: Shopping can brutalize your budget in Scandinavia. Good budget travelers find that this category has little to do with assembling a trip full of lifelong and wonderful memories.

When to Go

Summer is a great time to go. Scandinavia bustles and glistens under the July and August sun; it's the height of the tourist season, when all the sightseeing attractions are open and in full swing. In many cases, things don't kick into gear until midsummer—about June 20—when Scandinavian schools let out. Most local industries take July off, and the British and southern Europeans tend to visit Scandinavia in August. You'll notice crowds during these times, but up here "crowds" mean fun and action rather than congestion. At these northern latitudes, the days are long—on June 21 the sun comes up around 4:00 in Oslo and sets around 23:00. Things really quiet down when the local kids go back to school, around August 20.

"Shoulder-season" travel—in late May, early June, and September—lacks the vitality of summer but offers occasional good weather and minimal crowds.

Winter is a bad time to explore Scandinavia unless winter sports are high on your agenda. Like a bear, Scandinavia's metabolism goes down, and many sights and accommodations are closed or open on a limited schedule (especially in remote fjord towns). Business travelers drive hotel prices way up. Winter weather can be cold and dreary. Days are short, and nighttime will draw the shades on your sightseeing well before dinner. Christmastime activities (such as colorful markets and Copenhagen's festively decorated Tivoli Gardens) offer a warm experience at a chilly time of year.

Know Before You Go

Your trip is more likely to go smoothly if you plan ahead. Check this list of things to arrange while you're still at home.

You need a **passport**—but no visa or shots—to travel in Scandinavia. You may be denied entry into certain European countries if your passport is due to expire within three to six months of your ticketed date of return. Get it renewed if you'll be cutting it close. It can take up to six weeks to get or renew a passport (for more on passports, see www.travel.state.gov). Pack a photocopy of your passport in your luggage in case the original is lost or stolen.

Border crossings between Norway, Sweden, Denmark, and Finland are a wave-through. Getting into and out of Estonia, even though it's in the European Union, takes a little longer, but still goes relatively quickly. When you change countries, you change money, phone cards, and postage stamps.

Book your rooms well in advance, especially if you'll be traveling during peak season (July and August) and any major **holidays** (see sidebar on previous page).

Call your **debit- and credit-card companies** to let them know the countries you'll be visiting so they won't deny your international charges. Confirm your daily withdrawal limit; consider asking to have it raised so you can take out more cash at each ATM stop. Ask about international transaction fees.

If you're interested in **travel insurance**, do your homework before you buy. Compare the cost of the insurance to the likelihood of your using it and your potential loss if something goes wrong. For details on the many kinds of travel insurance, see www.ricksteves.com/plan/tips/insurance.htm.

If you're planning on **renting a car** in Scandinavia, bring your US driver's license.

Consider buying a **railpass** after researching your options (see page 567 and www.ricksteves.com/rail for all the specifics).

If you want to take an **overnight boat** between major Scandinavian cities in summer or on weekends, book it in advance

Scandinavia at a Glance

Denmark

▲▲▲Copenhagen Vibrant Danish capital city, with *The Little Mermaid,* old-time Tivoli Gardens amusement park, excellent National Museum, Renaissance King Christian IV's Rosenborg Castle, delightful pedestrian Strøget, and eye-opening hippie enclave at Christiania.

▲Near Copenhagen Great day-trip options: West to the Viking Ship Museum and Royal Cathedral at Roskilde, and north to Frederiksborg Castle—the "Danish Versailles"—in Hillerød, the Louisiana modern-art museum in Humlebæk, the Karen Blixen Museum in Rungsted, and Kronborg Castle in Helsingør.

▲▲Central Denmark Peaceful isle of Ærø—perfect for a loop tour by bike or car—and home to Denmark's best-preserved 18th-century village—Ærøskøbing; and the busy town of Odense, with the Hans Christian Andersen Hus and the nearby Funen Village open-air folk museum.

▲Jutland Family-friendly region with Legoland kids' adventure park, and Denmark's second-largest city, Århus, with its stroll-able pedestrian center, ARoS art museum, and Den Gamle By open-air folk museum.

Norway

▲▲▲Oslo Norway's sharp capital city, with its historic and walkable core, mural-lined City Hall, Vigeland sculptures at Frogner Park, and inspiring Nobel Peace Center, while the nearby Bygdøy district hosts museums dedicated to ships (Viking, *Fram,* and *Kon-Tiki*), the Holocaust, and traditional folk life.

▲▲Norway in a Nutshell A combination train, bus, and ferry trip to and through Norway's most spectacularly beautiful fjord, the Sognefjord, passing pristine waterfalls, verdant forests, and take-your-breath-away scenery.

▲More on the Sognefjord Fjordside hamlet of Balestrand, a cozy home-base for exploring nearby sights (including a medieval stave church), plus the serene Lustrafjord, with more stave churches and a glacier you can walk on.

▲Gudbrandsdal Valley and Jotunheimen Mountains Lush green valley connecting northern and southern Norway, with touristy Lillehammer, the excellent Maihaugen Open-Air Folk Museum, and a rugged mountain range with some of this country's finest hikes and drives.

▲▲Bergen Salty port town and medieval capital of Norway, with lively fish market, colorful Hanseatic quarter (Bryggen), and a funicular to the top of Mount Fløyen with great views.

▲South Norway Harborside Stavanger—with its Norwegian Emigration Center, Petroleum Museum, and Pulpit Rock, time-passed and remote Setesdal Valley, and the resort town of Kristiansand with ferry connections to Denmark.

Sweden

▲▲▲Stockholm Bustling capital of Sweden, with its charming island core of Gamla Stan, Europe's original—and unsurpassed—Skansen open-air folk museum, the *Vasa* museum (17th-century warship), and the Nordic Museum's look at five centuries of Swedish lifestyles.

▲Stockholm's Archipelago Sweden's rocky garden of more than 30,000 islands, best seen on a boat trip from Stockholm.

▲Southeast Sweden Växjö, with a first-rate emigration museum/research center and the Smålands Museum of glass-making; Kalmar, with its massive 12th-century Kalmar Castle and nearby holiday island of Öland; and the touristy "Kingdom of Crystal" Glass Country.

Finland

▲▲Helsinki Finland's capital city—an architectural delight for its Neoclassical and Art Nouveau buildings and churches—with the stirring "Chapel in the Rock," fine National Museum of Finland, and island fortress and open-air folk museum.

Estonia

▲▲Tallinn Russian-influenced, full-of-life capital of Estonia, with quaint Old Town center, remarkably intact medieval walls, and stirringly patriotic sights (Estonian art museum and the historic Song Festival Grounds).

(Copenhagen to Oslo, page 111; Stockholm to Helsinki, page 470; or Stockholm to Tallinn, page 514). If you're doing the Norway in a Nutshell in mid-July or August, make reservations for the Oslo–Bergen train and the Flåm-Gudvangen fjord cruise (see page 240).

If you plan to trace your Swedish or Norwegian **heritage,** bring along basic genealogical information (for details, see the Norwegian Emigration Center in Stavanger, Norway, page 329; or the House of Emigrants in Växjö, Sweden, page 429).

Because airline **carry-on restrictions** are always changing, visit the Transportation Security Administration's website (www.tsa.gov/travelers) for an up-to-date list of what you can bring on the plane with you...and what you have to check. Remember to arrive with plenty of time to get through security.

Sightseeing Priorities

Depending on the length of your trip, here are my recommended priorities. Assuming you're traveling by public transportation, I've taken geographical proximity into account.

4 days:	Copenhagen, Stockholm (connected by a 5.5-hour express train)
6 days, add:	Oslo
8 days, add:	Norway in a Nutshell fjord trip, Bergen
10 days, add:	Overnight cruise from Stockholm to Helsinki
14 days, add:	Ærø, Odense, Roskilde, Frederiksborg (all in Denmark)
17 days, add:	Århus (Denmark), Kalmar (Sweden)
21 days, add:	Tallinn (Estonia) and more time in capitals
24 days, add:	More Norwegian countryside or Stockholm's archipelago

The map on page 7 and the three-week itinerary on page 6 include most of the stops in the first 21 days.

Practicalities

Emergency Telephone Numbers: In all the countries in this book, dial 112 for medical or other emergencies. For police, dial 112 in Denmark, Norway, and Sweden; call 10022 in Finland; and dial 110 in Estonia.

Time: In Europe—and in this book—you'll use the 24-hour clock. It's the same through 12:00 noon, then keep going—13:00, 14:00, and so on. For anything after 12, subtract 12 and add p.m. (14:00 is 2:00 p.m.)

Norway, Sweden, and Denmark, which share the same time zone as continental Europe, are six/nine hours ahead of the East/

Where Do I Find Information On...?

Credit Card Theft	See page 16.
Packing Light	See the packing list on page 585.
Phoning	See "Telephones" on page 558.
Language	See page 580.
Making Hotel Reservations	See page 24.
Tipping	See page 17.
Tourist Information Offices	See page 557.
Updates to This Book	See www.ricksteves.com/update

West Coasts of the US. Finland and Estonia are one hour ahead of continental Europe. The exceptions are the beginning and end of Daylight Saving Time: Europe "springs forward" the last Sunday in March (two weeks after most of North America) and "falls back" the last Sunday in October (one week before North America). For a handy online time converter, try www.timeanddate.com/worldclock.

Watt's Up? Europe's electrical system is different from North America's in two ways: the shape of the plug (two round prongs) and the voltage of the current (220 volts instead of 110 volts). For your North American plug to work in Europe, you'll need an adapter, sold inexpensively at travel stores in the US. As for the voltage, most newer electronics or travel appliances (such as hair dryers, laptops, and battery chargers) automatically convert the voltage—if you see a range of voltages printed on the item or its plug (such as "110–220"), it'll work in Europe. Otherwise, you can buy a converter separately in the US (about $20).

Discounts: While discounts are generally not listed in this book, note that liberal Scandinavia is Europe's most generous corner when it comes to youths (under 18), students (with International Student Identity Cards, www.isic.org), seniors, and families. Children usually sleep and sightsee for half-price or free.

News: Americans keep in touch in Europe with the *International Herald Tribune* (published almost daily throughout Europe and online at www.iht.com). Other newsy sites are http://news.bbc.co.uk and www.europeantimes.com. Every Tuesday, the European editions of *Time* and *Newsweek* hit the stands with articles of particular interest to travelers in Europe. Sports addicts can get their fix from *USA Today.* News in English will be sold only where there's enough demand: in big cities and tourist centers. Many hotels have CNN or BBC television channels.

Money

This section offers advice on getting cash, using credit and debit cards, dealing with lost or stolen cards, and tipping.

Cash from ATMs

Throughout Europe, cash machines (ATMs) are the standard way for travelers to get local currency. Bring plastic—credit and/or debit cards. It's smart to bring two cards, in case one gets demagnetized or eaten by a temperamental machine. As an emergency backup, bring several hundred dollars in hard cash (in $20 bills rather than hard-to-exchange $100 bills). Don't use traveler's checks—they're a waste of time (long waits at slow banks) and a waste of money in fees.

Because Scandinavian countries have different currencies, you'll likely wind up with leftover cash when you're leaving a country. Coins can't be exchanged once you leave the country, so try to spend them before you cross the border. But bills are easy to convert to the "new" country's currency. When changing cash, use exchange bureaus rather than banks. The Forex desks (easy to find at major train stations and airports) are considered reliable and fair.

You'll find cash machines all over Scandinavia, always open and providing quick transactions. To withdraw money, you'll need a debit card—ideally with a Visa or MasterCard logo for maximum usability—plus a PIN (Personal Identification Number). Know your PIN code in numbers; there are only numbers—no letters—on European keypads.

Before you go, confirm with your bank that your card will work overseas, and alert them that you'll be making withdrawals in Europe; otherwise, the bank may not approve transactions if it perceives unusual spending patterns. (Your credit-card company may do the same thing—let them know about your travel plans, too.) Also ask about international transaction fees; see "Credit and Debit Cards," opposite page.

When using a cash machine, try to take out large sums of money to reduce your per-transaction bank fees. If the machine refuses your request, try again and select a smaller amount (some cash machines limit the amount you can withdraw—don't take it personally). If that doesn't work, try a different machine.

To keep your cash safe, use a money belt—a pouch with a strap that you buckle around your waist like a belt, and wear under your clothes. Even in safe, orderly Scandinavia, thieves target tourists. A money belt provides peace of mind, allowing you to carry lots of cash safely. Don't waste time every few days tracking down a cash machine—withdraw a week's worth of money, stuff it in your money belt, and travel!

Exchange Rates

I've priced things in local currencies throughout the book.

$1 equals about...
5 Danish kroner (1 krone equals about $0.20)
6 Norwegian kroner (1 krone equals about $0.17)
7 Swedish kronor (1 krona equals about $0.14)
0.60 euro in Finland (€1 equals about $1.40)
11 Estonian krooni (1 kroon equals about $0.09)

In Scandinavia, kroner are decimalized: 100 øre = 1 krone. Kroner from one Scandinavian country are not accepted in the next (except at foreign-exchange services and banks, and then only bills).

Standard abbreviations are Danish krone, DKK; Swedish krona, SEK; and Norwegian kroner, NOK. I'll keep it simple. For all three countries, I'll use the krone abbreviation "kr."

Here are the rough exchange rates for each country. Because of currency fluctuations, and to make things easier to convert in your head, these are very loose estimates (for the latest, see www.oanda.com):

To roughly translate Danish prices into US dollars, multiply by two, then drop a zero (e.g., 15 kr = $3, 100 kr = $20). In Norway, divide prices by 6 (100 kr = about $16); in Sweden, divide prices by 7 (100 kr = about $14). So, that 250-kr Norwegian sweater is about $40, and your 525-kr five-course dinner in Stockholm is about $75.

Finland's currency is the euro (€). To roughly convert prices in euros to dollars, add 40 percent (€20 = about $28).

Estonia's kroon, officially abbreviated as EEK, also appears as "kr" in this book. To roughly convert prices from krooni into dollars, drop the last two digits and multiply by nine (500 kr = about $45; 1,255 kr = about $108). Anything under 100 kr is less than $10.

Credit and Debit Cards

For purchases, Visa and MasterCard are more commonly accepted than American Express. Just like at home, credit or debit cards work easily at larger hotels, restaurants, and shops, but smaller businesses prefer payment in local currency (in small bills—break big bills at a larger store or a bank). If receipts show your credit-card number, don't toss these thoughtlessly.

In Denmark, many places charge a fee for using a credit card, so it's a good idea to ask before using your card. These fees aren't the only reason you should keep plenty of cash in your money belt: Many Danish businesses, even large ones, do not accept foreign-issued credit cards at all.

Fees: Credit- and debit-card transactions—whether used for purchases or ATM withdrawals—often charge additional, tacked-on "international transaction" fees of up to 3 percent plus $5 per transaction. Note that if you use a credit card for ATM transactions, it's technically a "cash advance" rather than a "withdrawal"—and subject to an additional cash-advance fee.

To avoid unpleasant surprises, call your bank or credit-card company before your trip to ask about these fees. Ask your bank if it has agreements with any Scandinavian banks for lower withdrawal fees. If the fees are too high, consider getting a card just for your trip: Capital One (www.capitalone.com) and most credit unions have low-to-no international transaction fees.

If merchants offer to convert your purchase price into dollars (called dynamic currency conversion, or "DCC"), refuse this "service." You'll pay even more in fees for the expensive convenience of seeing your charge in dollars.

Dealing with "Chip and PIN": Some parts of Europe (especially Scandinavia, France, Great Britain, Ireland, and the Netherlands) are adopting a "chip and PIN" system for their credit and debit cards. These "smartcards" come with an embedded microchip, and cardholders enter a PIN code instead of signing a receipt. In most cases, you can still use your credit or debit card at the cashier and sign the receipt the old-fashioned way. A few merchants might insist on the PIN code—making it helpful for you to know the PIN code for your credit card (ask your credit-card company); in a pinch, use cash or your debit card and PIN code instead.

US credit or debit cards don't work at many automated machines (such as ticket machines in a train station, or a pay-at-the-pump gas station). But in most of these situations, there's a cashier nearby who can take your credit or debit card and make it work.

Damage Control for Lost Cards

If you lose your credit, debit, or ATM card, you can stop people from using it by reporting the loss immediately to the respective global customer-assistance centers. Call these 24-hour US numbers collect: Visa (410/581-9994), MasterCard (636/722-7111), and American Express (623/492-8427).

At a minimum, you'll need to know the name of the financial institution that issued you the card, along with the type of card (classic, platinum, or whatever). Providing the following information will allow for a quicker cancellation of your missing card: full card number, whether you are the primary or secondary cardholder, the cardholder's name exactly as printed on the card, billing address, home phone number, circumstances of the loss or theft, and identification verification (your birth date, your mother's maiden name, or your Social Security number—memorize this, don't carry a copy). If you are the secondary cardholder, you'll also need to provide the primary cardholder's identification-verification details. You can generally receive a temporary card within two or three business days in Europe.

If you promptly report your card lost or stolen, you typically won't be responsible for any unauthorized transactions on your account, although many banks charge a liability fee of $50.

Tipping

Tipping in Europe isn't as automatic and generous as it is in the US—but for special service, tips are appreciated, if not expected. As in the US, the proper amount depends on your resources, tipping philosophy, and the circumstance, but some general guidelines apply.

Restaurants: Tipping is an issue only at restaurants that have table service. If you order your food at a counter, don't tip.

Throughout Scandinavia, a service charge is included in your bill, so there's no need to leave an additional tip. In fancier restaurants or for great service, round up the bill (about 5 percent of the total check). It's generally good form to tip about 5 percent at any restaurant in Estonia, where servers earn low wages and rely on tips.

Taxis: To tip the cabbie, round up about five percent (for an 85-kr fare, pay 90 kr). If the cabbie hauls your bags and zips you to the airport to help you catch your flight, you might want to toss in a little more. But if you feel like you're being driven in circles or otherwise ripped off, skip the tip.

Special Services: Tour guides at public sights sometimes hold out their hands for tips after they give their spiels. If I've already paid for the tour, I don't tip extra unless they've really impressed me (10–20 kr). At hotels, porters expect a few kroner for each bag they carry (another reason to pack light). Leaving the maid ten kroner per overnight at the end of your stay is a nice touch. In general, if someone in the service industry does a super job for you, a small tip (the equivalent of a few dollars) is appropriate...but not required.

When in doubt, ask. If you're not sure whether (or how much) to tip for a service, ask your hotelier or the TI; they'll fill you in on how it's done on their turf.

VAT Refunds for Shoppers

Wrapped into the purchase price of your Scandinavian souvenirs is a Value-Added Tax (VAT) of 20–25 percent (among the highest rates in Europe). You're entitled to get most of that tax back if you make a purchase of a certain amount (300 kr in Denmark, 315 kr in Norway, 200 kr in Sweden, €40 in Finland, and 2,001 kr in Estonia) at a store that participates in the VAT refund scheme. In

Denmark, for instance, look for the Danish Tax-Free Shopping emblem. VAT is called MVA in Norway and MOMS in Denmark, Finland, and Sweden. Note that you can't get refunds on meals, hotel stays, or transportation in Scandinavia.

Getting your refund is usually straightforward and, if you buy a substantial amount of souvenirs, well worth the hassle. If you're lucky, the merchant will subtract the tax when you make your purchase. (This is more likely to occur if the store ships the goods to your home.) Otherwise, you'll need to:

Get the paperwork. Have the merchant completely fill out the necessary refund document, called a "cheque." You might be asked for your passport at the store.

Get your stamp at the border or airport. If you've made purchases in Denmark, Sweden, Finland, and/or Estonia, get your cheque(s) stamped at your last stop in the European Union by the customs agent who deals with VAT refunds. If you've shopped hard in Norway (a non-EU country), get your cheque(s) stamped at the border or at your point of departure from Norway. It's best to keep your purchases in your carry-on for viewing, but if they're too large or dangerous (such as knives) to carry on, track down the proper customs agent to inspect them before you check your bag. You're not supposed to use your purchased goods before you leave. If you show up at customs wearing your new Norwegian sweater, officials might look the other way—or deny you a refund.

Collect your refund. You'll need to return your stamped document to the retailer or its representative. Many merchants work with a service that has offices at major airports, ports, and border crossings, such as Global Refund (www.globalrefund.com) or Premier Tax Free (www.premiertaxfree.com). These services, which extract a 4 percent fee, can usually refund your money immediately in your currency of choice, or credit your card (within two billing cycles). If the retailer handles VAT refunds directly, it's up to you to contact the merchant for your refund. You can mail the documents from home, or quicker, from your point of departure (using a stamped, addressed envelope you've prepared or one that's been provided by the merchant). You'll then have to wait—it could take months.

Customs for American Shoppers

You are allowed to take home $800 worth of items per person duty-free, once every 30 days. The next $1,000 is taxed at a flat 3 percent. After that, you pay the individual item's duty rate. You can also bring home duty-free a liter of alcohol (slightly more than a standard-size bottle of wine; you must be at least 21), 200 cigarettes, and up to 100 non-Cuban cigars. You may take home vacuum-packed cheeses; dried herbs, spices, or mushrooms; and canned fruits or vegetables, including jams and vegetable spreads. Baked goods, candy, chocolate, oil, vinegar, mustard, and honey are OK. Fresh fruits or vegetables are not. Meats, even if canned, are generally not allowed. Remember that you'll need to carefully pack any bottles of *akvavit* and other liquid-containing items in your checked luggage, due to the three-ounce limit on liquids in carry-on baggage. To check customs rules and duty rates before you go, visit www.cbp.gov, and click on "Travel," then "Know Before You Go."

Sightseeing

Sightseeing can be hard work. Use these tips to make your visits to Scandinavia's finest sights meaningful, fun, efficient, and painless.

Plan Ahead

Set up an itinerary that allows you to fit in all your must-see sights. For a one-stop look at opening hours in the bigger cities, see the "At a Glance" sidebars. Most sights keep stable hours in the summer months, but hours tend to fluctuate in the winter. If you have your heart set on visiting particular sights, it's always smart to confirm the latest hours by checking their websites or asking at the local TI.

When possible, visit major sights first thing (when your energy is best) and save other activities for the afternoon. Hit the highlights first, then go back to other things if you have the stamina and time.

Study up. To get the most out of the self-guided walks and sight descriptions in this book, read them before your visit. In some cities, you can buy a combo-ticket for discounted entry to two or more sights. I've noted these in this book.

At Sights

Here's what you can typically expect:

At churches—which often offer interesting art (usually free) and a welcome seat—a modest dress code (no bare shoulders or shorts) is encouraged.

Major museums and sights require you to check daypacks and coats. They'll be kept safely. If you have something you can't bear to part with, stash it in a pocket or purse. To avoid checking a small backpack, carry it under your arm like a purse as you enter. From a guard's point of view, a backpack is generally a problem, while a purse is not.

Photography is sometimes banned at major sights. Look for signs or ask. If cameras are allowed, video cameras are as well, but flashes or tripods usually are not. Flashes damage oil paintings and distract others in the room. Even without a flash, a handheld camera will take a decent picture (or buy postcards or posters at the museum bookstore).

Many sights rent audioguides, which generally offer excellent recorded descriptions in English (about $7.50). If you bring along your own pair of headphones and a Y-jack, you can sometimes share one audioguide with your travel partner and save money.

Guided tours at sights range from free to $12. Throughout Scandinavia, make a point to take the free tours that come with steep admission prices. Though tours range widely in quality, many of the sights are quite dull until a local guide brings them to life. Monolingual Americans are in luck—tours are often conducted only in English. Tours are most likely to occur during peak season; however, there is often a guide on duty ready to whip into teaching mode—but only when engaged by a curious tourist. Many sights also have videos about the attraction. These are generally well worth your time. I make it standard operating procedure to ask when I arrive at a sight if there is a video in English.

Major sights often have an on-site café or cafeteria (usually a good place to rest and have a snack or light meal). The WCs at many sights are free and clean. Many places sell postcards that highlight their attractions. Before you leave, scan the postcards and thumb through the biggest guidebook (or skim its index) to be sure you haven't overlooked something that you'd like to see.

Most sights stop admitting people 30–60 minutes before closing time, and some rooms close early (often 45 minutes before the actual closing time). Guards usher people out, so don't save the best for last.

Every sight or museum offers more than what is covered in this book. Use the information in this book as an introduction—not the final word.

Sleeping

Accommodations in Scandinavia are fairly expensive, but they are normally very comfortable and come with breakfast. Plan on spending about $150 per hotel double in big cities, and $70 to $100 in towns and in private homes. An overall average of $100 per night in humble doubles is possible using this book's listings.

I favor accommodations (and restaurants) handy to your sightseeing activities. Rather than list hotels scattered throughout a city, I choose two or three favorite neighborhoods and recommend the best accommodation values in each, from $30 bunk beds to fancy-for-my-book $270 doubles.

A triple is much cheaper than a double and a single. While hotel singles are most expensive, private accommodations have a flat per-person rate. Hostels and dorms always charge per person. Especially in private homes, where the boss changes the sheets,

Sleep Code

To help you sort easily through the listings, I've divided the rooms into three categories based on the price for a standard double room with bath:

$$$ Higher Priced
$$ Moderately Priced
$ Lower Priced

To give maximum information in a minimum of space, I use the following code to describe the accommodations. Prices listed are per room, not per person. Unless otherwise noted, English is spoken and breakfast is included. You can assume a hotel takes credit cards unless you see "cash only" in the listing.

When a price range is given for a type of room, that means the prices fluctuate with the season, room size, or length of stay.

S = Single room (or price for one person in a double).
D = Double or Twin. Double beds are usually big enough for non-romantic couples.
T = Triple (often a double bed with a single bed moved in).
Q = Quad (usually two double beds).
b = Private bathroom with toilet and shower or tub.
s = Private shower or tub only (the toilet is down the hall).

According to this code, a couple staying at a "Db-1,050 kr" hotel in Sweden would pay a total of 1,050 kr (about $150) for a double room with a private bathroom.

If I mention "Internet access" in a hotel listing, there's a public terminal in the lobby for guests to use. If I mention "Wi-Fi," you can generally access it in your room (usually for free), but only if you have your own laptop.

people staying several nights are most desirable. One-night stays are sometimes charged extra.

I look for places that are friendly; clean; a good value; located in a central, safe, quiet neighborhood; English-speaking; and not mentioned in other guidebooks. I'm more impressed by a handy location and a fun-loving philosophy than hair dryers and shoeshine machines.

I also like local character and simple facilities that don't cater to American "needs." Obviously, a place meeting every criterion is rare, and all of my recommendations fall short of perfection—sometimes miserably. But I've listed the best values for each price category, given the above criteria. I've also thrown in a few hostels, private rooms, and other cheap options for budget travelers.

Room-finding services offered by tourist information offices, if you have no place in mind, can be worth the booking fee (about \$8–10). Be very clear about what you want. (Mention if you have sheets or a sleeping bag, whether you will take a twin or double, if a bathroom down the hall is acceptable, and so on.) They know the hotel quirks and private-room scene better than anybody. Official "rack rates" (the highest rates a hotel charges) are often misleading; they omit cheaper oddball rooms and special clearance deals.

To save money, bring your own sheet or sleeping bag and offer to provide it in low-priced establishments. This can save \$20 per person per night, especially in rural areas. Families can get a price break; normally a child can sleep free or for very little in Mom and Dad's room.

During these times of economic uncertainty, many hotels will likely be discounting deeply to snare what customers they can. Try to avoid paying rack rates. If you email several places and ask for their best prices, you'll find that some are eager to discount. This can save you big bucks—with prices potentially far below those listed in this guidebook.

To get the most sleep for your dollar at these northern latitudes, pull the dark shades (and even consider bringing your own night shades) to keep out the early-morning sun.

For environmental reasons, towels are often replaced in hotels only when you leave them on the floor. In private accommodations and some cheap hotels, they aren't replaced at all, so hang them up to dry and reuse. The cord that dangles over the tub or shower in big Scandinavian resort hotels is not a clothesline—you pull it if you've fallen and can't get up.

Before accepting a room, confirm your understanding of the complete price (including, for example, extra fees for short stays). Pay your bill the evening before you leave to avoid the time-wasting crowd at the reception desk in the morning, especially if you need to rush off to catch your train. And, as always, I appreciate feedback on your experiences.

Types of Accommodations

Hotels

Hotels are expensive (\$100–200 doubles), with some exceptions. Business-class hotels drop prices to attract tourists with summer rates (late June–early Aug) and weekend rates (Fri, Sat, and sometimes Sun). You need to ask about these—receptionists don't volunteer the information.

To sleep in a fancy hotel in a big city, it can sometimes be cheapest to arrive without a reservation and let the local tourist

office book you a room. When a classy, modern $200 place has a $100 summer special that includes two $10 buffet breakfasts, the dumpy $80 hotel room without breakfast becomes less exciting.

Most hotels have several tiers of rates, including tourist office referral, weekend, summer, summer weekend, and walk-in. Walk-ins at the end of a quiet day can often get a room even below the summer rate. Some hotels also have lower rates for online bookings, so check the Web for deals. Many modern hotels have "combi" rooms (singles with a sofa that turns the room into a perfectly good double), which are cheaper than a full double. Also, many places have low-grade older rooms, considered unacceptable for the general public and often used by workers on weekdays outside of summer. If you're on a budget, ask for cheaper rooms with no windows or no water. And if a hotel is not full, any day can bring out summer discounts.

Hostels

Scandinavian hostels, Europe's finest, are open to travelers of all ages. They offer classy facilities, members' kitchens, cheap hot meals (often breakfast buffets), plenty of doubles (for a few extra kroner), and great people experiences. Hostels are also a tremendous source of local and budget travel information. Receptionists will hold a room if you promise to arrive by 18:00. Note that many hostels close in the off-season.

Hosteling only saves money if you come prepared. Buy a hostel membership card before you leave home ($28 a year, free if you're younger than 18 and $15 if you're older than 54; sold at your local student travel office, any hostel office, Hostelling International—US tel. 301/495-1240, or online at www.hiayh.org). Those without hostel cards pay about $7-per-night extra. Many hostels in Norway regularly promote nonmember prices—if you have a membership card, be sure to ask about a discount. To increase your options, consider the many independent hostels that don't require a membership card (some of them are at www.hostels.com).

Bring a hosteling sleep sack or bed sheets from home, or else plan on renting them for about $10 per stay. Making your meals in the hostel kitchen is a great way to save money.

You'll find lots of Volvos in hostel parking lots, as Scandinavians know that hostels provide the best (and usually only) $30 beds in town. Hosteling is ideal for families who fit into two sets of bunk beds (4-bed rooms, kitchens, washing machines, discount family memberships). Pick up each country's free hostel directory at any hostel or TI.

Private Rooms

Throughout Scandinavia, people rent rooms in their homes to travelers for about $80 per double (or about $90 for a double with private bath). While some put out a *Værelse, Rom, Rum,* or *Hus Rum* sign, most operate solely through the local TI (which occasionally keeps these B&Bs a secret until all hotel rooms are taken). You'll get your own key to a clean, comfortable, but usually simple private room (sometimes without a sink), with free access to the family shower and WC (unless the room has a private bath). Booking direct saves both you and your host the cut the TI takes. The TIs are very protective of their lists. If you enjoy a big-city private home that would like to be listed in this book, I'd love to hear from you.

Camping

Scandinavian campgrounds are practical, comfortable, and cheap (about $8 per person with $20 camping card, available on the spot). This is the middle-class Scandinavian family way to travel: safe, great social fun, and no reservation problems. Campgrounds are friendly, safe, more central and convenient than rustic, and rarely full.

The national tourist office has a fine brochure/map listing all their campgrounds, or ask the local TI for a list of regional campgrounds. Your hometown travel bookstore should also have guidebooks on camping in Europe. You'll find campgrounds just about everywhere you need them.

Most campgrounds provide **huts** *(hytter)* for wannabe campers with no gear. Huts normally sleep four to six in bunk beds, come with blankets and a kitchenette, and charge one fee (about 400 kr or $65, plus extra if you need sheets). Because locals typically move in for a week or two, many campground huts are booked for summer long in advance. If you're driving and arrive late with no place to stay, find a campground and try to grab a hut.

Phoning

To make international calls to Scandinavia to line up hotel reservations, you'll need to know the country codes. For detailed instructions on telephoning, see page 558 in the appendix.

Making Reservations

Given the quality of the places I've found for this book, I'd recommend that you reserve your rooms in advance, particularly if you'll be traveling during peak season (especially in the capitals during conventions—early June is packed in Oslo and Stockholm). Book several weeks ahead, or as soon as you've pinned down your travel dates. Note that some holidays jam things up and merit your making reservations far in advance (see the "Major Holidays and Weekends" sidebar on page 8). Just like at home, holidays that fall on a Monday, Thursday, or Friday can turn the weekend into a long holiday, so book the entire weekend well in advance.

Requesting a Reservation: To make a reservation in advance, contact hotels directly by email, phone, or fax. Email is the clearest and most economical way to make a reservation. Or you can go straight to the hotel website; many have secure online reservation forms and can instantly inform you of availability and any special deals. But be sure you use the hotel's official site and not a booking agency's site—otherwise you may pay higher rates than you should. If phoning from the US, be mindful of time zones (see page 12). Most hotels listed are accustomed to guests who speak only English.

The hotelier wants to know these key pieces of information (also included in the sample request form on page 584):

- number and type of rooms
- number of nights
- date of arrival
- date of departure
- any special needs (e.g., bathroom in the room or down the hall, twin beds vs. double bed, air-conditioning, quiet, view, ground floor, etc.)

When you request a room, use the European style for writing dates: day/month/year. Hoteliers need to know your arrival and departure dates. For example, for a two-night stay in July, I would request: "2 nights, arrive 16/07/11, depart 18/07/11." (Consider in advance how long you'll stay; don't just assume you can tack on extra days once you arrive.)

If you don't get a reply to your email or fax, it usually means the hotel is already fully booked (but you can try sending the message again, or call to follow up).

Confirming a Reservation: If the hotel's response includes its room availability and rates, it's not a confirmation. You must tell them that you want that room at the given rate. Many hoteliers will request your credit-card number for a one-night deposit to hold the room. While you can email your credit-card information (I do), it's safer to share that personal info via phone call, fax, two successive emails, or secure online reservation form (if the hotel has one on its website).

Canceling a Reservation: If you must cancel your reservation, it's courteous to do so with as much advance notice as possible—at least three days. Simply make a quick phone call or send an email. Family-run hotels and B&Bs lose money if they turn away customers while holding a room for someone who doesn't show up. Understandably, many hotels bill no-shows for one night.

Hotels in larger cities sometimes have strict cancellation policies. For example, you might lose a deposit if you cancel within two weeks of your reserved stay, or you might be billed for the entire reserved visit if you leave early. Ask about cancellation policies before you book.

If canceling via email, request confirmation that your cancellation was received to avoid being accidentally billed.

Reconfirm Your Reservation: Always call to reconfirm your room reservation a day or two in advance from the road. Smaller hotels appreciate knowing your time of arrival. If you'll be arriving after 17:00, be sure to let your hotelier know. On the small chance that a hotel loses track of your reservation, bring along a hard copy of your emailed or faxed confirmation. Don't have the TI reconfirm rooms for you; they'll take a commission.

Reserving Rooms as You Travel: If you enjoy having a flexible itinerary, you can make reservations as you travel, calling hotels a few days to a week before your visit. If you prefer the flexibility of traveling without any reservations at all, you'll have greater success snaring rooms if you arrive at your destination early in the day. When you anticipate crowds (weekends are worst), call hotels at about 9:00 on the day you plan to arrive, when the hotel clerk knows who'll be checking out and just which rooms will be available.

Eating

Breakfast

Hotel breakfasts are a huge and filling buffet, generally included but occasionally a $10-or-so option. This features fruit, cereal, and various milks (look for words like *skummet* for skim, *lett* for low-fat, *sød* or *hel* for whole, *filmjölk* for buttermilk). Grab a drinkable yogurt and go local by pouring it in the bowl and sprinkling your cereal over it. The great selection of breads and crackers comes with jam, butter *(smør)*, margarine (same word), and cheese *(ost)*. And

you'll get cold cuts, pickled herring, caviar paste (in a squeeze tube), and boiled eggs *(æg—bløt* is soft-boiled, *kokt* is hard-boiled); use the plastic egg cups and small spoons provided to eat your soft-boiled egg Scandinavian-style.

The brown cheese with the texture of earwax and a slightly sweet taste is *geitost* (goat cheese). Popular in Norway, it's usually made from a mixture of cow's milk and goat's milk. Try to develop a taste for this odd but enjoyable cheese.

For beverages, it's orange juice (the word for orange is *appelsin,* so OJ is AJ) and coffee or tea. Coffee addicts can buy a thermos and get it filled in most hotels and hostels for around $5. While it is bad form to take freebies from the breakfast buffet to eat later, many hotels will provide you with wax paper and a plastic bag to pack yourself a lunch, legitimately, for $7 or $8. Ask for a *matpakke.*

If you skip your hotel's breakfast, you can visit a bakery to get a sandwich and cup of coffee. Bakeries have wonderful inexpensive pastries. The only cheap breakfast is the one you make yourself. Many simple accommodations provide kitchenettes or at least coffeepots with heated bases.

Lunch

Many restaurants offer cheap daily lunch specials *(dagens rett)* and buffets for office workers. Scandinavians, not big on lunch, often just grab a sandwich *(smørrebrød)* and a cup of coffee at their work desk.

Especially in Denmark, you'll find *smørrebrød* shops turning sandwiches into an art form. These open-face delights taste as good as they look. My favorite is the one piled high with *rejer* (shrimp). The roast beef is good, too. Shops will wrap sandwiches up for a perfect picnic in a nearby park.

If you want to enjoy a combination of picnics and restaurant meals on your trip, you'll save money by eating in restaurants at lunch (when there's usually a special and food is generally cheaper) and picnicking for dinner.

Picnics

Scandinavia has colorful markets and economical supermarkets. Picnic-friendly mini-markets at gas and train stations are open late. Samples of picnic treats: *Wasa* cracker bread (Sport is my favorite; Ideal *flatbrød* is ideal for munchies), packaged meat and cheese, brown goat cheese *(geitost),* drinkable yogurt, freshly cooked or smoked fish from markets, fresh fruit and vegetables,

lingonberries, squeeze tubes of mustard and sandwich spreads (shrimp, caviar), rye bread, and boxes of juice and milk. Grocery stores sell a cheap, light breakfast: a handy yogurt with cereal and a spoon. Most places offer cheap ready-made sandwiches. If you're bored with sandwiches, some groceries and most delis have hot chicken, salads by the portion, and picnic portables.

Dinner

The large meal of the Nordic day is an early dinner. Most Scandinavians eat dinner at home, and restaurant dinners are expensive treats. Alternate between picnic dinners (outside or in your hotel or hostel); cheap, forgettable, but filling cafeteria or fast-food dinners ($20); and atmospheric, carefully chosen restaurants popular with locals ($35 and up). One main course and two salads or soups fill up two travelers without emptying their pocketbooks. If potatoes came with your main dish, most servers are happy to give you a second helping. Booze is pricey: A beer costs about $8 in Oslo. Water is served free with an understanding smile at most restaurants (though in Denmark, there is a charge for water if you don't order another beverage).

In Scandinavia, a $30 meal in a restaurant is not that much more than a $20 American meal, since tax and tip are included in the menu price.

Most Scandinavian nations have one inedible dish that is cherished with a perverse but patriotic sentimentality. These dishes, which often originated during a famine, now remind the young of their ancestors' suffering. Norway's penitential food, lutefisk (dried cod marinated for days in lye and water), is used for Christmas and for jokes.

Smörgåsbord

The *smörgåsbord* (known in Denmark and Norway as the *store koldt bord*) is a revered Scandinavian culinary tradition. Though locals reserve the *smörgåsbord* for certain holidays and other festive occasions, travelers can dig into this all-you-can-eat buffet any time of year. *Smörgåsbord* translates to something like "bread

and butter table." It has evolved over the centuries to the elaborate spread popular today. A modern *smörgåsbord* is best accented with a local firewater (see "Drinking," below).

Seek out a *smörgåsbord* at least once during your trip to sample the culinary delights of the Nordic lands. Good *smörgåsbord* opportunities covered in this book are at the Grand Hotels in Stockholm and Oslo; on the overnight boats between Stockholm and Helsinki or Copenhagen and Oslo; and at Kviknes Hotel in the Norwegian fjordside town of Balestrand.

Follow these simple steps to enjoy a *smaklig* (tasty) *smörgåsbord*:

1. Browse the buffet before you begin, so you can budget your stomach space. Think of the *smörgåsbord* as a five- or six-course meal.

2. Don't overload your plate. Instead, make several trips, taking a fresh plate and cutlery each time. To signal the waiter that you're finished with each round, lay your fork and knife side-by-side on the plate. If you're getting up but are not finished with your plate, place your fork and knife in the shape of an X on the plate.

3. Begin with the herring dishes, along with boiled potatoes and *knäckebröd* (Swedish crisp bread).

4. Next, sample the other fish dishes (warm and cold) and more potatoes. *Gravlax* is salt-cured salmon flavored with dill, served along with a sweet mustard sauce *(gravlax senap)*.

5. Move on to salads, egg dishes, and various cold cuts.

6. Now for the meat dishes—it's meatball time! Pour on some gravy as well as a spoonful of lingonberry sauce, and have more potatoes. Reindeer and other roast meats and poultry may also tempt you.

7. Still hungry? Make a point to sample the Nordic cheeses—try creamy Havarti, mild Castello (a soft bleu cheese), and in Norwegian buffets, goat cheese. Sample the delicious seasonal fruits and *franskbrød* white bread. And there are racks of traditional desserts, cakes, and custards (see "Dessert," later). Cap the meal with coffee.

Smaklig måltid! Enjoy your meal!

Drinking

Purchasing wine, beer, and spirits in Scandinavia can put a dent in your vacation budget. In Sweden and Norway, spirits, wine, and strong beer (more than 3.5 percent alcohol) are sold in state-run liquor stores: Systembolaget in Sweden, and Vinmonopolet in Norway. (Rumor has it, though, that Sweden will soon liberalize its booze sales.) Buying a beer or glass of wine in a bar or restaurant in Sweden or Norway is particularly expensive. Therefore, many Scandinavians will have a drink or a glass of wine at home (or in their hotel room) before going out, then limit themselves to one or two glasses at the restaurant. If taking an overnight cruise during your trip, you can get a good deal on a bottle of wine or spirits in the onboard duty-free shop. Liquor laws are much more relaxed in Denmark, where you can buy wine, beer, and spirits at any supermarket or corner store. Prices are a bit lower as well. Public drinking is acceptable in Denmark, while it is illegal (although often done) in Norway and Sweden. Throughout Scandinavia, drinking and driving is not tolerated.

Some local specialties are *akvavit,* a strong, vodka-like spirit distilled from potatoes and flavored with anise, caraway, or other herbs and spices—then drunk ice-cold (common in Norway, Sweden, and Denmark). *Lakka* is a syrupy-sweet liqueur made from cloudberries, the small orange berries grown in the Arctic (popular in Norway, Sweden, and Finland). *Salmiakka* is a nearly black licorice-flavored liqueur (Finland, Norway, and Denmark). *Gammel Dansk* can be described as Danish bitters for the adventurous (Denmark only).

Dessert

Scandinavians love sweets. A meal is not complete without a little treat and a cup of coffee at the end. Bakeries *(konditori)* fill their window cases with all varieties of cakes, tarts, cookies, and pastries. The most popular ingredients are marzipan, almonds, hazelnuts, chocolate, and fresh berries. Many cakes are covered with entire sheets of solid marzipan. To find the neighborhood bakery, just look for a golden pretzel hanging above the door or windows.

Scandinavian chocolate is some of the best in Europe. In Denmark, seek out Anthon Berg's dark chocolate and marzipan treats as well as Toms' chocolate-covered caramels (Toms Guld are

How Was Your Trip?

Were your travels fun, smooth, and meaningful? If you'd like to share your tips, concerns, and discoveries, please fill out the survey at www.ricksteves.com/feedback. I value your feedback. Thanks in advance—it helps a lot.

the best). Sweden's biggest chocolate producer, Maribou, makes huge bars of solid milk chocolate, as well as some with dried fruits or nuts. *Daim* are milk chocolate-covered hard toffees, sold in a variety of sizes, from large bars to bite-size pieces, all in bright-red wrappers. The Freia company, Norway's chocolate goddess (named for the Norse goddess Freya), makes a wonderful assortment of delights, from *Et lite stykke Norge* ("A little piece of Norway"—bars of creamy milk chocolate wrapped in pale-yellow paper) and *Smil* (chocolate-covered soft caramels sold in rolls) to *Firkløver* (bars of milk chocolate with hazelnuts). For those who can't decide on one type, the company sells bags of assorted chocolates called *Twist* and red gift boxes of chocolates called *Kong Haakon,* named after Norway's first king.

While chocolate rules, licorice and gummy candies are also popular. Black licorice *(lakrits)* is at its best here, except for *salt lakrits* (salty licorice), which is not for the timid. Black licorice flavors everything from ice cream to chewing gum to liqueur (see "Drinking," above). Throughout Scandinavia, you'll find stores selling all varieties of candy in bulk. Fill your bag with a variety of candies and pay by the gram. Look around at the customers in these stores...they aren't all children.

Traveling as a Temporary Local

We travel all the way to Scandinavia to enjoy differences—to become temporary locals. You'll experience frustrations. Certain truths that we find "God-given" or "self-evident," such as cold beer, ice in drinks, bottomless cups of coffee, hot showers, and bigger being better, are suddenly not so true. One of the benefits of travel is the eye-opening realization that there are logical, civil, and even better alternatives.

While the materialistic culture of the US is sneaking into these countries, simplicity has yet to become subversive. Scandinavians are into "sustainable affluence." They have experimented aggressively in the area of social welfare—with mixed results. Travel in high-tax/high-government service Scandinavia can rattle capitalist Americans. The people seem so happy and the society seems so genteel. Fit in, don't look for things American on the other side of the Atlantic, and you're sure to enjoy some thought-provoking stimulation and a full dose of Scandinavian hospitality.

Americans are enjoying a surge in popularity in Europe these days. But if there is a negative aspect to the image Europeans have of Americans, it is that we are big, loud, aggressive, impolite, rich, superficially friendly, and a bit naive.

Americans tend to be noisy in public places, such as restaurants and trains. My European friends place a high value on speaking quietly in these same places. Listen while on the bus or in a restaurant—the place can be packed, but the decibel level is low. Try to remember this nuance, and soften your speaking voice as a way of respecting their culture.

While Europeans look bemusedly at some of our Yankee excesses—and worriedly at others—they nearly always afford us individual travelers all the warmth we deserve. Judging from all the happy feedback I receive from travelers who have used this book, it's safe to assume you'll enjoy a great, affordable vacation—with the finesse of an independent, experienced traveler.

Thanks, and happy travels!

Back Door Travel Philosophy

From *Rick Steves' Europe Through the Back Door*

Travel is intensified living—maximum thrills per minute and one of the last great sources of legal adventure. Travel is freedom. It's recess, and we need it.

Experiencing the real Europe requires catching it by surprise, going casual..."Through the Back Door."

Affording travel is a matter of priorities. (Make do with the old car.) You can travel—simply, safely, and comfortably—anywhere in Europe for $120 a day plus transportation costs. In many ways, spending more money only builds a thicker wall between you and what you came to see. Europe is a cultural carnival, and, time after time, you'll find that its best acts are free and the best seats are the cheap ones.

A tight budget forces you to travel close to the ground, meeting and communicating with the people, not relying on service with a purchased smile. Never sacrifice sleep, nutrition, safety, or cleanliness in the name of budget. Simply enjoy the local-style alternatives to expensive hotels and restaurants.

Connecting with people carbonates your experience. Extroverts have more fun. If your trip is low on magic moments, kick yourself and make things happen. If you don't enjoy a place, maybe you don't know enough about it. Seek the truth. Recognize tourist traps. Give a culture the benefit of your open mind. See things as different but not better or worse. Any culture has much to share.

Of course, travel, like the world, is a series of hills and valleys. Be fanatically positive and militantly optimistic. If something's not to your liking, change your liking.

Travel can make you a happier American as well as a citizen of the world. Our Earth is home to six and a half billion equally important people. It's humbling to travel and find that people don't have the "American Dream"—they have their own dreams. Europeans like us, but, with all due respect, they wouldn't trade passports.

Thoughtful travel engages us with the world. In tough economic times, it reminds us what is truly important. By broadening perspectives, travel teaches new ways to measure quality of life.

Globe-trotting destroys ethnocentricity, helping you understand and appreciate different cultures. Rather than fear the diversity on this planet, celebrate it. Among your prized souvenirs will be the strands of different cultures you choose to knit into your own character. The world is a cultural yarn shop, and Back Door travelers are weaving the ultimate tapestry. Join in!

SCANDINAVIA

SCANDINAVIA

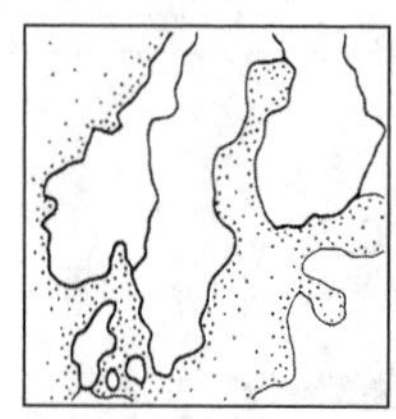

Scandinavia is Western Europe's least populated, most literate, most prosperous, most demographically homogeneous, most highly taxed, most socialistic, and least churchgoing corner. For the visitor, it's a land of Viking ships, brooding castles, salty harbors, deep green fjords, stave churches, and farmhouses—juxtaposed with the sleek modernism of its people-friendly cities.

The name "Scandinavia" technically means only the two countries—Sweden and Norway—that inhabit the Scandinavian Peninsula. But historically and culturally, it includes neighbors Denmark and Finland (and the term is often extended to Iceland and others). "Scandinavia" may be Old German for "dangerous island," as ancient mariners thought the treacherous coasts to be. Separated from the continent by water, distance, and cold weather, Scandinavia evolved on a course parallel to the rest of Europe—but while much of Europe was Latinized and Christianized in Roman times, Scandinavia stayed closer to its pagan, tribal roots. (For more background, see the Scandinavian History chapter.)

Scandinavia is blessed with natural beauty. The cavernous fjords of Norway's west coast are famous. Much of the region has mountains, lakes, green forests, and waterfalls. By contrast, low-lying Denmark has its rugged islands, salty harbors, and windswept sandy coasts.

Climate-wise, Scandinavia has four distinct seasons. With Alaska-like latitudes, it's the "land of the midnight sun" in summer (18 hours of daylight) and of midafternoon darkness in winter (six hours of daylight).

Most of Scandinavia is sparsely populated and very big. Sweden is the size of California, but has only a quarter the people (9 million). Nearly 5 million Norwegians stretch out in Norway, where Oslo is as far from the northern tip of Norway as it is from Rome. The exception is Denmark, which packs 5.5 million fun-loving Danes into a flat land the size of Switzerland.

Scandinavian society is carefully organized to maximize

prosperity and happiness for everyone. With its wealth, Scandinavia is the home of cradle-to-grave security. Residents pay hefty taxes but get a hefty return. Children are educated. The old and sick are cared for. Cities are carefully planned to be clean, green, crime-free, and built on a human scale—with parks, fountains, public art, and pedestrian zones.

Generally speaking, citizens willingly share the burden for the common good. High taxes mean there's less of a gap between the very rich and the very poor, resulting in a less class-oriented society. Scandinavians are proud of this. If they seem a bit smug, you can't fault them, because statistics verify that they live longer, healthier, happier lives. In the UN Human Development Index for 2008, Norway, Sweden, Denmark, and Finland all ranked in the top 15 most livable countries.

Scandinavians are united by their common ethnicity, though recent immigration is changing that. Also, though each of the Scandinavian countries has its own language, there are some common threads. Danes and Norwegians can read each other's newspapers and can converse somewhat (but with difficulty because of thick accents). Swedes (whose written language is different) have a hard time with printed Danish and Norwegian, but can carry on simple conversations. Many Finns (whose language is not related at all) can talk with Swedes because of Sweden's long historical presence in Finland. Despite these common denominators, communication can be difficult due to one more factor—national pride. A Dane may simply pretend not to understand a Swede's request, and vice versa. If there's ever a language barrier, though, most Scandinavians can easily revert to their common second language—English.

It's not easy (and probably unwise) to make sweeping generalizations about a region's people, but here goes: In general, Scandinavians are confident, happy, healthy, and tall. They speak their minds frankly, even about taboo subjects like sex. They're strong individualists who cut others slack for their own eccentricities. They don't fawn on the rich and famous or look down on the down and out. At work, they're efficient and conscientious. They don't take cuts in line. They're well-educated, well-traveled, and worldly. Though reserved and super-polite at first, they have a good sense of humor and don't take life or themselves too seriously.

Scandi-hoovians You Might Know

Famous Norwegians

Leif Eriksson, Viking discoverer of America
Edvard Grieg, Romantic composer
Edvard Munch, *The Scream* painter
Henrik Ibsen, playwright
Roald Amundsen, Antarctic explorer
Gustav Vigeland, sculptor
Sonja Henie, figure skater and movie actress
Thor Heyerdahl, explorer of *Kon-Tiki* fame
Jan Stenerud, NFL placekicker
Liv Ullman, movie actress and director
Rick Steves, travel writer

Famous Danes

Hans Christian Andersen, writer of *The Ugly Duckling, The Little Mermaid,* etc.
Søren Kierkegaard, proto-existentialist philosopher
Bertel Thorvaldsen, sculptor
Karen Blixen, wrote *Out of Africa* under pen name Isak Dinesen
Niels Bohr, physicist who described the atom as a tiny planetary system
Victor Borge, classical-music comedian
Arne Jacobsen, architect
Lars Ulrich, drummer for rock band Metallica
Brigitte Nielsen and Viggo Mortensen (half Danish), movie actors

Scandinavians work hard, but they guard their leisure time fiercely. They like the out-of-doors, perhaps in keeping with the still-rural landscape they live in. For many, a weekend with the family at a (well-furnished) country cottage is all they need. Cycling, boating, and fishing are popular. Internationally, they're known for skiing, speed skating, hockey, and other winter sports. And, as with the rest of Europe, they're wild about football (soccer).

The region is a leader in progressive lifestyles, including recognizing same-sex partnerships. More than half the heterosexual couples in Denmark are "married" only because they've lived together for so long and have children. Families are small, with one or two children. Wives and mothers generally have a job outside the home. While the state religion is Lutheran, only a small percentage of Scandinavians actually attend church other than at Easter or Christmas. Most are either indifferent or assertively secular.

Scandinavia is rich, with a very high standard of living (as

Lars von Trier, movie director
Morten Andersen, NFL placekicker and all-time leading scorer

Famous Swedes

Anders Celsius, inventor of the temperature scale
Carolus Linnaeus, botanist who developed taxonomic naming system
August Strindberg, playwright
Alfred Nobel, inventor of dynamite and the Nobel Peace Prize
Carl Milles, sculptor
Astrid Lindgren, children's author who created *Pippi Longstocking*
Greta Garbo, actress
Ingmar Bergman, movie director
Max von Sydow, actor
Dag Hammarskjöld, UN Secretary General
Björn Borg and Stefan Edberg, tennis players
Hans Blix, UN weapons inspector
Annika Sörenstam and Jesper Parnevik, golfers
ABBA, pop-rock supergroup

Famous Finns

Jean Sibelius, Romantic composer
Alvar Aalto and Eero Saarinen, Modernist architects
Esa-Pekka Salonen, classical conductor

American tourists learn the hard way). Norway has been blessed with offshore oil, Denmark with farmland, and Sweden and Finland with lush forests. They are all fish-rich. Alternative energy sources are important, especially hydroelectric and wind power. Given such pristine natural surroundings, the Scandinavians are environmentalists, committed to preserving their resources for future generations (except for the Norwegians' stubborn appetite for whaling).

Scandinavia is also on the high-tech edge of the global economy. They practice a mix of free-market capitalism and enlightened socialism. Internationally, they make their mark with telecommunications (Nokia from Finland, Ericsson from Sweden), Ikea furniture (originally from Sweden), and Electrolux appliances (Sweden).

Politically, Scandinavia's four countries are all democracies, ruled by a parliament, a prime minister, and a president. Denmark, Norway, and Sweden are constitutional monarchies with a figurehead monarch who cuts ribbons, works with parliament, and tries to stay out of the tabloids. The Scandinavian nations maintain close ties with each other. To some degree or other, they all participate in the European Union (though Norway is not a member, and only Finland uses the euro). Every election brings another debate about how close they want to tie themselves with the rest of Europe. The Scandinavian nations have a tradition of neutrality in wars and a reputation for international cooperation, exemplified by Sweden and Norway's Nobel Peace Prize.

All of Scandinavia's monarchs are descended from Oscar I, King of Sweden and Norway (and son of King Karl Johan XIV), through the House of Bernadotte: Denmark's Queen Margrethe II and Crown Prince Frederik (b. 1968), Sweden's King Carl XVI Gustaf and Crown Princess Victoria (b. 1977), and Norway's King Harald V and Crown Prince Håkon (b. 1973).

Artistically, Scandinavia is known for its serious playwrights (Henrik Ibsen and August Strindberg), brooding filmmakers (Ingmar Bergman), and gloomy painters (Edvard Munch). Nordic mythology is familiar to the English-speaking world for its *Lord of the Rings*–style roots. Hans Christian Andersen and Astrid Lindgren (creator of *Pippi Longstocking*) brought us children's tales. Less familiar are Scandinavia's people-friendly sculptors—Bertel Thorvaldsen, Gustav Vigeland, and Carl Milles—whose noble, realistic statues evoke the human spirit. Architecturally, Scandinavia continues to lead the way, with sleek modern buildings that fit in with the natural landscape. Late–20th-century Modernism (or Functionalism) had several Scandinavian champions, including Eero Saarinen and Alvar Aalto (Finland) and Arne Jacobsen (Denmark). Musically, Scandinavia is known for classical composers like Grieg (Norway) and Sibelius (Finland) who celebrate the region's nature and folk tunes. Scandinavia's cities have thriving jazz scenes that rival America's. Oh yes, and then there's Scandinavia's biggest musical export—the '70s pop band from Sweden named ABBA.

The Scandinavian flair for art shines best in the design of everyday objects. They fashion chairs, lamps, and coffeemakers to be both functional and beautiful: sleek, with no frills, where the "beauty" comes from how well it works. In their homes,

Scandinavians strive for a coziness that mixes modern practicality with traditional designs—carved wood and old flower-and-vine patterns.

Despite its ultra-modern, progressive outlook, Scandinavia still honors its traditions. Parents tell kids the old folk tales about grumpy, clever trolls, and gardeners dot their yards with friendly garden gnomes. At midsummer, you'll see locals in traditional clothes dancing around a maypole to the tunes of a folk band. At winter solstice and Christmas, they enjoy Yule cakes and winter beer. Scandinavia is sailing into the high-tech future on the hardy ship of its Viking past.

DENMARK

DENMARK

Danmark

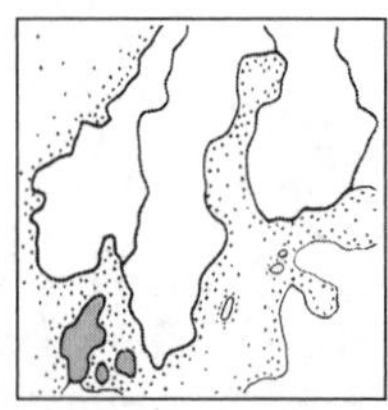

Denmark is by far the smallest of the Scandinavian countries, but in the 16th century, it was the largest—at one time, Denmark ruled all of Norway and the three southern provinces of Sweden. Danes are proud of their mighty history and are the first to remind you that they were a lot bigger and a lot stronger in the good old days.

In the 10th century, before its heyday as a Scan-superpower, Denmark was, like Norway and Sweden, home to the Vikings. More than anything else, these fierce warriors were known for their great shipbuilding, which enabled them to travel far. Denmark's Vikings journeyed west to Great Britain and Ireland (where they founded Dublin) and brought back various influences, including Christianity.

Denmark is composed of many islands, a peninsula (Jutland) that juts up from northern Germany, Greenland, and the Faroe Islands. The two main islands are Zealand, where Copenhagen is located, and Funen, where H. C. Andersen was born. Out of the hundreds of smaller islands, ship-in-bottle cute Æro is my favorite. Danes like to say you can stand on a beer crate anywhere in the country and see the sea, and in fact, no part of the country is more than 30 miles from the ocean. The Danish landscape is gentle compared to the dramatic fjords, mountains, and vast lakes of other Scandinavian nations. Denmark's highest point in Jutland is only 560 feet above sea level. In contrast to the rest of Scandinavia, much of Denmark is arable. The landscape consists of rolling hills, small thatched-roof farmhouses, beech forests, and whitewashed churches with characteristic stairstep gables.

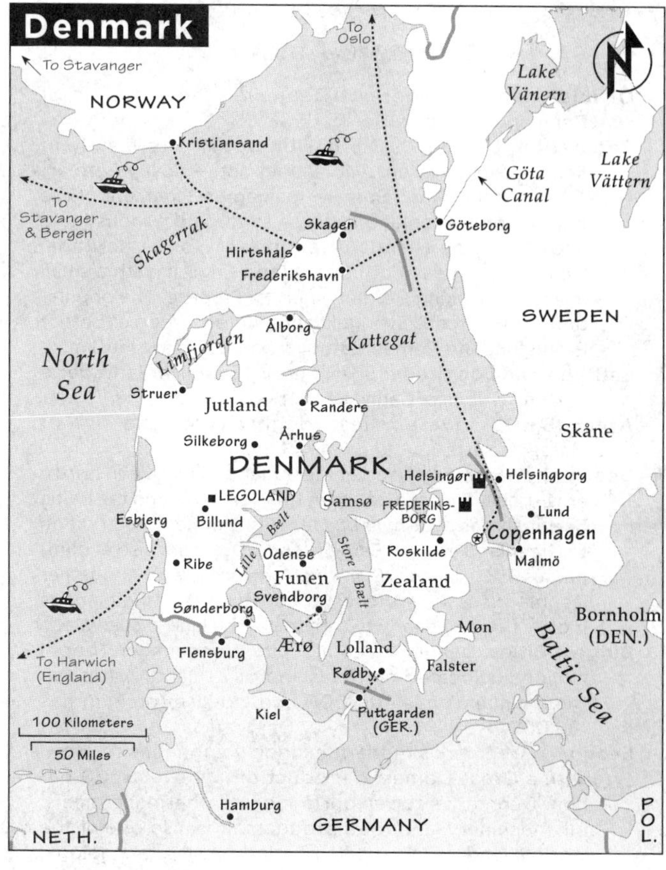

Like the other Scandinavian countries, Denmark is predominantly Lutheran, but only a small minority attend church regularly. The majority are ethnic Danes, and many (but certainly not all) of them have the stereotypical blond hair and blue eyes. Two out of three Danes have last names ending in "-sen." The assimilation of ethnic groups into this homogeneous society, which began in earnest in the 1980s, is a source of some controversy. But in general, most Danes have a live-and-let-live attitude and enjoy one of the highest standards of living in the world. Taxes are high in this welfare state, but education is free and medical care highly subsidized. Generous maternity leave extends to both men and women.

Denmark, one of the most environmentally conscious European countries, is a front-runner in renewable energy, recycling, and organic farming. You'll see lots of modern windmills dotting

Denmark Almanac

Official Name: Kongeriget Danmark—the Kingdom of Denmark—or simply Denmark.

Population: Denmark's 5.5 million people are mainly of Scandinavian descent, with immigrants—mostly German, Turkish, Iranian, and Somali—making up 9 percent of the population. Greenland is home to the indigenous Inuit, and the Faroe Islands to people of Nordic heritage. Most Danes speak both Danish and English, with a small minority speaking German, Inuit, or Faroese. The population is 95 percent Evangelical Lutheran, 3 percent other Protestant and Roman Catholic, and 2 percent Muslim.

Latitude and Longitude: 56°N and 10°E, similar latitude to northern Alberta, Canada.

Area: 16,600 square miles, roughly twice the size of Massachusetts.

Geography: Denmark includes the Jutland peninsula in northern Europe. Situated between the North Sea and the Baltic Sea, it shares a 42-mile border with Germany. In addition to Greenland and the Faroe Islands, Denmark also encompasses 400 islands (78 of which are inhabited). Altogether Denmark has 4,544 miles of coastline. The mainland is mostly flat, and nearly two-thirds of the land is cultivated.

Biggest Cities: Denmark's capital city, Copenhagen (pop. 1 million), is located on the island of Zealand. Århus (on the mainland) has 400,000 and Odense (on Fyn) has 186,000.

Economy: Denmark's modern economy continues to grow, with a Gross Domestic Product of just over $200 billion. Denmark's top exports include pharmaceuticals, oil, machinery, and food products. It is also one of the world's leaders in exports of wind turbine technology. The GDP per capita is about $37,000.

Currency: 5 Danish kroner (kr) = about $1.

Government: Denmark is a constitutional monarchy. Queen Margrethe II is the head of state, but the head of government is the prime minister, a post held since April 2009 by Lars Løkke Rasmussen. The 179-member parliament (Folketinget) is elected every four years.

Flag: The Danish flag is red with a white cross.

The Average Dane: The average Dane is 40 years old, has 1.74 children, and will live to be 78. About 71 percent of Danish women are employed outside the home. About 53 percent of Danes own a home or apartment, 83 percent own a mobile phone, and 78 percent have Internet access.

the countryside. Since the country lacks other sources of power, wind power accounts for 20 percent of Denmark's energy today, with a goal of 50 percent by 2030. Half of all waste is recycled. In grocery stores, organic products are shelved right alongside nonorganic ones—for the same price.

Denmark's Queen Margrethe II is a very popular and talented woman who, along with her royal duties, has designed coins, stamps, and book illustrations. Danes gather around the TV on New Year's Eve to hear her annual speech to the nation and flock to the Royal Palace in Copenhagen on April 16 to sing her "Happy Birthday." Her son, Crown Prince Frederik, married Australian Mary Donaldson in 2004. Their son Christian's birth in 2005 was cause for a national celebration.

The Danes are proud of their royal family and of the flag, a white cross on a red background. Legend says it fell from the sky during a 13th-century battle in Estonia, making it Europe's oldest continuously used flag. You'll see it everywhere—decorating cakes, on clothing, or fluttering in the breeze atop government buildings. It's as much a decorative symbol as a patriotic one.

From an early age, Danes develop a passion for soccer. You may see red-and-white-clad fans singing on their way to a match. Despite the country's small size, the Danish national team does well in international competition. Other popular sports include sailing, cycling, badminton, and team handball.

The Danish language, with its three extra vowels (Æ, Ø, and Å), is notoriously difficult for foreigners to pronounce. Luckily for us, almost everyone also speaks English. Danes have playful fun teasing tourists who make the brave attempt to say Danish words. The hardest phrase, *rød grød med fløde* (a delightful red fruit porridge topped with cream), is nearly impossible for a non-Dane to pronounce. Ask a local to help you.

Sample Denmark's sweet treats at one of the many bakeries you'll see. The pastries that we call "Danish" in the US are called *wienerbrød* in Denmark. Bakeries line their display cases with several varieties of *wienerbrød* and other delectable sweets. Try *kringle, snegle,* or *Napoleonshatte,* or find your own favorite. (Chances are it will be easier to enjoy than to pronounce.)

For a selection of useful Danish survival phrases, see page 591. Two important words to know are *skål* ("cheers," a ritual always done with serious eye contact) and *hyggelig* (pronounced HEW-glee), meaning warm and cozy. Danes treat their home like a sanctuary and spend a great deal of time improving their gardens and houses—inside and out. Cozying up one's personal space (a national obsession) is something the Danes do best. If you have the opportunity, have some Danes adopt you while you are in Denmark so you can enjoy their warm hospitality.

Heaven to a Dane is returning home after a walk in a beloved beech forest to enjoy open-faced sandwiches washed down with beer among good friends. Around the *hyggelig* candlelit table, there will be a spirited discussion of the issues of the day, plenty of laughter, and probably a few good-natured jokes about the Swedes or Norwegians. *Skål!*

COPENHAGEN

København

Copenhagen, Denmark's capital, is the gateway to Scandinavia. And now that the Øresund Bridge connects Sweden and Denmark (creating the region's largest metropolitan area), Copenhagen is energized and ready to dethrone Stockholm as Scandinavia's powerhouse city. A busy day cruising the canals, wandering through the palace, and taking an old-town walk will give you your historical bearings. Then, after another day strolling the Strøget (STROY-et, Europe's first and greatest pedestrian shopping mall), biking the canals, and sampling the Danish good life, you'll feel right at home. Live it up in Scandinavia's cheapest and most fun-loving capital.

In 2010, *The Little Mermaid*, Copenhagen's most-photographed statue, will be traveling just like you. For much of the year, she'll be absent from her rock in the city's harbor, as she visits Shanghai, China, to represent Denmark at the World Expo. You may see a temporary version created by Chinese sculptors in her place, and can visit a replica of *The Little Mermaid* at Tivoli Gardens.

Planning Your Time

A first visit deserves a minimum of two days.

Day 1: Catch a 10:30 city walking tour (mid-May–mid-Sept daily except Sun; described later under "Tours in Copenhagen"). After lunch at Riz-Raz, catch the relaxing canal-boat tour out to *The Little Mermaid* site and back. Enjoy the rest of the afternoon tracing Denmark's cultural roots in the National Museum and visiting the Ny Carlsberg Glyptotek art gallery (Impressionists and Danish artists). Spend the evening strolling the Strøget (follow my self-guided walk).

Day 2: At 10:00, go Neoclassical at Thorvaldsen's Museum (closed Mon). At 11:00, take the 50-minute guided tour of Denmark's royal Christiansborg Palace (daily May–Sept). After a *smørrebrød* lunch, spend the afternoon seeing the Rosenborg Castle/crown jewels and the Museum of Danish Resistance. Spend the evening at Tivoli Gardens.

Christiania—the hippie squatters' community—is not for everyone. But it's worth considering if you're intrigued by alternative lifestyles, or simply want a break from the museums. During a busy trip, Christiania fits best in the evening.

Budget Itinerary Tip: Remember the efficiency and cost-effectiveness of sleeping while traveling in and out of town (saving time and hotel costs). Consider taking an overnight train (via Malmö) to Stockholm or Oslo, or cruise up to Oslo on a night boat. Kamikaze sightseers see Copenhagen as a useful Scandinavian bottleneck. They sleep in and out heading north into Scandinavia, and in and out heading south at the end of their Scandinavian travels, with two days and no nights in Copenhagen (you can check your bag and take a shower at the train station). Considering the joy of Oslo and Stockholm, this isn't all that crazy if you have limited time and can sleep on a moving train or boat.

Orientation to Copenhagen

For most visitors, the core of Copenhagen is the axis formed by the train station, Tivoli Gardens, Rådhuspladsen (City Hall Square), and the Strøget pedestrian street, ending at the colorful old Nyhavn sailors' harbor. Bubbling with street life, colorful pedestrian zones, and most of the city's sightseeing, this main drag is fun (and most of it is covered by my self-guided walk in this chapter). But also be sure to get off the Strøget and explore. By doing things by bike or on foot, you'll stumble onto some charming bits of Copenhagen that many miss.

Outside of the old city center are three areas of interest to tourists:

1. To the north are Rosenborg Castle and *The Little Mermaid* area (Amalienborg Palace and Museum of Danish Resistance).

2. To the east are Christianshavn (Copenhagen's "Little Amsterdam" district) and the alternative enclave of Christiania.

3. To the west is Vesterbro, a young and trendy part of town with lots of cafés, bars, and boutiques; the picnic-friendly Frederiksberg park; and the Carlsberg Brewery.

All of these sights are walkable from the Strøget, but taking a bike, bus, or taxi is more efficient. I rent a bike for my entire visit

The Story of Copenhagen

If you study your map carefully, you can read the history of Copenhagen in today's street plan. København (literally, "Merchants' Harbor") was born on the little island of Slotsholmen—today home of Christiansborg Palace—in 1167. What was Copenhagen's medieval moat is now a string of pleasant lakes and parks, including Tivoli Gardens. You can still make out some of the zigzag pattern of the moats and ramparts in the city's greenbelt.

Many of these fortifications—and several other landmarks—were built by Denmark's most memorable king. You need to remember one character in Copenhagen's history: Christian IV. Ruling from 1588 to 1648, he was Denmark's Renaissance king and a royal party animal (see the "King Christian IV" sidebar, later). The personal energy of this "Builder King" sparked a Golden Age when Copenhagen prospered and many of the city's grandest buildings were erected. In the 17th century, Christian IV extended the city fortifications to the north, doubling the size of the city, while adding a grid plan of streets and his Rosenborg Castle. This old "new town" has the Amalienborg Palace and *The Little Mermaid* site.

In 1850, Copenhagen's 140,000 residents all lived within this defensive system. Building in the no-man's-land outside the walls was only allowed with the understanding that in the event of an attack, you'd burn your dwellings to clear the way for a good defense.

Most of the city's historic buildings still in existence were built within the medieval walls, but conditions became too crowded, and outbreaks of disease forced Copenhagen to spread outside the walls. Ultimately those walls were torn down and replaced with "rampart streets" that define today's city center: Vestervoldgade (literally, "West Rampart Street"), Nørrevoldgade ("North"), and Østervoldgade ("East"). The fourth side is the harbor and the island of Slotsholmen, where København was born.

(for about the cost of a single cab ride per day) and park it safely in my hotel courtyard. I get anywhere in the town center literally faster than by taxi (nearly anything is within a 10-minute pedal). The city is an absolute delight by bike (for more on biking in Copenhagen, see "Getting Around Copenhagen: By Bike," later).

Tourist Information

Copenhagen This Week is a free, handy, and misnamed monthly guide to the city, worth reading for its good maps, museum hours with telephone numbers, sightseeing tour ideas, shopping suggestions, and calendar of events, including free English tours and

concerts (online at www.ctw.dk). This is *the* essential listing of everything in town, and it's always the most up-to-date information in print. You can pick it up at some information offices, most hotels and many sites, but it's often unavailable at the city's poor excuse for a tourist office (self-dubbed "Wonderful Copenhagen"—see below). The Danish Tourist Board's website also has a wealth of information on activities and events in Copenhagen (www.visitdenmark.com).

Copenhagen offers its visitors no real tourist information office. An advertising bureau called **"Wonderful Copenhagen"** bills itself as the TI, but is actually a blatantly for-profit company—providing information only about businesses that pay a hefty display fee (thousands of dollars a year). This colors the advice and information the office provides. As you can get the free city map and *Copenhagen This Week* almost anywhere, the office is worthwhile only as a big rack of advertising brochures (July–Aug Mon–Sat 9:00–20:00, less on Sun and off-season, across from train station at Vesterbrogade 4A, tel. 70 22 24 42, www.visitcopenhagen.com).

The **Copenhagen Card,** which includes free entry to many of the city's sights and all local transportation, can save you some money if you're sightseeing like crazy (225 kr/24 hours, 450 kr/72 hours, sold at Wonderful Copenhagen, airport TI, and some hotels).

Arrival in Copenhagen

By Train

The main train station is called Hovedbanegården (HOETH-bahn-gorn; look for *København H* on signs). It's a temple of travel and a hive of travel-related activity, offering **lockers** (30–40 kr/day), a **checkroom** (*garderobe,* 35–45 kr/day per bag, Mon–Sat 5:30–24:00, Sun 6:00–24:00), a **post office** (Mon–Fri 8:00–21:00, Sat–Sun 10:00–16:00), **Internet terminals** (19 kr/hr), **ATMs, Forex** exchange desks (the least expensive place in town to change money, daily 8:00–21:00), 24-hour thievery, and the best **bike-rental shop** in town (see "Getting Around Copenhagen: By Bike," page 58). **Showers** for 15 kr are available in the public restrooms at the back of the station.

While you're in the station, you can plan for your departure by reserving your overnight train seat or *couchette* at the *Billetsalg* office (daily 9:30–18:00). Some international rides and high-speed InterCity trains require reservations (usually 25–55 kr), but railpass-holders can ride any Danish train without a reservation. The *Kviksalg* office sells tickets within Denmark (plus the regional train to Malmö, Sweden). This "quick sale" office will also help you with reservations for international trips if the *Billetsalg* office is closed, or if you're departing by train within one hour or early the next day (daily 5:45–23:30).

By Plane

Kastrup, Copenhagen's international airport, is a traveler's dream, with a TI, baggage check, bank, ATMs, post office, shopping mall, grocery store, and bakery. You can use dollars or euros at the airport, but you'll get change back in kroner (airport info tel. 32 31 32 31, www.cph.dk; SAS info tel. 70 10 20 00).

Getting from the Airport to Downtown: Options include the Metro, trains, and taxis. There are also buses into town, but the Metro or trains generally are better.

The Metro runs directly from the airport to Christianshavn,

Kongens Nytorv, and Nørreport, making it the best choice for getting into town if you're staying in any of these areas (31.50-kr three-zone ticket, yellow M2 line, direction: Vanløse, 4–10/hr, 11 min to Christianshavn). The Metro station is located at the end of Terminal 3 and is covered by the roof of the terminal.

Convenient trains also connect the airport with downtown (31.50-kr three-zone ticket, covered by railpass, 3/hr, 12 min). Buy your ticket from the ground-level ticket booth before riding the escalator down to the tracks. Trains going from the airport into the city stop at the main train station (signed *København H*), as well as the Nørreport and Østerport stations. At Nørreport, you can connect to the Metro for Kongens Nytorv and Christianshavn.

Taxis are fast, civil, accept credit cards, and, at about 250 kr to the town center, are a reasonable deal for foursomes.

Helpful Hints

Emergencies: Dial 112 and specify fire, police, or ambulance. Emergency calls from public phones are free.

US Embassy: It's at Dag Hammerskjölds Allé 24 (passport services open Mon–Tue and Thu–Fri 9:00–12:00, tel. 33 41 71 00, fax 35 43 02 23, after-hours tel. 35 55 92 70, www.denmark.usembassy.gov).

Pharmacy: Steno Apotek is across from the train station (open 24 hours, Vesterbrogade 6c, tel. 33 14 82 66).

Blue Monday: As you plan, remember that most sights close on Monday, but these attractions remain open: Rosenborg Castle (closed Mon Nov–April), Tivoli Gardens (generally closed late Sept–mid-April), a canal tour, walking or bike tours, and Christiania.

Telephones: Use the telephone liberally—everyone speaks English. Calls anywhere in Denmark are cheap; calls to Norway and Sweden cost 6 kr per minute from a booth (half that from a private home). Get a phone card (sold at newsstands, starting at 30 kr). To make inexpensive international calls, buy an international phone card. There are a variety to choose from, varying in price. "Call to All" and "Lotus" are two of many and cost 40 kr for 50 minutes of calls to the US. (7-Eleven stores give you a receipt that acts as the calling card, with instructions and your PIN code.)

Internet Access: Boom Town Netcafé, opposite the main Tivoli entrance (on the corner of Vesterbrogade and Axeltorv), is the biggest Internet and video gaming center in town (open 24 hours daily, 30 kr/hr, 25 kr minimum). Copenhagen's for-profit Internet cafés are expensive, but several places offer free Internet access (designed for quick info and email checks): **Copenhagen Central Library** (most terminals, least wait, midway between

Nørreport and the Strøget at Krystalgade 15, Mon–Fri 10:00–19:00, Sat 10:00–14:00, closed Sun); **"Black Diamond" library** (2 stand-up terminals on the skyway over the street nearest the harbor, see page 82); and the main **university building** (corner of Nørregade and Sankt Peders Stræde, 2 terminals just inside the door). Many cafés offer free Wi-Fi.

Laundry: Pams Møntvask is a good coin-op laundry near Nørreport (45 kr/load wash and dry, daily 6:00–21:00, 50 yards from Ibsens Hotel at 86 Nansensgade). **Tre Stjernet Møntvask** ("Three Star Laundry") is a half-mile behind the train station at Istedgade 45 (45 kr/load wash and dry, daily 6:00–21:00). *Vaskel* is wash, *torring* is dry, and *sæbe* is soap.

Ferries: Book any ferries now that you plan to take later in Scandinavia. Visit a travel agent or call direct. For the Copenhagen–Oslo overnight ferry described on page 111, call **DFDS** (Mon–Fri 9:30–17:00, tel. 33 42 30 00, www.dfds.com) or visit the **DSB Resjebureau** at the main train station. For the cruise from Stockholm to Helsinki described on page 470, call **Silja Line** (tel. 08 22 21 40 www.silja.com).

Jazz Festival: The Copenhagen Jazz Festival—10 days starting the first Friday in July—puts the town in a rollicking slide-trombone mood. The Danes are Europe's jazz enthusiasts, and this music festival fills the town with happiness. Wonderful Copenhagen prints up an extensive listing of each year's festival events, or get the latest at www.jazzfestival.dk. There's also an autumn jazz festival the first week of November.

Getting Around Copenhagen

By Bus, Metro, and S-tog: It's easy to navigate Copenhagen with its fine buses, Metro, and S-tog (a suburban train system with stops in the city; Eurail valid on S-tog).

The same **tickets** are used throughout the system. A 21-kr two-zone ticket gets you an hour's travel within the center (pay as you board buses, or buy from station ticket offices or vending machines for the Metro). Other options include the blue two-zone *klippekort* (130 kr for ten 1-hour rides; note this can be shared—e.g., two people can take five rides each), the 24-hour pass (120 kr, validate by stamping in yellow machine on bus or at station), or the seven-day pass (205 kr, can be a good value even for less than a week). All passes are sold at stations, Wonderful Copenhagen, 7-Elevens, and other kiosks. Assume you'll be within the middle two zones unless traveling to or from the airport, which is in zone 3 (and requires a 31.50-kr three-zone ticket).

Buses go every five to eight minutes during daytime hours. Bus drivers are patient, have change, and speak English. City maps list bus routes. Locals are usually friendly and helpful. There's also

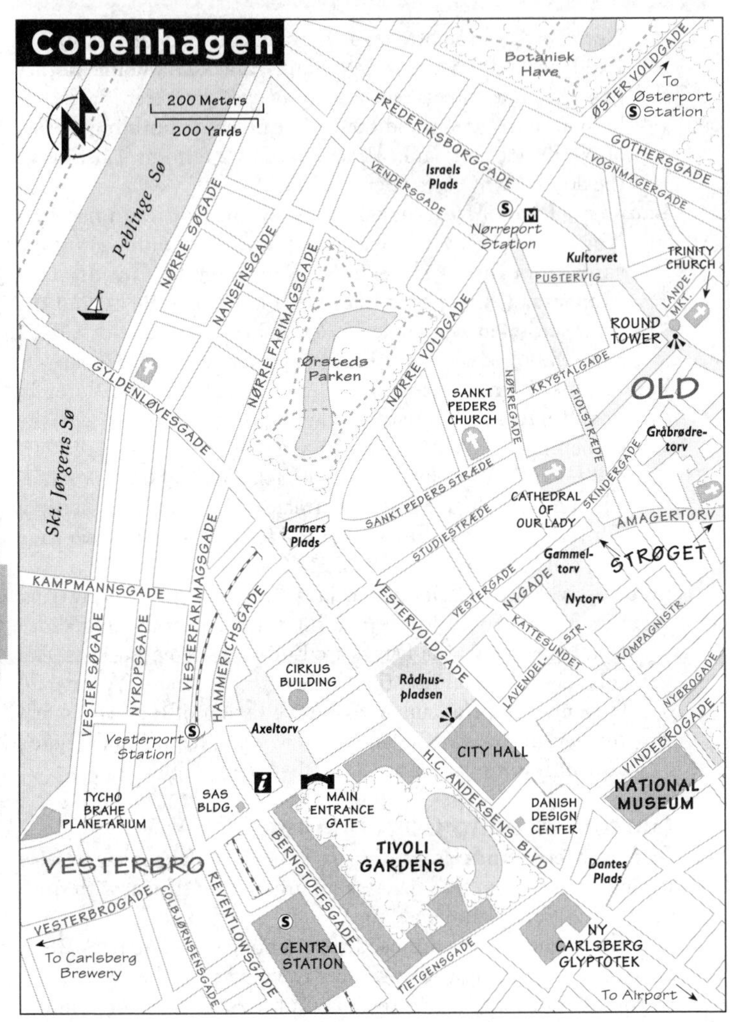

a floating "Harbor Bus" (described below).

Copenhagen's **Metro** line, while simple, is super-futuristic and growing. It now runs to the airport, and eventually will extend to Ørestad, the industrial and business center created after the Øresund Bridge was built between Denmark and Sweden (for the latest on the Metro, see www.m.dk). For most tourists' purposes, only the airport and three consecutive stops within the city matter: Nørreport (connected every few minutes by the S-tog to the main train station), Kongens Nytorv (near Nyhavn and the Strøget's north end), and Christianshavn. All three stops are connected to the airport by the yellow M2 line. Nearly all recommended hotels are within walking

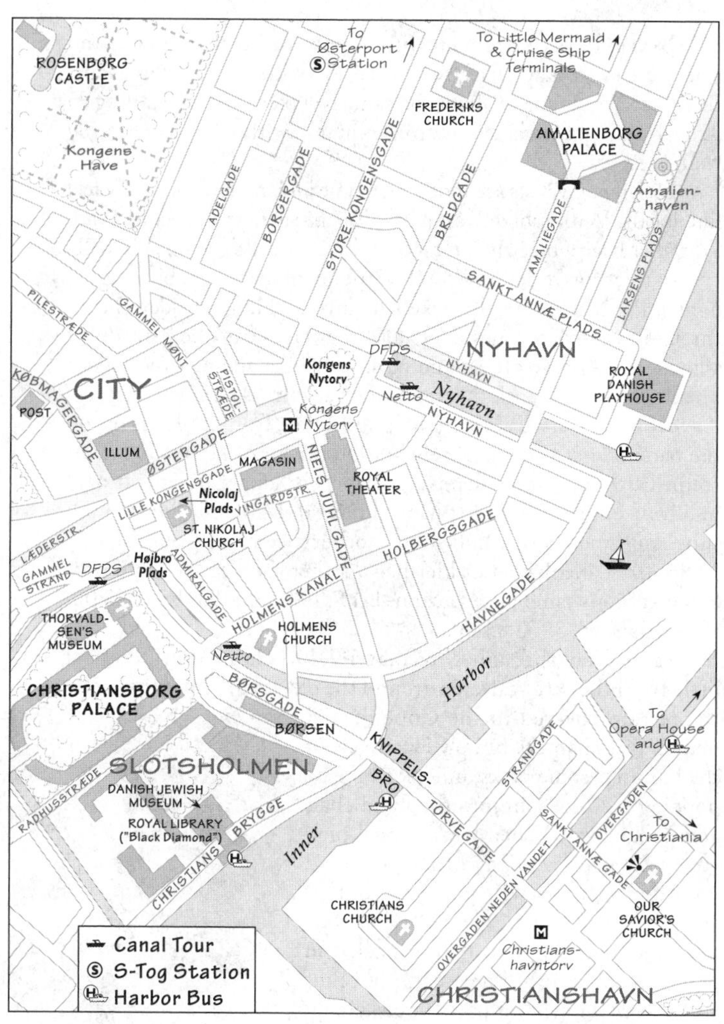

distance of the main train station or these three stops.

By Boat: The hop-on, hop-off **"Harbor Bus"** (Havnebus) boat stops at the "Black Diamond" library, Christianshavn (near Knippels Bridge), Nyhavn, the Opera House, and *The Little Mermaid* site (part of the city bus system—lines #901 and #902—and covered by the tickets described above, runs 6:00–19:00). For sightseeing rather than transportation, consider a harbor cruise (described later under "Tours in Copenhagen").

By Tour Bus: Both **CityCirkel** and **Open Top Tour** buses do a hop-on, hop-off one-hour circle connecting the city's top sights (for details, see "Tours in Copenhagen," later).

By Taxi: Taxis are plentiful, easy to call or flag down, and pricey (26-kr pickup charge and then 13 kr/kilometer). For a short ride, four people spend about the same by taxi as by bus. Calling 35 35 35 35 will get you a taxi within minutes...with the meter already well on its way.

By Bike: Cyclists see more, save time and money, and really feel like locals. With a bike, you have Copenhagen at your command. I'd rather have a bike than a car and driver at my disposal. Virtually every street has a dedicated bike lane (complete with bike signal lights). Police issue 500-kr tickets to anyone riding on sidewalks or through pedestrian zones. Note also that bikes can't be parked just anywhere. Observe others and park your bike among other bikes. The simple built-in lock that binds the back tire is adequate.

Københavns Cykler rents good bikes from its location on the back side of the main train station (85 kr/24 hours, 500 kr or credit-card imprint for deposit, cheaper for longer periods if paid in advance, helmets-20 kr; Mon–Fri 8:00–17:30, Sat 9:00–13:00; July–Aug open Sun 10:00–13:00, otherwise closed Sun; tel. 33 33 86 13). Københavns Cykler has another shop at the Østerport S-tog station (same prices, Mon–Fri 8:00–18:00, Sat 9:00–13:00, closed Sun, tel. 33 33 85 13).

From May through November, 2,400 clunky but practical little **free bikes** are scattered around the old-town center (basically the terrain covered in the Copenhagen map in this chapter). Simply locate one of the hundred-some racks, unlock a bike by popping a 20-kr coin into the handlebar, and pedal away. When you're done, plug your bike back into any other rack, and your deposit coin will pop back out (if you can't find a rack, just abandon your bike and someone will take it back and pocket your coin). These simple bikes come with theft-proof parts (unusable on regular bikes) and—they claim—embedded computer chips so that bike patrols can trace and retrieve strays. The bikes are funded by advertisements painted on the wheels and by a progressive electorate. Copenhagen's radical city-bike program is a clever idea, but in practice, it doesn't work great for sightseers. It's hard to find bikes in working order, and when you get to the sight and park your bike, it'll be gone by the time you're ready to pedal on. (The 20-kr deposit coin acts as an incentive for any kid or homeless person to pick up city bikes not plugged back into their special racks.) Use the free bikes for a one-way pedal here and there. For efficiency, pay to rent one.

Tours in Copenhagen

On Foot

Copenhagen is an ideal city to get to know by foot. You have two good options:

▲▲Richard Karpen's Tours—Once upon a time, American Richard Karpen visited Copenhagen and fell in love with the city (and one of its women). Now, dressed as Hans Christian Andersen, he leads daily 90-minute tours that wander in and out of buildings, courtyards, backstreets, and unusual parts of the old town. Along the way, he gives insightful and humorous background on the history and culture of Denmark, Copenhagen, and the Danes.

Richard offers three entertaining walks: "Castles and Kings," "Royal Copenhagen," and "Romantic Copenhagen." Each walk is a little more than a mile with breaks and covers different parts of the historic center (100 kr apiece, kids under 12 free, departs from Wonderful Copenhagen, mid-May–mid-Sept Mon–Sat at 10:30). Richard's tours, while all different, complement each other and are of equal introduction value. Go whichever day is convenient for you. The earlier you take this tour, the earlier you'll have a good historic orientation.

Richard also does excellent tours of Rosenborg Castle (75 kr, doesn't include castle entry, mid-May–mid-Sept Mon and Thu at 13:30, 90 min, led by dapper Renaissance "Sir Richard," meet outside castle ticket office). You can also hire him for a private tour of the city and Rosenborg Castle (1,000 kr, or save a bit by paying $180 in US dollars, March–Sept, advance notice required, tel. 32 84 74 35).

For details, look for Richard's schedule in *Copenhagen This Week*, at Wonderful Copenhagen, or see www.copenhagenwalks.com. No reservations are needed for Richard's scheduled tours—just show up.

▲▲Copenhagen History Tours—Christian Donatzky, a charming young Dane with a master's degree in history, runs a weekly walking tour. "Danish History 1600–1800" covers the king's Copenhagen and the city's rise as an international business center (March–Oct Sat at 10:00). "Danish History 1800–2000" covers Hans Christian Andersen's Copenhagen and the modern democratic age, March–Oct Sun at 10:00. The tours are thoughtfully designed, and those with a serious interest in Danish history find them time well spent. Strolling with Christian is like walking with your own private Danish encyclopedia (80 kr, approximately

90 min each in small groups of 5–15 people, tours depart from statue of Bishop Absalon on Højbro Plads between the Strøget and Christiansborg Palace, English only, no advance booking necessary—just show up, tel. 28 49 44 35, www.historytours.dk, info@historytours.dk).

By Boat

For many, the best way to experience the city's canals and harbor is by boat. Two companies offer essentially the same live, three-language, one-hour cruises. Both boats leave at least twice an hour from Nyhavn and Christiansborg Palace, cruise around the palace and Christianshavn area, and then proceed into the wide-open harbor. It's a relaxing way to see *The Little Mermaid* (when she's not off in China) and munch on a lazy picnic during the slow-moving narration.

▲Netto-Bådene—These inexpensive cruises cost only half the price of their rival, DFDS. Go with Netto; there's no reason to pay double (30 kr, mid-March–mid-Oct daily 10:00–17:00, later in summer, sign at dock shows next departure, 2–5/hr, dress warmly—boats are open-top until Sept, tel. 32 54 41 02, www.havnerundfart.dk).

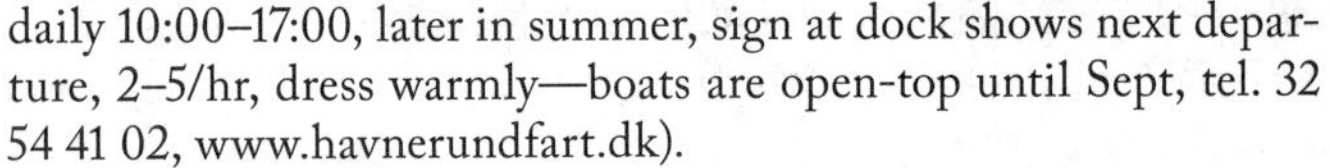

Don't mix up the cheaper Netto and pricier DFDS boats: At Nyhavn, the Netto dock is midway down the canal (on the city side), while the DFDS dock is at the head of the canal. At Christiansborg Palace, the Netto boats leave from Holmen's Bridge in front of the palace, while DFDS boats depart from Gammel Strand, 200 yards away.

DFDS Canal Tours—This more expensive option does the same cruise as Netto for 60 kr (daily March–mid-Oct 9:30–17:00, late June–late Aug until 20:00, mid-Oct–mid-Dec 10:00–15:00, boats are covered if it's raining, tel. 32 96 30 00, www.canaltours.com).

In summer, DFDS also runs unguided hop-on, hop-off **"water bus"** tours (60 kr, late May–Aug daily 10:15–16:45) and two-hour evening **jazz cruises** (see "Nightlife in Copenhagen," page 96).

By Bus

Here are two hop-on, hop-off options, with the cheaper (and unnarrated) option listed first:

CityCirkel Bus #11—Providing an inexpensive and easy overview of the city, bus #11 takes you on a one-hour loop past many of the major sights. You can get on and off anywhere along the route. The quiet, eco-friendly, electric buses are smaller than normal buses, allowing access into the narrower streets of the old town (21 kr, covered by Copenhagen Card, ticket valid one hour and also works on Metro and regular city buses; runs every 7 min, Mon–Fri 9:00–20:00, Sat 10:00–16:00, Sun 11:00–15:00; buy ticket from driver or at any ticket office, kiosk, information office, or Metro vending machine; www.citycirkel.dk). These buses use regular bus stops (shown as #11 with green dots on schedules posted at bus stops) near tourist sights such as Rådhuspladsen, Christiansborg Palace, and Nyhavn. They also have their own special stops, marked with green dots painted on the curb. Just wave one down when you see it coming.

Open Top Tour—City Sightseeing's hop-on, hop-off **Open Top Tour** does the basic one-hour circle of the city sights: Tivoli Gardens, the royal Christiansborg Palace, National Museum, *The Little Mermaid* site, Rosenborg Castle, Nyhavn sailors' quarter, and more, with recorded narration (120 kr, 2/hr, 150 kr includes Carlsberg and Christiana tours, ticket good for 48 hours, April–Oct daily 9:30–17:00; you can get off, see a sight, and catch a later bus; bus departs City Hall below the *Lur Blowers* statue—to the left of City Hall—or at many other stops throughout city, pay driver, run by Copenhagen Excursions, tel. 32 66 00 00, www.citysightseeing.dk).

City Sightseeing also runs jaunts into the countryside, with themes such as Vikings, castles, and Hamlet. There are other companies as well; a variety of guided bus tours depart from Rådhuspladsen in front of the Palace Hotel.

By Bike

▲Bike Copenhagen with Mike—Mike offers a good three-hour, guided tour of the city daily at 10:30 (Mon, Wed, and Fri–Sat also at 15:00). A Copenhagen native, Mike enjoys showing off his city to visitors by biking at a leisurely pace, "along the high roads, low roads, in-roads, and off-roads of Copenhagen." All tours are in English, and depart from the Baisikeli bike shop at Turesensgade 10, off Nansensgade—see the map on page 98 (165 kr, doesn't include bike rental, 85 kr for 24-hour rental, show up 15 min early if you need to rent a bike). Mike also offers a night tour, a countryside tour, and private tours; see the details at www.bikecopenhagenwithmike.dk.

▲City Safari—This three-hour guided bike tour of Copenhagen is seasoned with a little history. Managed by Jon Martin, a fun-loving young historian, the tour covers Christianshavn and comes with a great pedal through the community of Christiania (starting at 250 kr, price depends on size of group, 1,500-kr minimum per-group charge, price includes bike, in English and Danish as needed, generally at 10:00 and 13:30, book by email or phone, then show up 10 min in advance at the Danish Architecture Center, Gammel Dok Storehouse, Strandgade 27B, tel. 33 23 94 90, www.citysafari.dk, basictours@citysafari.dk).

Self-Guided Walk

The Strøget and Copenhagen's Heart and Soul

Start from Rådhuspladsen (City Hall Square), the bustling heart of Copenhagen, dominated by the tower of the City Hall. Today this square always seems to be hosting some lively community event, but it was once Copenhagen's fortified west end. For 700 years, Copenhagen was contained within its city walls. By the mid-1800s, 140,000 people were packed inside. The overcrowding led to hygiene problems. (A cholera outbreak killed 5,000.) It was clear: The walls needed to come down...and they did. Those formidable town walls survive today only in echoes—a circular series of roads and the remnants of moats, now people-friendly city lakes (see "The Story of Copenhagen" sidebar, earlier).

• *Stand 50 yards in front of City Hall and turn clockwise for a...*

Rådhuspladsen Spin-Tour

The **City Hall,** or Rådhus, is worth a visit (described on page 76). Old **Hans Christian Andersen** sits to the right of City Hall, almost begging to be in another photo (as he used to in real life). Climb onto his well-worn knee. (While up there, you might take off your shirt for a racy photo, as many Danes enjoy doing.)

The wooded area behind Andersen is **Tivoli Gardens.** In 1843, magazine publisher Georg Carstensen convinced the king to let him build a pleasure garden outside the walls of crowded Copenhagen. The king quickly agreed, knowing that happy people care less about fighting for democracy. Tivoli became Europe's first great public amusement park. When the train lines came, the station was placed just beyond Tivoli.

The big, broad boulevard is **Vesterbrogade** ("Western Way"), which led to the western gate of the medieval city (behind you, where the pedestrian boulevard begins). Here, in the traffic hub of this huge city, you'll notice...not many cars. Denmark's 180 percent tax on car purchases makes the bus, Metro, or bike a sweeter option.

Down Vesterbrogade towers the **SAS building,** Copenhagen's only skyscraper. Locals say it seems so tall because the clouds hang so low. When it was built in 1960, Copenhageners took one look and decided—that's enough of a skyline.

The golden **weather girls** (on the corner, high above Vesterbrogade) indicate the weather: on a bike (fair weather) or

Hans Christian Andersen (1805–1875)

The author of such classic fairy tales as *The Ugly Duckling* was an ugly duckling himself—a misfit who blossomed. Hans Christian Andersen (called H. C., pronounced "hoe see" by the Danes) was born to a poor shoemaker in Odense. As a child he was gangly, high-strung, and effeminate. He avoided school because the kids laughed at him, so he spent his time in a fantasy world of books and plays. When his father died, the 11-year-old was on his own, forced into manual labor. He moved to Copenhagen and worked as a boy soprano for the Royal Theater. When his voice changed, the director encouraged him to return to school. He dutifully attended—a teenager among boys—and eventually went on to the university.

After graduation, Andersen toured Europe, the first of many trips he'd make and write about. Still in his twenties, he published an (obviously autobiographical) novel, *The Improvisatore,* about a poor young man who comes into his own while traveling in Italy. The novel launched his writing career, and soon he was hobnobbing with the international crowd—Charles Dickens, Victor Hugo, Franz Liszt, Richard Wagner, Henrik Ibsen, and Edvard Grieg.

Though he wrote novels, plays, and travel literature, it was his fairy tales, including *The Ugly Duckling, The Emperor's New Clothes, The Princess and the Pea, The Little Mermaid,* and *The Red Shoes,* that made him famous in Denmark and abroad. They made him Denmark's best-known author, the "Danish Charles Dickens." Some stories are based on earlier folk tales, and others came straight from his inventive mind, all written in conversational language.

The tales appeal to children and adults alike. They're full of magic and touch on strong, universal emotions—the pain of being different, the joy of self-discovery, and the struggle to fit in. The ugly duckling, for example, is teased by his fellow ducks before he finally discovers his true identity as a beautiful swan. In *The Emperor's New Clothes*, a boy is derided by everyone for speaking the simple, self-evident truth that the emperor is fooling himself. (For more on Andersen's famous story *The Little Mermaid*—and what it might tell us about his life—see page 74.)

By the time of his death, the poor shoemaker's son was wealthy, cultured, and had been knighted. His rise through traditional class barriers mirrors the social progress of the 19th century.

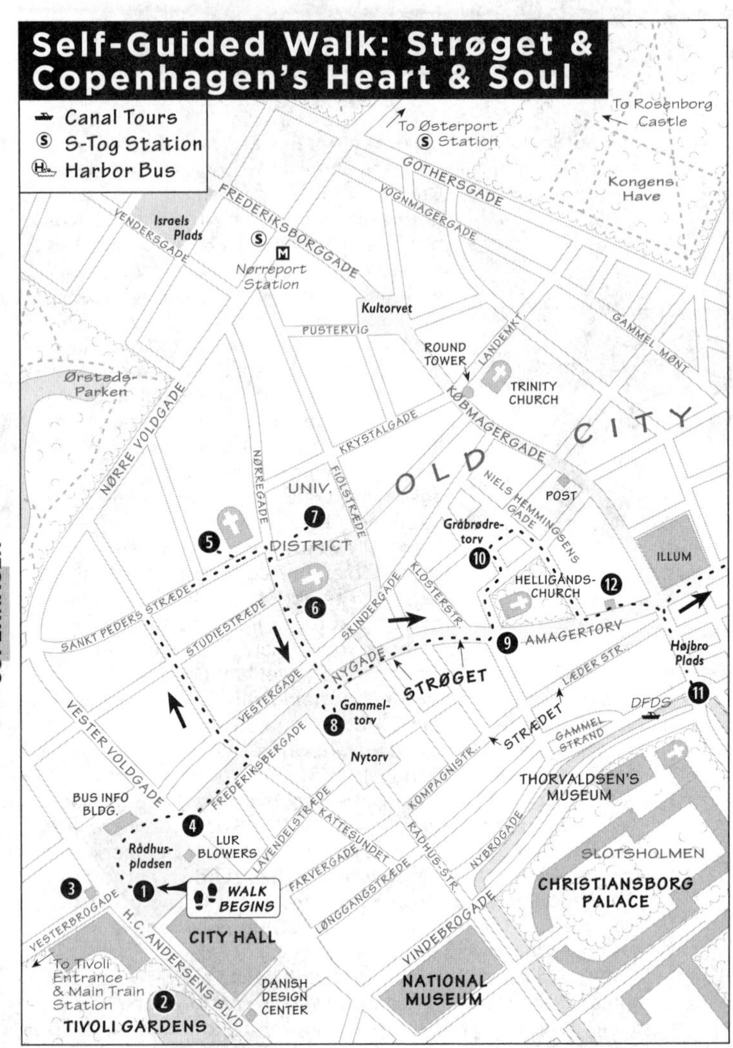

with an umbrella. These two have been called the only women in Copenhagen you can trust, but for years they've been stuck in almost-sunny mode...with the bike just peeking out. Notice that the red temperature dots max out at 28° Celsius (that's 82° Fahrenheit).

To the right, just down the street, is the Tiger Store (a popular local dime store...everything is priced at 10 or 20 kr). The next street (once the local Fleet Street, with the big newspapers) still has the offices for *Politiken* (the leading local newspaper) and the best bookstore in town, Boghallen.

Three fast-food joints stand at the entry to the Strøget

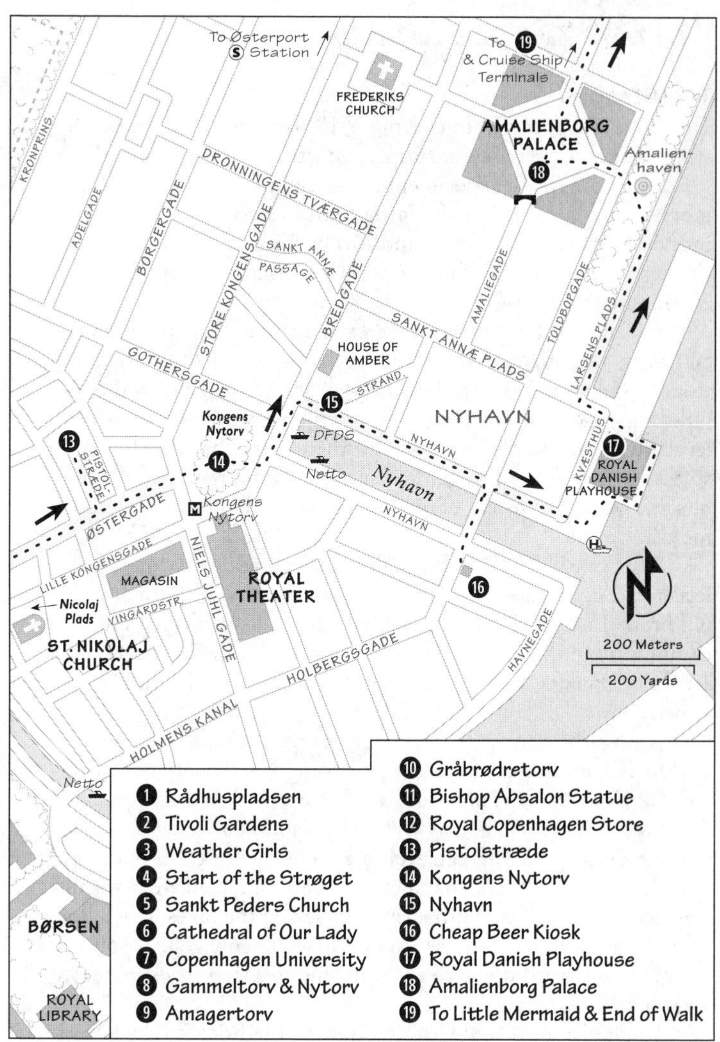

(STROY-et), Copenhagen's grand pedestrian boulevard—where we're heading next. Just beyond that and the Art Deco–style Palace Hotel (with a tower to serve as a sister to the City Hall) is the ***Lur Blowers* sculpture,** which honors the earliest warrior Danes. The *lur* is a curvy, trombone-sounding horn that was used to call soldiers to battle or to accompany pagan religious processions. The earliest bronze *lurs* date as far back as 3,500 years ago. Later, the Vikings used a wood version of the *lur*. The ancient originals, which still play, are displayed in the National Museum. (City tour buses leave from below these Vikings.)

• *Now head down the pedestrian boulevard.*

The Strøget

The American trio of Burger King, 7-Eleven, and KFC marks the start of this otherwise charming pedestrian street. Finished in 1962, Copenhagen's experimental, tremendously successful, and much-copied pedestrian shopping mall is a string of lively (and individually named) streets and lovely squares that bunny-hop through the old town from City Hall to the Nyhavn quarter, a 20-minute stroll away.

As you wander down this street, remember that the commercial focus of a historic street like the Strøget drives up the land value, which generally trashes the charm and tears down the old buildings. Look above the modern window displays and street-level advertising to discover bits of 19th-century character that still survive. Though the Strøget has become hamburgerized, historic bits and attractive pieces of old Copenhagen are just off this commercial cancan.

After one block (at Kattesundet), make a side-trip three blocks left into Copenhagen's colorful **university district.** Formerly the old brothel neighborhood, later the heart of Copenhagen's hippie community in the 1960s, today this "Latin Quarter" is Soho chic. At Sankt Peders Stræde, turn right and walk to the end of the street.

Along the way, look for large mansions that once circled expansive **courtyards.** As the population grew, the city walls constricted Copenhagen's physical size. The courtyards were gradually filled with higgledy-piggledy secondary buildings. Today throughout the old center, you can step off a busy pedestrian mall and back in time into these characteristic half-timbered time-warps. Replace the parked car with a tired horse and the bikes with a line of outhouses, and you're in 19th-century Copenhagen. If you see an open courtyard door, you're welcome to discreetly wander in and look around.

You'll also pass funky shops, and the big brick Sankt Peders church—the old German merchant community's church, which still holds services in German. Its crypt (filling a ground-floor building out back due to the boggy nature of the soil) is filled with fancy German tombs (fee to enter).

• *When Sankt Peders Stræde intersects with Nørregade, look right to find the big, Neoclassical...*

Cathedral of Our Lady (Vor Frue Kirche)

The **Reformation Memorial** in front of the cathedral celebrates Denmark's break from the Roman Catholic Church to become Lutheran in 1536. Walk around and study the reliefs of great

Danish reformers protesting from their pulpits. The relief facing the church shows King Christian III presiding over the pivotal town council meeting when they decided to break away from Rome. As a young man, Prince Christian had traveled to Germany, where he was influenced by Martin Luther. He returned to take the Danish throne by force, despite Catholic opposition. Realizing the advantages of being the head of his own state church, Christian confiscated church property and established the state Lutheran Church. King Christian was crowned inside this cathedral. Because of the reforms of 1536, there's no Mary in the Cathedral of Our Lady.

The cathedral's **facade** looks like a Greek temple. (Two blocks to the right, in the distance, notice more Neoclassicism—the law courts.) You can see why Golden Age Copenhagen (early 1800s) fancied itself a Nordic Athens. Old Testament figures (King David and Moses) flank the cathedral's entryway. Above, John the Baptist stands where you'd expect to see Greek gods. He invites you in...to the New Testament.

The **interior** is a world of Neoclassical serenity. Go inside (free, open daily 8:00–17:00). This pagan temple now houses Christianity. The nave is lined by the 12 apostles, clad in classical robes—masterpieces by the great Danish sculptor Bertel Thorvaldsen (see sidebar, page 81). Each strikes a meditative pose, carrying his identifying symbol: Peter with keys, Andrew with the X-shaped cross of his execution, Matthew and John writing their books, and so on. They lead to a statue of the *Risen Christ,* standing where the statue of Zeus would have been: inside a temple-like niche, flanked by columns, and topped with a pediment. Rather than wearing a royal robe, Jesus wears his burial shroud, opens his arms wide, and says, "Come to me." (Mormons will recognize this statue—a replica stands in the visitors center at Salt Lake City's Temple Square and is often reproduced in church publications.) The marvelous acoustics are demonstrated in free organ concerts Saturdays in July and August at noon.

• *Head back outside. If you face the facade and look to the left (across the square called Frue Plads), you'll see...*

Copenhagen University

Now home to 30,000 students, this university was founded by the king in the 15th century to stop the Danish brain drain to Paris. Today tuition is free (but room, board, and beer are not). Locals say it's easy to get in, but, given the wonderful lifestyle, very hard to get out.

Step up the middle steps of the university's big building and enter a colorful lobby, starring Athena and Apollo. The frescoes celebrate high thinking, with themes such as the triumph of wisdom over barbarism. Notice how harmoniously the architecture, sculpture, and painting work together. (Just inside the door are two stand-up terminals offering free Internet access.)

Outside, busts honor great minds from the faculty, including (at the end) Niels Bohr, a professor who won the 1922 Nobel Prize for theoretical physics. He evaded the clutches of the Nazi science labs by fleeing to America in 1943, where he helped develop the atomic bomb.

• *Rejoin the Strøget (down where you saw the law courts) at the twin squares called...*

Gammeltorv and Nytorv

This was the old town center. In Gammeltorv ("Old Square"), the Fountain of Charity (Caritas) is named for the figure of Charity on top. It has provided drinking water to locals since the early 1600s. Featuring a pregnant woman squirting water from her breasts next to a boy urinating, this was just too much for people of the Victorian Age. They corked both figures and raised the statue to what they hoped would be out of view. The Asian-looking kiosk was one of the city's first community telephone centers from the days before phones were privately owned. Look at the reliefs ringing its top: an airplane with bird wings (c. 1900) and two women talking on the newfangled phone. (It was thought business would popularize the telephone, but actually it was women.)

While Gammeltorv was a place of happiness and merriment, Nytorv ("New Square") was a place of severity and judgment. Walk to the small raised area in front of the old ancient-Greek–style former City Hall. Do a 360. The square is Neoclassical (built mostly around 1800). Read the old Danish on the City Hall facade: "With Law Shall Man Build the Land." Look down at the pavement and read the plaque: "Here stood the town's *Kag* (whipping post) until 1780."

• *Now walk down the next stretch of the Strøget to reach...*

Amagertorv

This is prime real estate for talented street entertainers and pickpockets. Walk to the stately brick Holy Ghost church. The fine spire is typical of old Danish churches. Under the stepped gable was a medieval hospital run by monks (one of the oldest buildings in town, dating from the 12th century).

A block behind the church (walk down Valkendorfsgade and through a passage under the rust-colored building at #32) is the leafy and caffeine-stained **Gråbrødretorv.** This "Grey Friars' Square," surrounded by fine old buildings, is a popular place for an outdoor meal or drink in the summer. At the end of the square, the street Niels Hemmingsens Gade returns (past the recommended Copenhagen Jazz House, a good place for live music nightly) to the Strøget.

Once at the Strøget, turn left and continue down Amagertorv, with its fine inlaid Italian granite stonework, to the next square with the stork fountain (actually a heron). From the fountain, you can see the imposing Parliament building, Christiansborg Palace (with its "three crowns" spire) and an equestrian statue of Bishop Absalon, the city's founder (canal boat tours depart nearby). The Victorian WCs here (steps down from fountain, 2 kr, free urinals) are a delight.

Amagertorv is a highlight for shoppers, with the Royal Copenhagen store—stacked with three floors of porcelain—and Illums Bolighus' three floors of modern Danish design (see "Shopping in Copenhagen," later). A block toward the canal—running parallel to the Strøget—starts Strædet, which is a "second Strøget" featuring cafés, antique shops, and no fast food.

North of Amagertorv, a broad pedestrian mall called **Købmagergade** leads past a fine modern bakery (Illum Bager, next to McDonald's; salads, sandwiches, and traditional pastries) to Christian IV's Round Tower and the Latin Quarter (university district). The recommended Café Norden overlooks the fountain—a good place for a meal or coffee with a view. The second floor offers the best vantage point.

The final stretch of the Strøget leads to **Pistolstræde** (leading off the Strøget to the left from Østergade at #24), a cute lane of shops in restored 18th-century buildings. Wander back into the half-timbered section.

• *Continuing along the Strøget, passing major department stores (see "Shopping in Copenhagen," later), you'll come to the biggest square in town...*

Kongens Nytorv

The "King's New Square" is home to the National Theater, French embassy, and venerable Hotel d'Angleterre. In the mid-1600s the city expanded, pushing its wall farther east. The equestrian statue in the middle of the square celebrates Christian V, who made this square the city's geographical and cultural center. In 1676, King Christian rode off to reconquer the southern tip of Sweden and reclaim Denmark's dominance. He returned empty-handed and broke. Denmark became a second-rate power, but Copenhagen prospered. In the winter this square becomes a popular ice-skating rink.

Before entering the square, walk right toward the small glass pyramids (marking the Metro). Wander into **Hviids Vinstue,** the town's oldest wine cellar (from 1723, before the Metro station, at

Copenhagen at a Glance

▲▲▲**Tivoli Gardens** Copenhagen's classic amusement park, with rides, music, food, and other fun. **Hours:** Mid-April–late Sept daily 11:00–23:00, later on Fri–Sat and mid-June–late Aug, also open daily 11:00–22:00 for a week in mid-Oct and mid-Nov–late Dec. See page 75.

▲▲▲**National Museum** History of Danish civilization with tourable 19th-century Victorian Apartment. **Hours:** Museum Tue–Sun 10:00–17:00, closed Mon; Victorian Apartment tours June–Sept Sat at 11:00. See page 78.

▲▲▲**Rosenborg Castle and Treasury** Renaissance castle of larger-than-life "warrior king" Christian IV. **Hours:** June–Sept daily 10:00–17:00; May and Oct daily 10:00–16:00; Nov–April Tue–Sun 11:00–14:00, closed Mon. See page 83.

▲▲▲**Christiania** Colorful counterculture squatters' colony. **Hours:** Always open. See page 91.

▲▲**Christiansborg Palace** Royal reception rooms with dazzling tapestries. **Hours:** Daily 10:00–16:00 except closed Mon Oct–April. See page 79.

▲▲**Museum of Danish Resistance** Chronicle of Denmark's struggle against the Nazis. **Hours:** May–Sept Tue–Sun 10:00–17:00, closed Mon; Oct–April Tue–Sun 10:00–15:00, closed Mon. See page 83.

▲**City Hall** Copenhagen's landmark, packed with Danish history and symbolism and topped with a tower. **Hours:** Mon–Fri 8:00–17:00, open Sat only for tours, closed Sun. See page 76.

#19, under the Bali Restaurant) to check out its characteristic interior and fascinating old Copenhagen photos. It's a colorful spot for an open-face sandwich and a beer (three sandwiches and a beer for 60 kr at lunchtime). Their wintertime *gløgg* (hot spiced wine) is legendary. Across the street, towering above the Metro station, is Magasin du Nord, the grandest old department store in town.

Pop into the futuristic **Metro station.** Ride the escalators down and up to see the latest in Metro design (circa 2002, automated cars, no driver...sit in front to watch the tracks coming at you). As the cars come and go without drivers, compare this system to the public transit in your town.

▲**Ny Carlsberg Glyptotek** Scandinavia's top art gallery, featuring Egyptians, Greeks, Etruscans, French, and Danes. **Hours:** Tue-Sun 11:00-17:00, closed Mon. See page 77.

▲**Museum of Copenhagen** The story of Copenhagen, displayed in an old house. **Hours:** Thu-Tue 10:00-16:00, Wed 10:00-21:00. See page 79.

▲**Thorvaldsen's Museum** Works of the Danish Neoclassical sculptor. **Hours:** Tue-Sun 10:00-17:00, closed Mon. See page 80.

▲**Danish Jewish Museum** Exhibit tracing the 400-year history of Danish Jews, in a unique building by American architect Daniel Libeskind. **Hours:** June-Aug Tue-Sun 10:00-17:00; Sept-May Tue-Fri 13:00-16:00, Sat-Sun 12:00-17:00; closed Mon year-round. See page 82.

▲**Amalienborg Palace Museum** Quick and intimate look at Denmark's royal family. **Hours:** May-Oct daily 10:00-16:00; Nov-April Tue-Sun 11:00-16:00, closed Mon. See page 83.

▲**Rosenborg Gardens** Park surrounding Rosenborg Castle, filled with statues and statuesque Danes. **Hours:** Always open. See page 88.

▲**National Art Museum** Good Danish and Impressionist collections. **Hours:** Tue-Sun 10:00-17:00, Wed until 20:00, closed Mon. See page 89.

▲**Our Savior's Church** Spiral-spired church with bright Baroque interior. **Hours:** April-Aug Mon-Sat 11:00-16:30, Sun 12:00-16:30, off-season until 15:30, spire closed in bad weather and Nov-March. See page 90.

• *Back up at ground level, walk across the square to the trendy harbor of...*

Nyhavn

Established in the 1670s along with Kongens Nytorv, Nyhavn ("New Harbor") is a recently gentrified sailors' quarter. (Hong Kong is the last of the nasty bars from the rough old days.) With its trendy cafés, jazz clubs, and tattoo shops (pop into Tattoo Ole at #17—fun photos, very traditional), Nyhavn is a wonderful place to hang out. The canal is filled with glamorous old sailboats of all sizes. Historic sloops are welcome to moor here in Copenhagen's ever-changing boat museum. Hans Christian Andersen lived and wrote his first stories here (in the red double-gabled building on the right at #20). A miniscule amber museum is above the House of Amber at the head of the canal (see "Shopping in Copenhagen," page 95).

Wander the quay, enjoying the frat-party parade of tattoos (hotter weather reveals more tattoos). Celtic and Nordic mythological designs are in (as is bodybuilding, by the looks of things). The place thrives—with the cheap-beer drinkers dockside and the richer and older ones looking on from comfier cafés.

A note about all this public beer-drinking: There's no more beer consumption here than in the US; it's just out in public. Many young Danes can't afford to drink in a bar, so they "picnic drink" their beers in squares and along canals, spending a quarter of the bar price for a bottle from a nearby kiosk. Consider grabbing a cold 10-kr beer yourself and joining the scene (the kiosk is on Holbergsgade, just over the bridge on the right, open daily until 24:00).

Just past the bridge, a line of people wait for the best ice cream around—packed into fresh-baked waffles (look through the window to see the waffle iron in action).

From the end of Nyhavn canal, turn left around the Royal Danish Theatre's new Playhouse. Continuing north along the harbor, you'll stroll a delightful waterfront promenade to the modern fountain of Amaliehaven Park, immediately across the harbor from Copenhagen's slick new Opera House. The **Opera House** is bigger than it looks because much of it is underground. Its striking design is controversial. Completed in 2005 by Henning Larsen, it was a $400 million gift to the nation from an oil-shipping magnate.

• *A block inland (behind the fountain) is the orderly...*

Amalienborg Palace and Square

Queen Margrethe II and her husband live in the mansion to your immediate left as you enter the square from the harborside. (If the flag's flying, she's home.) Her son and heir to the throne, Crown Prince Frederik,

recently moved into the mansion across the street with his wife, Australian businesswoman Mary Donaldson, and their young son and daughter.

Though the guards change with royal fanfare at noon only when the queen is in residence, they shower every morning. The royal guard often has a police escort when it marches through town on special occasions—leading locals to joke that theirs is "the only army in the world that needs police protection."

The small Amalienborg Palace Museum offers an intimate look at royal living (far side of square, described on page 83).

The equestrian statue of Frederick V is a reminder that this square was the centerpiece of a planned town he envisioned in 1750. It was named for him—Frederikstaden. During the 18th century, Denmark's population grew and the country thrived (as trade flourished and its neutrality kept it out of the costly wars impoverishing much of Europe). Frederikstaden, with its strong Neoclassical harmony, was designed as a luxury neighborhood for the city's business elite. Nobility and other big shots moved in, but the king came here only after his other palace burned down in a 1794 fire. Just inland, the striking Frederikskirke (better known as the Marble Church) was designed to fit this ritzy new quarter.

• *From the square, Amaliegade leads two blocks north to...*

Kastellet Park

In this park, you'll find some worthwhile sightseeing. Just before the park's entrance, look for Denmark's fascinating WWII-era **Museum of Danish Resistance** (see page 83). Nearby is the 1908 **Gefion Fountain,** which illustrates the myth of the goddess who was given one night to carve a hunk out of Sweden to make into Denmark's main island, Sjælland (or "Zealand" in English), which you're on. Gefion transformed her four sons into oxen to do the job, and the chunk she removed from Sweden is supposedly Vänern, Sweden's largest lake. If you look at a map showing Sweden and Denmark, the island and the lake are, in fact, roughly the same shape.

Beyond the fountain is an Anglican church built of flint and, finally, the site of the overrated, overfondled, and overphotographed symbol of Copenhagen, ***Den Lille Havfrue—The Little Mermaid.*** If you visit in 2010, you may instead see a temporary Chinese version of the mermaid, as the statue itself will take a trip to Shanghai, China, for the World Expo. (A copy of *The Little Mermaid* will be on display at Tivoli Gardens during her China trip.)

The Little Mermaid statue was a gift to the city of Copenhagen in 1909 from brewing magnate Carl Jacobsen (whose art collection forms the basis of the Ny Carlsberg Glyptotek). Inspired by a ballet performance of Andersen's story, Jacobsen hired the young

The Little Mermaid and Hans Christian Andersen

"Far out in the ocean, where the water is as blue as a cornflower, as clear as crystal, and very, very deep..." there lived a young mermaid. So begins one of Hans Christian Andersen's (1805-1875) best-known stories. The plot line starts much like the Disney children's movie, but it's spiced with poetic description and philosophical dialogue about the immortal soul.

The mermaid's story goes like this: One day, a young mermaid spies a passing ship and falls in love with a handsome human prince. The ship is wrecked in a storm, and she saves the prince's life. To be with the prince, the mermaid asks a sea witch to give her human legs. In exchange, she agrees to give up her voice and the chance of ever returning to the sea. And, the witch tells her, if the prince doesn't marry her, she will immediately die heartbroken and without an immortal soul. The mermaid agrees, and her fish tail becomes a pair of beautiful but painful legs. She woos the prince—who loves her in return—but he eventually marries another. Heartbroken, the mermaid prepares to die. She's given one last chance to save herself: She must kill the prince on his wedding night. She sneaks into the bedchamber with a knife...but can't bear to kill the man she loves. The mermaid throws herself into the sea to die. Suddenly, she's miraculously carried up by the mermaids of the air, who give her an immortal soul as a reward for her long-suffering love.

The tale of unrequited love mirrors Andersen's own sad love life. He had two major crushes—one of them for the famous opera singer, Jenny Lind—but he was turned down both times, and he never married. Scholars with access to Andersen's diary believe he was bisexual and died a virgin. The great author is said to have feared he'd lose his artistic drive if he ever actually made love to another person. His dearest male friend (in the Romantic 19th century, when men tended to have more emotional and intimate friendships than is common today) inherited Andersen's entire estate.

sculptor Edvard Eriksen to immortalize the mermaid as a statue. Ericksen used his wife Eline as the model.

For the non-Disneyfied *Little Mermaid* story—and insights into Hans Christian Andersen—see the sidebar.

• *Our walking tour is finished. You can get back downtown on foot, by taxi, or on bus #1A, #15, or #19 from Store Kongensgade on the other side of Kastellet Park, or bus #29 from behind the Museum of Danish Resistance on Langelinie Street.*

Sights in Copenhagen

Near the Train Station

Copenhagen's great train station, the Hovedbanegården, is a fascinating mesh of Scandinavian culture and transportation efficiency. Even if you're not a train traveler, check it out (see "Arrival in Copenhagen," earlier). From the station, wonderful sights fan out into the old city. The following attractions are listed roughly in order from the train station to Slotsholmen Island.

▲▲▲Tivoli Gardens—The world's grand old amusement park—since 1843—is 20 acres, 110,000 lanterns, and countless ice cream cones of fun. You pay one admission price and find yourself lost in a Hans Christian Andersen wonderland of rides, restaurants, games, marching bands, roulette wheels, and funny mirrors. Tivoli doesn't try to be Disney. It's wonderfully and happily Danish. I find it worth the admission just to see Danes—young and old—at play. In 2010, Tivoli Lake hosts a special guest—a copy of *The Little Mermaid.* The family of *The Little Mermaid*'s sculptor are loaning their copy to the park while the original is in China for the World Expo.

Cost, Hours, Location: Admission is 85 kr. The park is open from mid-April to late September (daily 11:00–23:00, later on Fri–Sat and mid-June–late Aug, tel. 33 15 10 01, www.tivoli.dk). Rides range in price from 20 to 80 kr (210 kr all-day pass). It's a children's fantasyland midday, but it becomes more adult-oriented later on. In winter, Tivoli opens for a week in mid-October, then for a Christmas market with *gløgg* (hot spiced wine) and ice skating on Tivoli Lake (daily 11:00–22:00 for a week in Oct and mid-Nov–just before Christmas). Dress warm for chilly evenings any time of year. There are lockers by each entrance.

Tivoli is across Bernstoffsgade from the train station. If you're catching an overnight train, this is *the* place to spend your last Copenhagen hours.

Entertainment in Tivoli: Upon arrival (through main entrance, on left in the service center), pick up a map and events schedule. Take a moment to sit down and plan your entertainment for the evening. Events are spread between 15:00 and 23:00; the 19:30 concert in the concert hall can be as little as 50 kr or as much as 1,200 kr, depending on the performer (box office tel. 33 15 10 12).

If the Tivoli Symphony is playing, it's worth paying for. The ticket box office is outside, just to the left of the main entrance (daily 10:00–20:00; if you buy a concert ticket you get into Tivoli for free). You'll also find the daily events schedule on the posts outside the main entrance.

Free concerts, pantomime theater, ballet, acrobats, puppets, and other shows pop up all over the park, and a well-organized visitor can enjoy an exciting evening of entertainment without spending a single krone beyond the entry fee. Friday evenings feature a (usually free) rock or pop show at 22:00. People gather around the lake 30 minutes before closing time for the "Tivoli Illuminations" (except on Fri, when there's no show). Fireworks blast each Saturday in summer at 23:45. The park is particularly romantic at dusk, when the lights go on.

Eating at Tivoli: Inside the park, expect to pay amusement-park prices for amusement-park-quality food. Still, a meal here is part of the fun. **Søcafeen** serves only traditional open-face sandwiches in a fun beer garden with lakeside ambience. They allow picnics if you buy a drink (and will rent you plates and silverware for 10 kr per person). The *pølse* (sausage) stands are cheap, and there's a bagel sandwich place in the amusements corner. **Færgekroen** offers a quiet, classy lakeside escape from the amusement-park intensity, with traditional dishes washed down by its own microbrew. They host live piano on Thursday, Friday, and Saturday evenings from 20:00, often resulting in an impromptu sing-along with a bunch of very happy Danes. **Wagamama** is a modern pan-Asian slurpathon serving healthy noodle dishes (at the far back side of the park). **Georg,** to the left of the concert hall, has tasty 60-kr sandwiches and a lake view.

▲City Hall (Rådhus)—This city landmark, between the train station/Tivoli and the Strøget, offers private tours and trips up its 345-foot-tall tower. It's draped, inside and out, in Danish symbolism. The city's founder, Bishop Absalon, stands over the door. Absalon (c. 1128–1201)—bishop, soldier, and foreign-policy wonk—was King Valdemar I's right-hand man. In Copenhagen, he drove out pirates and built a fort to guard the harbor, turning a miserable fishing village into a humming Baltic seaport. The polar bears climbing on the rooftop symbolize the giant Danish protectorate of Greenland. Six night-watchmen flank the city's gold-and-green seal under the Danish flag.

Step inside. The lobby has racks of tourist information (city maps and *Copenhagen This Week*). The building and its huge tower were inspired by the City Hall in Siena, Italy (with the necessary bad-weather addition of a glass roof). Huge functions fill this grand hall (the iron grill in the center of the floor is an elevator for bringing up 1,200 chairs) while the busts of four illustrious local boys—fairy-tale writer Hans Christian Andersen, sculptor Bertel

Thorvaldsen, physicist Niels Bohr, and the building's architect, Martin Nyrop—look on. Underneath the floor are national archives dating back to 1275, popular with Danes researching their family roots. City Hall is free and open to the public (Mon–Fri 8:00–17:00, open on Sat only with a tour—see below, closed Sun). You can wander throughout the building and into the peaceful garden out back. Guided English-language **tours** get you into more private, official rooms (30 kr, 45 min, year-round Mon–Fri at 15:00, Sat at 10:00).

Tourists romp (in groups with an escort) up the **tower**'s 300 steps for the best aerial view of Copenhagen (20 kr; June–Sept Mon–Fri at 10:00, 12:00, and 14:00, Sat at 12:00; Oct–May Mon–Sat at 12:00; tel. 33 66 25 82).

Danish Design Center—This center, its building a masterpiece in itself, shows off the best in Danish design as well as top examples from around the world, including architecture, fashion, and graphic arts. A visit to this low-key display case for sleek Scandinavian design offers an interesting glimpse into a culture that takes pride in functionalism and minimalism. The basement features fun special exhibits (50 kr, Mon–Fri 10:00–17:00, Wed until 21:00—free after 17:00, Sat–Sun 11:00–16:00, across from Tivoli Gardens and down the street from City Hall at H. C. Andersen Boulevard 27, tel. 33 69 33 69, www.ddc.dk). The boutique next to the ticket counter features three themes: travel light (chic travel accessories and gadgets), modern Danish classics, and books and posters. The café on the main level, under the atrium, serves light lunches (65–120 kr).

▲Ny Carlsberg Glyptotek—Scandinavia's top art gallery is an impressive example of what beer money can do. Brewer Carl Jacobsen was an avid collector and patron of the arts (he donated *The Little Mermaid* statue to the city). His namesake museum has intoxicating artifacts from Egypt (mummy cases, a 5,000-year-old hippo statue), Greece (red-and-black painted vases, statues), the Etruscan world (Greek-looking vases), and Rome (grittily realistic statues and portrait busts). The sober realism of 19th-century Danish Golden Age painting reflects the introspection of a once-powerful nation reduced to second-class status. The "French Wing" (just inside the front door) has Rodin statues. A heady, if small, exhibit of 19th-century French paintings (in a modern building within the back courtyard) shows how Realism morphed into Impressionism and Post-Impressionism, and includes works by Géricault, Delacroix, Manet, Degas, Pissarro, and Gauguin—from before Tahiti (when he lived in Copenhagen with his Danish wife and their five children) and after Tahiti. Linger with marble gods under the palm leaves and glass dome of the very soothing winter garden. Designers, figuring Danes would be more interested in a lush garden than in classical art, used this wonderful space as leafy bait to cleverly introduce locals to a few Greek and Roman statues. (It works for tourists, too.) One of the original *Thinker* sculptures by Rodin (wondering how to scale the Tivoli fence?) is in the museum's backyard. The next time you sip on a Carlsberg beer, drink a toast to Carl Jacobsen and his marvelous collection. *Skål!* (60 kr, free Sun, open Tue–Sun 11:00–17:00, closed Mon, classy cafeteria under palms, behind Tivoli at Dantes Plads 7, tel. 33 41 81 41, www.glyptoteket.dk).

▲▲▲National Museum—Focus on this museum's excellent and curiously enjoyable Danish collection, which traces this civilization from its ancient beginnings. Exhibits are laid out chronologically and described in English. Pick up the museum map as you enter.

Cost, Hours, Location: Free, Tue–Sun 10:00–17:00, closed Mon, mandatory 10-kr bag check, enter at Ny Vestergade 10, tel. 33 13 44 11, www.nationalmuseet.dk. The café overlooking the entry hall serves coffee, pastries, and lunch (55-135 kr).

➲Self-Guided Tour: Start before history did, with Stone Age tools, oak coffins, and still-clothed skeletons of Scandinavia's reindeer-hunters. The Bronze Age "Chariot of the Sun"—a small statue of a horse pulling the sun across the sky—likely had religious significance for early Scandinavians (whose descendants continue to celebrate the solstice with fervor). You'll also see still-playable *lur* horns (see page 65) and horned helmets. Contrary to popular belief (and countless tourist shops), these helmets were not worn by the Vikings, but by their predecessors—for ceremonial purposes, centuries earlier. This leads to the Iron Age and an object that's neither Iron nor Danish: the 2,000-year-old Gundestrup Cauldron of art-textbook fame. This 20-pound, soup-kitchen-size bowl made of silver was found in a Danish bog, but its symbolism suggests it was originally from Thrace (in northeast Greece) or Celtic Ireland. On the sides, hunters slay bulls, and gods cavort with stags, horses, dogs, and dragons. It's both mysterious and fascinating. There's also lots of Viking stuff on view and a bitchin' collection of well-translated rune stones proclaiming heroic deeds.

Next, go upstairs to see the coming of Christianity—golden altars and *aquamaniles*, pitchers used for ritual hand-washing. The Dagmar Cross is the prototype for a popular form of crucifix worn by many Danes. Carry on to find fascinating material on the Reformation, an exhibit on everyday town life in the 16th and 17th centuries, and, in Room 126, a unique "cylinder perspective" of the noble family (from 1656) and two peep shows.

The next floor takes you into modern times, with historic toys and a slice-of-Danish-life (1600–2000) gallery where you'll see everything from rifles and old bras to early jukeboxes. Capping off the collection is a stall that, until recently, was used for selling marijuana in the squatters' community of Christiania.

▲National Museum's Victorian Apartment—The National Museum (listed above) inherited an incredible Victorian apartment just around the corner. The wealthy Christensen family managed to keep its plush living quarters a 19th-century time capsule until the granddaughters passed away in 1963. Since then, it's been part of the National Museum, with all but two of its rooms looking just as they did around 1890 (50 kr, required 45-min tours in English leave from museum reception desk, June–Sept Sat only at 11:00).

▲Museum of Copenhagen (Bymuseet)—This fine old house is filled with an entertaining and creative exhibit telling the story of Copenhagen. The 25-minute video (in English at 11:15, 12:45, and 14:15) is worth planning ahead for. The ground floor covers the city's origins, the upper floor is dedicated to the 19th century, and the top floor includes a fun year-by-year walk through Copenhagen's 20th century, with lots of fun insights into contemporary culture (20 kr, free on Fri, open Thu–Tue 10:00–16:00, Wed 10:00–21:00, Vesterbrogade 59, www.bymuseum.dk).

On Slotsholmen Island

This island, where Copenhagen began in the 12th century, is a short walk from the train station and Tivoli, just across the bridge from the National Museum. It's dominated by Christiansborg Palace and several other royal and governmental buildings.

▲▲Christiansborg Palace—A complex of government buildings stands on the ruins of Copenhagen's original 12th-century fortress: the Parliament, Supreme Court, prime minister's office, royal reception rooms, royal library, several museums, and royal stables.

Although the current palace dates only from 1928 and the royal family moved out 200 years ago, this building—the sixth to stand here in 800 years—is rich with tradition. The information-packed 50-minute English tours of the royal reception rooms are excellent. As you slip-slide on protect-the-floor slippers through 22 rooms, you'll gain a good feel for Danish history, royalty, and politics. (For instance, the family portrait of King Christian IX shows why he's called the "father-in-law of Europe"—his children eventually became or married royalty in Denmark, Russia, Greece, Britain, France, Germany, and Norway.) The highlight is the dazzling set of modern tapestries—Danish-designed but Gobelin-made in Paris. This gift, given to the queen on her 60th birthday in 2000, celebrates 1,000 years of Danish history, from the Viking age to our chaotic times (60 kr; daily 10:00–16:00 except closed Mon Oct–April, English tours daily at 15:00, palace sometimes closes without notice for royal functions—call or check website before you go; from equestrian statue in front, go through wooden door, past entrance to Christiansborg Castle ruins, into courtyard, and up stairs on right; tel. 33 92 64 92, www.ses.dk/christiansborg).

Christiansborg Castle Ruins—An exhibit in the scant remains of the first fortress built by Bishop Absalon, the 12th-century founder of Copenhagen, lies under the palace. There's precious little to see, but it is old and well-described. A video covers more recent palace history (40 kr, daily 10:00–16:00 except closed Mon Oct–April).

Old Stock Exchange (Børsen)—The eye-catching red-brick stock exchange was inspired by the Dutch Renaissance, like much of 17th-century Copenhagen. Built to promote the mercantile ambitions of Denmark in the 1600s, it was the "World Trade Center" of Scandinavia. The facade reads, "For the profitable use of buyer and seller." The dragon-tail spire with three crowns represents the Danish aspiration to rule a united Scandinavia—or at least be its commercial capital. The Børsen (which is not open to tourists) symbolically connected Christianshavn (the harbor, also inspired by the Dutch) with the rest of the city, in an age when trade was a very big deal.

▲Thorvaldsen's Museum—This museum, which has some of the best swoon-worthy art you'll see anywhere, tells the story and shows the monumental work of the great Danish Neoclassical sculptor Bertel Thorvaldsen (see sidebar). Considered Canova's equal among Neoclassical sculptors, Thorvaldsen spent 40 years in Rome. He was lured home to Copenhagen with the promise to showcase his work in a fine museum, which opened in the revolutionary year of 1848 as Denmark's first public art gallery. Of the 500 or so sculptures Thorvaldsen completed in his life—including 90 major statues—this museum has most of them, in one form or another (the plaster model used to make the original, the original marble, or a copy done in marble or bronze). The ground floor showcases his statues (pull open the little black "information" cases for descriptions). Upstairs, get into the mind of the artist by perusing his personal possessions and the private collection of paintings from which he drew inspiration (20 kr, free Wed, open Tue–Sun 10:00–17:00, closed Mon, well-described, located in Neoclassical building with colorful walls next to Christiansborg Palace, tel. 33 32 15 32, www.thorvaldsensmuseum.dk).

Bertel Thorvaldsen
(1770-1844)

Bertel Thorvaldsen was born, raised, educated, and buried in Copenhagen, but his most productive years were spent in Rome. There he soaked up the prevailing style of the time: Neoclassical. He studied ancient Greek and Roman statues, copying their balance, grace, and impassive beauty. The simple-but-noble style suited the patriotism of the era, and Thorvaldsen got rich off it. Public squares throughout Europe are dotted with his works, celebrating local rulers, patriots, and historical figures looking like Greek heroes or Roman conquerors.

In 1819, at the height of his fame and power, Thorvaldsen returned to Copenhagen. He was asked to decorate the most important parts of the recently bombed, newly rebuilt Cathedral of Our Lady: the main altar and nave. His *Risen Christ* on the altar (along with the 12 apostles lining the nave) became his most famous and reproduced work.

The prolific Thorvaldsen depicted a range of subjects. His grand statues of historical figures (Copernicus in Warsaw, Maximilian I in Munich) were intended for public squares. Portrait busts of his contemporaries were usually done in the style of Roman emperors. Thorvaldsen carved the *Lion Monument,* depicting a weeping lion, into a cliff in Luzern, Switzerland. He did religious statues, like the *Risen Christ*. Thorvaldsen's most accessible works are from Greek mythology—*The Three Graces,* naked *Jason with the Golden Fleece,* or Ganymede crouching down to feed the eagle Jupiter.

Though many of his statues are of gleaming white marble, Thorvaldsen was not a chiseler of stone. Like Rodin and Canova, Thorvaldsen left the grunt work to others. He fashioned a life-sized model in plaster, which could then be reproduced in marble or bronze by his assistants. Multiple copies were often made, even in his lifetime.

Thorvaldsen epitomized the Neoclassical style. His statues assume perfectly balanced poses—maybe even a bit stiff, say critics. They don't flail their arms dramatically or emote passionately. As you look into their faces, they seem lost in thought, as though contemplating deep spiritual truths.

In Copenhagen, catch Thorvaldsen's *Risen Christ* at the Cathedral of Our Lady, his portrait bust at City Hall, and the full range of his long career at the Thorvaldsen Museum.

Royal Library—Copenhagen's "Black Diamond" library is a striking, supermodern building made of shiny black granite, leaning over the harbor at the edge of the palace complex. From the inviting lounge chairs, you can ponder this stretch of harborfront, which serves as a showcase for architects. Inside, wander through the old and new sections, catch the fine view from the "G" level, read a magazine, surf the Internet (free terminals in the skyway lobby over the street nearest the harbor), and enjoy a classy—and pricey—lunch (library is free, special exhibitions generally 30 kr; reading room open May–Aug Mon–Fri 9:00–21:00, Sat 10:00–17:00, closed Sun; different parts of the library have varying hours, tel. 33 47 47 47, www.kb.dk).

▲Danish Jewish Museum (Dansk Jødisk Museum)—This museum, which opened in 2004 in a striking building by American architect Daniel Libeskind, offers a small but well-exhibited display of 400 years of the life and impact of Jews in Denmark. Libeskind—who created the equally conceptual Jewish Museum in Berlin, and whose design is the basis for redeveloping the World Trade Center site in New York City—has literally written Jewish culture into this building. The floor plan, a seemingly random squiggle, is actually in the shape of the Hebrew characters for *Mitzvah*, which loosely translated means "act of kindness."

Be sure to watch the 12-minute introductory film about the Jews' migration to Denmark (plays continuously). As you tour the collection, the uneven floors and asymmetrical walls give you the feeling that what lies around the corner is completely unknown... much like the life and history of Danish Jews. Another interpretation might be that the uneven floors give you the sense of motion, like waves on the sea—a reminder that despite Nazi occupation in 1943, nearly 7,000 Danish Jews were ferried across the waves by fishermen to safety in neutral Sweden (40 kr; June–Aug Tue–Sun 10:00–17:00; Sept–May Tue–Fri 13:00–16:00, Sat–Sun 12:00–17:00; closed Mon year-round, behind the Royal Library's "Black Diamond" branch at Proviantpassagen 6, tel. 33 11 22 18, www.jewmus.dk).

Near the Strøget

Round Tower—Built in 1642 by Christian IV, the tower connects a church, library, and observatory (the oldest functioning observatory in Europe) with a ramp that spirals up to a fine view of Copenhagen (25 kr, nothing to see inside but the ramp and the view; June–Aug daily 10:00–20:00; Sept–May Mon–Sat 10:00–17:00, Sun 12:00–17:00 plus mid-Oct–mid-March Tue–Wed 19:00–22:00; just off the Strøget on Købmagergade). The view from atop Our Savior's Church is far better (see page 90).

Amalienborg Palace and Nearby

For more information on this palace and nearby attractions, including the famous *Little Mermaid* statue, see the end of my self-guided walk (page 73).

▲Amalienborg Palace Museum—While Queen Margrethe II and her husband live quite privately in one of the four mansions that make up the palace complex, another mansion has been open to the public since 1994. It displays the private studies of four kings of the House of Glucksborg, who ruled from 1863–1972. Your visit is short—six or eight rooms on one floor—but it affords an intimate and unique peek into Denmark's royal family (55 kr; May–Oct daily 10:00–16:00; Nov–April Tue–Sun 11:00–16:00, closed Mon; with your back to the harbor, the entrance is ahead on the right; tel. 33 12 21 86, www.rosenborg-slot.dk).

Amalienborg Palace Changing of the Guard—This noontime event is boring in the summer, when the queen is not in residence—the guards just change places. If the queen's at home (indicated by a flag flying above her home), the changing of the guard is accompanied by a military band.

▲▲Museum of Danish Resistance (Frihedsmuseet)—On April 9, 1940, Hitler's Nazis violated a peace treaty and invaded Denmark, overrunning the tiny nation in mere hours. This museum tells what happened next. The compelling story of Denmark's heroic Nazi-resistance struggle (1940–1945) is well-explained in English, from Himmler's eye patch to fascinating tricks of creative sabotage (free; May–Sept Tue–Sun 10:00–17:00, closed Mon; Oct–April Tue–Sun 10:00–15:00, closed Mon; guided tours at 14:00 Tue, Thu, and Sun in the summer; on Churchillparken between Amalienborg Palace and *The Little Mermaid* site, bus #26 from Langelinie or bus #1, #1A, #19, or #29 from farther away, tel. 33 13 77 14, www.frihedsmuseet.dk).

Rosenborg Castle and Nearby

▲▲▲Rosenborg Castle (Rosenborg Slot) and Treasury—This finely furnished Dutch Renaissance–style castle was built by King Christian IV in the early 1600s as a summer residence. Rosenborg was his favorite residence and where he chose to die. Open to the public since 1838, it houses the Danish crown jewels and 500 years of royal knickknacks. For more on Christian, read the sidebar on page 85.

Cost, Hours, Location: 70 kr; June–Sept daily 10:00–17:00; May and Oct daily 10:00–16:00; Nov–April Tue–Sun 11:00–14:00, closed Mon; S-tog: Nørreport, then 5-min walk on Østervoldgade, tel. 33 15 32 86, www.rosenborgslot.dk.

Tours: Richard Karpen leads fascinating 90-minute tours in princely garb (mid-May–mid-Sept Mon and Thu at 13:30, 75 kr plus your entrance fee, see "Tours in Copenhagen" on page 59). Or take the following self-guided tour that I've woven together from the highlights of Richard's walk.

➲ **Self-Guided Tour:** You'll tour the ground floor room by room, then climb to the third floor for the big throne room. After a quick sweep of the middle floor, finish in the basement (enter from outside) for the jewels. Begin the tour on the palace's ground floor, in the Audience Room.

Ground Floor: Here in the wood-paneled **Audience Room,** all eyes were on King Christian IV. Today, your eyes should be on him, too. Take a close look at his bust by the fireplace. Check this guy out—earring and fashionable braid, hard drinker, hard lover, energetic statesman, and warrior king. Christian IV was dynamism in the flesh, wearing a toga: a true Renaissance guy. During his reign, Copenhagen doubled in size. You're surrounded by Dutch paintings (the Dutch had a huge influence on 17th-century Denmark). Note the smaller statue of the 19-year-old king, showing him jousting jauntily on his coronation day. The astronomical clock—with musical works and moving figures—did everything you can imagine.

The **study** (nearest where you entered) was small (and easy to heat). Kings did a lot of corresponding. We know a lot about Christian because 3,000 of his handwritten letters survive. The painting shows Christian at age eight. Three years later, his father died, and little Christian technically ascended the throne, though Denmark was actually ruled by a regency until Christian was 19. A portrait of his mother hangs above the boy, and opposite is a portrait of Christian in his prime—having just conquered Sweden—standing alongside the incredible coronation crown you'll see later.

In the **bedroom,** paintings show the king as an old man... and as a dead man. (Christian died in this room.) In the case are the clothes he wore at his finest hour. During a naval battle against Sweden (1644), Christian stood directing the action when an explosion ripped across the deck, sending him sprawling and

King Christian IV: A Lover and a Fighter

King Christian IV (1577–1648) inherited Denmark at the peak of its power, lived his life with the exuberance of the age, and went to his grave with the country in decline. His legacy is obvious to every tourist—Rosenborg Castle, Frederiksborg Palace, the Round Tower, Christianshavn, and on and on. Look for his logo adorning many buildings: the letter "C" with a "4" inside it and a crown on top. Thanks to both his place in history and his passionate personality, Danes today regard Christian IV as one of their greatest monarchs.

During his 60-year reign, Christian IV reformed the government, rebuilt the army, established a trading post in India, and tried to expand Denmark's territory. He took Kalmar from Sweden and captured strategic points in Germany. The king was a large man and lived large as well. A skilled horseman and avid hunter, he could drink his companions under the table. He spoke several languages and gained a reputation as outgoing and humorous. His lavish banquets were legendary, and his romantic affairs were numerous.

But Christian's appetite for war proved destructive. In 1626, Denmark again attacked Germany, but was beaten back. In 1643, Sweden launched a sneak attack, and despite Christian's personal bravery (he lost an eye), the war went badly. By the end of his life, Christian was tired and bitter, and Denmark was drained.

The heroics of Christian and his sailors live on in the Danish national anthem, "King Christian Stood by the Lofty Mast."

riddling him with shrapnel. Unfazed, the 67-year-old monarch bounced right back up and kept going, inspiring his men to carry on the fight. Christian's stubborn determination during this battle is commemorated in Denmark's national anthem. Shrapnel put out Christian's eye. No problem: The warrior king with a knack for heroic publicity stunts had the shrapnel bits removed from his eye and forehead and made into earrings as a gift for his mistress. The earrings hang in the case above the blood-stained cloth. Christian lived to be 70 and fathered 25 children (with two wives and three mistresses).

The next room displays **wax casts** of royal figures. This was the way famous and important people were portrayed back then.

The **chair** is a forerunner of the whoopee cushion. When you sat on it, metal cuffs pinned your arms down, allowing the prankster to pour water down the back of the chair (see hole)—making you "wet your pants." When you stood up, the chair made embarrassing tooting sounds.

The next room has a particularly impressive inlaid **marble floor.** Imagine the king meeting emissaries here in the center, with the emblems of Norway (right), Denmark (center), and Sweden (left) behind him.

The end room was a **dining room** used by Christian's first mistress. Study the box made of amber (petrified tree resin, 30–50 million years old). The tiny figures show a healthy interest in sex. (You might want to shield children from the more graphic art in the case next to the door you just passed.) By the window (opposite where you entered), a hole in the wall let the music performed by the band in the basement waft in. (Who wants the actual musicians in the dining room?) The audio hole was also used to call servants.

The long **hall** leading to the staircase exhibits an intriguing painting showing the crowds at the coronation of Christian's son, Frederick III. After Christian's death, a weakened Denmark was invaded, occupied, and humiliated by Sweden (Treaty of Roskilde, 1658). Copenhagen alone held out through the long winter of 1658–1659 (the Siege of Copenhagen), and Sweden eventually had to withdraw from the country. During the siege, Frederick III distinguished himself with his bravery. He seized upon the resulting surge of popularity as his chance to be anointed an absolute, divinely ordained monarch (1660). This painting marks that event—study it closely for slice-of-life details. Next, a sprawling family tree makes it perfectly clear that Christian IV comes from good stock. Notice the tree is labeled in German—the second language of the realm.

The queen had a hand-pulled elevator, but you'll need to hike up two flights of stairs to the throne room.

Throne Room (Third Floor): The **Long Hall**—considered one of the best-preserved Baroque rooms in Europe—was great for banquets. The decor trumpets the accomplishments of Denmark's great kings. The four corners of the ceiling feature the four continents known at the time. (America was still considered pretty untamed—notice the decapitated head with the arrow sticking out of it.) In the center, of course, is the proud seal of the Danish Royal Family. The tapestries, designed for this room, are from the late 1600s. Effective propaganda, they show the Danes defeating their Swedish rivals on land and at sea. The king's throne—still more propaganda for two centuries of "absolute" monarchs—was made of "unicorn horn" (actually narwhal tusk from Greenland).

Believed to bring protection from evil and poison, the horn was the most precious material in its day. The queen's throne is of hammered silver. The 150-pound lions are 300 years old.

The small room to the left holds a delightful **royal porcelain** display with Chinese, French, German, and Danish examples of the "white gold." For five centuries, Europeans couldn't figure out how the Chinese made this stuff. The difficulty in just getting it back to Europe in one piece made it precious. The Danish pieces, called "Flora Danica" (on the left as you enter), are from a huge royal set showing off the herbs and vegetables of the realm.

On your way back down, the middle floor is worth a look.

Middle Floor: Circling counterclockwise, you'll see more fine clocks, fancy furniture, and royal portraits. In the first room, notice the double portrait of the king and his sister. The queen enjoyed her royal lathe (with candleholders for lighting and pedals to spin it hidden away below). The small mirror room (on the side) was where the king played Hugh Hefner—using mirrors on the floor to see what was under those hoop skirts. In hidden cupboards, he had a fold-out bed and a handy escape staircase.

Back outside, find the stairs leading down to the...

Royal Danish Treasury (Castle Basement): The palace was a royal residence for a century and has been the royal vault right up until today. As you enter, peek into the **wine cellar,** with thousand-liter barrels, to the right of the ticket checker. Then continue into the treasury where you can browse through exquisite royal knickknacks.

The diamond- and pearl-studded **saddles** were Christian IV's—the first for his coronation, the second for his son's wedding. When his kingdom was nearly bankrupt, Christian had these constructed lavishly—complete with solid-gold spurs—to impress visiting dignitaries and bolster Denmark's credit rating.

The next case displays **tankards.** Danes were always big drinkers, and to drink in the top style, a king had narwhal steins (#4030). Note the fancy Greenland Inuit (Eskimo) on the lid (#4023). The case is filled with exquisitely carved ivory. On the other side of that case, what's with the mooning snuffbox (#4063)? Also, check out the amorous whistle (#4064).

Drop by the case on the wall in the back-left of the room: The 17th century was the age of **brooches.** Many of these are made of freshwater pearls. Find the fancy combination toothpick and ear spoon (#4140). Look for #4146: A queen was caught having an affair after 22 years of royal marriage. Her king gave her a special present: a golden ring—showing the hand of his promiscuous queen shaking hands with a penis.

Step downstairs, away from all this silliness. Passing through the serious vault door, you come face-to-face with a big, jeweled

sword. The tall, two-handed, 16th-century coronation sword was drawn by the new king, who cut crosses in the air in four directions, symbolically promising to defend the realm from all attacks. The cases surrounding the sword contain everyday items used by the king (all solid gold, of course). What looks like a trophy case of gold records is actually a collection of dinner plates with amber centers (#5032).

Go down the steps. In the center case is Christian IV's **coronation crown** (from 1596, seven pounds of gold and precious stones, #5124), which some consider to be the finest Renaissance crown in Europe. Its six tallest gables radiate symbolism. Find the symbols of justice (sword and scales), fortitude (a woman on a lion with a sword), and charity (a woman nursing—meaning the king will love God and his people as a mother loves her child). The pelican, which famously pecks its own flesh to feed its children, symbolizes God sacrificing his son, just as the king would make great sacrifices for his people. Climb the footstool to look inside—it's as exquisite as the outside. The shields of various Danish provinces remind the king that he's surrounded by his realms.

Circling the cases along the wall (right to left), notice the fine enameled lady's goblet with traits of a good woman spelled out in Latin (#5128); and above that, an exquisite prayer book (with handwritten favorite prayers, #5134). In the fifth window, the big solid-gold baptismal basin (#5262) hangs above tiny oval silver boxes that contained the royal children's umbilical chords (handy for protection later in life, #5272); and royal writing sets with wax, seals, pens, and ink (#5320).

Go down a few more steps into the lowest level of the treasury and last room. The two **crowns** in the center cases are more modern (from 1670), lighter, and more practical—just gold and diamonds without all the symbolism. The king's crown is only four pounds, the queen's a mere two.

The cases along the walls show off the **crown jewels.** These were made in 1840 of diamonds, emeralds, rubies, and pearls from earlier royal jewelry. The saber (#5540) shows emblems of the realm's 19 provinces. The sumptuous pendant features a 19-carat diamond cut (like its neighbors) in the 58-facet "brilliant" style for maximum reflection (far-left case, #5560). Imagine these on the dance floor. The painting shows the coronation of Christian VIII at Frederiksborg Chapel in 1840. The crown jewels are still worn by the queen on special occasions several times a year.

▲Rosenborg Gardens—Rosenborg Castle is surrounded by the royal pleasure gardens and, on sunny days, a minefield of sunbathing Danish beauties and picnickers. While "ethnic Danes" grab the shade, the rest of the Danes worship the sun. When the royal family is in residence, there's a daily changing-of-the-guard mini-parade from the Royal Guard's barracks adjoining Rosenborg Castle (at 11:30) to Amalienborg Castle (at 12:00). The Queen's Rose Garden (across the moat from the palace) is a royal place for a picnic. The fine statue of Hans Christian Andersen in the park—erected while he was still alive (and approved by him)—is meant to symbolize how his stories had a message even for adults.

▲**National Art Museum (Statens Museum for Kunst)**—This museum fills an impressive building with Danish and European paintings from the 14th century through today. Of most interest are the Danish Golden Age paintings, and those from the late 19th and early 20th centuries. Its collection of early French Modernism is impressive (with works by Matisse, Picasso, Braque, and more). This is complemented with works by Danish artists, who, inspired by the French avant-garde, introduced new, radical forms and colors to Scandinavian art. Make a point to meet the "Skagen" artists. They gathered in the fishing village of Skagen on the northern tip of Denmark, surrounded by the sea and strong light, and painted heroic folk fishermen themes in the late 1800s (permanent collection-free, special exhibits-80 kr, Tue–Sun 10:00–17:00, Wed until 20:00, closed Mon, Sølvgade 48, tel. 33 74 84 94, www.smk.dk).

Christianshavn

Across the harbor from the old town, Christianshavn is one of the most delightful districts in town to explore. A little background helps explain what you'll see.

Copenhagen's planned port, Christianshavn, was vital to Danish power in the 17th and 18th centuries. Denmark had always been second to Sweden when it came to possession of natural resources, so the Danes tried to make up for it by acquiring resource-rich overseas colonies. They built Christianshavn (with Amsterdam engineering help) to run the resulting trade business.

Since Denmark's economy was so dependent on trade, the port town was the natural target of enemies. When the Danes didn't support Britain against Napoleon in 1807, the Brits bombarded Christianshavn. In this "blackest year in Danish history," Christianshavn burned down. That's why today there's hardly a building here that dates from before 1807.

Christianshavn remained Copenhagen's commercial center until the 1920s, when a modern harbor was built. Suddenly, Christianshavn's economy collapsed and it became a slum. Chea prices attracted artsy types, giving it a bohemian flavor.

In 1971, several hundred squatters took over an unus military camp and created the Christiania commune (descri below). City officials looked the other way because back then one cared about the land. But by the 1980s, the neighborhoo become gentrified, and today it's some of priciest real est town. (A small flat costs around $300,000.) Suddenly developers are pushing to take back the land from squatters, and the very existence of Christiania is threatened.

Christianshavn prices are driven up by wealthy locals (who pay about 60 percent of their income in taxes) paying too much for flats, renting them cheap to their kids, and writing off the loss. Demand for property is huge. Prices have skyrocketed. Today the neighborhood is inhabited mostly by rich students and young professionals. Apart from pleasant canalside walks and trendy restaurants to enjoy, there are two things to see in Christianshavn: Our Savior's Church (with its fanciful tower) and Christiania (before it's gone).

▲Our Savior's Church (Vor Frelsers Kirke)

The church reopens in 2010 after restoration. Its bright Baroque interior (1696), with its pipe organ supported by the royal elephants, is worth a look (free, helpful English flier, April–Aug Mon–Sat 11:00–16:30, Sun 12:00–16:30, off-season closes at 15:30, bus #2A, #19, or Metro: Christianshavn, Sankt Annægade 29, tel. 32 57 27 98). You can climb the unique spiral spire for great views of the city and of the Christiania commune below (25 kr, 400 steps, 311 feet high, tower open daily 11:00–20:00, closed in bad weather and Nov–March).

➲ **Spin-Tour from the Top of Our Savior's Church:** Climb up until you run out of stairs. As you wind back down, look for these landmarks:

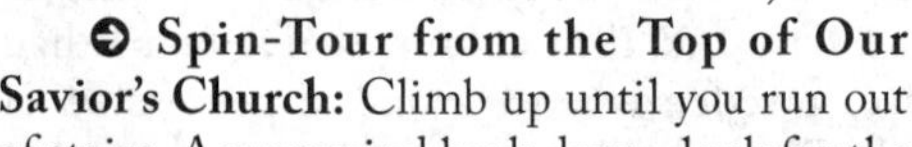

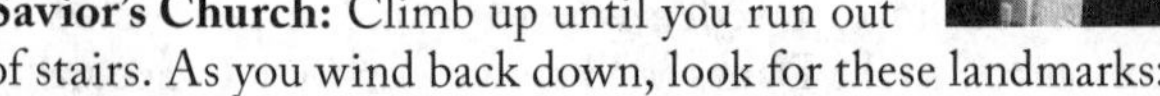

The modern windmills are a reminder that Denmark generates 20 percent of its power from wind. Below the windmills is a great aerial view of the Christiania commune. Beyond the windmills, across Øresund (the strait that separates Denmark and Sweden), stands a shuttered Swedish nuclear power plant. The lone skyscraper in the distance—the first and tallest skyscraper in Scandinavia—is in Malmö, Sweden. The Øresund Bridge made Malmö an easy 35-minute bus or train ride from Copenhagen (it's ...come a bedroom community, with much cheaper apartments ...ing the commute worthwhile).

...rther to the right, the big red-roof zone is Amager Island. ...dred years as the city's dumping grounds earned Amager ...me "Crap Island." Circling on, you come to the tower... ...n SAS hotel. The area beyond it is slated to become a ...rapers—the center of Europe's biomedical industry.

... Copenhagen is decorated with several striking ...s. The tower capped by the golden ball is a ride in

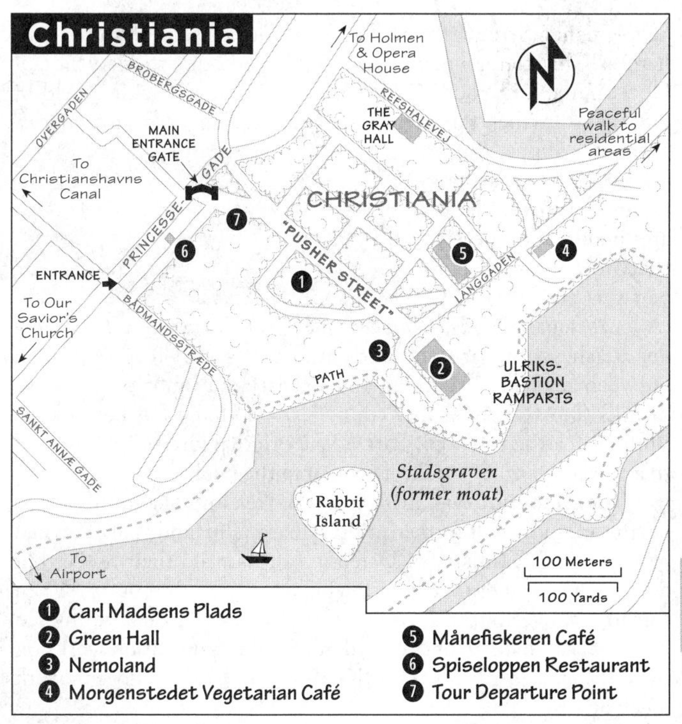

Tivoli Gardens. Next is City Hall's pointy brick tower. The biggest building, with the three-crown tower, is Christiansborg Palace. The Børsen (old stock exchange) is just beyond, with its unique dragon-tail tower. Behind that is Nyhavn. Just across from that and the new Playhouse is the dramatic new Opera House (with the flat roof and big, grassy front yard).

Christiania

If you're interested in visiting a free-wheeling community of alternative living, Christiania is a ▲▲▲ sight.

In 1971, the original 700 Christianians established squatters' rights in an abandoned military barracks just a 10-minute walk from the Danish parliament building. A generation later, this "free city" still stands—an ultra-human mishmash of idealists, hippies, potheads, non-materialists, and happy children (60[illegible] adults, 200 kids, 200 cats, 200 dogs, 2 parrots, and 17 horses[illegible] There are even a handful of Willie Nelson–type seniors amo[illegible] the 180 remaining here from the original takeover. And[illegible] amazing thing has happened: The place has become the th[illegible] most-visited sight among tourists in Copenhagen. Move [illegible] *Little Mermaid.*

"Pusher Street" (named for the former sale of soft drugs here) is Christiania's main drag. Get beyond this touristy side of Christiania, and you'll find a fascinating, ramshackle world of moats and earthen ramparts, alternative housing, cozy tea houses, carpenter shops, hippie villas, children's playgrounds, peaceful lanes, and people who believe that "to be normal is to be in a straightjacket."

(A local slogan claims, *"Kun døde fisk flyder med strømmen"*—"Only dead fish swim with the current.") Be careful to distinguish between real Christianians and Christiania's motley guests—drunks (mostly from other countries) who hang out here in the summer for the freedom. Part of the original charter guaranteed that the community would stay open to the public.

The Community: Christiania is broken into 14 administrative neighborhoods on a former military base. The land is still owned by Denmark's Ministry of Defense. Locals build their homes but don't own the land; there's no buying or selling of property. When someone moves out, the community decides who will be invited in to replace that person. A third of the adult population works on the outside, a third works on the inside, and a third doesn't work much at all.

There are nine rules: no cars, no hard drugs, no guns, no explosives, and so on. The Christiania flag is red and yellow because when the original hippies took over, they found a lot of red and yellow paint onsite. The three yellow dots in the flag are from the three "i"s in Christiania (or, some claim, the "o"s in "Love, Love, Love").

The community pays the city about $1 million a year for utilities and has about $1 million a year more to run its local affairs. A few "luxury hippies" have oil heat, but most use wood or gas. The ground here was poisoned by its days as a military base, so nothing is grown in Christiania. There's little industry within the commune (Christiania Cykler, which builds fine bikes, is an xception—www.pedersen-bike.dk). The community has one iling address (for 25 kr/month, you can receive mail here). A e chain provides a system of communal security (they have d experiences calling the police). Each September 26, the first squatters took over the barracks in 1971, Christiania irthday bash.

are entirely welcome here, because they've become f the economy. Visitors react in very different ways me see dogs, dirt, and dazed people. Others see e, freedom, and no taboos. Locals will remind judgmental Americans (whose country incarcerates more than a quarter of the world's prison inmates) that a society must make the choice: Allow for alternative lifestyles...or build more prisons.

Even since its inception, Christiania has been a political hot potato. No one in the Danish establishment wanted it. And no one had the nerve to mash it. In the last decade, Christiania has connected better with the rest of society—such as paying for its utilities and taxes. But Denmark's conservative government, which took over in 2001, has vowed to "normalize" Christiania (with pressure from the US), and in recent years police have regularly conducted raids on pot sellers. There's talk about opening the commune to market forces and developing posh apartments to replace existing residences, according to one government plan. But Christiania has a legal team, and litigation will likely drag on for many years.

Many predict that Christiania will withstand the government's challenge, as it has in years past. The community, which also calls itself Freetown, fended off a similar attempt in 1976 with the help of fervent supporters from around Europe. *Bevar Christiania*—"Save Christiania"—banners fly everywhere, and locals are confident that their free way of life will survive. As history has shown, the challenge may just make this hippie haven a bit stronger.

Orientation Tour: Passing under the gate, take Pusher Street directly into the community. The first square—a kind of market square (souvenirs and marijuana-related stuff)—is named Carl Madsens Plads, honoring the lawyer who took the squatters' case to the Danish supreme court in 1976 and won. Beyond that is Nemoland (a food circus, on the right). A huge warehouse called the Green Hall (Den Gronne Hal) is a recycling center (where people get most of their building material) that does double duty at night as a concert hall and as a place where children work on crafts. On the left, a lane leads to the Månefiskeren café, and beyond that, to the Morgenstedet vegetarian restaurant. Going straight on Pusher Street takes you to the ramparts that overlook the lake. A walk or bike ride through Christiania is a great way to see how this community lives. (When you leave, look up—the sign above the gate says, "You are entering the EU.")

Smoking Marijuana: Pusher Street was once lined with stalls selling marijuana, joints, and hash. Residents intentionally destroyed the stalls in 2004 to reduce the risk of Christiania being disbanded by the government. (One stall was spared and is on display at the National Museum.) Walking along Pusher Street today, you may witness policemen or covert deals being made—but never at the same time. You may also notice wafts of marijuana smoke and whispered offers of "hash" during your visit. However, purchasing and smoking may buy you more time in Denmark than you'd planned—possession of marijuana is illegal. With the recent police crackdown on marijuana sales, the street price has skyrocketed, crime has crept into the scene, and someone was actually murdered recently in a drug scuffle near Christiania—problems unthinkable in mellower times.

About hard drugs: For the first few years, junkies were tolerated. But that led to violence and polluted the mellow ambience residents envisioned. In 1979, the junkies were expelled—an epic confrontation in the community's folk history now—and since then the symbol of a fist breaking a syringe is as prevalent as the leafy marijuana icon. Hard drugs are emphatically forbidden in Christiania.

Eating in Christiania: The people of Christiania appreciate good food and count on tourism as a big part of their economy. Consequently, there are plenty of decent eateries. Most of the restaurants are closed on Monday (the community's weekly holiday). **Pusher Street** has a few grungy but tasty falafel stands, as well as a popular burger bar. **Nemoland** is the hangout zone—a fun collection of stands peddling Thai food and fast hippie food with great tented outdoor seating. Its stay-a-while atmosphere comes with backgammon, foosball, bakery goods, and fine views from the ramparts. **Morgenstedet** ("Morning Place") is a good, cheap vegetarian café with a mellow, woody interior and a rustic patio outside (70–90-kr meals, Tue–Sun 12:00–21:00, closed Mon, left after Pusher Street). **Månefiskeren** ("Moonfisher Bar") looks like a Brueghel painting—from 2009—with billiards, chess, snacks, and drinks. **Spiseloppen** is *the* classy, good-enough-for-Republicans restaurant in the community (closed Mon, described on page 108).

Hours and Tours: Christiania is open all the time (main entrance is down Prinsessegade behind the Our Savior's Church spiral tower in Christianshavn). You're welcome to snap photos, but ask residents before you photograph them. Guided tours leave from the front entrance of Christiania at 15:00 (just show up, 30 kr, 90 min, daily late June–Aug, only Sat–Sun rest of year, in English and Danish, tel. 32 57 96 70).

Greater Copenhagen

Carlsberg Brewery—Denmark's beloved source of legal intoxicants, Carlsberg welcomes you to its Visitors Center for a self-guided tour and a half-liter of beer (60 kr, Tue–Sun 10:00–17:00, Thu until 19:30, closed Mon, last entry one hour before closing; catch the local train to Enghave, or bus #18, #26, or #6A; enter at Gamle Carlsbergvej 11 around corner from brewery entrance, tel. 33 27 13 14, www.visitcarlsberg.dk).

Open-Air Folk Museum (Frilandsmuseet)—This park is filled with traditional Danish architecture and folk culture (free, mid-April–Oct Tue–Sun 10:00–17:00, closed Mon and Nov–mid-April, outside of town in the suburb of Lyngby, S-tog: Sorgenfri and 10-min walk to Kongevejen 100, tel. 33 13 44 11).

Bakken—Danes gather at Copenhagen's *other* great amusement park, Bakken (free; late June–mid-Aug daily 12:00–24:00, shorter hours April–late June and mid-Aug–mid-Sept; closed mid-Sept–March; S-tog: Klampenborg, then walk 10 min through the woods; tel. 39 63 73 00, www.bakken.dk).

Dragør—If you don't have time to get to the idyllic island of Ærø (see Central Denmark chapter), consider a trip a few minutes out of Copenhagen to the fishing village of Dragør (bus #30 from the main train station or bus #350S from Nørreport). For information, see www.dragoer.dk.

Shopping in Copenhagen

Shops are generally open Monday through Friday from 10:00 to 19:00 and Saturday from 9:00 to 16:00 (closed Sun). While the big department stores dominate the scene, many locals favor the characteristic, small artisan shops and boutiques.

Uniquely Danish souvenirs to look for include intricate paper cuttings with idyllic motifs of swans, flowers, or Christmas themes; mobiles with everything from bicycles to Viking ships (look for the quality Flensted brand); and the colorful artwork (posters, postcards, T-shirts, and more) by Danish artist Bo Bendixen.

For a street's worth of shops selling **"Scantiques,"** wander down Ravnsborggade from Nørrebrogade.

Copenhagen's colorful **flea markets** are small but feisty and surprisingly cheap (Sat May–Nov 8:00–14:00 at Israels Plads; Fri and Sat May–Sept 8:00–17:00 along Gammel Strand and on Kongens Nytorv). For other street markets, ask at Wonderful Copenhagen.

The city's top **department stores** (Illum at Østergade 52, and Magasin du Nord at Kongens Nytorv 13) offer a good, if expensive, look at today's Denmark. Both are on the Strøget and have fine cafeterias on their top floors. The department stores and the Politiken Bookstore on Rådhuspladsen have a good selection of maps and English travel guides.

The section of the Strøget called **Amagertorv** is a highlight for shoppers. The Royal Copenhagen store here sells porcelain on three floors (Mon–Fri 10:00–19:00, Sat–Sun 12:00–17:00). The first floor up features figurines and collectables. The second floor has a free museum with demonstrations and a great video (10 min, plays continuously, English only). In the basement, proving that "even the best painter can miss a stroke," you'll find the discounted seconds. Next door, Illums Bolighus shows off three floors of modern Danish design (Mon–Fri 10:00–19:00, Sat 9:00–17:00, Sun 10:00–17:00, shorter hours off-season).

Shoppers who like jewelry look for amber, known as "gold of the North." Globs of this petrified sap wash up on the shores of all the Baltic countries. **House of Amber** has a shop and a tiny two-room museum with about 50 examples of prehistoric insects trapped in the amber (remember *Jurassic Park*?) under magnifying glasses (25 kr, daily May–Aug 10:00–19:30, Sept–April 10:00–18:00, 50 yards off Nyhavn at Kongens Nytorv 2; 4 other locations sell amber, but only the Nyhavn location houses a museum as well).

If you buy anything substantial (more than 300 kr, about $60) from a shop displaying the **Danish Tax-Free Shopping** emblem, you can get a refund of the Value-Added Tax, roughly 20 to 25 percent of the purchase price (VAT is "MOMS" in Danish). If you have your purchase mailed, the tax can be deducted from your bill. For details, call 32 52 55 66, and see "VAT Refunds for Shoppers" in the Introduction.

Nightlife in Copenhagen

Copenhagen Jazz House is a good bet for live jazz (about 80–125 kr, Tue–Thu and Sun at 20:00, Fri–Sat at 21:00, closed Mon, Niels Hemmingsensgade 10, tel. 33 15 26 00, check website for schedule, www.jazzhouse.dk). For blues, try the **Mojo Blues Bar** (70 kr Fri–Sat, otherwise no cover, nightly 20:00–5:00, music starts at 21:30, Løngangsstræde 21c, tel. 33 11 64 53, schedule in Danish on website, www.mojo.dk). (For locations, see the map on page 98.) **Christiania** always seems to have something musical going on after dark. **Tivoli** has evening entertainment daily from mid-April through mid-September until 23:00 (see page 75).

DFDS Canal Tours offers two-hour **jazz cruises** along the canals of Copenhagen. You can bring a picnic dinner and drinks on board and enjoy a lively night on the water surrounded by Danes (120 kr, June–Aug Thu and Sun at 19:00, Sept–Dec and April–May and Sun at 15:00, no tours Jan–March; departs from DFDS dock at Nyhavn, tel. 32 96 30 00). Call to reserve on July and August evenings; otherwise try arriving 20 to 30 minutes in advance.

Event and Live Music Listings: For complete event listings, see the Friday edition of the *Politiken* newspaper. For the latest on the city's hopping jazz scene, inquire at Wonderful Copenhagen or study your *Copenhagen This Week* booklet.

Sleeping in Copenhagen

I've listed a few big business-class hotels, the best budget hotels in the center, cheap rooms in private homes in great neighborhoods an easy bus ride from the station, and a few backpacker dorm options.

Big Copenhagen hotels have an exasperating pricing policy. Their high rack rates are actually charged only about 20 or 30 days a year (unless you book in advance and don't know better). As hotels are swamped at certain times, they like to keep their gouging options open. Therefore, you'll need to check their website for deals or be bold enough to simply show up and use Wonderful Copenhagen's self-service booking system to find yourself a room on their push list. Wonderful Copenhagen swears that, except for maybe 10 days a year, you can land yourself a deeply discounted room in a three- or four-star business-class hotel in the center. That means a 1,400-kr double with American-style comfort for about 900 kr, including a big buffet breakfast.

Hotels in Central Copenhagen

Prices include breakfast unless noted otherwise. All of these hotels are big and modern, with elevators and non-smoking rooms upon request, and all accept credit cards (remember, you'll need a PIN to use it—see page 16 of the Introduction for details). Beware: Many hotels have rip-off phone rates even for local calls.

$$$ Ibsens Hotel is an elegant 118-room hotel in a charming neighborhood away from the main train station commotion and a short walk from the old center (Sb-1,280–1,380 kr, Db-1,480–1,680 kr; ask about discounts when booking, or check their website for the latest offers; higher prices are for larger rooms, third

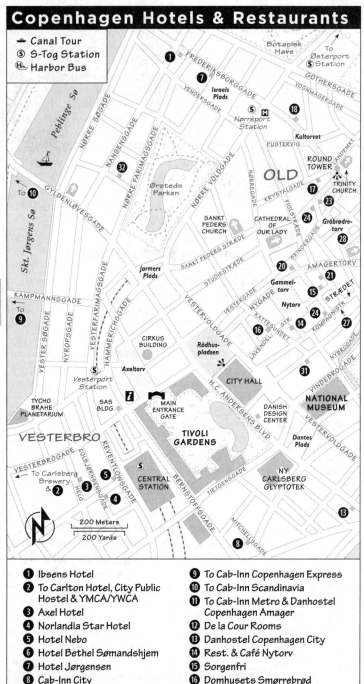

1 Ibsens Hotel
2 To Carlton Hotel, City Public Hostel & YMCA/YWCA
3 Axel Hotel
4 Norlandia Star Hotel
5 Hotel Nebo
6 Hotel Bethel Sømandshjem
7 Hotel Jørgensen
8 Cab-Inn City
9 To Cab-Inn Copenhagen Express
10 To Cab-Inn Scandinavia
11 To Cab-Inn Metro & Danhostel Copenhagen Amager
12 De la Cour Rooms
13 Danhostel Copenhagen City
14 Rest. & Café Nytorv
15 Sorgenfri
16 Domhusets Smørrebrød

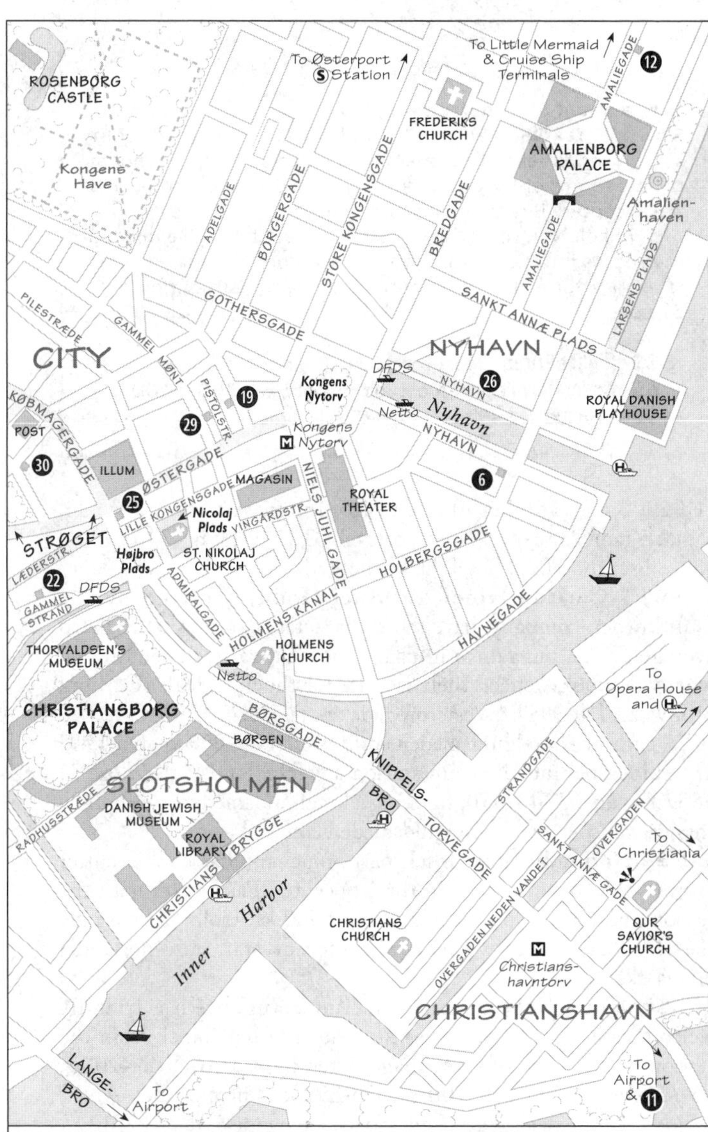

- 17 Café Halvvejen
- 18 Slagteren ved Kultorvet
- 19 Kransekagehuset Bakery
- 20 Conditori La Glace
- 21 Københavner Caféen
- 22 Gammel Strand Restaurant
- 23 Det Lille Apotek
- 24 Riz-Raz Veg. Buffet (2)
- 25 Café Norden
- 26 Nyhavn Eateries
- 27 Kompagnistræde Eateries
- 28 Gråbrødretorv Eateries
- 29 Netto Supermarket
- 30 Copenhagen Jazz House
- 31 Mojo Blues Bar
- 32 Baisikeli Bike Shop

Sleep Code

(5 kr = about $1, country code: 45)
S = Single, **D** = Double/Twin, **T** = Triple, **Q** = Quad, **b** = bathroom, **s** = shower. Breakfast is generally included at hotels but not at private rooms or hostels. Unless otherwise noted, credit cards are accepted. Everybody speaks English.

To help you sort easily through these listings, I've divided the rooms into three categories, based on the highest rack-rate price for a standard double room with bath during high season:

$$$ Higher Priced—Most rooms 1,000 kr or more.
$$ Moderately Priced—Most rooms between 600–1,000 kr.
$ Lower Priced—Most rooms 600 kr or less.

bed-200 kr, great bikes-10 kr/day, free Internet access and Wi-Fi, Vendersgade 23, S-tog: Nørreport, tel. 33 13 19 13, fax 33 13 19 16, www.ibsenshotel.dk, hotel@ibsenshotel.dk).

$$$ Carlton Hotel and **Axel Hotel,** operated by the Guldsmeden company, have more character than most. I've listed average prices, but rates can change dramatically, depending on when you book—check their website for the best deals (Carlton: Sb-895 kr, Db-995 kr, Vesterbrogade 66, tel. 33 22 15 00, fax 33 22 15 55, carlton@hotelguldsmeden.com; Axel: Sb-1,095 kr, Db-1,495 kr, a block behind the train station at Helgolandsgade 7, tel. 33 31 32 66, fax 33 31 69 70, booking@hotelguldsmeden.com). They share a website: www.hotelguldsmeden.com.

$$ Norlandia Star Hotel, part of a chain, has cookie-cutter rooms at reasonable prices in the city center. Prices vary with the season and online specials (Db-800–1,250 kr, Colbjornsensgade 13, tel. 33 22 11 00, www.norlandiahotels.dk/star, star@norlandiahotels.dk).

$$ Hotel Nebo, a secure-feeling refuge with a friendly welcome and 88 comfy, spacious rooms, is a half-block from the station on the edge of Copenhagen's red light district (S-420 kr, Sb-650–700 kr, D-650–700 kr, Db-899 kr, cheaper Oct–April, periodic online deals, extra bed-150 kr, Istedgade 6, tel. 33 21 12 17, fax 33 23 47 74, www.nebo.dk, nebo@email.dk).

$$ Hotel Bethel Sømandshjem, run by a Lutheran association, is a calm and stately former seamen's hotel facing the boisterous Nyhavn canal and offering 30 somewhat tired rooms at the most reasonable rack rates in town. A third of their rooms are more modern and non-smoking, but the older rooms are a bit more spacious. Book long in advance (Sb-645 kr, Db-845 kr, big Db on corner-945 kr, extra bed-200 kr, Metro to Kongens Nytorv, facing bridge over the canal at Nyhavn 22, tel. 33 13 03 70, fax 33 15 85 70, www.hotel-bethel.dk, info@hotel-bethel.dk).

$$ Hotel Jørgensen is a friendly little 30-room hotel in a great location just off Nørreport with some cheap, depressing, and grungy rooms and some good-value, nicer rooms. A good budget option, it's a bit worn around the edges. While the lounge is welcoming, the halls are a narrow, tangled maze. Prices here don't flex with demand (basic S-575 kr, Sb-675 kr, very basic D-675 kr, nicer Db-800 kr, extra bed-200 kr, Rømersgade 11, tel. 33 13 81 86, fax 33 15 51 05, www.hoteljoergensen.dk, hoteljoergensen@mail.dk). They also rent 150-kr dorm beds to those under 35 (4–12 beds per room, sheets-30 kr).

A Danish Motel 6

$$ Cab-Inn is a radical innovation and a great value, with several locations in Copenhagen: identical, mostly collapsible, tiny but comfy, cruise-ship–type staterooms, all bright, molded, and shiny, with TV, coffeepot, shower, and toilet. Each room has a single bed that expands into a twin-bedded room with one or two fold-down bunks on the walls. It's tough to argue with this kind of efficiency (generally Sb-545 kr, Db-675 kr, Tb-805 kr, Qb-935 kr, breakfast-60 kr, easy parking-60 kr, free Internet access in lobby, some have in-room Wi-Fi, www.cabinn.com). The best of the bunch is **Cab-Inn City,** with 350 rooms and a great central location (three levels of Db rooms: bunks-675 kr, tight standard-775 kr, spacious "Captain's" room-875 kr, a short walk south of the main train station and Tivoli at Mitchellsgade 14, tel. 33 46 16 16, fax 33 46 17 17, city@cabinn.com). Two more, nearly identical Cab-Inns are a 15-minute walk northwest of the station: **Cab-Inn Copenhagen Express** (86 rooms, Danasvej 32–34, tel. 33 21 04 00, fax 33 21 74 09, express@cabinn.com) and **Cab-Inn Scandinavia** (201 rooms, some quads, "Commodore" rooms have a real double bed for 100 kr extra, Vodroffsvej 55, tel. 35 36 11 11, fax 35 36 11 14, scandinavia@cabinn.com). The newest and largest is **Cab-Inn Metro,** near the Ørestad Metro station (710 rooms, some quads, on the airport side of town at Arne Jakobsens Allé 2, tel. 32 46 57 00, fax 32 46 57 01, metro@cabinn.com).

Rooms in Private Homes

At about 600 kr or so per double, staying in a private home can be a great value. While B&Bs offer a fine peek into Danish domestic life, the experience can be as private or as social as you want it to be. Hosts generally speak English, and you'll get a key and can come and go as you like. Rooms generally have no sink, and the bathroom's down the hall. They usually don't include breakfast, but you'll have access to the kitchen.

I've listed an agency with a great website that represents scores of fine places and—if you'd rather book direct—two good (cash only) B&Bs. One (run more like a small boarding house) is in Christianshavn, and the other is a block from Amalienborg Palace.

$ Bed & Breakfast Denmark has served as a clearinghouse for local B&Bs since 1992. Peter Eberth and his staff take a 20 percent cut (the "deposit" you pay) but monitor quality. Given the high cost of hostels and hotels and the way local B&B hosts come and go, this is a fine and worthwhile service. Peter's user-friendly website lets you choose the type and location of place best for you and gives you the necessary details when you pay. He has piles of good local rooms in central apartments (D-400 kr, Db-500–600 kr). He's located near the station at Sankt Peders Stræde 41, but there's no reason to visit his office (tel. 39 61 04 05, www.bbdk.dk).

$ Chicken's Private Pension rents five basic rooms in a funky old house, with steep stairs and rustic furniture. It's right on Christianshavn's main drag (S-400 kr, D-550 kr, T-675 kr, Q-800 kr, extra bed-150 kr, kitchen available for breakfast on your own, Torvegade 36, Metro: Christianshavntorv, tel. 32 95 32 73, www.chickens.dk, morten@chickens.dk, Morton Frederiksen).

$ Puk and Holger De la Cour and their friends are artistic and professional folks renting rooms in their utilitarian, modern, sometimes smoky, very Danish flats on Amaliegade, a stately cobbled street in a quiet neighborhood (a 10-min walk north of Nyhavn and the Strøget). You can look out your window and see the palace guard changing. They rent rooms to travelers April through September and include a do-it-yourself breakfast (2–3 rooms, S-425 kr, D-500 kr, extra bed-150 kr, kitchen/lounge available, catch bus #1A or #15 from the station to Fredericiagade, Amaliegade 34, fourth floor, tel. 33 12 04 68, mobile 23 72 96 45, www.delacour-bed-and-breakfast.eu, delacour@mail.dk). Puk and Holger can also put you in touch with five friends who rent decently priced rooms nearby.

$ Esben Juhl rents two spic-and-span, bright rooms in his charming Christianshavn apartment, close to the harbor and canal (S-400 kr, D-500 kr, extra bed-150 kr, includes light breakfast, David Balfours Gade 5, Metro: Christianshavntorv, tel. 32 57 39 08, mobile 27 40 12 15, mail@esju.dk).

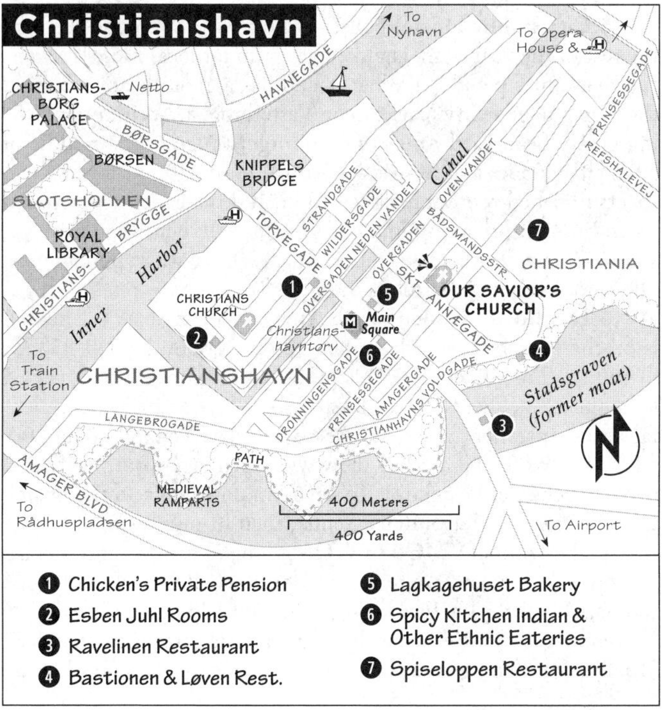

Christianshavn

1. Chicken's Private Pension
2. Esben Juhl Rooms
3. Ravelinen Restaurant
4. Bastionen & Løven Rest.
5. Lagkagehuset Bakery
6. Spicy Kitchen Indian & Other Ethnic Eateries
7. Spiseloppen Restaurant

Hostels

Copenhagen energetically accommodates the young vagabond on a shoestring. Hostels are the best value for those who travel alone, bring their own sheets, and make their own breakfast. Otherwise they can cost 250 kr per night per person.

$ Danhostel Copenhagen City, an official HI hostel, is the hostel of the future. This huge harborside skyscraper (1,000 beds on 16 stories) opened in 2005 and is clean, modern, non-smoking, and a 10-minute walk from the train station and Tivoli. Some rooms on higher floors have panoramic views over the city (available on a first-come, first-served basis). This is your best bet for a clean, basic, and inexpensive room in the city center (dorm beds in 6-bed rooms with bathrooms-130–195 kr—some co-ed, some separate; Sb/Db/Qb-600 kr, sheets and towel-60 kr, breakfast-70 kr, nonmembers pay 35 kr/night extra, lockers available, kitchen facilities, rental bikes, H. C. Andersen Boulevard 50, tel. 33 11 85 85, www.danhostel.dk/copenhagencity, copenhagencity@danhostel.dk).

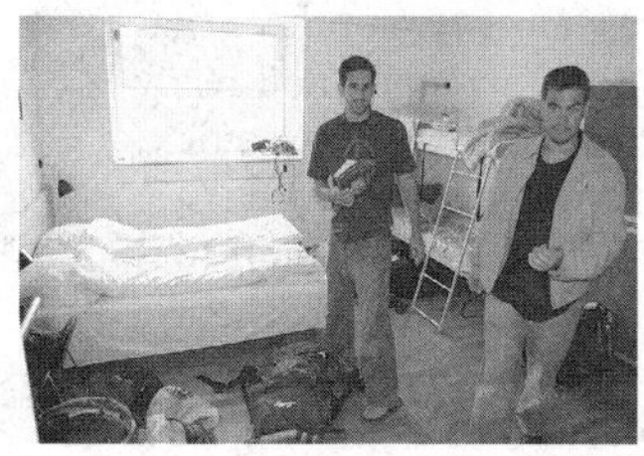

$ City Public Hostel houses travelers May through August; the rest of the year, it's a latchkey program for local kids. It's well-run, welcomes people of all ages, and has a great location behind the Copenhagen City Museum on Vesterbrogade. With its sprawling grassy front yard, you can even forget you're in the middle of a big city (125 kr/bed in massive 70-bed room; 200 kr for bed and sheets in 6-bed room; breakfast-40 kr, 10 kr cheaper if purchased when booking; relaxing lounge, 10-min walk behind main train station at Absalonsgade 8, tel. 33 31 20 70, www.citypublichostel.dk, info@citypublichostel.dk).

$ Danhostel Copenhagen Amager, an official HI hostel, is on the edge of town (dorm bed-120 kr, D-360 kr, Db-450 kr, T-460 kr, Tb-530 kr, Q-530 kr, Qb-590 kr, nonmembers pay 35 kr/night extra, sheets-40 kr, breakfast-50 kr, no curfew, excellent facilities, Internet access, self-serve laundry, Vejlands Allé 200, tel. 32 52 29 08, fax 32 52 27 08, www.copenhagenyouthhostel.dk, copenhagen@danhostel.dk). To get from downtown to the hostel, take the Metro (Metro: Bella Center, then 10-min walk).

$ The **Danish YMCA/YWCA** is a big, grungy, central crash pad open in July and August only (dorm bed-105 kr, 4- to 10-bed rooms, sheets-15 kr, blankets-25 kr, towel-15 kr, no breakfast, Valdemarsgade 15, 10-min walk from train station or bus #6, tel. 33 31 15 74, www.ymca-interpoint.dk, info@ymca-interpoint.dk).

Eating in Copenhagen

Cheap Meals

For a quick lunch, try a *smørrebrød,* a *pølse,* or a picnic. Finish it off with a pastry.

Smørrebrød

Denmark's 300-year-old tradition of open-face sandwiches survives. Find a *smørrebrød* take-out shop and choose two or three that look good (about 20 kr each). You'll get them wrapped and ready for a park bench. Add a cold drink, and you have a fine, quick, and very Danish lunch. Tradition calls for three sandwich courses: herring first, then meat, and then cheese. Downtown, you'll find these handy local alternatives to Yankee fast-food chains:

Near Gammeltorv/Nytorv: **Restaurant and Café Nytorv** has pleasant outdoor seating (with indoor tables available nearby) and a great deal on a *smørrebrød* sampler for about 160 kr—perfect for two people to share. This "Copenhagen City Plate" gives you a selection of the traditional sandwiches and extra bread on request (daily 11:30–22:00, Nytorv 15, tel. 33 11 77 06). **Sorgenfri** offers a local experience in a dark, woody spot just off the Strøget (daily 11:00–21:00, Brolæggerstræde 8, tel. 33 11 58 80). Or consider **Domhusets**

Smørrebrød (Mon–Fri 7:00–15:00, closed Sat–Sun, off the City Hall end of the Strøget at Kattesundet 18, tel. 33 15 98 98).

Near Copenhagen University: **Café Halvvejen** is a small mom-and-pop place serving traditional lunches and open-face sandwiches in a woody and smoke-stained café, lined with portraits of Danish royalty. You can eat inside or at an outside table in good weather (45-70 kr *smørrebrød*, Mon–Thu 11:00–14:00, Fri–Sat 11:00–15:00, closed Sun, next to public library at Krystalgade 11).

Slagteren ved Kultorvet, a few blocks northwest of the university, is a small butcher shop selling good, inexpensive sandwiches to go for about 30 kr. Choose from ham, beef, or pork (sorry—no vegetarian options, Mon–Thu 8:00–17:30, Fri 8:00–19:00, Sat 8:00–14:00, closed Sun, just off Kultorvet square at #4 Frederiksborggade, look for gold bull's head hanging outside).

The *Pølse*

The famous Danish hot dog, sold in *pølsevogne* (sausage wagons) throughout the city, is another typically Danish institution that has resisted the onslaught of our global, Styrofoam-packaged, fast-food culture. Study the photo menu for variations. These are fast, cheap, tasty, and, like their American cousins, almost worthless nutritionally. Even so, what the locals call the "dead man's finger" is the dog Danish kids love to bite.

There's more to getting a *pølse* than simply ordering a "hot dog" (which in Copenhagen simply means a sausage with a bun on the side, generally the worst bread possible). The best is a *ristet* (or grilled) hot dog *med det hele* (with the works). Employ these other handy phrases: *rød* (red, the basic boiled weenie), *medister* (spicy, better quality), *knæk* (short, stubby, tastier than *rød*), *brød* (a bun, usually smaller than the sausage), *svøb* ("swaddled" in bacon), *Fransk* (French style, buried in a long skinny hole in the bun with sauce). *Sennep* is mustard and *ristet løg* are crispy, fried onions. Wash everything down with a *sodavand* (soda pop).

By hanging around a *pølsevogn,* you can study this institution. Denmark's "cold feet cafés" are a form of social care: People who have difficulty finding jobs are licensed to run these wiener-mobiles. As they gain seniority, they are promoted to work at more central locations. Danes like to gather here for munchies and *pølsesnak*—the local slang for empty chatter (literally, "sausage talk"). And traditionally, guys stop here after getting drunk for a hot dog and chocolate milk on the way home—that's why the stands stay open until wee hours.

Picnics

Throughout Copenhagen, small delis *(viktualiehandler)* sell fresh bread, tasty pastries, juice, milk, cheese, and yogurt (drinkable, in tall liter boxes). Two of the largest supermarket chains are **Irma** (in arcade on Vesterbrogade next to Tivoli) and **Super Brugsen. Netto** is a cut-rate outfit with the cheapest prices.

Pastry

The golden pretzel sign hanging over the door or windows is the Danes' age-old symbol for a bakery. Danish pastries, called *wienerbrød* ("Vienna bread") in Denmark, are named for the Viennese bakers who brought the art of pastry-making to Denmark, where the Danes say they perfected it. Try these bakeries: **Nansens** (on corner of Nansensgade and Ahlefeldtsgade, near Ibsens Hotel), **Kransekagehuset** (just off the Strøget, near Kongens Nytorv at Ny Ostergade 9), and **Lagekagehuset** (on Torvegade in Christianshavn, and next to the Wonderful Copenhagen office). For a genteel bit of high-class 1870s Copenhagen, pay a lot for a coffee and a fresh danish at **Conditori La Glace,** just off the Strøget at Skoubogade 3.

Dine with the Danes

For a unique experience and a great opportunity to meet locals in their homes, consider having this organization arrange a dinner for you with a Danish family. You get a homey two-course meal with lots of conversation. Some effort is made to match your age and interests, but not occupations. Book online at least a week in advance (400 kr per person, www.dinewiththedanes.dk, tel. 26 85 39 61). Fill out an online questionnaire, and you'll be contacted by email a day or two later.

Restaurants

Due to the high cost of water in Denmark, it's common to be charged for tap water with your meal if you do not order any other beverage. You'll often save money by paying with cash; many Danish restaurants charge a fee for credit-card transactions.

Dining in the Center

Københavner Caféen, cozy yet classy, is a plush and convivial place that feels like a ship captain's dining room. The staff is enthusiastically traditional, serving fine local dishes and elegant open-face sandwiches for a good value. Lunch specials are served until 17:00, when the more expensive dinner menu kicks in (plates for 109–189 kr, daily, kitchen closes at 22:00, at Badstuestræde 10, tel. 33 32 80 81).

Gammel Strand, which serves "Danish-inspired French cuisine," is ideal for a dressy splurge in the old center. Outdoor tables come with an enjoyable view of the canal and people strolling by, while indoor tables are white-tablecloth elegant. Reservations are wise (200–350-kr entrées, daily 12:00–15:30 & 18:00–22:00, across from DFDS Canal Tours tour boats at Gammel Strand 42, tel. 33 91 21 21). They also serve traditional Danish lunch specials (145–195 kr).

Eating Inexpensively in the Center

Det Lille Apotek ("The Little Pharmacy") is a reasonable, candle-lit place. It's been popular with locals for 200 years, and now it's also quite touristy. Their specialty is "Stone Beef," a big slab of tender, raw steak plopped down and cooked in front of you on a scalding-hot soapstone. Cut it into smaller pieces and it's cooked within minutes (sandwich lunches, traditional dinners for 100–190 kr, nightly from 17:30, just off the Strøget, between Frue Church and Round Tower at St. Kannikestræde 15, tel. 33 12 56 06).

Riz-Raz Vegetarian Buffet has two locations in Copenhagen: around the corner from the canal boat rides at Kompagnistræde 20 (tel. 33 15 05 75) and across from Det Lille Apotek at Store Kannikestræde 19 (tel. 33 32 33 45). At both places, you'll find a healthy all-you-can-eat Mediterranean/vegetarian buffet lunch for 79 kr (cheese but no meat, daily 9:30–16:00) and an even bigger dinner buffet for 99 kr (16:00–23:00). The wonderfully varied and very filling dinner buffet has to be the best deal in town. Use lots of plates and return to the buffet as many times as you like. They also offer à la carte and meat options for 100–190 kr. Tap water is 8 kr per jug.

Café Norden, very Danish with modern "world cuisine" and fine pastries, is a big, venerable institution overlooking Amagertorv by the swan fountain. They have good light meals and salads, and great people-watching from window seats on the second floor (90–140-kr entrées, huge splittable portions, daily 9:00–24:00, order at bar, Østergade 61, tel. 33 11 77 91).

Illum and **Magasin du Nord** department stores serve cheery, reasonable meals in their cafeterias. At Illum, eat outside at tables along the Strøget, or head to the elegant glass-domed top floor (Østergade 52). Magasin du Nord (Kongens Nytorv 13) also has a great grocery and deli in the basement.

Also try **Restaurant and Café Nytorv** at Nytorv 15 or **Sorgenfri** at Brolæggerstræde 8 (both are described under "*Smørrebrød*," earlier).

In Christianshavn

This neighborhood is so cool, it's worth combining an evening wander with dinner, even if you're not staying here. It's a 10-minute walk across the bridge from the old center, or a 3-minute ride on the

Metro. Choose one of my listings (for locations, see map on page 103), or simply wander the blocks between Christianshavntorv, the main square, and the Christianshavn Canal—you'll find a number of lively neighborhood pubs and cafés.

Ravelinen Restaurant, on a tiny island on the big road 100 yards south of Christianshavn, serves traditional Danish food at reasonable prices to happy local crowds. Dine indoors or on the lovely lakeside terrace (which is tented and heated, so it's comfortable even on blustery evenings). This is like Tivoli without the kitsch and tourists (50–80-kr *smørrebrød,* 80–100-kr lunch dishes, 150–180-kr dinners, April–mid-Dec daily 11:30–20:00, closed off-season, Torvegade 79, tel. 32 96 20 45).

Bastionen & Løven, at the little windmill (Lille Mølle), serves gourmet Danish nouveau cuisine with a French inspiration from a small but fresh menu, on a Renoir terrace or in its Rembrandt interior. The classiest and most gourmet of all my listings, this restaurant fills a classic old mansion (65–165-kr lunches, 145–200-kr dinners, 335-kr three-course meal, daily 12:00–22:00, walk to end of Torvegade and follow ramparts up to restaurant, at south end of Christianshavn, Christianshavn Voldgade 50, tel. 32 95 09 40 for reservations indoors—required on Fri and Sat, no reservations for outdoor seating, as weather is unpredictable).

Lagkagehuset is everybody's favorite bakery in Christianshavn. With a big selection of pastries, sandwiches, excellent fresh-baked bread, and award-winning strawberry tarts, it's a great place for breakfast or picnic fixings (take-out coffee and pastries for 20 kr, Torvegade 45).

Ethnic Strip on Christianshavn's Main Drag: Torvegade, which is within a few minutes' walk of the Christianshavn Metro station, is lined with appealing and inexpensive ethnic eateries, including Italian, cheap kebabs, Mexican (thriving with a nightly 99-kr buffet), Chinese, and more. **Spicy Kitchen** serves cheap and good Indian food—tight and cozy, it's a hit with locals (50–70-kr plates, nightly until 23:00, Torvegade 56).

In Christiania: **Spiseloppen** ("The Flea Eats") is a wonderfully classy place in Christiania. It serves great 140-kr vegetarian meals and 160–250-kr meaty ones by candlelight. It's gourmet anarchy—a good fit for Christiania, the free city/squatter town (Tue–Sun 17:00–22:00, closed Mon, occasional live music on weekends, reservations often necessary Fri–Sat; 3 blocks behind spiral spire of Our Savior's Church, on top floor of old brick warehouse, turn right just inside Christiania's gate, enter the wildly empty warehouse, and climb the graffiti-riddled stairs; tel. 32 57 95 58). Other, less-expensive Christiania eateries are listed on page 94.

Near Nørreport

The following eateries are near the recommended Ibsens and Jørgensens hotels.

Café Klimt is a tight and thriving place, noisy and lit with candles. A young, hip crowd gathers here under the funky palm tree for modern world cuisine—salads, big pastas, burgers, omelets, and brunch until 16:00 (70–150 kr, daily 10:00–24:00, later Fri–Sat, Frederikborggade 29, tel. 33 11 76 70).

Café Marius, with a jazzy elegance, dressy indoor tables, and casual sidewalk seating, is popular for its homemade pasta, hearty burgers, and big salads. Marius is from Chicago, so don't expect traditional Danish here (100–145-kr plates and lunch specials, Tue–Fri 12:00–23:00, Sat 11:00–2:00 in the morning, Sun 11:00–16:00, weekend brunch with American-style pancakes served until 15:00, closed Mon, Nørre Farimagsgade 55, tel. 33 11 83 83).

Other Central Neighborhoods to Explore

To find a good restaurant, try simply window-shopping in one of these inviting districts.

Nyhavn's harbor canal is lined with a touristy strip of restaurants set alongside its classic sailboats. Here thriving crowds are served mediocre, overpriced food in a great setting. On any sunny day, if you want steak and fries (120 kr) and a 50-kr beer, this can be fun. On Friday and Saturday, the strip becomes the longest bar in the world.

Kompagnistræde is home to a changing cast of great little eateries. Running parallel to the Strøget, this street has fewer tourists and lower rent, and encourages places to compete creatively for the patronage of local diners.

Gråbrødretorv ("Grey Friars' Square") is perhaps the most popular square in the old center for a meal. It's like a food court, especially in good weather. Choose from Italian, Danish, or a meal in the old streetcar #14. **Jensen's Bofhus** and the pricier **Bof & Ost** are both respected steakhouses. **Skildpadden** ("The Turtle") is a student hit, with make-it-yourself sandwiches and salads (69 kr) and draft beer (30 kr) in a cozy cellar with three little tables on the lively square (Mon–Sat 11:30–21:30, Sun 12:00–20:00, Gråbrødretorv 9, tel. 33 13 05 06).

Istedgade and the surrounding streets behind the train station are home to an assortment of inexpensive ethnic restaurants. You will find numerous kebab, Chinese, Thai, and pizza places. The area can be a bit seedy, especially right behind the station, but walk a few blocks away to take your pick of inexpensive, ethnic eateries frequented by locals.

Copenhagen Connections

Trains

Malmö, Sweden—just a 35-minute train trip across the Øresund Bridge from Copenhagen (3/hr)—has become the regional hub for international trains. To reach destinations from Copenhagen such as Stockholm or Berlin, you'll usually have to transfer at the Malmö Central Station; be sure to get off the train at Malmö C (for "Central"). If you get off at Malmö Syd, you'll miss your connection.

From Copenhagen by Train to: Hillerød/Frederiksborg (6/hr, 40 min on S-tog), **Roskilde** (1–3/hr, 30 min), **Humlebæk** (Louisiana modern-art museum; 4/hr, 45 min), **Helsingør** (3/hr, 50 min), **Odense** (3/hr, 1.5–2 hrs), **Ærøskøbing** (5/day, 2.75 hrs to Svendborg with a transfer in Odense, then 75-min ferry crossing to Ærøskøbing—see page 138 for info on ferry), **Billund/Legoland** (hourly, 2.25 hrs to Vejle, then take bus #244 to Billund, allow 3.5 hrs total), **Århus** (1–2/hr, 3 hrs), **Stockholm** (almost hourly, 5.5 hrs on X2000 high-speed train, most with a transfer at Malmö Central Station, reservation required; see below for night-train option), **Växjö** (8/day, 2.5–3 hrs), **Kalmar** (8/day, 3.5–4 hrs, transfer in Alvesta), **Oslo** (4/day, 8 hrs, usually with transfer at Göteborg; see below for night-train option and overnight boat), **Berlin** (5/day, 6.5 hrs, reservation required, change in Hamburg; plus 1 direct night train from Malmö Central, 20:56–6:01), **Amsterdam** (9/day, 11–18 hrs, most require multiple changes, 1 night train with change in Duisburg at 6:00), and **Frankfurt/Rhine** (4/day, 9–11 hrs, most change in Hamburg). National train info tel. 70 13 14 15. International train info tel. 70 13 14 16.

By Night Train to Stockholm and Oslo: There are no direct night trains from Copenhagen to Oslo or Stockholm. However, you can connect to these cities via Malmö, across the Øresund Bridge in Sweden. First take a 35-minute regional train from Copenhagen to **Malmö Central Station,** then transfer to the night train bound for **Stockholm** (23:08–5:54) or **Oslo** (23:08–8:00, June–Aug only). Always confirm schedules locally.

By Bus: Taking the bus to **Stockholm** is cheaper but more time-consuming than taking the train (2/day, 9 hrs, www.swebusexpress.se).

Cruise Ships

More than half a million people visit Copenhagen via cruise ship each year. For a wealth of online information for cruise-ship passengers, see www.cruisecopenhagen.com.

Terminals: Most cruise ships use one of two main terminals—**Freeport Terminal,** about an hour's walk from the city center, and **Langelinie Pier** (near *The Little Mermaid* site). Contact your cruise-ship line to find out which terminal your cruise will use.

A third terminal, **Marmokai**, is located between the Freeport and Langelinie piers, and serves DFDS ferries to and from Oslo (see "Overnight Cruise to Oslo," below).

From Freeport Terminal to Copenhagen's City Center: Most cruise lines run shuttle buses between the port and town, usually stopping at Kongen Nytorv, Østerport, and/or Rådhuspladsen (coordinated with ship arrivals and departures; contact your cruise line for details). A taxi costs about 125 kr.

When ships are in port, City Sightseeing's **tour buses** often wait at the terminal and link to the company's regular hop-on, hop-off Open Top Tour (timed to arrivals and departures, 120 kr for 48-hour ticket, buy from driver, see page 61 for details).

Public bus #26 runs three times an hour between the port and Rådhuspladsen (21 kr, buy ticket from driver, 26 min). This option only works Monday through Friday (public buses don't stop at Freeport Terminal Sat–Sun). To reach the bus stop from the dock, exit the terminal following the blue painted lines on the sidewalk and *Port Entrance* signs (10-min walk). At the port entrance, cross Sundkrogsgade to the bus stop.

From Langelinie Pier to Copenhagen's City Center: The pier is just a few minutes' walk north of *The Little Mermaid* site. A good option for those traveling light or here only for the day is to do my self-guided walk in reverse, starting at *The Little Mermaid* and ending at Rådhuspladsen (see page 62).

Otherwise, the easiest option is to take a **taxi** (about 120 kr, 15 min) or the cruise ship **shuttle bus** (timed to ship arrivals and departures) to Rådhuspladsen.

City Sightseeing's hop-on, hop-off **Open Top Tour buses** stop at the Langelinie terminal (near *The Little Mermaid* site) and Rådhuspladsen, on a circular "Mermaid Tour" with stops at most major sights (120 kr for 48-hour ticket, buy from driver, 2/hr, see page 61 for details).

Public bus #26 connects Langelinie with Rådhuspladsen (21 kr, buy ticket from driver, 3/hr, 22 min).

Overnight Cruise to Oslo

Luxurious DFDS Seaways cruise ships leave nightly from Copenhagen for Oslo, and from Oslo for Copenhagen. The 16-hour sailings leave at 17:00 and arrive at 9:30 the next day. So you can spend seven hours in Norway's capital and then return to Copenhagen, or take this cruise from Oslo and do Copenhagen as a day trip...or just go one-way in either direction (see page 231 for info on departing from Oslo).

Cruise Costs

Cabins vary dramatically in price depending on the day and season (most expensive on weekends and late June–mid Aug; cheapest on weekdays and Oct–April). For example, a bed in a four-berth "Seaways" shoehorn economy cabin starts at 250 kr per person one-way for four people traveling together (425 kr with a window); a luxurious double "Commodore class" cabin higher on the ship starts at 825 kr per person one-way (and includes a TV, minibar, and free breakfast buffet). A "mini-cruise" round-trip with a day in Oslo and no meals starts at 598 kr per person in an economy double cabin. All cabins have private bathrooms inside.

Onboard Services

DFDS Seaways operates two ships on this route—the MS *Pearl of Scandinavia* and the MS *Crown of Scandinavia*. Both offer all the cruise-ship luxuries: big buffets for breakfast (129 kr) and dinner (239 kr), gourmet restaurants (359-kr three-course meals), a kids' playroom, pool (indoor on the *Crown*, indoor and outdoor on the *Pearl*), sauna, nightclubs, pay Wi-Fi, satellite phone, and tax-free shopping. There are no ATMs on board. Cash advances are available at the shipboard exchange desk. All shops and restaurants accept credit cards as well as euros, dollars, and Danish, Swedish, and Norwegian currency.

Reservations

Reservations are smart in summer and on weekends. Advance bookings get the best prices. Book online or call DFDS Seaway's Danish office at 33 42 30 00 (Mon–Fri 9:30–17:00, www.dfds.com), or, in the US, call 800-533-3755 (www.seaeurope.com).

Terminal and Transportation Connections

In Copenhagen, the Marmokai Terminal is a short walk north of *The Little Mermaid* site. The terminal is open daily 9:00–17:00 (luggage lockers available).

Getting from Copenhagen City Center to the Terminal: The cruise line operates a shuttle bus, marked *#20E*, from Kongens Nytorv and Østerport station (free for cruise passengers, coordinated with sailing schedule; daily 14:00–16:00, departs every 10–30 min, arrives at the terminal 11 min later). Or take the S-tog from downtown in the direction of Hellerup or Hillerød to the Nordhavn station. Exit the station, cross under the tracks, and hike toward the water. Follow the *til Marmokai* signs (you'll see the ship).

Getting from the Terminal to Copenhagen City Center: Shuttle bus #20E meets arriving ships from Oslo (daily 9:30–10:15) and will drop you at Østerport station or Kongens Nytorv.

NEAR COPENHAGEN

Roskilde • Frederiksborg Castle • Louisiana • Karen Blixen Museum • Kronborg Castle

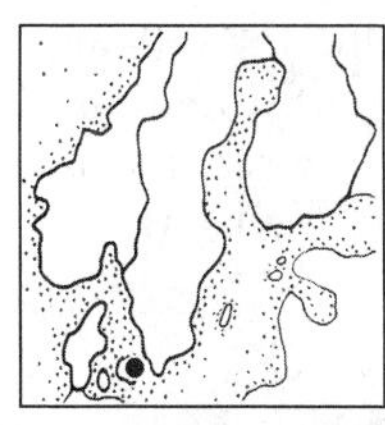

Copenhagen's the star, but there are several worthwhile sights nearby, and the public transportation system makes side-tripping a joy. Visit Roskilde's great Viking ships and royal cathedral. Tour Frederiksborg, Denmark's most spectacular castle, and slide along the cutting edge at Louisiana—a superb art museum with a coastal setting as striking as its art. Blixen fans can get *Out of Africa* at the author's home. At Helsingør, do the dungeons of Kronborg Castle before heading on to Sweden.

Planning Your Time

Roskilde's Viking ships and Frederiksborg Castle are the area's essential sights. Each one takes a half-day, and each one is an easy commute from Copenhagen (30–45-min train ride, then 20-min walk). You'll find fewer tour-bus crowds in the afternoon. While you're in Roskilde, you can also pay your respects to the tombs of the Danish royalty.

If you're choosing between castles, Frederiksborg is the beautiful showpiece, and Kronborg—darker and danker—is more typical of the way most castles really were.

Louisiana is the obvious choice for art-lovers; the Karen Blixen Museum is for her admirers.

By car, you can see these sights on your way into or out of Copenhagen. By train, do day trips from Copenhagen, then sleep while traveling to and from Copenhagen to Oslo (by boat, or by train via Malmö, Sweden) or Stockholm (by train via Malmö). Consider getting a Copenhagen Card (see page 53), which covers your transportation and admission to—or discounts on—many major sights.

Roskilde

Denmark's roots, both Viking and royal, are on display in Roskilde (ROSS-killa), a pleasant town 18 miles west of Copenhagen. Eight hundred years ago, Roskilde was the seat of Denmark's royalty—its center of power. Today the town that introduced Christianity to Denmark in A.D. 980 is most famous for hosting northern Europe's biggest annual rock/jazz/folk festival (July 1–4 in 2010, June 30–July 3 in 2011, www.roskilde-festival.dk). Wednesday and Saturday are flower/flea/produce market days (8:00–14:00).

Getting There: Roskilde is an easy side-trip from Copenhagen by train (1–3/hr, 30 min). Trains headed to Ringsted, Nykøbing, or Lindholm all stop in Roskilde (which is an intermediate stop you won't see listed on departure boards).

Tourist Information: Roskilde's TI is helpful (April–mid-Aug Mon–Fri 10:00–17:00, Sat 10:00–13:00; open Sat until 14:00 July–mid-Aug; shorter hours off-season, closed Sun year-round, 3 blocks from cathedral, follow signs to *Turistbureau,* Gullandsstræde 15, tel. 46 31 65 65, www.visitroskilde.com).

Sights in Roskilde

▲▲Roskilde Cathedral

Roskilde's imposing 12th-century, twin-spired cathedral houses the tombs of 38 Danish kings and queens (pick up a map as you enter). It's a stately, modern-looking old church with great marblework, paintings (notice the impressive 3-D piece with Christian IV looking like a pirate, in the room behind the small pipe organ), wood carvings in and around the altar, a great 16th-century Baroque organ, and a silly little glockenspiel that plays high above the entrance at the top of every hour.

Cost and Hours: 25 kr, good 25-kr guidebook; open April–Sept Mon–Sat 9:00–17:00, Sun 12:30–17:00; Oct–March Tue–Sat 10:00–16:00, Sun 12:30–16:00, closed Mon; often closed Sat and Sun afternoons for baptisms and weddings. Tel. 46 35 58 14, www.roskildedomkirke.dk.

Tours and Concerts: 20-kr tours run Mon–Fri at 11:00 and 14:00, Sat at 11:00, Sun at 14:00, fewer off-season. Free organ concerts offered July–Aug Thu at 20:00.

Near Copenhagen

Location: From the train station, cross the road and head down the pedestrian street, following signs (10-min walk). From the cathedral, it's a pleasant walk through a hillside park down to the harbor and Viking ships.

▲▲▲Viking Ship Museum (Vikingeskibshallen)

Vik literally means "shallow inlet," so "Vikings" are people who lived along those inlets. Roskilde—and this award-winning museum—are strategically located along one such inlet. The collection displays five different Viking ships. One boat is like the one Leif Eriksson took to America 1,000 years ago. Another is like those depicted in the Bayeux Tapestry in Normandy, France. These ships were deliberately sunk a thousand years ago to block a nearby harbor and were only recently excavated, preserved, and pieced together. The ships aren't as intact or as ornate as those in Oslo (see page 208), but this museum does a better job of explaining shipbuilding. The English descriptions are excellent—it's the kind of museum where you want to read everything.

As you enter, check the board for the day's activities and demonstrations (including shipbuilding, weaving, blacksmithing, and minting). Buy the 20-kr guidebook, and request the 13-minute English movie introduction.

Exhibits in the main hall and museum café describe the re-creation of the 100-foot-long, eight-man long boat *Sea Stallion,* constructed by modern shipbuilders using ancient techniques. A crew of 65 sailed the replica Viking war ship to Dublin, Ireland, in 2007, and then back to Roskilde in the summer of 2008.

Cost, Hours, Location: 95 kr, cheaper off-season, daily 10:00–17:00, free tours daily in summer at 12:00 and 15:00; from station catch bus #216 or #607 toward Boserup, 2/hr, 7-min ride; or, from cathedral, it's a 10-min walk downhill; tel. 46 30 02 00, www.vikingeskibsmuseet.dk.

Cruise: For an extra 75 kr, you can go for a fun hour-long sail around Roskilde's harbor in a replica Viking ship.

Frederiksborg Castle

Frederiksborg Castle, rated ▲▲, is located in the cute town of Hillerød. This grandest castle in Scandinavia is often called the "Danish Versailles." Built from 1602 to 1620, Frederiksborg was the castle of Denmark's King Christian IV. Much of it was reconstructed after an 1859 fire, with the normal Victorian over-the-top flair, by the brewer J. C. Jacobsen and his Carlsberg Foundation.

A museum since 1878, today's castle takes you on a chronological walk through the story of Denmark from 1500 until today (the third floor covers modern times). Many rooms have a handy English-language information sheet. The countless musty paintings are a fascinating scrapbook of Danish history.

The traffic-free center of Hillerød is also worth a wander (just outside the gates of the castle, toward train station).

Tourist Information: Pick up a city map and brochures about the area at Hillerød's TI (Mon–Wed 10:30–17:00, Thu–Fri 10:30–16:30, Sat 10:30–14:00, closed Sun, inside the library at Christiansgade 1, tel. 48 24 26 26, www.hillerodturist.dk, turistbureau@c4.dk).

Getting There: From Copenhagen, take the S-tog to Hillerød (line E, 6/hr, 40 min). From the Hillerød station, you can enjoy a pleasant 20-minute walk to the castle, or catch bus #701 or #702 (free with S-tog ticket or Copenhagen Card, buses are to the right as you exit station). Drivers will find easy parking at the castle.

Cost and Hours: 60 kr, daily April–Oct 10:00–17:00, Nov–March 11:00–15:00. Tel. 48 26 04 39, www.frederiksborgmuseet.dk.

➲ **Self-Guided Tour:** From the entrance of the castle complex, it's an appropriately regal approach to the king's residence. You can almost hear the clopping of royal hooves as you walk over the moat and through the first island (which housed the stables and small businesses needed to support a royal residence). Then walk down the winding (and therefore easy-to-defend) lane to the second island, which was home to the domestic and foreign ministries. Finally, cross over the last moat to the main palace, where the king lived.

Main Courtyard: Survey the castle exterior from the Fountain of Neptune in the main courtyard. Christian IV imported Dutch architects to create this "Christian IV style," which you'll see all over Copenhagen. The brickwork and sandstone are products of the local clay and sandy soil. The building, with its horizontal lines, triangles, and squares, is generally in Renaissance style, but notice how this is interrupted by a few token Gothic elements on the church's facade. Some say this homey touch was to let the villagers know the king was "one of them."

Royal Chapel: Christian IV wanted to have the grandest royal chapel in Europe. For 200 years the coronation place of Danish kings, this chapel is still used for royal weddings (and is extremely popular for commoner weddings—book long in advance). The chapel is nearly all original, dating back to 1620. As you walk around the upper level, notice the graffiti scratched on the windows by the diamond rings of royal kids visiting for the summer back in the 1600s. Most of the coats of arms show off noble lineage (Eisenhower's, past the organ, is an exception). The organ is from 1620, with its original hand-powered bellows. (If you like music, listen for hymns on the old carillon at the top of each hour.) Leaving the chapel, you step into the king's oratory, with evocative romantic paintings (restored after a fire) from the mid-19th century.

Audience Room: Here, where formal meetings took place, a grand painting shows the king as a Roman emperor firmly in command (with his two sons prominent for extra political stability). Christian's military victories line the walls, and the four great continents—Europe, North America, Asia, and Africa—circle the false cupola.

Dutch Reformation: In Room 26, note the effort noble families put into legitimizing themselves with family trees and family seals. Over the door to the next room is the image of a monk invited by the king to preach the new thinking of the Reformation. In the case is the first Bible translated into Danish (from 1550—access to the word of God was a big part of the Reformation).

Time for Lunch: You can picnic in the castle's moat park or enjoy the elegant **Spisestedet Leonora** at the moat's edge (59–99-kr *smørrebrød* and sandwiches, 70-kr salads, 90–160-kr hot dishes, 128-kr brunch buffet Sun until 13:00, open daily 10:00–17:00, slow service, tel. 48 26 75 16).

Louisiana

This is Scandinavia's most-raved-about modern-art museum. Located in the town of Humlebæk, beautifully situated on the coast 18 miles north of Copenhagen, Louisiana is a holistic place that masterfully mixes its art, architecture, and landscape. Wander from famous Chagalls and Picassos to more obscure art. Poets spend days here nourishing their creative souls with new angles, ideas, and perspectives. Frequent special exhibitions offer visitors an extra treat (visit www.louisiana.dk for the latest). The views over the Øresund, one of the busiest passages in the nautical world, are nearly as inspiring as the art. The cafeteria, with indoor and outdoor seating, is reasonable and welcomes picnickers who buy a drink.

Cost and Hours: 90-kr museum admission, free with Copenhagen Card, included in a special 166-kr round-trip tour ticket from Copenhagen—ask at any train station, open Tue–Fri 11:00–22:00, Sat–Sun 11:00–18:00, closed Mon, Gammel Strandvej 13, www.louisiana.dk, tel. 49 19 07 19.

Getting There: Take the train from Copenhagen toward Helsingør, get off at Humlebæk (4/hr, 45 min), and follow the signs to Louisiana along a busy road about 15 minutes. Or walk 10 minutes through the woods: Exit the station and immediately go left onto Hejreskor Allé, a residential street, and then along a path through the trees. After you exit the trail, the museum is across the street.

If you're coming from Frederiksborg Castle, you have two options: You can catch the Lille Nord train at Hillerød station toward Helsingør, then change there to a regional train heading south to Humlebæk (2/hr, 45 min). Or you can take the S-tog toward Copenhagen and Køge, get off at Hellerup, then catch a regional train north toward Helsingør to reach Humlebæk (4/hr, about 1 hour, longer distance but runs more frequently).

Karen Blixen Museum

Danish writer Karen Blixen, a.k.a. Isak Dinesen of *Out of Africa* fame, lived most of her life in Rungstedlund—her family house in Rungsted, on the Øresund coast. The house, one of the area's finest mansions, is now a museum about her life and writing. For fans of Blixen's works, the house is a ▲▲ sight, though Blixen's dramatic life story and the house's beautiful setting are enough to make a visit enjoyable even for those who've never heard of *Out of Africa*.

Unlike many houses-turned-museums that file you past roped-off doorways, you'll don slippers to pad through the house, mostly unchanged from the time of Blixen's life. Over headphones, listen to Blixen read selections from her own stories as you look out at the same views she enjoyed. She wrote her best-known books (including *Babette's Feast*) in this house, surrounded by mementos of her 17 years in Kenya. Her simple grave is a short walk away through the mansion's backyard gardens.

Cost and Hours: 50 kr; May–Sept Tue–Sun 10:00–17:00, closed Mon; Oct–April Wed–Fri 13:00–16:00, Sat–Sun 11:00–16:00, closed Mon–Tue; tel. 45 57 10 57, www.karen-blixen.dk.

Getting There: From Copenhagen, take the train 30 minutes to Rungsted Kyst (3/hr). From the station, take bus #388, or simply walk 15–20 minutes (follow signs to the house). Rungsted is a short hop away from Humlebæk (7 min by train) and Helsingør (20 min).

Kronborg Castle

Kronborg Castle is located in Helsingør, a small, pleasant little Danish town that's often confused with its Swedish sister, Helsingborg, just two miles across the channel. Helsingør has a TI (tel. 49 21 13 33, www.visithelsingor.dk), a medieval center, Kronborg Castle, and lots of Swedes who come over for the lower-priced alcohol.

Kronborg Castle (also called Elsinore) is a ▲▲ sight famous for its questionable (but profitable) ties to Shakespeare. Most of the "Hamlet" castle you'll see today—a darling of every big bus tour and travelogue—was built long after the historical Hamlet died (more than a thousand years ago), and Shakespeare never saw the place. But this Renaissance castle existed when a troupe of English actors performed here in Shakespeare's time (Shakespeare may have known them). To see or not to see? The castle is most impressive from the outside. The free grounds between the walls and sea are great for picnics, with a pleasant view of the strait between Denmark and Sweden. If you're heading to Sweden, Kalmar Castle (described in the Southeast Sweden chapter) is a better medieval castle. But you're here, and if you like castles, see Kronborg.

Duck into the creepy casements under the castle, where the servants and guards lived. Take a free tour of the casements (daily at 11:00 and 13:00), or use the 20-kr guide available at the ticket counter. The royal apartments include English explanations. In the basement, notice the statue of Holger Danske, a mythical Viking hero revered by Danish children. The story goes that if the nation is ever in danger, this Danish superman will awaken and restore peace and security to the land.

Cost and Hours: 90 kr; May–Sept daily 10:30–17:00; Oct–April Tue–Sun 11:00–16:00, until 15:00 Nov–March, closed Mon. Tel. 49 21 30 78, www.kronborgcastle.com.

Getting There: Helsingør is a 50-minute train ride from Copenhagen (3/hr). Exit the station at track 3, then look for the sign for the TI, where you can pick up a free map or use the WC. The castle is a 10-minute walk around the harbor.

Near Copenhagen Connections

Route Tips for Drivers

Copenhagen to Hillerød (45 min) to Helsingør (30 min) to Kalmar (4 hrs): Just follow the town-name signs. Leave Copenhagen, following signs for *E-4* and *Helsingør*. The freeway is great. *Hillerød* signs lead to the Frederiksborg Castle (not to be confused with the nearby Fredensborg Palace) in the pleasant town of Hillerød. Follow signs to *Hillerød C* (for "center"), then *slot* (for "castle"). Though the E-4 freeway is the fastest, the Strandvejen coastal road (152) is pleasant, passing some of Denmark's grandest mansions (including that of Karen Blixen, described earlier.)

The 10-mile Øresund Bridge linking Denmark with Sweden (261-kr toll) lets drivers and train travelers skip nonstop from one country to the next.

If you're nostalgic for the pre-bridge days, the Helsingør–Helsingborg ferry still putters across the Øresund Channel twice hourly (follow the signs to *Helsingborg, Sweden*—freeway leads to dock). Buy your ticket as you roll on board (275 kr one-way for

Øresund Region

When the Øresund (UH-ra-soond) Bridge, which connects Denmark and Sweden, opened in July 2000, it created Europe's most dynamic new metropolitan area. Almost overnight, the link forged an economic power with the 12th-largest gross domestic product in Europe. The Øresund region has surpassed Stockholm as the largest metro area in Scandinavia. Now 3.5 million Danes and Swedes—a highly trained and highly technical workforce—are within a quick commute of each other.

The bridge opens up new questions of borders. Historically, southern Sweden (the area across from Copenhagen, called Skåne) had Danish blood. It was Danish for a thousand years before Sweden took it in 1658. Notice how Copenhagen is the capital on the fringe of its realm—at one time it was in the center.

The 10-mile-long link, which has a motorway for cars (261-kr toll) and a two-track train line, ties together the main islands of Denmark with Europe and Sweden. The $4 billion project consisted of a 2.5-mile-long tunnel, an artificial island called Peberholm, and a 5-mile-long bridge. With speedy connecting trains, Malmö in Sweden is now an easy half-day side-trip from Copenhagen (78 kr each way, 3/hr, 35 min). The train drops you at the "Malmö C" (central) station right in the heart of Malmö, and all the important sights are within a short walk. The *Malmö This Week* publication (free from Copenhagen Right Now tourist office) has everything you need for a well-organized visit.

car, driver, and up to nine passengers). Reservations are free but not usually necessary, as ferries depart every 30 minutes (tel. 33 15 15 15, or book online at www.scandlines.dk; also see www.hhferries.se). If you arrive early, you can probably drive onto any ferry. The 20-minute Helsingør–Helsingborg ferry ride gives you just enough time to enjoy the view of the Kronborg "Hamlet" castle, be impressed by the narrowness of this very strategic channel, and exchange any leftover Danish kroner into Swedish kronor (the ferry exchange desk's rate is decent).

In Helsingborg, follow signs for *E-4* and *Stockholm*. The road is good, traffic is light, and towns are all clearly signposted. At Ljungby, road 25 takes you to Växjö and Kalmar. Entering Växjö, skip the first Växjö exit and follow the freeway into *Centrum*, where it ends. It takes about four hours total to drive from Copenhagen to Kalmar.

CENTRAL DENMARK

Ærø • Odense

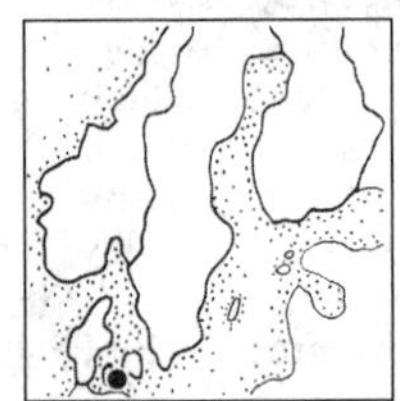

The sleepy isle of Ærø is the cuddle after the climax. It's the perfect time-passed world in which to wind down, enjoy the seagulls, and take a day off. Wander the unadulterated cobbled lanes of Denmark's best-preserved 18th-century town. Get Ærø-dynamic and pedal a rented bike into the essence of Denmark. Settle into a world of sailors, who, after the invention of steam-driven boat propellers, decided that building ships in bottles was more their style.

Between Ærø and Copenhagen, drop by bustling Odense, home of Hans Christian Andersen and a fine open-air folk museum.

Planning Your Time

Allow four hours to get from Copenhagen to Ærø. All trains stop in Roskilde (with its Viking Ship Museum—see previous chapter) and bustling Odense (see the end of this chapter). On a quick trip, you can leave Copenhagen in the morning and do justice to both towns en route to Ærø. (With just one day, Odense and Roskilde together make a long but doable day trip from Copenhagen.)

While out of the way, Ærø is worth the journey. Once there, you'll want two nights and a day to properly enjoy it (for details, see "Planning Your Time" for Ærøskøbing, page 124).

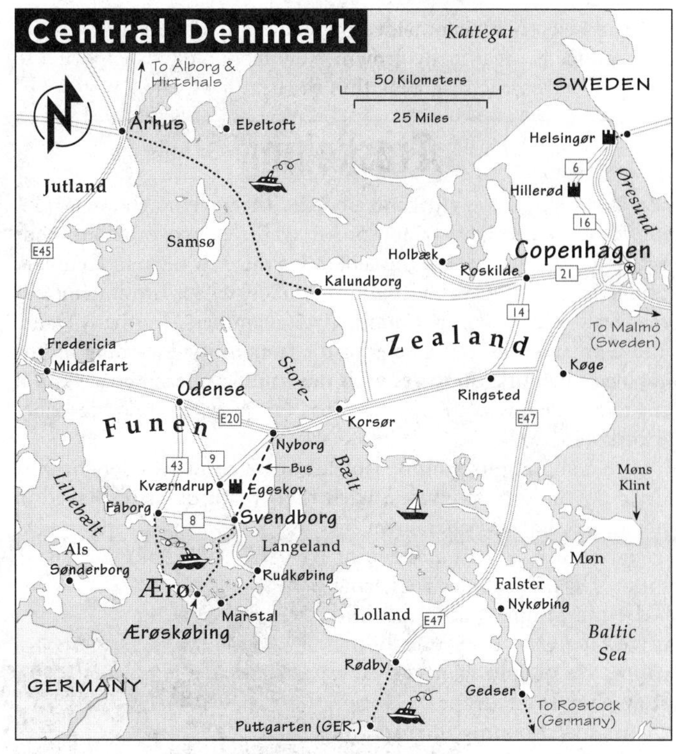

Ærø

This small (22 by 6 miles) island on the south edge of Denmark is as salty and sleepy as can be. A typical tombstone reads: "Here lies Christian Hansen at anchor with his wife. He'll not weigh until he stands before God." It's the kind of island where baskets of strawberries sit in front of houses—for sale on the honor system.

Ærø statistics: 7,000 residents, 500,000 visitors, and 80,000 boaters annually, 350 deer, seven priests, no crosswalks, and three police officers. The three big industries are farming (wheat and dairy), shipping, and tourism—in that order. Twenty percent of the Danish fleet still resides on Ærø, in the town of Marstal. But jobs are scarce, the population is slowly dropping, and family farms are consolidating into larger units.

Ærø, home to several windmills and one of the world's largest solar power plants, is going "green." They hope to become completely wind- and solar-powered. Currently, nearly half the island's heat and electricity is provided by renewable sources, and most of its produce is organically grown. New technology is expected to bring Ærø closer to its goal within the next few years.

Ærøskøbing

Ærøskøbing is Ærø's village in a bottle. The government, recognizing the value of this amazingly preserved little town, prohibits modern building anywhere in the center. It's the only town in Denmark protected in this way. Drop into the 1680s, when Ærøskøbing was the wealthy home port of a hundred windjammers. The many Danes and Germans who come here for the tranquility—washing up the cobbled main drag in waves with the landing of each boat—call it the fairy-tale town. The Danish word for "cozy," *hyggelig,* describes Ærøskøbing well.

Ærøskøbing is simply a pleasant place to wander. Stubby little porthole-type houses, with their birth dates displayed in proud decorative rebar, lean on each other like drunk, sleeping sailors. Wander under flickering old-time lamps. Snoop around town. It's OK. Peek into living rooms (if people want privacy, they shut their drapes). Notice the many "snooping mirrors" on the houses—antique locals are following your every move. The harbor now caters to holiday yachts, and on midnight low tides you can almost hear the crabs playing cards.

The town economy, once rich with the windjammer trade, hit the rocks in modern times. Kids 15 to 18 years old go to a boarding school in Svendborg; many don't return. It's an interesting discussion: Should the island folk pickle their culture in tourism, or forget about the cuteness and get modern?

Planning Your Time

You'll regret not setting aside a minimum of two nights for your Ærøskøbing visit. In a busy day you can "do" everything you like—except relax. If ever a place was right for recreating, this is it. I'd arrive in time for an evening stroll, dinner, and the Night Watchman's tour (21:00 in summer). The next morning, do the island bike tour, returning by mid-afternoon. You can see the town's three museums in less than two hours, then browse the rest of your daylight away. Your second evening is filled with options: Stroll out to the summer huts for sunset, watch the classic sailing ships come in to moor for the evening (mostly Dutch and German boats crewed by vacationers), watch a movie in the pint-sized town cinema, go bowling with local teens, or check out live music in the pub.

Orientation to Ærøskøbing

Ærøskøbing is tiny. Everything's just a few cobbles from the ferry landing.

Tourist Information

The TI, which faces the ferry landing, is a clearinghouse for brochures promoting sights and activities on the island, has info on other Danish destinations, can help book rooms, rents small electric cars (300 kr/half-day, 500 kr/day, reserve a day or two in advance in summer), and offers Internet access and Wi-Fi (late-June–mid-Aug Mon–Fri 9:00–18:00, Sat–Sun 10:00–18:00; off-season Mon–Fri 10:00–16:00, closed Sat–Sun; tel. 62 52 13 00, www.aeroeisland.com).

Helpful Hints

Money: The town has two cash machines (at the top of Vestergade and on Torvet Square).

Internet Access: Try the TI (steady hours) or the library on Torvet Square (sketchy hours).

Laundry: A self-service launderette is on Gyden. Instructions are posted in English, and soap is available (bring one 50-kr note, two or three 5-kr coins, and three 2-kr coins; daily 7:30–21:00). Beware: The doors automatically lock at 21:00.

Ferries: See "Ærøskøbing Connections," page 138.

Bike Rental: Pilebækkens Cykler rents bikes year-round at the gas station at the top of the town. Manager Janne loans readers of this book the 25-kr island *cykel* map so they won't get lost (three-speed bikes-55 kr/24 hours, seven-speed bikes-75 kr/24 hours; Mon–Fri 9:00–16:30, Sat 9:00–13:00, closed Sun except in July—when it's open 10:00–13:00; from Torvet Square, go through green door at Søndergade end of square, past garden to next road, Pilebækken 7; tel. 62 52 11 10). **Hotel Ærøhus** rents seven-speed bikes (75 kr/24 hours, open very long hours). The campground also rents bikes (see "Sleeping in Ærøskøbing," later). There are no deposits and few locks on Ærø.

Self-Guided Walk

▲▲▲Welcome to Ærøskøbing

Ideally, take this stroll with the sun low, the shadows long, and the colors rich. Start at the harbor.

Harbor: Loiter around the harbor a bit first. German and Dutch vacationers on grand old sailboats come into port each evening. Because Ærø is only nine miles across the water from Germany, the island is popular with Germans who regularly return to this peaceful retreat.

• *From the harbor and TI, walk up the main street a block and go left on...*

Smedegade: This is the poorest street in town, with the most architectural and higgledy-piggledy charm. Have a close look at the "street spies" on the houses—clever mirrors letting old women inside keep an eye on what's going on outside. The ship-in-a-bottle Bottle Peter Museum is on the right (described on page 129). Notice the gutters—some protect only the doorway. Locals find the rounded modern drainpipes less charming than the old-school ones with hard angles. Appreciate the finely carved old doors. Each is proudly unique—try to find two the same. Number 37, from the 18th century, is Ærøskøbing's cutest house. Its tiny dormer is from some old ship's poop deck. The plants above the door have a traditional purpose—to keep this part of the house damp and slow to burn in case of fire.

Smedegade ends at the Folkehojskole (folks' high school). Inspired by the Danish philosopher, Nikolaj Gruntvig—who wanted people to be able to say "I am good at being me"—it offers people of any age the benefit of government-subsidized cultural education (music, art, theater, and so on).

• *Jog left and stroll along the peaceful, harborside...*

Molestien Lane: This street is lined with gardens, a quiet beach, and a row of small-is-beautiful houses—beginning with humble and progressing to captain's class. These fine buildings are a reminder that through the centuries, Ærøskøbing has been the last town in Germany, independent, the first town in Denmark... and always into trade—legal and illegal. (The smuggling spirit survives in residents' blood even today. When someone returns from a trip, friends eagerly ask, "And what did you bring back?") Each garden is cleverly and lovingly designed. The harborfront path, nicknamed "Virgin's Lane," was where teens could court within view of their parents.

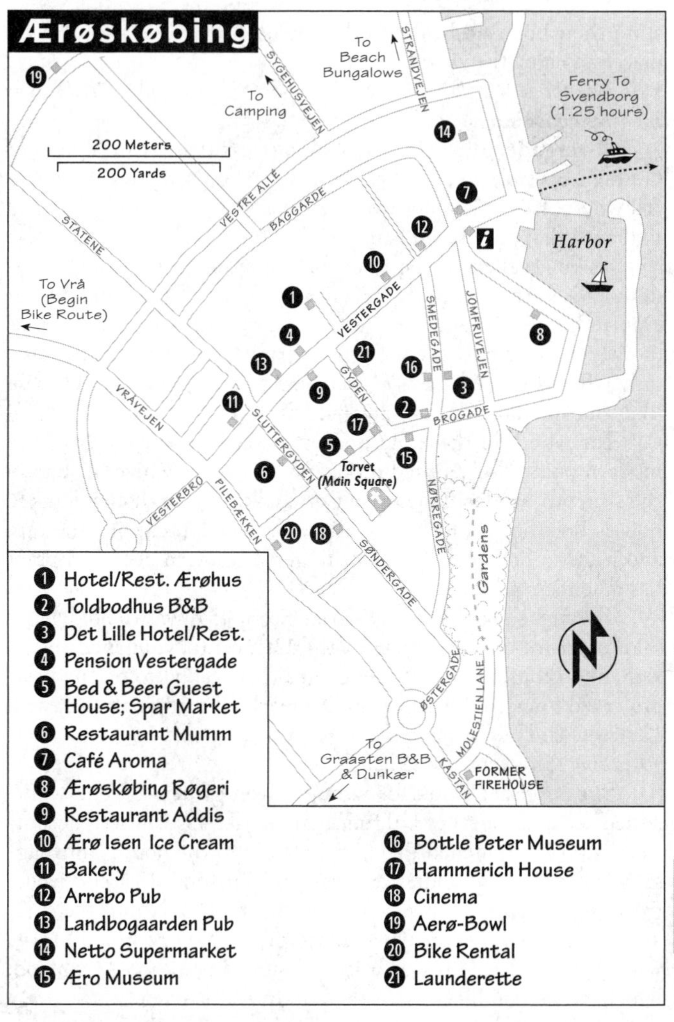

The dreamy-looking island immediately across the way is a nature preserve and a resting spot for birds making their long journey from the north to the Mediterranean. There's one lucky bull here (farmers raft over their heifers, who return as cows). Rainbows often end on this island—where plague victims were once buried. In the winter, when the water freezes (about once a decade), locals slip and slide over for a visit.

At the end of the lane stands the former firehouse (now a place for the high school garage band to practice). Twenty yards before the firehouse, a trail cuts left about 100 yards along the shore to a place the town provides for fishermen to launch and store their boats and tidy up their nets. A bench is strategically placed to enjoy the view.

• *Follow the rutted lane inland, back past the firehouse. At the first intersection, take a right onto...*

Østergade: This was Ærøskøbing's east gate. In the days of German control, all island trade was legal only within the town. All who passed this point would pay various duties and taxes at a tollbooth that once stood here.

As you walk past the traditional houses, look through windows to see the sea. Peer into living rooms. Catch snatches of Danish life. Ponder the beauty of a society with such a keen sense of civic responsibility that fishing permits commit you "to catch only what you need." You're welcome to pick berries where you like...but "no more than what would fit in your hat."

The wood on these old houses prefers organic coverings to modern paint. Tar painted on beams as a preservative blisters in the sun. An old-fashioned paint of chalk, lime, and clay lets old houses breathe and feel more alive. (It gets darker with the rain and leaves a little color on your fingers.) Modern chemical paint has much less personality.

The first square (actually a triangle, at #55) was the old goose market. Ærøskøbing—born in the 13th century, burned in the 17th, and rebuilt in the 18th—claims (believably) to be the best-preserved town from that era in Denmark. The original plan, with 12 streets laid out by its founder, survives.

• *Leaving the square, stay left on...*

Søndergade: Look for wrought-iron girders on the walls, added to hold together bulging houses. (At #55, notice the nuts that could be tightened like a corset to keep the house from sagging.) Ærøskøbing's oldest houses—the only ones that survived a fire during a war with Sweden—are #36 and #32. Notice the dates and the hatches upstairs where masts and sails were stored for the winter. The red on #32's door is the original paint job—ox blood, which, when combined with the tannin in the wood, really lasts. The courtyard behind #18 was a parking lot in pre-car days. Farmers, in town for their shopping chores, would leave their horses here. Even today, the wide-open fields are just beyond.

• *Wander down to Torvet, Ærøskøbing's main square.*

Torvet (Main Square): Notice the two pumps. Until 1951, townspeople came here for their water. The linden tree is the town symbol. The rocks around it celebrate the reunion of a big chunk of southern

Denmark (including this island), which was ruled by Germany from 1864 to 1920. See the town seal featuring a linden tree, over the door of the old City Hall (now the library, with Internet stations in former prison cells). Read the Danish on the wall: "With law shall man a country build."

• *Our walk is over. Continue straight (popping into recommended Restaurant Mumm, the best place in town, to make a reservation for dinner). You'll return to the main street (Vestergade) and—just when you need it—the town bakery.*

Sights in Ærøskøbing

Museums

Ærøskøbing's three tiny museums cluster within a few doors of each other just off the main square (30 kr each, or 75 kr for a combo-ticket to all three, tel. 62 52 29 50, www.arremus.dk). In July, they organize daily chatty tours. While quirky and fun (and with sketchy English handouts), these museums would be much more interesting and worthwhile if they translated their Danish descriptions for the rare person on this planet who doesn't speak *Dansk*. (Your gentle encouragement might help get results.)

▲Ærø Museum—This museum presents the island's local history, from seafaring to farming. Explore the collection, featuring 19th-century outfits, household objects, and an actual old-time pharmacy. A fun diorama shows an aerial view of Ærøskøbing in 1862—notice the big gardens behind nearly every house. This museum carries on the tradition with its own garden out back (June–July Mon–Fri 10:00–16:00, Aug–May Mon–Fri 10:00–13:00, always closed Sat–Sun).

▲Bottle Peter Museum—This fascinating house has 750 different bottled ships. Old Peter Jacobsen, who made his first bottle at 16 and his last at 85, bragged that he drank the contents of each bottle...except those containing milk. He died in 1960 (and is most likely buried in a glass bottle), leaving a lifetime of tedious little creations for visitors to squint and marvel at (mid-June–mid-Aug daily 10:00–17:00, off-season daily 10:00–16:00, even less in winter).

▲Hammerich House—These 12 funky rooms in three houses are filled with 200- to 300-year-old junk (mid-June–Aug Wed–Mon 11:00–15:00, closed Tue and off-season).

More Sights

Many of these activities can be done in the evening, after a day of biking around the island.

▲Town Walk with Night Watchman—Each evening in July and August, Mr. Jan Pedersen becomes the old night watchman and leads visitors through town. The hour-long walk is likely in

Danish and English—and often in German, too—so you'll hang around a lot. But it's a fine time to be out, meet other travelers, and be charmed by gentle Jan (25 kr; July–Aug Tue–Sun, not Mon or off-season; meet on Torvet near the church at 21:00, Jan also available as private guide, tel. 62 58 17 57, www.aeroe-turguide.dk, jan.leby@mail.dk).

▲▲Beach Bungalow Sunset Stroll—At sunset, stroll to Ærøskøbing's sand beach. Facing the ferry dock, go left, following the harbor. Upon leaving the town, you'll pass the Netto supermarket (convenient for picking up snacks, beer, or wine), a mini-golf course, and a children's playground. In the rosy distance, past a wavy wheat field, is Vestre Strandvejen—a row of tiny, Monopoly-like huts facing the sunset. These tiny beach escapes are privately owned on land rented from the town (no overnight use, WCs at each end). Each is different, but all are stained with merry memories of locals enjoying themselves Danish-style. Bring a beverage or picnic. It's perfectly acceptable—and very Danish—to borrow a porch for your sunset sit. From here, it's a fine walk out to the end of Urehoved (as this spit of land is called).

CENTRAL DENMARK

Cinema—The cute little 30-seat Andelen Theater (a former grain warehouse near Torvet Square) plays movies in their original language (Danish subtitles, closed Mon and in July, new titles begin every Tue). It's run in a charming community-service kind of way. The management has installed heat, so tickets no longer come with a blanket.

Bowling—Ærø-Bowl is a six-lane alley in a modern athletic club at the edge of town (hot dogs, junk food, arcade games, local kids on dates; Tue–Thu 16:00–22:00, later on Fri–Sat, closed Sun–Mon, Søndergade 28, tel. 62 52 23 06).

Shopping—The town is speckled with cute little shops, including a funky flea market shop next to the bakery. Each July, local artisans show their creations in a warehouse facing the ferry landing.

Ice Cream—Halfway up the main drag, you'll smell fresh-baked waffles and see benches filled with happy ice-cream lickers. **Ærø Isen** serves good ice cream in fresh waffle cones, with whipped

cream and jam topping. Their "Ærø-Isen Special" (walnut-maple syrup ice cream topped with whipped cream and maple syrup) is 9 kr more than the other flavors (daily 11:00–21:00). Be sure to check out the gallery behind the shop to see paintings and sculptures featuring local artists.

Bakery—This old-school little bakery sells homemade bread, cheese, yogurt, and tasty pastries (Tue–Fri 7:00–17:00, Sat–Sun 7:00–14:00, closed Mon, top of Vestergade).

Pubs—Ærøskøbing's two bars are at the top and bottom of Vestergade. **Arrebo Pub,** near the ferry landing, attracts a young crowd and is *the* place for live music. **Landbogaarden** is a classic pub filled with the "old boys"—it feels a little uninviting, but they don't bite (top of Vestergade, only place serving food in the winter).

Ærø Island Bike Ride (or Car Tour)

This 15-mile trip shows you the best of this windmill-covered island's charms. The highest point on the island is only 180 feet above sea level, but the wind can be strong and the hills seem long. This ride is good exercise. Rent a bike in town (see "Helpful Hints," page 125). While my map and instructions work, a local cycle map is helpful (free loaner maps if you rent from Pilebækkens Cykler—see page 125, or buy one at the TI). Or it could be fun and easy—though pricier—to rent an electric car from the TI (see page 125).

• *Leave Ærøskøbing to the west on the road to Vrå (Vråvejen, signed* Bike Route #90*).*

Leaving Ærøskøbing: You'll see the first of many U-shaped farms, typical of Denmark. The three sides block the wind and store cows, hay, and people. *Gaard* (farm) shows up on many local surnames.

At Osemarksvej, bike along the coast in the protection of the dike built in 1856 to make the once-salty swampland to your left farmable. While the weak soil is good for hay and little else, they get the most out of it. Each winter, certain grazing areas flood with seawater. (Some locals claim this makes their cows produce fatter milk and meat.) As you roll along the dike, the land on your left is about eight feet below sea level. The little white pump house—alone in the field—is busy each spring and summer.

• *At the T-junction, go right (over the dike) toward Borgnæs.*

Borgnæs: The traditional old "straw house" (50 yards down, on left) is a café and shop selling fresh farm products. Just past that, a few roadside tables sell farm goodies on the honor system. Borgnæs is a cluster of modern summer houses. In spite of huge demand, a weak economy, and an aging population, development like this is no longer allowed.

• *Keep to the right (passing lots of wheat fields and two* Vindeballe *turnoffs), following signs to* Bregninge. *After a secluded beach, head inland (direction: O. Bregninge). Pass the island's only water mill, and climb uphill over the island's 2,700-inch-high summit toward Bregninge. The tallest point on Ærø is called Synes Høj ("Seems High").*

Gammelgaard: Take a right turn marked only by a *Bike Route #90* sign. The road deteriorates as you wind scenically through "Ærø's Alps," past classic "old farms" (hence the name of the lane—Gammelgaard).

• *At the modern road, turn left (leaving Bike Route #90) and bike to the big village church. Before turning right to roll through Denmark's "second-longest village," visit the church.*

Bregninge Church: The interior of the 12th-century Bregninge church is still painted as a Gothic church would have been. Find the painter's self-portrait (behind the pulpit, right of front pew). Tradition says that if the painter wasn't happy with his pay, he'd paint a fool's head in the church (above third pew on left). Note how the fool's mouth—the hole for a rope tied to the bell—has been worn wider and wider by centuries of ringing. (During services, the ringing bell would call those who were ill and too contagious to be allowed into the church to come for communion—distributed through the square hatches flanking the altar.)

The altarpiece—gold leaf on carved oak—is from 1528, six years before the Reformation came to Denmark. The cranium carved into the bottom indicates it's a genuine masterpiece by Claus Berg (from Lübeck, Germany). This Crucifixion scene is such a commotion, it seems to cause Christ's robe to billow up. The soldiers who traditionally gambled for Christ's robe have traded their dice for knives. Even the three wise men (each perhaps a Danish king) made it to this Crucifixion. Notice the escaping souls of the two thieves—the one who converted on the cross being carried happily to heaven, and the other, with its grim-winged escort, heading straight to hell. The scene at lower left—a bare-breasted, dark-skinned woman with a disciple feeding her child—symbolizes the Great Commission: "Go ye to all the world." Since this is a Catholic altarpiece, a roll

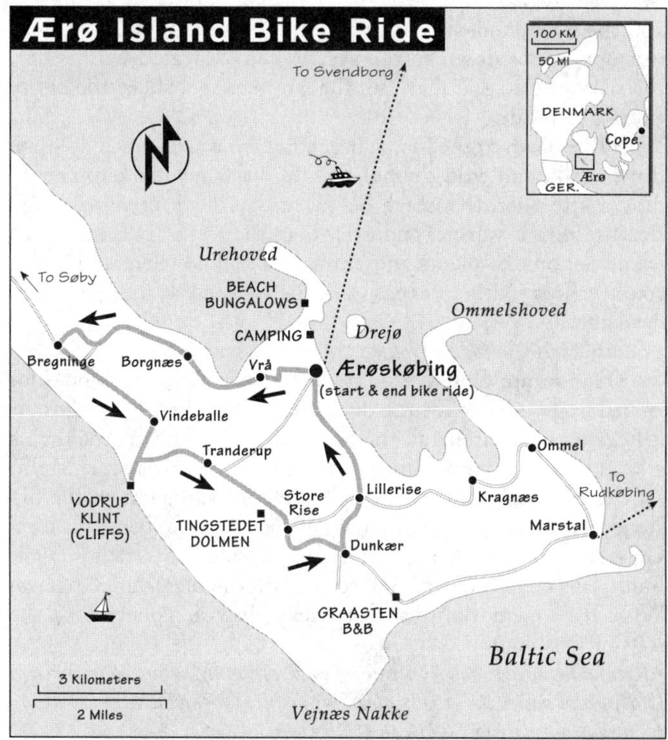

call of saints lines the wings. During the restoration, the identity of the two women on the lower right was unknown, so the lettering—even in Latin—is clearly gibberish. Take a moment to study the 16th-century art on the ceiling (for example, the crucified feet ascending, leaving only footprints on earth). In the narthex, a list of pastors goes back to 1505. The current pastor (Agnes) is the first woman on the list.

• *Now's the time for a bathroom break (public WC in the churchyard). Then roll downhill through Bregninge past many more U-shaped* gaards. *Notice how the town is in a gully. Imagine pirates trolling along the coast, looking for church spires marking unfortified villages. Ærø's 16 villages are all invisible from the sea—their church spires carefully designed not to be viewable from sea level.*

About a mile down the main road is Vindeballe, which has a traditional kro *(inn) if you're hungry or thirsty. Just before the village (past the* din fart *sign—which tells you "your speed"), take the* Vodrup Klint *turnoff to the right.*

Vodrup Klint: A road leads downhill (with a well-signed jog to the right) to dead-end at a rugged bluff called Vodrup Klint (WC, picnic benches). If I were a pagan, I'd worship here—the sea, the wind, and the chilling view. Notice how the land steps in sloppy slabs down to the sea. When saturated with water, the slabs of clay that make up the land here get slick, and entire chunks can slide.

Hike down to the foamy beach (where you can pick up some flint, chalk, and wild thyme). While the wind at the top could drag a kite-flier, the beach below can be ideal for sunbathing. Because Ærø is warmer and drier than the rest of Denmark, this island is home to plants and animals found nowhere else in the country. This southern exposure is the warmest area. Germany is dead ahead.

• *Backtrack 200 yards and follow the signs to* Tranderup.

Tranderup: On the way, you'll pass a lovely pond famous for its bell frogs and happy little duck houses. Still following signs for *Tranderup*, stay parallel to the big road through town. You'll pass a lovely farm and a potato stand. At the main road, turn right. At the Ærøskøbing turnoff, side-trip 100 yards left to the big stone (commemorating the return of the island to Denmark from Germany in 1750) and a grand island panorama. Seattleites might find Claus Clausen's rock interesting (in the picnic area, next to WC). It's a memorial to an extremely obscure pioneer from the state of Washington.

• *Return to the big road (continuing in direction: Marstal), pass through Olde, pedal past FAF (the local wheat farmers' co-op facility), and head toward Store Rise (STOH-reh REE-zuh), the next church spire in the distance. Think of medieval travelers using spires as navigational aids.*

Store Rise Prehistoric Tomb, Church, and Brewery: Thirty yards after the Stokkeby turnoff, follow the rough, tree-lined path on the right to the Langdysse (Long Dolmen) Tingstedet, just behind the church spire. This is a 6,000-year-old dolmen, an early Neolithic burial place. Though Ærø once had more than 200 of these prehistoric tombs, only 13 survive. The site is a raised mound the shape and length (about 100 feet) of a Viking ship, and archeologists have found evidence that indicates a Viking ship may indeed have been burned and buried here.

Ting means assembly spot. Imagine a thousand years ago: Viking chiefs representing the island's various communities gathering here around their ancestors' tombs. For 6,000 years, this has been a holy spot. The stones were considered fertility stones. For centuries, locals in need of virility chipped off bits and took them home (the nicks in the rock nearest the information post are mine).

Tuck away your chip and carry on down the lane to the Store Rise church. Inside you'll find little ships hanging in the nave, a fine 12th-century altarpiece, a stick with offering bag and a ting-a-ling bell to wake those nodding off (right of altar), double seats (so worshippers can flip to face the pulpit during sermons), and Martin Luther in the stern keeping his Protestant hand on the rudder. The list in the church allows today's pastors to trace their pastoral lineage back to Doctor Luther himself. (The current pastor, Janet, is the first woman on the list.) The churchyard is circular—a reminder of how churchyards provided a last refuge for humble communities under attack. Can you find anyone buried in the graveyard whose name doesn't end in "-sen"?

The buzz lately in Ærø is its brewery, located in a historic brewery 400 yards beyond the Store Rise church. Follow the smell of the hops (or the *Rise Bryggeri* signs). It welcomes visitors with free samples of its various beers. The *Ærø* traditional brews are available in pilsner (including the popular walnut pilsner), light ale, dark ale, and a typical dark English-like stout. The *Rise* organic brews come in light ale, dark ale, and walnut (mid-June–Aug daily 10:00–14:00, Sept–mid-June open Thu only 10:00–14:00, tel. 62 52 11 32, www.risebryggeri.dk).

• *From here, climb back to the main road and continue (direction: Marstal) on your way back home to Ærøskøbing. The three 330-foot-high modern windmills on your right are communally owned and, as they are a nonpolluting source of energy, state-subsidized. At Dunkær (3 miles from Ærøskøbing), take the small road, signed* Lille Rise, *past the topless windmill. Except for the Lille Rise, it's all downhill from here, as you coast past great sea views back home to Ærøskøbing.*

Huts at the Sunset Beach: Still rolling? Bike past the campground along the Urehoved beach (*strand* in Danish) for a look at the coziest little beach houses you'll never see back in the "big is beautiful" US. This is Europe, where small is beautiful, and the concept of sustainability is neither new nor subversive. (For more details, see "Beach Bungalow Sunset Stroll" earlier.)

Sleeping in Ærøskøbing

The accommodations scene here is boom or bust. Summer weekends and all of July are packed (book long in advance). It's absolutely dead in the winter. These places come with family-run personality, and each is an easy stroll from the ferry landing.

In Ærøskøbing

$$$ Hotel Ærøhus is big and sprawling, with 33 rooms. Although it is less personal and cozy than some of the other listings here, it's the closest thing to a grand hotel in this capital of quaint (S-600 kr,

Sleep Code

(5 kr = about $1, country code: 45)
S = Single, **D** = Double/Twin, **T** = Triple, **Q** = Quad, **b** = bathroom, **s** = shower. Credit cards are accepted (with a 4 percent surcharge), and breakfast is included unless otherwise noted.

To help you sort easily through these listings, I've divided the rooms into three categories, based on the price for a standard double room with bath during high season:

$$$ Higher Priced—Most rooms 800 kr or more.
$$ Moderately Priced—Most rooms between 450-800 kr.
$ Lower Priced—Most rooms 450 kr or less.

Sb-990 kr, D-800 kr, Db-1,250 kr, free Internet access and Wi-Fi, bike rentals-75 kr/day, possible noise from large dinner parties—ask for a quiet room, tel. 62 52 10 03, fax 62 52 21 23, www.aeroehus-hotel.dk, mail@aeroehus.dk, Ole Jensen and family). Their modern holiday apartments nearby are used as overflow accommodations and can be a fine value for groups and families (details on their website).

$$$ Toldbodhus B&B, a tollhouse from 1770 to 1906, now rents four delightful rooms. Three rooms share two bathrooms in the main house, and a small garden house has a double room with a detached bathroom. Karin and John Steenberg—who, as avid travelers, understand your needs—named and decorated each room after cities they've lived in: Amsterdam, København, London, and Hong Kong (D-850 kr with this book, cash only, near harbor on corner of Smedegade at Brogade 8, tel. 62 52 18 11, www.toldbodhus.com, toldbodhus@mail.dk).

$$$ Det Lille Hotel, a former 19th-century captain's home with six tidy rooms, is warm, modern, and shipshape (S/D-850 kr, extra bed-265 kr, Smedegade 33, tel. & fax 62 52 23 00, www.det-lille-hotel.dk, mail@det-lille-hotel.dk).

$$ Pension Vestergade is your best home away from home in Ærøskøbing. It's lovingly run by Susanna Greve and her daughters, Henrietta and Celia. Susanna is a wealth of knowledge about the town's history and takes good care of her guests. Built in 1784 for a sea captain's daughter, this creaky, sagging, and venerable eight-room place—with each room named for its particular color scheme—is on the main street in the town center. Picnic in the back garden and get to know Hector, the live-in hound. Reserve well in advance (July: S-600 kr, D-850 kr; outside of July: S-600 kr, D-750 kr; 2-night minimum, cash only, cuddly hot-water bottles, shared bathrooms, free Internet access and Wi-Fi, Vestergade 44, tel. 62 52 22 98, www.vestergade44.com, pensionvestergade44@post.tele.dk).

$$ Bed & Beer Guest House, while sloppily run, is good in a pinch, with six big, modern, apartment-like rooms on the main square (Db-750 kr, no breakfast, Torvet 7, tel. 40 29 40 50, www.bedandbeer.dk).

Outside of Ærøskøbing

$$ Vindeballe Kro, about three miles from Ærøskøbing, is a traditional inn in Vindeballe at the island's central crossroads. Maria and Steen rent 10 fine little rooms (S-400 kr, D-600 kr, tel. 62 52 16 13, www.vindeballekro.dk, vindeballe.kro@get2net.dk, restaurant closed Mon).

$$ Graasten B&B, also about three miles out, is a cattle farm 300 yards from the sea run by a British/Danish couple, Julie and Aksel Hansen (D-550 kr for 1 night, D-1000 kr for 2 nights, extra bed-250 kr, four-person apartment with kitchen, bath, and separate entrance-235 kr/person, cash only, Østermarksvej 20, short ride on bus #990—direction Marstal, tel. 23 26 11 38, www.greyfarm.dk, greyfarm@adr.dk). Julie requires a bank wire to secure a reservation.

$ Ærø Campground is set on a fine beach a few minutes' walk out of town. This three-star campground offers a lodge with a fireplace, campsites, and cabins (camping-69 kr/person, 4- to 6-bed cabins-125–200 kr plus per-person fee, bedding-75 kr/person, open May–Sept, facing the water, follow waterfront to the left, tel. 62 52 18 54, www.aeroecamp.dk).

Eating in Ærøskøbing

Ærøskøbing has a handful of charming and hardworking little eateries. Business is so light that chefs and owners come and go constantly, making it tough to predict the best value for the coming year. As each place has a distinct flavor, I'd spend 20 minutes enjoying the warm evening light and do a strolling survey before making your choice. While there are several simple burger-type joints, I've listed only the serious kitchens. The only places in town serving food during the winter are Restaurant Addis and the Landbogaarden bar (see "Pubs," page 131).

Restaurant Mumm is where visiting yachters go for a good and classy meal. Portions are huge, and on balmy days their garden terrace out back is a hit. Call ahead to reserve (daily specials-180 kr, main courses-170–212 kr, daily 16:30–21:00, near Torvet Square, tel. 62 52 12 12, Peter Sorensen).

Café Aroma, an inexpensive Danish café that feels like a rustic old diner, has a big front porch filled with tables and good, reasonably priced entrées, sandwiches, and burgers for 60–175 kr. Ask about the daily special, which will save you money and is not listed on the confusing menu. Order at the bar (May–Aug daily 11:00–21:00, closed Sept–April, on Vestergade).

Ærøskøbing Røgeri serves wonderful smoked fish meals on paper plates and picnic tables. Facing the harbor, it's great for a light meal (60-kr fish with potato salad and bread). Eat there or find a pleasant picnic site at the beach or at the park behind the fish house. A smoked fish dinner and a couple of cold Carlsbergs are a well-earned reward after a long bike ride (May–Sept daily 11:00–18:00, until 20:00 in July, Havnen 15, tel. 62 52 40 07).

Restaurant Addis is one of two places open all year, serving fresh seafood and meat dishes. Eat in the main dining room among portraits of Danish royalty, or in the larger side room (daily lunch and dinner specials, lunch main courses-48–85 kr, dinner main courses-169–180 kr, daily 12:00–15:00 & 18:00–21:00, across street from Pension Vestergade, Vestergade 39, tel. 62 52 21 43).

Other Places Worth Considering: **Det Lille Hotel** serves meals in an inviting dining room or garden (daily 12:00–21:00, Smedegade 33, tel. 62 52 23 00, Klaus cooks with attitude). **Hotel Ærøhus,** serving creative French-inspired modern fare, is the closest thing to nouvelle cuisine in town (open daily, on Vestergade, tel. 62 52 10 03).

Grocery: Buy picnic fixings plus wine and beer at the **Spar Market** (Mon–Fri 9:00–18:00, Sat–Sun 10:00–14:00, on Torvet Square) or the bigger **Netto** supermarket (cold beer and wine—handy for walks to the little huts on the beach at sunset, Mon–Fri 9:00–19:00, Sat 8:00–17:00, closed Sun, across street from ferry dock).

Ærøskøbing Connections

Ærø-Svendborg Ferry

The ferry ride between **Svendborg,** with connections to Copenhagen, and **Ærøskøbing,** on the island of Ærø, is a relaxing 75-minute crossing (cash only, 166 kr round-trip per person, 370 kr round-trip per car—not including driver/passengers, crew collects fares on ferry after departure, you'll save a little money with round-trip tickets, you can leave the island via any of the three different Ærø ferry routes, ferry not covered by railpass).

The ferry always has room for walk-ons, but drivers should reserve a spot in advance, especially on weekends and in summer (car reservations by phone or email are free and easy—simply give name and license-plate number, office open Mon–Fri 8:00–16:00, Sat–Sun 9:00–15:00, tel. 62 52 40 00, www.aeroe-ferry.dk, info @aeroe-ferry.dk).

Ferries depart Svendborg daily at 10:30, 13:30, 16:30, 19:30, and 22:30 (plus a 7:30 departure Mon–Fri). Ferries depart

Ærøskøbing daily at 8:55, 11:55, 14:55, 17:55, and 20:55 (plus a 5:55 departure Mon–Fri). Drivers with reservations just drive on (be sure to get into the *med* reservations line). If you won't use your car in Ærø, park it in Svendborg (big, safe lot two blocks in from ferry landing). On Ærø, parking is free.

Trains Connecting with Ærø-Svendborg Ferry

The train from **Odense** dead-ends at the Svendborg harbor (2/hour, 45 min). Train departures and arrivals are coordinated with the ferry schedule.

Arriving in Svendborg: The ferry leaves Svendborg about five minutes after your train arrives. Since trains run every half-hour during summer, I recommend leaving Odense on an earlier train, so you have a little more time. To get from the Svendborg train station (more like an open-air subway stop) to the dock, turn left after exiting the train, following the sidewalk between the tracks and the station, then take a left at the first street, Brogade. Head a block downhill to the harbor, make a right, and the ferry dock is ahead, across from Hotel Ærø. If you arrive early, you can head to the waiting room in the little blue building across the street from the hotel.

Departing from Svendborg: All Svendborg trains go to Odense (where you can connect to Copenhagen or Århus). Trains leave shortly after the ferry arrives (tight connections for hurried commuters). To reach the train from the Svendborg ferry dock, pass Hotel Ærø, walk up Brogade one block, then take a right and follow the sidewalk between the tracks and the train station. A train signed *Odense* should be waiting on the single track (departs at :22 or :52 past each hour).

Buses Connecting with Ærø-Svendborg Ferry

If you're going from Ærø to Copenhagen, a ferry/bus/train combo shaves about 30 minutes off the ferry/train journey covered earlier. Bus #910, which coordinates with the ferry, runs from Svendborg to the town of Nyborg, which is linked by direct train to Copenhagen. The twice-hourly bus trip takes 45 minutes, arriving and departing Nyborg within 15–20 minutes of the Copenhagen train (2/hr, 1.25 hours). Note that if you have a railpass, or if you're going to Odense or to points west, taking the train from the ferry is a better option.

For a complete schedule of buses and trains in Denmark, visit www.rejseplanen.dk.

Odense

Founded in A.D. 988 and named after Odin (the Nordic Zeus), Odense is the birthplace of storyteller Hans Christian Andersen (whom the Danes call simply H. C., pronounced "hoe see"). He is Odense's favorite son—you'll find his name and image all over town. He once said, "Perhaps Odense will one day become famous because of me." Today, Odense (OH-then-za) is one of Denmark's most popular tourist destinations. As Denmark's third-largest city, with 186,000 people, it is big and industrial. But its old center retains some of the fairy-tale charm it had in the days of H. C. A.

Orientation to Odense

Tourist Information

The TI is in the Town Hall (Rådhuset; July–Aug Mon–Fri 9:30–18:00, Sat 10:00–15:00, Sun 11:00–14:00; Sept–June Mon–Fri 9:30–16:30, Sat 10:00–13:00, closed Sun; tel. 63 75 75 20, www.visitodense.com). To get from the train station to the TI, cross through the Kongens Have (King's Garden) park and head south (away from train station) down Jernabanegade. When you come to Vestergade, take a left and follow this fine pedestrian street 100 yards to the TI. For all the information needed for a longer stop, pick up their excellent and free ***Go Odense*** guide.

Arrival in Odense

The train station is located in the Bånegard Center, a big shopping complex, which also holds the bus station, library (with free Internet access), shops, eateries, and a movie theater. For a quick visit, check your luggage at the train station (20/40 kr lockers at top of escalators, outside DSB Resjebureau office), pick up a free map inside the ticket office, jot down the time your train departs, and hit the town (follow signs to *Odense Centrum*).

Sights in Odense

▲▲Hans Christian Andersen Hus—To celebrate Hans Christian Andersen's 100th birthday in 1904, the city founded this museum in the house where he was born. Today the humble (and rebuilt) house is the corner of an expansive, high-tech museum packed with mementos from the writer's life and hordes of children and tourists. You could spend several delightful hours here getting into his life story and work. Exhibits include a display on the era in which Andersen lived (1805–1875), a 13-minute introductory film about his life (plays every 15 minutes, alternates between Danish

and English), a library of Andersen's books from around the world (his tales were translated into nearly 150 languages), and headsets and benches throughout for you to listen to a selection of fairy tales. It's fun if you like the man and his tales (60 kr, free for kids under 17; daily mid-June–mid-Aug 9:00–18:00; off-season Tue–Sun 10:00–16:00, closed Mon; Bangs Boder 29, tel. 65 51 46 01). Because the museum includes good descriptions in English, the guidebook is unnecessary (but pick up the *Go Odense* guide next to entrance turnstiles if you aren't stopping by the TI). For more on the author, see the sidebars on pages 63 and 74.

The garden fairy-tale **theater**—with pleasing vignettes—thrills kids daily in July and early August in the museum garden at 11:00, 13:00, and 15:00 (30-minute show in Danish, but fun regardless of language). The museum gift shop is full of mobiles, cut-paper models, and English versions of Andersen's fairy tales. The café next door offers seating indoors and out with sandwiches, burgers, and pancakes (50–100 kr).

Next door to the café is the **Fyrtøjet** ("Tinderbox"), a modern and fun hands-on center for children based on works by Hans Christian Andersen. Kids can dress up in costumes, act out a fairy tale, and paint in the art studio (70 kr, 115-kr combo-ticket sold here includes Hans Christian Andersen Hus and Funen Village, July–mid-Aug daily 9:00–18:00; off-season Tue–Sat 10:00–16:00, closed Sun–Mon; Hans Jensens Stræde 21, tel. 66 14 44 11, www.fyrtoejet.com).

▲Møntergården Urban History Museum—This humble little museum, three blocks from the Hans Christian Andersen Hus, offers Odense history, medieval buildings, and early town photos (25 kr, Tue–Sun 10:00–16:00, closed Mon, Overgade 48, tel. 65 51 46 01, www.museum.odense.dk).

▲Funen Art Museum—This small, pleasant museum collects Danish art from 1750 to the present, paying particular attention to artists of the island of Funen, or *Fyn* in Danish (40 kr, Tue–Sun 10:00–16:00, closed Mon, Jernbanegade 13, tel. 65 51 46 01, www.museum.odense.dk).

▲Funen Village/Den Fynske Landsby Open-Air Museum—The sleepy gathering of 26 old buildings located about two miles out of town preserves the 18th-century culture of this region. There are no explanations in the buildings, because many school groups who visit play guessing games. Pick up the 15-kr guidebook (60 kr; July–mid-Aug daily 10:00–19:00; April–June and mid-Aug–late Oct Tue–Sun 10:00–17:00, closed Mon; late Oct–March Sun only 11:00–15:00; tel. 65 51 46 01, www.museum.odense.dk).

Sleeping in Odense

(5 kr = about $1, country code: 45)

$$$ Radisson H. C. A. Hotel is big, comfortable, and impersonal, with 145 rooms a block from the Hans Christian Andersen Hus. It offers great rates every day through the summer (Sb-1,375 kr, Db-1,575 kr, special summer deal mid-June–Aug: Db-925 kr, free Wi-Fi, Claus Bergs Gade 7, tel. 66 14 78 00, fax 66 14 78 90, www.radissonblu.com/hotel-odense, hcandersen@radissonsas.com).

$$ Cab-Inn Odense brings its no-frills minimalist economy to town, with 200 simple, comfy, and modern rooms (economy Sb-485 kr, standard Db-675 kr, larger "Captains Class" Db-805 kr, Tb-110 kr, breakfast-60 kr, free Internet and Wi-Fi, next to the station at Øster Stationsvej 7, tel. 63 14 57 00, www.cabinn.com, odense@cabinn.com). For more about this chain, see page 101.

$$ Hotel Domir, recently remodeled with new bathrooms, has 35 tidy, basic little rooms along its tiny halls. It's located on a quiet side-street just a few minutes from the train station (Sb-595 kr, twin Db-695 kr, Db-795 kr, Tb-845 kr, free Internet access, Hans Tausensgade 19, tel. 66 12 14 27, fax 66 12 14 13, www.domir.dk). They also run **Ydes Hotel,** just down the street, with industrial and metallic simplicity (50 kr cheaper).

$ Jytte Gamdrup (pronounced "U-ter") rents two well-appointed rooms in her 17th-century home a few doors down from the Hans Christian Andersen Hus. This is probably your best Odense home, located on a fairy-tale street (D-450 kr, Ramsherred 17, tel. 21 45 49 72).

$ Danhostel Odense City is a huge and efficient hostel towering above the train station, with 140 beds in 4- and 6-bed rooms with baths. "Better" rooms have "better beds and a TV;" prices reflect standard/better rooms (dorm bed-240 kr, Sb-465/515 Db-630/680 kr, Tb-695/745 kr, Qb-760/810 kr, nonmembers pay 35 kr/night extra, sheets-60 kr, breakfast-60 kr—it can add up, Stationsvej 31, tel. 63 11 04 25, www.cityhostel.dk, info@cityhostel.dk).

$ Blommenslyst B&B rents two rooms in its private guest house just outside Odense (S-300 kr, D-440 kr, breakfast-60 kr, 15-min drive from town center, Ravnebjerggyden 31, tel. 65 96 81 88, www.blommenslyst.dk, ingvartsen-speth@post.tele.dk, Marethe and Poul Erik Speth).

Eating in Odense

If you are in town for just a short stopover to visit the Hans Christian Andersen Hus, consider the café at the museum for lunch. Otherwise, Odense's main pedestrian shopping streets, **Vestergade** and **Kongensgade,** offer the best atmosphere and most options for lunch and dinner.

Vintapperstræde is an alleyway full of restaurants just off Vestergade. Choose from Danish, Mexican, Italian, and more. Study the menus posted outside each restaurant to decide, then grab a table inside or join the locals at an outdoor table.

Odense Connections

From Odense by Train to: Copenhagen (3/hr, 1.5–2 hrs, some go direct to the airport), **Århus** (2/hr, 1.5 hrs), **Billund/Legoland** (2/hr, 50-min train to Vejle, transfer to bus #244, allow 2 hrs total), **Svendborg/Ærø ferry** (2/hr, 45 min, to Ærø ferry—75-min crossing), **Roskilde** (2/hr, 70 min).

Route Tips for Drivers

Århus or Billund to Ærø: Figure about two hours to drive from Billund (or 2.5 hours from Århus) to Svendborg. The freeway takes you over a suspension bridge to the island of Funen (or *Fyn* in Danish); from Odense, take the highway south to Svendborg.

Leave your car in Svendborg (at the convenient long-term parking lot two blocks from the ferry dock) and sail for Ærø. It's an easy 75-minute crossing; note there are only five or six boats a day (see page 138). Cars need reservations but walk-on passengers don't. A ferry/bus combo-ticket gives you the whole island with stopovers.

Ærø to Copenhagen via Odense: From Svendborg, drive north following signs to *Fëborg*, past Egeskov Castle, and on to Odense. For the open-air folk museum (Den Fynske Landsby), leave Route 9 just south of town at Højby, turning left toward Dalum and the Odense campground (on Odensevej). Look for *Den Fynske Landsby* signs (near the train tracks, south edge of town). If you're going directly to the Hans Christian Andersen Hus, follow the signs.

Continuing toward Copenhagen, you'll take the world's second-longest suspension bridge (200-kr toll, 12.5 miles long, free exhibition center on bridge in Halsskov, July–Aug Wed–Sun 11:00–16:00, closed Tue and off-season, take exit 43 off E-20). Follow signs marked *København* (Copenhagen). At Ringsted, signs point you to Roskilde. Aim toward the twin church spires and follow signs for *Vikingskibene* (Viking ships).

Copenhagen is 30 minutes from Roskilde. If you're heading to the airport, stay on the freeway to the end, following signs to *København C,* then to *Dragør/Kastrup Airport.*

JUTLAND

Legoland • Århus

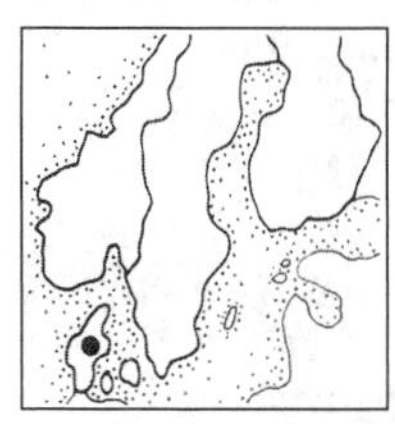

Jutland (Jylland—pronounced "YEW-lan"—in Danish) is the part of Denmark that juts up from Germany. It's a land of sand dunes, Lego toys, moated manor houses, and fortified old towns. This region is particularly family friendly. Make a pilgrimage to the most famous land in all of Jutland: the pint-sized kids' paradise, Legoland. In Århus, the lively capital of Jutland, wander the pedestrian street of this busy port, tour its boggy prehistory, and visit centuries-old Danish town life in its open-air folk museum.

Legoland

Legoland is Scandinavia's top kids' sight. If you have a child (or are a child at heart), it's a fun stop. This huge park is a happy combination of rides, restaurants, trees, smiles, and 33 million Lego bricks creatively arranged into such wonders as Mount Rushmore, the Parthenon, "Mad" King Ludwig's castle, and the Statue of Liberty. It's a Lego world here, as everything is cleverly related to this popular toy. If your time in Denmark is short, or if your family has already visited a similar Legoland park in California, England, or Germany, consider skipping the trip. But if you're in the neighborhood, a visit to

the "Mothership" of all things Lego will be a hit with kids ages two through the pre-teens.

Cost: 275 kr, 245 kr for kids ages 3–12 and over 60 (entry fee gets you on all the rides). To bypass the ticket line, purchase tickets online at www.legoland.dk (reduced-price family tickets also available). Legoland generally doesn't charge in the evening (free after 19:30 in July and late Aug, otherwise after 17:30).

Hours: Generally open April–Oct daily 10:00–18:00, until 20:00 Sat–Sun and most of Aug, until 21:00 daily in July, closed Nov–March and Wed–Thu in Sept–mid-Oct (tel. 75 33 13 33). Activities close an hour before the park, but it's basically the same place after dinner as during the day, with fewer tour groups.

Getting There: Legoland, located in the town of Billund, is easiest to visit by car (see "Route Tips for Drivers" at the end of the chapter), but doable by public transportation. The nearest train station to Billund is Vejle. Trains arrive at Vejle from **Copenhagen** (hourly, 2.25 hrs), **Odense** (2/hr, 50 min), and **Århus** (3/hr, 45 min). At Vejle, catch the #244 bus to travel the remaining 25 miles to Billund (1.25 hours). For details on transportation, see www.legoland.dk or www.rejseplanen.dk.

Background: Lego began in 1932 in the workshop of a local carpenter who named his wooden toys after the Danish phrase *leg godt* ("play well"). In 1949, the company started making the plastic interlocking building bricks for which they are world famous. Since then, Lego has continued to expand its lineup and now produces everything from motorized models and "Bionicles" to Clikits jewelry and video games—making kids drool in many languages all around the world. According to the company, each person on this planet has, on average, 62 Lego blocks.

➲ **Self-Guided Tour:** Legoland is divided into eight different "worlds" with fun themes such as Adventure Land, Pirate Land, and Knight's Kingdom. Pick up a brochure at the entrance and make a plan using the colorful 3-D map. You can see it all in a day, but you'll be exhausted. The Legoredo section (filled with Wild West clichés Europeans will enjoy more than Americans) merits just a quick look, though your five-year-old might enjoy roasting a biscuit-on-a-stick around the fire with a tall, blond park employee wearing a Native American headdress.

A highlight is Mini Land, where landscaped gardens are filled with carefully constructed Lego landscapes and cityscapes. Alongside representations of

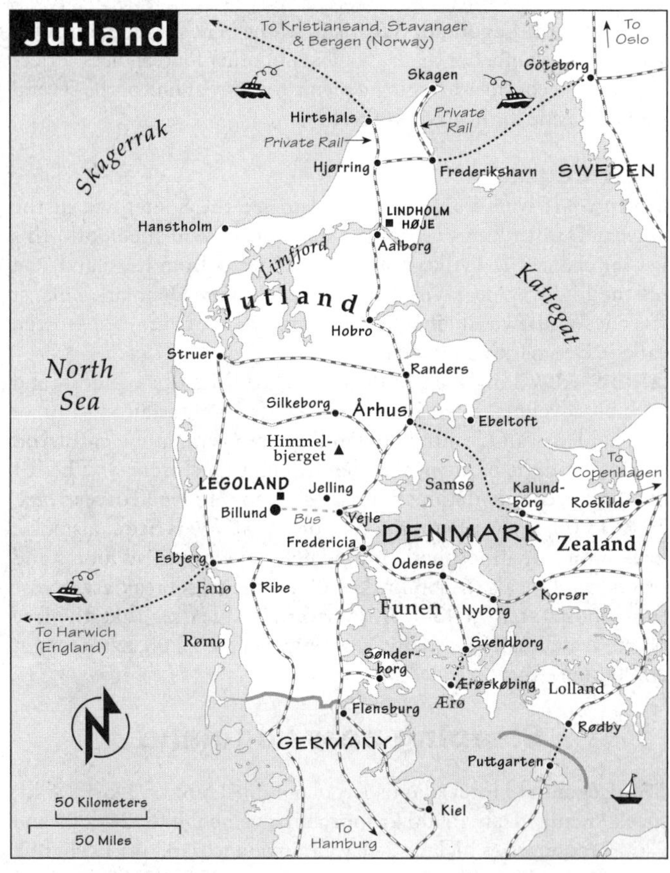

the world's famous sights, you'll see Danish monuments, Dutch windmills, and an amazing representation of the Norwegian harbor of Bergen. Children joyfully watch as Lego boats ply the waters and Lego trains chug merrily along the tracks. Also in Mini Land is the Traffic School, where little drivers can learn the rules of the road.

Rides scattered throughout the park are included with admission. While the rides aren't thrilling by Disneyland standards, most kids will find something to enjoy (parents should check the brochure for height restrictions).

The indoor museum features company history, high-tech Lego creations, a great doll collection, and a toy museum full of mechanical wonders from the early 1900s, many ready to jump into action with the push of a button. A Lego playroom encourages hands-on fun, and a campground is across the street if your kids refuse to move on.

Eating at Legoland: Surprisingly, the park's restaurants don't serve Leg-o-lamb, but there are plenty of other food choices. Prices are high, so consider bringing a picnic to enjoy at one of the several spots set aside for bring-it-yourselfers.

Near Legoland

Jelling—If you've always wanted to see the hometown of the ancient Danish kings Gorm the Old and Harald Bluetooth, this is your chance. The village of Jelling (12 miles from Legoland, just off the highway near Vejle) has a church with Denmark's oldest frescoes and two ancient runic stones in its courtyard—often called "Denmark's birth certificate."

▲Ribe—A Viking port 1,000 years ago, Ribe is the oldest, and possibly loveliest, town in Denmark. It's an entertaining mix of cobbled lanes and leaning medieval houses, with a fine **cathedral** (12 kr, modern paintings under Romanesque arches). The **TI** can find accommodations for a 25-kr booking fee (Torvet 3, tel. 75 42 15 00, www.ribetourist.dk), or try **$$ Weis Stue**, a smoky, low-ceilinged, atmospheric inn, which rents primitive rooms and serves good meals (S-450 kr, D-600 kr, includes breakfast, across from church, tel. 75 42 07 00, www.weis-stue.dk). Take the free Night Watchman tour (daily May–mid-Sept at 22:00, extra tour at 20:00 June–Aug).

Sleeping near Legoland

$$$ Legoland Hotel adjoins Legoland (Sb-1,500 kr, Db-1,875 kr, special family deals: 2,300 kr for room big enough for 2 adults and 2 kids, room prices include 2-day admission to park, prices slightly lower Sept–May or for 2 or more nights, tel. 75 33 12 44, fax 75 35 38 10, www.hotellegoland.dk, hotel@legoland.dk).

Sleep Code

(5 kr = about $1, country code: 45)
S = Single, **D** = Double/Twin, **T** = Triple, **Q** = Quad, **b** = bathroom, **s** = shower. You can assume credit cards are accepted unless otherwise noted.

To help you sort easily through these listings, I've divided the rooms into three categories based on the price for a standard double room with bath during high season:

$$$ Higher Priced—Most rooms 1,000 kr or more.
$$ Moderately Priced—Most rooms between 500–1,000 kr.
$ Lower Priced—Most rooms 500 kr or less.

$$$ Hotel Svanen is close by, in Billund (Sb-1,095–1,795 kr, Db-1,195–1,895 kr, extra bed-100 kr, Nordmarksvej 8, tel. 75 33 28 33, fax 75 35 35 15, www.hotelsvanen.dk, info@hotelsvanen.dk).

$$ Legoland Village is a family youth hostel offering inexpensive rooms that sleep one to five people (Db-695–925 kr, Tb-895–1,045 kr, Qb-975–1,135 kr, 5b-1,045–1,225 kr, higher prices are for peak season, sheets and towels-60 kr, includes breakfast, Ellehammers Alle 2, tel. 75 33 27 77, fax 75 33 28 77, www.legoland-village.dk, info@legoland-village.dk).

$ Private rooms are the key to a budget visit here. In a forest just outside of town, **Erik and Mary Sort** have a great setup: a cottage that sleeps up to six people and six double rooms. Their guests enjoy a huge living room, a kitchen, lots of Lego toys, and a kid-friendly yard (Ss-240 kr, Sb-300 kr, Ds-340 kr, Db-380 kr, 580 kr for the cottage—towels and sheets extra, breakfast-35 kr, free Internet access, rental bikes-15 kr, cash only, leave Billund on Grindsted Road, turn right on Stilbjergvej, go a half-mile to Stilbjergvej 4B, tel. 75 33 23 27, www.gregersminde.dk).

Århus

Århus (OAR-hoos), Denmark's second-largest city, has a population of 400,000 and calls itself the "World's Smallest Big City." I'd argue it's more like the world's biggest little town: easy to handle and easy to like. Århus is Jutland's capital and cultural hub. Its Viking founders settled here—where a river hit the sea—in the eighth century. Today, Århus bustles with a lively port, an important university, a Strøget-like pedestrian boulevard, and an adorable "Latin Quarter" filled with people living very, very well. Århus, a scenic three-hour train ride from Copenhagen, is well worth a stop.

JUTLAND

Orientation to Århus

Tourist Information

The TI is across the street from the train station (July–mid-Sept Mon–Fri 10:00–17:30, Sat 10:00–15:00, closed Sun; mid-Sept–June Mon–Fri 10:00–16:30, closed Sat–Sun; tel. 87 31 50 10, www.visitaarhus.com). They sell the **Århus Card,** which provides free or discounted entry to sights and includes public transportation. This can be a money-saver for busy sightseers (120 kr/1 day, 150 kr/2 days).

Guided City Walks: In peak season, the TI offers three different two-hour historic town walks, each offering a worthwhile education for curious travelers (125 kr, mid-June–mid-Aug: Mon—The Old Town, Wed—Architecture and Art, Fri—The Latin Quarter; tours depart at 14:00, in Danish and English, book at TI).

Getting Around Århus

The sights mentioned in my self-guided walk and the Århus Art Museum are all within a 15-minute walk. The Moesgård Museum (prehistory), Den Gamle By (open-air folk museum), and Tivoli Friheden (amusement park) can be reached by bus from the train station or around the corner at Park Alle (18-kr tickets are good for 2 hours, buy from coin-op machine in bus). Bus drivers are friendly and speak English. Taxis are easy to flag down but pricey (30-kr drop fee).

Helpful Hints

Internet Access: Boomtown Netcafé, a busy cyber-game arcade with lots of terminals, faces the canal in the city center (25 kr/30 min, daily 11:00–24:00, Åboulevarden 21). Also, many hotels, cafés, and restaurants offer free Wi-Fi. Ask the TI for a list of hotspots.

Laundry: A launderette *(møntvask)* is four blocks south of the TI, at M.P. Bruunsgade 64 (daily 7:30–21:00, 60 kr for wash and dry, on the square in front of St. Paul's Church).

Self-Guided Walk

Welcome to Århus

This quick little walk acquaints you with the historic center, covering everything of sightseeing importance except the three big museums (modern art, prehistory, and open-air folk). You'll begin at the cathedral, check out the modest sights in its vicinity, wander the cute Latin Quarter, take a stroll down the "most beautiful street" in Århus, and end at the canal. After touring the impressive cathedral, the rest of the walk should take about an hour.

• *Start at the cathedral.*

Århus Cathedral: Go inside Scandinavia's biggest church (330 feet long and tall; free entry, daily May–Sept 9:30–16:00, Oct–April 10:00–15:00). The cathedral was finished in 1520 in all its Catholic glory. Imagine it with 55 side chapels, each dedicated to a different saint and wallpapered with colorful frescos. Bad timing. Just 16 years later, in 1536, the Reformation hit and Protestants cleaned out the church—side altars gone, paintings whitewashed over—and added a pulpit mid-nave so parishioners could hear the sermon. The front pews were even turned away from the altar to face the pulpit (a problem for weddings today).

Ironically, that Lutheran whitewash protected the fine 16th-century Catholic art. When it was peeled back in the 1920s, the frescoes were found perfectly preserved. In 1998, the surrounding whitewash was redone, making the old original paintings, which have never been restored, pop. Noble tombs that once lined the floor (worn smooth by years of traffic) now decorate the walls. The fancy text-filled wall medallions are epitaphs, originally paired with tombs. Ships hang from the ceilings of many Danish churches. In this nation of seafarers, there were invariably women praying for the safe return of their sailors.

The altarpiece, dating from 1479, features the 12 apostles surrounding John the Baptist, St. Anne, and St. Clement (the patron saint of Århus and sailors—his symbol is the anchor). On top, Jesus is crowning Mary in heaven. This is a polyptych (a many-paneled altarpiece). A model in the apse demonstrates how it flips to different scenes throughout the church year.

The fresco in the aisle (right of altar, facing windows) shows a three-part universe: heaven, earth (at Mass), and—under the thick black line—purgatory...an ugly land with angels and devils fighting over souls. The kid on the gallows illustrates how the medieval Church threatened even little children with ugly damnation. Notice the angels trying desperately to save the damned. Just a little more money to the Church and...I...think...we...can...pull... Grandpa...OUT.

An earlier Romanesque church—just as huge—once stood on this spot. As you exit, notice the tiny window in the back-right. It survives with its circa-1320 fresco from that earlier church. Even back then—when the city had a population of 1,000—the church seated 1,200. Imagine the entire community (and their dogs) assembled here to pray and worship their way through the darkness and uncertainty of medieval life.

• *Standing at the cathedral door, survey the...*

Cathedral Square: The long, triangular square is roughly the shape of the original Viking town from A.D. 770. Århus is the Viking word for "mouth of river." The river flows to your left to the beach, which—before modern land reclamation—was just behind the church. The green spire peeking over the buildings dead ahead is the Church of Our Lady (which we'll visit later on this walk). Fifty yards to the right, the nubile caryatids by local artist Hans Krull decorate the entry to the **Hotel Royal** and town casino. (Krull's wildly decorated bar is just beyond, on the corner.)

• *Fifty yards to the left of the church, in the basement of the Nordea Bank, is the tiny...*

Århus Center
Self-Guided Walk
1 Århus Cathedral
2 Cathedral Square
3 Hotel Royal
4 Viking Museum
5 Århus Theater
6 Church of Our Lady
7 Møllestien
8 Canal (Åboulevarden)
200 Yards
200 Meters
Botanical Gardens
DEN GAMLE BY FOLK MUSEUM
MAIN ENTRANCE
LANGELANDSGADE
NY MUNKEGADE
SAMSØGADE
THUNØGADE
LOLLANDSGADE
GRØNNEGADE
SEJRØGADE
MØLLEVEJEN
HJORTENSGADE
SALTHOLMSGADE
MØNSGADE
NØRRE ALLÉ
VIBORGVEJ
VESTERBROGADE
VESTERGADE
SILKEBORGVEJ
MØLLESTIEN
MØLLEGADE
Mølleparken
Canal
THORVALDSENSGADE
CARL BLOCHS GADE
LUNDBYESGADE
MAR. STRANDSGATE
VESTER ALLÉ
CHRISTIANSGADE
FREDERIKSGADE
ARoS ART MUSEUM
GODSBANEGÅRD
SONNESGADE
CONCERT HALL
Rådhuspladsen
TOWN HALL
PARK ALLÉ
Banegårds-pladsen
To 23
Hotels, Restaurants & Services
9 Scandic Plaza Hotel
10 Best Western Hotel Ritz
11 Villa Provence
12 Hotel Guldsmeden
13 Cab-Inn
14 To Danhostel Århus
15 City Sleep In
16 Bryggeriet Sct. Clemens
17 Jacob's barBQ & Pita Bar
18 Le Coq
19 Teaterbodega
20 Carlton Brasserie
21 Åboulevarden Canal Eateries
22 Internet Café
23 To Launderette

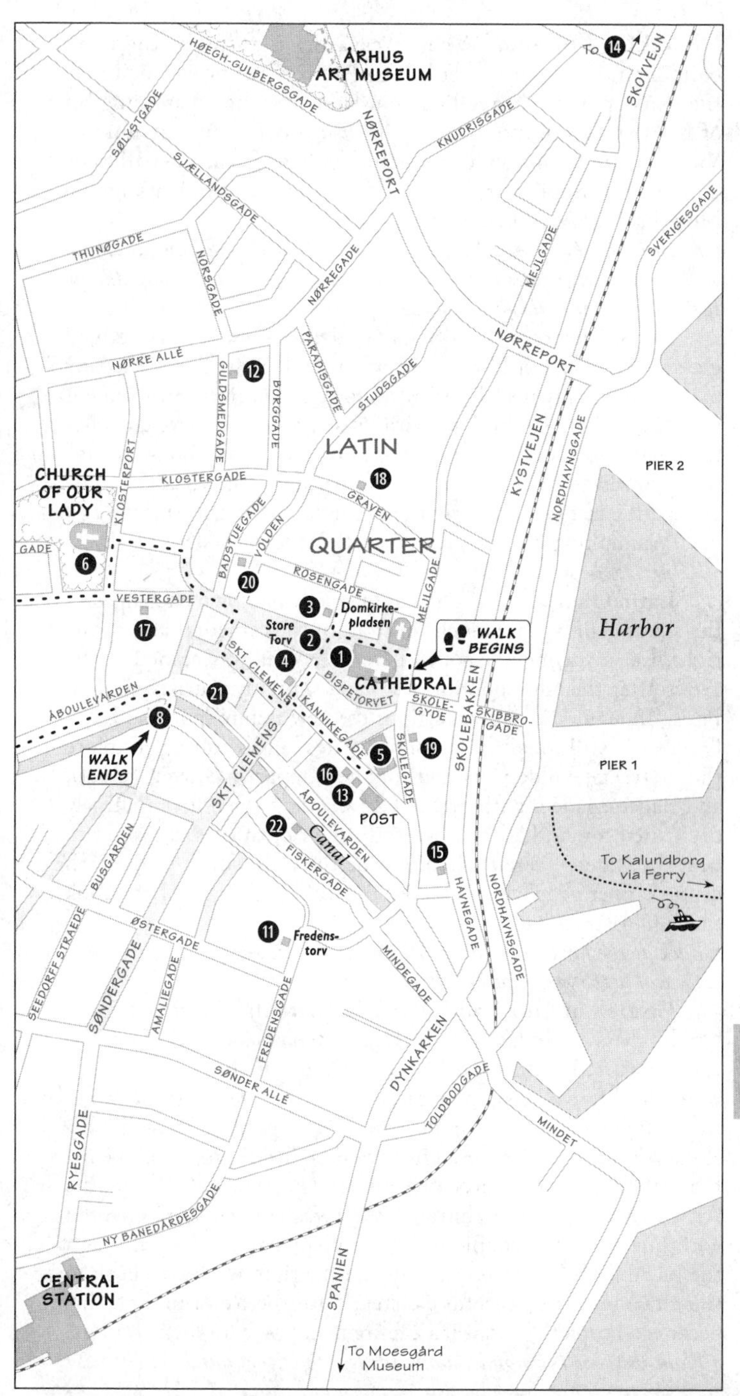
ÅRHUS
ART MUSEUM
HØEGH-GULBERGSGADE
To 14
SKOVVEJN
SØLYSTGADE
SJÆLLANDSGADE
NØRREPORT
KNUDRISGADE
SVERIGESGADE
THUNØGADE
NØRSGADE
NØRREGADE
MEJLGADE
NØRREPORT
NØRRE ALLÉ
GULDSMEDGADE
BORGGADE
PARADISGADE
STUDSGADE
LATIN
QUARTER
KYSTVEJEN
NORDHAVNSGADE
PIER 2
CHURCH
OF OUR
LADY
KLOSTERPORT
KLOSTERGADE
GRAVEN
GADE
BADSTUEGADE
VOLDEN
ROSENGADE
MEJLGADE
VESTERGADE
Domkirke-
pladsen
Store
Torv
WALK
BEGINS
Harbor
CATHEDRAL
SKT. CLEMENS
BISPETORVET
SKOLE-
GYDE
SKIBBRO-
GADE
SKOLEBAKKEN
ÅBOULEVARDEN
KANNIKEGADE
SKOLEGADE
PIER 1
WALK
ENDS
SKT. CLEMENS
POST
ÅBOULEVARDEN
Canal
FISKERGADE
HAVNEGADE
NORDHAVNSGADE
To Kalundborg
via Ferry
BUSGARDEN
Fredens-
torv
ØSTERGADE
MINDEGADE
SEEDORFF STRAEDE
SØNDERGADE
AMALIEGADE
FREDENSGADE
DYNKARKEN
SØNDER ALLÉ
TOLDBODGADE
MINDET
RYESGADE
NY BANEDÅRDESGADE
CENTRAL
STATION
SPANIEN
To Moesgård
Museum

Viking Museum: When excavating the site for the bank building in 1960, remains of Viking Århus were uncovered. Today the bank sponsors a free little museum showing a surviving bit of the town's original boardwalk *in situ* (where it was found), Viking artifacts, and a murder victim (missing his head)—all well-described in English (ride the escalator down, open bank hours: Mon–Fri 10:00–16:00, closed Sat–Sun).

• *Leaving the bank, walk straight ahead along the substantial length of the cathedral (brides have plenty of time to reconsider things during their procession) to the fancy facade opposite.*

Århus Theater: This ornate facade, with its flowery stained glass, is Danish Art Nouveau from around 1900. Under the tiny balcony is the town seal, featuring towers, the river, St. Clement with his anchor, and St. Paul with his sword. High above crouches the devil. The local bishop made a stink when this "house of sin" was allowed to be built facing the cathedral. The theater builders had the last say, finishing their structure with this smart-aleck devil triumphing (this was a hit with the secular modern locals).

• *Return to the square in front of the cathedral.*

Latin Quarter: The higgledy-piggledy old town encompasses the six or eight square blocks in front of the cathedral and to the right. Latin was never spoken here—the area was named in the 1960s after the cute, boutique-ish, and similarly touristy zone in Paris. Though Århus' canal strip is the new trendy spot, the Latin Quarter is still great for shopping, cafés, and strolling. Explore these streets: Volden (named for the rampart), Graven (moat), and Badstuegade ("Bath Street"). In the days when fires routinely decimated towns, bathhouses—with their open fires necessary to heat the water—were located outside the walls. Back in the 15th century, finer people bathed monthly, while everyday riff-raff took their "Christmas bath" once a year.

• *Back at the far end of the cathedral square, side-trip away from the cathedral to the green spire of the...*

Church of Our Lady (Vor Frue Kirke): The smart brick building you see today is in the Dutch Renaissance style from the 15th century, but this local "Notre-Dame" is the oldest church in town. After Christianity came to Viking Denmark in 965, a tiny wooden church was built here. The crypt of its 11th-century stone rebuild was discovered in 1955. Step inside and climb below the main altar into an evocative arcaded space (c. 1060). Like the Århus Cathedral, the church's whitewashed walls are covered with fine epitaph medallions with family portraits. Step through the low door behind the rear pew (on the right with your back to the altar) into the peaceful cloister. With the Reformation, this became a hospital. Today, it's a retirement home for lucky seniors.

• *Walk west on Vestergade, along the length of the church, to the next street, Grønnegade. Turn left, then take the next right onto...*

Møllestien: Locals call this quiet little cobbled lane the "most beautiful street in Århus." The small, pastel cottages—draped in climbing roses and hollyhock in summer—date from the 18th century. Notice the small mirrors on some of the windows. Known as "street spies," they allow old women inside to inconspicuously watch what's going on outside.

• *At the end of the lane, head left toward the canal (the park on your right, Mølleparken, is a good spot for a picnic). When you reach the canal, turn left and walk until you get to the white bridge.*

Canal (Åboulevarden): You're standing on the site of the original Viking bridge. The open sea was to the left. A protective harbor was to the right. When attacked, the bridge on this spot was raised, ships were tucked safely away, and townsmen stood here to defend their fleet. Given the choice, they'd let the town burn and save their ships.

In the 1930s, the Århus River was covered over to make a new road—an event marked by much celebration. In the 1980s, locals reconsidered the change, deciding that the road cut a boring, people-mean swath through the center of their town. They removed the road, artfully canalized the river, and created a trendy new people zone—the town's place to see and be seen. This strip of modern restaurants ensures the street stays as lively as possible even after the short summer, providing heaters and even blankets to outdoor diners if necessary.

• *Your walk is over. Following the canal to the right takes you to Den Gamle By (open-air folk museum). Following it to the left takes you past the best of the Århus canal zone. Crossing the canal and going straight (with a one-block jog left) gets you to the major pedestrian boulevard that leads all the way to the train station (where you can catch a bus to the Moesgård Museum or open-air folk museum).*

Sights in Århus

▲▲▲ARoS—The Århus Art Museum is a must-see sight, if only for the building's architecture. Square and unassuming from the outside, the bright white interior, with its spiral staircase winding up the museum's three floors, is surprising. The building has two sections, one for the exhibits and one for administration. The halves are divided by a passageway, which is free to enter if you just want to peek at the building itself. You'll also see the squatting sculpture called *Boy* (by Australian artist Ron Mueck)—realistic, yet 15 feet high.

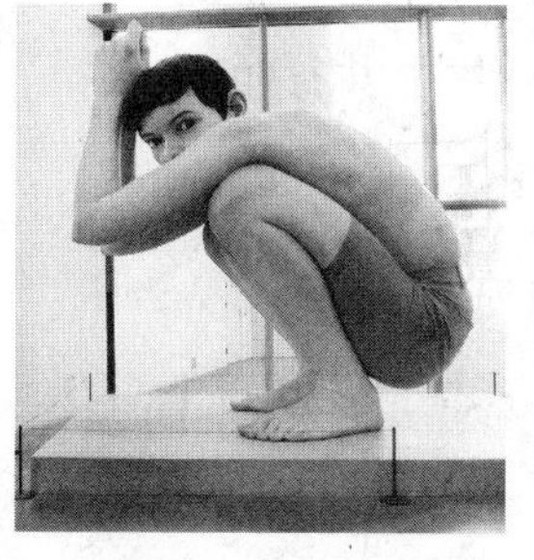

Pick up a museum floor plan at the ticket counter. The permanent collection features paintings dating from the Danish Golden Age (1800–1850) to modern art, including many multimedia installations and works by Bill Viola, James Turrell, and others such as Danish artist Per Kirkeby. In the basement (amid black walls), artists from around the world exhibit their works of light and sound in each of nine rooms *(De 9 Rum)*. On the rooftop, the *Rainbow Panorama* is a large, circular, glass walkway featuring the different colors of the spectrum. Scheduled for completion by summer 2010, the piece provides 360-degree views over the city.

Cost, Hours, Location: 90 kr, Tue–Sun 10:00–17:00, until 22:00 on Wed, closed Mon, lunch café on ground floor, exclusive restaurant on top floor, ARoS Allé 2, tel. 87 30 66 00, www.aros.dk.

▲▲▲Den Gamle By—"The Old Town" open-air folk museum has 75 half-timbered houses and craft shops. Unlike other Scandinavian open-air museums that focus on rural folk life, Den Gamle By is designed to give you the best possible look at Danish urban life in centuries past. Highlights include Torvet (the main square), the Mayor's House (#28, from 1597, facing Torvet), the toy museum (#41, Legetoj, a block beyond Torvet), and the recently completed Mintmaster's Mansion, the residence of a Copenhagen noble (#33, from 1683, facing Torvet). Your ticket comes with a flier of special events throughout the park—consider these as you plan your time. Though each building is described with a plaque, and there are maps throughout the park, the 10-kr guidebooklet is a worthwhile investment.

For a light meal or drink, the cheery indoor/outdoor Simonsens Have is an inviting cafeteria. In the basement of the Mintmaster's Mansion, you'll find Wineke's Cellar, an 18th-century public house serving beer, wine, and sandwiches. After hours, the buildings of the open-air museum are locked, but the peaceful park is open. A fine botanical garden is next door.

Cost and Hours: 100 kr, daily July–early Sept 9:00–18:00, April–June and early Sept–Nov 10:00–17:00, until 19:00 most of Dec, shorter hours off-season, tel. 86 12 31 88, www.dengamleby.dk.

Getting There: Stroll 15 minutes up the canal, or catch bus #3, #14, or #25 from near the train station (around the corner on Park Alle, on the Ritz Hotel side).

▲▲Moesgård Museum—This prehistory museum, just outside of town at Moesgård, has three sections: Stone Age, Iron Age (500 B.C. to A.D. 800), and Viking Age. Its state-of-the-art exhibits, with lots of real artifacts, are well-described in English. The museum's highlight and claim to fame is its incredibly intact Grauballe Man—the world's best-preserved "bog-corpse." Reclining in his stately glass tomb, the more than 2,000-year-old "bog man" looks like a fellow half his age. You'll see his skin, nails, hair, and even the slit in his throat he got at the sacrificial banquet (back in 300 B.C.). Sit, as if in a big, sleek, dark-wood sauna, and enjoy some private time with this visitor from the past. The story of his discovery (in a peat field in 1952) and conservation is also interesting.

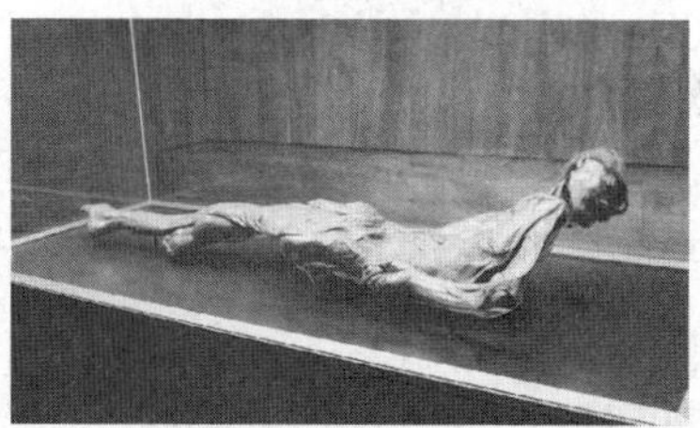

Behind the museum, a two-mile-long circular trail stretches down to a fine beach. This "Prehistoric Trackway" runs past a few model Viking buildings, including a 12th-century stave church (included in museum admission, essential 15-kr guidebooklet).

Cost and Hours: 60 kr; April–Sept daily 10:00–17:00; Oct–March Tue–Sun 10:00–16:00, closed Mon; cafeteria, tel. 89 42 11 00, www.moesmus.dk.

Getting There: The museum is located outside Århus in a lush, wooded park sprawling down to the sea (200 kr by taxi, easy 18-kr bus ride: #6 leaves from the curb in front of the train station twice hourly at :20 and :50 past the hour, ride 20 min to end of line—about 100 yards from the museum; return buses depart from museum at :15 and :45 past the hour).

Tivoli Friheden Amusement Park—The local Tivoli offers great fun for the family (65-kr entry only, 195 kr includes rides, daily 12:00–22:00, shorter hours off-season; bus #1, #4, #6, #8, or #18 to edge of town; tel. 86 14 73 00, www.tivoli-friheden.dk).

Sleeping in Århus

(5 kr = about $1, country code: 45)

My recommendations include the following: two tired business hotels facing the station with rates that flex with demand (a good value if booked in advance and arriving on a weekend or in the summer); two charming hotels with personality; a stripped-down, functional, Motel 6-type place; and two backpacker/student-friendly hostels. For a 50-kr fee, the TI can set you up in a 500-kr double (with shared bath) in a private home. They also have summer deals on ritzy hotels (Db-around 800 kr).

$$$ Scandic Plaza Hotel rents 162 well-furnished, business-class rooms 100 yards from the station (Db-1,100 kr weekends and summer, Db-1,600 kr weekdays, check website for best deals, kids under age 12 free, includes breakfast, sauna/gym/hot tub, Banegårdspladsen 14, tel. 87 32 01 00, fax 87 32 01 99, www.scandic-hotels.com, plaza.aarhus@scandic-hotels.com). They offer a 20 percent discount for nonrefundable advance bookings on their website.

$$$ Best Western Hotel Ritz, also across the street from the station, has similar-quality rooms but is less welcoming (Sb-850–1,100, Db-1,000–1,300 kr, Banegårdspladsen 12, tel. 86 13 44 44, fax 86 13 45 87, www.hotelritz.dk, mail@hotelritz.dk).

$$$ Villa Provence, named for owners Steen and Annette's favorite vacation destination, is a *petit* taste of France in the center of Århus. Its 39 fun-yet-tasteful rooms, decorated with antique furniture and old French movie posters, surround a quiet courtyard. Prices vary depending on the size and elegance of the room (Db-1,295–2,800 kr, includes breakfast, parking-110 kr/day, 10-min walk from station, near Åboulevarden at the end of Fredensgade, Fredens Torv 12, tel. 86 18 24 00, fax 86 18 24 03, www.villaprovence.dk, hotel@villaprovence.dk).

$$$ Hotel Guldsmeden is a small, welcoming, and sparkling-clean hotel with 27 rooms, fluffy comforters, and a young, disarmingly friendly staff. A steep staircase takes you to the best rooms, while the cheaper rooms (without private facilities) are in a ground-floor annex behind the stay-awhile garden (S-745 kr, Sb-1,175 kr, D-945 kr, Db-1,295 kr, extra bed-250 kr, 10 percent off rooms with private bath with this book based on availability, includes breakfast, 15-min walk or 70-kr taxi from the station, in Århus' quiet Latin Quarter at Guldsmedgade 40, tel. 86 13 45 50, fax 86 13 76 76, www.hotelguldsmeden.com, aarhus@guldsmeden.com).

$$ Cab-Inn, overlooking the atmospheric Åboulevarden canal, is extremely practical. Its simple, minimalist-yet-comfy little rooms each come with a single bed that expands into a twin and one or two fold-down bunks on the walls. The service, like the rooms, is no-nonsense (Sb-485 kr, Db-705–805 kr, Tb-805 kr, Qb-935 kr, breakfast-60 kr, easy parking-80 kr, rooms overlook canal or quieter courtyard, Kannikegade 14, tel. 86 75 70 00, fax 86 75 71 00, www.cabinn.dk, aarhus@cabinn.dk). For more on this chain, see page 101.

$-$$ Danhostel Århus, an official HI hostel with six-bed dorms and plenty of two- and four-bed rooms, is near the water two miles out of town (dorm bed-160 kr, S/D-506 kr, Sb/Db-620 kr, sheets-45 kr, towels-10 kr, breakfast-55 kr, nonmembers pay 35 kr/night extra, take bus #1 to the end and follow signs, Marienlundsvej 10, tel. 86 16 72 98, www.aarhus-danhostel.dk, info@aarhus-danhostel.dk).

$ City Sleep In, a creative and independent hostel open 24 hours a day year-round, has a kitchen, fun living and games room, laundry service, and lockers. It's on a busy road facing the harbor, a 10-minute hike from the station (140 kr/bunk in 4- to 6-bed dorms, D-400 kr, Db-460 kr, sheets-50 kr, breakfast-65 kr, Havnegade 20, tel. 86 19 20 55, fax 86 19 18 11, www.citysleep-in.dk, sleep-in@citysleep-in.dk).

Eating in Århus

Affluent Århus has plenty of great little restaurants. All of these are in the old town, within a five-minute stroll from the cathedral. Choose between a good-time steak house/brewpub (St. Clement's Brewery); a more intimate steak house (Jacob's barBQ); a hot French place (Le Coq Restaurant); classy, traditional Danish (Teaterbodega); lost in the Latin Quarter (Carlton Brasserie); or any number of places among the trendy crowd on the canal.

Bryggeriet Sct. Clemens (St. Clement's Brewery), facing the church, is a bright, convivial, fun-loving, and woody land of happy eaters and drinkers. Choose from a hearty menu and eat amid shiny copper vats. If dropping by for just a beer, they have enticing beer snacks—including little *Nürnberger* bratwurst (75–115-kr lunch and light meals; 170–270-kr hearty dinners such as steak, ribs, and fish; Mon–Sat 11:30–24:00, closed Sun, Kannikegade 10–12, tel. 86 13 80 00).

Jacob's barBQ is another welcoming steak house, but without the microbrew fun and with a bit more class. Behind a nondescript café zone is a popular summer garden, set under a house with two floors of happy eaters and a big sizzling grill. Their piano bar (live music Tue–Sat from 21:00) is a popular place to nurse an after-dinner drink (hearty 150-kr plates, famous steak dinners starting at 200 kr, restaurant open nightly until the wee hours, Vestergade 3, tel. 87 32 24 20). The same owners also run **Jacob's Pita Bar,** next door, serving pita sandwiches that are a cut above the average *shawarma.* Choose from grilled beef, chicken, lamb, or ground beef. The sandwiches are great for an inexpensive, quick meal—get an order to go and head to the nearby square, along the canal, or Møllerparken (42-kr pita sandwiches, "menu" with fries and a drink-76 kr, Mon–Thu 11:00–21:00, Fri–Sat 11:00 until really late, Sun 17:00–21:00).

Le Coq is a local favorite in the Latin Quarter. Chef/owner Troels Thomsen and his youthful gang (proud alums from a prestigious Danish cooking school) serve up a fresh twist on traditional French cuisine in a single Paris-pleasant yet unassuming 10-table room. The set-price meals (218 kr for three courses) are not described—Troels likes his staff to talk with individual guests and come up with a meal plan that fits both the kitchen and diner. Reservations are smart (165-kr main dishes, daily 17:00–24:00, Graven 14, tel. 86 19 50 74).

Teaterbodega is the venerable best bet for traditional Danish—where local men go for "food their wives won't cook." Facing the theater and cathedral, it's dressy and draped in theater memorabilia (150–200-kr main dishes, open-face sandwiches at lunch only, Mon–Sat 11:30–22:30, closed Sun, Skolegade 7, tel. 86 12 19 17).

Carlton Brasserie, facing a pretty square in the Latin Quarter, is a solid bet for good Danish and international food in relaxing yet classy surroundings. The restaurant has tables on the square, with more formal seating in back (inviting menu, 135–225 kr plates, 230-kr formal 2-course dinner, closed Sun, Rosensgade 23, tel. 86 20 21 22). The Latin Quarter streets are teeming with other hardworking and popular eateries.

The Åboulevarden Canal is lined with trendy eateries—all overpriced unless you value making the scene with the locals (and all open daily until late). They have indoor and canalside seating with heaters and blankets, so diners can eat outdoors even when it's cold. Before settling in, cruise the entire strip, with special consideration for the **Ziggy Sidewalk** and **Cross Café** (both popular for salads, sandwiches, burgers, and drinks), and **Grappa** (a classy Italian place with 100-kr pastas and pizzas, as well as pricier plates).

Århus Connections

From Århus by Train to: Odense (2/hr, 1.5 hrs), **Copenhagen** (1–2/hr, 3 hrs), **Ærøskøbing** (5–6/day, transfer to ferry in Svendborg, total trip-4.25 hrs, sample schedules: 10:27–14:45 or 13:27–17:45), **Hamburg, Germany** (2 direct/day, more with transfers, 5 hrs), **Hirtshals/Ferry to Kristiansand, Norway** (hourly, 2.5–3 hrs; to meet the Color Line ferry, transfer at Hjørring and continue to Hirtshals Havn; note that Eurail passes don't cover the Hjørring-Hirtshals train, but do give a 50 percent discount; buy your ticket in Hjørring or on board—12 kr with railpass, 23 kr without; for the latest ferry schedule, see www.colorline.com).

Route Tips for Drivers

From the Ferry Dock at Hirtshals to Århus to Billund: From the dock in Hirtshals, drive south (signs to *Hjørring*, *Ålborg*). It's about 2.5 hours to Århus. (To skip Århus, skirt the center and follow E-45 south.) To get to downtown Århus, follow signs to the center, then *Domkirke*. Park in the pay lot across from the cathedral. Signs all over town direct you to Den Gamle By open-air folk museum. From Århus, it's 60 miles to Billund/Legoland (go south on Skanderborg Road; follow signs to *Vejle*, *Kolding*). For Legoland, take the *Vejle S* (after *Vejle N*) exit for Billund.

NORWAY

NORWAY

Norge

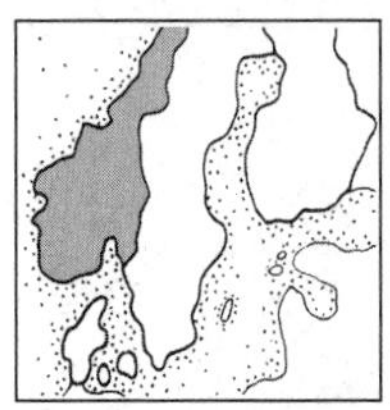

Norway is stacked with superlatives—it's the most mountainous, most scenic, and most prosperous of all the Scandinavian countries. Perhaps above all, Norway is a land of intense natural beauty, its famously steep mountains and deep fjords carved out and shaped by an ancient ice age.

Norway is also a land of rich harvests—timber, oil, and fish. In fact, its wealth of resources is a major reason why Norwegians have voted *"nei"* to membership in the European Union. They don't want to be forced to share fishing rights with EU countries.

The country's relatively recent independence (in 1905, from Sweden) makes Norwegians notably patriotic and proud of their traditions and history.

Norway's Viking past (c. A.D. 800–1050) can still be seen today in the country's 28 remaining stave churches—with their decorative nods to Viking ship prows—and the Viking artifacts housed in Oslo's Viking Ship Museum.

The Vikings, who also lived in present-day Denmark and Sweden, were great traders, shipbuilders, and explorers. However, they are probably best known for their infamous invasions, which terrorized much of Europe. The sight of their dragon-prowed ships on the horizon struck fear into the hearts of people from Ireland to the Black Sea.

Named for the Norse word *vik*, which means fjord or inlet, the Vikings sailed their sleek, seaworthy ships on extensive voyages, laden with amber and furs for trading—and weapons for fighting. They traveled up the Seine and deep into Russia, through the Mediterranean east to Constantinople, and across the Atlantic to Greenland and even "Vinland" (Canada). In fact, they touched the soil of the Americas centuries before Columbus, causing proud "ya sure ya betcha" Scandinavian immigrants in the US to display bumper stickers that boast, "Columbus used a Viking map!"

Both history and Hollywood have painted a picture of the Vikings as fierce barbarians, an image reinforced by the colorful names of leaders like Sven Forkbeard, Erik Bloodaxe, and Harald Bluetooth. Unless you're handy with an axe, these don't sound

like the kind of men you want to hoist a tankard of mead with. They kept slaves and were all-around cruel (though there is no evidence that they forced their subjects to eat lutefisk). But the Vikings also had a gentle side. Many were farmers, fishermen, and craftsmen who created delicate works with wood and metal. Faced with a growing population constrained by a lack of arable land, they traveled south not just to rape, pillage, and plunder, but in search of greener pastures. Sometimes they stayed and colonized, as in northeast England, which was called the "Danelaw," or in northwest France, which became known as Normandy ("Land of the North-men").

The Vikings worshipped many gods and had a rich tradition of mythology. Epic sagas were verbally passed down through generations or written in angular runic writing. The sagas told the heroic tales of the gods, who lived in Valhalla, the Viking heaven, presided over by Odin, the god of both wisdom and war. Like the

Norway Almanac

Official Name: Kongeriket Norge—"The Kingdom of Norway"—or simply Norge (Norway).

Population: Norway's 4.6 million people (about 30 per square mile) are mainly of Nordic and Germanic heritage, with a small population of indigenous Sami people in the north. The rapidly growing immigrant population is primarily from Pakistan, Sweden, Denmark, Iraq, Vietnam, and Somalia. Most Norwegians speak one of two official forms of Norwegian (Bokmål and Nynorsk), and the majority speak English as a second language. While church attendance is way down, the vast majority of Norwegian Christians consider themselves Lutheran.

Latitude and Longitude: 62°N and 10°E, similar latitude to Canada's Northwest Territories.

Area: 148,900 square miles, slightly larger than New Mexico.

Geography: Sharing the Scandinavian Peninsula with Sweden, Norway also has short northern borders with Finland and Russia. Its 51,575-mile coastline extends from the Barents Sea in the Arctic Ocean to the Norwegian Sea and North Sea in the North Atlantic. Shaped by glaciers, Norway has a rugged landscape of mountains, plateaus, and deep fjords. In the part of Norway that extends north of the Arctic Circle, the sun never sets at the height of summer, and never comes up in the deep of winter.

Biggest Cities: Norway's capital city, Oslo, has a population of 580,000; over a million live in its metropolitan area.

Economy: The Norwegian economy grows around 4 percent each year, contributing to a healthy $215 billion Gross Domestic Product and a per capita GDP of $46,200. Its

Egyptians, the Vikings believed in life after death, and chieftains were often buried in their ships within burial mounds, along with prized possessions such as jewelry, cooking pots, food, and Hagar the Horrible cartoons.

Like the Greeks and Etruscans before them, the Vikings never organized on a large national scale and eventually faded away due to bigger, better-organized enemies and the powerful influence of Christianity. By 1150, the Vikings had become Christianized and assimilated into European society. But their memory lives on in Norway.

Beginning in the 14th century, Norway came under Danish rule for more than 400 years, until the Danes took the wrong side in the Napoleonic Wars. The Treaty of Kiel forced Denmark to cede Norway to Sweden in 1814. Sweden's rule of Norway lasted until 1905, when Norway voted to dissolve the union. Like many European countries, Norway was taken over by Germany during primary export is oil—Norway ranks behind only Saudi Arabia and Russia in the amount of oil exported, making it one of the world's richest countries. Thanks to this oil wealth, and the country's generally prudent approach to debt, the recent economic crisis has been relatively easy on Norway.

Currency: 6 Norwegian kroner (kr) = about $1.

Government: As the leader of Norway's constitutional monarchy, King Harald V has largely ceremonial powers. The head of state since October 2005 has been Prime Minister Jens Stoltenberg, who survived a narrow election in 2009. The legislative body is the Stortinget, with 169 members elected for four-year terms. The Labor Party currently holds 61 seats, followed by the Progress Party with 38, the Conservative Party with 23, and the Socialist Left Party with 15. The remaining seats are divided among smaller political parties.

Flag: The Norwegian flag is red with a blue Scandinavian cross outlined in white.

The Average Norwegian: The average Norwegian is 38 years old, has 1.78 children, and will live to be 79. One in three Norwegians is employed in the service sector, one in four in industry, and only 4 percent in agriculture.

World War II. April 1940 marked the start of five years of Nazi occupation, during which a strong resistance movement developed and hindered some of the Nazi war efforts.

Each year on May 17, Norwegians celebrate their ill-fated but idealistic 1814 constitution with fervor and plenty of flag-waving. Men and women wear folk costumes *(bunads),* each specific to a region of Norway. Parades are held throughout the country. The parade in Oslo marches past the Royal Palace, where the royal family waves to the populace from their balcony. While the king holds almost zero political power (Norway has a parliament chaired by a prime minister), the royal family is still highly revered and respected.

Four holidays in early summer disrupt transportation schedules: Constitution Day (May 17, mentioned above), Ascension Day (May 13 in 2010, June 2 in 2011), and Whitsunday and Whitmonday (a.k.a. Pentecost and the following day, May 23–24 in 2010, June 12–June 13 in 2011).

High taxes contribute to Norway's high standard of living. Norwegians receive cradle-to-grave social care: university education, health care, nearly yearlong maternity leave, and an annual six weeks of vacation. Norwegians feel there is no better place than home. Norway regularly shows up in first place on the annual UN Human Development Index.

Visitors enjoy the agreeable demeanor of the Norwegian people—friendly but not overbearing, organized but not uptight, and with a lust for adventure befitting their gorgeous landscape. Known for their ability to suffer any misfortune with an accepting (if a bit pessimistic) attitude, Norwegians are easy to get along with.

Despite being looked down upon as less sophisticated by their Scandinavian neighbors, Norwegians are proud of their rich folk traditions—from handmade sweaters and folk costumes to the small farms that produce sweet goat cheese, called *geitost.* Less than 7 percent of the country's land is arable, resulting in numerous small farms. The government recognizes the value of farming, especially in the remote reaches of the country, and provides rich subsidies to keep this tradition alive. These subsidies would not be allowed if Norway joined the European Union—yet another reason the country remains an EU holdout.

Appropriate for a land with countless fjords and waterfalls, Norway is known for its pristine water. Norwegian bottled artisan water has an international reputation for its crisp, clean taste. Although the designer Voss water (www.vosswater.com)—the H_2O of choice for Hollywood celebrities—comes with a high price tag, the blue-collar Olden is just as good. (The tap water is actually wonderful, too—and much cheaper.)

While the Norwegian people speak a collection of mutually understandable dialects, the Norwegian language has two official forms: *bokmål* (book language), and *nynorsk* (New Norse). During the centuries of Danish rule, people in Norway's cities and upper classes adopted a Danish-influenced style of speech and writing (called Dano-Norwegian), while rural language remained closer to the Old Norse. After independence, Dano-Norwegian was renamed *bokmål,* and the rural dialects were formalized as *nynorsk,* as part of a nationalistic drive for a more purely Norwegian language. Despite later efforts to combine the two forms, *bokmål* remains the most commonly used, especially in urban areas, books, newspapers, and government agencies. Students learn both.

The majority of the population under 70 years of age also speak English, but a few words in Norwegian will serve you well. For starters, see the Norwegian Survival Phrases on page 590. If you visit a Norwegian home, be sure to leave your shoes at the door; indoors is usually meant for stocking-feet only. At the end of a meal, it's polite to say "Thanks for the food"—*"Takk for maten"* (tahk for MAH-ten). Norwegians rarely feel their guests have eaten enough food, so be prepared to say *"Nei, takk"* (nigh tahk; "No, thanks"). You can always try *"Jeg er met"* (yigh ehr met; "I am full"), but be careful not to say *"Jeg er full"*—"I am drunk."

Stave Churches

Norway's most distinctive architecture is the stave church. These medieval houses of worship—tall, skinny, wooden pagodas with dragon's-head gargoyles—are distinctly Norwegian and palpably historic, transporting you right back to the Viking days. On your visit, make it a point to visit at least one stave church.

Stave churches are the finest architecture to come out of medieval Norway. Wood was plentiful and cheap, and locals had an expertise with woodworking (from all that boat-building). In 1300, there were as many as 1,000 stave churches in Norway. After a 14th-century plague, Norway's population dropped and many churches fell into disuse or burned down. By the 19th century, only a few dozen stave churches survived. Fortunately, they became recognized as part of the national heritage and were protected. Virtually all of Norway's surviving stave churches have been rebuilt or renovated, with painstaking attention to the original details.

A distinguishing feature of the "stave" design is its frame of tall, stout vertical staves (Norwegian *stav,* or "staff"). The churches typically sit on stone foundations, to keep the wooden structure away from the damp ground (otherwise it would rot). Most stave churches were made of specially grown pine, carefully prepared before being felled for construction. As the trees grew, the tips and most of the branches were cut off, leaving the trunks just barely alive to stand in the woods for about a decade. This allowed the sap to penetrate the wood and lock in the resin, strengthening the wood while keeping it elastic. Once built, a stave church was slathered with black tar to protect it from the elements.

Stave churches are notable for their resilience and flexibility. Just as old houses creak and settle over the years, wooden stave churches can flex to withstand fierce winds and the march of time. When the wind shifts with the seasons, stave churches groan and moan for a couple of weeks...until they've adjusted to the new influences, and settle in.

Even after the Vikings stopped raiding, they ornamented

the exteriors of their churches with warlike, evil spirit–fighting dragons reminiscent of their ships. Inside, a stave church's structure makes you feel like you're huddled under an overturned ship. The churches are dark, with almost no windows (aside from a few small "portholes" high up). Typical decorations include carved, X-shaped crossbeams; these symbolize the cross of St. Andrew (who was crucified on such a cross). Round, Romanesque arches near the tops of the staves were made from the "knees" of a tree, where the roots bend to meet the trunk (typically the hardest wood in a tree). Overall, these churches are extremely vertical: the beams inside and the roofline outside both lead the eye up, up, up to the heavens.

Most surviving stave churches were renovated during the Reformation (16th and 17th centuries), when they acquired more horizontal elements such as pews, balconies, pulpits, altars, and other decorations to draw attention to the front of the church. In some (such as the churches in Lom and Urnes), the additions make the church feel almost cluttered. But the most authentic (including Hopperstad near Vik) feel truly medieval. These time-machine churches take visitors back to early Christian days: no pews (worshippers stood through the service), no pulpit, and a barrier between the congregation and the priest, to symbolically separate the physical world from the spiritual one. Incense filled the church, and the priest and congregation chanted the service back and forth to each other, creating an otherworldly atmosphere that likely made worshippers feel close to God. (If you've traveled in Greece, Russia, or the Balkans, Norway's stave churches might remind you of Orthodox churches, which reflect the way all Christians once worshipped.)

When traveling through Norway, you'll be encouraged to see stave church after stave church. Sure, they're interesting, but there's no point in spending time seeing more than a few of them. Of Norway's 28 remaining stave churches, seven are described in this book. The easiest to see are the ones that have been moved to open-air museums in Oslo and Lillehammer. But I prefer to appreciate a stave church in its original fjords-and-rolling-hills setting. My two favorites are both near Sognefjord: Borgund and Hopperstad. They are each delightfully situated, uncluttered by more recent additions, and evocative as can be. Borgund is in a pristine wooded valley, while Hopperstad is situated on a fjord. Borgund comes with the only good adjacent stave church museum. (Most stave churches on the Sognefjord are operated by the same preservation society; for more details, see www.stavechurch.com.)

Other noteworthy stave churches include the one in Lom, near the Jotunheimen Mountains, which is one of Norway's biggest, and is indeed quite impressive. The Urnes church, across from Solvorn, is technically the oldest of them all—but it's been thoroughly renovated in later ages (it is still worth considering, however, if only for its exquisite carvings and the fun excursion to get to it; see the More on the Sognefjord chapter). The Fantoft church, just outside Bergen, recently burned down, and the replica built to replace it has none of the original's magic. The stave church in Undredal (see the Norway in a Nutshell chapter) advertises itself as the smallest. I think it's also the dullest, and unless you're in tiny Undredal with time to kill, I recommend skipping it.

OSLO

While Oslo is the smallest and least earth-shaking of the Scandinavian capitals, this brisk little city offers more sightseeing thrills than you might expect. As an added bonus, you'll be inspired by a city that simply has its act together.

Sights of the Viking spirit—past and present—tell an exciting story. Prowl through the remains of ancient Viking ships, and marvel at more peaceful but equally gutsy modern boats (the *Kon-Tiki, Ra,* and *Fram*). Dive into the traditional folk culture at the Norwegian open-air folk museum, and get stirred up by the country's heroic spirit at the Norwegian Resistance Museum.

For a look at modern Oslo, tour the striking City Hall, take a peek at sculptor Gustav Vigeland's people pillars, climb the newly rebuilt Holmenkollen Ski Jump (opening in spring of 2010), walk all over the new Opera House, and then celebrate the world's greatest peacemakers at the Nobel Peace Center.

Situated at the head of a 60-mile-long fjord, surrounded by forests, and populated by more than a half-million people, Oslo is Norway's cultural hub. For 300 years (1624–1924), the city was called Christiania, after Danish King Christian IV. With independence, it reverted to the Old Norse name of Oslo. As an important port facing the Continent, Oslo has been one of Norway's main cities for a thousand years and the de facto capital since around 1300. Still, Oslo has always been small by European standards; in 1800, Oslo had 10,000 people, while cities such as Paris and London had 50 times as many.

Today the city sprawls out from its historic core to encompass over a million people in its metropolitan area, about one in

five Norwegians. Oslo's port hums with international shipping and a sizeable cruise industry. Its waterfront, once traffic-congested and slummy, is undergoing a huge change: Cars and trucks now travel in tunnels, a string of upscale condos and restaurants is taking over, and the neighborhood has a splashy new Opera House. Oslo is full of rich Norwegians and is, understandably, expensive. Its streets are a mix of grand Neoclassical facades and boxy 60s-style modernism. But overall, the feel of this major capital is green and pastoral—spread out, dotted with parks and lakes, and surrounded by hills and forests. For the visitor, Oslo is an all-you-can-see *smörgåsbord* of historic sights, trees, art, and Nordic fun.

Planning Your Time

Oslo offers an exciting two-day slate of sightseeing thrills. Ideally, spend two days, and leave on the night boat to Copenhagen or on the scenic "Norway in a Nutshell" train to Bergen the third morning. Spend the two days like this:

Day 1: Take my self-guided introductory walk. Tour the Akershus Fortress and the Norwegian Resistance Museum. Catch the City Hall tour. Spend the afternoon at the National Gallery and at the Holmenkollen Ski Jump and museum.

Day 2: Ferry across the harbor to Bygdøy and tour the *Fram, Kon-Tiki,* and Viking Ship museums. Spend the afternoon at the Norwegian Folk Museum. Finish the day at Frogner Park, enjoying the Vigeland statues (two recommended restaurants are nearby).

Orientation to Oslo

Oslo is easy to manage. Its sights cluster around the main boulevard, Karl Johans Gate (with the Royal Palace at one end and the train station at the other), and in the Bygdøy district, a 10-minute ferry ride across the harbor.

The monumental, homogenous city center contains most of the sights, but head out of the core to see the more colorful neighborhoods. Choose from Majorstuen and Frogner (chic boutiques, trendy restaurants), Grünerløkka (bohemian cafés, hipsters), and Grønland (multiethnic immigrants' zone).

Tourist Information

Oslo has two TIs: The **Oslo Information Center** faces City Hall (June–Aug daily 9:00–19:00, shorter hours and closed Sat–Sun off-season, Fridtjof Nansens Plass 5, www.visitoslo.com, info @visitoslo.com). Another TI is in front of the **train station** (Mon–Fri 7:00–20:00; Sat–Sun 8:00–18:00, until 20:00 May–Sept). Go early or late to avoid lines; otherwise, grab a number as you enter and wait. They answer the phone only on weekdays from 9:00 to 16:00 (tel. 24 14 77 00).

At either TI, pick up these freebies: an Oslo map, the helpful public transit map, the annual *Oslo Guide* (with plenty of details on sightseeing, shopping, and eating), the *What's On in Oslo* monthly (for the most accurate listing of museum hours and special events), and *Streetwise* magazine (an insightful, worthwhile student guide that's fun to read and full of offbeat ideas). If you're traveling on, pick up the *Bergen Guide* and information for the rest of Norway. The annual *Fjord Norway Travel Guide* is very useful. Consider buying the Oslo Pass (described below), unless you get the Oslo Package, which includes your hotel accommodation and an Oslo Pass (described under "Sleeping in Oslo," page 219).

Use It, a hardworking information center, is officially geared for those under age 26 but is generally happy to offer anyone its solid, money-saving, experience-enhancing advice (July–mid-Sept daily 9:00–18:00; off-season Mon–Fri 11:00–17:00, closed Sat–Sun; Møllergata 3, look for *Ungdomsinformasjonen* sign, tel. 24 14 98 20, www.unginfo.oslo.no). They can find you the cheapest beds in town (no booking fee), and offer free Internet access (30-min limit, may have to wait for a computer). Their free *Streetwise* magazine—packed with articles on Norwegian culture, ideas on eating and sleeping cheap, good nightspots, the best beaches, and so on—is a must for young travelers and worthwhile for anyone curious to probe the Oslo scene.

Oslo Pass: This pass covers the city's public transit, ferry boats, and entry to nearly every major sight—all described in a useful handbook (220 kr/24 hours, 320 kr/48 hours, 410 kr/72 hours; kids ages 4–15 and seniors over age 67 save 30 percent). Do the arithmetic carefully before buying; add up the individual costs of the sights you want to see to determine whether an Oslo Pass will save you money. (Here are some sample charges: 8-ride transit pass-180 kr, Nobel Peace Center-80 kr, three boat museums at Bygdøy-140 kr, National Gallery-free. These sights alone justify the cost of a 48-hour pass). Students with an ISIC card may be better off without the Oslo Pass. The TI's Oslo Package (see "Sleeping in Oslo," later) includes an Oslo Pass with your discounted hotel room.

Entertainment Listings: The periodical *What's On in Oslo* has an extensive listing of happenings every day. Pick it up free at the TI, and review the busy lineup of special events, tours, and concerts. *Streetwise* magazine is also good.

Arrival in Oslo

By Train

The central train station (Oslo Sentralstasjon, or "Oslo S" for short) is slick and helpful. You'll find Internet cafés, ATMs, and a Forex exchange desk. The station is plugged into a lively modern shopping mall called Byporten (Mon–Fri 10:00–21:00, Sat 10:00–18:00, closed Sun). You'll also find a Bit sandwich shop with seating for a cheap meal, an ICA supermarket (near the escalator, Mon–Fri 7:00–21:00, Sat–Sun 9:00–18:00), and a Vinmonopolet liquor store (Oslo's most central place to buy wine or liquor, sold only at Vinmonopolet stores). The TI is across the square in front of the station.

For tickets and train info, you can go to the station's ticket office (Mon–Fri 6:30–19:00, Sat 7:00–18:00, Sun 10:00–18:00) or to the helpful train office at the National Theater railway and T-bane station, which can have shorter lines (Mon–Fri 7:00–21:00, Sat–Sun 10:00–19:00, Ruseløkkveien, southwest of National Theater). There's also an after-hours full-service ticket desk at the train station, located between tracks 8 and 9 (open until 23:15). At each office, you can buy domestic, international, and Norway in a Nutshell tickets, and pick up leaflets on the Flåm and Bergen Railway. The TI also sells train tickets—likely friendlier and faster—for the same price.

By Plane

Oslo Airport: Oslo Lufthavn, also called Gardermoen, is about 30 miles north of the city center and has a helpful 24-hour information center (www.osl.no). For SAS, dial tel. 05400.

The speedy **Flytoget** train zips travelers between the airport and the central train station in 20–25 minutes (170 kr, less for students and seniors, 4/hr, runs roughly 5:00–24:00, not covered by railpasses, buy and validate ticket before boarding, keep it to exit, tel. 81 50 07 77, www.flytoget.no). Note that Flytoget trains alternate between those that go only to the central train station, and others that also continue on through Oslo, stopping at the National Theater station (which is closer to some recommended hotels and uses the same ticket).

Local trains cost less than Flytoget and take only a little longer (102 kr, hourly, 40 min, covered by railpasses, some also serve National Theater station). You'll save about 50 percent on this trip with an Oslo Pass because the pass covers transportation within Oslo; you only need to pay the fare for the stretch between the airport and the edge of town.

To reach the Flytoget and local train counters at the airport, exit right after you leave customs, and walk all the way to the far corner; you'll see two separate ticket counters (one for Flytoget,

NSB for the cheaper local trains) and separate TV screens showing the timetables for Flytoget and the "lokal–InterCity–fjerntog" trains.

Flybus airport buses stop directly outside the arrival hall and make several downtown stops, including the central train station (140 kr one-way, 4/hr, 40 min).

Taxis run to and from the airport (670-kr fixed rate, confirm price before you commit, some companies have cheaper special deals). If you start your ride after 17:00, there's a 200-kr extra charge (get in at 17:01 and suddenly it costs 870 kr). I prefer the slick and faster Flytoget train, but the taxi can be a good value for families and those with lots of luggage.

Sandefjord Airport Torp: Ryanair and other discount airlines use this airport, 70 miles sounds of Oslo (trains run hourly between Sandefjord station and Oslo, fewer Sat–Sun, 1.75 hours, www.nsb.no; 219-kr train fare includes shuttle bus between airport and Sandefjord station—2/hr, 4 min). Airport info: tel. 33 42 70 00, www.torp.no.

Helpful Hints

Pickpocket Alert: They're a problem in Oslo, particularly in crowds on the street and in subways and buses. Always wear your money belt. To call the police, dial 112.

Street People and Drug Addicts: Oslo's street population loiters around the train station. While a bit unnerving to some travelers, locals consider this rough-looking bunch harmless. The police have pretty much corralled them to the square called Christian Frederiks Plass, south of the station.

US Embassy: It's the big place behind all the fortifications (passport services open Mon–Fri 9:00–12:00, Henrik Ibsens Gate 48, tel. 22 44 85 50, norway.usembassy.gov).

Currency Exchange: Banks don't change money. Use ATMs or Forex exchange offices (outlets near City Hall at Fridtjof Nansens Plass 6, at train station, and at Egertorget at the crest of Karl Johans Gate, hours vary by location but generally Mon–Fri 9:00–18:00, Sat 9:00–16:00, closed Sun).

Internet Access: You have two options at the train station. **Sidewalk Express,** the budget choice, has locations on the mezzanine level under the escalators and near the city center entrance (29 kr/1.5 hours, open 24/7, coin-op). **@rctic Internet Café,** in the station's main hall and above track 13, is quieter but pricey (60 kr/hr, daily 9:00–22:00, sells international phone cards).

Post Office: It's in the train station.

Pharmacy: Jernbanetorgets Vitus Apotek is open 24 hours daily (across from train station on Jernbanetorget, tel. 23 35 81 00).

Laundry: Selva Laundromat is on the corner of Wessels Gate and Ullevålsveien at Ullevålsveien 15, a half-mile north of the train station (daily self-serve 8:00–21:00, full-serve 10:00–19:00, walk or catch bus #37 from station, tel. 41 64 08 33).

Bike Rental: Bikes are tough to rent in Oslo. A public system lets you grab simple city bikes out of locked racks at various points around town (80 kr/24 hours, rent card at TI, must leave credit-card number as deposit). A more expensive conventional bike rental company delivers bikes to your hotel (details at TI). To rent a bike in the countryside, see page 212.

Getting Around Oslo

By Public Transit: Commit yourself to taking advantage of Oslo's excellent transit system, made up of buses, trams, ferries, and a subway (*Tunnelbane*, or T-bane for short). Use the TI's free public transit map to navigate. The system runs like clockwork, with schedules clearly posted and followed. Many stops have handy electronic reader boards showing the time remaining before the next tram arrives (usually less than 10 min). **Trafikanten,** the public-transit information center, faces the train station under the glass tower (same building as TI; Mon–Fri 7:00–20:00, Sat–Sun 8:00–20:00, tel. 177 or 81 50 01 76, www.trafikanten.no).

Individual **tickets** work on buses, trams, ferries, and T-bane for one hour (25 kr if bought at a Narvesen kiosk/convenience store, or 36 kr if bought on board). Other options include the **Flexicard** (180 kr for 8 rides, shareable, can buy from driver), the 24-hour **Dagskort Tourist Ticket** (65 kr, pays for itself in three rides), and the **Oslo Pass** (free run of entire system; pass described earlier).

By Taxi: Taxis come with a 105-kr drop charge that covers you for three or four kilometers—about two miles (134 kr on evenings and weekends). To get a taxi, wave one down, find a taxi stand, or call 02323.

Tours in Oslo

By Boat, Bus, and Foot

Oslo Fjord Tours—A fascinating world of idyllic islands sprinkled with charming vacation cabins is minutes away from the Oslo harborfront. For locals, the fjord is a handy vacation getaway. Tourists can get a glimpse of this island world by public ferry or tour boat. Cheap ferries regularly connect the nearby islands with downtown (covered by Oslo Pass or transit pass).

Several tour boats leave regularly from pier 3 in front of City Hall. Båtservice has a relaxing and scenic 50-minute mini-cruise, with a live-but-boring multilanguage commentary, that departs on the hour (130 kr, daily late May–June 10:00–16:00, July–Aug until 19:00, no boats Sept–late May, tel. 23 35 68 90, www.boatsightseeing.com). They won't scream if you bring something to munch. They also offer two-hour fjord tours (230 kr, 3–4/day late April–Sept) and a "Summer Evening on the Fjord" dinner cruise (390 kr; joyride without narration that includes a "shrimp buffet"—just shrimp, bread, and butter; daily late June–mid-Sept 19:00–22:00). The 72-hour Oslo Pass gets you Båtservice's two-hour lunch cruise for free (normally costs 390 kr, 10:30–12:30 summer only, seats limited so reserve far in advance).

Bus Tours—Båtservice, which runs the harbor cruises (above), also offers three-hour bus tours of Oslo, with stops at the ski jump, Bygdøy museums, and Frogner Park (380 kr, 2/day late May–Aug, departs from ticket office on pier 3, longer tours also available, tel. 23 35 68 90, www.boatsightseeing.com). HMK also does daily city bus tours (215 kr/2 hours, 300 kr/3 hours, departs from TI across from City Hall, tel. 22 78 94 00, www.hmk.no). While there is a hop-on, hop-off bus service for Oslo (225 kr/24 hours), the city doesn't really work well with this kind of tour bus. Again, commit yourself to public transit to save lots of time, and try the self-guided tram tour described below.

Guided Walking Tour—The local guides' union offers 90-minute historic "Oslo Promenade" walks (from 100 kr, free with Oslo Pass; Mon, Wed, Fri at 17:30 in summer; leaves from sea side of City Hall, confirm departures at TI, tel. 22 42 70 20, www.guideservice.no).

Local Guide—To hire a private guide, call the guides' association at tel. 22 42 70 20 (1,150 kr/2 hours, www.guideservice.no). Another local guide bureau is at tel. 22 42 28 18.

Self-Guided Tram Tour

Tram #11/#12: A Hop-On, Hop-Off Introduction to Oslo

Tram #12, which becomes tram #11 halfway through its loop (at Majorstuen), circles the city from the train station, lacing together many of Oslo's main sights. Apart from the practical value of being able to hop on and off as you sightsee your way around town (trams come by at least every 10 minutes), this 40-minute trip gives you a fine look at parts of the city you wouldn't otherwise see.

The route starts at the main train station, at the traffic-island tram stop located immediately in front of the transit office tower. The route finishes at Stortorvet (the cathedral square), making 90 percent of a circle, and dropping you a three-minute walk from where you began the tour. Confirm with your driver that the tram #12 you're boarding becomes tram #11, and finishes at Stortorvet. Here's what you'll see and ideas on where you might want to hop out:

From the **station,** you'll go through the old grid streets of 16th-century Christiania, King Christian IV's planned Renaissance town. After the city's 17th fire, in 1624, the king finally got fed up. He decreed that only brick and stone buildings would be permitted in the city center, with wide streets to serve as fire breaks.

You'll turn a corner at the **fortress** (Christiana Torv stop; get off here for the fortress and Norwegian Resistance Museum), then head for **City Hall** (Rådhus stop). Next comes the harbor and upscale **Aker Brygge** waterfront neighborhood (jump off at the Aker Brygge stop for the harbor and restaurant row). Passing the harbor, you'll see on the left a few old shipyard buildings that still survive. Then the tram goes uphill, past the **House of Oslo** (a mall of 20 shops highlighting Scandinavian interior design; Vikatorvet stop) and into a district of ugly 1960s buildings (when elegance was replaced by "functionality"). The tram then heads onto the street Norwegians renamed **Henrik Ibsens Gate** in 2006 to commemorate the centenary of Ibsen's death, honoring the man they claim is the greatest playwright since Shakespeare.

After Henrik Ibsens Gate, the tram follows Frognerveien through the chic **Frogner neighborhood.** Behind the fine old facades are fancy shops and spendy condos. Here and there you'll see 19th-century mansions built by aristocratic families who wanted to live near the Royal Palace. Today many of these house foreign embassies. Turning the corner, you roll along the edge of **Frogner Park,** stopping at its grand gate (hop out at the Vigelandsparken stop for Frogner Park and Vigeland statues).

Ahead on the left, a statue of 1930s ice queen Sonja Henie marks the arena where she learned to skate. Turning onto Bogstadveien, the tram becomes #11 at the Majorstuen stop. **Bogstadveien** is lined with trendy shops, restaurants, and cafés—it's a fun place to stroll and window-shop. (You could get out here and walk along this street all the way to the Royal Palace park and the top of Karl Johans Gate.) The tram veers left before the palace, passing the **National Historical Museum** and stopping at the **National Gallery** (Tullinløkka stop). As you trundle along, you may notice that lots of roads are ripped up for construction. It's too cold to fix the streets in the winter, so, when possible, that work is done in the summer. Jump out at **Stortorvet** (a big square filled with flower stalls and fronted by the cathedral and the big GlasMagasinet department store). From here, you're a three-minute walk from the station, where this tour began.

Self-Guided Walk

▲▲Hello Oslo

This stroll covers the heart of Oslo—the zone most tourists find themselves walking—from the train station, up the main drag, and past City Hall to the harborfront. It takes a brisk 30 minutes if done nonstop.

Train Station: Start at the main entrance of Oslo's central train station (Oslo Sentralstasjon)—still marked *Østbanehallen,* or "East Train Station," from when Oslo had two stations. The statue of the tiger commemorates the 1,000th birthday of Oslo's founding, celebrated in the year 2000. The statue alludes to the town's nickname of Tigerstaden ("Tiger Town"). In the 1800s, Oslo was considered an urban tiger, leaving its mark on the soul of simple country folk who ventured into the wild and crazy New York City of Norway. (These days, the presence of so many beggars, or *tigger,* has prompted the nickname "Tiggerstaden.")

With your back to the train station, look for the glass Trafikanten tower that marks the **public transit office** (and TI);

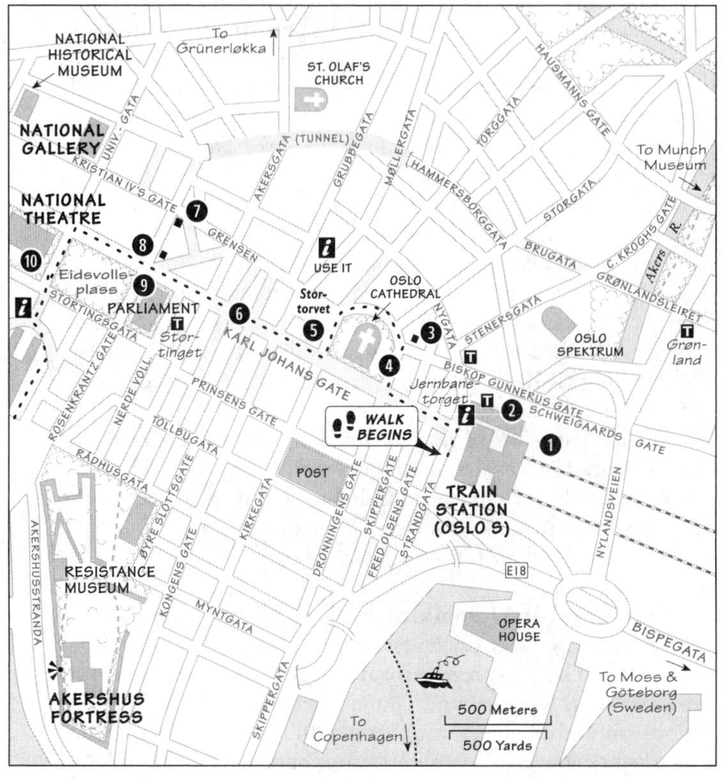

from here, trams zip to City Hall (harbor, boat to Bygdøy), and the underground subway (T-bane, or *Tunnelbane*—look for the *T* sign to your right) goes to Frogner Park (Vigeland statues) and Holmenkollen. Tram #12—featured in the self-guided tram tour described above—leaves from directly across the street.

The green building behind the Trafikanten tower is a shopping mall called **Byporten** (literally, "City Gate," see big sign on rooftop), built to greet those arriving from the airport on the shuttle train. Oslo's 37-floor pointed-glass **skyscraper,** the Radisson/SAS Plaza Hotel, looms behind that. Its 34th-floor pub welcomes the public with air-conditioned views and pricey drinks (daily 16:00–24:00). The tower was built with reflective glass so that, from a distance, it almost disappears. The area behind the Radisson—the lively and colorful "Little Karachi," centered along a street called Grønland—is where most of Oslo's immigrant population settled. It's become a vibrant nightspot, offering a fun contrast to the predictable homogeneity of Norwegian cuisine and culture (see "Immigration in Norway" sidebar).

Oslo allows hard-drug addicts and prostitutes to mix and mingle in the station area. (While it's illegal to buy sex in Norway, those who sell it are not breaking the law.) Troubled young people come here from small towns in the countryside for anonymity and community. The two cameras near the top of the Trafikanten tower monitor drug deals. Signs warn that this is a "monitored area," but victimless crimes proceed while violence is minimized.

• *Turn your attention to Norway's main drag...*

Karl Johans Gate: This grand boulevard leads directly from the train station to the Royal Palace. The street is named for the French prince Jean Baptiste Bernadotte, who was given a Swedish name, established the current Swedish dynasty, and ruled as a popular king (1818–1844) during the period after Sweden took Norway from Denmark.

Walk three blocks up Karl Johans Gate. This stretch is referred to as **"Desolation Row"** by locals because it has no soul. (Shoppers can detour to the recommended Oslo Sweater Shop, a block to the right down Skippergata, at Biskop Gunnerusgata 3.)

• *Hook around the curved old brick structure of an old market and walk to the...*

Oslo Cathedral (Domkirke): This Lutheran church, from 1697, is where Norway celebrates and mourns its royal marriages and deaths. The most recent royal wedding here was of Crown Prince Håkon Magnus and commoner Mette-Marit Tjessem Høiby—an unwed mom—in August 2001. Her father was a pensioner, poor enough to be a cheap source of gossip for the tabloids. It's a win-win situation, since locals enjoyed all the blather...and he got new teeth and a free mobile phone paid for by Oslo's tabloids.

Look for the cathedral's cornerstone (right of entrance), a thousand-year-old carving from Oslo's first and long-gone cathedral showing how the forces of good and evil tug at each of us. Step inside beneath the red, blue, and gold seal of Oslo and under an equally colorful ceiling. The box above on the right is for the royal family. Back outside, notice the tiny square windows midway up the copper cupola—once the lookout quarters of the fire watchman.

Walk behind the church. The **courtyard** is lined by a circa-1850 circular row of stalls from an old market. Rusty meat hooks now decorate the lamps of a peaceful café, which has quaint tables around a fountain. The atmospheric **Café Bacchus,** at the far left end of the arcade, serves food outside and in a classy café downstairs (light 120-kr meals, Mon–Sat 11:00–22:00, closed Sun, salads, good cakes, coffee, tel. 22 33 34 30).

• *The big square that faces the cathedral is called...*

Stortorvet: In the 17th century, when Oslo's wall was about here, this was the point where farmers were allowed to enter and

Immigration in Norway

Oslo has a big and growing immigrant community. About 10 percent of today's Norwegians are not ethnic Norwegians, and one in four of Oslo's residents is an immigrant. The border was closed to immigration in 1975. But because immigrants already in Norway have been allowed to sponsor relatives—and because Norway still allows refugees to enter for humanitarian reasons (for instance, Iranians can claim they are gay and can't safely return)—its immigrant population continues to grow.

These "new Norwegians" have provided a much-needed and generally appreciated labor force, filling jobs that wealthy Norwegians would rather not do. Immigrants are critical in the booming construction industry. Cab companies, restaurants, and hotels employ large numbers of immigrant workers. And entrepreneurial immigrants have opened wonderful ethnic restaurants, literally adding spice to the otherwise pretty drab local cuisine.

But in some parts of Oslo (such as near the train station), you'll see some of the downside of a country that is disinclined to be a melting pot. There have been scuffles between gangs and immigrant groups. Locals complain that the Norwegian government gives refuge to various ethnic groups who are historic enemies and then houses them side by side. Another source of friction is the tough love Norwegians feel they get from their government compared to the easy ride offered to needy immigrants: "They even get pocket money in jail!"

While Norway is a leader among rich nations in per-capita giving to the developing world, the immigrant issue is an awkward one for locals to discuss. While many aren't eager to have their country become the next melting pot, they're also careful not to object too strenuously, wary of being labeled racist.

sell their goods. Today it's still lively as a flower and produce market (Mon–Fri). The statue shows Christian IV, the Danish king who ruled Norway around 1600, dramatically gesturing that-a-way. He named the city, immodestly, Christiania. (Oslo took back its old Norse name only in 1924.) Christian was serious about Norway. During his 60-year reign, he visited it 30 times (more than all other royal visits combined during 300 years of Danish rule). The big GlasMagasinet department store is a landmark on this square.

• *Return to Karl Johans Gate, and continue up the boulevard past street musicians, cafés, shops, and hordes of people. Kongens Gate leads left, past the 17th-century grid-plan town to the fortress. Continue hiking straight up to the crest of the hill, pausing to enjoy some of the street musicians along the way. If you're here early in the morning (Mon–Fri) you may see a commotion at #14. This is the studio of a big TV station (channel 2) where the Norwegian version of the* Today *show is taped, and as in New York, locals gather here, clamoring to get their mug on TV.*

The Crest of Karl Johans Gate: Look back at the train station. A thousand years ago, the original (pre-1624) Oslo was located at the foot of the wooded hill behind the station. Now look ahead to the Royal Palace in the distance, which was built in the 1830s "with nature and God behind it and the people at its feet." If the flag flies atop the palace, the king is in the country. Karl Johans Gate is a parade ground from here to the palace—the axis of modern Oslo. Each May 17th, Norway's Independence Day, an annual children's parade turns this street into a sea of marching student bands and costumed young flag-wavers, while the royal family watches from the palace balcony. Since 1814, Norway has preferred peace. Rather than celebrating its military on the national holiday, it celebrates its children.

King Harald V and Queen Sonja moved back into the palace in 2001, after extensive (and costly) renovations. To quell the controversy caused by this expense, the public is now allowed inside to visit each summer with a pricey one-hour guided tour (95 kr, daily late June–mid-Aug at 14:00, Mon–Thu and Sat also at 12:00, buy tickets in advance at any post office or by calling 81 53 31 33, www.kongehuset.no).

From here, the *T* sign marks a stop of the T-bane (Oslo's subway). Let W. B. Samson's bakery tempt you with its pastries (and short cafeteria line; WC in back). Next to that, David Andersen's jewelry store displays traditional silver art and fine enamel work. Inside, halfway down the wall on the right (next to the free water dispenser), is a display of Norwegian folk costumes *(bunader)* with traditional jewelry—worn on big family occasions and church holidays. From here, the street called Akersgata kicks off a worthwhile stroll past the national cemetery and through a park-like river gorge to the trendy Grünerløkka quarter (an hour-long walk, described on page 215).

People-watching is great along Karl Johans Gate, but remember that if it's summer, half of the city's regular population is gone—vacationing in their cabins or farther away—and the city center is filled mostly with visitors.

Hike two blocks down Karl Johans Gate, past the big brick Parliament building (on the left). In this section, the sidewalk is heated so it won't be icy in the frigid winter. On the right is a statue of the painter Christian Krohg. Farther down Karl Johans Gate, just past the Freia shop (Norway's oldest and best chocolate), the venerable **Grand Hotel** (Oslo's celebrity hotel—Nobel Peace Prize winners sleep here) overlooks the boulevard.

• Ask the waiter at the Grand Café if you can pop inside for a little sightseeing (he'll generally let you).

Grand Café: This historic café was for many years the meeting place of Oslo's intellectual and creative elite. The playwright Henrik Ibsen was a regular here. Notice the photos and knick-knacks on the wall. At the back of the café, a mural shows Norway's literary and artistic clientele—from a century ago—enjoying this fine hangout. On the far left, find Ibsen, coming in as he did every day at 13:00. Edvard Munch is on the right, leaning against the window, looking pretty drugged. Names are beneath the mural.

• For a cheap bite with prime boulevard seating, continue next door to Deli de Luca, a convenience store with a super selection of take-away food and a great people-watching perch. Across the street, a little park faces Norway's...

Parliament Building (Stortinget): Norway's Parliament meets here (along with anyone participating in a peaceful protest outside). Built in 1866, the building seems to counter the Royal Palace at the other end of Karl Johans Gate. If the flag's flying, Parliament's in session. Today the king is a figurehead, and Norway is run by a unicameral Parliament and a prime minister. Guided tours of the Stortinget are offered for those interested in Norwegian government (free; mid-June–Aug Mon–Fri at 10:00, 11:30, and 13:00; enter on Karl Johans Gate side, tel. 23 31 35 96, www.stortinget.no).

• Continue walking toward the palace through the park, past the fountain, to the...

Statue of Wergeland: The poet Henrik Wergeland helped inspire the movement for Norwegian autonomy. In the winter, the pool here is frozen and covered with children happily ice-skating. Across the street behind Wergeland stands the **National Theater** and statues of Norway's favorite playwrights: Ibsen and Bjørnstjerne Bjørnson. Across Karl Johans Gate, the pale yellow building is the first university building in Norway, dating from 1854. A block behind that is the National Gallery, with Norway's best collection of paintings (free entry; see self-guided tour on page 195).

• Follow Roald Amundsens Gate left, to the towering brick...

City Hall (Rådhuset): Built in the 1930s with contributions from Norway's leading artists, City Hall is full of great art and is worth touring (see page 189). The mayor has his office here (at the base of one of the two 200-foot towers), and every December 10, this building is where the Nobel Peace Prize is presented. For the best exterior art, circle the courtyard clockwise, studying the colorful woodcuts in the arcade.

Oslo at a Glance

▲▲▲**Frogner Park** Sprawling park with works by Norway's greatest sculptor, Gustav Vigeland, and the studio where he created them (now a museum). **Hours:** Park—always open; Museum—June-Aug Tue-Sun 10:00-17:00, closed Mon; Sept-May Tue-Sun 12:00-16:00, closed Mon. See page 201.

▲▲▲**Norwegian Folk Museum** Norway condensed into 150 historic buildings in a large open-air park. **Hours:** Daily mid-May-mid-Sept 10:00-18:00, off-season park open daily 11:00-15:00 but most historical buildings closed. See page 207.

▲▲▲**City Hall** Oslo's artsy 20th-century government building, lined with huge, vibrant, municipal-themed murals, best visited with included tour. **Hours:** Daily 9:00-18:00; tours daily at 10:00, 12:00, and 14:00, no tours Sat-Sun in winter. See page 189.

▲▲▲**National Gallery** Norway's cultural and natural essence, captured on canvas. **Hours:** Tue-Fri 10:00-18:00, Thu until 19:00, Sat-Sun 11:00-17:00, closed Mon. See page 193.

▲▲**Norwegian Resistance Museum** Gripping look at Norway's tumultuous WWII experience. **Hours:** June-Aug Mon-Sat 10:00-17:00, Sun 11:00-17:00; Sept-May Mon-Fri 10:00-16:00, Sat-Sun 11:00-16:00. See page 192.

▲▲**Viking Ship Museum** An impressive trio of ninth-century Viking ships, with exhibits on the people who built them. **Hours:** Daily May-Sept 9:00-18:00, Oct-April 11:00-16:00. See page 208.

▲▲**Fram Museum** Captivating exhibit on the Arctic exploration ship. **Hours:** Daily June-Aug 9:00-18:00, May and Sept 10:00-17:00, Oct-April 10:00-16:00. See page 209.

▲▲**Holmenkollen Ski Jump and Ski Museum** Dizzying vista and schuss through skiing history. **Hours:** Reopens spring of 2010 after big rebuild; museum open daily June-Aug 9:00-20:00, May and Sept 10:00-17:00, Oct-April 10:00-14:00. See page 210.

Each shows a scene from Norwegian mythology, well-explained in English: Thor with his billy-goat chariot, Ask and Embla (a kind of Norse Adam and Eve), Odin on his eight-legged horse guided by ravens, the swan maidens shedding their swan disguises, and so on. Circle around City Hall on the right to the front. The statues (especially the six laborers on the other side of the building, facing the harbor, who seem to guard the facade) celebrate the nobility of the working class.

▲▲***Kon-Tiki* Museum** Adventures of primitive *Kon-Tiki* and *Ra II* ships built by Thor Heyerdahl. **Hours:** Daily June-Aug 9:30-17:30, April-May and Sept 10:00-17:00, Oct-March 10:30-16:00. See page 210.

▲**Nobel Peace Center** Exhibit celebrating the ideals of the Nobel Peace Prize and the lives of those who have won it. **Hours:** June-Aug daily 10:00-18:00; Sept-May Tue-Sun 10:00-18:00, closed Mon. See page 191.

▲**Akershus Fortress Complex and Tours** Historic military base and fortified old center, with guided tours, a ho-hum castle interior, and a couple of museums (including the excellent Norwegian Resistance Museum, listed above). **Hours:** Park open daily 6:00-21:00; 45-minute tours of the grounds generally offered May-Aug Mon-Fri at 11:00, 12:00, 13:00, 14:00, and 15:00, Sat-Sun at 13:00 and 15:00, no tours off-season. See page 192.

▲**Norwegian Holocaust Center** High-tech walk through rise of anti-Semitism, the Holocaust in Norway, and racism today. **Hours:** Daily summer 10:00-18:00, off-season 11:00-16:00. See page 209.

▲**Norwegian Maritime Museum** Dusty cruise through Norway's rich seafaring heritage. **Hours:** Mid-May-Aug daily 10:00-18:00; Sept-mid-May daily 10:30-16:00, Thu until 18:00. See page 210.

▲**Edvard Munch Museum** Works of Norway's famous Expressionistic painter. **Hours:** June-Aug daily 10:00-18:00; Sept-May Tue-Fri 10:00-16:00, Sat-Sun 11:00-17:00, closed Mon. See page 211.

▲**Opera House** Stunning performance center that's helping revitalize the harborfront. **Hours:** Mon-Fri 10:00-23:00, Sat 11:00-23:00, Sun 12:00-22:00. See page 191.

▲**Grünerløkka** Oslo's bohemian district, with bustling cafés and pubs. **Hours:** Always open. See page 213.

• *Walk to the...*

Harbor: A few years ago, you would have dodged several lanes of busy traffic to get to the harborfront. But in Oslo today, most cars cross the city underground in tunnels. The city has made its town center relatively quiet and pedestrian-friendly by levying a traffic-discouraging 25-kr toll for every car entering town. (This system, like a similar one in London, subsidizes public transit and the city's infrastructure.)

Browsing

Oslo's pulse is best felt by strolling. Three good areas are along and near the central Karl Johans Gate, which runs from the train station to the palace (see my self-guided walk on page 180); in the trendy harborside Aker Brygge mall, a glass-and-chrome collection of sharp cafés, fine condos, and polished produce stalls (really lively at night, trams #10 and #12 from train station); and along Bogstadveien, a lively shopping street with no-nonsense modern commerce, lots of locals, and no tourists (T-bane to Majorstuen and follow this street back toward the palace and tourist zone). While most tourists never get out of the harbor/Karl Johans Gate district, the real, down-to-earth Oslo is better seen elsewhere, such as Bogstadveien. The bohemian, artsy Grünerløkka district, described on page 213, is good for a daytime wander.

At the water's edge, find the shiny metal plaque (just left of center) listing the contents of a time capsule planted in the harbor for 1,000 years. You can see the little lighthouse in the harbor ahead. Go to the end of the stubby pier (on the right). This is the ceremonial "enter the city" point for momentous occasions. One such occasion was in 1905 when Norway gained its independence from Sweden, and a Danish prince sailed in from Copenhagen to become the first modern king of Norway. Another milestone event occurred at the end of World War II, when the king returned to Norway after the country was liberated from the Nazis.

• *Stand at the harbor and give it a sweeping counterclockwise look.*

Harborfront Spin-Tour: Oslofjord is a playground, with 40 city-owned, park-like islands. Big white cruise ships—a large part of the local tourist economy—dock just under the Akershus Fortress on the left. Just past the fort's impressive 13th-century ramparts, a statue of FDR grabs the shade. He's here in gratitude for the safe refuge the US gave to members of the royal family (including a young prince who is now Norway's king) during World War II—while the king and his government-in-exile waged Norway's fight against the Nazis from London.

Enjoy the grand view of City Hall. The yellow building farther to the left was the old West Train Station; today it houses the Nobel Peace Center, which celebrates the work of Nobel Peace Prize winners (see page 191). The next pier is the launch pad for harbor boat tours and the shuttle boat to the Bygdøy museums. A fisherman often moors his boat here, selling shrimp from the back. Shrimp doesn't get fresher: He catches them, and while making the four-hour sail back into Oslo, cooks them up (40 kr/half-liter, 80 kr/liter, Tue–Sat from 8:00 until sold out; no fishing allowed on weekends so closed Sun–Mon). He often sells smaller shrimp for about 25 percent less; they're considered tastier, but you'll find them less easy to shell. At the other end of the harbor, shipyard buildings (this was the heart of Norway's once important ship-building industry) have been transformed into Aker Brygge—Oslo's thriving restaurant/shopping/nightclub zone (see "Eating in Oslo").

• *From here, you can tour City Hall (cheap lunches Mon–Fri 12:30–13:30 only), visit the Nobel Peace Center, hike up to Akershus Fortress, take a harbor cruise (see "Tours in Oslo," earlier), or catch a boat across the harbor to the museums at Bygdøy (from pier 3). The sights just mentioned are described in detail in the following section.*

Sights in Oslo

Near the Harborfront

▲▲▲City Hall (Rådhuset)—In 1931, Oslo tore down a slum and began constructing its richly decorated City Hall. It was finished—after a WWII delay—in 1950 to celebrate the city's 900th birthday. Norway's leading artists all contributed to the building, an avant-garde thrill in its day.

City halls, rather than churches, are the dominant buildings in Scandinavian capitals. The prominence of this building on the harborfront makes sense in this most humanistic, yet least churchgoing, end of the Continent. Up here, people pay high taxes, have high expectations, and are generally satisfied with what their governments do with their money.

At Oslo's City Hall, the six statues facing the waterfront—dating from a period of Labor Party rule in Norway—celebrate the nobility of the working class. The art implies a classless society, showing everyone working together. The theme continues inside, with 20,000 square feet of bold and colorful Social Realism murals showing town folk, country folk, and people from all walks of life working harmoniously for a better society. The huge murals take you on a voyage through the collective psyche of Norway, from its simple rural beginnings through the scar tissue of the Nazi occupation and beyond. Filled with significance and symbolism—and well-described in English—they become more meaningful only with the excellent, 50-minute guided **tours** (free tours daily at 10:00, 12:00, and 14:00, no tours Sat–Sun in winter).

The main hall feels like a temple to good government, with its altar-like mural celebrating "work, play, and civic administration."

The mural emphasizes Oslo's youth participating in community life—and rebuilding the country after Nazi occupation. Across the bottom, the slum that once cluttered up Oslo's harborfront is being cleared out to make way for this building. Above that, scenes show Norway's pride in its innovative health care and education systems. Left of center, near the top, Mother Norway rests on a church—reminding viewers that the Lutheran Church of Norway (the official state religion) provides a foundation for this society. On the right, four forms represent the arts; they illustrate how creativity springs from children. And in the center, the figure of Charity is surrounded by Culture, Philosophy, and Family.

The "Mural of the Occupation" lines the left side of the hall. It tells the story of Norway's WWII experience. Looking left to right, you'll see the following: The German blitzkrieg overwhelms the country. Men head for the mountains to organize a resistance movement. Women huddle around the water well, traditionally where news is passed, while Quislings (traitors named after the Norwegian fascist who ruled the country as a Nazi puppet) listen in. While Germans bomb and occupy Norway, a family gathers in their living room. As a boy clenches his fist (showing determination) and a child holds the beloved Norwegian flag, the Gestapo steps in. Columns lie on the ground, symbolizing how Germans shut down the culture by closing newspapers and university. Two resistance soldiers are executed. A cell of resistance fighters (wearing masks and using nicknames so if tortured they can't reveal their compatriots' identities) plan a sabotage mission. Finally, prisoners are freed, the war is over, and Norway celebrates its happiest day: May 17, 1945—the first Independence Day after five years under Nazi control.

While gazing at these murals, keep in mind that the Nobel Peace Prize is awarded in this central hall each December (though the general Nobel Prize ceremony occurs in Stockholm's City Hall). You can see videos of the ceremony and acceptance speeches in the adjacent Nobel Peace Center (see below).

City Hall is free and open daily (9:00–18:00; enter on Karl Johans Gate side, tel. 23 46 12 00). There's a free WC and a wonderful budget lunch cafeteria downstairs that offers a simple hot meal and salad bar at a no-profit price; it's primarily for the building's workers, but the public is also welcome (Mon–Fri 12:30–13:30 only).

Fans of the explorer Fridtjof Nansen might enjoy a coffee or beer across the street at Fridtjof, an atmospheric bar filled with memorabilia from Nansen's Arctic explorations (Mon–Sat 12:00 until late, Sun 14:00–22:00, Nansens Plass 7, near Forex).

▲Nobel Peace Center (Nobels Fredssenter)—This thoughtful and thought-provoking museum, housed in the former West Train Station (Vestbanen), poses the question, "What is the opposite of conflict?" It celebrates the 120-some past and present Nobel Peace Prize winners with engaging audio and video exhibits and high-tech gadgetry (all with good English explanations). Allow time for reading about past prizewinners and listening to acceptance speeches by recipients from President Carter to Mother Theresa. Check out the interactive book detailing the life and work of Alfred Nobel, the Swedish inventor of dynamite, who initiated the prizes—perhaps to assuage his conscience (80 kr; June–Aug daily 10:00–18:00; Sept–May Tue–Sun 10:00–18:00, closed Mon; included guided tours at 11:00, 12:00, and 15:00; Brynjulfs Bulls Plass 1, tel. 48 30 10 00, www.nobelpeacecenter.org).

▲Opera House—Opened in 2008, Oslo's striking Opera House is the talk of the town and a huge hit. The Opera House rises from the water on the city's eastern harbor, across the highway from the train station. Its boxy, low-slung, glass center holds a state-of-the-art, 1,400-seat main theater. The jutting white marble planes of its roof double as a public plaza. When visiting, you feel a need to walk all over it. The Opera House is part of larger harbor redevelopment that includes rerouting traffic into tunnels and turning a once-derelict industrial zone into an urban park.

In summer, the Opera House offers guided tours of the auditorium and backstage area (daily at 14:00, 100 kr) and foyer concerts (daily at 13:00, 50 kr). For tours, reserve by email at omvisninger@operaen.no, or use the website, www.operaen.no (foyer and café/restaurant open Mon–Fri 10:00–23:00, Sat 11:00–23:00, Sun 12:00–22:00, just a short walk via a sky-bridge from train station, tel. 21 42 21 00).

▲Akershus Fortress Complex

This park-like complex of sights scattered over Oslo's fortified old center is still a military base. But as you dodge patrol guards and vans filled with soldiers, you'll see the castle, a prison, war memorials, the Norwegian Resistance Museum, the Armed Forces Museum, and cannon-strewn ramparts affording fine harbor views and picnic perches. There's an unimpressive changing of the guard daily at 13:30 (at the parade ground, deep in the castle complex). The park is open daily 6:00–21:00. From the harbor, follow the stairs (which lead past the FDR statue) to the park.

Fortress Visitors Center: Located immediately inside the gate, the information center has an interesting exhibit tracing the story of Oslo's fortifications from medieval times through the environmental struggles of today. Stop here to pick up a castle overview booklet, quickly browse through the museum, watch the quick video, and consider catching a tour (see below; museum entry free, mid-June–mid-Aug Mon–Fri 9:00–18:00, Sat–Sun 11:00–17:00, shorter hours off-season, tel. 23 09 39 17, www.mil.no/felles/ak).

▲Fortress Tours—The free 45-minute, English-language walking tours of the grounds help you make sense of the most historic piece of real estate in Oslo (generally offered May–Aug Mon–Fri at 11:00, 12:00, 13:00, 14:00, and 15:00; Sat–Sun at 13:00 and 15:00; no tours off-season; depart from Fortress Visitors Center, call center in advance to confirm times, phone number above).

Akershus Castle—Although it's one of Oslo's oldest buildings (c. 1300), the castle overlooking the harbor is mediocre by European standards; the big, empty rooms recall Norway's medieval poverty. From the old kitchen, where the ticket desk and gift shop are located, you'll follow a one-way circuit of rooms open to the public. Descend through a secret passage to the dungeon, crypt, and royal tomb. Emerge behind the altar in the chapel, then walk through echoing rooms including the Daredevil's Tower, Hall of Christian IV, and Hall of Olav I. The castle is more interesting with the included tour (65 kr, sparse English descriptions throughout; May–Aug Mon–Sat 10:00–16:00, Sun 12:30–16:00; castle tours in English Mon–Sat at 11:00, 12:00, 13:00, 14:00, and 15:00; Sun at 13:00 and 15:00; closed Sept–April except tours in English Thu at 12:00, 13:00, and 14:00; tel. 22 41 25 21). There are terrific harbor views from the rampart just outside.

▲▲Norwegian Resistance Museum (Norges Hjemmefrontmuseum) —This fascinating museum tells the story of Norway's WWII experience: appeasement, Nazi invasion (they made Akershus their headquarters), resistance, liberation, and, finally, the return of the king. It's a one-way, chronological, can't-get-lost route—enter through the 1940 door.

You'll see propaganda posters attempting to get Norwegians to join the Nazi party, and the German ultimatum to which the king gave an emphatic "No." Various displays show secret radios, transmitters, underground newspapers, crude but effective homemade weapons, and the German machine that located clandestine radio stations. Exhibits explain how the country coped with 350,000 occupying troops; how airdrops equipped a home force of 40,000 ready to coordinate with the Allies when liberation was imminent; and the happy day when peace and freedom returned to Norway.

The museum is particularly poignant because many of the patriots featured inside were executed by the Germans right outside the museum's front door. (At war's end, the traitor Vidkun Quisling was also executed here.) With good English descriptions, this is an inspirational look at how the national spirit can endure total occupation by a malevolent force.

Cost, Hours, Location: 50 kr, 100-kr family ticket covers two adults plus one or two kids; June–Aug Mon–Sat 10:00–17:00, Sun 11:00–17:00; Sept–May Mon–Fri 10:00–16:00, Sat–Sun 11:00–16:00; next to castle, overlooking harbor, tel. 23 09 31 38, www.mil.no/felles/nhm.

Armed Forces Museum (Forsvarsmuseet) —Across the fortress parade ground, a too-spacious museum traces Norwegian military history from Viking days to post–World War II. The early stuff is sketchy, but the WWII story is compelling (free, May–Aug Mon–Fri 10:00–17:00, Sat–Sun 11:00–17:00, shorter hours and closed Mon off-season, tel. 23 09 35 82).

▲▲▲National Gallery (Nasjonalgalleriet)

While there are many schools of painting and sculpture displayed in Norway's National Gallery, focus on what's uniquely Norwegian. Paintings come and go in this museum, but you're sure to find plenty that showcase the harsh beauty of Norway's landscape and people. A thoughtful visit here gives those heading into the mountains and fjord country a chance to pack along a little of Norway's cultural soul. Tuck these images carefully away with your goat cheese—they'll sweeten your explorations.

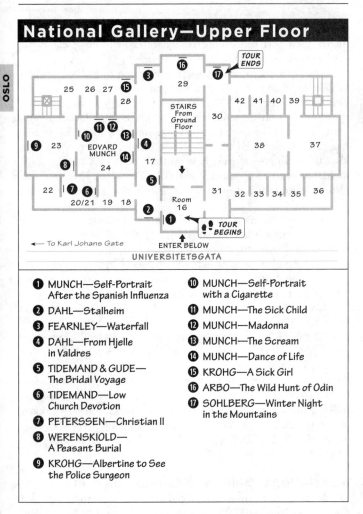

National Gallery—Upper Floor

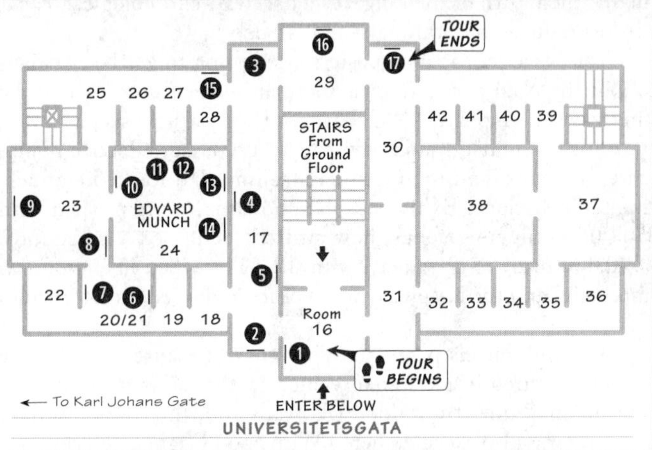

1. MUNCH—Self-Portrait After the Spanish Influenza
2. DAHL—Stalheim
3. FEARNLEY—Waterfall
4. DAHL—From Hjelle in Valdres
5. TIDEMAND & GUDE—The Bridal Voyage
6. TIDEMAND—Low Church Devotion
7. PETERSSEN—Christian II
8. WERENSKIOLD—A Peasant Burial
9. KROHG—Albertine to See the Police Surgeon
10. MUNCH—Self-Portrait with a Cigarette
11. MUNCH—The Sick Child
12. MUNCH—Madonna
13. MUNCH—The Scream
14. MUNCH—Dance of Life
15. KROHG—A Sick Girl
16. ARBO—The Wild Hunt of Odin
17. SOHLBERG—Winter Night in the Mountains

The gallery also has several Picassos, a noteworthy Impressionist collection, and some Vigeland statues. Its many raving examples of Edvard Munch's work, including one of his famous *Scream* paintings, make a trip to the Munch Museum unnecessary for most (see page 211).

Cost, Hours, Location: Free, Tue–Fri 10:00–18:00, Thu until 19:00, Sat–Sun 11:00–17:00, closed Mon, chewing gum prohibited, Universitets Gata 13, tel. 22 20 04 04, www.nationalmuseum.no. The 25-kr audioguide covers 15 paintings, has a poetic narrative with quotes from artists, and forces you to linger at each work of art—but doesn't have much more information than my tour below.

Self-Guided Tour

This easy-to-handle museum gives an effortless tour back in time and through Norway's most beautiful valleys, mountains, and fjords, with the help of its Romantic painters (especially Johan Christian Dahl). The paintings are organized roughly chronologically, from 1814 through 1950.

• *Go up the stairs into Room 16, where you're treated to a nibble of the misery that was Munch.*

❶ **Munch—*Self-Portrait After the Spanish Influenza* (1919):** Norway's long, dark winters and social isolation have produced many gloomy artists, but none gloomier than Edvard Munch (1863–1944, see sidebar on page 198). Here he paints himself suffering from the effects of the devastating influenza pandemic that ravaged the globe at the end of World War I, killing tens of millions. Drained, rigid, and glassy-eyed, Munch personifies the weary disillusionment of postwar Europe.

• *We'll get back to Munch later. But for now, let's head somewhere more idyllic. Enter Room 17.*

Landscape Paintings and Romanticism

Landscape painting has always played an important role in Norwegian art, perhaps because Norway provides such an awesome and varied landscape to inspire artists. The style reached its peak during the Romantic period in the late 1800s, which stressed the beauty of unspoiled nature. (This passion for landscapes sets Norway apart from Denmark and Sweden.) After 400 years of Danish rule, the soul of the country was almost snuffed out. But with semi-independence and a constitution in the early 1800s, there was a national resurgence. Romantic paintings featuring the power of Norway's natural wonders and the toughness of its salt-of-the-earth folk came in vogue.

❷ **Johan Christian Dahl—*Stalheim* (1842):** This painting epitomizes the Norwegian closeness to nature. It shows the same view 21st-century travelers enjoy on their Norway in a Nutshell excursion (see page 232): the mountains at the head of the Sognefjord as seen from the venerable Stalheim Hotel. Painted in 1842, it's textbook Romantic style. Nature rules—the background is as detailed as the foreground, and you are sucked in.

Johan Christian Dahl (1788–1857) is considered the father of Norwegian Romanticism. Romantics such as Dahl (and Turner, Beethoven, and Lord Byron) put emotion over rationality. They reveled in the power of nature—death and pessimism ripple through their work. The rainbow says it all: This is God's work. Nature is big. God is great. Man is small...and he's gonna die. The birch tree—standing boldly front and center—is a standard symbol for the politically downtrodden Norwegian people: hardy, cut down, but defiantly sprouting new branches. The tiny folks are in traditional dress. In the mid-19th century, Norwegians were awakening to their national identity. Throughout Europe, nationalism and Romanticism went hand in hand.

Find four typical Norse farms. They remind us that these are hardworking, independent, small landowners. There was no feudalism in medieval Norway. People were poor...but they owned their own land. You can almost taste the *geitost.*

• *Look at the other works in Room 17 (the biggest room in the gallery). Dahl's paintings and those by his Norwegian contemporaries, showing heavy clouds and glaciers, repeat these same themes—drama over rationalism, nature pounding humanity. Human figures are melancholy. Norwegians, so close to nature, are fascinated by those plush, magic hours of dawn and twilight. The dusk makes us wonder: What will the future bring?*

In particular, focus on....

❸ **Thomas Fearnley—*Waterfall* (1817):** Man cannot control nature or his destiny. Lumberjacks are working. But the eagle says, "While you can cut these logs, they'll always be mine."

❹ **Dahl—*From Hjelle in Valdres* (1851):** Another typical Dahl setting: romantic nature and an idealized scene. The characters are wearing the *bunad* (national folk costume of Norway). This isn't everyday work wear, but it fits just fine in this nationalistic tableau.

❺ **Adolph Tidemand and Hans Gude—*The Bridal Voyage* (1848):** This famous painting shows the ultimate Norwegian scene: a wedding party with everyone decked out in traditional garb, heading for the stave church on the quintessential fjord (Hardanger). It's a studio work (not real) and a collaboration: Hans Gude painted the landscape, and Adolph Tidemand painted the people. Study their wedding finery. This work trumpets the greatness of both the landscape and Norwegian culture.

• *Continue through Rooms 18 and 19 to Room 20.*

The Photographic Eye

At the end of the 19th century, Norwegian painters traded the emotions of Romanticism for more slice-of-life detail. This was the end of the Romantic period and the beginning of Realism. With the advent of photography, painters went beyond simple realism and into extreme realism.

❻ **Tidemand—*Low Church Devotion* (1848):** This scene shows a dissenting Lutheran church group (of which there were many in the 19th century) worshipping in a smokehouse. The light of God powers through the chimney, illuminating salt-of-the-earth people with strong faiths. Rather than accept the Norwegian king's "High Church," they worshipped in their homes in a more ascetic style. Later, many of these people emigrated to America for greater religious freedom.

❼ **Eilif Peterssen—*Christian II* (1875):** The Danish king signs the execution order for the man who'd killed the king's beloved mistress. With camera-like precision, the painter captures the whole story of murder, anguish, anger, and bitter revenge in the king's set jaw and steely eyes.

• *Enter Room 23 and browse the paintings.*

Modern Life

In the 1880s, Europe's artistic community (which included a few Norwegians) turned to Paris. Impressionism took the art world by storm. French artists abandoned reality, using the physical object only as a rack upon which to hang light and color—their true subject matter. Inhibited Norwegians couldn't go quite that far. While their Naturalism (parallel to Impressionism) came with a new appreciation of light, their subjects remained real things.

❽ **Erik Werenskiold—*A Peasant Burial* (1885):** While Monet and the Impressionists were busy abandoning the realistic style, Norwegian artists continued to embrace it. In this painting, you're invited to participate. The poor man's funeral is attended by not many more than his family, the preacher, and the gravediggers. Your presence completes the half-circle at the grave site. The simple scene is set before a majestic, perfectly lit mountain backdrop that dwarfs the deceased man's legacy. Rough Impressionistic brush strokes have replaced the tedious detail of earlier Romantic Age painters, but you still have earthy people immersed in nature. Their hands speak volumes about the life of toil here. A common thread in Norwegian art is the cycle—the tough cycle—of life. There's also an interest in everyday experiences.

❾ **Christian Krohg—*Albertine to See the Police Surgeon* (c. 1885–1887):** Christian Krohg (1852–1925) is known as Edvard Munch's inspiration, but to Norwegians, he is famous in his own right for his artistry and giant personality. Krohg had a sharp interest in social justice. In this painting, Albertine, a sweet girl from the countryside, has fallen into the world of prostitution in the big city. She's the new kid on the red light block in the 1880s,

Edvard Munch (1863–1944)

Edvard Munch (pronounced "moonk") is Norway's most famous and influential painter. His life was rich, complex, and sad. His father was a doctor who had a nervous breakdown. His mother and sister both died of tuberculosis. He knew suffering. And he gave us the enduring symbol of 20th-century pain, *The Scream*.

He was also Norway's most forward-thinking painter, a man who traveled extensively through Europe, soaking up the colors of the Post-Impressionists and the curves of Art Nouveau. He helped pioneer a new style—Expressionism—using lurid colors and wavy lines to "express" inner turmoil and the angst of the modern world.

After a nervous breakdown in 1908, Munch emerged less troubled—but a less powerful painter. His late works were as a colorist: big, bright, less tormented...and less noticed.

as Oslo's prostitutes are pulled into the police clinic for their regular checkup. Note her traditional dress and the disdain she gets from the more experienced girls. Krohg has buried his subject in this scene. His technique requires the viewer to find her, and that search helps humanize the prostitute.

• *Continue into Room 24, the Munch room.*

Turmoil

Room 24 is filled with works by Norway's single most famous painter, Edvard Munch (see sidebar). Munch infused his work with emotion and expression at the expense of realism. After viewing the paintings in general, take a look at these in particular (listed in clockwise order).

⑩ **Edvard Munch—*Self Portrait with a Cigarette* (1895):** In this self-portrait, Munch is spooked, haunted—an artist working, immersed in an oppressive world. Indefinable shadows inhabit the background. His hand shakes as he considers his uncertain future. (Ironic, considering he created his masterpieces during this depressed period.) After a 1909 visit to a Danish clinic, he found peace—and lost his painting power. Afterward, Munch never again painted another strong example of what we love most about his art.

⓫ **Munch—*The Sick Child* (1896):** The death of Munch's sister in 1877 due to tuberculosis likely inspired this painting. The girl's face melts into the pillow. She's becoming two-dimensional, halfway between life and death. Everything else is peripheral, even her despairing mother saying good-bye. You can see how Munch scraped and repainted the face until he got it right.

⓬ **Munch—*Madonna* (1894–1895):** Munch had a tortured relationship with women. He never married. He dreaded and struggled with love, writing that he feared if he loved too much, he'd lose his painting talent. This painting is a mystery: Is she standing or lying? Is that a red halo or some devilish accessory? Munch wrote that he would strive to capture his subjects at their holiest moment. His alternative name for this work: *Woman Making Love.* What's more holy than a woman at the moment of conception?

⓭ **Munch—*The Scream* (1893):** Munch's most famous work shows a man screaming, capturing the fright many feel as the human "race" does just that. The figure seems isolated from the people on the bridge—locked up in himself, unable to stifle his scream. Munch made four versions of this scene, which has become *the* textbook example of Expressionism. On one, he graffitied: "This painting is the work of a madman." He explained that the painting "shows today's society, reverberating within me... making me want to scream." He's sharing his internal angst. In fact, this Expressionist masterpiece is a breakthrough painting; it's angst personified.

⓮ **Munch—*Dance of Life* (1899–1900):** In this scene of five dancing couples, we glimpse Munch's notion of femininity. To him, women were a complex mix of Madonna and whore. We see Munch's take on the cycle of women's lives: She's a virgin (discarding the sweet flower of youth), a whore (a jaded temptress in red), and a widow (having destroyed the man, she is finally alone, aging, in black). With the phallic moon rising on the lake, Munch demonizes women as they turn men into green-faced, lusty monsters.

• *Go back through Room 23 to reach Room 28.*

Vulnerability

Death, disease, and suffering were themes seen again and again in art from the late 1800s. The most serious disease during this period was tuberculosis (which killed Munch's mother and sister).

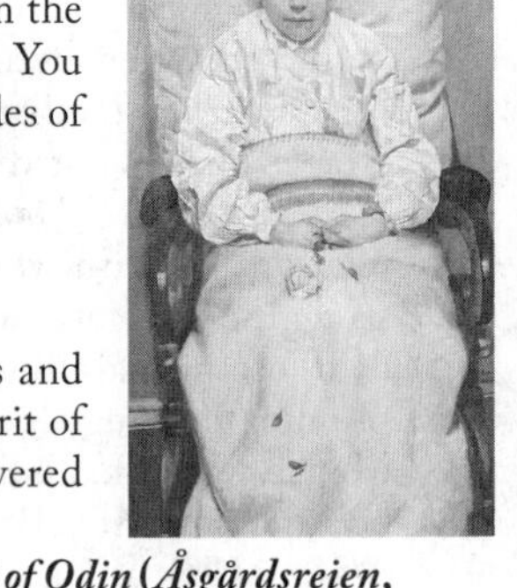

⓯ **Krohg—*A Sick Girl* (1880):** This extremely realistic painting shows a child dying of tuberculosis, as so many did in Norway in the 19th century. The girl looks directly at you. You can almost feel the cloth, with its many shades of white.

• *Cross through Room 17 into Room 29.*

Mythology

The folk legends of Thor and Odin, heroes and dwarves, predate the Christian era. In a spirit of nationalism, 19th-century painters rediscovered Norway's pagan roots.

⓰ **Peter Nicolai Arbo—*The Wild Hunt of Odin* (*Åsgårdsreien*, 1872):** A rowdy horde of Viking-like warriors gallop across the sky, snatching up unsuspecting maidens and the souls of sleepers. These supernatural hunters of folklore, led by Odin (the king of the gods, in billowing cape), represent the uncontrolled life force of Nature that fights the encroachment of civilization. Lit by moonlight and a fiery sunset, the huge band blends into the cloudy distance, suggesting the wild party goes on forever.

• *Continue to Room 30.*

Atmosphere

Landscape painters were often fascinated by the phenomena of nature, and the artwork in this room takes us back to this ideal from the Romantic Age. Painters were challenged by capturing atmospheric conditions at a specific moment, since it meant making quick sketches outdoors, before the weather changed yet again.

⓱ **Harald Sohlberg—*Winter Night in the Mountains* (1914):** Harald Sohlberg was inspired by this image while skiing in the mountains in the winter of 1899. Over the years, he attempted to re-create the scene that inspired this remark: "The mountains in winter reduce one to silence. One is overwhelmed, as in a mighty, vaulted church, only a thousand times more so."

Near the National Gallery

National Historical Museum (Historisk Museum)—Directly behind the National Gallery and just below the palace is a fine Art Nouveau building offering a free and easy (if underwhelming) peek at Norway's history. The ground floor offers a walk through the local history from prehistoric times. It includes the country's top collection of Viking artifacts, displayed in low-tech, old-school exhibits with barely a word of English to give it meaning. There's also some medieval church art. The museum's highlight is upstairs: an exhibit (well-described in English) about life in the Arctic for the Sami people (also previously known to outsiders as Laplanders). In this overview of the past, a few Egyptian mummies and Norwegian coins through the ages are tossed in for good measure. The museum offers free 45-minute Viking tours daily at noon in the summer (free; mid-May–mid-Sept Tue–Sat 10:00–17:00, Sun 11:00–16:00, closed Mon; mid-Sept–mid-May Tue–Sun 11:00–16:00, closed Mon; Frederiks Gate 2, tel. 22 85 99 12, www.khm.uio.no).

▲▲▲Frogner Park

This 75-acre park contains a lifetime of work by Norway's greatest sculptor, Gustav Vigeland (see sidebar on next page). In 1921, he made a deal with the city. In return for a great studio and state support, he'd spend his creative life beautifying Oslo with this sculpture garden. From 1924 to 1943 he worked on-site, designing 192 bronze and granite statue groupings—600 figures in all, each nude and unique. Vigeland even planned the landscaping. Today the park is loved and respected by the people of Oslo (no police, no fences, and no graffiti). The garden is always open and free (buses #20 and #45, and trams #12 and #19 all stop immediately in front of the main entry; or T-bane: Majorstuen and a 5-min walk). The Frognerbadet swimming pool is also at Frogner Park. The park is safe (cameras monitor for safety) and lit in the evening.

Vigeland's park is more than great art: It's a city at play. Appreciate its urban Norwegian ambience. The park is huge, but this visit is a snap. Here's a quick, four-stop, straight-line, gate-to-monolith tour:

1. Enter the Park from Kirkeveien: For an illustrated guide and fine souvenir, pick up the 75-kr book in the Visitors Center (Besøkssenter) on your right as you enter. The modern cafeteria has sandwiches (indoor/outdoor seating, daily 9:00–20:30, shorter hours Sun and off-season), plus books, gifts, and WCs. Look at the statue of Gustav Vigeland (hammer and chisel in hand,

Gustav Vigeland
(1869–1943)

As a young man, Vigeland studied sculpture in Oslo, then supplemented his education with trips abroad to Europe's art capitals. Back home, he carved out a successful, critically acclaimed career feeding newly independent Norway's hunger for homegrown art.

During his youthful trips abroad, Vigeland had frequented the studio of Auguste Rodin, admiring Rodin's naked, restless, intertwined statues. Like Rodin, Vigeland explored the yin/yang relationship of men and women. Also like Rodin, Vigeland did not personally carve or cast his statues. Rather, he formed them in clay or plaster, to be executed by a workshop of assistants. Vigeland's sturdy humans capture universal themes of the cycle of life—birth, childhood, romance, struggle, child-rearing, growing old, and death.

drenched in pigeon poop) and consider his messed-up life. He lived with his many models. His marriages failed. His children entangled his artistic agenda. He didn't age gracefully. He didn't name his statues, and refused to explain their meanings. While those who know his life story can read it clearly in the granite and bronze, I'd forget Gustav's troubles and see his art as observations on the bittersweet cycle of life in general—from a man who must have had a passion for living.

2. Bridge: The 300-foot-long bridge is bounded by four granite columns: Three show a man fighting a lizard, the fourth shows a woman submitting to the lizard's embrace. Hmmm. (Vigeland was familiar with medieval mythology, where dragons represent man's primal—and sinful—nature.) But enough lizard love; the 58 bronze statues along the bridge are a general study of the human body. Many deal with relationships between people. In the middle, on the right, find the circular statue of a man and woman going round and round—perhaps the eternal attraction and love between the sexes. But directly opposite, another circle feels like a prison—man against the world, with no refuge. From the man escaping, look down at the children's playground: eight bronze infants circling a head-down fetus.

On your left, see the famous *Sinnataggen*, the hot-headed little boy. It's said Vigeland gave him chocolate and then took it away to get this reaction. The statues capture the joys of life (and, on a sunny day, so do the Norwegians filling the park around you).

3. Fountain: Continue through a rose garden to the earliest sculpture unit in the park. Six giants hold a fountain, symbolically toiling with the burden of life, as water—the source of life—cascades steadily around them. Twenty tree-of-life groups surround the fountain. Four clumps of trees (on each corner) show humanity's relationship to nature and the seasons of life: childhood, young love, adulthood, and winter.

Take a quick swing through life, starting on the right with youth. In the branches you'll see a swarm of children (Vigeland called them "geniuses"): A boy sits in a tree, boys actively climb while most girls stand by quietly, and a girl glides through the branches wide-eyed and ready for life...and love. Circle clockwise to the next stage: love scenes. In the third corner, life becomes more complicated: a sad woman in an animal-like tree, a lonely child, a couple plummeting downward (perhaps falling out of love), and finally an angry man driving away babies. The fourth corner completes the cycle, as death melts into the branches of the tree of life and you realize new geniuses will bloom.

The 60 bronze reliefs circling the basin develop the theme further, showing man mixing with nature and geniuses giving the carousel of life yet another spin. Speaking of another spin, circle again and follow these reliefs.

The sidewalk surrounding the basin is a maze—life's long and winding road with twists, dead ends, frustrations, and, ultimately, a way out. If you have about an hour to spare, enter the labyrinth (on the side nearest the park's entrance gate, there's a single break in the black border) and follow the white granite path until (on the monolith side) you finally get out. (Tracing this path occupies older kids, affording parents a peaceful break in the park.) Or you can go straight up the steps to the monolith.

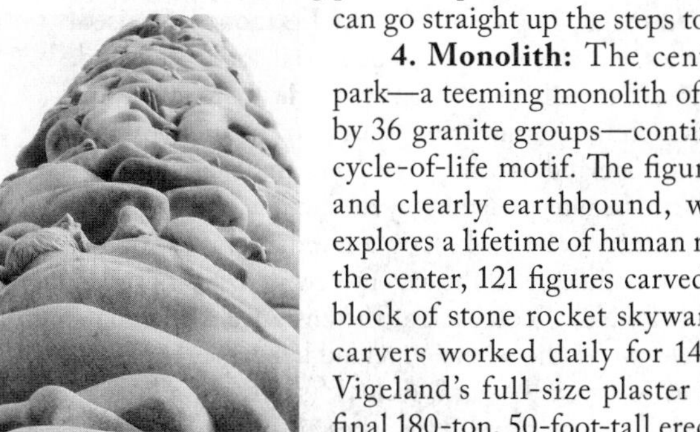

4. Monolith: The centerpiece of the park—a teeming monolith of life surrounded by 36 granite groups—continues Vigeland's cycle-of-life motif. The figures are hunched and clearly earthbound, while Vigeland explores a lifetime of human relationships. At the center, 121 figures carved out of a single block of stone rocket skyward. Three stone carvers worked daily for 14 years, cutting Vigeland's full-size plaster model into the final 180-ton, 50-foot-tall erection.

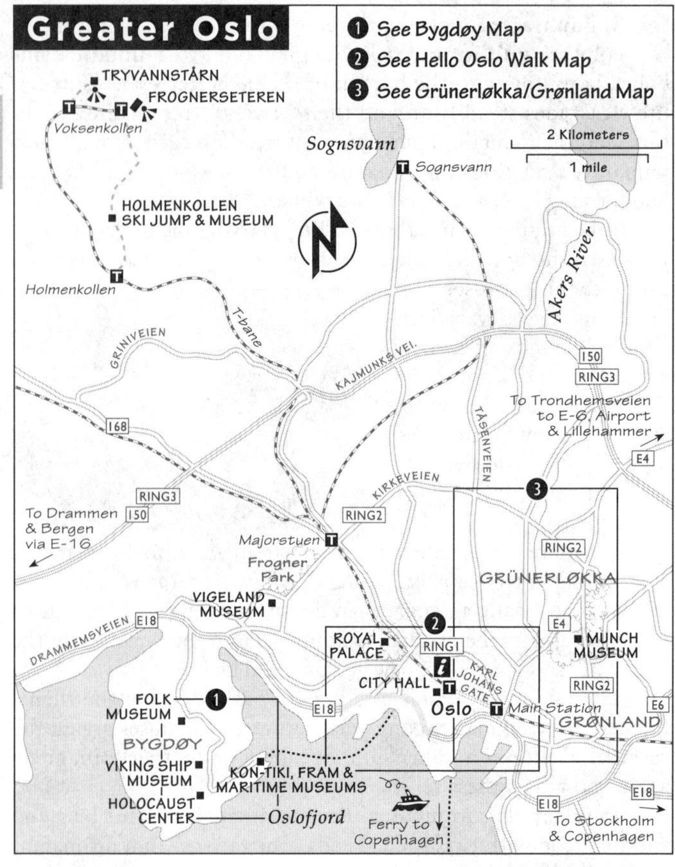

Circle the plaza, once to trace the stages of life in the 36 statue groups, and a second time to enjoy how Norwegian kids relate to the art. The statues—both young and old—seem to speak to children.

Vigeland lived barely long enough to see his monolith raised. Covered with bodies, it seems to pick up speed as it spirals skyward. Some people seem to naturally rise. Others struggle not to fall. Some help others. Although the granite groups around the monolith are easy to understand, Vigeland left the meaning of the monolith itself open. Like life, it can be interpreted many different ways.

From this summit of the park, look a hundred yards farther, where four children and three adults are intertwined and spinning in the Wheel of Life. Now, look back at the entrance. If the main gate is at 12 o'clock, the studio where Vigeland lived and worked—now the Vigeland Museum—is at 2 o'clock (see the green copper tower poking above the trees). His ashes sit in the top of the tower in clear view of the monolith. If you liked the park, visit the museum—it's a delightful five-minute walk—for an intimate look at the art and how it was made.

▲▲Vigeland Museum—Filled with original plaster casts and well-described exhibits on his work, this palatial city-provided studio was Vigeland's home and workplace. The high south-facing windows provided just the right light.

Vigeland, who had a deeply religious upbringing, saw his art as an expression of his soul. He once said, "The road between feeling and execution should be as short as possible." Here, immersed in his work, Vigeland supervised his craftsmen like a father, from 1924 until his death in 1943 (50 kr; June–Aug Tue–Sun 10:00–17:00, closed Mon; Sept–May Tue–Sun 12:00–16:00, closed Mon; bus #20 or #45 or tram #12 to Frogner Plass, Nobels Gate 32, tel. 23 49 37 00, www.vigeland.museum.no).

Oslo City Museum (Oslo Bymuseum)—This hard-to-be-thrilled-about little museum tells the story of Oslo (50 kr, free on Sat, open Tue–Sun 11:00–16:00, closed Mon, shorter hours off-season, borrow English description sheet, located in Frogner Park at Frogner Manor Farm across street from Vigeland Museum, tel. 23 28 41 70, www.oslobymuseum.no).

▲▲Oslo's Bygdøy Neighborhood

This thought-provoking and exciting cluster of sights is on a park-like peninsula just across the harbor from downtown. It provides a busy and rewarding half-day (at a minimum) of sightseeing. Here, within a short walk, are six important sights (listed in order of importance):

- **Norwegian Folk Museum,** an open-air park with traditional log buildings from all corners of the country.
- **Viking Ship Museum,** showing off the best-preserved Viking longboats in existence.
- ***Fram* Museum,** showcasing the modern Viking spirit with the ship of arctic-exploration fame.
- ***Kon-Tiki* Museum,** starring the *Kon-Tiki* and the *Ra II,* in which Norwegian explorer Thor Heyerdahl proved that early civilizations—with their existing technologies—could have crossed the oceans.

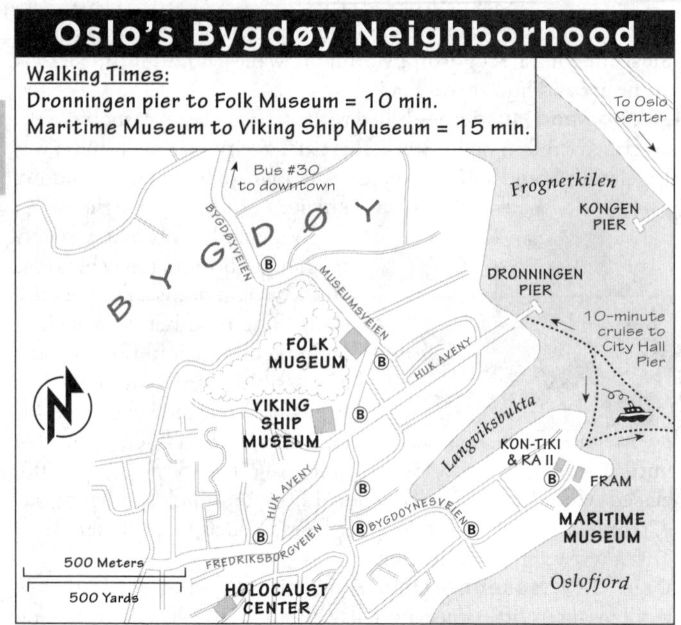

• **Norwegian Maritime Museum,** interesting mostly to old salts, has a wonderfully scenic movie of Norway.

• **Norwegian Holocaust Center,** a high-tech look at the Holocaust in Norway and contemporary racism.

Getting There: Sailing from downtown to Bygdøy is fun, and it gets you in a seafaring mood. Ride the Bygdøy ferry—marked *Public Ferry Bygdøy Museums*—from pier 3 in front of City Hall (36 kr one-way, covered by city transit ticket or Oslo Pass, May–Sept daily 8:45–21:00, usually 3/hr; doesn't run Oct–April). Avoid the nearby, and much more expensive, tour boats. Boats generally leave from downtown and from the museum dock at :05, :25, and :45 past each hour. For a less memorable approach, you can take bus #30 (from train station or National Theater).

Getting Around Bygdøy: The Norwegian Folk and Viking Ship museums are a 10-minute walk from the ferry's first stop (Dronningen). The other boating museums (*Fram, Kon-Tiki,* and Maritime) are at the second ferry stop (Bygdøynes). The Holocaust Center is off Fredriksborgveien, about halfway between these two museum clusters. All Bygdøy sights are within a pleasant (when sunny) 15-minute walk of each other. The walk gives you a picturesque taste of small-town Norway. A city bus (#30) connects the sights four times hourly, making the following stops in this order: the Norwegian Folk Museum, Viking Ship Museum, *Kon-Tiki* Museum, Norwegian Holocaust Center (the stop is a long block away), then passing the ships and folk museum again on its way back to the city center. If you take the bus within an hour of having taken the public ferry, your ticket is still good on the bus. Note that after 17:00, bus and boat departures are sparse. Get there a little early—otherwise the boat is likely to be filled, and you'll have to wait for the next sailing.

Eating at Bygdøy: Lunch options near the *Kon-Tiki* are a sandwich bar (relaxing picnic spots along the grassy shoreline) and a cafeteria (with tables overlooking the harbor). The Norwegian Folk Museum has a decent cafeteria inside and a fun little farmers' market stall across the street from the entrance. The Holocaust Center has a small café on its second floor (daily 11:00–22:00).

▲▲▲Norwegian Folk Museum (Norsk Folkemuseum)—Brought from all corners of Norway, 150 buildings have been reassembled on these 35 acres. While Stockholm's Skansen was the first to open to the public (see page 375), this museum is a bit older, started in 1882 as the king's private collection (and the inspiration for Skansen).

Think of the visit in three parts: the park sprinkled with old buildings, the re-created old town, and the folk-art museum. In peak season, the park is lively, with craftspeople doing their traditional things and costumed guides all around. (They're paid to happily answer your questions—so ask many.) The evocative Gol stave church, at the top of a hill at the park's edge, is a must-see (built in 1212 in Hallingdal and painstakingly reconstructed here; for more on stave churches, see page 169). Across the park, the old town comes complete with apartments from various generations (including some reconstructions of actual people's homes) and offers an intimate look at lifestyles here in 1905, 1930, 1950, 1979, and even a modern-day Norwegian-Pakistani apartment.

The museum beautifully presents woody, colorfully painted folk art (ground floor), exquisite-in-a-peasant-kind-of-way folk costumes (upstairs), and temporary exhibits. Everything is thoughtfully explained in English. Don't miss the best Sami culture exhibit I've seen in Scandinavia (across the courtyard in the green building, behind the toy exhibit).

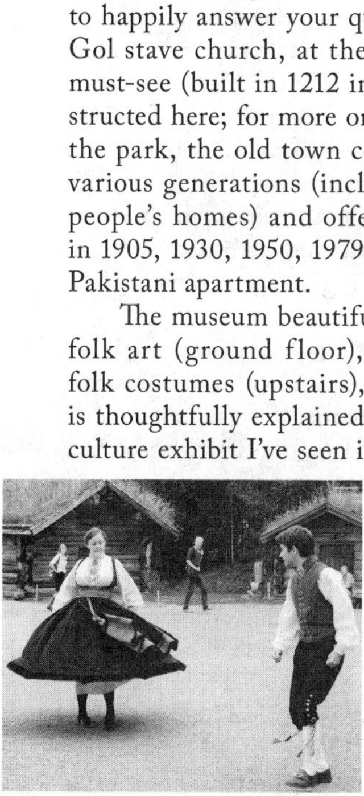

Upon arrival, pick up the site map and review the list of activities, concerts, and guided tours on that day. In summer, guided tours go daily at 12:00 and 14:00; the Telemark Farm hosts a small daily fiddle-and-dance show on the hour; and a folk music-and-dance show is held each

Sunday at 14:00. The folk museum is lively only June through mid-August, when buildings are open and staffed. Otherwise, the indoor museum is fine, but the park is just a walk past lots of locked-up log cabins. If you don't take a tour, glean information from the 10-kr guidebook and the informative attendants stationed in buildings throughout the park.

Cost, Hours, Location: 95 kr, 70 kr off-season, daily mid-May–mid-Sept 10:00–18:00, off-season daily 11:00–15:00 but most historical buildings closed, free lockers, Museumsveien 10. Bus #30 stops immediately in front.

▲▲Viking Ship Museum (Vikingskiphuset)—In this impressive museum you'll gaze with admiration at two finely crafted, majestic oak Viking ships dating from the 9th and 10th centuries. Along with the well-preserved ships, you'll see remarkable artifacts that may cause you to consider these notorious raiders in a different light. Over a thousand years ago, three things drove Vikings on their far-flung raids: hard economic times in their bleak homeland, the lure of prosperous and vulnerable communities to the south, and a mastery of the sea. There was a time when most frightened Europeans closed every prayer with, "And deliver us from the Vikings, Amen." Gazing up at the prow of one of these sleek, time-stained vessels, you can almost hear the screams and smell the armpits of those redheads on the rampage.

The *Oseberg* ship, from A.D. 834, is the first ship you see. With its ornate carving and impressive rudder, it was likely a royal pleasure craft. It seems designed for sailing on calm inland waters during festivals, but not in the open sea.

The *Gokstad* ship, from A.D. 950, is a practical working boat, capable of sailing the high seas. A boat like this brought settlers to the west of France (Normandy was named for the Norsemen). And in a boat like this, explorers such as Eric the Red hopscotched from Norway to Iceland to Greenland and on to what they called Vinland—today's Newfoundland in Canada. Imagine 30 men hauling on long oars out at sea for weeks and months. In 1892, a replica of this ship sailed from Norway to America in 44 days to celebrate the 400th anniversary of Columbus *not* discovering America.

The ships tend to steal the show, but don't miss the hall displaying **jewelry and personal items** excavated along with the ships. The ships and related artifacts survived so well because they were buried in clay as part of a gravesite. Many of the finest items were not actually Viking art, but goodies they brought home after raiding more advanced (but less tough) people. Still, there are lots of actual Viking items, such as metal and leather goods, that give an insight into their culture. Highlights are the cart and sleighs, ornately carved with scenes from Viking sagas.

The museum doesn't offer tours, but it's easy to eavesdrop on the many guides leading big groups through the museum. Everything is well-described in English. You probably don't need the little museum guidebook—it repeats exactly what's already posted on the exhibits.

Cost, Hours, Location: 50 kr, daily May–Sept 9:00–18:00, Oct–April 11:00–16:00, Huk Aveny 35, tel. 22 13 52 80, www.khm.uio.no.

▲Norwegian Holocaust Center (HL-Senteret)—Located in the former home of Nazi collaborator Vidkun Quisling, this museum and study center offers a high-tech look at the racist ideologies that fueled the Holocaust. To show the Holocaust in a Norwegian context, the first floor displays historical documents about the rise of anti-Semitism and personal effects from Holocaust victims. Downstairs, the names of 760 Norwegian Jews killed by the Nazis are listed in a bright, white room. The *Innocent Questions* glass-and-neon sculpture shows an old-fashioned punch card, reminding viewers of how the Norwegian puppet government collected seemingly innocuous information before deporting its Jews. The *Contemporary Reflections* video is a reminder that racism and genocide continue today.

Cost, Hours, Location: 50 kr, ask for free English audioguide, daily in summer 10:00–18:00, off-season 11:00–16:00, Huk Aveny 56—follow signs to *HL-Senteret*, tel. 22 84 21 00, www.hlsenteret.no.

▲▲*Fram* Museum (Frammuseet) —This museum holds the 125-foot, steam- and sail-powered ship that took modern-day Vikings Roald Amundsen and Fridtjof Nansen deep into the Arctic and Antarctic, farther north and south than any ship had gone before. For three years, the *Fram*—specially designed to survive the pressure of a frozen-over sea—drifted as part of the Arctic ice. The exhibit is engrossing. Read the ground-floor displays, check out the videos below the bow of the ship, then climb the steps to the third-floor gangway to explore the *Fram*'s claustrophobic but fascinating interior. The building also tells the chilling tales of other Arctic and Antarctic adventures undertaken beneath the Norwegian flag. The polar sloop *Gjøa*, dry-docked outside next to the ferry dock, is the boat

Amundsen and a crew of six used from 1903 to 1906 to "discover" the Northwest Passage.

Cost, Hours, Location: 40 kr, daily June–Aug 9:00–18:00, May and Sept 10:00–17:00, Oct–April 10:00–16:00, Bygdøynesveien 36, tel. 23 28 29 50, www.fram.museum.no.

▲▲*Kon-Tiki* Museum (*Kon-Tiki* Museet)—Next to the *Fram* is a museum housing the *Kon-Tiki* and the *Ra II*, the boats built by Thor Heyerdahl (1914–2002). In 1947, Heyerdahl and five crewmates constructed the *Kon-Tiki* raft out of balsa wood, using only pre-modern tools and techniques. They set sail from Peru on the tiny craft, surviving for 101 days on fish, coconuts, and sweet potatoes. About 4,300 miles later, they arrived in Polynesia. The point was to show that early South Americans could have settled Polynesia. (While Heyerdahl proved they could have, anthropologists doubt they did.) The *Kon-Tiki* story became a best-selling book and award-winning documentary (and helped spawn the "Tiki" culture craze in the USA). In 1970, Heyerdahl's *Ra II* made a similar 3,000-mile journey from Morocco to Barbados to prove that Africans could have populated America. Both boats are well-displayed and described in English. Various 10-minute clips from the *Kon-Tiki* movie (winner of 1951 Oscar for best documentary) play constantly in a small theater at the end of the exhibit

Cost, Hours, Location: 50 kr, daily June–Aug 9:30–17:30, April–May and Sept 10:00–17:00, Oct–March 10:30–16:00, Bygdøynesveien 36, tel. 23 08 67 67, www.kon-tiki.no.

▲Norwegian Maritime Museum (Norsk Sjøfartsmuseum)—If you like the sea, this museum is a salt lick, providing a wide-ranging look at Norway's maritime heritage. Its dusty collection includes the charred remains of Norway's oldest boat (2,200 years old), artifacts from the immigration days, and a case devoted to World War II. Don't miss the movie *The Ocean: A Way of Life*, included with your admission. It is a breathtaking widescreen film swooping you scenically over Norway's dramatic sea and fishing townscapes from here all the way to North Cape in a comfy theater (20 min, shown at the top and bottom of the hour, follow signs to Supervideografen).

Cost, Hours, Location: 40 kr, kids under 16 free; mid-May–Aug daily 10:00–18:00; Sept–mid-May daily 10:30–16:00, Thu until 18:00; Bygdøynesveien 37, tel. 24 11 41 50, www.norsk-sjofartsmuseum.no.

Outer Oslo

▲▲Holmenkollen Ski Jump and Ski Museum—The site of one of the world's oldest ski jumps (from 1892), Holmenkollen has hosted many championships, including the 1952 Winter Olympics. In order to win the privilege of hosting the 2011 World Ski Jump

Championship, Oslo agreed to build a bigger jump to match modern ones. In 2008, they tore down the old Olympic ski jump and started construction of a futuristic, cantilevered, Olympic-standard new **ski jump** with a tilted elevator. The jump empties into a 50,000-seat amphitheater, and spectators can witness ski-jumpers' launches into flight from a glass-enclosed viewing platform. The jump also offers some of the best possible views of Oslo.

While due to open in the spring of 2010, escalating costs have threatened the timetable and project design. Check with the TI or call before you visit to be sure it's open. For the latest updates on construction and the world championships, visit www.oslo2011.no.

The **ski museum,** a must for skiers, traces the evolution of the sport, from 4,000-year-old rock paintings to crude 1,500-year-old wooden sticks to the slick and quickly evolving skis of modern times, including a fun exhibit showing the royal family on skis. The museum should reopen with the ski jump, but if it's still closed, stop by the free visitors center in Kollenstua, at the gateway to the jump arena, to see some temporary exhibits.

Cost and Hours: Remember to confirm at the TI that everything's open; 90-kr ticket includes museum and jump; museum open daily June–Aug 9:00–20:00, May and Sept 10:00–17:00, Oct–April 10:00–14:00; ramp open same hours except Oct–April 10:00–16:00; tel. 22 92 32 64, www.holmenkollen.com or www.skiforeningen.no.

Simulator: To cap your Holmenkollen experience, step into the simulator and fly down the Olympic slopes of Lillehammer in a virtual downhill ski race. My legs were exhausted after the five-minute terror. This simulator (or should I say stimulator?), parked in front of the ski museum, costs 50 kr (if you pay for four tickets, try getting a fifth one free).

Getting There: The T-bane gets you out of the city, through the hills, forests, and mansions that surround Oslo, and to the jump (take any westbound train—that's *tog mot vest*—to Majorstuen, then line #1 to Holmenkollen, and hike up the road 10 min). For an easy downhill jaunt through the Norwegian forest, with a woodsy coffee or meal break in the middle, stay on the T-bane past Holmenkollen to the end of the line (Frognerseteren) and walk 10 minutes downhill to the recommended **Frognerseteren Hovedrestaurant,** a fine traditional eatery with sod roof, reindeer meat on the griddle, and a city view. Continue on the same road another 20 minutes downhill to the ski jump, and then to the Holmenkollen T-bane stop.

▲Edvard Munch Museum (Munch Museet)—The only Norwegian painter to have had a serious impact on European art, Munch (pronounced "moonk") is a surprise to many who visit this fine museum, located one mile east of Oslo's center. The emotional, disturbing, and powerfully Expressionistic work of this strange and perplexing man is arranged chronologically. You'll see an extensive collection of paintings, drawings, lithographs, and photographs. Note that Oslo's centrally located—and free—National Gallery, which also displays many Munch works, can be a good alternative if you find the Munch Museum too expensive or time-consuming to reach (75 kr; June–Aug daily 10:00–18:00; Sept–May Tue–Fri 10:00–16:00, Sat–Sun 11:00–17:00, closed Mon; 25-kr audioguide, guided tours daily July–Aug at 13:00, T-bane or bus #20 to Tøyen, Tøyengata 53, tel. 23 49 35 00, www.munch.museum.no). For more on Munch, see page 198.

The Munch Museum was in the news in August 2004, when two Munch paintings, *Madonna* and a version of his famous *Scream,* were brazenly stolen right off the walls in broad daylight. Two men in black hoods simply entered through the museum café, waved guns at the stunned guards and tourists, ripped the paintings off the wall, and sped off in a black Audi station wagon. Happily, in 2006, the thieves were caught and the stolen paintings recovered. Today they are on display behind glass with heightened security.

Forests, Lakes, and Beaches—Oslo is surrounded by a vast forest dotted with idyllic little lakes, huts, joggers, bikers, and sun-worshippers. Mountain-biking possibilities are endless (as you'll discover if you go exploring without a good map). Consider taking your bike on the T-bane (for the cost of a child's ticket) to the end of line #1 (Frognerseteren, 30 min from National Theater) to gain the most altitude possible. Then follow the gravelly roads (mostly downhill but with some climbing) past several dreamy lakes to Sognsvann at the end of T-bane line #3. Farther east, from Maridalsvannet, a bike path follows the Akers River all the way back into town. (The TI has details.) While Oslo isn't much on bike rentals, you can rent them in summer at Skiservice, located at the Voksenkollen stop on T-bane line #1, at the high end of the woods. Keep in mind that you'll need to bring your bike back here—via T-bane if you like (tel. 22 13 95 00, www.skiservice.no).

For plenty of trees and none of the exercise, ride T-bane line #3 to its last stop, Sognsvann (with a beach towel rather than a bike), and join the lakeside scene. A pleasant trail leads around the lake.

Other popular beaches are located on islands in the harbor (such as Bygdøy Huk—direct boat from pier 3 in front of City Hall). The various island getaways are described in Use It's *Streetwise* magazine.

Tusenfryd—This giant amusement complex just out of town offers a world of family fun. It's sort of a combination Norwegian Disneyland/Viking Knott's Berry Farm, with more than 50 rides, plenty of entertainment, and restaurants.

Cost and Hours: Admission is based on your height: under 95 centimeters (3 feet)—free, under 1.2 meters (4 feet)—240 kr, over 1.2 meters (4 feet)—290 kr (daily June–late Aug 10:30–19:00, closed in winter, tel. 64 97 66 99, www.tusenfryd.no).

Getting There: Bus #541 takes fun-seekers to the park from behind Oslo's train station (30 kr, 2/hr, 20-min ride, departs Oslo 10:00–16:00, departs Tusenfryd 14:30–17:30).

Wet Fun—Oslo offers a variety of water play. In Frogner Park, the **Frognerbadet** has three outdoor pools, a waterslide, high dives, a cafeteria, and lots of young families (69 kr, students-50 kr, mid-May–late Aug Mon–Fri 7:00–19:00, Sat–Sun 10:00–18:00, last entry one hour before closing, closed late Aug–mid-May, Middelthunsgate 28, tel. 23 27 54 50).

Tøyenbadet, a modern indoor/outdoor pool complex with a 330-foot-long waterslide, also has a gym and sauna (73 kr, children-35 kr, Mon–Fri 7:00–19:30, Sat–Sun 10:00–18:00, 10-min walk from Edvard Munch Museum, Helgengate 90, tel. 23 30 44 70). Oslo's free botanical gardens are nearby.

From Akers River to the Grünerløkka District

Connect the dots by following the self-guided "Walk up the Akers River to Grünerløkka" (below).

Akers River—This river, though only about five miles long, powered Oslo's early industry: flour mills in the 1300s, sawmills in the 1500s, and Norway's Industrial Revolution in the 1800s. A walk along the river not only spans Oslo's history, but also shows the contrast the city offers. The bottom of the river (where this walk doesn't go)—bordered by the high-rise Oslo Radisson/SAS Plaza Hotel and the "Little Pakistan" neighborhood of Grønland—has its share of drunks and drugs, reflecting a new urban reality in Oslo. Farther up, the river valley becomes a park as it winds past decent-size waterfalls and red-brick factories. The source of the river (and Oslo's drinking water) is the pristine Lake Maridal, situated at the edge of the Nordmarka wilderness. The idyllic recreation scenes along Lake Maridal are a world apart from the rougher reality downstream.

▲Grünerløkka—The Grünerløkka district is the largest planned urban area in Oslo. It was built in the latter half of the 1800s to house the legions of workers employed at the factories powered by the Akers River. The first buildings were modeled on similar places built in Berlin. (German visitors observe that there's now more turn-of-the-20th-century Berlin here than in present-day Berlin.) While slummy in the 1980s, today it's trendy. Locals sometimes refer to it as "Oslo's Greenwich Village." Although that's way over the mark, it is a bustling area with lots of cafés, good spots for a fun meal, and few tourists.

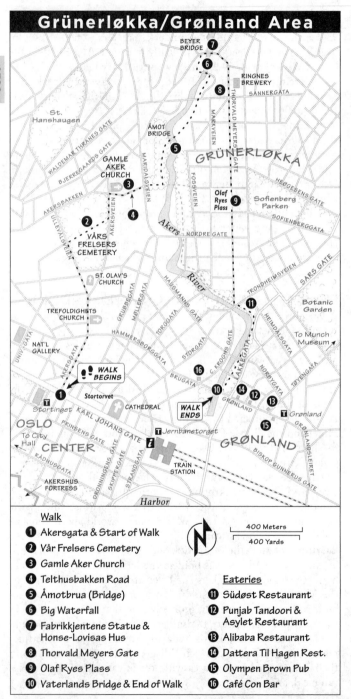

Grünerløkka/Grønland Area

400 Meters
400 Yards

Walk

1. Akersgata & Start of Walk
2. Vår Frelsers Cemetery
3. Gamle Aker Church
4. Telthusbakken Road
5. Åmotbrua (Bridge)
6. Big Waterfall
7. Fabrikkjentene Statue & Honse-Lovisas Hus
8. Thorvald Meyers Gate
9. Olaf Ryes Plass
10. Vaterlands Bridge & End of Walk

Eateries

11. Südøst Restaurant
12. Punjab Tandoori & Asylet Restaurant
13. Alibaba Restaurant
14. Dattera Til Hagen Rest.
15. Olympen Brown Pub
16. Café Con Bar

Grünerløkka can be reached from the center of town by a short ride on tram #11, #12, or #13, or by taking the short but interesting walk described next.

▲Walk up the Akers River to Grünerløkka—While every tourist explores the harborfront and main drag of Oslo, few venture into this neighborhood that evokes the Industrial Revolution. Once housing poor workers, it now attracts hip professionals. A hike up the Akers River, finishing in the stylish Grünerløkka district, shines a truly different light on Oslo. Allow about an hour at a brisk pace, including a fair bit of up and down. Navigate with the TI's free city map and the map in this chapter. This walk is best during daylight hours.

Begin the walk by leaving Karl Johans Gate at the top of the hill, and head right up Akersgata, which becomes Ullevålsveien. Akersgata is Oslo's "Fleet Street" (lined with major newspaper companies) and home to some big government buildings. On the right, notice the red-brick Supreme Court building and then the Department of Finance—an example of Jugendstil, or Art Nouveau, architecture. Then you'll pass the massive brick Trefoldighets Church and St. Olav's Church before reaching the **Vår Frelsers (Our Savior's) Cemetery.** Enter the cemetery across from the Baby Shop store (where Ullevålsveien meets Wessels Gate).

Stop at the big metal map just inside the gate to chart your course through the cemetery: Go through the light-green Æreslunden section—with the biggest plots and highest elevation—and out the opposite end (#13 on the metal map) onto Akersveien. En route, check out some of the tombstones of the illuminati and literati buried in the honorary Æreslunden section. They include Munch, Ibsen, Bjørnson, and many of the painters whose works you can see in the National Gallery (all marked on a map posted at the entrance). Exiting on the far side of the cemetery, walk left 100 yards up Akersveien to the church.

The Romanesque **Gamle Aker Church** (from the 1100s), the oldest building in Oslo, is worth a look inside (free, Mon–Fri 12:00–16:00). The church, which fell into ruins and has been impressively rebuilt, is pretty bare except for a pulpit and baptismal font from the 1700s.

From the church, backtrack 20 yards, head left at the playground, and go downhill on the steep **Telthusbakken Road** toward the huge, gray former grain silos (now student housing). The cute lane is lined with colorful old wooden houses: The people who constructed these homes were too poor to meet the no-wood fire-safety building codes within the city limits, so they built in what used to be suburbs. At the bottom of Telthusbakken, cross the busy Maridalsveien and walk directly through the park to the Akers River. The lively Grünerløkka district is straight across the river from here, but if you have 20 minutes and a little energy, detour upstream first and hook back down. Don't cross the river yet.

Walk along the riverside bike lane upstream through the river gorge park. Just above the first waterfall, cross **Åmotbrua,** the big white springy suspension footbridge from 1852 (moved here in 1958). Keep hiking uphill along the river. At the base of the next big waterfall, cross over again to the large brick buildings, hiking up the stairs to the Beyer bridge (above the falls) with ***Fabrikkjentene,*** a statue of four women laborers. They're pondering the textile factory where they and 700 like them toiled long and hard. This gorge was once lined with the water mills that powered Oslo through its 19th-century Industrial Age boom. The tiny red house next to the bridge—the **Honse-Lovisas Hus** cultural center—makes a good rest-stop (Tue-Sun 11:00–18:00, closed Mon, coffee and cake). Cross over to the red-brick Ringnes Brewery and follow **Thorvald Meyers Gate** downhill directly into the heart of Grünerløkka. The main square, called **Olaf Ryes Plass,** is a happening place to grab a meal or drink. Trams take you from here back to the center.

• *To continue exploring, you could keep walking (always going straight) until you reach a T-intersection with a busy road (Trondheimsveien). From there (passing the recommended Südøst Restaurant), you can catch a tram back to the center, or drop down to the riverside path and follow it downstream to Vaterlands bridge in the Grønland district. From here the train station is a five-minute walk down Stenersgata. (The last section, around Grønland, is a bit seedy and best done in daylight.)*

Near Oslo

▲Eidsvoll Manor—During the Napoleonic period, control of Norway went from Denmark to Sweden. This ruffled the patriotic feathers of Norway's Thomas Jeffersons and Ben Franklins, and on May 17, 1814, Norway's constitution was written and signed in this stately mansion (in the town of Eidsvoll Verk, north of Oslo). While Sweden still ruled, Norway had more autonomy than ever. The mansion is full of elegant furnishings and stirring history.

Cost and Hours: 75 kr; May–Aug daily 10:00–17:00; April and Sept Tue–Fri 10:00–15:00, Sat–Sun 12:00–17:00, closed Mon; Oct–March Wed–Fri 10:00–15:00, Sat–Sun 12:00–17:00, closed Mon–Tue; tel. 63 92 22 10, www.eidsvoll1814.no.

Getting There: Eidsvoll is 45 minutes from Oslo by car (take road E6 toward Trondheim, turn right at *Eidsvolls Bygningen* sign, free parking) or bus (direct bus #854 runs hourly from Oslo Airport). You can also take the train to Eidsvoll (hourly, 45 min plus 15-min walk). If you're driving from Oslo to Lillehammer and the Gudbrandsdal Valley, it's right on the way and worth a stop.

Drøbak—This delightful fjord town is just an hour from Oslo by bus (70 kr one-way, 2/hr, bus #541 or #542 from behind the train station) or ferry (70 kr one-way, sporadic departures, check at pier 1 or ask at Oslo TI). Consider taking the 75-minute boat trip down, exploring the town, having dinner, and taking the bus back.

For holiday cheer year-round, stop into **Tregaarden's Julehuset** Christmas shop, right off Drøbak's main square (generally Mon–Fri 10:00–17:00, Sat 10:00–15:00, variable hours on Sun, longer hours in Dec, closed Jan–Feb, tel. 64 93 41 78, www.julehus.no). Then wander out past the church and cemetery on the north side of town to a pleasant park. Looking out into the fjord, you can see the old **Oscarsborg Fortress,** where Norwegian troops fired their cannons to sink Hitler's battleship, *Blücher*. The attack bought enough time for Norway's king and Parliament to escape capture and eventually set up a government-in-exile in London during the Nazi occupation of Norway (1940–1945). Nearby, a monument is dedicated to the commander of the fortress, and the *Blücher*'s anchor rests aground. (A 70-kr round-trip summer ferry shuttles visitors from the town harbor.)

If you want to spend the night, the **TI** can recommend accommodations (June–Aug Mon–Fri 8:00–18:00, Sat–Sun 10:00–16:00; Sept–May Mon–Fri 8:00–16:00, closed Sat–Sun; tel. 64 93 50 87, www.visitdrobak.no). **Restaurant Skipperstuen** is a good option for dinner, with outdoor seating that overlooks the fjord and all the Oslo-bound boat traffic (entrées from 200 kr, Mon–Sat 11:00–21:00, closed Sun, tel. 64 93 07 03).

Shopping in Oslo

Shops in Oslo are generally open 10:00–18:00. Many stay open until 20:00 on Thursday and close early on Saturday and all day Sunday. Shopping centers are open Monday through Friday 10:00–21:00, Saturday 10:00–18:00, and are closed Sunday. Remember, when you make a purchase of 310 kr or more, you can get the 25 percent tax refunded when you leave the country if you hang on to the paperwork (see page 17).

Oslo's fanciest department store is **GlasMagasinet** (top end, near the cathedral on Stortorvet, good souvenir shop). The big, splashy **Byporten** mall, adjoining the central train station, is more youthful and hip (Mon–Fri 10:00–21:00, Sat 10:00–18:00, closed Sun). The trendiest boutiques and chic, high-quality shops lie along the street named **Bogstadveien** (running from behind the Royal Palace to Frogner Park). And on Saturday mornings, you can browse the **flea market** at Vestkanttorvet.

Sweaters and colorful Norwegian folk crafts are on many visitors' shopping lists. The **Husfliden shop,** in the basement of the GlasMagasinet department store, is much appreciated for its traditional yarn and Norsk folk items (Mon–Fri 10:00–18:00, Thu until 19:00, Sat 10:00–16:00, closed Sun, tel. 22 42 10 75). For a superb selection of sweaters and other Norwegian crafts (top quality at high prices), visit **Heimen Husfliden** (Mon–Fri 10:00–17:00, Thu until 18:00, Sat 10:00–15:00, closed Sun, Rosenkrantz Gate 8, tel. 22 41 40 50). The **Oslo Sweater Shop** has good prices for sweaters (Mon–Fri 10:00–18:00, Sat 10:00–15:00, closed Sun, off Skippergata at Biskop Gunnerusgata 3, tel. 22 42 42 25). For flags (a long, skinny *vimple* dresses up a boat or cabin wonderfully), pop into **Oslo Flaggfabrikk** (Mon–Fri 9:00–17:00, Sat 10:00–16:00, closed Sun, near City Hall, across the street from Heimen Husfliden shop, at Rosenkrantz Gate 18).

Vinmonopolet stores are the only place where you can buy wine and spirits in Norway. The most convenient location is at the central train station (Mon–Thu 10:00–18:00, Fri 9:00–18:00, Sat 9:00–15:00, closed Sun). The bottles used to be kept behind the counter, but now you can actually touch the merchandise. Locals say it went from being a "jewelry store" to "grocery store."

Sleeping in Oslo

In Oslo, the season and type of hotel dictate the best deals. The basic formula: In midsummer and on weekends, discounted business-class hotels offer the best value; otherwise, consider a cheap hotel, a room in a private home, or a hostel.

Like those in its sister Scandinavian capitals, Oslo's hotels are mostly designed for business travelers; they're expensive during the tourists' off-season (autumn through spring), full in May and June for conventions, and wide open otherwise. From July through mid-August—and weekends (Fri–Sat but not Sun) year-round—fancy business-class hotels deeply discount their rooms. At half-price (about 800–900 kr for a double), you get a huge breakfast and a lot of extra comfort for little more than the cost of a cheap hotel or hostel.

During business days (Sun–Thu) outside of summer, business hotels hold out for their inflated "rack rates," and budget travelers opt for Oslo's dumpy-for-Scandinavia (but still nice by European standards) cheapie options: doubles for about 800 kr in central "cheap" hotels, or 350 kr in private homes on the outskirts of the city. For experience and economy—but not convenience—go for a private home. For convenience and modern comfort, I like the Thon Budget Hotels (described later).

Only the TI can sort through all of the confusing hotel specials and get you the best deal going on fancy hotel rooms on the push list. If it's late in the day, the TI's prices get even better. With the uncertain economy these days, it's tough to get a hotel to give a straight price in advance. If booking on your own and on

Sleep Code

(6 kr = about $1, country code: 47)
S = Single, **D** = Double/Twin, **T** = Triple, **Q** = Quad, **b** = bathroom, **s** = shower. You can assume credit cards are accepted and breakfast is included unless otherwise noted. Everyone speaks English.

To help you sort through these listings easily, I've divided the rooms into three categories, based on the price for a standard double room with bath:

$$$ Higher Priced—Most rooms 1,000 kr or more.
$$ Moderately Priced—Most rooms between 600–1,000 kr.
$ Lower Priced—Most rooms 600 kr or less.

a budget, email several places and see who's willing to offer the most aggressive discount.

The most predictable special is the TI's **Oslo Package,** which offers business-class rooms plus an Oslo Pass for 500–800 kr per person (based on double occupancy); prices vary depending on the hotel you choose. The Oslo Package is offered daily year-round. It's a good deal for couples and ideal for families with young children. Two kids under 16 sleep free, breakfast is included, and up to four family members get free Oslo Passes, covering admission to sights and all public transportation (worth as much as 135 kr per person per day—see page 174). These passes are valid for four days, even if you only stay one night at the hotel (allowing you to squeeze two days of sightseeing out of a one-night stay—for example, if you take an overnight train or boat out of town on your second evening). Buy the Oslo Package through your travel agent at home, ScanAm World Tours in the US (US tel. 800-545-2204), or—easiest—upon arrival in Oslo at the TI. Even if you show up late in the day when prices are most deeply discounted, you still get the Oslo Pass along with your room. For details on the Oslo Package, see www.visitoslo.com.

Near the Train Station and Karl Johans Gate

These accommodations are within a 15-minute walk of the station. While evidence of an earlier shady time survives in some places, the hotels feel secure and comfortable. Parking in a central garage will run you about 170 kr per day.

Thon Hotels

This chain of business-class hotels (found in big cities throughout Norway) knows which comforts are worth paying for and which are not. They offer little character, but provide maximum comfort per

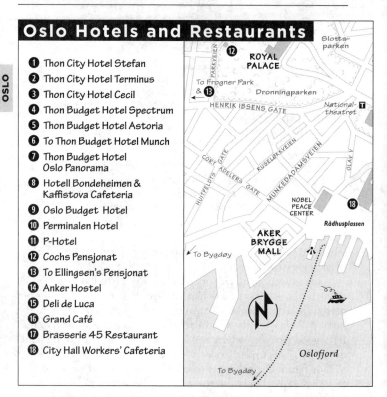

Oslo Hotels and Restaurants

1. Thon City Hotel Stefan
2. Thon City Hotel Terminus
3. Thon City Hotel Cecil
4. Thon Budget Hotel Spectrum
5. Thon Budget Hotel Astoria
6. To Thon Budget Hotel Munch
7. Thon Budget Hotel Oslo Panorama
8. Hotell Bondeheimen & Kaffistova Cafeteria
9. Oslo Budget Hotel
10. Perminalen Hotel
11. P-Hotel
12. Cochs Pensjonat
13. To Ellingsen's Pensjonat
14. Anker Hostel
15. Deli de Luca
16. Grand Café
17. Brasserie 45 Restaurant
18. City Hall Workers' Cafeteria

krone in big, modern, conveniently located buildings. Each hotel has a cheery staff and lobby, tight but well-designed rooms, non-smoking floors, free Internet access, and a big buffet breakfast.

Thon Hotels come in categories: Their "City Hotels" are a cut above their "Budget Hotels." While City Hotels are much more expensive during business times (weekdays outside of summer), Budget Hotels have nearly the same rack rates all year. That means City Hotels can be a better value in low season. City Hotels generally offer free juice and coffee all day. In Budget Hotels (which have no phones or mini-fridges in the rooms), rooms with double beds are a bit bigger than twin-bedded rooms for the same price.

Thon Hotels share a similar price structure: **Thon City Hotels**—Sb-1,525, Db-1,825 kr; discounted rates: Fri–Sat year around and daily mid-June–mid-Aug Sb-900 kr, Db-1,100; **Thon Budget Hotels**—Sb-750 kr, Db-1,075 kr, no weekend deals; summer rates: Sb-650 kr, Db-875 kr. These rates include breakfast (you have the option of saving 50 kr per day per person by not taking breakfast). Extra beds are 300 kr for an adult and 150 kr for a child under 17 (kids under 6 stow away for free). Book by phone or online (central booking tel. 23 08 02 00, www.thonhotels.no).

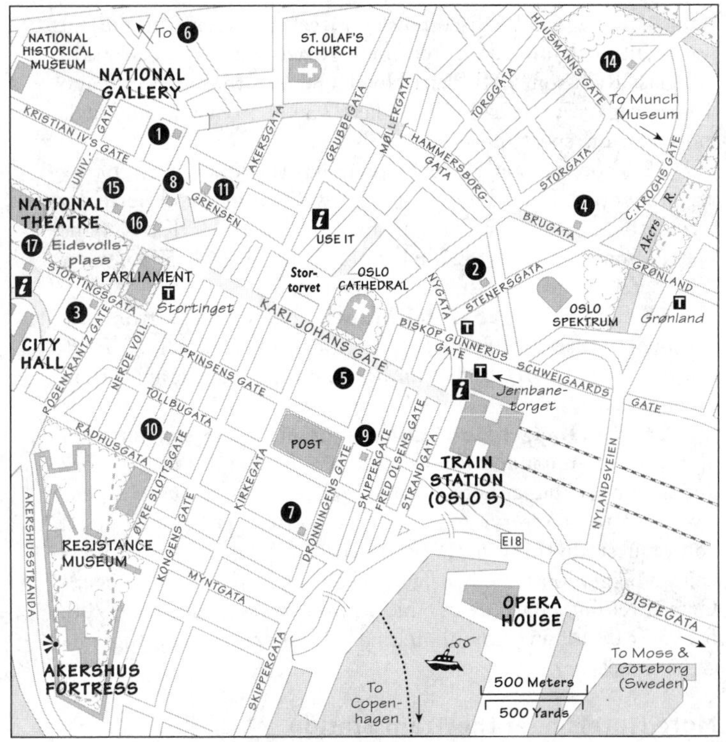

Thon Hotels generally offer a 10 percent discount for those who prepay via their website with no option to change or cancel their booking. The free Thon Membership Card offers a 10 percent discount off-season (doesn't apply to summer/weekend rates). My price ratings for Thon Hotels are based on their summer/weekend rates. Of the 14 Thon Hotels in Oslo, I find the following most convenient:

$$$ Thon City Hotel Stefan, in a classy and central location two blocks off Karl Johans Gate, is a cut above its sisters in comfort and charm (Rosenkrantz Gate 1, entrance on Kristian Augusts Gate side, tel. 23 31 55 00, fax 23 31 55 55, www.thonhotels.no/stefan, stefan@thonhotels.no).

$$$ Thon City Hotel Terminus is similar but closer to the station (Steners Gate 10, tel. 22 05 60 00, fax 22 17 08 98, www.thonhotels.no/terminus, terminus@thonhotels.no).

$$$ Thon City Hotel Cecil is near the Parliament building a block below Karl Johans Gate (Stortingsgata 8, tel. 23 31 48 00, fax 23 31 48 50, www.thonhotels.no/cecil, cecil@thonhotels.no).

$$ Thon Budget Hotel Spectrum is four blocks from the station near the Grønland Torg shopping street. A quarter of its rooms are plagued by disco noise on weekends (leave station out north entrance toward bus terminal, go across footbridge toward tall glass Radisson/SAS Plaza Hotel, and pass through Grønland Torg, Brugata 7; tel. 23 36 27 00, fax 23 36 27 50, www.thonhotels.no/spectrum, spectrum@thonhotels.no).

$$ Thon Budget Hotel Astoria has the least charm of my recommended Thon Hotels, but it's well-located and perfectly serviceable (3 blocks in front of station, 50 yards off Karl Johans Gate, Dronningens Gate 21, tel. 24 14 55 50, fax 22 42 57 65, www.thonhotels.no/astoria, astoria@thonhotels.no).

$$ Thon Budget Hotel Munch, a few blocks from the National Gallery, is like its sisters (Munchs Gate 5, tel. 23 21 96 00, fax 23 21 96 01, www.thonhotels.no/munch, munch@thonhotels.no).

$$ Thon Budget Hotel Oslo Panorama is a 15-story attempt at a downtown condominium building. The condos didn't work and now it's a budget hotel. While higher rooms are more expensive, even those reserving a cheap room often get bumped up. If you request anything higher than the fourth floor, you'll likely enjoy a bigger room, perhaps with a balcony (just off Dronningens Gate at Rådhusgata 7, about 6 blocks from station, tel. 23 31 08 00, fax 23 31 08 10, www.thonhotels.no/oslopanorama, oslopanorama@thonhotels.no).

More Hotels near the Train Station

$$$ Hotell Bondeheimen ("Farmer's Home") is a historic hotel run by the farmers' youth league, *Bondeungdomslaget.* It once housed the children of rural farmers attending school in Oslo. Now a Best Western, its 127 rooms have all the comforts of a modern hotel (weekday rates too high, Fri–Sat all year and July Db-900 kr, Aug Db-1,100 kr; you generally save money by booking on their website; non-smoking rooms, elevator, Rosenkrantz Gate 8, tel. 23 21 41 00, www.bondeheimen.com, booking@bondeheimen.com). This almost-100-year-old building is also home to the Kaffistova cafeteria (see "Eating in Oslo") and the Heimen Husfliden shop (see "Shopping in Oslo").

$$ Oslo Budget Hotel has clean, basic, and well-worn but homey rooms (many with bunks), in a somewhat seedy fourth-floor location handy to the train station. The hotel originated 100 years ago as a cheap place for Norwegians to sleep while they waited to sail to their new homes in America. It now serves the opposite purpose. With prices the same throughout the year, this hotel is a good value on off-season weekdays (Sun–Thu), when other hotels are at their most expensive (S-490 kr, Sb-590 kr, D-590 kr, Db-790 kr, T-690 kr, Tb-890 kr, Q-790 kr, Qb-990 kr, 10 percent discount with this book—mention when you reserve, breakfast-65 kr, free waffles in afternoon, non-smoking rooms, Prinsens Gate 6, tel. 22 41 36 10, fax 22 42 24 29, www.budgethotel.no, oslo@budgethotel.no).

$$ Perminalen Hotel, a place for military personnel on leave, is perfectly central, spartan, inexpensive, and welcoming to civvies. They have the same fair prices all year. Spliced invisibly into a giant office block on a quiet street, it has sleek woody furniture and a no-nonsense reception desk (Sb-620 kr, twin Db-820 kr, some seventh-floor rooms have balconies, entirely non-smoking, elevator, tram #12 from station to Øvre Slotts Gate 2, tel. 23 09 30 81, fax 23 41 18 58, www.perminalen.com, post.perminalen@iss.no). Single beds in shared quads segregated by sexes (with lockers and breakfast) rent for 360 kr each. Its cheap mess hall is open all day.

$$ P-Hotel, the latest thing in economic hotels in Oslo, rents 92 comfortable rooms—some with hardwood-slick floors—for the same great price every day of the year. You get a boxed breakfast delivered each morning, as well as free Internet access and Wi-Fi. Avoid late-night street noise by requesting a room high up or in the back (Sb-795 kr, Db-895 kr, bigger rooms add 150 kr per person up to five, some sixth-floor rooms have balconies, pay by credit card—no cash accepted, Grensen 19, T-bane: Storting, tel. 23 31 80 00, www.p-hotels.com, oslo@p-hotels.no).

The West End

$$ Cochs Pensjonat has 88 characteristic rooms (20 remodeled doubles), many with kitchenettes. It's right behind the Royal Palace (S-460 kr, Sb-610 kr, D-660 kr, Db-760 kr, newly refurnished Db-820 kr, Q-1,020 kr, Qb-1,180 kr, breakfast-65 kr at nearby café, non-smoking rooms, elevator; T-bane to National Theater, exit to Parkveien, and walk through park; or ride tram #11, #17, or #18 to Høgskolen/Dalsbergsstien; Parkveien 25; tel. 23 33 24 00, fax 23 33 24 10, www.cochspensjonat.no, booking@cochs.no, three generations of the Skram family).

$$ Ellingsen's Pensjonat rents 18 clean, bright rooms with fluffy down comforters. It's in a residential neighborhood four blocks behind the Royal Palace (S-330 kr, Sb-460 kr, D-540 kr, Db-650 kr, extra bed-150 kr, no breakfast, cash only, non-smoking, back rooms have less street noise, tram #19 from central station to Uranienborgveien, near Uranienborg church at Holtegata 25, tel. 22 60 03 59, fax 22 60 99 21, www.ellingsenspensjonat.no, post@ellingsenspensjonat.no).

Private Homes

The central station TI can find you a 350-kr double for a 45-kr fee (minimum two-night stay, likely a tram ride out of the center).

Hostels

$ Anker Hostel, a huge student dorm open to travelers of any age, offers 250 of Oslo's best cheap doubles. Though it comes with the ambience of a bomb shelter, each of its rooms is spacious, simple, and clean. There are kitchens, free parking, and elevators (bed in 6-bed room-210 kr, bed in quad-230 kr, Db-550 kr, sheets-50 kr, towel-20 kr, breakfast-75 kr at adjacent Best Western hotel, self-serve laundry; tram #12, #13, or #15, or bus #30, #31, or #32 from central station, bus and tram stop: Hausmanns Gate; or 10-min walk from station; Storgata 55, tel. 22 99 72 00, fax 22 99 72 20, www.ankerhostel.no, hostel@anker.oslo.no).

$ Haraldsheim Youth Hostel (IYHF), a huge, modern hostel open all year, comes with a grand view, laundry, self-service kitchen, 270 beds...and a long commute (2.5 miles out of town). Beds in the fancy quads with private showers and toilets are 250 kr per person (bed in simple quad with bathroom down the hall-220 kr). They also offer private rooms (S-415 kr, Sb-470 kr, bunk-bed D-540 kr, Db-625 kr; all include breakfast, members get 15 percent off, sheets-50 kr, catch bus #31 or tram #17 or T-bane lines #4 or #6 from Oslo's central train station to Sinsenkrysset, then 5-min uphill hike to Haraldsheimveien 4, tel. 22 22 29 65, fax 22 22 10 25, www.haraldsheim.oslo.no, post@haraldsheim.oslo.no). Eurailers can train to the hostel with their railpass (2/hr, to Grefsen and walk 10 min).

Sleeping on the Train or Boat

Norway's trains and ferries offer ways to travel while sleeping. The eight-hour night train between Bergen and Oslo leaves at about 23:00 in each direction (nightly except Sat). Eurail hobos sleep cheap, if not well, for the cost of a 50-kr train reservation (sleep on a train ride out, cross platform, and sleep back)—for example, Oslo–Vinstra (direction: Trondheim) 23:05–2:55, Vinstra–Oslo 3:14–6:43. Overnight trains connect Oslo with Copenhagen June–August only (leaves nightly at 20:30, arrives at Malmö Central Station at 6:42 the next morning, easy transfers to Copenhagen). The overnight cruise between these Nordic capitals is a clever way to avoid a night in a hotel and to travel while you sleep, saving a day in your itinerary (see "Oslo Connections," later).

Eating in Oslo

Eating Cheaply

How do the Norwegians afford their high-priced restaurants? They don't eat out much. This is one city in which you might just settle for simple or ethnic meals—you'll save a lot and miss little. Many menus list small and large plates. Because portions tend to be large,

Oslo's One-Time Grills

Norwegians are experts at completely avoiding costly restaurants. "One-time grills," or *engangsgrill,* are the rage for locals on a budget. For about 20 kr, you get a disposable outdoor cooker consisting of an aluminum tray, easy-to-light charcoal, and a flimsy metal grill. All that's required is a sunny evening, a grassy park, and a group of friends. During balmy summer evenings, the air in Oslo's city parks is thick with the smell of disposable (and not terribly eco-friendly) grills. It's fun to see how prices for this kind of "dining" aren't that bad in the supermarket: Norwegian beer-12 kr/bottle, potato salad-20 kr/tub, cooked shrimp-75 kr/half kilo, "ready for grill" steak-two for 110 kr, *grill polse* hot dogs-60 kr per dozen, *lomper* (Norwegian tortillas for wrapping hot dogs)-15 kr per stack, and the actual grill itself.

Bars are also too expensive for the average Norwegian. Young night owls drink at home before *(forspiel)* and after *(nachspiel)* an evening on the town, with a couple of hours, generally around midnight, when they go out for a single drink in a public setting. A beer in a bar costs about $8-10 (compared to $6 in Ireland and $2 in the Czech Republic), while they can get an entire six-pack for that price in a grocery store.

choosing a small plate or splitting a large one makes some otherwise pricey options reasonable. You'll notice many locals just drink free tap water, even in fine restaurants. For a description of Oslo's classic (and expensive) restaurants, see the TI's *Oslo Guide* booklet.

Splurge for a hotel that includes breakfast, or pay for it if it's optional. At 75 kr, a Norwegian breakfast fit for a Viking is a good deal. Picnic for lunch or dinner. Basements of big department stores have huge, first-class supermarkets with lots of alternatives to sandwiches for picnic dinners. The little yogurt tubs with cereal come with collapsible spoons. Wasa crackers and meat, shrimp, or cheese spread in a tube are cheap and pack well. The central station has an ICA supermarket with long hours (Mon–Fri 7:00–22:00, Sat–Sun 9:00–18:00).

You'll save 12 percent by getting take-away food from a restaurant rather than eating inside. (The VAT on take-away food is 12 percent; restaurant food is 24 percent.) Fast-food restaurants ask if you want to take away or not before they ring up your order on the cash register. Even McDonald's has a two-tiered price list.

Oslo is awash with little budget eateries (modern, ethnic, fast food, pizza, department-store cafeterias, and so on). **Deli de Luca,** a cheery convenience store chain, notorious for having a store on every key corner in Oslo, is a step up from the similarly ubiquitous 7-Elevens. Most are open 24/7, selling sandwiches, pastries, sushi, and to-go boxes of warm pasta or Asian noodle dishes. You can fill your belly here for about 60 kr. Some outlets (such as the one at the corner of Karl Johans Gate and Rosenkrantz Gate) have seating on the street or upstairs. Beware: Because this is still a *convenience* store, not everything is well-priced. Convenience stores—while convenient—charge double what supermarkets do.

Eating on or near Karl Johans Gate

Consider the restaurants and eateries listed below. They're grouped by those that are from Karl Johans Gate and slightly to the north (between this main boulevard and the National Gallery) and to the south (between Karl Johans Gate and City Hall).

Strangely, **Karl Johans Gate** itself—the most Norwegian of boulevards—is lined with a strip of good-time American chain eateries where you can get ribs, burgers, and pizza, including T.G.I. Fridays and the Hard Rock Cafe. Egon Pizza offers a daily 100-kr all-you-can-eat pizza deal (11:00–18:00). Each place comes with great sidewalk seating and essentially the same prices.

Grand Café is perhaps the most venerable place in town. At lunchtime, they set up a sandwich buffet (100-kr single sandwich, 300-kr all-you-like). Lunch plates are 150 kr, and dinner plates run about 250 kr. Reserve a window, and if you hit a time when there's no tour group, you're suddenly a posh Norwegian (Karl Johans Gate 31, tel. 23 21 20 18).

Deli de Luca, just across from the Grand Café, offers good-value food and handy seats on Karl Johans Gate. For a fast meal with the best people-watching view in town, you may find yourself dropping by here repeatedly (Karl Johans Gate 33, tel. 22 33 35 22).

Kaffistova is where my thrifty Norwegian grandparents always took me. After remaining unchanged for 30 years, it got a facelift in 2007. This alcohol-free cafeteria still serves simple, hearty, and typically Norwegian (read: bland) meals for a good price (Mon–Fri 6:30–21:00, Sat–Sun 7:00–19:00; Rosenkrantz Gate 8, tel. 23 21 42 10).

Brasserie 45, overlooking Stortingsgata and the National Theater from its second-floor perch, is a modern eatery offering decent and affordable Continental cuisine with energetic service. While larger entrées go for about 180 kr, their "light plates" (about 100 kr) are plenty for me. It's worth calling ahead to reserve a window seat with a view of Karl Johans Gate (Mon–Thu 15:00–23:00,

Fri–Sat 14:00–24:00, Sun 14:00–22:00, always a veggie option, Stortingsgata 20, tel. 22 41 34 00).

City Hall workers' cafeteria, just steps off the harborfront, welcomes the public with the cheapest lunch I've found in Oslo. It has soup, an inexpensive salad bar measured by weight (35 kr for a meal-sized bowl), and a daily hot dish for 30–45 kr (12:30–13:30 Mon–Fri only). While City Hall workers get access to the place before 12:30 and the food can be pretty picked over, it's still a fine, handy value. From the grand harbor entrance, it's up one flight of stairs above the city info desk and WC. From the tour entrance on its inland courtyard, it's just downstairs.

Harborside Dining in Aker Brygge

The **Aker Brygge** harborfront mall is popular with businesspeople and tourists. While it isn't cheap, its inviting cafés and restaurants with outdoor, harborview tables make for a memorable waterfront meal. Before deciding where to eat, you might want to walk the entire lane (including the back side), considering both the regular places (some with second-floor view seating) and the various floating options. Nearly all are open for lunch and dinner.

Druen, the first restaurant on the strip—while not a particularly good food value—is best for people-watching. I like the balcony seats upstairs, under outside heaters and with a harbor view. They serve international dishes—spicy Asian, French, and seafood—in small plates for 150 kr, hearty salads for 130 kr, and big meals for 220–260 kr (daily from 11:00, Stranden 1, Aker Brygge, tel. 23 11 54 60).

Two restaurants are right on the water with a view of the harbor rather than the river of strolling people. **Lekter'n,** a trendy bar with a floating dining area open only when the weather is warm, has the best harbor view. It serves hamburgers, pizza, and shrimp buckets. Budget eaters can split a 160-kr pizza (all outdoors, Stranden 3, tel. 22 83 76 46). Farther out, **Herbern Marina** is *the* place for shrimp on a balmy evening. In the midst of lots of pleasure boats, couples enjoy the fun, laid-back, dockside ambience, and fill up by splitting a 200-kr liter bucket of shrimp with bread. Request a free peeling lesson; rinse in the finger bowl (pizzas, burgers, and salads from 130 kr; daily 11:00–22:00, Stranden 30, tel. 22 83 19 90).

Rorbua, the "Fisherman's Cabin," is a lively yet cozy eatery tucked into this mostly modern stretch of restaurants. Inside, it's extremely woody with a rustic charm and candlelit picnic tables surrounded by harpoons and old B&W photos. Grab a stool at one of the wooden tables, and choose from a menu of meat-and-potato dishes (100–200 kr) and seafood offerings (150–200 kr). There's a hearty daily special with coffee for 125 kr (daily 12:30–23:00, Stranden 71, tel. 22 83 53 86).

Lofoten Fiskerestaurant serves fish amid a dressy yacht-club atmosphere at the end of the strip. While it's beyond the people-watching action, it's comfortable even in cold and blustery weather because of its heated atrium, which makes a meal here practically outdoor dining. Reservations are a must, especially if you want a harborside window table (lunch-150–225 kr, dinner from 275 kr, open daily, Stranden 75, tel. 22 83 08 08).

Budget Tips: If you're on a budget, get a take-out meal from the fast-food stands and grab a bench along the boardwalk. The **ICA "Gourmet"** grocery store—in the middle of the mall a few steps behind all the fancy restaurants—has salads, warm take-away dishes, and more (turn in about midway down the boardwalk, Mon–Fri 9:00–22:00, Sat 9:00–20:00, closed Sun).

Dining near Frogner Park

Lofotstua Restaurant feels transplanted from the far northern islands it's named for. Kjell Jenssen and his son, Jan Hugo, proudly serve up fish Lofoten-style. Evangelical about fish, they will patiently explain to you the fine differences between all the local varieties, with the help of a photo-filled chart. They serve only the freshest catch, perfectly—if simply—prepared. If you want meat, they've got it—whale or seal (180–250-kr plates, Mon–Fri 15:00–22:00, generally closed in July, 5-min walk from gate of Vigeland statue garden, tram #12, in Majorstuen at Kirkeveien 40, tel. 22 46 93 96). This place is packed daily in winter for their famous lutefisk.

Curry and Ketchup Indian Restaurant is filled with in-the-know locals enjoying tasty and hearty meals for 90 kr. This happening place requires no reservations and feels like an Indian market. If you want a reasonable Indian meal in Oslo, this is hard to beat (daily 14:00–23:00, cash only, a 5-min walk from gate of Vigeland statue garden, tram #12, in Majorstuen at Kirkeveien 51, tel. 22 69 05 22).

Trendy Dining at the Bottom of Grünerløkka

Südøst Restaurant, once a big bank, now fills its vault with wine (which makes sense, given Norwegian alcohol prices). Today it's popular with young Norwegian professionals as a place to see and be seen. It's a fine mix of Norwegian-chic woody ambience inside with a formal and expensive menu, and a big riverside terrace outdoors with a more casual menu. Diners enjoy its open-fire grill, smart service, and modern Continental cuisine (Mon–Sat 11:00–22:00, Sun 12:00–18:00, at bottom of Grünerløkka, tram #17 to Trondheimsveien 5, tel. 23 35 30 70).

Eating Cheap and Spicy in Grønland

The street called Grønland leads through this colorful immigrant neighborhood (a short walk behind the train station or T-bane: Grønland). After the cleanliness and orderliness of the rest of the city, the rough edges and diversity of people here can feel like a breath of fresh air. Whether you eat here or not, the street is fun to explore. In Grønland, backpackers and immigrants munch street food for dinner. Cheap and tasty *börek* (feta, spinach, mushroom) is sold hot and greasy to go for 20 kr.

Punjab Tandoori is friendly and serves hearty meals (lamb and chicken curry, tandoori specials) for 70 kr. They're open late when other places aren't. I like eating outside here with a view of the street scene (daily 11:00–23:00, Grønland 24).

Alibaba Restaurant is clean, inviting, filled with smart locals, and cheap for Turkish food. They have good indoor or outdoor seating (99-kr fixed-price meal Mon-Thu only, open daily 12:30–22:30, corner of Grønlandsleiret and Tøyengata at Tøyengata 2, tel. 22 17 22 22). The 99-kr special is much cheaper than the menu items, but isn't advertised very clearly; you may need to request it.

Asylet is more expensive and feels like it was here long before Norway ever saw a Pakistani. This big, traditional eatery—like a Norwegian beer garden—has a rustic, cozy interior and a gravelly backyard filled with picnic tables (150–170-kr plates and hearty dinner salads, daily 11:00–24:00, Grønland 28, tel. 22 17 09 39).

Dattera Til Hagen feels like a college party. It's a lively scene filling a courtyard with picnic tables and benches under strings of colored lights. Locals like it for the tapas, burgers, and salads (140-kr plates, pricey beers, Grønland 10, tel. 22 17 18 61). After 22:00 it becomes a disco.

Olympen Brown Pub is a dressy dining hall that's a blast from the past. You'll eat in a spacious woody saloon with big dark furniture, faded paintings of circa-1920 Oslo lining the walls, and huge chandeliers. They serve hearty 180-kr plates and offer a huge selection of beers. The grill restaurant upstairs comes with music and can be more fun (daily 11:00–2:00 in the morning, Grønlandsleiret 15, tel. 22 17 28 08).

Café Con Bar is a trendy yuppie eatery on the downtown edge of Grønland. Locals consider it to have the best burgers in town (150 kr). While the tight interior seating is very noisy, the sidewalk tables are great for people-watching (open daily, but only drinks served after 20:00; where Grønland hits Brugata).

Roasted Rudolph Under a Thatched Roof High on the Mountain

Frognerseteren Hovedrestaurant, nestled high above Oslo (and 1,400 feet above sea level), is a classy, sod-roofed old restaurant. Its terrace, offering a commanding view of the city, is a popular stop for famous apple cake and coffee. The café is casual and less expensive, with indoor and outdoor seating (75-kr sandwiches and cold dishes, 125-kr entrées, daily 11:00–22:00, reservations unnecessary). The elegant view restaurant is pricier (250–300-kr plates, 555-kr three-course meal, Mon–Sat 12:00–22:00, Sun 13:00–21:00, reindeer specials, reserve for evening dining, tel. 22 92 40 40).

You can combine a trip into the forested hills surrounding the city with lunch or dinner and get a chance to see the famous Holmenkollen Ski Jump up close (see page 210).

Oslo Connections

For train information, call 81 50 08 88 and press 4 for English. For international trains, dial 81 56 81 00. Even if you have a railpass, reservations are required for long rides (e.g., a reservation to Stockholm in first class costs 140 kr, second class for 60 kr). First class often comes with a hot meal, fruit bowl, and unlimited juice and coffee.

Be warned that international connections from Oslo are often in flux. Schedules can vary depending on the day of the week, so carefully confirm the specific train you need and purchase any required reservations in advance. Aside from the occasional direct train to Stockholm, most trips from Oslo to Copenhagen or Stockholm require a change in Sweden. From June through August only, direct night trains run from Oslo to Stockholm and to Malmö, Sweden (which is very close to Copenhagen).

From Oslo by Train to Bergen: Oslo and Bergen are linked by a spectacularly scenic train ride (3–5/day, 7 hrs, overnight possible daily except Sat). Many travelers take it as part of the **Norway in a Nutshell** route, which combines train, ferry, and bus travel in an unforgettably beautiful trip. For information on times and prices, see the next chapter.

By Train to: Lillehammer (hourly, 2.5 hrs), **Kristiansand** (4/day, 4.5 hrs), **Copenhagen** (4/day, 8 hrs, transfer at Göteborg and likely Malmö; for night train—which runs June–Aug only—sleep on the direct train to Malmö, Sweden, arrive Malmö Central Station around 6:40, easy transfer to Copenhagen, www.sj.se), **Stockholm** (2/day direct InterCity trains, 6 hrs; 2/day with changes in Karlestad or Katrineholm, 7 hrs; plus a direct 9-hour night train June–Aug only).

By Bus to Stockholm: Taking the bus to Stockholm is cheaper but slower than the train (2/day, 8 hrs, www.swebusexpress.se).

By Car to the Jotunheimen Mountains: See "Route Tips for Drivers" on page 294.

Overnight Cruise to Copenhagen

Consider connecting Oslo and Copenhagen by cruise ship. The boat leaves daily from Oslo at 17:00 (arrives in Copenhagen at 9:30 the following morning; going the other way, it departs Copenhagen at 17:00 and arrives in Oslo at 9:30; about 16 hours sailing each way). The boat leaves Oslo from the far (non-City Hall) side of the Akershus Fortress peninsula (get there via bus #60 from the train station, 2–3/hr, get off at Vippetangen stop and follow signs to DFDS ticket office). Boarding is from 15:30 to 16:00. From Oslo, you'll sail through the Oslofjord—not as dramatic as Norway's western fjords, but impressive if you're not going to Bergen. On board are three gourmet restaurants, dinner and breakfast buffets, cafés, nightclubs, shops, a sauna, hot tub, and swimming pool. This is fun and convenient, but more expensive and not as swanky as the Stockholm–Helsinki cruise (see page 470).

You can take this cruise one-way or do a round-trip from either city. Book online or call DFDS Seaways' Norwegian office at 22 41 90 90 (Mon–Fri 8:00–17:00, closed Sat–Sun, www.dfdsseaways.com), or in the US, call 800-533-3755 (www.seaeurope.com). Book in advance for the best prices. For more specifics and sample prices, see "Overnight Cruise to Oslo" on page 111.

NORWAY IN A NUTSHELL

A Scenic Journey to the Sognefjord

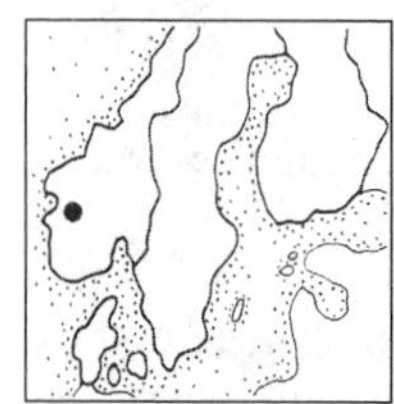

While Oslo and Bergen are the big draws for tourists, Norway is first and foremost a place of unforgettable natural beauty. There's a certain mystique about the "land of the midnight sun," but you'll get the most scenic travel thrills per mile, minute, and dollar by going west from Oslo rather than north.

Norway's greatest claims to scenic fame are her deep, lush fjords. Three million years ago, an ice age made this land as inhabitable as the center of Greenland. As the glaciers advanced and cut their way to the sea, they gouged out long grooves—today's fjords.

The entire west coast is slashed by stunning fjords, and the Sognefjord—Norway's longest (120 miles) and deepest (1 mile)—is tops. Anything but the Sognefjord is, at best, foreplay. The seductive Sognefjord has tiny but tough ferries, towering canyons, and isolated farms and villages marinated in the mist of countless waterfalls.

A series of well-organized and spectacular bus, train, and ferry connections—appropriately nicknamed "Norway in a Nutshell"—lays Norway's beautiful fjord country before you on a scenic platter. With the Nutshell, you'll delve into two offshoots of the Sognefjord, which make an upside-down "U" route: the Aurlandsfjord and the Nærøyfjord. You'll link the ferry ride to the rest of Norway with two trains and a bus: The main train is an express route that takes you through stark polar scenery above the tree line. To get from the express train down to the ferry, you'll catch an old-fashioned slow train one way (passing waterfalls and forests) and a bus the other way (offering fjord views and more waterfalls). All connections are designed for tourists, explained in

English, convenient, and easy. At the fjord you'll go through the town of Flåm (a transit hub), stop briefly at the workaday town of Aurland, and pass the hamlet of Undredal (by taking the Nutshell trip segments at your own pace, you can visit the latter two fjord towns on your own; all are described in this chapter).

This region enjoys mild weather for its latitude, thanks to the warm Gulf Stream. (When it rains in Bergen, it just drizzles here.) Recently the popularity of the Nutshell route has skyrocketed. And the 2005 completion of the longest tunnel in the world (15 miles between Flåm and Lærdal) rerouted the main E16 road between Bergen and Oslo through this idyllic fjord corner. All of this means that July and August come with a crush of crowds, dampening some of the area's magic. Unfortunately, many tourists are overcome by Nutshell tunnel-vision, and spend so much energy scurrying between boats, trains, and buses that they forget to simply enjoy the fjords. Relax—you're on vacation.

Planning Your Time

Even the blitz tourist needs a day for the Norway in a Nutshell trip. With more time, sleep in a town along the fjord, and customize your fjord experience to include sights outside the Nutshell.

Day 1: The Nutshell works well as a single day (one-way between Oslo and Bergen in either direction, or as a long day trip from either city). Those with a car and only one day should leave the car in Oslo and do the Nutshell by train, bus, and boat. If you're using public transportation and want to make efficient use of your time, organize your trip so that it ends in Bergen, or return to Oslo on a night train (sleeping through all the scenery you saw westbound).

Day 2: If you have enough time, spend the night somewhere on the Sognefjord—either along the Nutshell route itself (in Flåm or Aurland; accommodations listed later), or in another, even more appealing fjordside town (such as Balestrand or Solvorn, both described in the next chapter).

With More Time: The Sognefjord deserves more than a day. If you can spare the time, venture off the Nutshell route. You can easily connect to some non-Nutshell towns (such as Balestrand) via the handy express boat. Drivers can improve on the Nutshell by taking a northern route: From Oslo, drive through the Gudbrandsdal Valley, go over the Jotunheimen Mountains, then along Lustrafjord to Balestrand; from there, you can cross the Sognefjord on a car ferry (such as Kaupanger–Gudvangen) and drive the Nutshell route on to Bergen. (Most of these sights, and the car ferry connection, are covered in the next two chapters.) For more tips, see the "Beyond the Nutshell" sidebar.

Beyond the Nutshell

The Sognefjord is the ultimate natural thrill Norway has to offer, and there's no doubt that the Nutshell route outlined in this chapter is the most efficient way to see it quickly. Unfortunately, its trains, buses, and boats are thronged with other visitors who have the same idea. Those who stick with the Nutshell crowd enjoy it, but—as they spend the day jostling with a United Nations of tourists for the best photo—can't shake that lemming feeling.

Travelers with a bit more time, and the willingness to chart their own course, often have a more rewarding Sognefjord experience. It's surprisingly easy to break out of the Nutshell and hit the northern part of the Sognefjord (for example, using the Bergen-Vik-Balestrand-Aurland-Flåm express boat, described on page 267).

In the next chapter, you'll find some tempting stopovers on the north bank of the Sognefjord, including adorable fjordside villages (such as Balestrand and Solvorn), evocative stave churches (including Hopperstad and Urnes), and a chance to get up close to a glacier (at the Nigard Glacier).

Read up on your options, then be adventurous about mixing and matching the fjordside attractions that appeal to you most. Use the Nutshell as a springboard for diving into the Back Door fjords of your travel dreams.

Orientation

The most exciting single-day trip you could make from Oslo or Bergen is this circular train/boat/bus/train jaunt through fjord country. Everybody does this famous trip... and if you're looking for a delicious slice of Norway's scenic grandeur, so should you.

Local TIs (listed throughout this chapter) are well-informed about your options, and they sell tickets for various segments of the trip. At TIs, train stations, and hotels, look for souvenir-worthy brochures with photos, descriptions, and exact times (a sidebar later in this chapter has sample schedules).

Route Overview: The route works round-trip from Oslo or Bergen, or one-way between Oslo and Bergen (going in either direction). The basic idea is this: Take a train halfway across the mountainous spine of Norway, make your way down to the Sognefjord for a boat cruise, then climb back up out of the fjord and get back on the main train

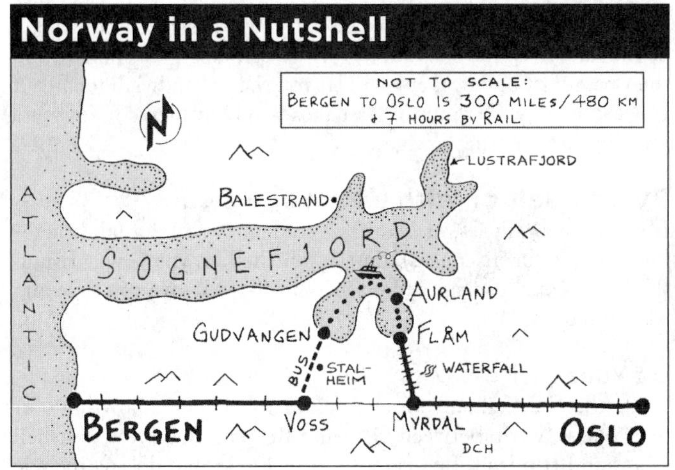

line. Each of these steps is explained in the self-guided tour, below. Transportation along the Nutshell route is carefully coordinated. If any segment of the journey is delayed, your transportation for the next segment will wait (because everyone on board is catching the same connection).

When to Go: The Nutshell trip is possible all year. In the summer (late June–late Aug), the connections are most convenient, the weather is most likely to be good...and the route is at its most crowded. Outside of this time, sights close and schedules become more challenging. Some say the Nutshell is most beautiful in winter, though schedules are severely reduced (and you can't do it as a day trip from Oslo). It's easy to confirm schedules, connections, and prices locally or online (latest info posted each May on www.ruteinfo.net).

Express Boat to Balestrand and Bergen: If you don't want to do the Nutshell Route, take note of this very handy and speedy express boat connecting this area (Aurland and Flåm) with two other worthwhile destinations: Balestrand (on the Sognefjord's northern bank) and Bergen. While this boat misses the best fjord (Nærøyfjord), many travelers use it to craft their own itinerary that escapes the Nutshell rut. For more on this boat, see page 267.

Eating: Options along the route aren't great—on the Nutshell I'd consider food just as a source of nutrition and forget about fine dining. You can buy some food on the fjord cruises (30–60-kr hot dogs, burgers, and pizza) and the Oslo–Bergen train (50–100-kr hot meals, 110-kr daily specials). Depending on the timing of your layovers, Myrdal or Flåm are your best lunch-stop options (both train stations have decent cafeterias, and other eateries surround the Flåm station)—although you won't have a lot of time there if making the journey all in one day. Your best bet is to pack a picnic lunch. While some hotels sell a sack lunch assembled from their breakfast buffet, many will let you snag a sandwich for free if you ask politely. Or you can plan ahead and buy picnic fixings at a grocery store to bring along.

By Yourself or with a Package Deal?

If you have a railpass, or if you're a student or a senior (and therefore eligible for discounts), do the Nutshell on your own. If not, the Fjord Tours packages (described below) will save you time and a bit of money.

On Your Own

To do the Nutshell on your own without a railpass, allow 1,300 kr for a one-way trip between Oslo and Bergen. Doing the Nutshell as a round-trip from Bergen costs only 900 kr, but doesn't include the majestic train ride between Myrdal and Oslo. Likewise, the 2,000-kr round-trip from Oslo doesn't go all the way to Bergen, but does include all the must-sees (the Voss-Bergen stretch is the least-thrilling stretch).

Railpass Discounts: If you have any railpass that includes Norway, the Oslo–Bergen train is covered (except a 50-kr reservation fee for second class; free for first-class passholders) and the Myrdal–Flåm Flåmsbana train is discounted (to 140 kr). You still have to pay full fare for the Gudvangen–Voss bus (86 kr) and the boat cruise (230 kr). Your total one-way cost between Oslo and Bergen: about 450 kr with a first-class pass, 500 kr with a second-class pass.

Buying Tickets: You can get Nutshell train tickets, including the Myrdal–Flåm segment, at the train station in Oslo or Bergen. In summer it's smart to reserve the Oslo–Myrdal segment in advance (see below). Purchase your fjord-cruise ticket on the boat or from the TI in Flåm (or reserve a day ahead in peak season; see below), and buy the tickets for the Gudvangen bus on board from the driver. Always ask about senior and student discounts.

Reservations: At the busiest part of peak season (July–mid-Aug), the Oslo–Bergen train—especially the segment between Oslo and Myrdal—can fill up well in advance: *It's very important to reserve a seat at least a week ahead.* Do it as soon as your itinerary is set: Dial 81 50 08 88 (from the US: 011-47-81-50-08-88), press 4 for English, and book with a credit card. It can be difficult to get through to this number in peak season—keep trying. Once connected, you can buy a ticket or, if you have a railpass, make a seat reservation. You can also buy tickets—but not make railpass reservations—online at www.nsb.no.

It's also wise to reserve ahead for the Flåm–Gudvangen fjord cruise (see page 240). Although you can't make a reservation for

Sample Norway in a Nutshell Schedules

Here are several one-day options for doing the Nutshell in the summer (late June-late Aug). Confirm specific times before your trip (www.ruteinfo.net).

Oslo-Bergen: Train departs Oslo-8:11, arrives Myrdal-12:53; Flåmsbana train departs Myrdal-13:02, arrives Flåm-14:00; boat departs Flåm-15:10, arrives Gudvangen-17:00; bus departs Gudvangen upon arrival, arrives Voss-19:05; train departs Voss-19:20, arrives Bergen-20:34. (Several departures allow you to stop over in Voss.)

Bergen-Oslo: Train departs Bergen-8:40, arrives Voss-9:54; bus departs Voss-10:00, arrives Gudvangen-11:10; boat departs Gudvangen-11:30, arrives Flåm-13:40; Flåmsbana train departs Flåm-16:05, arrives Myrdal-17:03; train departs Myrdal-17:52, arrives Oslo-22:32.

Day Trip from Oslo: Train departs Oslo-6:33, arrives Myrdal-11:41; Flåmsbana train departs Myrdal-12:11, arrives Flåm-13:05; boat departs Flåm-13:20, arrives Gudvangen-15:20; bus departs Gudvangen-15:30, arrives Voss-16:50; train departs Voss-17:10, arrives Oslo-22:32.

Day Trip from Bergen: Train departs Bergen-8:40, arrives Voss-9:54; bus departs Voss-10:00, arrives Gudvangen-11:10; boat departs Gudvangen-11:30, arrives Flåm-13:40; Flåmsbana train departs Flåm-14:50, arrives Myrdal-15:47; train departs Myrdal-15:56, arrives Bergen-17:52.

Variations: If you spend a night (or more) on the fjords, you have many options other than the speedy itineraries outlined above. One popular variation is to take the express boat from Bergen to Balestrand for an overnight, then plunge into the Nutshell the next day (or vice versa—do the Nutshell partway, then boat to Bergen; for express boat information, see page 267).

the Myrdal–Flåm train or the Gudvangen–Voss bus, this won't pose a problem for you.

Package Deals

Fjord Tours sells the Nutshell package and other package trips at all Norwegian State Railways stations, including Oslo and Bergen, or through their customer-service line in Norway (tel. 81 56 82 22, www.fjordtours.no). The costs of the Nutshell packages are as follows: one-way from Bergen or Oslo-1,295 kr; round-trip from Oslo via Voss (but not Bergen)-1,800 kr; round-trip from Oslo via Bergen-2,055 kr; round-trip from Bergen via Myrdal (but not Oslo)-935 kr. They also sell a "Sognefjord in a Nutshell" tour, which takes an express boat from Bergen to Flåm, then picks up the Nutshell route from there (round-trip back to Bergen-1,115 kr; one-way to Oslo-1,470 kr). Note that the trip only goes once daily in winter (Oct–April).

Self-Guided Tour

▲▲▲Norway in a Nutshell

If you only have one day for this region, it'll be a thrilling day. The following segments of the Nutshell route are narrated from Oslo to Bergen. If you're going the other way, hold the book upside down.

▲▲Oslo–Bergen Train

This is simply the most spectacular train ride in northern Europe. The scenery crescendos as you climb over Norway's mountainous spine. After a mild three hours of deep woods and lakes, you're into the barren, windswept heaths and glaciers. These tracks were begun in 1894 to link Stockholm and Bergen, but Norway won its independence from Sweden in 1905, so the line served to link the two main cities in the new country—Oslo and Bergen. The entire railway, an amazing engineering feat completed in 1909, is 300 miles long; peaks at 4,266 feet, which, at this Alaskan latitude, is far above the tree line; goes under 18 miles of snow sheds; trundles over 300 bridges; and passes through 200 tunnels in just under seven hours.

Here's what you'll see traveling westward from Oslo: Leaving Oslo, you pass through a six-mile-long tunnel and stop in Drammen, Norway's fifth-largest town. The scenery stays low-key and woodsy up Hallingdal Valley until you reach Geilo, a popular ski resort. Then you enter a land of big views and tough little cabins. Finse, at about 4,000 feet, is the highest stop on the line. From here, you enter the longest high-mountain stretch of railway in Europe. Much of the line is protected by snow tunnels. The scenery gets more dramatic as you approach Myrdal (MEER-doll). Just before Myrdal, look to the right and down into the Flåm Valley (Flåmsdalen), where the branch line winds its way down to the fjord. Nutshell travelers get off at Myrdal.

Cost: Note that the Nutshell route includes only part of this train ride (as a day trip from Oslo, for instance, you take the Oslo–Myrdal and Voss–Oslo segments). Here are the one-way fares for various segments: Oslo–Bergen-788 kr, Oslo–Myrdal-637 kr, Myrdal–Voss-105 kr, Myrdal–Bergen-250 kr, Voss–Bergen-170 kr.

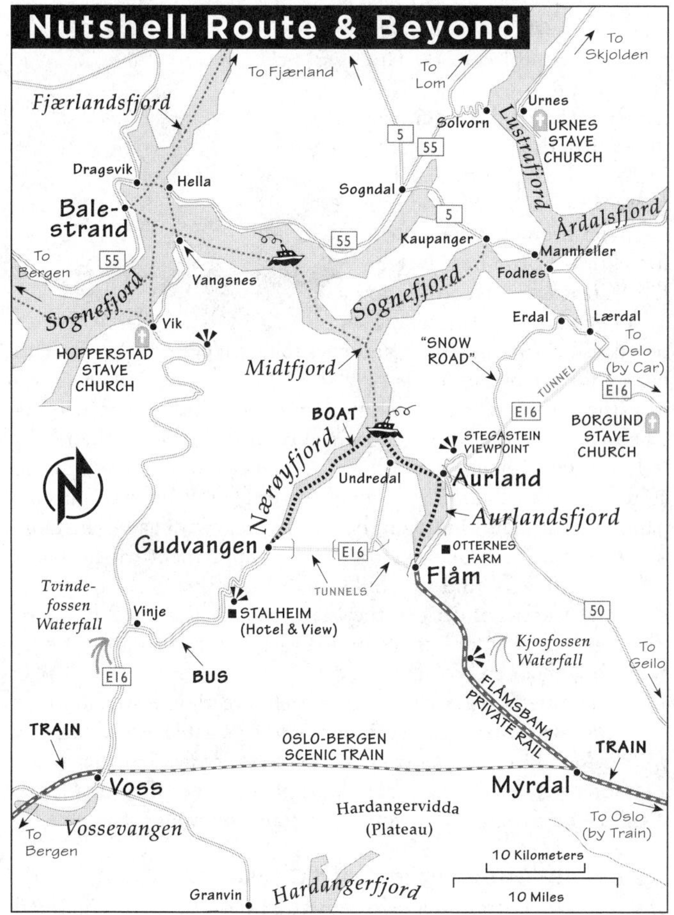

Remember, second-class railpass-holders pay just 50 kr to reserve, and first-class passholders pay nothing. Anyone can pay 90 kr extra to upgrade to "Komfort" class, with more legroom, reclining seats, free coffee and tea, and an electrical socket for your laptop (reserve ahead or ask the conductor when you board).

Schedule: This train runs three to five times per day (overnight possible daily except Sat). The segment from Oslo to Myrdal takes 4.75–5.5 hrs; going all the way to Bergen takes 7–7.5 hours.

Reservations: In peak season, remember to get reservations for this train at least a week in advance (see page 236).

▲▲Myrdal-Flåm Train (Flåmsbana)

The little 12-mile spur line leaves the Oslo–Bergen line at Myrdal (2,800 feet), which is nothing but a scenic high-altitude train junction with a decent cafeteria. From Myrdal, the train winds down to Flåm (sea level) through 20 tunnels (more than three miles' worth) in 55 thrilling minutes. It's party time on board, and the engineer even stops the train for photos at the best waterfall, Kjosfossen. According to a Norwegian legend, a temptress lives behind these falls and tries to lure men to the rocks with her singing...look out for her.

The train line is an even more impressive feat of engineering when you realize it's not a cogwheel train—it's held to the tracks only by steel wheels, though it does have five separate braking systems. Before boarding, pick up the free, multilingual souvenir pamphlet with lots of info on the trip (or see www.flaamsbana.no).

Cost: 230 kr one-way (or 140-kr supplement for railpass-holders), 330 kr round-trip (280 kr with a railpass). You can buy tickets at the ticket desk in the Flåmsbana stations in Myrdal or Flåm, at local TIs, or—if you're in a rush to make a tight connection—buy them on board.

Schedule: The train departs in each direction nearly hourly.

Reservations: Reservations are not possible—you can buy your ticket ahead (at any train station in Norway), but that won't guarantee you a seat on a particular train. (Ticket-sellers assure me it's exceedingly rare not to get on the train you want.)

▲▲▲Flåm-Gudvangen Fjord Cruise

The Flåmsbana train deposits you at **Flåm,** a scenic, functional transit hub at the far end of the Aurlandsfjord. If you're doing the Nutshell route nonstop, follow the crowds and hop on the sightseeing boat that'll take you to **Gudvangen** (listen for the train conductor to announce which pier number to go to). With minimal English narration, the boat takes you close to the goats, sheep, waterfalls, and awesome cliffs.

You'll cruise up the lovely **Aurlandsfjord,** stop at the town of **Aurland** (a good home base), pass **Undredal,** and hang a left at the stunning **Nærøyfjord** ("Narrow Fjord"). The cruise ends at the apex of the Nærøyfjord, in **Gudvangen.**

The Facts on Fjords

The process that created the majestic Sognefjord began during an ice age about three million years ago. A glacier up to 6,500 feet thick slid downhill at an inch an hour, following a former river valley on its way to the sea. Rocks embedded in the glacier gouged out a steep, U-shaped valley, displacing enough rock material to form a mountain 13 miles high. When the climate warmed up, the ice age came to an end. The melting glaciers retreated and the sea level rose nearly 300 feet, flooding the valley now known as the Sognefjord. The fjord is more than a mile deep, flanked by 3,000-foot mountains—for a total relief of 9,300 feet. Waterfalls spill down the cliffs, fed by runoff from today's glaciers. Powdery sediment tinges the fjords a cloudy green, the distinct color of glacier melt.

Why are there fjords on the west coast of Norway, but not, for instance, on the east coast of Sweden? The creation of a fjord requires a setting of coastal mountains, a good source of moisture, and a climate cold enough for glaciers to form and advance. Due to the earth's rotation, the prevailing winds in higher latitudes blow from west to east, so chances of glaciation are ideal where there is an ocean to the west of land with coastal mountains. When the winds blow east over the water, they pick up a lot of moisture, then bump up against the coastal mountain range, and dump their moisture in the form of snow—which feeds the glaciers that carve valleys down to the sea.

You can find fjords along the northwest coast of Europe—including western Norway and Sweden, Denmark's Faroe Islands, Scotland's Shetland Islands, Iceland, and Greenland; the northwest coast of North America (from Puget Sound in Washington state north to Alaska); the southwest coast of South America (Chile); the west coast of New Zealand's South Island; and on the continent of Antarctica.

As you travel through Scandinavia, bear in mind that, while we English-speakers use the word "fjord" to mean only glacier-cut inlets, Scandinavians often use it in a more general sense to include bays, lakes, and lagoons that weren't formed by glacial action.

The trip is breathtaking in any weather. For the last hour, as you sail down the Nærøyfjord, camera-clicking tourists scurry around the drool-stained deck like nervous roosters, scratching fitfully for a photo that will catch the magic. Waterfalls turn the black cliffs into bridal veils, and you can nearly reach out and touch the cliffs of the Nærøyfjord. It's the world's narrowest fjord: six miles long and as little as 820 feet wide and 40 feet deep. On a sunny day, the ride is one of those fine times—like when you're high on the tip of an Alp—when a warm camaraderie spontaneously combusts between the strangers who've come together for the experience.

Cost: For the whole route (Flåm–Gudvangen), you'll pay 245 kr one-way (123 kr for students with ISIC cards, 340 kr round-trip). Taking the boat for just the 20-min hop between Flåm and Aurland costs 78 kr (more than twice as expensive and twice as slow as the bus—see "Getting There," page 250). There are no rail-pass discounts.

Schedule: From late June through late August, boats leave Flåm daily at 9:00, 11:00, 13:20, and 15:10; and leave Gudvangen daily at 10:30, 11:30, 13:20, and 16:00. But note that frequency drops off-season (3/day early June and late Aug–mid-Sept; 2/day May and late Sept; only 1/day Oct–April).

Reservations: It's possible to reserve, but only necessary in the very peak of the season (July–mid-Aug), when the boats can occasionally fill up. To reserve, email fylkesbaatane@fjord1.no or call 55 90 70 70 by 14:00 one business day before.

Other Ways to Cruise Nærøyfjord: While most visitors thunder onto the state-run ferry described above, consider taking a round-trip on a Sognefjorden Cruise ship, or a thrilling ride on little inflatable FjordSafari speedboats (both described later, under "Sights near Flåm"; see page 245).

▲Gudvangen–Voss Bus

Gudvangen is little more than a boat dock and giant tourist kiosk. Nutshellers get off the boat at Gudvangen and take the one-hour bus to Voss (buses meet each ferry—but confirm this in advance if you plan to take the last boat of the day, which arrives in Gudvangen at about 20:00—the ferry crew can call ahead to be sure the bus waits for you). Most buses take the extra-scenic route via Stalheim (described below).

First the bus takes you up the **Nærøydal.** After crossing a river, the bus climbs up a corkscrew series of switchbacks flanked

by a pair of dramatic waterfalls. At the top of this road, most buses stop at the landmark **Stalheim Hotel** for a last grand view back into fjord country. Though this hotel dates from 1885, there's been an inn here since about 1700, where the royal mailmen would change horses. The hotel is geared for tour groups (genuine trolls sew the pewter buttons on the sweaters), but the priceless view from the backyard is free. Stop in the living room to survey the art showing this perch in the 19th century.

The bus rejoins the main road and heads through pastoral countryside to Voss. Just before Voss, look to the right for the wide and tumbling **Tvindefossen waterfall.** Drivers will find the grassy meadow and flat rocks at its base ideal for letting the mist fog their glasses and enjoying a drink or snack (be discreet, as "picnics are forbidden").

Cost: 76 kr, pay on board, no railpass discounts.

Reservations: Not possible or necessary.

Voss

The Nutshell bus from Gudvangen drops you at the Voss train station, which is on the Oslo–Bergen train line. Drivers should zip right through, and Nutshellers should catch the next train out. A plain town in a lovely lake-and-mountain setting, Voss lacks the striking fjordside scenery of Flåm, Aurland, or Undredal, and is basically a home base for summer or winter sports (Norway's Winter Olympics teams often practice here).

Voss has a **TI** (June–Aug Mon–Fri 8:00–19:00, Sat 9:00–19:00, Sun 12:00–19:00; Sept–May Mon–Fri 8:30–15:30, closed Sat–Sun; in the center of town at Uttrågata 9, tel. 56 52 08 00), a 13th-century church, and little else. Fans of American football will want to see the humble monument to player and coach Knute Rockne, who was born in Voss in 1888; look for the metal memorial plaque on a rock near the train station. Two miles outside town, the Mølstertunet Folk Museum has 16 buildings showing off farm life in the 17th and 18th centuries (50 kr; mid-May–mid-Sept daily 10:00–17:00; mid-Sept–mid-May Mon–Fri 10:00–15:00, Sun 12:00–15:00, closed Sat; Mølstervegen 143, tel. 56 51 15 11).

▲Voss-Bergen Train

The least exciting segment of the trip—but still pleasantly scenic—this train chugs along the valley between the midsize town of Voss (described above) and Bergen. For the best scenery, sit on the right side of the train if coming from Oslo/Voss, or the left side if coming from Bergen. Between Voss and Dale, you'll pass several scenic lakes; near Bergen, you'll go along the Veafjord.

Cost: The train costs 170 kr between Voss and Bergen and is fully covered by railpasses that include Norway.

Schedule and Reservations: Unlike the long-distance Oslo–Bergen journey, this line is also served by more frequent commuter trains (about hourly, 1–1.25 hrs), and reservations aren't necessary.

Voss-Oslo Train: Note that if you're doing the Nutshell round-trip from Oslo, you can catch the train from Voss (rather than Bergen) back to Oslo. The trip takes 5.5–6 hours and costs 683 kr; reservations are strongly recommended in peak season.

Flåm

Flåm (sometimes spelled Flaam, pronounced "flome")—where the boat and Flåmsbana train meet, at the head of the Aurlandsfjord—feels more like a transit junction than a village. But its striking setting, easy transportation connections, and touristy bustle make it appealing as a home base for exploring the nearby area.

Orientation to Flåm

Most of Flåm's services are inside the train station, including the TI (see below), train ticket desk, several Internet terminals, post office, public WC, cafeteria, and souvenir shops hawking overpriced reindeer pelts (cheaper in Bergen). Just outside the station, the little red shed at the head of the tracks serves as a left-luggage desk (25 kr, daily 8:00–19:45, on your right as you depart the train, ring bell if nobody's there), and displays a chart of the services you'll find in the station. The boat dock for fjord cruises is just beyond the end of the tracks. Surrounding the station are a grocery store (Mon–Thu 9:00–17:00, Fri 9:00–18:00, Sat 9:00–15:00, closed Sun) and a smattering of hotels, hostels, travel agencies, and touristy restaurants. Aside from a few scattered farmhouses and some homes lining the road, there's not much of a town here. (The old town center—where tourists rarely venture, and which you'll pass on the Flåm–Myrdal train—is a few miles up the river, in the valley.)

Tourist Information

At the TI inside the train station, you can purchase your boat tickets and load up on handy brochures (daily May–Sept 8:30–16:00, June–Aug also 16:30–20:00, closed Oct–April, tel. 57 63

21 06, www.visitflam.com or www.alr.no, very helpful Vladimir). Answers to most of your questions can be found on the walls and at the counter here. Bus schedules, boat and train timetables, maps, and more are photocopied and available for your convenience (and the staff's).

Sights near Flåm

Flåm's village activities are all on the pier. There's a free historic train museum next to track 1, a fjord "panorama" movie (50 kr, 23 min), and the Aegir Bryggeri, a micro-brewery offering tastes of its five beers (65 kr) in a great woody brew-pub setting. But the main reason people come to Flåm is to leave it. If you want to linger, consider renting a rowboat or kayak to go out on the usually calm, peaceful waters of the fjord. You can paddle near the walls of the fjord and really get a sense of the immensity of these mountains.

Because Aurland and Flåm are close together (10 minutes away by car or bus, or 20 minutes by boat), I've also listed attractions "Near Aurland," below.

▲▲▲Cruising Nærøyfjord

The most scenic fjord I've seen anywhere in Norway is about an hour from Flåm (basically the last half of the 2-hour Flåm–Gudvangen trip). There are several ways to cruise it: You can take the state-run ferry, described above as part of the Norway in a Nutshell trip (4-hour round-trips departing Flåm at 9:00, 11:00, and 13:20, 340 kr; these also stop in Aurland, and the cruise ends in Gudvangen). Two other Flåm-based options follow:

Sognefjorden Cruise—This private company runs round-trip cruises—from Flåm to Gudvangen and back to Flåm—daily from mid-June through August (330 kr, 660 kr for family of four, 10:00–13:00 or 13:15–16:30 with a 45-min stop in Undredal, tel. 57 66 00 55).

▲▲FjordSafari to Nærøyfjord—FjordSafari takes little groups out onto the fjord in small, open Zodiac-type boats with an English-speaking guide. Participants wear full-body weather suits, furry hats, and spacey goggles (making everyone on the boat look like crash-test dummies). As the boat rockets across the water, you'll be thankful for the gear, no matter what the weather. You'll get the same scant information and stops as on the slow ferry, except that Safari boats stop right under a towering rock cliff—a magnificent experience. Their two-hour Flåm–Gudvangen–Flåm tour focuses on the Nærøyfjord, and gets you all the fjord magnificence you can imagine (500 kr). Their three-hour tour (640 kr) is the same as the two-hour tour, except that it includes a stop in Undredal, where you can see goat cheese being made and wander that sleepy village. They run several departures daily from June through August (fewer off-season, kids get discounts, tel. 99 09 08 60, www.fjordsafari.no, Johanna). They also offer a 90-minute "mini" tour that costs 430 kr and misses the Nærøyfjord...so what's the point?

▲Flåm Valley Bike Ride or Hike

For the best single-day, non-fjord activity from Flåm, take the train to Myrdal, then hike or mountain-bike along the road (part gravel but mostly paved) back down to Flåm (2–3 hours by bike, gorgeous waterfalls, great mountain scenery, and a cute church with an evocative graveyard, but no fjord views). The Flåm TI rents mountain bikes (50 kr/hr, 250 kr/day) as does the youth hostel (50 kr/hr, 200 kr/day). It costs 80 kr to take a bike to Myrdal on the train. You can hike just the best two hours from Myrdal to Berekvam, where you can catch the train into the valley. Pick up the helpful map with this and other hiking options (easy to strenuous) at the Flåm TI.

▲▲Otternes Farms

This humble but magical cluster of four centuries-old farms, realistically accessible only to drivers, is perched high on a ridge, up a twisty gravel road midway between Flåm and Aurland. Laila Kvellestad runs this low-key sight, valiantly working to save and share traditional life as it was back when butter was the farmers' gold. (That was before emigration decimated the workforce, coinage replaced barter, and industrialized margarine became more popular than butter, leaving farmers to eke out a living relying only on their goats and the cheese they produce.) Until 1919 the only road between Aurland and Flåm passed between this huddle of 27 buildings, high above the fjord. First settled in 1522, farmers lived here until the 1990s. Laila gives 45-minute English tours through several time-warp houses and barns at 10:00, 12:00, 14:00, and 16:00 (50 kr, June–Sept daily 10:00–17:00, tel. 57 63 11 32, www.otternes.no). It's wise to call first to confirm tour times and that it's open. For 170 kr, Laila serves a traditional lunch with your tour (sour-cream porridge, dried meat, dessert, and a drink).

Over (or Under) the Mountains, to Lærdal and Borgund

To reach these sights, you'll first head along the fjord to Aurland (described on page 250). Of the sights below, the Lærdal Tunnel,

Stegastein viewpoint, and Aurlandsvegen "Snow Road" are best for drivers. The Borgund Stave Church can be reached by car, or by bus from Flåm or Aurland.

For more specifics on driving through the Lærdal Tunnel or on the Aurlandsvegen "Snow Road," see below.

Lærdal Tunnel

Drivers find that this tunnel makes connecting Flåm and Lærdal a snap. It's the world's longest road-vehicle tunnel, stretching 15 miles between Aurland and Lærdal as part of the E16 highway. It also makes the wonderful Borgund Stave Church (described below) less than an hour's drive from Aurland. The downside to the tunnel is that it goes beneath my favorite scenic drive in Norway (the Aurlandsvegen "Snow Road," described next). But with a little more than an hour, you can drive through the tunnel to Lærdal and then return via the "Snow Road," with the Stegastein viewpoint as a finale, before dropping back into Aurland.

▲▲Stegastein Viewpoint and Aurlandsvegen "Snow Road"

With a car and clear weather, consider twisting up the mountain behind Aurland on route 243 for about 20 minutes for a fine view over the Aurlandsfjord. A new viewpoint called Stegastein—which looks like a giant, wooden, inverted number "7"—provides a platform from which you can enjoy stunning views across the fjords. Immediately beyond the viewpoint, you leave the fjord views and enter the mountaintop world of the Aurlandsvegen "Snow Road." When you finally hit civilization on the other side, you're a mile from the Lærdal tunnel entrance and about 30 minutes from the fine Borgund Stave Church.

▲▲Borgund Stave Church

About 16 miles east of Lærdal, in the village of Borgund, is Norway's most-visited and one of its best-preserved stave churches. Borgund's church comes with one of Norway's best stave-church history museums, which beautifully explains these icons of medieval Norway. Dating from around 1180, the interior features only a few later

additions, including a 16th-century pulpit, 17th-century stone altar, painted decorations, and crossbeam reinforcements.

The oldest and most authentic item in the church is the stone baptismal font. In medieval times, priests conducting baptisms would go outside to shoo away the evil spirits from an infant before bringing it inside the church for the ritual. (If infants died before being baptized, they couldn't be buried in the churchyard, so parents would put them in little coffins and hide them under the church's floorboards to get them as close as possible to God.)

Explore the dimly lit interior, illuminated only by the original, small, circular windows up high. Notice the X-shaped crosses of St. Andrew (the church's patron), carvings of dragons, and medieval runes.

Cost and Hours: 70 kr, buy tickets in museum across street, daily mid-June–mid-Aug 8:00–20:00, May–mid-June and mid-Aug–Sept 10:00–17:00, closed Oct–April. The museum has a shop and a fine little cafeteria serving filling and tasty lunches (70 kr soup with bread, tel. 57 66 81 09).

Getting There: It's about a 30-minute **drive** east of Lærdal, on E16 (the road to Oslo—if coming from Aurland or Flåm, consider taking the scenic route via the Stegastein viewpoint, described above). There's also a convenient **bus** connection: The bus departs Flåm and Aurland around midday and heads for the church, with a return bus departing Borgund in mid-afternoon (240 kr, get ticket from driver, about 1 hour each way, about 2 hours at the church, bus runs daily May–Sept).

Sleeping and Eating in Flåm

My recommended accommodations are away from the tacky train-station bustle, but a close enough walk to be convenient. The first two places are located along the waterfront a quarter-mile from the station: Walk around the little harbor (with the water on your left) for about 10 minutes. It's more enjoyable to follow the level, gravel waterfront path than to hike up the main road.

Dining options beyond your hotel's dining room or kitchenette are sparse. The cafeteria section of Furukroa Restaurant in the station complex has reasonably priced food.

$$$ Flåm Marina and Apartments, perched right on the fjord, is ideal for families and longer stays. They offer 10 new-feeling, self-catering apartments that sleep 2–4 people each. All units offer views of the fjord with a balcony, kitchenette, and small dining area (Db-1,095 kr June–late Sept, less off-season, 300 kr more for each additional adult, 150 kr more for each additional child, save 150 kr/person by using your own sheets, check online or ask about specials for longer stays, no breakfast, boat rental,

Sleep Code

(6 kr = about $1, country code: 47)
S = Single, **D** = Double/Twin, **T** = Triple, **Q** = Quad, **b** = bathroom, **s** = shower. All of these places accept credit cards.

To help you sort easily through these listings, I've divided the rooms into three categories, based on the price for a standard double room with bath:

$$$ Higher Priced—Most rooms 1,000 kr or more.
$$ Moderately Priced—Most rooms 600–1,000 kr.
$ Lower Priced—Most rooms 600 kr or less.

Note that the season is boom or bust here. It can be dead in June and packed in July and August.

laundry facilities, next to the guest harbor just below Heimly Pensjonat—see next, tel. 57 63 35 55, fax 57 63 35 44, www.flammarina.no, booking@flammarina.no).

$$ Heimly Pensjonat, with 23 straightforward rooms, is clean, efficient, and the best small hotel in town. Sit on the porch with new friends and watch the clouds roll down the fjord (Sb-895 kr, Db-995 kr, view Db costs 100 kr more in summer, extra bed-325 kr for adult or 225 kr for child, includes breakfast, cheaper Oct–May, Db rooms are mostly twins, try to reserve a room with a view at the standard price, bike and car rental, tel. 57 63 23 00, fax 57 63 23 40, www.heimly.no, post@heimly.no). The budget annex out back has more rooms that share bathrooms (D-470 kr, sheets and towels-90 kr/person, breakfast-95 kr).

$–$$ Flåm Youth Hostel and Camping Bungalows, voted Scandinavia's most beautiful campground, is run by the friendly Haland family, who rent the cheapest beds in the area (hostel: bunk in 4-bed room-190 kr, S-330 kr, D-470–570 kr; newer, fancier building: bunk in 4-bed room-265 kr, Db-755; 4-bed cabins-600–930 kr; for all beds: sheets-65 kr, towels-15 kr, showers-10 kr, 15 percent discount for members, no meals but kitchen access, laundry, apple grove, tel. 57 63 21 21, www.flaam-camping.no, camping@flaam-camping.no). It's a five-minute walk toward the valley from the train station: Cross the bridge and turn left up the main road; then look for the hostel on the right.

Aurland

A few miles north of Flåm, Aurland is more of a real town and less of a tourist depot. While it's nothing exciting (Balestrand is more lively and appealing, and Solvorn is cuter—see next chapter), it's a good, easygoing fjordside home base. And thanks to its location—on the main road and boat lines, near Flåm—it's relatively handy for those taking public transportation.

Getting There: Aurland is an easy 10-minute drive or bus trip from Flåm. If you want to stay overnight in Aurland, note that every train (except the late-night one) arriving in Flåm connects with a bus or boat to Aurland. Eleven buses and at least four ferries link the towns daily in summer (bus-30 kr, 10 min; boat-79 kr, 20 min). The Flåm–Gudvangen boat stops at Aurland en route, so it's possible to continue the Nutshell route from Aurland without backtracking to Flåm. Boat tickets bought at the Aurland TI come with a reservation (helpful on the busiest days in July and August, when the boats can fill up in Flåm). The Bergen–Balestrand–Flåm express boat stops in Aurland (for details, see page 267).

Orientation to Aurland

From Aurland's dingy boat dock area, walk one block up the paved street into the heart of town. On your right is the Spar supermarket (handy for picnic supplies) and Aurlandskafeen, the best restaurant in town (at the bridge). To your left is the Vangsgården Guest House and, behind it, Aurland Fjordhotel. To reach the TI, go straight ahead and bear right, then look behind the white church (800 years old and worth a peek). The bus stop, with buses to Flåm, is in front of the TI. For attractions near Aurland, see page 245.

Tourist Information

The TI stocks English-language brochures about hikes and day trips from the area, offers Internet terminals, and hosts a small history exhibit (mid-June–Aug Mon–Fri 9:00–18:00, Sat 10:00–17:00, closed Sun; Sept–mid-June Mon–Fri 8:30–15:30, closed Sat–Sun; behind the white church—look for green-and-white *i* sign; tel. 57 63 33 13, www.alr.no).

Sleeping in Aurland

$$$ Aurland Fjordhotel is big, modern, and centrally located. While a bit faded, many of its 30 rooms come with gorgeous fjord-view balconies (Sb-945 kr, Db-1,190 kr, Tb-1,290, check website for deals, includes breakfast, free Wi-Fi, tel. 57 63 35 05, fax 57

63 36 22, www.aurland-fjordhotel.com, post@aurland-fjordhotel.com, Steinar and Dorte Kjerstein).

$$ Vangsgården Guest House, closest to the boat landing, is a complex of old buildings dominating the old center of Aurland and run from one reception desk (tel. 57 63 35 80, www.vangsgaarden.no, vangsgaarden@alb.no, open all year, Astrid). The main building is a simple, old guest house offering basic rooms, a large self-serve kitchen, and a fine old-timey living room (Sb-550 kr, Db-875 kr). Their old-fashioned **Aabelheim Pension** is Aurland's best *koselig* (cozy)-like-a-farmhouse place (same prices). And lining the waterfront are their six adorable, woody cabins, each with a kitchen, bathroom, and two bedrooms (2–6 people, 1,075 kr, sheets-60 kr/person). The optional 75-kr breakfast is served in a wonderfully traditional dining room. The owners also run the Duehuset Pub (see "Eating in Aurland," below).

Near Aurland

$$ Skahjem Gard is an active farm run by Aurland's former deputy mayor, Nils Tore, and his wife Dagrun. They've converted their old sheep barn into seven spick-and-span family apartments with private bathrooms and kitchenettes, each sleeping up to four people (600 kr for studio, 700 kr with separate bedroom; rustic, cozy fishing cottage with a separate bathroom-450 kr; sheets and towels-70 kr/person, two miles up the valley—road #50, follow *Hol* signs, tel. 57 63 33 29, mobile 95 17 25 67, www.skahjemgard.com, nskahjem@online.no). It's a 25-minute walk from town, but Nils will pick up and drop off travelers at the ferry. This is best for families and foursomes with cars.

$ Winjum Huts, 500 yards toward the "Snow Road" from Aurland, rents 14 very basic cabins on a peaceful perch overlooking the majestic fjord (300–400 kr for up to 4 people, sheets-50 kr/person, no food available—just beer, tel. 57 63 34 61).

Eating in Aurland

Aurlandskafeen is a basic little café/diner serving the best-value food in town from its inviting cafeteria line. It's a block from the main square, at the bridge over the river. Sit upstairs or on its riverside terrace (90-kr daily plates, open daily 10:00–19:00—provided there are customers, tel. 57 63 36 66).

Duehuset Pub ("The Dove's House"), run by Vangsgården Guest House, serves up decent food in the center of town (190–240-kr pizzas big enough for four, 155–240-kr main dishes; June–Sept daily 15:00–23:00; Oct–May Fri–Sun 18:00–23:00, closed Mon–Thu). For cheap eats on dockside benches, gather a picnic at **Spar supermarket** (Mon–Fri 9:00–20:00, Sat 9:00–18:00, closed Sun).

Undredal

This almost impossibly remote community is home to about 75 people (and 400 goats). A huge percentage of the town's former population (300 people) emigrated to the US between 1850 and 1925. Undredal was accessible only by boat until 1988, when the road from Flåm opened. There's not much in the town, which is famous for its church and its goat cheese, but I'll never forget the picnic I had on the ferry wharf. While appealing, Undredal is quiet (some say better from the boat) and difficult to reach—you'll have to be patient to connect to other towns. For more information on the town, see www.undredal.no.

Undredal has Norway's smallest still-used **church,** seating 40 people for services every fourth Sunday. The original church was built in 1147 (look for the four original stave pillars inside). It was later expanded, pews added, and the interior painted in the 16th century in a way that resembles the traditional Norwegian *rosemaling* style (which came later). You can get in only with an overpriced 15-minute tour (60 kr, mid-June–mid-Aug daily 9:30–18:30, less in shoulder season, closed Oct–April).

Undredal's farms exist for cheese. The beloved local cheese comes in two versions: brown and white. The brown version is unaged and slightly sweet, while the white cheese has been aged and is mild and a bit salty. For samples, visit the Undredalsbui grocery store at the harbor (Mon–Fri 9:00–17:00, Sat 9:00–15:00, Sun 12:00–16:00).

The 15-minute drive from Flåm is mostly through a new tunnel. By sea, you'll sail past Undredal on the Flåm–Gudvangen boat (you can request a stop). To get the ferry to pick you up in Undredal, turn on the blinking light (though some express boats will not stop).

This sleepy town can accommodate about eight visitors a night. **$$ Undredal Overnatting** rents four modern, woody, comfortable rooms. The reception is at the café on the harbor, while the rooms are at the top of town (Db-700 kr, sheets-50 kr/person, tel. 57 63 30 80 or 57 63 31 00, visit@undredal.no).

MORE ON THE SOGNEFJORD

Balestrand • The Lustrafjord • Scenic Drives

Norway's world of fjords is decorated with medieval stave churches, fishing boats, cascading waterfalls, dramatic glaciers, and brightly painted shiplap villages. Travelers in a hurry zip through the fjords on the Norway in a Nutshell route (see previous chapter). Their heads spin from all the scenery, and most wish they had more time on the Sognefjord. If you can linger in fjord country, this chapter is for you.

Snuggle into the fjordside village of Balestrand, which has a variety of walking and biking options and a fun local arts scene. Balestrand is also a handy jumping-off spot for adventures great and small, including a day trip up the Fjærlandsfjord to gaze at a receding tongue of the Jostedal Glacier, or across the Sognefjord to the truly medieval-feeling Hopperstad Stave Church. Farther east is the Lustrafjord, a tranquil branch of the Sognefjord offering drivers an appealing concentration of visit-worthy sights. On the Lustrafjord, you'll enjoy enchanting hamlets with pristine fjord views (such as Solvorn), historic churches (including Norway's oldest stave church at Urnes and the humble village Dale Church in Luster), an opportunity to touch and even hike on a glacier (the Nigard), and more stunning fjord views.

This region is important to the people of Norway. After four centuries under Danish rule, the soul of the country was nearly lost. With independence and a constitution in the early 1800s, the country experienced a resurgence of national pride. Urban Norwegians headed for the fjord country here in the west. Norway's first Romantic painters and writers were drawn to Balestrand, inspired by the unusual light and dramatic views of mountains plunging

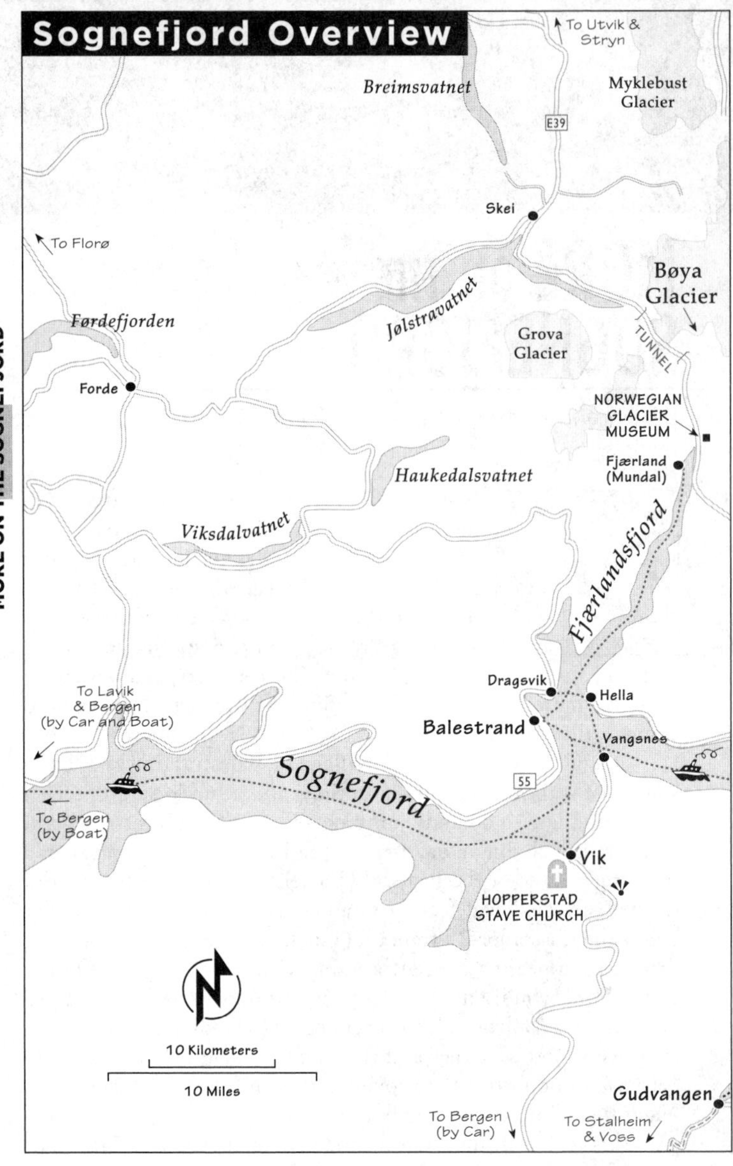
Sognefjord Overview
To Utvik & Stryn
Breimsvatnet
Myklebust Glacier
E39
Skei
To Florø
Bøya Glacier
Jølstravatnet
Førdefjorden
Grova Glacier
TUNNEL
Forde
NORWEGIAN GLACIER MUSEUM
Fjærland (Mundal)
Haukedalsvatnet
Viksdalvatnet
Fjærlandsfjord
Dragsvik
Hella
To Lavik & Bergen (by Car and Boat)
Balestrand
Vangsnes
Sognefjord
55
To Bergen (by Boat)
Vik
HOPPERSTAD STAVE CHURCH
10 Kilometers
10 Miles
Gudvangen
To Bergen (by Car)
To Stalheim & Voss

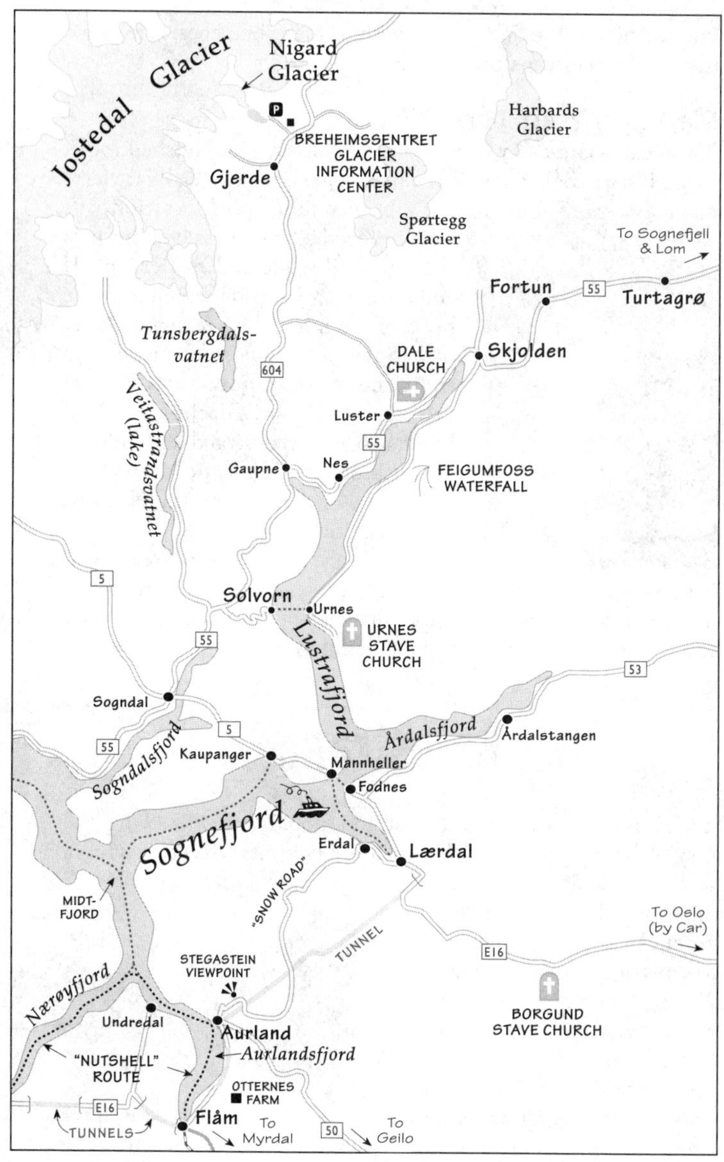
Jostedal Glacier
Nigard Glacier
BREHEIMSSENTRET GLACIER INFORMATION CENTER
Gjerde
Harbards Glacier
Spørtegg Glacier
To Sognefjell & Lom
Fortun
55
Turtagrø
Tunsbergdals-vatnet
604
DALE CHURCH
Skjolden
Veitastrandsvatnet (lake)
Luster
55
Gaupne
Nes
FEIGUMFOSS WATERFALL
5
Solvorn
Urnes
URNES STAVE CHURCH
55
Lustrafjord
53
Sogndal
5
Årdalsfjord
Årdalstangen
55
Sogndalsfjord
Kaupanger
Mannheller
Fodnes
Sognefjord
Erdal
Lærdal
"SNOW ROAD"
MIDT-FJORD
TUNNEL
To Oslo (by Car)
E16
STEGASTEIN VIEWPOINT
Nærøyfjord
Undredal
Aurland
Aurlandsfjord
BORGUND STAVE CHURCH
"NUTSHELL" ROUTE
OTTERNES FARM
E16
TUNNELS
Flåm
To Myrdal
50
To Geilo

into the fjords. The Sognefjord, with its many branches, is featured in more Romantic paintings than any other fjord.

Planning Your Time

If you can spare a day or two off the Norway in a Nutshell route, spend it here. Balestrand is the best home base, especially if you're relying on public transportation (it's well-connected by express boat both to the Nutshell scene and to Bergen). If you have a car, consider staying in the heart of the Lustrafjord region in sweet little Solvorn (easy ferry connection to the Urnes Stave Church and a short drive to the Nigard Glacier). As fjord home bases go, Balestrand and Solvorn are both better—but less convenient—than Flåm or Aurland on the Nutshell route (see previous chapter).

With one night in this area, you'll have to blitz the sights on the way between destinations; with two nights, you can slow your pace (and your pulse) to enjoy the fjord scenery and plenty of day-trip possibilities.

Balestrand

The pleasant fjord town of Balestrand (pop. 2,000) has a long history of hosting tourists, thanks to its landmark Kviknes Hotel. But it also feels real and lived-in, making Balestrand a nice mix of cuteness and convenience. The town is near, but not *too* near, the Nutshell bustle across the fjord—and yet it's an easy express-boat trip away if you'd like to dive into the Nuttiness. In short, consider Balestrand a worthwhile detour from the typical fjord visit—allowing you to dig deeper into the Sognefjord, just like the glaciers did during the last ice age.

With two nights, you can relax and consider some day trips: Cruise up the nearby Fjærlandsfjord for a peek at a distant tongue of the ever less-mighty Jostedal Glacier, or head across the Sognefjord to the beautiful Hopperstad Stave Church in Vik. Balestrand also has outdoor activities for everyone, from dreamy fjordside strolls and strenuous mountain hikes to wildly scenic bike

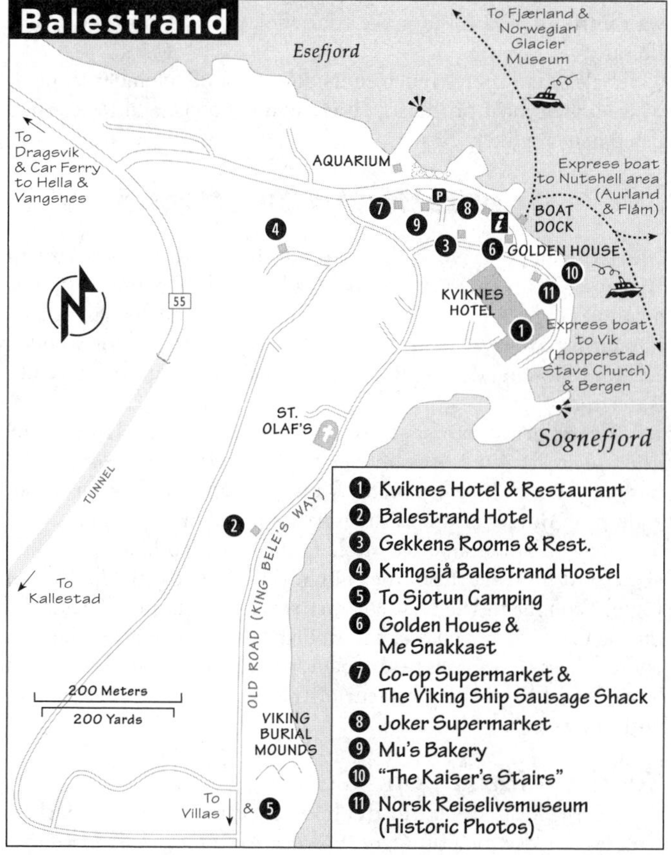

rides. For dinner, splurge on the memorable *smörgåsbord*-style *store koldt bord* dinner in the Kviknes Hotel dining room, then sip coffee from its balcony as you watch the sun set (or not) over the fjord.

Planning Your Time

Balestrand's key advantage is its easy express-boat connection to Bergen, offering an alternative route to the fjord from the typical Nutshell train-bus combo. Consider zipping here on the Bergen boat, then continuing on via the Nutshell route.

One night is enough to get a taste of Balestrand. But two nights buy you some time for day trips. Note that the first flurry of day trips depart early, around 7:30–8:05 (includes the boat to Vik/Hopperstad Stave Church, the full-day Fjærlandsfjord glacier excursion, and the Glacier Bus connection to Nigard Glacier), and the next batch departs around noon (the half-day Fjærlandsfjord glacier excursion and the boat to Flåm). If you wait until after 12:00 to make your choice, you'll miss the boat... literally.

Balestrand pretty much shuts down from September through May—when most of the activities, sights, hotels, and restaurants listed here are likely closed.

Orientation to Balestrand

Most travelers arrive in Balestrand on the express boat from Bergen or Flåm. The tidy harbor area has a TI, two grocery stores, a couple of galleries, a town history museum, and a small aquarium devoted to marine life found in the fjord. The historic wooden Kviknes Hotel and its ugly modern annex dominate Balestrand's waterfront.

Even during tourist season, Balestrand is quiet. How quiet? The police station closes on weekends. And it's tiny—from the harbor to the Balestrand Hotel is a five-minute stroll, and you can walk from the aquarium to the Kviknes Hotel in less than that.

Balestrand became accessible to the wider world in 1858 when an activist minister (from the church you see across the fjord from town) brought in the first steamer service. That put Balestrand on the Grand Tour map of the Romantic Age. Even the German Kaiser chose to summer here. Today, people from around the world come here to feel the grandeur of the fjord country and connect with the essence of Norway.

Tourist Information

At the TI, located next to the Joker supermarket at the harbor, pick up the free, helpful *Outdoor Activities in Balestrand* brochure. If you're planning on a longer hike, consider buying the good 70-kr hiking map. The TI has numerous brochures about the Sognefjord area and detailed information on the more challenging hikes. It offers terminals with Internet access (1 kr/min) and free Wi-Fi, rents bikes (40 kr/hr, 200 kr/day), sells day-trip excursions to the glacier, and more (late June–late Aug Mon–Sat 7:30–18:00, Sun 10:00–17:30, shorter hours in spring and fall, closed Oct–April, tel. 57 69 12 55—answered all year).

Local Guide: Bjørg Bjøberg, who runs the Golden House art gallery, knows the town well and is happy to show visitors around (500 kr/2 hours, tel. 91 56 28 42).

Sights in Balestrand

Balestrand Harborfront Stroll—The tiny harbor stretches from the aquarium to the big, old Kviknes Hotel. Stroll its length, starting at the aquarium (described later) and little marina. Across the street, at The Viking Ship shack, a German woman named Carola sells German sausages with an evangelical zeal (see "Eating in Balestrand," later). Next door, the Spindelvev ("Spider's Web") shop sells handicrafts made by people with physical and mental disabilities. A local home for the disabled was closed in the 1980s, but many of its former residents stayed in Balestrand because the government gave them pensions and houses in town.

Then, in the ugly modern strip mall, you'll find the TI, supermarket, and a community bulletin board with the schedule for the summer cinema (the little theater, 800 yards away, runs films nightly in their original language). On the corner is the Golden House art gallery and museum (described later). Just beyond that is the dock where the big Bergen-Sognefjord express catamaran ties up.

Across the street is a cute white house (at #8), which used to stand at the harborfront until the big Joker supermarket and Kviknes Hotel, with its modern annex, partnered to ruin the town center. This little house was considered historic enough to be airlifted 100 yards to this new spot. It's flanked by two other historic buildings, housing a gallery and an artisans' workshop.

Farther along, find the rust-red building that was the waiting room for the 19th-century steamer that first brought tourism to town. Today it houses the Norsk Reiselivsmuseum (Norwegian Travel Museum). It's filled with historic photos, described in English, that show this part of Norway over the last 150 years (free and open daily).

Walk a few steps farther, and stop at the tall stone monument erected to celebrate the North Bergen Steamship Company. Its boats first connected Balestrand to the rest of the world in 1858. In front of the monument, some nondescript concrete steps lead into the water. These are "The Kaiser's Stairs," built for the German emperor, Kaiser Wilhelm II, who made his first summer visit (complete with navy convoy) in 1899 and kept returning until the outbreak of World War I.

Behind the monument stands one of the largest old wooden buildings in Norway, the Kviknes Hotel. It was built in the 1870s and faces the rare little island in the fjord, which helped give the town its name: "Balestrand" means the strand or promenade in front of an island. (The island is now connected to the hotel's front yard and is part of a playground for its guests.) Hike up the black driveway that leads from the monument to the hotel's modern lobby. Go inside and find (to your left) the plush old lounge, a virtual painting gallery. All the pieces are by artists from this area, celebrating the natural wonder of the fjord country—part of the trend that helped 19th-century Norway reconnect with its heritage. (While you're here, consider making a reservation and choosing a table for a *smörgåsbord* dinner tonight.) Leave the hotel lobby (from the door opposite to the one you entered), and head up to St. Olaf's Church (300 yards, described next). To continue this stroll, take King Bele's Way (described later) up the fjord.

St. Olaf's Church—This distinctive wooden church was built in 1897. Construction was started by Margaret Sophia Kvikne, the wife of Knut Kvikne (of the Kviknes Hotel family; her portrait is in the rear of the nave), but she died in 1894, before the church was finished. This devout Englishwoman wanted a church in Balestrand where English services were held...and to this day, bells ring to announce services by British clergy (free, open daily, services in English every Sun late May–Aug). St. Olaf, who brought Christianity to Norway in the 11th century, was the country's patron saint in Catholic times. The church was built in a "Neo-stave" style, with lots of light from its windows and an altar painting inspired by the famous *Risen Christ* statue in Copenhagen's Cathedral of Our Lady. Here, Christ is flanked by fields of daisies (called "Priests' Collars" in Norwegian) and peace lilies. From the door of the church, enjoy a good view of the island in the fjord.

Golden House (Det Gylne Hus)—This golden-colored house facing the ferry landing was built as a general store in 1928. Today it houses an art gallery and a quirky museum created by local watercolorist and historian Bjørg Bjøberg, and her Scottish husband, Arthur Adamson.

On the ground floor, you'll find Bjørg's gallery, with her watercolors celebrating the beauty of Norway, and Arthur's paintings, celebrating the beauty of women. Upstairs is a free exhibit of historical knickknacks, contributed by locals wanting to preserve treasures from their own families' past. You'll see a medicine cabinet stocked with old-fashioned pills, an antiquated tourist map, lots of skis, and WWII-era mementos. A wheel in the wall once powered a crane that could winch up goods from the fjord below (before today's embankment was built, when this store was right on the waterfront). While there are no written English explanations, Bjørg is happy to explain things (free, May–Aug daily 10:00–22:00, shorter hours late April and Sept, tel. 91 56 28 42).

Unable to contain her creative spirit, Bjørg has put together an eccentric wonderland experience with her private tour of the Golden House's hidden rooms, which includes a 30-minute movie merging her art and local nature (50 kr/person, 100-kr minimum, 200-kr maximum, one hour). Bjørg and Arthur also run the recommended on-site café, Me Snakkast.

Strolling King Bele's Way up the Fjord—For a delightful walk (or bike ride), head west out of town up the "old road"—once the main road from the harbor—for about a mile. It follows the fjord's edge, passing numerous "villas" from the late 1800s. At the time, this Swiss style was popular with some locals, who hoped to introduce a dose of Romanticism into Norwegian architecture. Look for the dragons' heads (copied from Viking-age stave churches) decorating the gables. Along the walk, you'll pass a swimming area, a campground, and two burial mounds from the Viking age, marked by a ponderous statue of the Viking King Bele. Check out the wooden shelters for the mailboxes; some give the elevation (*m.o.h.* stands for "meters over *havet*"—the sea)—not too high, are they? The walk is described in the *Outdoor Activities in Balestrand* brochure (free at the TI or your hotel).

Aquarium—The tiny aquarium gives you a good look at marine life in the Sognefjord. For descriptions, borrow the English booklet at the front desk. While not thrilling, the well-explained place is a decent rainy-day option. A 15-minute slide show starts at the top and bottom of each hour. The last room is filled with wood carvings depicting traditional everyday life in the fjordside village of Munken (70 kr, June–Aug daily 9:30–17:00, closed Sept–May, tel. 57 69 13 03). The fish-filled tanks on the dock outside are also worth a look.

Biking—You can cycle around town, or go farther by circling the scenic Esefjord (north of town, en route to the ferry landing at Dragsvik—about 6 miles each way). Or pedal scenically west up Sognefjord along King Bele's Way (described above). The roads here are relatively flat. Rental bikes are available at the TI.

Kayaking—A local outfit offers three-hour tours (450 kr, daily at 10:00 and 15:00, see TI for details).

Near Balestrand

These two side-trips are possible only if you've got the better part of a day in Balestrand. With a car, you can see Hopperstad Stave Church on the drive to Bergen.

▲▲Hopperstad Stave Church (Hopperstad Stavkyrkje) in Vik

The most accessible stave church in the area—and perhaps the most scenically situated in all Norway—is located just a 15-minute express-boat ride across the Sognefjord, in the town of Vik. Hopperstad Stave Church boasts a breathtaking exterior, with several tiers of dragon heads overlooking rolling fields between fjord cliffs. The interior is notable for its emptiness. Instead of being crammed full of later additions, the church is blissfully uncluttered, as it was when built in the mid-12th century. (For more on stave churches, see page 169.)

Cost and Hours: 50 kr, good 30-kr color booklet in English, daily mid-June–mid-Aug 9:00–19:00, May–mid-June and mid-Aug–Sept 10:00–17:00, tel. 57 69 52 70.

Tours: The attendant will give you a free tour at your request, provided she's not too busy. (Ask where the medieval graffiti is, and she'll grab her flashlight and show you.)

Location: The church is a 20-minute walk up the valley from Vik's harbor. From the boat landing, walk up the main street from the harbor about 200 yards (past the TI, a grocery store, and hotel). Take a right at the sign for *Hopperstad Stavkyrkje,* walk 10 minutes, and you'll see the church perched on a small hill in the distance.

Getting There: Pedestrians can ride the express passenger boat between Balestrand and Vik (68 kr each way, 15 min). The only way to get to the church and back in one day (only possible Mon–Sat) is to take the 7:50 departure from Balestrand, then return on the 11:30 departure from Vik, arriving back in Balestrand at 11:50—just in time to join a 12:00 glacier excursion (described below). Since cars can't go on this express boat, **drivers** must go around the small Esefjord to the town of Dragsvik, then catch the ferry across the Sognefjord to Vangsnes (a 20-min drive from Vik and the church).

➲ **Self-Guided Tour:** Originally built around 1140 and retaining most of its original wood, Hopperstad was thoroughly restored and taken back to basics in the 1880s by renowned architect Peter Blix. Unlike the famous stave church at Urnes (described later), whose interior has been re-jiggered by centuries of engineers and filled with altars and pews, the Hopperstad church looks close to the way it did when it was built. You'll see only a few non-original features, including the beautifully painted canopy that once covered a side altar (probably dating from around 1300), and a tombstone from 1738. There are only a few colorful illustrations and some very scant medieval "graffiti" carvings and runic inscriptions. Notice the intact chancel screen (the only one surviving in Norway), which separates the altar area from the congregation. As with the iconostasis (panel of icons) in today's Orthodox faith, this screen gave priests privacy to do the spiritual heavy lifting. Because Hopperstad's interior lacks the typical adornments, you can really grasp the fundamentally vertical nature of stave church architecture, leading your gaze to the heavens. Follow that impulse and look up to appreciate the Viking-ship rafters. Imagine the comfort this ceiling brought the church's original parishioners, whose seafaring ancestors had sought refuge under overturned boats. For a unique angle on this graceful structure, lay your camera on the floor and shoot the ceiling.

▲Excursion to Fjærland and the Jostedal Glacier

From Balestrand, cruise up the Fjærlandsfjord to visit the Norwegian Glacier Museum in Fjærland and to see a receding tongue of the Jostedal Glacier (Jostedalbreen). Half-day (524 kr) and full-day (570 kr) excursions are sold by Balestrand's TI or on board the boat. Reservations are smart (daily May–Sept only, www.fjord1.no, fylkesbaatane@fjord1.no).

While the museum and the glacier's tongue are underwhelming, it's a pleasant excursion with a dreamy fjord cruise (80 min each way). The full-day trip is essentially the same price as the half-day version. To take the all-day trip, catch the 8:05 ferry; for the shorter trip, hop on the noon boat. They both return on the same boat, getting you back in Balestrand at 16:55 (in time to catch the fast boat back to Bergen). Both tours offer the same fjord ride, museum visit, and trip to the glacier. The all-day version, however, gives you a second glacier viewing point and 2.5 hours to hang out in the town of Fjærland. (This sleepy village, famous for its secondhand book shops, is about as exciting as Walter Mondale, the vice president whose ancestors came from here.)

The ferry ride (no stops, no narration) is just a scenic 80-minute glide with the gulls. Bring a picnic, as there's almost no food sold on board, and some bread to toss to the gulls (they do acrobatics to catch whatever you loft into the air). You'll be met at the ferry dock (labeled *Mundal*) by a bus—and your guide, who reads a script about the glacier as you drive up the valley for about 15 minutes. You'll stop for an hour at the **Norwegian Glacier Museum** (Norsk Bremuseum). After watching an 18-minute aerial tour of the dramatic Jostedal Glacier in the theater, you'll learn how glaciers were formed, experiment with your own hunk of glacier, weigh evidence of the woolly mammoth's existence in Norway, and learn about the effect of global climate change on the fjords (way overpriced at 110 kr, included in excursion price, daily June–Aug 9:00–19:00, April–May and Sept–Oct 10:00–16:00, tel. 57 69 32 88, www.bre.museum.no). From the museum, the bus runs you up to a café near a lake, at a spot that gives you a good look at the Boyabreen, a tongue of the Jostedal Glacier. Marvel at how far the glacier has retreated—10 years ago, the visit was more dramatic. With global warming, glacier excursions like this become more sad than majestic. I wonder how long they'll even be able to bill this as a "glacier visit."

Considering that the fjord trip is the highlight of this journey, you could save time and money by just riding the ferry up and back (8:05–11:30). At 310 kr for the round-trip boat ride, it's much cheaper than the 524-kr tour.

Note that if you're into glaciers, a nearby arm of the Jostedal, called the **Nigard Glacier,** is a more dramatic and boots-on experience (see page 271). It's easy for drivers. Non-drivers can catch the Glacier Bus in Sogndal for an all-day visit by public transportation. From Balestrand, the bus to Sogndal (to meet up with the Glacier Bus) departs Mon–Fri in July–Aug at 7:30, and returns at 20:00 (no bus connection Sat–Sun or Sept–June).

Sleeping in Balestrand

$$$ Kviknes Hotel is the classy grande dame of Balestrand, dominating the town and packed with tour groups. The picturesque wooden hotel—and five generations of the Kvikne family—have welcomed tourists to Balestrand since the late 19th century. The hotel has two parts: a new wing, and the historic wooden section, with 17 older, classic rooms, and no elevator. All rooms come with balconies. The elegant Old World public spaces in the old section make you want to just sit there and sip tea all afternoon (Db-1,700 kr in new building or 2,040 kr in old building, about 400 kr more with view; includes breakfast, mostly non-smoking, free Wi-Fi, family rooms available, closed Oct–April, tel. 57 69 42 00, fax 57 69 42 01, www.kviknes.no, booking@kviknes.no). Part of the Kviknes ritual is gorging on the *store koldt bord* buffet

Sleep Code

(6 kr = about $1, country code: 47)
S = Single, **D** = Double/Twin, **T** = Triple, **Q** = Quad, **b** = bathroom, **s** = shower. Unless otherwise noted, these accommodations accept credit cards.

To help you sort easily through these listings, I've divided the rooms into three categories, based on the price for a standard double room with bath:

$$$ Higher Priced—Most rooms 1,000 kr or more.
$$ Moderately Priced—Most rooms between 500–1,000 kr.
$ Lower Priced—Most rooms 500 kr or less.

dinner—open to non-guests, and a nice way to soak in the hotel's old-time elegance without splurging on an overnight (see "Eating in Balestrand," below; cheaper if you stay at the hotel for 2 or more nights).

$$ Balestrand Hotel, family-run by Unni-Marie Kvikne, her California-born husband Eric Palmer, and their three children, is your best fjordside home. Open late May through early September, this cozy, welcoming place has 30 well-appointed, comfortable, quiet rooms; a large, modern common area with lots of English paperbacks; laundry service, free Wi-Fi, balconies (in some rooms), and outdoor benches for soaking in the scenery. They also have a waterfront yard with inviting lounge chairs and a mesmerizing view. When reserving, let them know your arrival time, and they'll pick you up at the harborfront (non-view Sb-670 kr, view Sb-770 kr, non-view Db-990 kr, view Db-1,190 kr, includes breakfast, 5-min walk from dock, past St. Olaf's Church—or free pick-up, tel. 57 69 11 38, www.balestrand.com, info@balestrand.com).

$$ At **Gekken's Rooms,** Geir rents four homey rooms above his restaurant in the town center (D-550 kr, small D-450 kr, extra bed-150 kr, shared kitchen and WC, open June–Aug only, tel. 57 69 14 14, mobile 97 51 29 26, baleson2004@yahoo.com).

$–$$ Kringsjå Balestrand Hostel, a camp school for sixth-graders, rents beds and rooms to budget travelers from mid-June to mid-August. Half of their 58 beds are in doubles. All the four-bed rooms have private bathrooms and view balconies (bunk in 4-bed dorm-260 kr, Sb-510 kr, Db-790 kr, extra bed-120 kr, includes breakfast, discount for hostel members, sheets/towels-50 kr/person, free Wi-Fi, tel. 57 69 13 03, www.kringsja.no, kringsja@kringsja.no).

$ Sjotun Camping rents the cheapest beds around, in rustic huts (4-person hut-250 kr, no linen, a mile west of town, tel. 57 69 12 23, www.sjotun.com).

Eating in Balestrand

Balestrand's dining options are limited, but good.

Kviknes Hotel offers a splendid, spendy *store koldt bord* buffet dinner in a massive yet stately old dining room. For a memorable fjordside *smörgåsbord* experience, it doesn't get any better than this. Don't rush. Consider taking a preview tour—surveying the reindeer meat, lingonberries, and fjord-caught seafood—before you dive in, so you can budget your stomach space. Get a new plate with each course and save room for dessert. Each dish is labeled in English (500 kr/person, May–Sept daily 19:00–21:00, closed Oct–April). After dinner, head into the rich lounge to pick up your cup of coffee or tea (included), which you'll sip sitting on classy old-fashioned furniture and basking in fjord views. For tips on enjoying this feast, see page 28.

Me Snakkast ("Let's Talk"), inside the Golden House at the harbor, dishes up Norwegian home cooking and a variety of salads. Sit outside—or indoors, in a dining area built to resemble a traditional Norwegian kitchen. The restaurant upstairs shows off part of owner Bjørg's antique collection. They serve 30–100-kr light meals—sandwiches, soups, cakes, and more—throughout the day, and pricier meals after 15:00, such as 120–220-kr meat and fish dishes (May–Sept daily 9:30–21:30, closed off-season, tel. 91 56 28 42).

Gekkens is an informal summer restaurant serving good-value meat, fish, and vegetarian dishes, along with burgers, fish-and-chips, and other fried fare. Sit in the simply decorated interior, or out on the shaded little terrace. Geir Arne "Gekken" Bale can trace his family's roots back 400 years in Balestrand. He has filled his walls with fascinating historic photos and paintings, making his dining hall an art gallery of sorts (light dishes-60–100 kr, daily dinner plates-100–140 kr, June–Aug daily 12:00–22:00, closed Sept–May, above and behind the TI from the harbor, tel. 57 69 14 14).

The Viking Ship, the hot-dog stand facing the harbor, is proudly run by Carola. A bratwurst missionary from Germany,

Express Boat Between Bergen and the Sognefjord

The made-for-tourists express boat, called Fylkesbaatane, makes it a snap to connect Bergen with Balestrand and other Sognefjord towns (for foot passengers only—no cars). In summer, the boat goes twice each day in both directions, linking up Bergen, Vik, Balestrand, Aurland, and Flåm. You can also use this boat to connect towns on the Sognefjord, such as zipping from quiet Balestrand to busy Flåm, in the heart of the Nutshell action (reservations are smart—email fylkesbaatane@fjord1.no or call 55 90 70 70, discounts for students and seniors, tickets also sold on boat and at TI, www.fjord1.no).

Between Bergen and the Sognefjord: The boat trip between Bergen and **Balestrand** takes four hours (470 kr, departs Bergen May-Sept daily at 8:00, also Mon-Fri at 16:30, Sat at 14:15, some Sun at 16:30—but not mid-June-late Aug; Oct-April Mon-Fri at 8:00, Sun-Fri at 16:30, Sat at 14:15; departs Balestrand May-Sept daily at 16:55, Mon-Sat also at 7:50, some Sun at 11:30—but not mid-June-late Aug; Oct-April Mon-Sat at 7:50, Sun at 15:55). In summer, the 8:00 boat from Bergen continues to **Flåm** (645 kr). If you're traveling with two or more people, you'll save about 25 percent.

Between Flåm and Balestrand: Going by boat between Flåm and Balestrand takes about 1.5 hours (220 kr, departs Flåm May-Sept daily at 15:30, stops at Aurland, arrives in Balestrand at 16:55; second boat sometimes runs from Flåm Mon-Fri at 6:00, arrives Balestrand at 8:00; departs Balestrand daily at 11:50 arriving Flåm at 13:25; a different boat departs Balestrand Mon-Fri at 8:30 in July-early Aug; no express boats between Flåm and Balestrand Oct-April).

From Oslo to Balestrand via the Nutshell: This variation on the standard Norway in a Nutshell route is called "Sognefjord in a Nutshell" (Oslo-Myrdal-Flåm-Balestrand-Bergen). From **Oslo,** you can take an early train to Flåm (no later than the 8:11 train as part of the Norway in a Nutshell route—see previous chapter), then catch the 15:30 express boat to Balestrand. After your visit, you can continue on the express boat to Bergen, or return to the Nutshell route by taking the express boat to Midtfjord, and transferring to the next boat to Gudvangen (June-Aug only, otherwise transfer in Flåm).

she claims it took her years to get Norwegians to accept the tastier bratwurst over their beloved *pølser* weenies. Eat at her picnic tables or across the street on the harbor park (fine sausages, fish-and-chips, May–Sept daily 11:00–20:00, closed Oct–April).

Picnic: The delightful waterfront park next to the aquarium has benches and million-dollar fjord views. The Co-op and Joker **supermarkets** at the harbor have basic grocery supplies, including bread, meats, cheeses, and drinks. Co-op is bigger and has a wider selection (both open Mon–Fri 9:00–18:00, Sat 9:00–15:00, closed Sun). **Mu's Bakery** heats up baked goodies trucked here all the way from Germany (Mon–Sat 9:30–18:00, Sun 9:30–15:00, closed mid-Sept–early May, between Co-op and Joker supermarkets).

Balestrand Connections

Because Balestrand is separated from the Lustrafjord by the long Fjærlandsfjord, most Balestrand connections involve a boat trip.

From Balestrand by Express Passenger Boat

The easiest way to reach Balestrand is on the handy express boat, which connects to **Bergen, Vik** (near Hopperstad Stave Church), **Aurland,** and **Flåm** (see sidebar on previous page for schedules). Note that you can also use this boat to join the Nutshell trip mid-fjord (transferring at Midtfjord—literally from boat to boat, in the middle of the fjord—to the Kaupanger–Gudvangen ferry; possible only June–Aug). From here, continue on the Nutshell boat down the Nærøyfjord to Gudvangen, where you'll join the crowd onward to Voss, then Bergen or Oslo. As you're making schedule and sightseeing decisions, consider that the Balestrand–Flåm boat skips the Nærøyfjord, the most dramatic arm of the Sognefjord.

From Balestrand by Car Ferry

Balestrand's main car-ferry dock is at the village of **Dragsvik,** a six-mile, 15-minute drive around the adorable little Eselfjord. From Dragsvik, a car ferry makes the short crossing east to **Hella** (a 30-min drive from Sogndal and the Lustrafjord), then crosses the Sognefjord south to **Vangsnes** (a 20-min drive to Hopperstad Stave Church and onward to Bergen). The ferry goes at least once per hour (2/hr in peak times, fewer boats Sun, 74 kr for car and driver).

Note that you can also drive through Sogndal to catch the **Kaupanger–Gudvangen** or **Mannheller–Fodnes** ferries (described under "Lustrafjord Connections," near the end of this chapter).

The Lustrafjord

This arm of the Sognefjord is rugged country—only 2 percent of the land is fit to build or farm on. The Lustrafjord is ringed with tiny villages where farmers sell cherries and giant raspberries. A few interesting attractions lie along the Lustrafjord: the village Dale Church at Luster; the impressive Nigard Glacier (a 45-minute drive up a valley); the postcard-pretty village of Solvorn; and, across the fjord, Norway's oldest stave church at Urnes. While a bit trickier to explore by public transportation, this beautiful region is easy by car, but still feels remote. There are no ATMs between Lom and Gaupne—that's how remote this region is.

Suggested Route for Drivers

The Lustrafjord can be seen either coming from the north (over the Sognefjell pass from the Jotunheimen region—see next chapter) or from the south (from Balestrand or the Norway in a Nutshell route—see previous chapter). Note that public buses between Lom and Sogndal follow this same route (see "Lustrafjord Connections," later).

Here's what you'll see if you're driving from the north (if you're coming from the south, read this section backwards): Descending from Sognefjell, you'll hit the fjord at the village of Skjolden (decent TI in big community center, tel. 97 60 04 43). Follow Route 55 along the west bank of the fjord. In the town of Luster, consider visiting the beautifully decorated Dale Church (described next). Farther along, near the hamlet of Nes, you'll have views across the fjord of the towering Feigumfoss waterfall. Drops and dribbles come from miles around for this 650-foot tumble. Soon Route 55 veers along an inlet to the town of Gaupne, where you can choose to detour about an hour to the Nigard Glacier (up Route 604; described under "Sights on the Lustrafjord," next). After Gaupne, Route 55 enters a tunnel and cuts inland, emerging at a long, fjord-like lake at the town of Hafslo. Just beyond is the turnoff for Solvorn, a fine home-base town with the ferry across to Urnes and its stave church (Solvorn and Urnes Stave Church both described under "Sights on the Lustrafjord," next). Route 55 continues to Sogndal, where you can choose to turn off for the Kaupanger and Mannheller ferries across the Sognefjord, or continue on Route 55 to Hella and the boat across to either

Dragsvik (near Balestrand) or Vangsnes (across the Sognefjord, near Vik and Hopperstad Stave Church).

Route Timings: If you're approaching from Lom in the Gudbrandsdal Valley, figure about 1.5 hours over Sognefjell to the start of the Lustrafjord at Skjolden, then another 30 minutes to Gaupne (with the optional glacier detour: 2 hours to see it, 4 hours to hike on it). From Gaupne, figure 30 minutes to Solvorn or 40 minutes to Sogndal. Solvorn to Sogndal is about 30 minutes. Sogndal to Hella, and its boat to Balestrand, takes about 40 minutes. These estimated times are conservative, but they don't include photo stops.

Sights on the Lustrafjord

These attractions are listed as you'll reach them driving from north to south along the fjordside Route 55. If you're sleeping in this area, you could visit all four sights in a single day (but it'd be a busy, somewhat rushed day). If you're passing through, Dale Church and Solvorn are easy, but the other two involve major detours—choose one or skip them both.

▲Dale Church (Dale Kyrkje) in Luster

The namesake town of Luster, on the west bank of the Lustrafjord, boasts a unique 13th-century Gothic church. In a land of wooden stave churches, this stone church, with its richly decorated interior, is worth a quick stop as you pass through town (free entry but donation requested, good posted English info inside, 5-kr English brochure, open daily 10:00–20:00 but often closed for services and off-season, just off the main road—look for red steeple, WC in graveyard, fresh goodies at bakery across the street).

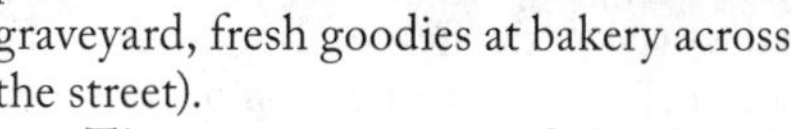

The soapstone core of the church dates from about 1250, but the wooden bell tower and entry porch were likely built around 1600. As you enter, on the left you'll see a tall, elevated platform with seating, surrounded by a wooden grill. Nicknamed a "birdcage" for the feathery fashions worn by the ladies of the time, this high-profile pew—three steps higher than the pulpit—was built in the late-17th century by a wealthy parishioner. The beautifully painted pulpit, decorated with faded images of the four evangelists, dates from the 13th century. In the chancel (altar area), restorers have uncovered frescoes from three different time periods: the 14th, 16th, and 17th centuries. Most of the ones you see here were likely created around the year 1500. The crucifix high over the pews, carved around 1200, predates the church, as does the old bench (with lots of runic carvings)—making them more than eight centuries old.

▲▲Jostedal's Nigard Glacier

The Nigard Glacier (Nigardsbreen) is the most accessible branch of mainland Europe's largest glacier (the Jostedalsbreen, 185 square miles). Hiking to or on this glacier offers Norway's best easy opportunity for a hands-on glacier experience. It's a 45-minute detour from the Lustrafjord up Jostedal Valley. Visiting a glacier is a quintessential Norwegian experience, bringing you face-to-face with the majesty of nature. If you can spare the time, it's worth the detour (even if you don't do a guided hike). But if glaciers don't give you tingles and you're feeling pressed, skip it.

Getting There: It's straightforward for **drivers.** When the main Route 55 along the Lustrafjord reaches Gaupne, turn onto Route 604, which you'll follow for 25 miles up the Jostedal Valley to the Breheimsenteret glacier information center. Access to the glacier itself is down the toll road past the information center (all described below).

In July and August, a **Glacier Bus** connects the Nigard Glacier to various home-base towns around the region (leaves Sogndal at 8:45, passes through Solvorn en route, arrives at the glacier around 10:30; departs glacier at 17:00, arrives back in Sogndal around 18:40; buses or boats from other towns—including Balestrand, Flåm, and Aurland—coordinate to meet this bus in Sogndal; combo-tickets include various glacier visits and hikes; no bus Sept–June; for complete timetable, see www.jostedal.com). While handy, the bus is designed for those spending the entire day at the glacier.

Breheimsenteret Glacier Information Center—This national park center, in a starkly modern building, stands at the entrance to the Nigard Glacier valley. The center has WCs, a gift shop, a cafeteria, free Wi-Fi, and a modest but pricey museum (50 kr). You'll watch a relaxing 20-minute film showing highlights of the glacier and region, then tour a gallery of glacier-related exhibits that use models and illustrations to explain these giant, slow-moving walls of ice. Even if you're not interested in the museum, drop by here to confirm your glacier plans—likely with Peter, who runs the place (daily mid-June–mid-Aug 9:00–19:00, May–mid-June and mid-Aug–Sept 10:00–17:00, closed Oct–April, tel. 57 68 32 50, www.jostedal.com).

Visiting the Glacier—The best quick visit is to walk to, but not on, the glacier. (If you want to walk *on* it, see "Hikes on the Glacier," next.) From the information center, a 25-kr toll road continues two miles to a lake facing the actual tongue of the glacier. About 75 years ago, the glacier reached all the way to today's parking lot. (It's named for the ninth farm—*ni gard*—where it finally stopped, after crushing eight farms higher up the valley.) From the lot, you can hike all the way to the edge of today's glacier (about 45 min each way); or, to save about 20 minutes of walking, take a special boat to a spot that's a 20-minute hike from the glacier (15 kr each way, 10-min boat trip, 4/hr, mid-June–mid-Sept 10:00–18:00).

The walk is uneven but well-marked—follow the red *T*'s and take your time. You'll hike on stone polished smooth by the glacier, and scramble over and around boulders big and small that were deposited by it. The path takes you right up to the face of the Nigardsbreen. Respect the glacier. It's a powerful river of ice, and fatal accidents do happen. If you want to walk on the glacier, read the next listing first.

Hikes on the Glacier—If you want to actually walk on top of the glacier, don't attempt it by yourself. The Breheimsenteret glacier information center offers guided family-friendly walks that include about one hour on the ice (200 kr, 100 kr for kids, minimum age 5, I'd rate the walks PG-13 myself, about 4/day, generally between 11:30–15:00, no need to reserve—just call glacier center to find out time and show up). Leave the information center one hour before your tour, then meet the group on the ice, where you'll pay and receive your clamp-on crampons. One hour roped up with your group gives you the essential experience. You'll find yourself marveling at how well your strap-on crampons work on the 5,000-year-old-ice. Even if it's hot, wear long pants, a jacket, and your sturdiest shoes. (Think ahead. It's awkward to empty your bladder after you're roped up.)

Longer, more challenging, and much more expensive hikes get you higher views, more exercise, and real crampons (starting at 410 kr, includes boots, June–Aug daily at 11:45 and 12:45, additional departure in July and Aug at 14:30, 4 hours including 2 hours on the ice, book by phone the day before—tel. 57 68 32 50, arrive at the information center 30 min early to pay for tickets and pick up your gear). If you're adventurous, ask about even longer hikes and glacier kayaking. While it's legal to go on the glacier on your own, it's dangerous and crazy to do so without crampons.

▲▲Solvorn

On the west bank of the Lustrafjord, 10 miles northeast of Sogndal, idyllic Solvorn is a sleepy little Victorian town with colorful wooden sheds lining its waterfront. My favorite town on the Lustrafjord is tidy and quaint, well away from the bustle of the Nutshell action. Its tiny ferry crosses the fjord regularly to Urnes and its famous stave church (see below). While not worth going far out of your way for, Solvorn is a mellow and surprisingly appealing place to kill some time waiting for the ferry...or just munching a picnic while looking across the fjord. A pensive stroll or photo shoot through the village's back lanes is a joy (look for plaques that explain historic buildings in English). Best of all, Solvorn also has a pair of excellent accommodations: a splurge (Hotel Walaker) and a budget place (Eplet Bed & Apple), described later under "Sleeping on the Lustrafjord."

Getting There: Solvorn is a steep five-minute **drive** down a switchback road from the main Route 55. The main road into town leads right to the Urnes ferry (see below) and dead-ends into a handy parking lot (free, 2-hour posted—but unmonitored—limit). It's a 30-minute drive or bus trip into Sogndal, where you can transfer to other **buses** (2–3 buses/day between Solvorn and Sogndal, including the Glacier Bus to the Nigard Glacier—described earlier).

▲▲Urnes Stave Church

The hamlet of Urnes (sometimes spelled "Ornes") has Norway's oldest surviving stave church, dating from 1129. While not easy to reach (it's across the Lustrafjord from other attractions), it's worth the scenic ferry ride. The exterior is smaller and simpler than most stave churches, but its interior—modified in fits and starts over the centuries—is uniquely eclectic. For more on stave churches, see page 169. If you want to pack along a bike (rentable in Solvorn), see "Bring a Bike?" at the end of this listing.

Cost and Hours: 50 kr, includes 25-minute English tour (departs at :40 past most hours, to coincide with ferry arrival—described below); June–Sept daily 10:30–17:45; closed Oct–May, tel. 57 68 39 45.

Services: A little café/restaurant is at the farm called Urnes Gard, across from the church (same hours as church, homemade apple cakes, tel. 57 68 39 44).

Getting There: Urnes is perched on the east bank of the Lustrafjord (across the fjord from Route 55 and Solvorn). Ferries running between Solvorn and Urnes depart Solvorn at the top of most hours and Urnes at the bottom of most hours (30 kr one-way passenger fare, 80 kr one-way for car and driver, no round-trip discount, 15-min ride). You can either drive or walk onto the boat—but, since you can't drive all the way up to the church, you might as well leave your car in Solvorn. Once across, it's about a five-minute uphill walk to the main road and parking lot (where drivers must leave their cars; parking lot at the church only for disabled visitors). From here, it's a steep 15-minute walk up a switchback road to the church (follow signs for *Urnes*).

Planning Your Time: Don't dawdle on your way up to the church, as the tour is scheduled to depart at :40 past most hours, about 25 minutes after the ferry arrives (giving most visitors just enough time to make it up the hill to the church). The first boat of the day departs Solvorn at 10:00; the last boat departs Solvorn at 16:00 (last tour at 16:40); and the last boat back to Solvorn departs Urnes at 18:00. Confirm the "last boat" time, and keep an eye on your watch to avoid getting stranded in Urnes.

➲ **Self-Guided Tour:** Most visitors to the church take the included 25-minute tour (scheduled to begin soon after the ferry arrives—described above). Here are some highlights:

Buy your ticket in the white house across from the church. Visit the little museum here after you see the church, so you don't miss the tour.

Many changes were made to the exterior to modernize the church after the Reformation (the colonnaded gallery was replaced, the bell tower was added, and modern square windows were cut into the walls). Go around the left side of the church, toward the cemetery. This is the third church on this spot, but the carved doorway embedded in the wall here was inherited from the second church. Notice the two mysterious beasts—a warm-blooded predator (standing) and a cold-blooded dragon—weaving and twisting around each other, one entwining the other. Yet, as they bite each other on the neck, it's impossible to tell which one is "winning"... perhaps symbolizing the everlasting struggle

of human existence. The door you see in the middle, however, has a very different message: the harmony of symmetrical figure-eights, an appropriately calming theme for those entering the church.

Now go around to the real entry door (with a wrought-iron lock and handle probably dating from the first church) and head inside. While it feels ancient and creaky, a lot of what you see in here is actually "new" compared to the 12th-century core of the church. The exquisitely carved, voluptuous, column-topping capitals are remarkably well-preserved originals. The interior initially was stark (no pews) and dark—lit not by windows (which were added much later), but by candles laid on the floor in the shape of a cross. Looking straight ahead, you see a cross with Mary on the left (where the women stood) and John the Baptist on the right (with the men). When they finally added seating, they kept things segregated: Notice the pews carved with hearts for women, crowns for men.

When a 17th-century wealthy family wanted to build a special pew for themselves, they simply sawed off some of the pinecone-topped columns to make way for it. When the church began to lean, it was reinforced with the clumsy, off-center X-shaped supports. Churchgoers learned their lesson, and never cut anything again.

The ceiling, added in the late 17th century, prevents visitors from enjoying the Viking-ship roof beams. But all of these additions have stories to tell. Experts can read various cultural influences into the church decorations, including Irish (some of the carvings) and Romanesque (the rounded arches).

Bring a Bike? To give your Lustrafjord excursion more dimension, take a bike on the ferry to Urnes (free passage, rentable for 150 kr/day with helmets from Eplet Bed & Apple hostel in Solvorn, where you can park your car for free). From the stave church, bike the super-scenic fjordside road (4.5 miles—with almost no traffic—to big Feigumfossen waterfall and back).

Sleeping on the Lustrafjord

These accommodations are along the Lustrafjord, listed from north to south.

In Nes

$$ Nes Gard Farmhouse B&B rents 15 homey rooms, offering lots of comfort in a grand 19th-century farmhouse for a good price (D-750 kr, Db-900 kr, rooms in main building more traditional, family apartment, tel. 95 23 26 94 or 61 36 23 45, www.nesgard.no, post@nesgard.no, Manum family). Mari and Asbjorn serve a three-course dinner for 280 kr.

$ Viki Fjord Camping has great fjordside huts—many directly on the water, with fjord views and balconies—located directly across from the Feigumfossen waterfall (230–450 kr without a private bathroom, 380–850 kr with bathroom, price depends on size and season, sheets-60 kr, tel. 57 68 64 20, mobile 99 53 97 30, http://home.c2i.net/sanaess, viki.camp@c2i.net, Berit and Svein).

In Solvorn

For more on this delightful little fjordside town—my favorite home base on the Lustrafjord—see the description earlier in this chapter. While it lacks the handy boat connections of Flåm, Aurland, or Balestrand, that's part of Solvorn's charm.

$$$ Walaker Hotel, a former inn and coach station, has been run by the Walaker family since 1690 (that's a lot of pressure on eighth-generation owner Ole Henrik, who has just taken over the reins from Oda and Hermod). The hotel, set right on the Lustrafjord (with a garden perfect for relaxing and, if necessary, even convalescing), is open May through September. In the main house, the halls and living rooms are filled with tradition. Notice the patriotic hymns on the piano. The 22 rooms are divided into two types: nicely appointed standard rooms in the modern annex (big Sb-1,400 kr, Db-1,600 kr); or recently renovated "historic" rooms with all the modern conveniences in two different old buildings: rooms with Old World elegance in the main house, and brightly painted rooms with countryside charm in the Tingstova house next door (Db-2,100 kr, 500 kr more for larger #20 and #23; all prices include breakfast, non-smoking, free Wi-Fi, sea kayak rental, tel. 57 68 20 80, fax 57 68 20 81, www.walaker.com, hotel@walaker.com). They serve excellent four-course dinners (525 kr plus drinks, nightly at 19:30, savor your dessert with fjordside setting on the balcony). Their impressive gallery of Norwegian art is in a restored, historic farmhouse out back (free for guests; Ole Henrik leads one-hour tours of the collection, peppered with some family history, nightly after dinner).

$-$$ Eplet Bed & Apple is my kind of hostel: innovative and friendly. It's creatively run by Trond, whose entrepreneurial spirit and positive attitude attract enjoyable guests. With welcoming public spaces and 22 beds in seven rooms (all with views, some with decks), this place is worth considering even if you don't normally sleep at hostels (open May–Sept only; camping space-90 kr, bunk in 7-bed dorm-140 kr plus 50 kr for sheets, S-450 kr, D-550 kr, T-750 kr, S/D/T cost 100 kr less for 2 nights or more, laundry-50 kr, kitchen, Wi-Fi, free loaner bikes for guests, tel. 41 64 94 69, www.eplet.net, trondhenrik@eplet.net). It's about 300 yards uphill from the boat dock—look for the white house with a giant red apple painted on it. It's surrounded by a raspberry and apple farm (they make and sell tasty juices from both). The hostel rents bikes and helmets to non-guests for 150 kr/day. If you plan to bike along the fjord from Urnes, consider that if you stay at the hostel, the free bikes will save you 300 kr (for two people).

Eating in Solvorn: Sleepy Solvorn is blessed with the cheery **Linahagen Kafé,** next door to Walaker Hotel, where delightful Signe and her family serve up good meals (120-kr dinner salads, 140-kr dinner plates, June–Aug daily 12:30–19:30, closed Sept–May).

In Sogndal

Sogndal is the only sizeable town in this region. While it lacks the charm of Solvorn and Balestrand, it's big enough to have a busy shopping street and a helpful **TI** (mid-June–mid-Aug Mon–Fri 9:00–18:00, Sat 10:00–16:00, closed Sun; shorter hours in May and Sept, closed in winter; in the Kulturhus at Hovevegen 2, tel. 97 60 04 43).

$$ Loftesnes Pensjonat, with 12 rooms, houses travelers mid-June through mid-August, and mostly students—reserving four rooms for travelers—during the school year (S-400 kr, Sb-420 kr, D-600 kr, Db-650 kr, no breakfast, kitchen, above a Chinese restaurant near the water, tel. & fax 57 67 15 77, mobile 90 93 51 71, loftesnes-pensjonat@hotmail.com).

$-$$ Sogndal Youth Hostel rents good, cheap beds (bunk in 4-bed room-200 kr, S-280 kr, D-480 kr, Db-660 kr, 15 percent less for members, breakfast included, sheets-60 kr, towel-30 kr, members' kitchen—B.Y.O. pots, mid-June–mid-Aug only, closed 10:00–17:00, at fork in the road as you enter town, tel. 57 62 75 75, mobile 90 93 51 71, fax 57 62 75 70, www.vandrerhjem.no, sogndal @hihostels.no).

Lustrafjord Connections

Sogndal is the transit hub for the Lustrafjord region.

From Sogndal by Bus

Buses go to **Lom** over the Sognefjell pass (2/day late June–Aug only, road closed off-season, 3.25 hrs), **Solvorn** (3/day in summer, 2/day in winter, fewer Sat–Sun, 30 min), **Balestrand** (3/day, fewer Sat–Sun, 1.25 hrs, includes ride on Hella–Dragsvik ferry), **Nigard Glacier** via the Glacier Bus (1/day, 1.5 hrs, departs Sogndal daily at 8:45, returns to Sogndal in the afternoon, also stops at Solvorn in each direction, July–Aug only). Most buses run less (or not at all) on weekends—check the latest at www.ruteinfo.net.

By Boat

Car ferries cost roughly $5 per hour for walk-ons and $20 per hour for a car and driver. Reservations are generally not necessary, and on many short rides, aren't even possible (for info and free and easy reservations for longer rides, call 55 90 70 70). Confirm schedules at www.ruteinfo.net. From near Sogndal, various boats fan out to towns around the Sognefjord. Most leave from two towns at the southern end of the Lustrafjord: **Kaupanger** (a 15-min drive from Sogndal) and **Mannheller** (a 5-min drive beyond Kaupanger, 20 min from Sogndal).

From Kaupanger: While Kaupanger is little more than a ferry landing, the small stave-type church at the edge of town merits a look. Boats go from Kaupanger all the way down the gorgeous Nærøyfjord to **Gudvangen,** which is on the Norway in a Nutshell route (where you catch the bus to Voss). Taking this boat allows you to see the best part of the Nutshell fjord scenery (the Nærøyfjord), but misses the other half of that cruise (Aurlandsfjord). The boat leaves Kaupanger daily in summer at 9:30, 12:05, 16:00, and 18:50 for the two-hour trip (these times are for June–Aug, only goes 1/day in May and Aug–mid-Sept departing Kaupanger at 9:30 and Gudvangen at 12:00, none mid-Sept–April; car and driver-565 kr, adult passenger-230 kr; reserve at least one day in advance—or longer in July–Aug, especially for the popular 12:05 departure; tel. 55 90 70 70). Prices are high because this route is mainly taken by tourists, not locals. Boats also connect Kaupanger to **Lærdal,** but the crossing from Mannheller to Fodnes is easier (described next).

From Mannheller: Ferries frequently make the speedy 15-minute crossing to **Fodnes** (63 kr for a car and driver, 3/hr, no reservations possible). From Fodnes, drive through the five-mile-long tunnel to Lærdal and the main E16 highway (near Borgund Stave Church, the long tunnel to Aurland, and the scenic overland road to the Stegastein fjord viewpoint—all described in the previous chapter).

To Balestrand: To reach Balestrand from the Lustrafjord, you'll take a short ferry trip (Hella–Dragsvik). For information on the car ferries to and from Balestrand, see "Balestrand Connections," earlier.

Scenic Drives from the Sognefjord

If you'll be doing a lot of driving, pick up a good local map. The 1:335,000-scale *Sør-Norge nord* map by Cappelens Kart is excellent (about 100 kr, available at local TIs and bookstores).

▲▲From the Lustrafjord to Aurland

The drive to the pleasant fjordside town of Aurland (see previous chapter) takes you either through the world's longest car tunnel, or over an incredible mountain pass. If you aren't going as far as Lom and Jotunheimen, consider taking the pass, as the scenery here rivals the famous Sognefjell pass drive.

From Sogndal, drive 20 minutes to the Mannheller–Fodnes ferry (described under "Lustrafjord Connections," earlier), float across the Sognefjord, then drive from Fodnes to Lærdal. From Lærdal, you have two options to Aurland: The speedy route is on E16 through the new 15-mile-long **tunnel** from Lærdal, or the Aurlandsvegen **"Snow Road"** over the pass.

The tunnel (described on page 247) is free, and impressively nonchalant—it's signed as if it were just another of Norway's countless tunnels. But driving it is a bizarre experience: A few miles in, as you find yourself trying not to be hypnotized by the monotony, it suddenly dawns on you what it means to be driving under a mountain for 15 miles. To keep people awake, three rest chambers, each illuminated by a differently colored light, break up the drive visually. Stop and get out—if no cars are coming, test the acoustics from the center.

The second, immeasurably more scenic route is a breathtaking one-hour, 30-mile drive that winds over a pass into Aurland, cresting at over 4,000 feet and offering classic aerial fjord views (it's worth the messy pants). From the Mannheller–Fodnes ferry, take the first road to the right (to Erdal), then leave E68 at Erdal (just west of Lærdal) for the Aurlandsvegen. This road, while well-maintained, is open only in summer, and narrow and dangerous during snowstorms (which can hit with a moment's notice, even in warm weather). You'll enjoy vast and terrifying views of lakes, snowfields, and remote mountain huts and farmsteads on what feels like the top of Norway. As you begin the 12-hairpin zigzag descent to Aurland, you'll reach the new "7"-shaped **Stegastein viewpoint**—well worth a stop. The "Snow Road" and viewpoint are both described on page 247.

▲From the Lustrafjord to Bergen, via the Nutshell Route (Nærøyfjord and Gudvangen)

Car ferries take tourists between Kaupanger and the Nutshell town of Gudvangen through an arm and elbow of the Sognefjord, including the staggering Nærøyfjord (for details on the ferry, see "Lustrafjord Connections," earlier). From Gudvangen, it's a 90-mile drive to Bergen, via Voss (figure about one hour to Voss, then another two hours into Bergen). This follows essentially the same route as the Norway in a Nutshell (Gudvangen–Voss bus, Voss–Bergen train). For additional commentary on the journey, see page 242.

Get off the ferry in Gudvangen and drive up the Nærøy valley past a river. You'll see the two giant falls just before the road marked *Stalheimskleiva*. Follow the sign (exiting left) to the little Stalheimskleiva road. This incredible road doggedly worms its way up into the ozone. My car overheated in a few minutes. Take it easy. (The main road gets you there more easily—through a tunnel and about a mile back up a smaller road—but you miss the twisty road and views.) As you wind up, you can view the falls from several turnouts. At the top, stop for a break at the touristy Stalheim Hotel (described on page 243).

The road rejoins E16 and continues into a mellower beauty, past lakes and farms, toward Voss. Soon before you reach Voss itself, watch the right side of the road for Tvindefossen, a waterfall with a handy campground/WC/kiosk picnic area that's worth a stop. Highway E16 takes you through Voss and into Bergen. If you plan to visit Edvard Grieg's home and the nearby Fantoft Stave Church, now is the ideal time, since you'll be driving near them and they're a headache to reach from downtown. Both are worth a detour if you're not rushed, and open until 18:00 in summer (see pages 312 and 313 of the Bergen chapter).

▲▲From Balestrand to Bergen, via Vik

If you're based in Balestrand and driving to Bergen, you have two options: Take the Dragsvik–Hella ferry, drive an hour to Kaupanger (via Sogndal), and drive the route described above; or, take the following slower, twistier, more remote, and more scenic route, with a stop at the beautiful Hopperstad Stave Church. This route is slightly longer, with more time on mountain roads and less time on the boat. Figure 20 minutes from Vangsnes to Vik, then about 1.5 hours to Voss, then another 2 hours into Bergen.

From Vagsnes, head into Vik on the main Route 13. In Vik, follow signs from the main road to Hopperstad Stave Church (described earlier in this chapter). Then backtrack to Route 13 and follow it south, to Voss. You'll soon begin a series of switchbacks that wind you up and out of the valley. The best views are from

the Storesvingen Fjellstove restaurant (on the left). Soon after, you'll crest the ridge, go through a tunnel, and find yourself on top of the world, in a desolate and harshly scenic landscape of scrubby mountaintops, snow banks, lakes, and no trees, scattered with vacation cabins. After cruising atop the plateau for a while, the road twists its way down (next to a waterfall) into a very steep valley, which it meanders through the rest of the way to Voss. This is an hour-long, middle-of-nowhere journey, with few road signs—you might feel lost, but keep driving toward Voss. When Route 13 dead-ends into E16, turn right (toward Voss and Bergen) and reenter civilization. From here, the route follows the same roads described in the Lustrafjord–Bergen drive described above (including the Tvindefossen waterfall).

GUDBRANDSDAL VALLEY AND JOTUNHEIMEN MOUNTAINS

Norway in a Nutshell is a great day trip, but with more time and a car, consider a scenic meander from Oslo to Bergen. You'll arc up the Gudbrandsdal Valley and over the Jotunheimen Mountains, then travel along the Lustrafjord (see previous chapter).

After an introductory stop in Lillehammer, with its fine folk museum, you might spend the night in a log-and-sod farmstead-turned-hotel, tucked in a quiet valley under Norway's highest peaks. Next, Norway's highest pass takes you on an exhilarating roller-coaster ride through the heart of the myth-inspiring Jotunheimen, bristling with Norway's biggest mountains. Then the road hairpins down into fjord country (see previous chapter).

Planning Your Time

While you could spend five or six days in this area on a three-week Scandinavian rampage, this slice of the region is worth three days. By car, I'd spend them like this:

Day 1: Leave Oslo early, and spend midday at Lillehammer's Maihaugen Open-Air Folk Museum for a tour and picnic. Drive up the Gudbrandsdal Valley, stopping at the stave church in Lom. Stay overnight in the Jotunheimen countryside.

Day 2: Drive the Sognefjell road over the mountains, then down along the Lustrafjord, stopping to visit the Dale Church and the Nigard Glacier (see previous chapter). Sleep in your choice of fjord towns, described in previous chapters (such as Solvorn—see page 276, Balestrand—see page 264, or Aurland—see page 250).

Day 3: Cruise the Aurland and/or Nærøy fjords and try to visit another stave church or two (such as Urnes—see page 273,

Hopperstad—see page 262, or Borgund—see page 247) before carrying on to Bergen.

This plan can be condensed into two days if you skip the Nigard Glacier side-trip.

Lillehammer and the Gudbrandsdal Valley

The Gudbrandsdal Valley is the tradition-steeped country of Peer Gynt, the Norwegian Huck Finn. This romantic valley of time-worn hills, log cabins, and velvet farms has connected northern and southern Norway since ancient times. While not as striking as other parts of the Norwegian countryside, Gudbrandsdal offers a suitable first taste of the natural wonders that crescendo farther north and west (in Jotunheimen and the Sognefjord). Throughout this region, the government subsidizes small farms to keep the countryside populated and healthy. (These subsidies would not be permitted if Norway were a member of the European Union.)

Orientation to Lillehammer

The de facto capital of Gudbrandsdal, Lillehammer, is a pleasant winter and summer resort town of 25,000. While famous for its brush with Olympic greatness (as host of the 1994 Winter Olympiad), Lillehammer is a bit disappointing—worthwhile only for its excellent Maihaugen Open-Air Folk Museum, or to break up the long drive between Oslo and the Jotunheimen region. If you do wind up here, Lillehammer has happy, old, woody pedestrian zones (Gågata and Storgata).

Tourist Information

Lillehammer's TI is inside the train station (mid-June–mid-Aug Mon–Fri 9:00–18:00, Sat–Sun 10:00–17:00; mid-Aug–mid-June Mon–Fri 9:00–16:00, Sat 10:00–14:00, closed Sun; Jernbanetorget 2, tel. 61 28 98 00, www.lillehammerturist.no).

Sights in Lillehammer

Lillehammer's two most worthwhile sights are up the hill behind the center of town. It's a fairly steep 15-minute walk from the train station to either sight and a 10-minute, mostly level walk between the two (follow the busy main road that connects them). Because

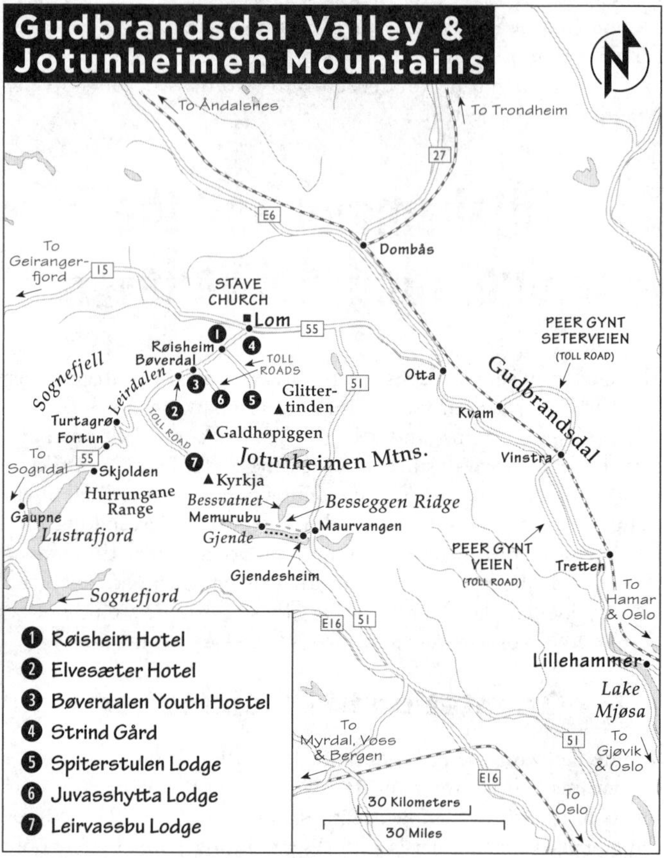

Gudbrandsdal Valley & Jotunheimen Mountains

1. Røisheim Hotel
2. Elvesæter Hotel
3. Bøverdalen Youth Hostel
4. Strind Gård
5. Spiterstulen Lodge
6. Juvasshytta Lodge
7. Leirvassbu Lodge

the walk from the station is uphill (and not very well-signed), consider catching the bus from in front of the train station (bus #005 or #003 to Olympics Museum, 2/hr; bus #007 to Maihaugen, 1/hr; 22 kr one-way for either bus).

▲▲Maihaugen Open-Air Folk Museum (Maihaugen Friluftsmuseet)—This idyllic park, full of old farmhouses and pickled slices of folk culture, provides a good introduction to what you'll see as you drive through the Gudbrandsdal Valley. Anders Sandvig, a "visionary dentist," started the collection in 1887. You'll divide your time between the fine indoor museum at the entrance and the sprawling exterior exhibits.

Upon arrival, ask about special

events, crafts, or musical performances. A TV monitor shows what's going on in the park.

Summer is busy with crafts in action and people reenacting life in the past, à la Colonial Williamsburg. There are no tours, so it's up to you to initiate conversations with the "residents." Off-season it's pretty dead, with no live crafts and most buildings locked up.

The outdoor section, with 200 buildings from the Gudbrandsdal region, is divided into three areas: the "Rural Collection," with old sod-roof log houses and a stave church; the "Town Collection," with reconstructed bits of old-time Lillehammer; and the "Residential Area," with 20th-century houses that look like most homes in today's Norway. The time trip can be jarring: In the 1980s house, a bubble-gum-chewing girl enthused about her new, "wireless" TV remote and played ABBA tunes from a cassette-tape player.

The museum's excellent "We Won the Land" exhibit (at the entry) sweeps you through Norwegian history from the Ice Age to the Space Age. The Gudbrandsdal art section shows village life at its best. And you can walk through Dr. Sandvig's old dental office and the original shops of various crafts- and tradespeople.

Because English descriptions are scant, the 95-kr English guidebook is worth considering (120 kr in summer, 80 kr off-season; 150-kr combo-ticket with Norwegian Olympics Museum; June–Aug daily 10:00–17:00; Sept–May Tue–Sun 11:00–16:00, closed Mon; paid parking, tel. 61 28 89 00; www.maihaugen.no).

Though the museum welcomes picnickers and has a simple cafeteria, Lillehammer's town center (a 10-min walk below the museum), with lots of fun eateries, is better for lunch (see "Eating in the Gudbrandsdal Valley," later).

Norwegian Olympics Museum (Norges Olympiske Museum)—This cute museum is housed in the huge Olympic ice-hockey arena, Håkon Hall. With brief English explanations, an emphasis on Norwegians and Swedes, and an endearingly gung-ho Olympic spirit, it's worth a visit on a rainy day or for sports fans. The ground-floor exhibit traces the ancient history of the Olympics, then devotes one wall panel to each of the summer and winter Olympiads of the modern era (with special treatment for the 1952 Oslo games). Upstairs, walk the entire concourse, circling the arena seating while reviewing the highlights (and lowlights) of the 1994 games (remember Tonya Harding?). While you're up there, check out the gallery of great Norwegian athletes and the giant egg used in the Lillehammer opening ceremony (75 kr, 150-kr combo-ticket with Maihaugen Open-Air Folk Museum; June–Aug daily 10:00–17:00; Sept–May Tue–Sun 11:00–16:00, closed Mon; tel. 61 25 21 00, www.ol.museum.no). With more time, see the 13-minute film on the 1994 Lillehammer Olympiad (included in museum ticket, 2/hr, usually in English, near ticket desk).

On the hillside above Håkon Hall (a 30-min hike or quick drive) are two ski jumps that host more Olympics sights, including a ski lift, the ski jump tower, and a bobsled ride (www.olympiaparken.no). In the summer, ski jumpers practice on the ski jumps, which are sprayed with water.

In the Gudbrandsdal Valley

If you're driving from Oslo to the Gudbrandsdal Valley, you'll go right past the historic Eidsvoll Manor (described on page 216).

Scenic Drives—The main E6 road north of Lillehammer (en route to Otta and Lom) passes through a bucolic valley with fine but unremarkable scenery. Along this road, a pair of toll-road side-trips (Gynt Veien and Peer Gynt Seterveien) loop off the E6 road. While they sound romantic, they're basically windy, curvy dirt roads over high, desolate heath and scrub-brush plateaus with fine mountain views. They're scenic, but pale in comparison to the Sognefjell road between Lom and the Lustrafjord (described later in this chapter).

GUDBRANDSDAL

Sleeping in the Gudbrandsdal Valley

I prefer sleeping in the more scenic and Norwegian-feeling Jotunheimen area (described later). But if you're sleeping here, Lillehammer and the surrounding valley offer several good options. My choices for Lillehammer are near the train station; the accommodations in Kvam provide a convenient stopping point in the valley.

In Lillehammer

$$$ Mølla Hotell, true to its name, is situated in an old mill along the little stream running through Lillehammer. The 58 rooms blend Old World charm with modern touches. It's more cutesy-cozy and less businesslike than other Lillehammer hotels in this price range (Db-1,200–1,400 kr depending on demand,

Sleep Code

(6 kr = about $1, country code: 47)

S = Single, **D** = Double/Twin, **T** = Triple, **Q** = Quad, **b** = bathroom, **s** = shower. You can assume credit cards are accepted unless otherwise noted.

To help you sort easily through these listings, I've divided the rooms into three categories, based on the price for a standard double room with bath:

$$$ Higher Priced—Most rooms 1,000 kr or more.
$$ Moderately Priced—Most rooms between 500–1,000 kr.
$ Lower Priced—Most rooms 500 kr or less.

elevator, free Internet access and Wi-Fi, a block below Gågata at Elvegata 12, tel. 61 05 70 80, fax 61 05 70 81, www.mollahotell.no, post@mollahotell.no).

$$ First Hotel Breiseth is a business-class hotel with 89 rooms in a handy location directly across from the train station (Db-1,300 kr, discounted to 1,000 kr for most of June–Aug, Sb costs 200 kr less, free parking, Jernbanegaten 1–5, tel. 61 24 77 77, www.firsthotels.no/breiseth, breiseth@firsthotels.no).

$ Vandrerhjem Stasjonen, Lillehammer's youth hostel, is actually upstairs inside the train station. With 75 beds in 28 institutional but new-feeling rooms—including 18 almost hotel-like doubles—it's a winner (325-kr bunk in a 3- to 4-bed dorm, Sb-700 kr, Db-840 kr, 15 percent cheaper for members, includes sheets and breakfast, elevator, free Wi-Fi, Jernbanetorget 2, tel. 61 26 00 24, www.stasjonen.no, post@stasjonen.no).

In Kvam

This is a popular vacation valley for Norwegians, and you'll find loads of reasonable small hotels and campgrounds with huts for those who aren't quite campers (*hytter* means "bungalows," *rom* is "private room," and *ledig* means "vacancy"). These huts normally cost about 400–600 kr, depending on size and amenities, and can hold from four to six people. Although they are simple, you'll have a kitchenette and access to a good WC and shower. When available, sheets rent for about an extra 60 kr per person. Here are a couple of listings in the town of Kvam, located midway between Lillehammer and Lom.

$$ Sinclair Vertshuset Motel has a quirky Scottish-Norwegian ambience. The 15 fine rooms are in old-fashioned motel wings, while the main building houses an inexpensive cafeteria, described below (Sb-790 kr, Db-990 kr, includes breakfast, family deals, free Internet access and Wi-Fi, tel. 61 29 54 50, fax 61 29 54 51, www.vertshuset-sinclair.no, post@vertshuset-sinclair.no). The motel was named after a Scotsman who led a band of adventurers into this valley, attempting to set up their own Scottish kingdom. They failed. All were kilt.

$-$$ Kirketeigen Ungdomssenter ("Church Youth Center"), behind the town church, welcomes travelers year-round (camping spots-120 kr/tent; small cabins without water-400 kr; cabins with kitchen and bath-700 kr, sleeps up to 5 people; simple 4-bed rooms in the main building-400 kr for 2–4 people with sheets; sheets and blankets-90 kr, Wi-Fi, tel. 61 21 60 90, www.kirketeigen.no, post@kirketeigen.no).

Eating in the Gudbrandsdal Valley

In Lillehammer: Good restaurants are scattered around the city center, but for the widest selection, head to where the main pedestrian drag (Gågata) crosses the little stream running downhill through town. Poke a block or two up and down **Elvegata,** which stretches along the river and hosts a wide range of tempting eateries—from pubs (both rowdy and upscale) to pizza and cheap sandwich stands.

In the Valley: Sinclair Vertshuset, described above, has a cafeteria handy for a quick and filling bite on the road between Lillehammer and Lom (50–70-kr sandwiches, 100–180-kr meals, daily 7:00–24:00).

Jotunheimen Mountains

Norway's Jotunheimen Mountains ("Giants' Home") feature the country's highest peaks and some of its best hikes and drives. This national park stretches from the fjords to the glaciers. You can play roller-coaster with mountain passes, take rugged hikes, wind up scenic toll roads, get up close to a giant stave church...and sleep in a time-passed rural valley. The gateway to the mountains is the unassuming town of Lom.

Lom

Pleasant Lom—the main town between Lillehammer and Sogndal—feels like a modern ski resort village. It's home to one of Norway's most impressive stave churches. While Lom has little else to offer, the church causes the closest thing to a tour-bus traffic jam this neck of the Norwegian woods will ever see.

Orientation to Lom

Park by the stave church—you'll see its dark spire just over the bridge. The church shares a parking lot with a gift shop/church museum and some public WCs. Across the street is the TI. If you're heading over the mountains, Lom's bank (at the Kommune building) has the last ATM until Gaupne.

Tourist Information

Lom's TI is an excellent source of information for hikes and drives in the Jotunheimen Mountains (mid-June–mid-Aug Mon–Fri 9:00–19:00, Sat–Sun 10:00–19:00; May–mid-June and mid-Aug–Sept Mon–Fri 9:00–16:00, Sat–Sun 10:00–17:00; Oct–April Mon–Fri 10:00–15:00, closed Sat–Sun; in the sod-roofed building across the busy road from the stave church parking lot, tel. 61 21 29 90, www.visitlom.com and www.visitjotunheimen.com).

The TI also serves as a national park office and hosts a worthwhile **Mountain Museum** (Norsk Fjellmuseum), tracing the history of the people who have lived off the land in Jotunheimen from the Stone Age to today. This is one of the better exhibits in fjord country. Its theater shows a 10-minute montage of images backed by Kenny G-type music, and the displays are well-presented with plenty of actual historic artifacts (50 kr, same hours as TI). The museum also has a computer with free Internet access for travelers.

Sights in Lom

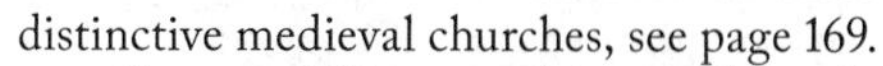

▲▲Lom Stave Church (Lom Stavkyrkje)

Despite extensive renovations, Lom's church (from 1158) remains a striking example of a Nordic stave church. For more on these distinctive medieval churches, see page 169.

Cost and Hours: 45 kr, daily mid-June–mid-Aug 9:00–20:00, mid-May–mid-June and mid-Aug–mid-Sept 10:00–16:00, closed in winter and during funerals, fine 10-kr leaflet.

Tours: Try to tag along with a guided tour—or, if it's not too busy, a docent can give you a quick private tour (included in ticket). Even outside of opening times—including winter—small groups can arrange a tour (40 kr/person, 300-kr minimum, call 97 07 53 97 in summer or 61 21 73 00 in winter).

➲ **Self-Guided Tour:** Buy your ticket and go inside to take in the humble **interior** (still used by locals for services—notice the posted hymnal numbers). Men sat on the right, women on the left, and prisoners sat with the sheriff in the caged area in the rear. Standing in the middle of the nave, look overhead to see the earliest surviving parts of the church, such as the circle of X-shaped St. Andrew crosses and the Romanesque arches above them. High above the door (impossible to see without a flashlight—ask a docent to show you) is an old painting of a dragon- or lion-like creature—likely an old Viking symbol, possibly drawn here to smooth the forced conversion local pagans made to Christianity. When King Olav II (later to become St. Olav) swept through this valley in 1021, he gave locals an option: convert or be burned out of house and home.

On the white town flag, notice the spoon—a symbol of Lom. Because of its position nestled in the mountains, Lom gets less rainfall than other towns, so large spoons were traditionally used to spread water over the fields. The apse (behind the altar) was added in 1240, when trendy new Gothic cathedrals made an apse a must-have accessory for churches across Europe. Lepers came to the grilled window in the apse for a blessing. When the Reformation hit in 1536, the old paintings were whitewashed over. The church has changed over the years: Transepts, pews, and windows were added in the 17th century. And the circa-1720 paintings were done by a local priest's son.

Drop into the **gift shop/church museum** in the big black building in the parking lot. Its one-room exhibit celebrates 1,000 years of the stave church—interesting if you follow the loaner English descriptions (10 kr, mid-July–mid-Aug daily 9:00–20:00, progressively shorter hours in shoulder season, in winter Mon–Sat 10:00–15:00, closed Sun, tel. 61 21 19 05). Inside you'll find a pair of beautiful model churches, headstones and other artifacts, and the only surviving stave-church dragon-head "steeple." In the display case near the early-1900s organ, find the little pencil-size stick carved with runes, dating from around 1350. It's actually a love letter from a would-be suitor. The woman rejected him, but she saved them both from embarrassment by hiding the stick under the church floorboards beneath a pew...where it was found in 1973. (Docents inside the church like to show off a replica of this stick.)

Before or after your church visit, explore the tidy, thought-provoking **graveyard** surrounding the church. Also, check out the precarious-looking little footbridge over the waterfall (the best view is from the modern road bridge into town).

Sleeping near Lom

(6 kr = about $1, country code: 47)
Lom itself has a handful of hotels, but the most appealing way to overnight in this area is at a rural rest stop in the countryside. All

of these are on Route 55 south of Lom, toward Sognefjord—Strind Gård first, then Bøverdalen, Røisheim, and finally Elvesæter (all within 20 minutes of Lom).

$$$ Røisheim, in a marvelously remote mountain setting, is an extremely expensive storybook hotel composed of a cluster of centuries-old, sod-roofed log farmhouses. Its posh and generous living rooms are filled with antiques. Each of the 20 rooms (in eight different buildings) is rustic but elegant, with fun "barrel bathtubs" and four-poster or canopy beds. Some rooms are in old, wooden farm buildings—*stabburs*—with low ceilings and heavy beams. The deluxe rooms are larger, with king beds and fireplaces. Call ahead so they'll be prepared for your arrival (open mid-May–Sept; standard Db-3,600 kr, deluxe Db-3,950 kr; includes breakfast, packed lunch, and an over-the-top four-course traditional dinner served at 19:30; non-smoking, Wi-Fi, 10 miles south of Lom on Route 55, tel. 61 21 20 31, fax 61 21 21 51, www.roisheim.no, booking@roisheim.dvgl.no, Haavard Lunde).

$$$ Elvesæter Hotel has its own share of Old World romance, but is bigger, cheaper, and more modest. Delightful public spaces bunny-hop through its traditional shell, while its 200 beds sprawl through nine buildings. The Elvesæter family has done a great job of retaining the historic character of their medieval farm, even though the place is big enough to handle large tour groups. The renovated "superior" rooms are new-feeling, but have sterile modern furniture; the older, cheaper "standard" rooms are well-worn but more characteristic (open May–Sept, standard Db-1,050 kr, superior Db-1,550 kr, extra bed-450 kr, family deals, includes breakfast, good 300-kr three-course dinners, strictly non-smoking, Wi-Fi, swimming pool, farther up Route 55, just past Bøverdal, tel. 61 21 99 00, fax 61 21 99 01, www.elveseter.no, post@elveseter.no). Even if you're not staying here, stop by to wander through the public spaces and pick up a flier explaining the towering Sagasøyla (Saga Column). It was started in 1926 to celebrate the Norwegian constitution, and was to stand in front of Oslo's Parliament Building—but the project stalled after World War II (thanks to the artist's affinity for things German and membership in Norway's fascist party). It was eventually finished and erected here in 1992.

$ Bøverdalen Youth Hostel offers 32 cheap-but-comfortable beds and a far more rugged clientele—real hikers rather than car hikers. While a bit institutional, it's well-priced and well-run (open late May–Sept, bunk in 4- to 6-bed room-175 kr, D-400 kr; 4-person cabins-600 kr with shower and toilet, 500 kr with toilet but no shower; 15 percent discount for members, sheets-65 kr, breakfast-70 kr, free Wi-Fi, kitchen, hot meals, self-serve café, tel. & fax 61 21 20 64, boverdalen@hihostels.no, Anna Berit). It's in the center of the little community of Bøverdal (store, campground, and toll road up to Galdhøpiggen area).

$ Strind Gård is your very rustic option if you can't spring for Røisheim or Elvesæter, but still want the countryside-farm experience. This 150-year-old farmhouse, situated by a soothing waterfall, rents two rooms and one apartment, plus four sod-roofed log huts. The catch: Many of the buildings have no running water, so you'll use the shared facilities at the main building. While not everyone's cup of tea, this place will appeal to romantics who always wanted to sleep in a humble log cabin in the Norwegian mountains—it's downright idyllic for those who like to rough it (2-person huts: without bathroom-220–450 kr depending on size, beautiful private hut with bathroom-700 kr; rooms in main house: D-300–450 kr depending on size, apartment for 4–6 with private bath-700 kr; no breakfast, free Wi-Fi, low ceilings, farm smells, valley views, 2 miles south of Lom on Route 55, tel. 61 21 12 37, www.strind-gard.no, Anne Jorunn and Trond Dalsegg).

Drives and Hikes in the Jotunheimen Mountains

Route 55, which runs between Lom and the Sognefjord to the south, is the sightseeing spine of this region. From this main (and already scenic) drag, other roads spin upwards into the mountains—offering even better views and exciting drives and hikes. Many of these get you up close to Norway's highest mountain, Galdhøpiggen (8,100 feet). I've listed these attractions from north to south, as you'll reach them driving from Lom to the Sognefjord; except for the first, they all branch off from Route 55. Another great high-mountain experience nearby—the hike to the Nigard Glacier near Lustrafjord—is covered on page 271.

Remember that the TI in Lom acts as a national park office, offering excellent maps and advice for drivers and hikers—a stop here is obligatory if you're planning a jaunt into the mountains (see "Orientation to Lom," earlier). For locations, see the map on page 284.

Besseggen

This trail offers an incredible opportunity to walk between two lakes separated by a narrow ridge and a 1,000-foot cliff. It's one of Norway's most beloved hikes, which can make it crowded in the summer. To get to the trailhead, drivers detour down Route 51 after Otta south to Maurvangen. Turn right to Gjendesheim to park your car. From Gjendesheim, catch the boat to Memurubu, where the path starts at the boat dock. Hike along the ridge—with a blue lake (Bessvatnet) on one side and a green lake (Gjende) on the other—and keep your balance. The six-hour trail loops back to Gjendesheim. Because the boat runs sporadically, time your visit to catch one (100 kr for 20-min ride, 3 morning departures daily, latest schedules at www.gjende.no, tel. 61 23 85 09). This is a thrilling but potentially hazardous hike, and it's a major detour: Gjendesheim is about 90 minutes and 50 miles from Lom.

Spiterstulen

From Røisheim, this 11-mile toll road (50 kr) takes you from Route 55 to the Spiterstulen mountain hotel/lodge in about 30 minutes (3,600 feet). This is the best destination for serious all-day hikes to Norway's two mightiest mountains, Glittertinden and Galdhøpiggen (a 5-hour hike up and a 3-hour hike down, doable without a guide). Or consider a guided, two-hour glacier walk (tel. 61 21 94 00, www.spiterstulen.no).

Juvasshytta

This toll road, starting from Bøverdal, takes you in about 40 minutes to the highest you can drive and the closest you can get to Galdhøpiggen by car (6,050 feet). At the end of the 85-kr toll road, daily, guided, six-hour hikes go across the glacier to the summit and back (150 kr, late June–late Sept daily at 10:00, July–mid-Aug also daily at 11:30, check in 30 min before, strict age limit—no kids under age 7, 4 miles each way, easy ascent but very dangerous without a guide, hiking boots required—possible to rent from nearby ski resort). You can sleep in the **$$ Juvasshytta lodge** (Db-660 kr with sheets, D without sheets-500 kr, sheets-100 kr, breakfast-100 kr, dinner-300 kr, tel. 61 21 15 50, www.juvasshytta.no).

Leirvassbu

This 11-mile, 40-kr toll road (about 30 min one-way from Bøverkinnhalsen, south of Elvesæter) is most scenic for car hikers. It takes you to a lodge at 4,600 feet with great views and easy walks. A serious (5-hr round-trip) hike goes to the lone peak, Kyrkja—"The Cathedral," which looms like a sanded-down mini-Matterhorn on the horizon (6,660 feet).

▲▲Sognefjell Drive to the Sognefjord

Norway's highest pass (at 4,600 feet, the highest road in northern Europe) is a thrilling drive through a cancan line of mountains, from Jotunheimen's Bøverdal Valley to the Lustrafjord (an arm of the Sognefjord—see previous chapter). Centuries ago, the farmers of Gudbrandsdal took their horse caravans over this difficult mountain pass on treks to Bergen. Today, the road (Route 55) is still narrow, windy, and otherworldly (and usually closed mid-Oct–May).

As you begin to ascend just beyond Elvesæter, notice the viewpoint on the left for the Leirdalen Valley—capped at the end with the Kyrkja peak (described earlier). Then you'll twist up into a lake-filled valley, then through a mild canyon with grand waterfalls. Before long, as you corkscrew up more switchbacks, you're above the tree line, enjoying a "top of the world" feeling. The best views (to the south) are of the cut-glass range called Hurrungane ("Noisy Children"). The 10 hairpin turns between Turtagrø and Fortun are exciting. Be sure to stop, get out, look around, and enjoy the lavish views. Treat each turn as if it were your last.

Just before you descend to the fjord, the terrain changes, and you reach a pullout on the right, next to a hilltop viewpoint—offering your first glimpse of the fjord. The Lustrafjord village of Skjolden is just around the bend (and down several more switchbacks). Entering Skjolden, continue following Route 55, which now traces the west bank of the Lustrafjord. For more on the sights from here on out, turn to page 270.

Connections

Cars are better, but if you're without wheels: **Oslo to Lillehammer** (trains almost hourly, 2.5 hrs, just 2 hrs from Oslo airport), **Lillehammer to Otta** (6 trains/day, 1.5 hrs); a bus meets some trains (confirm schedule at the train station in Oslo) for travelers heading on to **Lom** (2 buses/day, 1 hr) and onward from **Lom to Sogndal** (2 buses/day late June–Aug only, road closed off-season, 3.25 hrs).

Route Tips for Drivers

Use low gears and lots of patience both up (to keep the engine cool) and down (to save your brakes). Uphill traffic gets the right-of-way, but drivers, up or down, dive for the nearest fat part of the road whenever they meet. Ask backseat drivers not to scream until you've actually been hit or have left the road.

From Oslo to Jotunheimen: It's 2.5 hours from Oslo to Lillehammer and 3 hours after that to Lom. Wind out of Oslo following signs for *E6* (not to *Drammen*, but for *Stockholm* and then to *Trondheim*). In a few minutes, you're in the wide-open pastoral countryside of eastern Norway. Norway's Constitution Hall—Eidsvoll Manor—is a five-minute detour off E6, several miles south of Eidsvoll in Eidsvoll Verk (described on page 216;

follow the signs to *Eidsvoll Bygningen*). Then E6 takes you along Norway's largest lake (Mjøsa), through the town of Hamar, and past more lake scenery into Lillehammer. Signs direct you uphill from downtown Lillehammer to the Maihaugen Open-Air Folk Museum. From Lillehammer, signs to *E6/Trondheim* take you up the valley of Gudbrandsdal. At Otta, exit for Lom. Halfway to Lom, on the left, look for the long suspension bridge spanning the milky-blue river—a good opportunity to stretch your legs, and a scenic spot to enjoy a picnic.

BERGEN

Bergen is permanently salted with robust cobbles and a rich sea-trading heritage. Norway's capital in the 12th and 13th centuries, Bergen's wealth and importance came thanks to its membership in the heavyweight medieval trading club of merchant cities called the Hanseatic League. Bergen still wears her rich maritime heritage proudly.

Bergen gets an average of 80 inches of rain annually (compared to 30 inches in Oslo). A good year has 60 days of sunshine. The natives aren't apologetic about their famously lousy weather. In fact, they seem to wear it as a badge of local pride. "Well, that's Bergen," they'll say matter-of-factly as they wring out their raincoats. When I complained about an all-day downpour, a local cheerfully informed me, "There's no such thing as bad weather—just inappropriate clothing"...a local mantra that rhymes in Norwegian.

With 250,000 people, Bergen has big-city parking problems and high prices, but visitors sticking to the old center find it charming. Enjoy Bergen's salty market, then stroll the easy-on-foot old quarter, with cute lanes of delicate old wooden houses. From downtown Bergen, a funicular zips you up a little mountain for a bird's-eye view of this sailors' town.

Planning Your Time

Bergen can be enjoyed even on the tail end of a day's scenic train ride from Oslo before returning on the overnight train. But that teasing taste will make you wish you had more time. On a three-week tour of Scandinavia, Bergen is worth a whole day.

While Bergen's sights are visually underwhelming and pricey, nearly all come with thoughtful tours in English. If you dedicate the time to take advantage of these tours, otherwise barren attractions (such as Håkon's Hall and Rosenkrantz Tower, the Bryggen quarter, the Leprosy Museum, and Gamle Bergen) become surprisingly interesting. For a busy day, you could do this (enjoying tours at all but the last): 9:00—Stroll through the fish market; 10:00—Visit Håkon's Hall and Rosenkrantz Tower; 12:00—Take the Bryggen Walking Tour; 14:00—Take a harbor cruise or check out the Leprosy Museum; 16:00—Enjoy some free time in town (consider returning to the Bryggens Museum using your tour ticket), or catch the bus out to Gamle Bergen; 18:00—Ride up the Fløibanen funicular.

Although Bergen has plenty of attractions and charms of its own, it's most famous as the "Gateway to the Fjords." If you plan to use Bergen as a springboard for the fjord country, you have three options: Pick up a rental car here (fjord wonder is a three-hour drive away); take the express boat down the Sognefjord (about four hours to Balestrand and Flåm/Aurland); or do the "Norway in a Nutshell" as a scenic loop from Bergen. The "Nutshell" option also works well as a detour midway between Bergen and Oslo (hop the train from either city to Voss or Myrdal, then take a bus or spur train into the best of the Sognefjord; scenic ferry rides depart from there). While there are a million ways to enjoy the fjords, first-timers should start with this region (covered thoroughly in the Norway in a Nutshell and More on the Sognefjord chapters).

Also note that Bergen, a geographic dead-end, is actually an efficient place to begin or end your Scandinavian tour. Consider flying "open jaw"—for example, into Bergen and out of Helsinki (or vice versa).

Orientation to Bergen

Bergen clusters around its harbor—nearly everything listed in this chapter is within a few minutes' walk. The busy Torget (market square and fish market) is at the head of the harbor. As you face the sea from here, Bergen's TI is across the street behind you. The town's historic Hanseatic Quarter (Bryggen) lines the harbor on the right. Express boats to the Sognefjord (Balestrand and Flåm) and Stavanger dock at the harbor on the left.

Protected from the open sea by a lone sheltering island, Bergen is a place of refuge from heavy winds for the giant working boats that serve the North Sea oil rigs. (Much of Norway's current affluence is funded by the oil it drills just offshore.) Bergen is also one of the most popular cruise-ship ports in northern Europe, hosting 260 ships a year and up to 7 ships a day in peak season. Each morning is rush hour, as cruisers hike past the fortress and into town.

Charming cobbled streets surround the harbor and climb the encircling hills. Bergen's popular Fløibanen funicular climbs high above the city to the top of Mount Fløyen for the best view of the town. Surveying the surrounding islands and inlets, it's clear why this city is known as the "Gateway to the Fjords."

Tourist Information

The TI, filling the historic old Bergen Exchange building, is frescoed with old murals showing local and traditional life (June–Aug daily 8:30–22:00; May and Sept daily 9:00–20:00; Oct–April Mon–Sat 9:00–16:00, closed Sun; across from fish market at Vågsallmenningen 1, tel. 55 55 20 00, www.visitbergen.com). The TI covers Bergen and western Norway, provides information and tickets for tours, has a fjord information desk, books rooms, and maintains a very handy events board listing today's and tomorrow's slate of tours, concerts, and other events. Pick up this year's edition of the free *Bergen Guide* (also likely at your hotel), which has a fine map and lists all sights, hours, and special events. This booklet can answer most of your questions. If you need assistance and there's a line, take a number.

Bergen Card: This greedy little card gets cut back each year. You have to really work to make it pay. It gives you free use of the city buses, half off the Mount Fløyen funicular, free admission to most museums (but not the Hanseatic Museum), and discounts on some tours, events, and sights—such as a measly 10 percent discount on the Bryggen Walking Tour, and a 50 percent discount on Edvard Grieg's Home. It also covers the aquarium—if you're here in the winter (190 kr/24 hrs, 250 kr/48 hrs, sold at TI, train station, and most hotels).

Arrival in Bergen

By Train or Bus: Bergen's train and bus stations are on Strømgaten, facing a park-rimmed lake. The small, manageable train station has an office open long hours for booking all your travel in Norway—get your Nutshell reservations here if you haven't already (Mon–Fri 6:45–19:30, Sat 7:30–16:10, Sun 7:30–19:30). There are luggage lockers (30 kr/day, daily 6:30–23:30), pay toilets, a newsstand, sandwich shop, and coffee shop. (To get to the bus station, follow the covered walkway behind the Narvesen newsstand via the Storcenter shopping mall.) Taxis wait to the right (with the tracks at your back). From the train station, it's a 10-minute walk to the TI: Cross the street (Strømgaten) in front of the station and take Marken, a cobbled street (see map).

By Plane: Bergen's cute little Flesland Airport is 12 miles south of the city center. The airport bus runs between the airport and downtown Bergen, stopping at the SAS Radisson Hotel in Bryggen, the harborfront area near the TI (if you ask), the SAS Hotel Norge (in the modern part of town at Ole Bulls Plass), and the bus station (85 kr, pay driver, 4/hr at peak times, less in slow times, 30-min ride). Taxis take up to four people and cost about 400 kr for the 20-minute ride (depending on the time of day). Airport info: tel. 55 99 80 00; SAS info: tel. 81 52 04 00.

By Car: Driving is a headache in Bergen—avoid it if you can. Approaching town on E16 (from Voss and the Sognefjord area), follow signs for *Sentrum*, which spits you out near the big, modern bus station and parking garage. Parking is difficult and costly—ask at your hotel for tips. Note that all drivers entering Bergen must pay a 15-kr toll, but there are no toll-collection gates (since the system is entirely automated for locals). It's Norway's new way of collecting tolls: Assuming they bill you, it'll just show up on your credit card (which they access through your rental car company). For details, ask your rental company or see www.autopass.no.

Helpful Hints

Museum Tours: Many of Bergen's sights are hard to appreciate without a guide. Fortunately, many include a wonderful and intimate guided tour with admission. Make the most of the following sights by taking full advantage of their included tours: Håkon's Hall and Rosenkrantz Tower, Bryggens Museum, Hanseatic Museum, Leprosy Museum, Gamle Bergen, and Edvard Grieg's Home.

Laundry: Jarlens Vaskoteque is at Lille Øvregate 17, one block uphill from the church called Korskirken (2-hr drop-off service for 110 kr, self-service for 80 kr, Mon–Fri 10:00–18:00, Wed–Thu until 20:00, Sat 10:00–15:00, closed Sun, tel. 55 32 55 04).

Getting Around Bergen

Most in-town sights can easily be reached by foot; only the aquarium and Gamle Bergen (and the outlying sights of Fantoft Stave Church, Edvard Grieg's Home at Troldhaugen, and the Ulriken643 cable car) are more than a 10-minute walk from the TI.

By Bus: The free "Sentrum-VilVite bus" runs every 10 minutes from the big parking garage near the bus station, past the TI and fish market, and around Bryggen. It's designed to encourage people to park and ride. Hop on for a free circular joyride through town (Mon–Fri 7:30–21:00, no bus Sat–Sun).

City buses cost 24 kr per ride (pay driver). The best city buses for a city joyride are #20 (north along the coast) and #11 (into the hills).

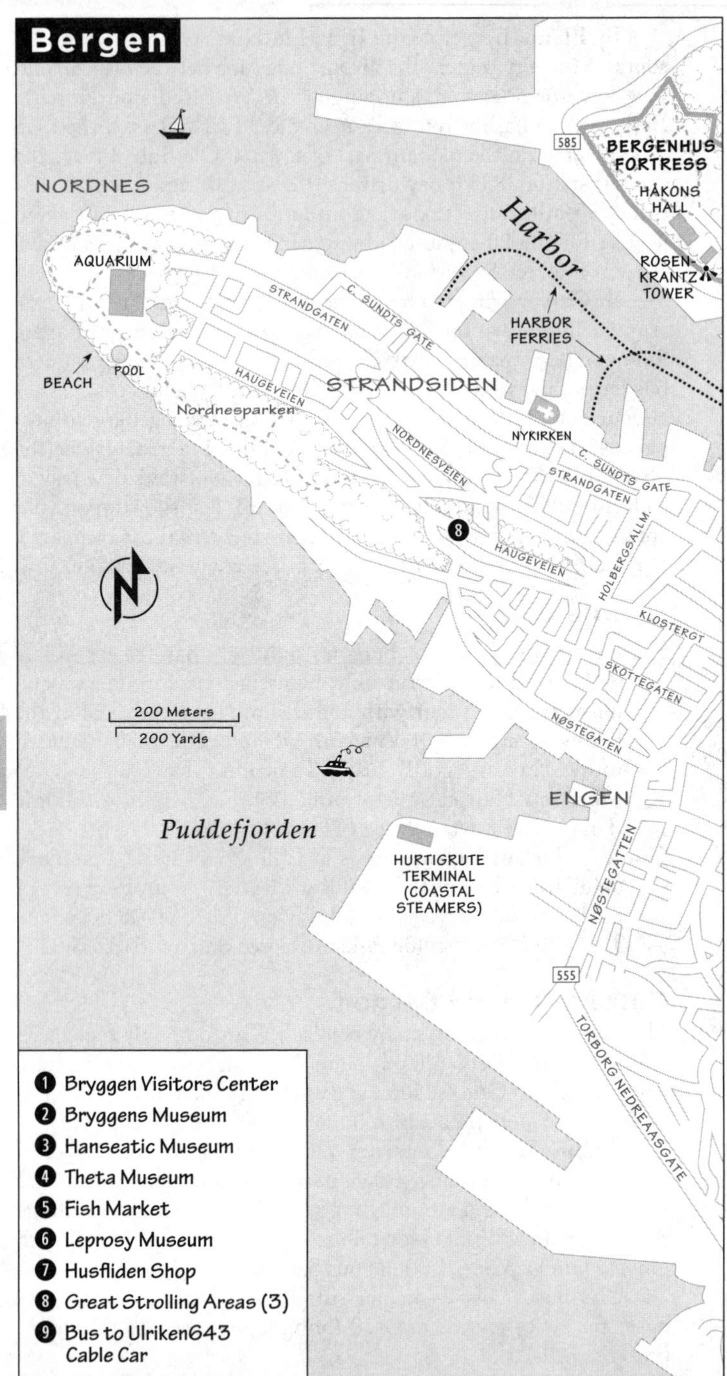
Bergen
NORDNES
AQUARIUM
BEACH
POOL
Nordnesparken
STRANDGATEN
C. SUNDTS GATE
HAUGEVEIEN
STRANDSIDEN
NORDNESVEIEN
NYKIRKEN
STRANDGATEN
C. SUNDTS GATE
HAUGEVEIEN
HOLBERGSALLM.
KLOSTERGT
SKOTTEGATEN
NØSTEGATEN
Harbor
HARBOR FERRIES
585
BERGENHUS FORTRESS
HÅKONS HALL
ROSEN-KRANTZ TOWER
200 Meters
200 Yards
Puddefjorden
ENGEN
HURTIGRUTE TERMINAL (COASTAL STEAMERS)
NØSTEGATEN
555
TORBORG NEDREAASGATE
1 Bryggen Visitors Center
2 Bryggens Museum
3 Hanseatic Museum
4 Theta Museum
5 Fish Market
6 Leprosy Museum
7 Husfliden Shop
8 Great Strolling Areas (3)
9 Bus to Ulriken643 Cable Car
BERGEN

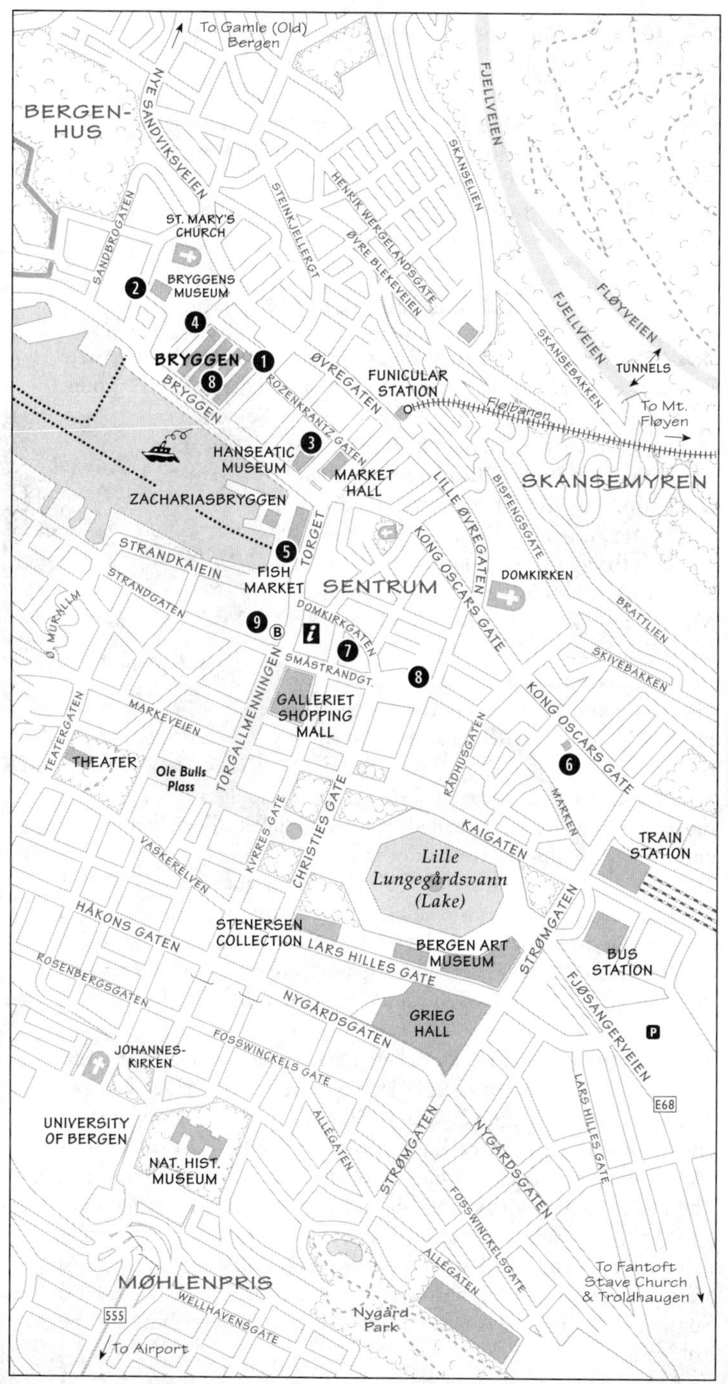

To Gamle (Old) Bergen
BERGEN-HUS
NYE SANDVIKSVEIEN
SANDBROGATEN
ST. MARY'S CHURCH
BRYGGENS MUSEUM
BRYGGEN
BRYGGEN
STEINKJELLERGT
HENRIK WERGELANDSGATE
ØVRE BLEKEVEIEN
SKANSELIEN
FJELLVEIEN
FJELLVEIEN
FLØYVEIEN
SKANSEBAKKEN
TUNNELS
To Mt. Fløyen
Fløibanen
FUNICULAR STATION
ØVREGATEN
ROZENKRANTZ GATEN
HANSEATIC MUSEUM
MARKET HALL
ZACHARIASBRYGGEN
SKANSEMYREN
LILLE ØVREGATEN
BISPENGSGATE
KONG OSCARS GATE
TORGET
FISH MARKET
STRANDKAIEIN
STRANDGATEN
SENTRUM
DOMKIRKEN
BRATTLIEN
DOMKIRKGATEN
SMÅSTRANDGT.
SKIVEBAKKEN
Ø. MURALLM
TORGALLMENNINGEN
GALLERIET SHOPPING MALL
KONG OSCARS GATE
TEATERGATEN
MARKEVEIEN
THEATER
Ole Bulls Plass
RÅDHUSGATEN
MARKEN
CHRISTIES GATE
KVRRES GATE
KAIGATEN
TRAIN STATION
VASKERELVEN
Lille Lungegårdsvann (Lake)
HÅKONS GATEN
STENERSEN COLLECTION
LARS HILLES GATE
BERGEN ART MUSEUM
STRØMGATEN
BUS STATION
ROSENBERGSGATEN
NYGÅRDSGATEN
GRIEG HALL
FJØSANGERVEIEN
FOSSWINCKELS GATE
JOHANNES-KIRKEN
E68
LARS HILLES GATE
UNIVERSITY OF BERGEN
ALLEGATEN
STRØMGATEN
NYGÅRDSGATEN
NAT. HIST. MUSEUM
FOSSWINCKELSGATE
ALLEGATEN
To Fantoft Stave Church & Troldhaugen
MØHLENPRIS
WELLHAVENSGATE
555
To Airport
Nygård Park
BERGEN

By Ferry: The *Beffen,* a little orange ferry, chugs across the harbor every half-hour (20 kr, Mon–Fri 7:30–16:30, no weekend runs). This three-minute "poor man's cruise" has good harbor views. The Vågen "Akvariet" ferry departs from in front of the fish market for the aquarium (40 kr one-way, 60 kr round-trip, 2/hr, daily May–Aug 10:00–18:00).

By Taxi: For a taxi, call 07000 or 08000 (not as expensive as you might expect).

Tours in Bergen

▲▲▲Bryggen Walking Tour—This tour of the historic Hanseatic district is one of Bergen's best activities. Local guides take visitors on an excellent 90-minute walk through 900 years of Bergen history via the old Hanseatic town (20 min in Bryggens Museum, 20-min visit to the medieval Hanseatic Assembly Rooms, 20-min walk through Bryggen, and 20 min in Hanseatic Museum). Tours leave from the Bryggens Museum (next to the big, modern SAS Radisson Hotel). When you consider that the tour price includes entry tickets to the Hanseatic and Bryggens museums and the Hanseatic Assembly Rooms, the tour more than pays for itself (100 kr, June–Aug daily at 11:00 and 12:00, none Sept–May, tel. 55 58 80 10). While the museum visits are a bit rushed, your tour ticket allows you to re-enter the museums for the rest of the day.

Other Walking Tours—Bergen Guide Service offers 1.5-hour bilingual walking tours of the city center daily in peak season (in Norwegian and English, 95 kr, mid-June–mid-Aug daily at 15:00, departs from TI, tel. 55 30 10 60, www.bergenguideservice.com). You can also contact Bergen Guide Service to hire your own local guide.

▲Bus Tours—The TI sells tickets for various bus tours. The 1.5-hour bus tour of the city center isn't very appealing, since you can enjoy everything better by foot (150 kr, June–Aug daily at 9:30 and 16:30). But the three-hour version that adds Edvard Grieg's Home at Troldhaugen is a handy way to reach that outlying sight. The bus is comfy, with big views and a fine recorded commentary (300 kr, May–Sept daily at 12:00, departs from curb across from fish market outside TI). There are also several full-day tour options from Bergen, including bus/boat tours to nearby Hardanger and Sogne fjords. The TI is packed with brochures describing all the excursions.

▲Harbor Tours—The *White Lady* leaves from the fish market daily in summer at 14:30 for a 50-minute cruise. The ride is both scenic and informative, with a relaxing sun deck and good—if scant—recorded narration (130 kr, June–late Aug). A four-hour fjord trip is also available (400 kr, May–Aug daily at 10:00, July–late Aug also daily at 15:30, sporadic departures in Sept, tel. 55 25 90 00).

Tourist Train—The tacky little "Bergen Express" train departs from in front of the Hanseatic Museum for a 55-minute loop around town (120 kr, May daily 10:00–16:00, June–Aug daily 10:00–19:00, Sept daily 11:00–15:00, 2/hr in peak season, otherwise hourly, headphone English commentary).

Sights in Bergen

▲▲Bergen Town Walk—For a quick and historic orientation walk through Bergen, start at the fortress and tower, head up to St. Mary's Church, peruse the old wooden Hanseatic Quarter, and loiter through the fish market. Then head into the modern center of town, the Torgallmenningen square, and finish with a stroll around the little lake. (These sights are all described below, in the order of this walk.) Ideally, you'll get side-tracked in the museums, and will take advantage of the excellent on-site tours (included with admission). As you explore, remember two points that shape the city you'll see:

While the city dates from 1070, little survives from before the last big fire in 1702. In its earlier heyday, Bergen was one of the largest wooden cities in Europe. Congested wooden buildings, combined with lots of small fires (to provide heat and light in this cold and dark corner of Europe), spelled disaster for Bergen. Over the centuries, the city suffered countless fires, including 10 devastating blazes. Each time the city burned, the destroyed material was tossed into the harbor, creating a haphazard landfill upon which much of the old town you see today was eventually built. After 1702, the city rebuilt using more stone and brick, and suffered fewer fires.

One of the biggest explosions of World War II, which occurred in the harbor on April 20, 1944, also shaped the city. An ammunition ship loaded with 120 tons of dynamite blew up just in front of the fortress. The blast leveled entire neighborhoods on either side of the harbor (notice the ugly 1950s construction opposite the fortress) and did serious damage to Håkon's Hall and Rosenkrantz Tower. How big was the blast? There's a hut called "the anchor cabin" a couple of miles away in the mountains. That's where the ship's anchor landed. While April 20 happened to be Hitler's birthday and the ship blew up about 100 yards away from the Nazi commander's headquarters (in the fortress), the blast is considered to be accidental.

▲Bergen's Fortress: Håkon's Hall and Rosenkrantz Tower—Back in the 13th century, Bergen was the Kingdom of Norway's first capital. (Prior to the 13th century, kings would circulate, staying on royal farms.) This fortress was a garrison, with a tower for the king's residence and a large hall for his banquets. Today the fortress grounds are used for big events (Bruce Springsteen filled it in 2009).

The tower and hall, sitting boldly out of place on the harbor just beyond Bryggen, are reminders of Bergen's medieval importance. Both sights feel vacant and don't really speak for themselves; the included guided tours, which provide a serious introduction to Bergen's history, are essential for grasping their significance. While each sight is covered by a separate ticket and tour, it's best to consider them as one and start at Håkon's Hall (tours leave at the top of the hour). Stick with your guide, as the Rosenkrantz Tower is part two of his tour.

Håkon's Hall, dating from the 13th century, is the largest secular medieval building in Norway. It's essentially a giant, grand reception hall (used today for banquets) under a ceiling that feels like an upturned Viking boat. While recently rebuilt, the ceiling's design is modeled after grand wooden roofs of that era. Beneath the hall is a whitewashed cellar. Banquets were a men-only affair. The raised seats gave royal, church, and military dignitaries the appropriate elevation.

Rosenkrantz Tower, the keep of a 13th-century castle, has a jumbled design, thanks to a Renaissance addition. The tour brings it to life. There's a good history exhibit on the top floors and a fine view from the rooftop.

Cost and Hours: The tower and hall cost 40 kr each and include a guided tour (leaves from Håkon's Hall at the top of each hour, last tour departs at 15:00). Both are open mid-May–Aug daily 10:00–16:00. The hall is also open Sept–mid-May daily 12:00–15:00, when the tower is closed (tel. 55 31 60 67).

St. Mary's Church (Mariakirken)—Dating from the 12th century, and still used for services today, this is Bergen's oldest building. This was the stately church of the Hanseatic merchants.

Its dour stone interior, enlivened by a colorful, highly decorated pulpit, is closed through 2014 while a 100-million-kroner renovation is under way. Behind the church is the back wall of the Hanseatic Quarter and the entrance to the communal Hanseatic Assembly Rooms (Schøtstuene).

Bergen's Hanseatic Quarter (Bryggen)—A horrific plague decimated the population and economy of Norway in 1350, killing about half of its people. A decade later, German merchants arrived and established a Hanseatic trading post (see sidebar), bringing order to that rustic society. For the next four centuries, the port of Bergen was German territory.

Bergen's old German trading center was called "the German wharf" until World War II, and is now just called "the wharf," or "Bryggen" (BREW-gun). From 1370 to 1754, German merchants controlled Bergen's trade. In 1550, it was a Germanic city of 1,000 workaholic merchants—surrounded and supported by some 5,000 Norwegians.

The German merchants were very strict and lived in a harsh, all-male world (except for Norwegian prostitutes). This wasn't a military occupation, but a mutually beneficial economic partnership. The Norwegian cod fishermen of the far north shipped their dried cod to Bergen, where the Hanseatic merchants marketed it to Europe. Norwegian cod provided much of Europe with food (a source of easy-to-preserve protein) and cod oil (which lit the lamps until about 1850).

The wharf area is mostly reclaimed from the sea. Each time the warehouses burned, the merchants would toss the refuse into the bay and rebuild. Gradually, the land crept out, and so did the buildings. (Looking at the Hanseatic Quarter from the harborfront, you can see how the buildings have settled. The foundations, composed of debris from the many fires, settle as they rot.) The long "tenements" (rows of warehouses) we see today date from the early 1700s—built after that last great fire in 1702. To prevent future fires, the Germans forbade all fires and candles for light or warmth except in isolated and carefully guarded communal houses behind each tenement. It was in these communal houses that apprentices studied, people dried out their soggy clothes, hot food was cooked, and the men drank and partied. One of these

The Hanseatic League and Cod

Middlemen in trade, the clever German merchants of the Hanseatic League ruled the waves of northern Europe for 500 years (c. 1250–1750). These sea-traders first banded together in a *Hanse*, or merchant guild, to defend themselves against pirates. As they spread out from Germany, they established trading posts in foreign lands, cut deals with local leaders for trading rights, built boats and wharves, and organized armies to protect ships and ports.

By the 15th century, these merchants had organized more than a hundred cities into the Hanseatic League, a free-trade zone that stretched from London to Russia. The League ran a profitable triangle of trade: Fish from Scandinavia were exchanged for grain from the eastern Baltic and luxury goods from England and Flanders. Everyone benefited, and the German merchants—the middlemen—reaped the profits.

At its peak in the 15th century, the Hanseatic League was the dominant force—economic, military, and political—in northern Europe. This was an age when much of Europe was fragmented into petty kingdoms and dukedoms. Revenue-hungry kings and robber-baron lords levied chaotic and extortionist tolls and duties. Pirates plagued shipments. It was the Hanseatic League, rather than national governments, that brought the stability that allowed trade to flourish.

Bergen's place in this Baltic economy was all about cod—a form of protein that could be dried, preserved, and shipped any-

medieval Hanseatic Assembly Rooms is preserved and open to the public (the Schøtstuene—separate entrance behind St. Mary's Church, included in Bryggen Walking Tour, difficult to appreciate without a guide).

Half of Bryggen (the stretch between the old wooden facades and the Hanseatic Museum—standing apart from the others at the head of the bay) was torn down around 1900. The man who owned the wooden building that now houses the Hanseatic Museum recognized the value of the city's heritage and kept his building as it was. Considered a nutcase back then, today he's celebrated as a visionary, as his decision left today's visitors with a fine example of an old merchant house to tour.

After World War II, Bryggen was again slated for destruction. Most of the locals wanted it gone—it reminded them of the Germans who had occupied Norway for several miserable years. Then excavators discovered rune stones indicating that the area predated the Germans. This boosted Bryggen's approval rating, and the quarter was saved.

From the front of Bryggen, look down at the Rosenkrantz

where. Though cursed by a lack of natural resources, the city was blessed with a good harbor conveniently located between the rich fishing spots of northern Norway and the markets of Europe. Bergen's port shipped dried cod and fish oil southward and imported grain, cloth, beer, wine, and ceramics.

Bryggen was one of four principal Hanseatic trading posts *(Kontors),* along with London, Bruges, and Novgorod. It was the last *Kontor* opened (c. 1360), the least profitable, and the last one closed (1754). Bryggen had warehouses, offices, and living quarters. Ships docked here were unloaded by counterpoise cranes. At its peak, as many as a thousand merchants, journeymen, and apprentices lived and worked here.

Bryggen was a self-contained German enclave within the city. The merchants came from Germany, worked a few years here, and retired back in the home country. They spoke German, wore German clothes, and attended their own churches. By law, they were forbidden to intermarry or fraternize with the Bergeners, except on business.

The Hanseatic League peaked around 1500, then slowly declined. Rising nation-states were jealous of the Germans' power and wealth. The Reformation tore apart old alliances. Dutch and English traders broke the Hanseatic monopoly. Cities withdrew from the League and *Kontors* closed. In 1754, Bergen's *Kontor* was taken over by the Norwegians. When it closed its doors on December 31, 1899, a sea-trading era was over, but the city of Bergen had become rich...by the grace of cod.

Tower. The little red holes at its top mark where cannons were once pointed at the German quarter by the Norwegian royalty. The threat was never taken seriously, however, because everyone knew that without German grain, the Norwegians would starve.

Bryggen is now touristy and boutiquey, but still lots of fun. Strolling through it, you feel swallowed up by history. Explore its wooden core, with medieval-style double-tenements—long rows of planky buildings leaning haphazardly across narrow alleys. Wander. You'll find plenty of art and artisan shops, sweater shops, atmospheric restaurants, and two worthwhile museums within a five-minute walk of each other (the Bryggens and Hanseatic museums, explained later). The little **visitors' center** plans to add exhibits about maintenance and restoration of the tenement houses (good 98-kr Bryggen guidebook, mid-May–mid-Sept daily 9:00–18:00, closed off-season, at the back end of the narrow wooden lane called Bellgården).

The **Bryggen Walking Tour** is your best bet for seeing Bryggen, the Bryggens Museum, and the Hanseatic Museum (100 kr, June–Aug daily at 11:00 and 12:00, none Sept–May, leaves from Bryggens Museum; for all the details, see "Tours in Bergen," earlier.)

▲▲Bryggens Museum—This modern museum explains the 1950s archaeological dig to uncover the earliest bits of Bergen (1050–1500). Brief English explanations are posted. From September through May, when there is no tour, ask to borrow the good museum guidebook (or buy it for 25 kr). The manageable, well-presented permanent exhibit occupies the ground floor. First you'll see foundations from original wooden tenements dating back to the 12th century (displayed right where they were excavated) and a giant chunk of the hull of a 100-foot-long, 13th-century ship that was found here. Then you'll enter an exhibit (roughly shaped like the long, wooden double-tenements outside) that shows off artifacts and explains lifestyles from medieval Bryggen. Behind that is a display of items you might have bought at the medieval market. You'll finish with exhibits about the church in Bergen, the town's role as a royal capital, and its status as a cultural capital. Upstairs are two floors of temporary exhibits (50 kr, included in summer with 100-kr Bryggen Walking Tour described earlier; open May–Aug daily 10:00–17:00; Sept–April Mon–Fri 11:00–15:00, Sat 12:00–15:00, Sun 12:00–16:00; in big modern building just beyond the end of Bryggen and the SAS Radisson Hotel, tel. 55 58 80 10, www.bymuseet.no). The museum has an inexpensive cafeteria with soup-and-bread specials.

▲▲Hanseatic Museum (Hanseatiske Museum)—This little museum was founded in the late 1900s to preserve a tenement interior. Its creaky old rooms—with hundred-year-old cod hanging from the ceiling—offer a time-tunnel experience back to Bryggen's glory days. It's located in an atmospheric old merchant house furnished with dried fish, antique ropes, an old oxtail (used for wringing spilled cod-liver oil back into the bucket), sagging steps, and cupboard beds from the early 1700s—one with a medieval pinup girl (50 kr, included in summer with 100-kr Bryggen Walking Tour, open daily June–Aug 9:00–17:00, Sept–May 11:00–14:00, tel. 55 54 46 96, www.museumvest.no).

BERGEN

Admission includes a good 45-minute guided tour (3/day in English, May–mid-Sept only). Even if you tour the museum with the Bryggen Walking Tour, you're welcome to revisit (same ticket) and take this longer tour.

Theta Museum—This small museum highlights Norway's resistance movement (specifically, a 10-person local group called Theta) during the Nazi occupation in World War II. It's housed in Theta's former headquarters—a small room in a wooden Bryggen building (30 kr, mid-May–mid-Sept Tue and Sat–Sun 14:00–16:00, closed Mon, Wed–Fri, and off-season, Enhjørningsgården, tel. 55 31 53 93).

▲▲Fish Market (Fisketorget)—A fish market has thrived here since the 1500s, when fishermen rowed in with their catch and haggled with the hungry locals. While it's now become a food circus of eateries selling fishy treats to tourists—no local would come here to actually buy fish—this famous market still offers lots of smelly photo fun and free morsels to taste. Many stands sell pre-made smoked-salmon *(laks)* sandwiches, fish soup, and other snacks ideal for a light lunch (confirm prices before ordering). To try Norwegian jerky, pick up a bag of dried cod snacks *(torsk)*. The red meat is minke whale, caught off the coast of northern Norway. You'll also find local fruit in season and hand-knit sweaters (June–Aug daily 8:00–19:00, less lively on Sun; Sept–May Mon–Sat 8:00–16:00, closed Sun). Watch your wallet: If you're going to get pickpocketed in Bergen, it'll likely be here.

Bergen's Main Square, Torgallmenningen—*Allmenningen* means "for all the people." *Torg* means "square." And, while this is the city's main gathering place, it was actually created as a fire break. The residents of this fire-plagued city—once one of the biggest wooden cities in Europe—knew fires were inevitable. The street plan was designed with breaks, or open spaces like this square, to help contain the destruction. In 1916, it stopped a fire, which is why it has a more modern feel today.

The **Seafarers' Monument** (which locals have nicknamed "the cube of goat cheese" for its shape) dates from about 1950. It celebrates Bergen's contact with the sea and remembers those who worked on it and died in it. Study the faces: All classes are represented. The statues relate to the scenes depicted in the reliefs above. Each side represents a century: 10th century—Vikings with a totem pole recalling the pre-Columbian Norwegian discovery of America; 18th century—equipping Europe's ships; 19th century—whaling; 20th century—shipping and war. For the 21st century, see the real people—a cross-section of today's Norway—sitting at the statue's base. Major department stores (Galleriet, Xhibition, and Telegrafen) are all nearby.

The "blue stone," a popular meeting point at the far end of the square, marks the center of a park-like swath known as **Ole Bulls Plass,** leading from the National Theater (above on right) to a little lake (below on left). The theater, built in Art Nouveau style in 1909, was founded by violinist Ole Bull in 1850, and was the first to host plays in the Norwegian language. After 450 years of Danish and Swedish rule, 19th-century Norway enjoyed a cultural awakening, and Bergen became an artistic power. Ole Bull (a pop idol and heartthrob in his day—women fainted when they heard him play his violin) collaborated with the playwright Henrik Ibsen. Ibsen commissioned Edvard Grieg to write the music for his *Peer Gynt*. These three lions of Norwegian culture all lived and worked together right here in Bergen. The park that spills downhill from the theater has a pleasantly bustling urban ambience. It leads past a popular fountain of Ole Bull (under the trees) to a cast-iron pavilion given to the city by Germans in 1889, and on to the little manmade lake (Lille Lungegårdsvann), which is circled by an enjoyable path. This green zone is considered a park, and is cared for by the local parks department.

▲▲Fløibanen—Bergen's popular funicular climbs 1,000 feet in seven minutes to the top of Mount Fløyen for the best view of the town, surrounding islands, and fjords all the way to the west coast. The top is a popular picnic or pizza-to-go dinner spot (a Peppe's Pizza is tucked behind the Hanseatic Museum, a block away from the base of the lift) and also has its own view restaurant in summer (affordable self-service all day, fancier dinners in evenings; see "Eating in Bergen," later). Sunsets are great here. The top is also the starting point for many peaceful hikes (ask for the *Fløyen Hiking Map* at the Fløibanen ticket window at the base). It's a pleasant but steep walk back down into Bergen. To save your knees, get off at the Promsgate stop halfway down, and then wander through the delightful cobbled and shiplap lanes (note that only the :00 and :30 departures stop at Promsgate). This funicular is regularly used by locals commuting into and out of downtown (70 kr round-trip, daily 7:30–23:00, May–Aug until 24:00, departures generally 4/hr—on the quarter-hour most of the day, tel. 55 33 68 00, www.floibanen.no).

Leprosy Museum (Lepramuseet)—Leprosy is also known as "Hansen's Disease" because in the 1870s a Bergen man named Armauer Hansen did groundbreaking work in understanding the ailment. This unique museum is in St. Jørgens Hospital, a leprosarium that dates back to about 1700. Up until the 19th century, as much as 3 percent of Norway's population had leprosy. This hospital—once called "a graveyard for the living" (its last patient died in 1946)—has a meager exhibit in a thought-provoking shell attached to a 300-year-old church. It's really only worth your time and money if you stick around for the free tour (40 kr, mid-May–Aug daily 11:00–16:00, tour generally at top of hour or by request, closed Sept–mid-May, between train station and Bryggen at Kong Oscars Gate 59, tel. 55 96 11 55, www.bymuseet.no).

▲Wandering—Bergen is a great strolling town. The harborfront is a fine place to kick back and watch the pigeons mate. Other good areas to explore are over the hill past Klostergate, Marken, Knosesmanet, Ytre Markevei, and the area behind Bryggen.

▲Aquarium (Akvariet)—Small, but great fun if you like fish, this aquarium claims to be the second-most-visited sight in Bergen. It's wonderfully laid out and explained in English. Check out the informative exhibit downstairs on Norway's fish-farming industry (150 kr, kids-100 kr, cheaper off-season, open daily May–Aug 9:00–19:00, Sept–April 10:00–18:00, feeding times at the top of most hours in summer, cheery cafeteria with light sandwiches, Nordnesbakken 4, tel. 55 55 71 71, www.akvariet.no). It's at the tip of the peninsula on the south end of the harbor—about a 20-minute walk or short ride on bus #11 from the TI. Or hop on the handy little Vågen "Akvariet" ferry that sails from the fish market to near the aquarium (60 kr round-trip, 2/hr). The lovely park behind the aquarium has views of the sea and a popular swimming beach (described next). The totem pole erected here was a gift from Bergen's sister city in the US—Seattle.

Swimming—Bergen has two seaside public swimming areas: one at the aquarium and the other in Gamle Bergen. Each is a great local scene on a hot sunny day. **Nordnes Sjøbad,** near the aquarium, offers swimmers an outdoor heated pool and a protected area of the sea (25 kr, kids-10 kr, mid-May–Aug Mon–Fri 7:00–19:00, Sat 7:00–14:00, Sun 10:00–14:00, Sat–Sun until 19:00 in good weather, closed off-season, Nordnesparken 30, tel. 55 90 21 70). **Sandviken Sjobad,** at Gamle Bergen (described next), is free. It comes with changing rooms, a roped-off bit of the bay (no pool), a high dive, and lots of sunbathing space.

BERGEN

▲Gamle Bergen (Old Bergen)—This Disney-cute gathering of fifty 18th- and 19th-century shops was founded in 1934 to save old buildings from destruction as Bergen modernized. Each of the houses was moved from elsewhere in Bergen and reconstructed here. Together, they create a virtual town that offers a cobbled look at the old life. It's free to wander through the town and park to enjoy the facades of the historic buildings. But to get into the 20 or so museum buildings, you'll need to join a 50-kr English tour, departing on the hour between 10:00–16:00 (open mid-May–early Sept daily 9:00–17:00, closed off-season, tel. 55 39 43 04, www.gamlebergen.museum.no). To get there, take any bus heading west from Bryggen (such as #20, direction: Lonborg) to Gamle Bergen (first stop after the tunnel). You'll get off at a freeway pullout and walk 200 yards, following signs to the museum. Any bus heading back into town takes you to the center (buses come by every few minutes). With the easy bus connection, there's no reason to taxi.

▲**Bergen Art Museum (Bergen Kunstmuseum)**—If you need to get out of the rain (and you enjoyed the National Gallery in Oslo), check out this collection of collections in several neighboring buildings on Rasmus Meyers allé. You'll see works by leading Norwegian painters such as Harriet Backer, J. C. Dahl, Christian Krohg, Edvard Munch, and an interesting modern art section. Small description sheets in English can be found in each room (60 kr, daily 11:00–17:00, closed Mon mid-Sept–mid-May, Rasmus Meyers allé 3, tel. 55 56 80 00, www.bergenartmuseum.no).

▲▲**The Bergen Folklore Show**—Enjoy an intimate and charming hour-long program of traditional music and dance in the historic Schøtstuene (Hanseatic Assembly Rooms). Dancers are accompanied by musicians playing the mouth organ and Hardanger fiddle (100-kr tickets sold by TI and at door, mid-June–late Aug, Tue at 21:00, a few steps below St. Mary's Church, tel. 55 55 20 06, mobile 97 52 86 30).

Near Bergen

▲**Ulriken643 Cable Car**—It's amazingly quick and easy to zip to the 643-meter-high (that's 2,110 feet) summit of Ulriken, the tallest mountain near Bergen. Stepping out of the cable car, you enter a different world, with views stretching to the ocean. A chart clearly shows the many well-marked and easy hikes that fan out over the vast rocky and grassy plateau above the tree line (circular walks of various lengths, a 40-minute hike down, and a 4-hour hike to the top of the **Fløibanen funicular**). For less exercise, you can simply sunbathe, crack open a picnic, or enjoy the Ulriken restaurant. Summiting involves a 10-minute bus ride (2/hr, departs a block from the fish market) followed by a 5-minute cable-car ride (every 7 minutes, 195 kr round-trip with bus, 145 kr round-trip without bus, 80 kr one-way without bus).

▲▲**Edvard Grieg's Home, Troldhaugen**—Norway's greatest composer spent his last 22 summers here (1885–1907), soaking up inspirational fjord beauty and composing many of his greatest works. Grieg fused simple Norwegian folk tunes with the bombast of Europe's Romantic style. In a dreamy Victorian setting, Grieg's "Hill of the Trolls" is pleasant for anyone and essential for

Grieg fans. The house (which you'll visit on an included 20-min tour) and adjacent museum (with a 20-min video; request an English viewing) are full of memories, including his Steinway. The walls are festooned with photos of the musical and literary superstars of his generation. Hugely popular in his time, Grieg's 1907 funeral attracted 40,000 mourners. His little studio hut near the water makes you want to sit down and modulate (60 kr, only by tour—departing 2/hr, open daily May–Sept 9:00–18:00, Oct–April 10:00–16:00, tel. 55 92 29 92, www.troldhaugen.com).

Ask the TI about piano concerts in the on-site concert hall—a gorgeous venue, with the fjord stretching out behind the big black grand piano (220-kr evening concerts, 160-kr matinees, free shuttle bus from TI if you show concert ticket; concerts scheduled roughly mid-June–late Aug Sun and Wed at 18:00, Sat at 14:00). Delightful 30-minute lunch piano concerts (40 kr plus entry ticket) are offered Monday through Friday at 13:00 in June, July, and August.

Getting to Troldhaugen: Public buses drop you a long 20-minute walk from Troldhaugen and a 10-minute walk from the Fantoft Stave Church (described next); just head south on buses #20, #21, #22, #23, or #24 for 15–20 minutes. The three-hour city bus tour promoted by the TI is worthwhile for the informative recorded narration and efficient transportation, getting you within a five-minute walk of Troldhaugen (300 kr, May–Sept daily at 12:00). If you're driving into Bergen from the east (such as from the Sognefjord), you'll drive right by Troldhaugen on your way into town.

Fantoft Stave Church—This huge, preserved-in-tar stave church burned down in 1992. It was rebuilt and reopened in 1997, but it will never be the same (for more on stave churches, see page 169). Situated in a quiet forest next to a mysterious stone cross, this replica of a 12th-century wooden church is bigger, though no better, than others covered in this book. But it's worth a look if you're in the neighborhood, even after-hours, for its evocative setting (40 kr, mid-May–mid-Sept daily 10:30–14:00 and 14:30–18:00, interior closed mid-Sept–mid-May, no English information, 3 miles south of Bergen on E39 in Paradis; for information on getting here, see the previous listing).

Shopping in Bergen

Most shops are open Mon–Fri 9:00–17:00, Thu until 19:00, Sat 9:00–15:00, and closed Sunday. Many of the tourist shops at the harborfront strip along Bryggen are open daily—even during holidays—until 20:00 or 21:00.

Bryggen is bursting with sweaters, pewter, and trolls. The **Husfliden** shop is popular for its handmade Norwegian sweaters and goodies (good variety and quality but expensive, just off the market square at Vågsalmenning 3).

The **Galleriet** shopping center on Torgalmenningen has six floors of shops, cafés, and restaurants. You'll find a pharmacy, photo shops, clothing, sporting goods, bookstores, and a basement grocery store (Mon–Fri 9:00–20:00, Sat 9:00–18:00, closed Sun).

Sleeping in Bergen

Busy with business travelers and increasingly popular with tourists, Bergen can be jammed any time of year. But with the economic crisis reaching Norway, once proud and pricey hotels may be willing to make deals. You might save a bundle by emailing the bigger hotels and asking for their best price. Otherwise, Bergen has some fine budget alternatives to normal hotels that can save you a bundle.

Hotels

$$$ Hotel Havnekontoret, with the best location in town, fills a grand old shipping headquarters dating from the 1920s. It's an especially fine value on weekends and in the summer, for those who will eat the included dinner. While part of a chain, it has a friendly spirit. Guests are welcome to climb its historic tower (with a magnificent view) or enjoy its free sauna and exercise room downstairs. The hotel's 116 rooms are expensive during weekdays, and half-price on weekends and through most of the summer. If you aren't interested in fancy dining, the room price includes virtually all your food—a fine breakfast, self-service waffles in the afternoon, fruit and coffee all day, and a light dinner buffet each evening. If you take advantage of them, these edible extras are easily worth 600 kr per day per couple,

Sleep Code

(6 kr = about $1, country code: 47)
S = Single, **D** = Double/Twin, **T** = Triple, **Q** = Quad, **b** = bathroom, **s** = shower. You can assume credit cards are accepted unless otherwise noted.

To help you sort easily through these listings, I've divided the rooms into three categories, based on the price for a standard double room with bath:

$$$ Higher Priced—Most rooms 1,200 kr or more.
$$ Moderately Priced—Most rooms between 850–1,200 kr.
$ Lower Priced—Most rooms 850 kr or less.

making the cost of this fancy hotel little more than a hostel (Db during business peak-2,300 kr, Db Fri-Sun and most of summer-1,200–1,500 kr, extra bed-300 kr, book online to save, free Wi-Fi, facing the harbor across the street from the SAS Radisson Hotel at Slottsgaten 1, tel. 55 60 11 00, www.choicehotels.no, cc.havnekontoret@choice.no).

$$$ Hotel Park Pension is classy, comfortable, and in a fine residential neighborhood a 15-minute uphill walk from the town center (10 min from the train station). It's tinseled in Old World, lived-in charm, yet comes with all of today's amenities (33 rooms—22 in classy old-fashioned hotel, 11 in modern annex across the street; Sb-1,050 kr, Db-1,250 kr, extra bed-350 kr, includes breakfast, winter weekend discounts, free Wi-Fi, Harald Hårfagres Gate 35, tel. 55 54 44 00, fax 55 54 44 44, www.parkhotel.no, booking@parkhotel.no).

$$$ Thon Hotel Rosenkrantz, with 129 rooms, is one block behind Bryggen, between the Bryggens Museum and the Fløibanen funicular station—right in the heart of Bergen's appealing old quarter. However, the next-door nightclub is noisy on Friday and Saturday nights—be sure to request a quiet room (rack rates: Sb-1,295 kr, Db-1,695 kr, these prices include light dinner Mon–Thu; mid-June–Aug: Db-1,200 kr without dinner; includes breakfast, elevator, free Internet access, pay Wi-Fi, Rosenkrantzgate 7, tel. 55 30 14 00, www.thonhotels.no/rosenkrantz, rosenkrantz@thonhotels.no).

$$ P-Hotel, a new, sleek budget hotel, has 43 basic rooms just up from Ole Bulls Plass. While it's not particularly charming and some rooms come with street noise, the price is right (Sb-795 kr, Db-895 kr, credit card only—no cash, box breakfast in your room, elevator, free Wi-Fi, Vestre Torggate, tel. 80 04 68 35, www.p-hotels.no, bergen@p-hotels.no).

Bergen Hotels & Restaurants

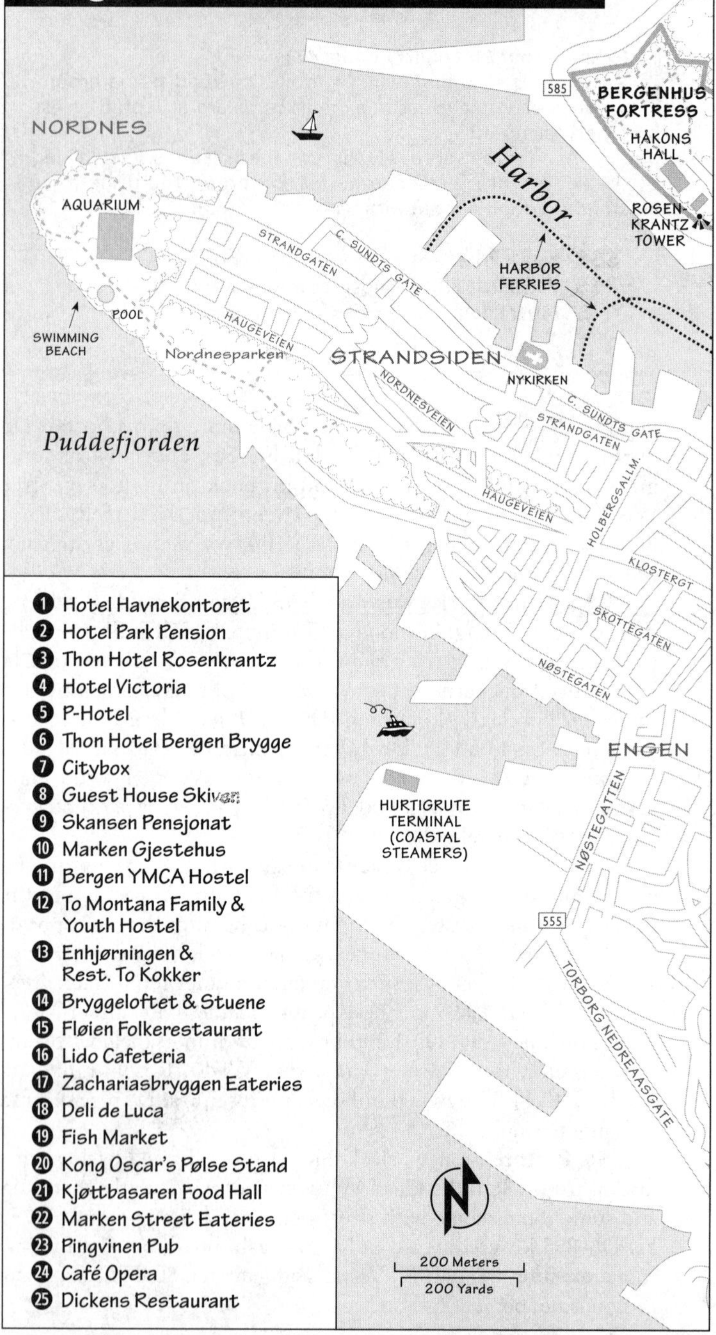

NORDNES
AQUARIUM
POOL
SWIMMING BEACH
Nordnesparken
Puddefjorden
STRANDGATEN
C. SUNDTS GATE
HAUGEVEIEN
STRANDSIDEN
NORDNESVEIEN
NYKIRKEN
Harbor
HARBOR FERRIES
585
BERGENHUS FORTRESS
HÅKONS HALL
ROSENKRANTZ TOWER
HOLBERGSALLM.
KLOSTERGT
SKOTTEGATEN
NØSTEGATEN
ENGEN
HURTIGRUTE TERMINAL (COASTAL STEAMERS)
NØSTEGATEN
555
TORBORG NEDREAASGATE
200 Meters
200 Yards

1. Hotel Havnekontoret
2. Hotel Park Pension
3. Thon Hotel Rosenkrantz
4. Hotel Victoria
5. P-Hotel
6. Thon Hotel Bergen Brygge
7. Citybox
8. Guest House Skiv[illegible]
9. Skansen Pensjonat
10. Marken Gjestehus
11. Bergen YMCA Hostel
12. To Montana Family & Youth Hostel
13. Enhjørningen & Rest. To Kokker
14. Bryggeloftet & Stuene
15. Fløien Folkerestaurant
16. Lido Cafeteria
17. Zachariasbryggen Eateries
18. Deli de Luca
19. Fish Market
20. Kong Oscar's Pølse Stand
21. Kjøttbasaren Food Hall
22. Marken Street Eateries
23. Pingvinen Pub
24. Café Opera
25. Dickens Restaurant

BERGEN

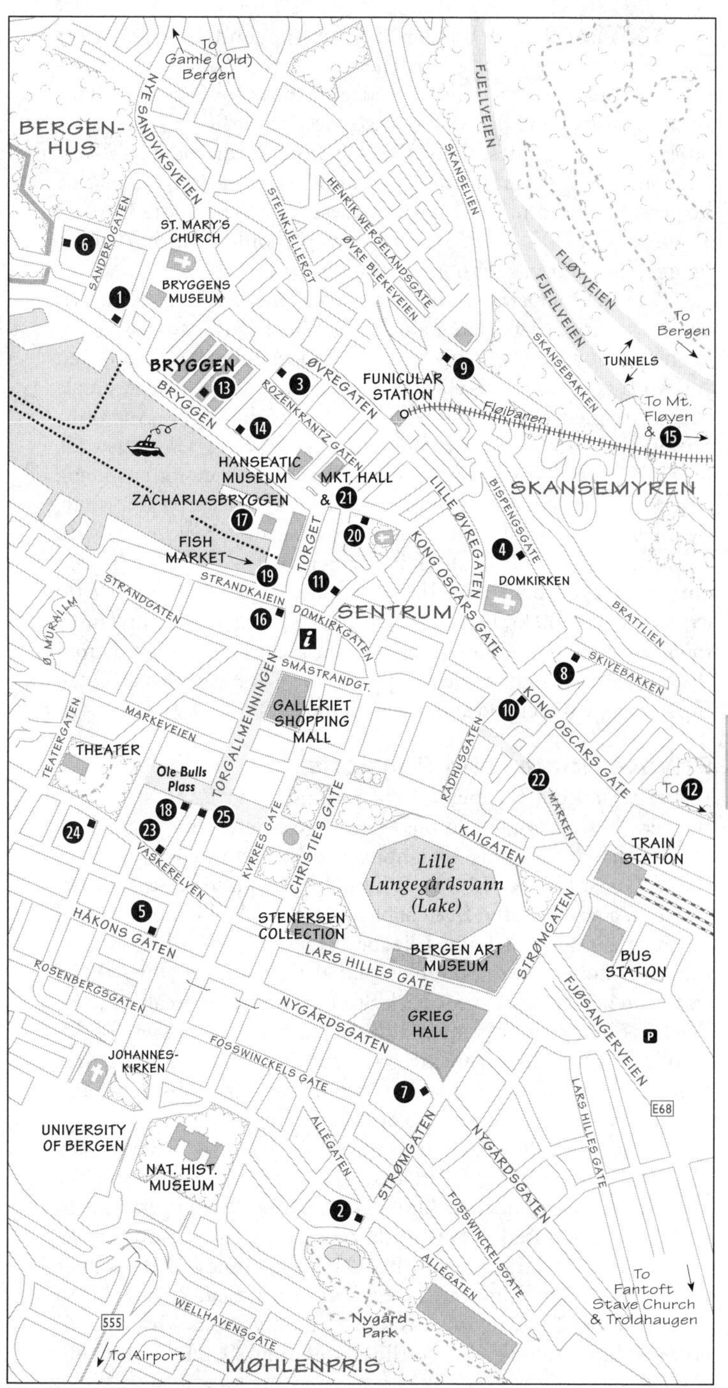
To Gamle (Old) Bergen
BERGEN-HUS
NYE SANDVIKSVEIEN
SANDBROGATEN
ST. MARY'S CHURCH
BRYGGENS MUSEUM
STEINKJELLERGT
HENRIK WERGELANDSGATE
ØVRE BLEKEVEIEN
SKANSELIEN
FJELLVEIEN
FLØYVEIEN
FJELLVEIEN
SKANSEBAKKEN
To Bergen
TUNNELS
BRYGGEN
BRYGGEN
ØVREGATEN
ROZENKRANTZ GATEN
FUNICULAR STATION
Fløibanen
To Mt. Fløyen & 15
HANSEATIC MUSEUM
MKT. HALL & 21
ZACHARIASBRYGGEN
SKANSEMYREN
LILLE ØVREGATEN
BISPENGSGATE
FISH MARKET
TORGET
KONG OSCARS GATE
DOMKIRKEN
STRANDKAIEIN
STRANDGATEN
SENTRUM
DOMKIRKGATEN
BRATTLIEN
Ø. MURALLM
TORGALLMENNINGEN
SMÅSTRANDGT.
SKIVEBAKKEN
GALLERIET SHOPPING MALL
KONG OSCARS GATE
TEATERGATEN
MARKEVEIEN
THEATER
Ole Bulls Plass
RÅDHUSGATEN
MARKEN
To 12
KYRRES GATE
CHRISTIES GATE
KAIGATEN
TRAIN STATION
VASKERELVEN
Lille Lungegårdsvann (Lake)
STRØMGATEN
HÅKONS GATEN
STENERSEN COLLECTION
BERGEN ART MUSEUM
BUS STATION
LARS HILLES GATE
ROSENBERGSGATEN
FJØSANGERVEIEN
NYGÅRDSGATEN
GRIEG HALL
JOHANNES-KIRKEN
FOSSWINCKELS GATE
E68
UNIVERSITY OF BERGEN
ALLEGATEN
STRØMGATEN
NYGÅRDSGATEN
LARS HILLES GATE
NAT. HIST. MUSEUM
FOSSWINCKELSGATE
ALLEGATEN
To Fantoft Stave Church & Troldhaugen
555
WELLHAVENSGATE
Nygård Park
To Airport
MØHLENPRIS
BERGEN

$$ Thon Hotel Bergen Brygge, beyond Bryggen near Håkon's Hall, is part of Thon's cheaper "Budget" chain. However, the 229 rooms are just about as nice as those in its sister hotels. Because of its good prices and great location, it fills up quickly—book ahead (rack rates: Sb-810 kr, Db-1,075 kr, discounts unlikely but you save 7 percent if you book online, skip breakfast to save 65 kr/person, elevator, free Internet access, pay Wi-Fi, Bradbenken 3, tel. 55 30 87 00, fax 55 32 94 14, www.thonhotels.com/bergen brygge, bergenbrygge@thonhotels.no).

$ Hotel Victoria is an old hotel turned into a college dorm that becomes a utilitarian, minimalist budget hotel each summer. There are no public spaces, the tiny reception is open only 9:00–23:00, and you won't get your towels changed. But its 40 modern, bright, simple rooms are plenty comfortable for the price (open June–Aug only, Sb-750 kr, Db-850 kr, Tb-1,150 kr, free Wi-Fi, Kong Oscarsgate 29, tel. 55 31 50 30, www.victoria-hotell.no, booking@victoria-hotell.no).

$ Citybox is a unique, no-nonsense hotel concept: plain, white, clean, and practical. It rents 52 rooms online and provides you with a confirmation number. Check-in is automated—just punch in your number and get your ticket. The reception is staffed daily 9:00–16:00 (S-400 kr, Sb-500 kr, D-600 kr, Db-700 kr, extra bed-150 kr, family room for up to four-1,000 kr, no breakfast, elevator, just away from the bustle in a mostly residential part of town at Nygårdsgate 31, tel. 55 31 25 00, www.citybox.no, post@citybox.no).

Private Homes and Pensions

If you're looking for local character and don't mind sharing a shower, these accommodations—far more quiet, homey, and convenient than hostel beds—might just be the best values in town.

$ Guest House Skiven is a humble little place beautifully situated on a steep, traffic-free cobbled lane called "the most painted street in Bergen." Alf and Elizabeth Heskja (who live upstairs) rent four non-smoking doubles that share a shower, two WCs, and a kitchen (D-500 kr for Rick Steves readers, no breakfast, free Wi-Fi, 4 blocks from station at Skivebakken 17, tel. 55 31 30 30, mobile 90 05 30 30, www.skiven.no, rs@skiven.no). From the station, go down Kong Oscars Gate, uphill on D. Krohns Gate, and up the stairs at the end of the block on the left.

$ Skansen Pensjonat (not to be confused with the nearby Skansen Guest House) is situated 100 yards directly behind the entrance to the Fløibanen funicular. Jannicke Alvær rents seven tastefully decorated rooms with views over town (small non-view S-400 kr, larger S-450 kr, D-650 kr, fancy D on corner with view and balcony-750 kr, includes breakfast, 2 showers on ground floor, 2 WCs, sinks in rooms, family room with TV; all non-smoking, free Wi-Fi, Vetrlidsalmenning 29, tel. 55 31 90 80, www.skansen-pensjonat.no, mail@skansen-pensjonat.no). Follow the switchback road behind the Fløibanen station to the paved plateau with benches, and look for the sign.

Dorms and Hostels

$ Marken Gjestehus is a quiet, tidy, and conveniently positioned 100-bed place between the station and the harborfront. Its rooms, while spartan, are modern and cheery. Breakfast is included, but you'll pay a one-time 65-kr fee for sheets (dorm bed in 8-bed room-175 kr, in 4-bed room-220 kr, S-450 kr, D-550 kr, Db-800 kr, extra bed-135 kr, towels-15 kr, free Wi-Fi, elevator, kitchen, laundry, open all year but with limited reception hours, fourth floor at Kong Oscars Gate 45, tel. 55 31 44 04, fax 55 31 60 22, www.marken-gjestehus.com, post@marken-gjestehus.com).

$ Bergen YMCA Hostel (IYHF), located a block in front of the TI and two blocks from the fish market, is the best location for the price, and its rooms are nicely maintained (bunk in 12- to 32-bed dorm with shared shower and kitchen-180 kr, bunk in 6-bed family room with private bathroom and kitchen-260 kr, Db with kitchen-900 kr, 15 percent cheaper for members June–Aug only, includes sheets, breakfast-60 kr, pay Internet access, free Wi-Fi, roof terrace, fully open June–Aug, no dorm beds off-season, Nedre Korskirkeallmenningen 4, tel. 55 60 60 55, www.bergenhostel.com, ymca@online.no).

BERGEN

Away from the Center: **$$ Montana Family & Youth Hostel (IYHF),** while one of Europe's best, is high-priced for a hostel and way out of town. Still, the bus connections (#31, 15 min from the center) and the facilities—modern rooms, classy living room, no curfew, huge free parking lot, and members' kitchen—are excellent (dorm bed in 20-bed room-200 kr—May–Sept only, bed in Q-265 kr, bed in Tb-300 kr; Sb-650 kr, Db-780 kr; 15 percent cheaper for members, sheets-70 kr, includes breakfast, 30 Johan Blytts Vei, tel. 55 20 80 70, www.montana.no, booking@montana.no).

Eating in Bergen

Bergen has numerous choices: restaurants with rustic, woody atmosphere, candlelight, and steep prices (entrées around 300 kr); chain restaurants that serve pizza, burgers, ribs, and chicken (150–250-kr entrées and pizzas); cafeterias and ethnic eateries with less ambience where you can get quality food at lower prices (100–200 kr); and take-away sandwich shops, bakeries, and cafés for a light bite (50–100 kr). You can always get a glass or pitcher of water for free, and fancy places give you seconds on potatoes for free—just ask. Remember, if you get your food to go, it's taxed at a lower rate and you'll save 12 percent.

Splurges in Bryggen

You'll pay a premium to eat at these three restaurants, but you'll have a memorable meal in a pleasant setting. If it's beyond your budget, remember that you can fill up on potatoes and drink tap water to dine for exactly the price of the dinner plate.

Enhjørningen Restaurant ("The Unicorn") is *the* place in Bergen for fish. With thickly painted walls and no right angles, this dressy-yet-old-time wooden interior wins my "Bryggen Atmosphere" award. The dishes, while not hearty, are close to gourmet and beautifully presented (275–320-kr main dishes, 500–600-kr multi-course meals, nightly 16:00–22:30, #29 on Bryggen harborfront—look for anatomically correct unicorn on the old wharf facade and dip into the alley and up the stairs, tel. 55 30 69 50).

Restaurant To Kokker, down the alley from Enhjørningen (and with the same owners), serves more meat and game. The prices and quality are equivalent, but even though it's also in an elegant old wooden building, I like the Unicorn's atmosphere much better (most main dishes around 300 kr, 500–650-kr multi-course meals, Mon–Sat 17:00–23:00, closed Sun, tel. 55 30 69 55).

Bryggeloftet & Stuene Restaurant, in a brick building just before the wooden stretch of Bryggen, is a vast eatery serving seafood and traditional meals. To dine memorably yet affordably, this is your best Bryggen bet. Upstairs feels more elegant and less touristy than the main floor—if there's a line downstairs, just head on up (100–150-kr lunches, 200–300-kr dinners, Mon–Sat 11:00–23:30, Sun 13:00–23:30, #11 on Bryggen harborfront, try reserving a view window upstairs, tel. 55 30 20 70).

Atop Mount Fløyen, at the Top of the Funicular

Fløien Folkerestaurant offers meals with a panoramic view. The cheaper cafeteria section has a light menu, with coffee, cake, and sandwiches for around 50 kr and a 115-kr soup buffet (May–Aug daily 10:00–22:00, Sept–April Sat–Sun only 12:00–17:00). The restaurant section has decent, expensive dinners with an emphasis on locally caught fish for about 250–350 kr (130–150-kr lighter dishes, May–Aug daily 17:00–23:00, restaurant closed Sept–April, tel. 55 33 69 99).

Cafeteria Overlooking the Fish Market

Lido offers basic, affordable food with great harbor and market views, better ambience than most self-serve places, and a museum's worth of old town photos on the walls. For cold items (such as open-face sandwiches and desserts, 50–80 kr), grab what you want, pay the cashier, and find a table. For hot dishes (120–170-kr Norwegian standards, including one daily special discounted to 105 kr), grab a table, order and pay at the cashier, and they'll bring your food to you (June–Aug Mon–Fri 10:00–21:00, Sat–Sun 13:00–20:00; Sept–May Mon–Fri 10:00–19:00, Sat 10:00–18:00, Sun 13:00–18:00; second floor at Torgalmenningen 1a, tel. 55 32 59 12).

Good Chain Restaurants

You'll find these tasty chain restaurants in Bergen and throughout Norway. All of these are open long hours daily (shorter off-season). Several are located at **Zachariasbryggen,** a modern restaurant complex lining a pier at the head of the harbor (on Torget), which also has an overpriced Tex-Mex restaurant.

Peppe's Pizza has cold beer and good pizzas (medium size for 1–2 people-175–200 kr, large for 2–3 people-200–250 kr, take-out possible; consider the Moby Dick, with curried shrimp, leeks, and bell peppers). There are six Peppe's in Bergen, including one behind the Hanseatic Museum near the Fløibanen funicular station and another inside the Zachariasbryggen harborfront dining complex, with views over the harbor.

Baker Brun makes 50–70-kr sandwiches, including wonderful shrimp baguettes, and pastries such as *skillingsbolle*—cinnamon rolls—warm out of the oven (open from 9:00, seating inside or take-away; locations include facing the fish market at Zachariasbryggen and in Bryggen).

Bon Appétit sells 60-kr baguette sandwiches and wraps, plus ice cream (locations include near Baker Brun at Zachariasbryggen and in Bryggen). Restaurant desserts run 100 kr; strolling with an ice-cream cone can save plenty.

Deli de Luca is a cut above other take-away joints, adding sushi and calzones to the normal lineup of sandwiches. While a bit more expensive than the others, the variety and quality are appealing (open long hours daily, on corner of Engen and Vaskerelven—a block off Ole Bulls Plass). With good weather, enjoy your meal with sun-worshipping locals in the great Theater Park across the street.

Budget Bets

The **Fish Market** has lots of stalls bursting with salmon sandwiches, fresh shrimp, fish-and-chips, and fish cakes. For a tasty, memorable, and inexpensive Bergen meal, assemble a seafood picnic here (ask for prices first; June–Aug daily 7:00–19:00, less lively Sun; Sept–May Mon–Sat 7:00–16:00, closed Sun).

Kong Oscar's Pølse Stand, your classic hot-dog stand, sells a wide variety of sausages (various sizes and flavors—including reindeer). The well-described English menu makes it easy to order your choice of artery-clogging guilty pleasures (15-kr tiny weenie, 45-kr medium-size weenie, 65-kr jumbo, open daily 11:00–5:00 in the morning, you'll see the little hot-dog shack a block up Kong Oscar Gate from the harbor, Kenneht is the boss).

Kjøttbasaren, the restored meat market of 1887, is a genteel-feeling food hall with stalls selling groceries such as meat, cheese, bread, and olives—a great opportunity to assemble a bang-up picnic (Mon–Fri 10:00–17:00, Thu until 18:00, Sat 9:00–16:00, closed Sun).

Marken Pedestrian Street Eateries

This cobbled lane, leading from the train station to the harbor, is lined with creative little restaurants and trendy cafés. Strolling along here, you can choose from cheap chicken and burgers, Vietnamese at **Bambus 33** (elegant, seating indoors and out, daily 14:00–23:00, Marken 33, tel. 55 56 00 60), the **Indian Palace** (with 70-kr lunch special, Marken 32), and the **Aura Café** (classy sandwiches and salads, indoors and out, daily until 20:00, weekends until 19:00, Marken 9).

From Ole Bulls Plass up to the Theater

Bergen's "in" cafés are stylish, cozy, small, and open very late—a great opportunity to experience the local yuppie scene. Around the cinema on Neumannsgate, there are numerous ethnic restaurants, including Italian, Middle Eastern, and Chinese.

Pingvinen Pub ("The Penguin") is a homey place in a charming neighborhood, serving traditional Norwegian home cooking to an enthusiastic local clientele. The pub has only indoor seating, with a long row of stools at the bar and five charming, living-room-cozy tables. After the kitchen closes, the place stays open very late as a pub. For unpretentious Norwegian cooking in a completely untouristy atmosphere, this is your best budget value (daily plates-120–150 kr, Sun–Thu 14:00–22:45, Fri–Sat 12:00–20:45, Vaskerelven 14 near the National Theater, tel. 55 60 46 46).

Café Opera, with a playful-slacker vibe, is the hip budget choice for its loyal, youthful following. With two floors of seating, and tables out front across from the theater, it's a winner (light 30–40-kr sandwiches until 16:00, 100–130-kr dinners, daily 11:00–24:00, occasional live music, live locals nightly, English newspapers in summer, chess, around the left side of the theater at Engen 18, tel. 55 23 03 15).

Dickens is a lively, checkerboard, turn-of-the-century–feeling place serving fish, chicken, and steak. The window tables in the atrium are great for people-watching, as is the fine outdoor terrace

(150-kr lunches, 250-kr dinners, Mon–Sat 11:00–24:00, later on Fri and Sat, Sun 13:00–24:00, reservations smart, Kong Olav V's Plass 4, tel. 55 36 31 30).

Bergen Connections

Bergen is conveniently connected to **Oslo** by plane and train (trains depart Bergen daily at 7:58, 10:28, 15:58, and 22:58—but no night train on Sat, arrive at Oslo seven scenic hours later, additional departures in summer and fall, confirm times at station, 50-kr seat reservation required—but free with first-class railpass, book well in advance if traveling mid-July–Aug). From Bergen, you can take the Norway in a Nutshell train/bus/ferry route; for information, see the Norway in a Nutshell chapter. Train info: tel. 81 50 08 88.

To get to **Stockholm** or **Copenhagen,** you'll go via Oslo (see "Oslo Connections" on page 230)...unless you fly. Before buying a ticket for a long train trip from Bergen, look into cheap flights.

By Express Boat to Balestrand and Flåm (on Sognefjord): The handy Fylkesbaatane express boat links Bergen with Balestrand (4 hrs) and Flåm (5.5 hrs). For details, see page 267.

By Bus to Kristiansand: If you're heading to Denmark on the ferry from Kristiansand, catch the Haukeli express bus (departing Bergen daily at 7:30). After a nearly two-hour layover in Haukeli, take the bus at 14:40, arriving at 18:50 in Kristiansand in time for the overnight ferry to Denmark (for boat details, see page 334 in the South Norway chapter).

By Boat to Stavanger: Flaggruten catamarans sail to Stavanger (2–4/day, 4 hrs, 720 kr one-way, 950 kr round-trip; nearly half-price for students and railpass-holders; tel. 55 23 87 00 or 05505, www.hsd.no). From Stavanger, trains run to Kristiansand and Oslo, and ships sail to Denmark (for Stavanger's transportation connections, see page 332 in the South Norway chapter).

By Boat to Denmark: Fjordline runs a boat from Bergen to Hirtshals, Denmark (17 hours; departs Mon, Wed, Fri generally at 12:30; boat from Hirtshals runs Sun, Tue, and Thu; seat in reclining chair-around 1,500 kr, tel. 81 53 35 00, www.fjordline.com).

By Boat to the Arctic: Hurtigruten coastal steamers depart nearly daily (mid-April–mid-Sept at 20:00, mid-Sept–mid-April at 22:00) for the seven-day trip north up the scenic west coast to Kirkenes on the Russian border.

This route was started in 1893 as a postal and cargo delivery service along the west coast of Norway. Although no longer delivering mail, their ships still fly the Norwegian postal flag by special permission and deliver people, cars, and cargo from Bergen to Kirkenes. A lifeline for remote areas, the ships call at 34 fishing villages and cities.

For the seven-day trip to Kirkenes, allow from $1,599 and up per person based on double occupancy (includes three meals per day, taxes, and port charges). Prices vary greatly depending on the season (highest June–July), cabin, and type of ship. Their fleet includes those with a bit of brass built in the 1960s, but the majority of the ships were built in the mid-1990s and later. Shorter voyages are possible (including even just a day trip to one of the villages along the route). Cabins should be booked well in advance. Ship services include a 24-hour cafeteria, a launderette on newer ships, and optional port excursions ($28–170). Check online for senior and off-season (Oct–March) specials at www.hurtigruten.com.

Call Hurtigruten in New York (US tel. 800-323-7436) or in Norway (tel. 81 00 30 30). For most travelers, the ride makes a great one-way trip, but a flight back south is a logical last leg (rather than returning to Bergen by boat—a 12-day round-trip).

SOUTH NORWAY

Stavanger • Setesdal Valley • Kristiansand

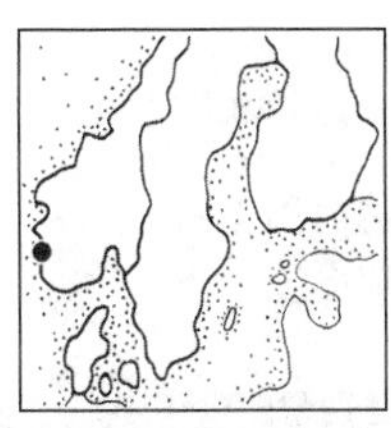

South Norway is not about must-see sights or jaw-dropping scenery—it's simply pleasant and pretty. Spend a day in the harborside town of Stavanger. Delve into your Scandinavian roots at the Norwegian Emigration Center or into the oil industry at the surprisingly interesting Petroleum Museum. Window-shop in the old town, cruise the harbor, or hoof it up Pulpit Rock for a fine view.

A series of time-forgotten towns stretch across the Setesdal Valley, with sod-roofed cottages and locals who practice fiddles and harmonicas, rose painting, whittling, and gold- and silver-work. The famous Setesdal filigree echoes the rhythmical designs of the Viking era and Middle Ages. Each town has a weekly rotating series of hikes and activities for the regular, stay-put-for-a-week visitor. The upper valley is dead in the summer but enjoys a bustling winter.

In Kristiansand, Norway's answer to a seaside resort, promenade along the strand, sample a Scandinavian zoo, or set sail to Denmark.

Planning Your Time

Even on a busy itinerary, Stavanger warrants a day. If you are an avid genealogist, consider two. The port town is connected by boat to Bergen (and Hirtshals, Denmark) and by train to Kristiansand.

Frankly, without a car, the Setesdal Valley is not worth the trouble. There are no trains in the valley, bus schedules are as sparse as the population, and the sights are best for joyriding. If you're in Bergen with a car, and want to get to Denmark, this route is more interesting than repeating Oslo. On a three-week Scandinavian trip, I'd do it in one long day, as follows: 7:00-Leave

Bergen; 9:00—Catch Kvanndal ferry to Utne; 10:00—Say goodbye to the last fjord at Odda; 13:00—Lunch in Hovden at the top of Setesdal Valley; 14:00—Frolic south with a few short stops in the valley; 16:30—Arrive in Kristiansand for dinner. Spend the night and catch the 9:00 boat to Denmark the next morning.

Kristiansand is not a destination town, but rather a place to pass through, conveniently connecting Norway to Denmark by ferry.

Stavanger

This burg of about 117,000 feels more cosmopolitan than most Norwegian cities. This is thanks in part to the oil industry, with its multinational workers and the money they bring into the city. Known as Norway's festival city, Stavanger hosts several lively events, including jazz in May (www.maijazz.no), chamber music in August (www.icmf.no), and a wooden boats festival in early September. With all of this culture, it's no surprise that Stavanger was named a European Capital of Culture for 2008.

Orientation to Stavanger

The most scenic and interesting parts of Stavanger surround its harbor. Here you'll find the Norwegian Emigration Center, lots of shops and restaurants, the indoor fish market, and a produce market (Mon–Fri 9:00–16:00, Sat 9:00–15:00, closed Sun). The artificial Lake Breiavatnet—bordered by Kongsgaten on the east and Olav V's Gate on the west—separates the train and bus stations from the harbor.

Tourist Information

The helpful staff at the TI can help you plan your time in Stavanger, and can also give you hiking tips and day-trip information. Pick up a free city guide and map (June–Aug daily 9:00–18:00; Sept–May Mon–Fri 9:00–16:00, Sat 9:00–14:00, closed Sun; Domkirkeplassen 3, tel. 51 85 92 00, www.regionstavanger.com).

Arrival in Stavanger

By Boat: Express boats from Bergen dock at Fiskepiren. From here, it's a five-minute walk to the center of town or to the train station. A taxi to a downtown hotel costs about 100 kr (tel. 51 90 90 90 or 51 90 90 50).

By Train and Bus: Stavanger's train and bus stations are a five-minute walk around Lake Breiavatnet to the harbor (train

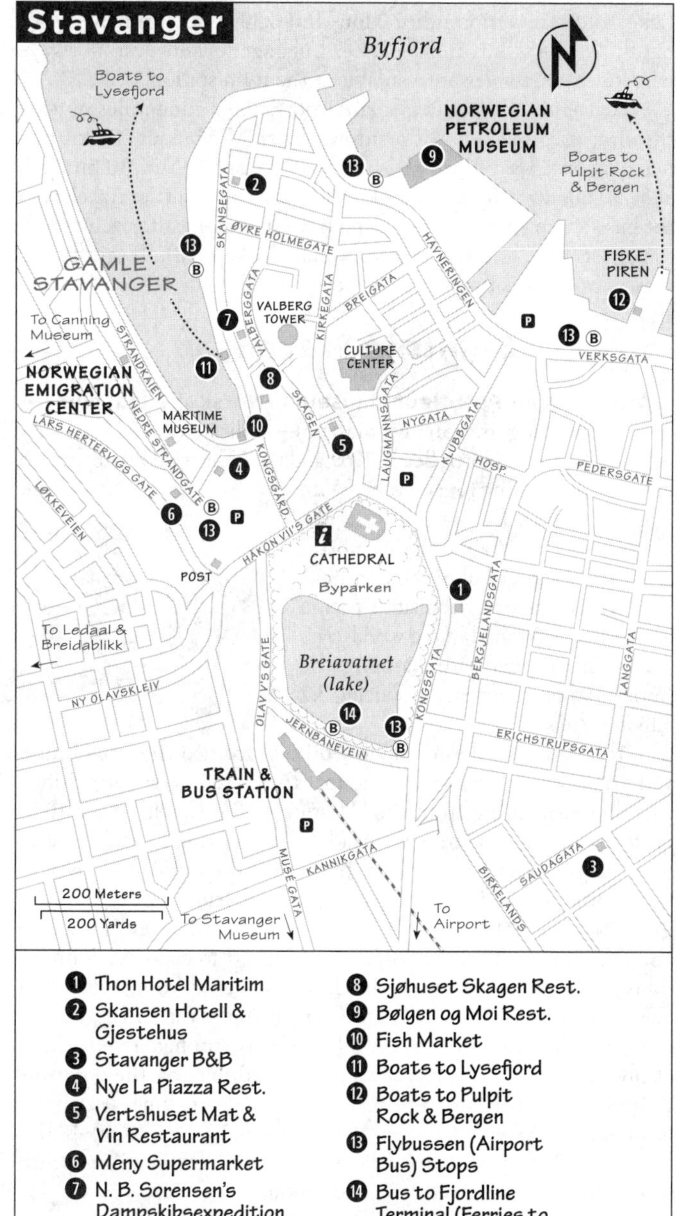

1. Thon Hotel Maritim
2. Skansen Hotell & Gjestehus
3. Stavanger B&B
4. Nye La Piazza Rest.
5. Vertshuset Mat & Vin Restaurant
6. Meny Supermarket
7. N. B. Sorensen's Dampskibsexpedition Pub & Rest.
8. Sjøhuset Skagen Rest.
9. Bølgen og Moi Rest.
10. Fish Market
11. Boats to Lysefjord
12. Boats to Pulpit Rock & Bergen
13. Flybussen (Airport Bus) Stops
14. Bus to Fjordline Terminal (Ferries to Hirtshals, Denmark)

ticket and reservation office Mon–Thu 6:30–17:45, Fri 6:30–19:45, Sat 9:00–16:45, Sun 10:30–17:45). Luggage lockers and Norway-wide train timetables are available at the train station.

By Plane: Stavanger's Sola Airport, about nine miles outside the city, is connected to downtown by the Flybussen (85 kr, buy ticket on bus, Mon–Fri 7:45–24:15, 3–4/hr, less Sat–Sun, 30 min, tel. 51 59 90 60, www.flybussen.no). This airport bus shuttles travelers to the bus station (Byterminalen) and train station (next to each other), the city center, and the boat terminal (Fiskepiren). To get to the airport from the city center, catch the shuttle at any of these stops.

Sights in Stavanger

▲▲Norwegian Petroleum Museum (Norskolje Museum)—This entertaining, informative museum—dedicated to the discovery of oil in Norway's North Sea in 1969 and the industry built up around it—offers something for everyone. With half of Western Europe's oil reserves, Norway is the Arabia of the North. Since the discovery of oil here in 1969, the formerly poor agricultural nation has been transformed into a world-class player. It's ranked third among the world's top oil exporters, producing 3.2 billion barrels a day.

This museum describes how oil was formed, how it's found and produced, and what it's used for. There are interactive exhibits covering everything from the "History of the Earth" (4.5 billion years displayed on a large overhead globe, showing how our planet has changed—stay for the blast that killed the dinosaurs), to day-to-day life on an offshore platform, to petroleum products in our lives. Kids love the model drilling platform that they can climb on. The museum's architecture was designed to echo the foundations of the oil industry—bedrock (the stone building), slate and chalk deposits in the sea (slate floor of the main hall), and the rigs (cylindrical platforms). While the museum has its fair share of propaganda, it also has several good exhibits on the environmental toll of drilling and consuming oil (80 kr; June–Aug daily 10:00–19:00; Sept–May Mon–Sat 10:00–16:00, Sun 10:00–18:00; tel. 51 93 93 00, www.norskolje.museum.no). The small museum shop sells various petroleum-based products.

Eating at the Museum: The **Bølgen og Moi** restaurant has an inviting terrace over the water for thirsty museum-goers. They also serve lunch (from 150 kr) and dinner (480–600 kr), with a fantastic view over the harbor (daily 11:00–17:00 and 16:00–22:00, reservations recommended for dinner, tel. 51 93 93 53).

▲Norwegian Emigration Center (Det Norske Utvandrer-senteret Ble)—This fine museum, in an old warehouse near the wharf where the first boats sailed with emigrants to "Amerika" in 1825, is worth ▲▲▲ for anyone seeking his or her Norwegian roots. On the second floor, you'll find a study center and library. It's free to use the computers and microfilm viewers to look up your relatives. The library is lined with shelves of *bygdebøker*—books from farm districts all over Norway, documenting the history of landowners and local families. For 300 kr per hour, the staff will give you a step-by-step consultation. Otherwise, they'll help answer questions and steer you in the right direction at no charge. The third floor has a small exhibit everyone will enjoy: It tells the story of the first emigrants who left for America—why they left, the journey, and what life was like in the New World (library—free, museum—20 kr, Mon–Fri 9:00–15:00, closed Sat–Sun, Standkaien 31, tel. 51 53 88 60, www.emigrationcenter.com). If you want to look up relatives, do some homework ahead of time and bring at least two or three of the following: family surname, farm name, birth year, and emigration year.

Stavanger Museum—This "museum" is actually five different buildings/museums covered by one 60-kr ticket: the **Stavanger Museum,** featuring the history of the city and a zoological exhibit (Muségate 16); Stavanger **Sjøfartsmuseum,** the maritime museum (Nedre Strandgate 17–19); **Norsk Hermetikkmuseum,** the Norwegian canning museum (*brisling*—herring—is smoked mid-June–mid-Aug Tue and Thu, Øvre Strandgate 88A); **Ledaal,** a royal residence and manor house (Eiganesveien 45); and **Breidablikk,** a wooden villa from the late 1800s (Eiganesveien 40A). Pick up the handy brochure and buy your ticket from the TI (museums open mid-June–mid-Aug daily 11:00–16:00; off-season Tue–Sun 11:00–16:00, closed Mon, except Ledaal and Breidablikk—open Sun only; www.stavanger.museum.no).

Gamle Stavanger—Stavanger's "old town" centers on Øvre Strandgate, on the west side of the harbor. Wander the narrow, winding back lanes and peek into a workshop or gallery to find ceramics, glass, jewelry, and more (free, shops and galleries open roughly daily 10:00–16:00, coinciding with the arrival of cruise ships).

Stavanger Cathedral (Domkirke)—The cathedral was originally built in 1125 in a Norman style, with basket-handle Romanesque arches. After a fire badly damaged the church in the 13th century, a new chancel was added in the pointy-arched Gothic style. Have a look inside and see where the architecture changes about three-quarters of the way up the aisle (free; June–Aug daily 11:00–19:00; Sept–May Tue–Thu and Sat–Sun 11:00–16:00, closed Mon and Fri; tel. 51 84 04 00).

Day Trips to Lysefjord and Pulpit Rock

The nearby Lysefjord is an easy day trip. Those with more time (and strong legs) can hike to the top of the 1,800-foot-high Pulpit Rock (Preikestolen). The dramatic 270-square-foot plateau atop the rock gives you a fantastic view of the fjord and surrounding mountains. The TI has brochures for several boat tour companies and sells tickets.

Boat Tour of Lysefjord—Rodne Clipper Fjord Sightseeing offers 3.5-hour round-trip excursions from Stavanger to Lysefjord (including a view of Pulpit Rock). Boats depart from the east side of the harbor, in front of Skansegaten, along Skagenkaien. Buy your ticket on board or at the TI (380 kr; July–Aug daily at 10:30 and 14:30, Thu–Sat also at 12:00; May–June and Sept daily at 12:00; Oct–April Fri–Sun only at 12:00; tel. 51 89 52 70, www.rodne.no).

Ferry and Bus to Pulpit Rock—The Pulpit Rock trail's starting point, about an hour from Stavanger by a ferry-and-bus combination, is easily reached in summer by public transit or tour. Then comes the hard part: the two-hour hike to the top. The total distance is 4.5 miles and the elevation gain is roughly 1,000 feet. Pack a lunch and plenty of water and wear good shoes.

Tide Reiser offers ferry-and-bus tours to the trailhead from Stavanger. The following are approximate departures—reconfirm all times at the TI before you go: Ferries leave from the Fiskepiren boat terminal to Tau (200-kr combo-ticket includes bus, mid-May–mid-Sept daily at 8:00 and 9:45, mid-April–mid-May and late Sept daily at 9:45 only; no tours Oct–mid-April, tel. 55 23 87 00, www.tidereiser.com). After you cross the fjord to Tau, buses meet the incoming ferries and head to Pulpit Rock cabin or to Preikestolen Fjellstue, the local youth hostel. Be sure to time your hike so that you can catch the last bus leaving Pulpit Rock cabin for the ferry (mid-May–mid-Sept last bus leaves daily at 18:15, mid-April–mid-May and late Sept last bus leaves at 15:45). Cheaper public transit options are also available; pick up the helpful leaflet and confirm details at the TI. They can also give you details about more strenuous hikes.

Sleeping in Stavanger

$$$ Thon Hotel Maritim, about two blocks from the train station, near the artificial Lake Breiavatnet, can be a good deal for a big-business class hotel (Sb-1,222 kr, Db-1,472 kr; weekends Sb-775 kr, Db-1,020 kr; includes breakfast, elevator, Kongsgaten 32, tel. 51 85 05 00, fax 51 85 05 01, www.thonhotels.no/maritim, maritim@thonhotels.no).

$$$ Skansen Hotell & Gjestehus splits 28 rooms between its hotel (newer, more expensive rooms) and guest house (less

Sleep Code

(6 kr = about $1, country code: 47)
S = Single, **D** = Double/Twin, **T** = Triple, **Q** = Quad, **b** = bathroom, **s** = shower. All of these places accept credit cards.

To help you sort easily through these listings, I've divided the rooms into three categories, based on the price for a standard double room with bath:

$$$ Higher Priced—Most rooms 1,000 kr or more.
$$ Moderately Priced—Most rooms between 600-1,000 kr.
$ Lower Priced—Most rooms 600 kr or less.

expensive for essentially the same quality). Most of the rooms are on the street and can be noisy, but you're just off the harbor in a great location (hotel: Sb-1,130 kr, Db-1,290 kr; guest house: Sb-1,030 kr, Db-1,190 kr; about 400 kr cheaper on Fri–Sun nights, includes breakfast, non-smoking floors, elevator to most floors, Skansengate 7, tel. 51 93 85 00, fax 51 93 85 01, www.skansenhotel .no, post@skansenhotel.no).

$$ Stavanger B&B is your best home-away-from-home in Stavanger. This large red house among a sea of white houses has 14 tidy rooms, each with its own shower (but the toilet's down the hall). Waffles, coffee, and friendly chatter are served up every evening at 21:00 (Ss-790 kr, Ds-890 kr, Ts-990 kr, extra bed-150 kr, includes breakfast, 10-min walk behind train station in residential neighborhood, Vikedalsgate 1A, tel. 51 56 25 00, fax 51 56 25 01, www.stavangerbedandbreakfast.no, peck@online.no). If you let them know in advance, they may be able to pick you up or drop you off at the boat dock or train station.

Eating in Stavanger

Casual Dining

Nye La Piazza, just off the harbor, has an assortment of pasta and other Italian dishes, including pizza, for 125–200 kr (Mon 13:00–24:00, Tue–Sat 12:00–24:00, Sun 12:00–22:00, Rosenkildettorget 1, tel. 51 52 02 52).

Vertshuset Mat & Vin, in an elegant setting, serves up big portions of traditional Norwegian food and pricier contemporary fare (200–270 kr, light meals-90–150 kr, open daily 11:00–22:00, a block behind main drag along harbor at Skagen 10 ved Prostbakken, tel. 51 89 51 12).

Meny is a large supermarket with a good selection and a fine deli for super-picnic shopping (Mon–Fri 9:00–20:00, Sat until 18:00, closed Sun, in Straen Senteret shopping mall, Lars Hertervigs Gate 6, tel. 51 50 50 10).

Dining Along the Harbor with a View

The harborside street of Skansegata is lined with lively restaurants and pubs, and most serve food. Here are a couple options:

N. B. Sorensen's Dampskibsexpedition consists of a lively pub on the first floor (150–200 kr for pasta, fish, meat, and vegetarian dishes, Mon–Sat 11:00–24:00, Sun 13:00–23:00) and a fine-dining restaurant on the second floor, with tablecloths, view tables overlooking the harbor, and entrées from 300 kr (Mon–Sat 18:00–23:00, closed Sun, Skagenkaien 26, tel. 51 84 38 20). The restaurant is named after an 1800s company that shipped from this building, among other things, Norwegians heading to the US. Passengers and cargo waited on the first floor, and the manager's office was upstairs. The place is filled with emigrant-era memorabilia.

Sjøhuset Skagen, with a woodsy interior, invites diners to its historic building for lunch or dinner. The building, from the late 1700s, housed a trading company. Today, you can choose from local seafood specialties with an ethnic flair, as well as plenty of meat options (100–150-kr lunches, 200–300-kr dinners, Mon–Sat 11:30–24:00, Sun 13:00–22:00, Skagenkaien 16, tel. 51 89 51 80).

Stavanger Connections

From Stavanger by Train to: Kristiansand (4–7/day, 3.5 hrs), **Oslo** (5/day, 8–9 hrs, overnight possible).

By Boat to Bergen: Flaggruten catamarans sail between Bergen and Stavanger (2–4/day, 4 hrs, 720 kr one-way, 950 kr round-trip; nearly half-price for students and railpass-holders; tel. 55 23 87 00, www.hsd.no).

By Boat to Hirtshals, Denmark: For details on this boat, see the "Sailing Between Norway and Denmark" sidebar.

The Setesdal Valley

Welcome to the remote, and therefore very traditional, Setesdal Valley. Probably Norway's most authentic cranny, the valley is a mellow montage of sod-roofed water mills, ancient churches, derelict farmhouses, yellowed recipes, and gentle scenery.

The Setesdal Valley joined the modern age with the construction of the valley highway in the 1950s. All along the valley you'll see the unique two-story storage sheds called *stabburs* (the top floor was used for storing clothes; the bottom, food) and many sod roofs.

The Setesdal Valley

To Kirkenes
Bergen
Voss
Kvanndal
Granvin
Utne
Kinsarvik
E16
To Oslo
Halhjem
Hardangerfjord
Hardangervidda
Odda
Sandvikvåg
Stord Island
Seljestad
Leirvik
9
Haukeligrend
11
Utbjoa
To Oslo
Hovden
Haugesund
Bykle
Valle
Skien
PULPIT ROCK
Setesdal
Larvik
Stavanger
Lysefjord
Bygland
Byglandsfjord
E39
Evje
Egersund
Arendal
North Sea
E18
Skagerrak
Flekkefjord
Kristiansand
50 Kilometers
25 Miles
To Hirtshals (Denmark)

Even the bus stops have rooftops the local goats love to munch.

In the high country, just over the Sessvatn summit (3,000 feet), you'll see herds of goats and summer farms. If you see an *ekte geitost* sign, that means genuine, homemade goat cheese is for sale. (It's sold cheaper and in more manageable sizes in grocery stores.) To some, it looks like a decade's accumulation of earwax. I think it's delicious. Remember, *ekte* means all-goat—really strong. The more popular and easier-to-eat regular goat cheese is mixed with cow's-milk cheese.

For more information on the Setesdal Valley, see www.setesdal.com.

Sailing Between Norway and Denmark

Two companies sail between the tips of Norway and Denmark. **Color Line** and **Fjordline** sail fast boats between Kristiansand, Norway, and Hirtshals, Denmark (2.25–3.5 hours). In addition, Fjordline boats connect Stavanger, Norway, and Hirtshals (12 hours, covered below). They also link Bergen with Hirtshals, though at 17 hours, it's a long haul. (For information on an Oslo-Copenhagen cruise—run by a different company—see page 231.)

Both Color Line and Fjordline offer car packages (covering up to 5 people and the car) and have various on-board amenities such as restaurants, coffee bars, duty-free shops, and several classes of travel.

Sailing Between Kristiansand and Hirtshals, Denmark: Color Line ships generally sail twice daily, all year, with a few more sailings added during summer, but mysteriously they sail only once a day in mid-April. Sailing from Norway to Denmark, Color Line boats usually leave Kristiansand at 8:00 and 16:30, arriving in Hirtshals at 11:15 and 19:45. Going from Denmark to Norway, the boats leave Hirtshals at 12:15 and 20:45, arriving in Kristiansand at 15:30 and midnight. Fares vary with day of week and season (cheaper weekdays and off-season). During the summer, passenger fares are €56/person mid-week, €62/person on weekends; car packages start at €204 mid-week and €237 on weekends.

Fjordline's seasonal ferry makes the crossing three times a day from late June to mid-August in a speedy 2.25 hours. The schedule is cut back to twice a day in late spring and early fall, with no ferries from October to April. In high season, sailing from Norway to Denmark, Fjordline boats leave Kristiansand at 7:00, 13:30, and 19:45, arriving in Hirtshals at 9:15, 15:45, and 22:00. Going from Denmark to Norway, the boats leave Hirtshals at

From Odda to Hovden

Attractions from here to Kristiansand are listed roughly from north to south.

Odda—At the end of the Hardanger Fjord, just past the huge zinc and copper industrial plant, you'll hit the industrial town of Odda (well-stocked **TI** for whole region and beyond; in summer Mon–Fri 7:30–19:00, Sat–Sun 11:00–17:00; off-season Mon–Fri 7:30–15:00, closed Sat–Sun; on market square at Torget 2–4, tel. 53 65 40 05, www.visitodda.com). Odda brags that Kaiser Wilhelm

10:15, 16:45, and 22:45, arriving in Kristiansand at 12:30, 19:00, and 1:00 in the morning. Passenger fares start at €79/person mid-week; car packages start at €165 mid-week.

Sailing Between Stavanger and Hirtshals, Denmark: Fjordline ships sailing from Norway to Denmark travel overnight, which can save you the cost of a hotel. Enjoy an evening in Stavanger, then sleep (or vomit) as you sail to Denmark. The boat generally sails four times a week (usually Mon, Wed, Fri, and Sat; departing Stavanger at either 19:00, 20:30, or 21:00; arriving in Hirtshals at either 7:00, 8:00, or 8:30 the next day). Ships sailing from Denmark to Norway leave Hirtshals in the morning or afternoon, arriving in Stavanger at night, not as desirable an option. These boats also sail four days a week (typically Tue, Thu, Sat, and Sun; departing Hirtshals at either 8:30, 12:30, or 14:30; arriving in Stavanger at either 20:30, 00:15, or 02:30 in the morning).

Fares vary, depending on how far in advance you book, the time of year, the day of the week, and the type of accommodation you want. Basic fares range from €13 to €102, plus the cost of meals (€14 breakfast, €38 dinner) and accommodations (an airline-type seat or cabin). A seat, referred to as a "sleeperette," starts at €8.50. But if you're efficient enough to spend a night traveling, you owe yourself the comfort of a private room. Cabins start at €71 for a basic, two-berth, inside cabin, and go up to €420 for a "Fjord Class" cabin with a double bed and ocean view. Car packages range from €38 to €438.

Reservations: To get the best fare, book online and early—as soon as you can commit to a firm date (http://fjordline.no and www.colorline.com). This is especially true for Fjordline. Many cheaper fares are non-refundable and non-changeable, so be sure to check the details carefully when you book. Days of the week and departure/arrival times can vary, so confirm specific schedules when you make your reservations.

Discounts: Color Line gives a discount off its regular fares to Eurailpass-holders, but you must call Color Line directly to book (Norway tel. 81 50 08 11 or 22 94 42 00; Denmark tel. 99 56 19 77). Fjordline doesn't offer discounts to Eurailers.

came here a lot, but he's dead and I'd drive right through. If you want to visit the tongue of a glacier, drive to Buar and hike an hour to Buarbreen. From Odda, drive into the land of boulders. The many mighty waterfalls that line the road seem to have hurled huge rocks (with rooted trees) into the rivers and fields. Stop at the giant double waterfall (on the left, pullout on the right, drive slowly through it if you need a car wash).

Røldal—Continue over Røldalsfjellet and into the valley below, where the old town of Røldal is trying to develop some tourism. Drive on by. Its old church isn't worth the time or money. Lakes are like frosted mirrors, making desolate huts come in pairs. Haukeliseter, a group of sod-roofed buildings filled with cultural clichés and tour groups, offers pastries, sandwiches, and reasonable hot meals (from 100 kr) in a lakeside setting. Try the traditional *rømmegrøt* porridge.

Haukeligrend—Haukeligrend is a bus/traffic junction, with daily bus service to/from Bergen and to/from Kristiansand (TI inside the café, open daily all year 10:00–19:00, brochures available all the time, TI staff available periodically, Internet access, tel. 35 07 03 67).

Hovden

Hovden is a ski resort at the top of the Setesdal Valley (2,500 feet). It's barren in the summer and painfully in need of charm. Still, it makes a good home base if you want to explore the area for a couple of days. Locals come here to walk and relax for a week.

Tourist Information: The TI is open all year (Mon–Fri 9:00–16:00, summer Sat 9:00–14:00, July also Sun 9:00–14:00, otherwise closed Sat–Sun, tel. 37 93 93 70, www.hovden.com, post@hovden.com).

Sights and Activities in Hovden

Canoe Rental—Hegni Center, on the lake at the south edge of town, rents canoes (230 kr/day, 120 kr/half-day, hourly rentals also possible, cash only, mid-June–mid-Aug daily 10:00–20:00, mid-Aug–early Sept daily 11:00–18:00, mid-Sept–mid-Oct Sat–Sun only 11:00–16:00, closed mid-Oct–mid-June, tel. 91 32 25 81).

Hikes near Hovden—Good walks offer you a chance to see reindeer, moose, arctic fox, and wabbits—so they say. The TI and most hotels stock brochures, maps, and other information about moderate to strenuous hikes in the area. Berry picking is popular in late August, when small, sweet blueberries are in season. A chairlift sometimes takes sightseers to the top of a nearby peak, with great views in clear weather (90 kr, July daily 11:00–14:00, Aug–mid-Oct Wed and Sat–Sun only). Hunting season starts in late August for reindeer (only in higher elevations) and later in the fall for grouse and moose.

Moose Safari—Per Johanson offers a 2.5-hour *Elg Safari* (that's Norwegian for "moose"). Learn more about this "king of the forest" during a late-night drive through Setesdal's back roads with a stop for moose-meat soup (340 kr, June–mid-Sept only; generally Tue, Fri, and Sun at 22:00—more often based upon demand; 50 percent money-back guarantee if you don't see a moose, tel. 37 93 93 70).

Museum of Iron Production (Jernvinnemuseum)—Learn about iron production from the late Iron Age (about 1,000 years ago) with the aid of drawings, exhibits, and recorded narration from a "Viking" (available in English; free, mid-June–mid-Aug daily 11:00–17:00, otherwise ask for the key at the TI or Hegni Center). The museum is about 100 yards behind the Hegni Center (look for the sign from the road to *Jernvinnemuseum*).
Swimming Pool—A super indoor spa/pool complex, the Hovden Badeland, provides a much-needed way to spend an otherwise dreary and drizzly early evening here (155 kr for 3 hours or more, cheaper for shorter visits, daily 10:00–19:00 in summer, shorter hours off-season, tel. 37 93 93 93).

Sleeping and Eating in Hovden

$$ Hovden Fjellstoge is a big, old ski chalet renting Hovden's only cheap beds. Even if you're just passing through, their café is a good choice for lunch or an early dinner. Check out the mural in the balcony overlooking the lobby—an artistic rendition of this area's history. Behind the mural is a frightening taxidermy collection (hotel: Sb-750 kr, bunk-bed Db-990 kr, includes breakfast; cabins: from 650 kr for 2–4 people with bathroom and kitchen; dorms: dorm bed-200 kr, D-500 kr, 25 kr extra if you're not a hostel member, breakfast-70 kr, sheets-100 kr, towel-20 kr; tel. 37 93 95 43, www.hovdenfjellstoge.no, post@hovdenfjellstoge.no).

From Hovden to Kristiansand

▲Dammar Vatnedalsvatn—Nine miles south of Hovden is a two-mile side-trip to a 400-foot-high rock-pile dam (look for the *Dammar* signs). Enjoy the great view and impressive rockery. This is one of the highest dams in northern Europe. Read the chart. Sit out of the wind a few rows down the rock pile and ponder the vastness of Norwegian wood.
▲Bykle—The most interesting folk museum and church in Setesdal are in the teeny town of Bykle. The 17th-century church has two balconies—one for men and one for women (free, late June–mid-Aug daily 11:00–17:00, tel. 37 93 85 00). Drivers should note that the Bykle toll booth accepts only exact change.
Grasbrokke—On the east side of the main road (at the *Grasbrokke* sign) is an old water mill (1630). A few minutes farther south, at the sign for *Sanden Såre Camping*, exit onto a little road to stretch your legs at another old water mill with a fragile, rotten-log sluice.
Flateland—The **Setesdal Museum** (Rygnestadtunet) offers more of what you saw at Bykle (30 kr, two buildings; late June–Aug daily

11:00–17:00; closed off-season; 1 mile east of the road, tel. 37 93 63 03, www.setesdalsmuseet.no). Unless you're a glutton for culture, I wouldn't do both.

Honneevje—Past Flateland is a nice picnic and WC stop, with a dock along the water for swimming...for hot-weather days or polar bears.

▲Valle—This is Setesdal's prettiest village (but don't tell Bykle). In the center, you'll find fine silver- and gold-work, homemade crafts next to the TI, and old-fashioned *lefse* cooking demonstrations (in the small log house by the Valle Motell). The fine suspension bridge attracts kids of any age (b-b-b-b-bounce) and anyone interested in a great view over the river to strange mountains that look like polished, petrified mudslides. European rock climbers, tired of the over-climbed Alps, often entertain spectators with their sport. Is anyone climbing? (TI tel. 37 93 75 27.)

Sleeping in Valle: **$$ Valle Motell** rents basic rooms (Sb-625 kr, Db-690 kr, includes breakfast, cabins with kitchen and bath but no breakfast-690–750 kr, tel. 37 93 77 00, www.valle-motell.no, post@valle-motell.no).

Nomeland—The Sylvartun silversmith shop sells Setesdal silver in a 17th-century log cabin (May–Sept daily 10:00–17:00, closed Oct–April, tel. 37 93 63 06).

Grendi—The Ardal Church (1827) has a rune stone in its yard. Three hundred yards south of the church is a 900-year-old oak tree.

Evje—A huge town by Setesdal standards (3,500 people), Evje is famous for its gems and mines. Fancy stones fill the shops here. Rock hounds find the nearby mines fun; for a small fee, you can hunt for gems. The TI is by Route 9 in the center of Evje (daily 10:00–15:00; tel. 37 93 14 00). The **Setesdal Mineral Park** is on the main road, two miles south of town (100 kr; July–mid-Aug daily 10:00–18:00, mid-Aug–Sept Mon–Sat 10:00–16:00, Sun 10:00–17:00; May–June Mon–Sat 10:00–16:00, Sun 10:00–17:00, closed Oct–April; tel. 38 00 30 70, www.mineralparken.no).

Kristiansand

This "capital of the south" has 80,000 inhabitants, a pleasant Renaissance grid-plan layout (Posebyen), a famous zoo with Norway's biggest amusement park (6 miles toward Oslo on the main road), a daily bus to Bergen, and lots of big boats going to Denmark. It's the closest thing to a beach resort in Norway. Markensgate is the bustling pedestrian market street—a pleasant place for good browsing, shopping, eating, and people-watching.

Stroll along the Strand Promenaden (marina) to Christiansholm Fortress.

Orientation to Kristiansand

The **TI** is at Rådhusgata 6, a few blocks south of the boat, bus, and train station (mid-June–mid-Aug Mon–Fri 9:00–18:00, Sat 10:00–18:00, Sun 12:00–18:00; mid-Aug–mid-June Mon–Fri 9:00–15:30, closed Sat–Sun; tel. 38 12 13 14, www.sorlandet.com). The bank at the Color Line terminal opens for each arrival and departure (even the midnight ones). The Fønix Kino cinema complex is within two blocks of the ferry and TI (70–100 kr, seven screens, movies shown in English, schedules at the entrance, tel. 38 10 42 00).

Sleeping in Kristiansand

(6 kr = about $1, country code: 47)
Kristiansand hotels are expensive and nondescript.

$$$ Rica Hotel Norge is a modern option (rack rates: Sb-1,375 kr, Db-1,575 kr; mid-June–mid-Aug: Sb-1,295 kr, Db-1,495 kr; weekend rates year-round: Sb-795 kr, Db-995 kr; Dronningensgate 5, tel. 38 17 40 00, fax 38 17 40 01, www.hotel-norge.no, firmapost@hotel-norge.no).

$$$ Thon Hotel Wergeland is inviting for a large chain hotel. It's within earshot of the church bells and busy Kirkegate, but quieter rooms away from the street are available (Sb-1,095, Db-1,395, includes breakfast, non-smoking rooms, no elevator, Internet access and Wi-Fi, Kirkegate 15, tel. 38 17 20 40, fax 38 02 73 21, www.thonhotels.no/wergeland, wergeland@thonhotels.no).

$$ At **Frobusdalen Rom,** Arild and Inger Nilssen rent seven clean, bright rooms and two apartments in a beautiful guest house. You'll have access to the garden, a full kitchen, and a large sitting room filled with lovely antiques and wooden wainscoting (Sb-400–500 kr, Db-600–800 kr, Db with balcony-1,200 kr, apartment for 4–6 people-1,200–2,400 kr, higher prices are for slightly larger room, no breakfast, laundry service available, free parking; 5-min walk from the boat, bus, and train terminals at Frobusdalen 2; tel. 91 12 99 06, www.gjestehus.no, imsan@start.no).

Eating in Kristiansand

The otherwise uninteresting harbor area has a cluster of wooden buildings called **Fiskebasaren** ("Fish Bazaar"). The indoor fish market is only open during the day, but numerous restaurants (serving fish, among other dishes) provide a nice atmosphere for dinner.

Follow Vester Strandgate past the Fønix movie theater to Østre Strandgate, take a right, and follow the signs to Fiskebrygga.

Kristiansand Connections

From Kristiansand by Train to: Stavanger (4–7/day, 3.5 hrs), **Oslo** (4/day, 4.5 hrs).

By Boat to Hirtshals, Denmark: For details on this boat, see the "Sailing Between Norway and Denmark" sidebar on page 334.

Route Tips for Drivers

Bergen to Kristiansand via the Setesdal Valley (10 hrs): Your first key connection is the Kvanndal–Utne ferry (departures hourly 6:00–23:00, less on weekends, reservations not possible or even necessary if you get there 20 min early, breakfast in cafeteria, www.hsd.no). If you make the 9:00, your day will be more relaxed. Driving comfortably, with no mistakes or traffic, it's two hours from your Bergen hotel to the ferry dock. Leaving Bergen is a bit confusing. Pretend you're going to Oslo on the road to Voss (Route E16, signs for *Nestune, Landås, Nattland*). About a half-hour out of town, after a long tunnel, leave the Voss road and take Route 7 heading for Norheimsund, and then Kvanndal. This road, treacherous for the famed beauty of the Hardanger Fjord it hugs as well as for its skinniness, is faster and safer if you beat the traffic (which you will with this plan).

The ferry drops you in Utne, where a lovely road takes you to Odda and up into the mountains. From Haukeligrend, turn south and wind up to Sessvatn at 3,000 feet. Enter the Setesdal Valley. Follow the Otra River downhill for 140 miles south to the major port town of Kristiansand. Skip the secondary routes. South of Valle, you'll have to pass a 25-kr tollbooth. The most scenic stretch is between Hovden and Valle. South of Valle, there is a lot more logging (and therefore less scenic). As you enter Kristiansand, pay a 10-kr toll and follow signs for Denmark.

SWEDEN

SWEDEN

Sverige

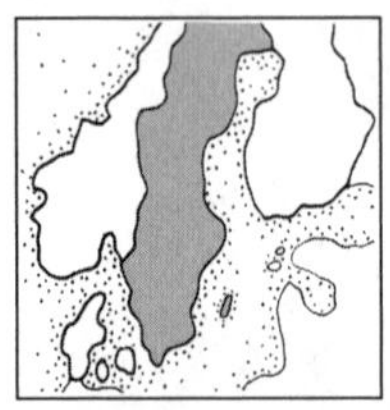

Scandinavia's heartland, Sweden is far bigger than Denmark and far flatter than Norway. This family-friendly land is home to Ikea, Volvo, ABBA, and long summer vacations at red-painted, white-trimmed summer cottages. Its capital, Stockholm, is Scandinavia's grandest city.

Once the capital of blond, Sweden is now home to a huge immigrant population. Sweden is committed to its peoples' safety and security, and proud of its success in creating a society with the lowest poverty rate in the world. Yet Sweden has thrown in its lot with the European Union, and locals debate whether to open their economy even further.

Swedes are often stereotyped as sex-crazed, which could not be further from the truth. Several steamy films and film stars from the 1950s and 1960s stuck Sweden with the sexpot stereotype, which still reverberates among male tourists. Italians continue to travel up to Sweden looking for those braless, loose, and lascivious blondes...but the real story is just that Sweden relaxed film censorship earlier than other European countries. Like other Scandinavians, Swedes are frank and open about sexuality. Sex education in schools is routine, living together before marriage is the norm (and has been common for centuries), and teenagers have easy access to condoms. But Swedes, who are the most unmarried people in the world, choose their partners carefully.

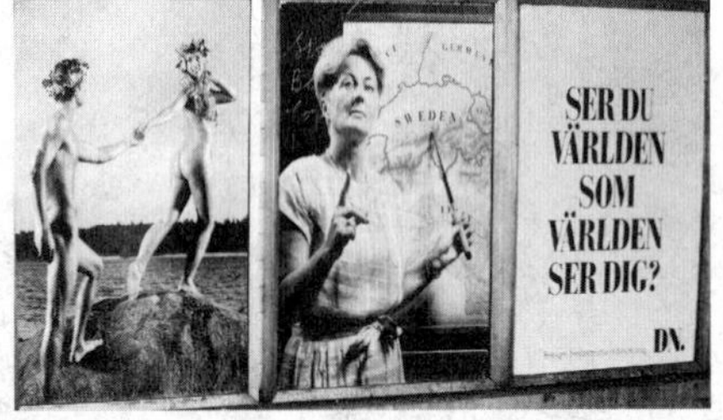

"Do you see the world as the world sees you?"

Before the year 2000, Sweden was a Lutheran state, with the Church of Sweden as its official church. Until 1996, Swedes automatically became members of the Lutheran Church at birth if one parent was Lutheran. Now you need to choose to join the church, and although the culture is nominally Lutheran, few people go to

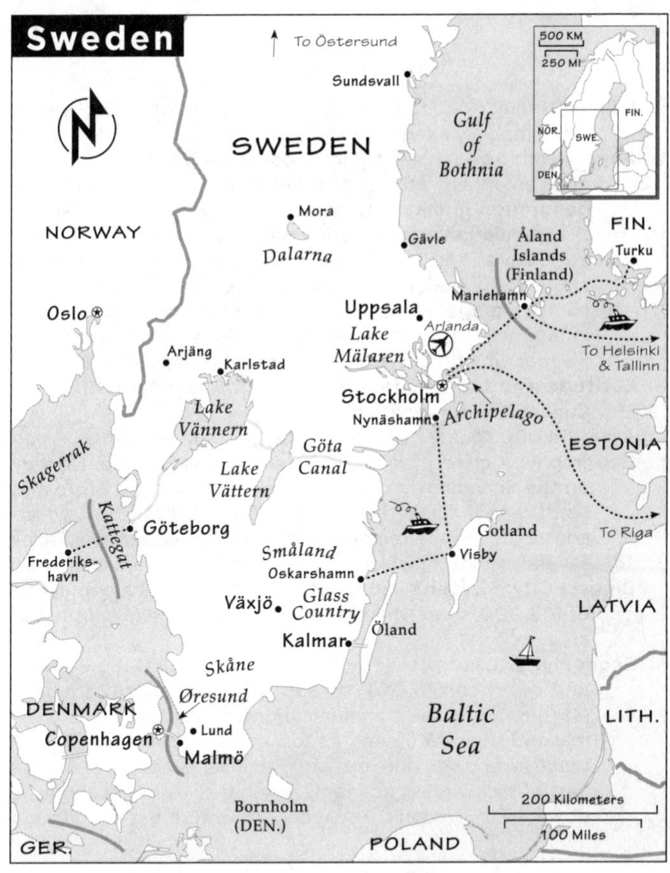

church regularly. While church is handy for Christmas, Easter, marriages, and burials, most Swedes are more likely to find religion in nature, hiking in the vast forests or fishing in one of the thousands of lakes or rivers.

Sweden is almost 80 percent wilderness, and modern legislation incorporates an ancient common law called *allemans rätt*, which guarantees people the right to move freely through Sweden's natural scenery without asking the landowner for permission, as long as they behave responsibly. In summer, Swedes take advantage of the long days and warm evenings for festivals such as Midsummer (in late June) and crayfish parties in August. Many Swedes have a summer cottage—or know someone who has one—where they spend countless hours swimming, soaking up the sun, and devouring boxes of juicy strawberries.

While Denmark and Norway look westward to Britain and the Atlantic, Sweden has always faced east, across the Baltic

Sweden Almanac

Official Name: Konungariket Sverige—the Kingdom of Sweden —or simply Sweden.

Population: Sweden's 9 million people (about 50 per square mile) are mostly ethnically Swedish. Foreign-born and first-generation immigrants account for about 10 percent of the population and are primarily from Finland, the former Yugoslavia, and the Middle East. Sweden is also home to about 17,000 indigenous Sami people. Swedish is the dominant language, with most speaking English as well. While immigrants bring their various religions with them, ethnic Swedes who go to church tend to be Lutheran.

Latitude and Longitude: 62°N and 15°E, similar latitude to Canada's Northwest Territories.

Area: 174,000 square miles (a little bigger than California).

Geography: A chain of mountains divides Sweden from Norway on the Scandinavian Peninsula. Sweden's mostly forested landscape is flanked to the east by the Baltic Sea, which contributes to the temperate climate. Sweden also includes several islands, of which Gotland and Öland are the largest.

Biggest City: Sweden's capital city, Stockholm, has a population of 818,000; more than 1.9 million live in the metropolitan area.

Economy: Sweden has a $344 billion Gross Domestic Product and a per capita GDP of $38,100—similar to Canada's. Manufacturing, telecommunications, automobiles, and pharmaceuticals rank among its top industries, along with timber, hydropower, and iron ore. Because exports are a huge part of the Swedish economy, when the world's economy is down, so is Sweden's. The recent downturn has been tough

Sea. As Vikings, Norwegians went west to Iceland, Greenland, and America; Danes headed south to England, France, and the Mediterranean; and the Swedes went east into Russia. (The word "Russia" has Viking roots.) In the early Middle Ages, Swedes founded the Russian cities of Nizhny Novgorod and Kiev, and even served as royal guards in Constantinople (modern-day Istanbul). During the later Middle Ages, German settlers and traders strongly influenced Sweden's culture and language. By the 17th century, Sweden was a major European power, with one of the largest naval fleets in Europe and an empire extending around the Baltic, including Finland, Estonia, Latvia, and parts of Poland, Russia, and Germany. But by the early 19th century, Sweden's war-weary empire had shrunk. The country's current borders date from 1809.

During a massive wave of emigration from the 1860s to World War II, about a quarter of Sweden's people left for the Promised for Sweden—the value of the krona decreased, and many workers have moved to Norway in search of employment (Norway, with its oil wealth, is less affected by global economics). Eighty-five percent of Swedish workers belong to a labor union.

Currency: 7 Swedish kronor (kr) = about $1.

Government: King Carl XVI Gustav is the ceremonial head of Sweden's constitutional monarchy. Elected every four years, the 349-member Swedish Parliament (Riksdag) is currently led by Prime Minister Fredrik Reinfeldt of the conservative Moderate Party (elected in October 2006). The Economist magazine—which considered factors such as participation, impact of people on their government, and transparency—ranked Sweden by far the world's most democratic country (followed by the other Scandinavian countries and the Netherlands, with North Korea coming in last.)

Flag: The Swedish flag is blue with a yellow Scandinavian cross. The colors are derived from the Swedish coat of arms, with yellow symbolizing the generosity of the people and blue representing vigilance, truth, loyalty, perseverance, and justice.

The Average Swede: The average Swede is 41.5 years old, has 1.67 children, and will live to be 81.

Land—America. Many emigrants were farmers from the southern region of Småland. The museum in Växjö tells their story (see the Southeast Sweden chapter), as does the movie *The Emigrants,* based on the book trilogy by Vilhelm Moberg.

The 20th century was good to Sweden. While other European countries were embroiled in the two World Wars, neutral Sweden grew stronger, finding a balance between the extremes of communism and the free market. After a recession hit in the early 1990s, and the collapse of Soviet communism reshaped the European political scene, some started to criticize Sweden's "middle way" as extreme and unworkable. But during the last decade, Sweden's economy improved, buoyed by a strong lineup of successful multinational companies. Saab, Volvo, Scania (trucks and machinery), Ikea, and Ericsson (the telecommunications giant) are leading the way in manufacturing, design, and technology.

Sweden has come a long way when it comes to accepting

immigrants. Less than a century ago, Swedes who traveled overseas were the only ones likely to ever see people of different ethnicities. In 1927 a black man worked in a Stockholm gas station, and people journeyed from great distances to fill up their car there...just to get a look. (Business boomed and his job was secure.)

Since the 1960s, however, Sweden (like Denmark and Norway) has accepted many immigrants and refugees from southeastern Europe, the Middle East, and elsewhere. This praiseworthy humanitarian policy has dramatically—and sometimes painfully—diversified a formerly homogenous country. The suburbs of Rinkeby, Tensta, and Botkyrka are Stockholm's ethnic neighborhoods, and are worth visiting. Many of the service-industry workers you will meet have come to Sweden from elsewhere.

For great electronic fact sheets on everything in Swedish society from health care to its Sami people, see www.sweden.se.

Most Swedes speak English, but a few Swedish words are helpful. "Hello" is *"Hej"* (hey) and "Good-bye" is *"Hej då"* (hey doh). "Thank you" is *"Tack"* (tack), which can also double for "Please." For a longer list of Swedish survival phrases, see page 589.

STOCKHOLM

If I had to call one European city home, it might be Stockholm. One-third water, one-third parks, one-third city, on the sea, surrounded by woods, bubbling with energy and history, Sweden's stunning capital is green, clean, and underrated.

The city is built on an archipelago of islands connected by bridges. Its location midway along the Baltic Sea made it a natural port, vital to the economy and security of the Swedish peninsula. In the 1500s, Stockholm became a political center when Gustav Vasa established the monarchy (1523). A century later, the expansionist King Gustavus Adolphus made it an influential European capital. The Industrial Revolution brought factories and a flood of farmers from the countryside. In the 20th century, the fuming smokestacks were replaced with steel-and-glass Modernist buildings housing high-tech workers and an expanding service sector.

Today, with nearly two million people in the greater metropolitan area (one in five Swedes), Stockholm is Sweden's largest city, as well as its cultural, educational, and media center. It's also the country's most ethnically diverse city. Despite its size, Stockholm is committed to limiting its environmental footprint. Development is strictly monitored, and pollution-belching cars must pay a toll to enter the city.

For the visitor, Stockholm offers both old and new. Crawl through Europe's best-preserved old warship and relax on a scenic harbor boat tour. Browse the cobbles and antique shops of the lantern-lit Old Town. Take a trip back in time at Skansen, Europe's first and best open-air folk museum. Marvel at Stockholm's glittering City Hall, slick shopping malls, and art museums.

While progressive and sleek, Stockholm respects its heritage. In summer, military bands parade daily through the heart of town to the Royal Palace, announcing the Changing of the Guard and turning even the most dignified tourist into a scampering kid.

Planning Your Time

On a two- to three-week trip through Scandinavia, Stockholm is worth two days. For the busiest and best two-day plan, I'd suggest this:

Day 1: 10:00—See *Vasa* warship (starting with video and tour); 12:00—Visit Nordic Museum; 13:00—Tour Skansen open-air museum and grab lunch there; 16:00—Ride boat to Nybroplan (summer only) and follow my self-guided walk through the modern city from Kungsträdgården; 18:30—Take Royal Canal tour (confirm times, last boat departs earlier Sept–April, 50-min tour from Grand Hotel).

Day 2: 10:00—Catch 90-minute bus tour from the Royal Opera House, or take the City Hall tour; 12:15—Catch the Changing of the Guard at the palace (13:15 on Sun); 13:00–Lunch on Stortorget; 14:00—Tour Royal Palace Museums and Armory and follow my Old Town self-guided walk; 18:30—Free evening (could take a harbor dinner cruise).

Day 3: With an extra day, add a cruise through the scenic island archipelago (easy to do from Stockholm), or spend more time in Stockholm (there's plenty left to do and experience).

Orientation to Stockholm

(area code: 08)

Greater Stockholm's 1.9 million residents live on 14 islands woven together by 54 bridges. Visitors need only concern themselves with these districts, most of which are islands:

• **Norrmalm** is downtown, with most of the hotels and shopping areas, and the combined train and bus station. Östermalm, to the east, is more residential.

• **Kungsholmen,** the island across from Norrmalm, is home to City Hall and several inviting lakefront eateries.

• **Gamla Stan** is the Old Town island of winding, lantern-lit streets, antiques shops, and classy cafés clustered around the Royal Palace.

• **Skeppsholmen** is the small, central, traffic-free park/island with the Museum of Modern Art and two fine youth hostels.

• **Djurgården** is the park island—Stockholm's wonderful green playground, with many of the city's top sights (bike rentals just over bridge as you enter island).

• **Södermalm,** just south of the others, is aptly called

"Stockholm's Brooklyn." Apart from its fine views and some good eateries, this residential island is of less interest to those on a quick visit. Its "SoFo" quarter is considered Stockholm's Greenwich Village, with a young, creative, trendy scene.

Tourist Information

Sweden House (Sverige Huset), Stockholm's official tourist office, is a six-block walk from the central train and bus station. The efficient staff provides free city maps, pamphlets on everything, Stockholm Cards (see below), transportation passes, a huge souvenir shop, day-trip and bus-tour information and tickets, and a room-booking service (75-kr fee for hotels, 25-kr/person fee for hostels). Avoid lines at the counter by looking up sightseeing details on one of the 10 user-friendly computer terminals (some with Internet access, 1 kr/min). Check out their helpful "today's events" board and grab a copy of *What's On Stockholm*, a free monthly magazine with hours and directions for most sights, special event listings, and details on public transportation (Mon–Fri 9:00–19:00, Sat 10:00–17:00, Sun 10:00–16:00, located in the basement of Hamngatan 27, but to enter

go around to Kungsträdgården side, T-bana: Kungsträdgården, tel. 08/5082-8508, www.stockholmtown.com). The TI has placed computer terminals with tourist information in many hotel lobbies and at Stockholm's central station.

Airport Visitor Information Center, a branch of the TI, is in Arlanda Airport's Terminal 5, where most international flights arrive. It offers many of the same services as Sweden House (staffed daily 6:00–24:00, brochures available 24 hours, tel. 08/797-6000).

The Stockholm Card, a 24-hour pass for 375 kr, includes all public transit, free entry to almost every sight (75 attractions), some free or discounted tours, and a handy sightseeing handbook. An added bonus is the substantial pleasure of doing everything without considering the cost (many of Stockholm's sights are worth the time but not the money). The card pays for itself if you just use public transportation and see Skansen, the *Vasa* Museum, and Millesgården. You can stretch it by entering Skansen on your 24th hour. A child's pass (age 7–17) costs about 60 percent less. The Stockholm Card also comes in 48-hour (495 kr) and 72-hour (595 kr) versions. Cards are sold at the Sweden House, airport TI, many hotels, hostels, larger subway stations, Pressbyrån newsstands, and at www.stockholmtown.com.

Arrival in Stockholm

By Train or Bus

Stockholm's combined train and bus station, at the southwestern edge of Norrmalm (six blocks from the Sweden House TI), is a hive of services, shops, exchange desks, and people on the move. The bus section (called Cityterminalen) is up the escalators from the train station's main hall. The station has a subway (T-bana) stop—signed *T-Centralen*—and taxi stands. Those sailing to Finland or Estonia will find cruise-ship offices in the bus terminal, and can catch a shuttle bus to the port from here. The best way to connect the city and its airport is via the Arlanda Express shuttle train, which leaves from here (see below).

By Plane

Arlanda Airport: Stockholm's Arlanda Airport is 28 miles north of town (airport info: tel. 08/797-6000, SAS toll-free tel. 0770-727-727). The airport TI (see "Airport Visitor Information Center," above) can advise you on getting into Stockholm and on your sightseeing plans.

The **airport shuttle train,** the Arlanda Express, is the fastest way to zip between the airport and the central train station (240 kr one-way, 460 kr round-trip, kids under 17 free with adult, covered by railpass; generally 4/hr—departing at :05, :20, :35, and :50 past the hour in each direction; even more frequent midday, 20-min trip, has its own dedicated platform in train station—follow signs to *Arlanda*, toll-free tel. 020-222-224, www.arlandaexpress.com). Buy your ticket either at the window near the track or from a ticket-vending machine, or pay an extra 50 kr to buy it on board. In summer and on weekends, a special fare lets two people travel for nearly half-price (two for 250 kr one-way, available daily mid-June–Aug, Sat–Sun year-round).

Airport shuttle buses (Flygbussarna) run between the airport and the train/bus station (110 kr, 6/hr, 40 min, may take longer at rush hour, buy tickets from ticket kiosks or at airport TI, www.flygbussarna.se).

Taxis between the airport and the city center take about 30–40 minutes (about 500 kr, depends on company, look for price printed on side of cab). Establish the price first. Reputable taxis accept credit cards.

The **cheapest airport connection** is to take bus #583 from the airport to Märsta, then switch to the *pendeltåg* (suburban train, 2/hr), which goes to Stockholm's central station (60 kr, total journey time 60 min, covered by Stockholm Card).

Skavsta Airport: Some discount airlines use Skavsta Airport, about 60 miles south of Stockholm (www.skavsta.se). Flygbussarna shuttle buses connect to the city (150 kr, timed to meet arriving flights, 80 min, www.flygbussarna.se).

By Boat

For information on Stockholm's cruise-ship terminals, see page 513 for boats to Tallinn, or page 470 for boats to Helsinki.

By Car

Only a Swedish meatball would drive his car in Stockholm. Park it and use public transit instead. The TI has a *Parking in Stockholm* brochure. Those sailing to Finland or Estonia should ask about long-term parking at the terminal when reserving their ticket; to minimize the risk of theft and vandalism, pay extra for the most secure parking garage.

Helpful Hints

Theft Alert: Even in Stockholm, when there are crowds, there are pickpockets (such as at the Royal Palace during the Changing of the Guard). Too-young-to-arrest teens—many from Eastern Europe—are hard for local police to control.

Museum Prices and Hours: Not long ago, many Stockholm museums were free. But since the Moderate Party took control of the government in 2006, state-run museums have reintroduced entrance fees. (The left wants to make culture

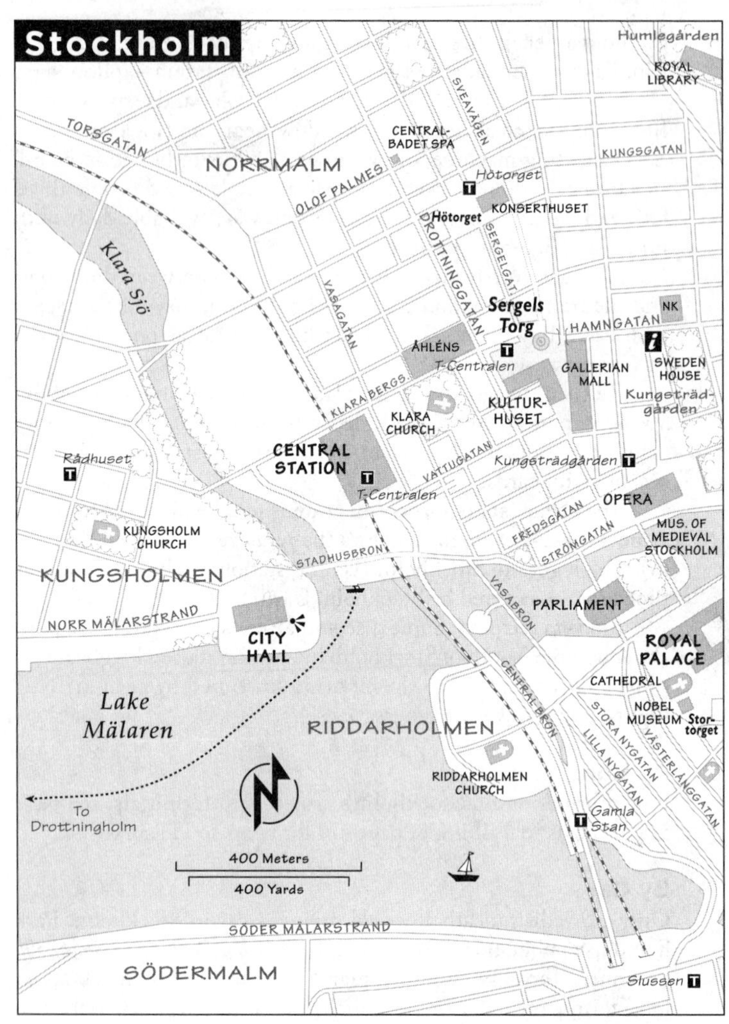

accessible to all, while the right believes you'll only appreciate what you have to pay for.) You can still save money by asking at ticket desks about reduced and free entry for seniors, students, or children. Many museums are open late (17:00–20:00) and are free one night a week. Most sights have consistent hours only in summer—off-season hours tend to vary. If planning an off-season trip, check websites or ask the TI for the most recent hours.

US Embassy: It's at Dag Hammarskjölds Väg 31 (passport services available Mon–Fri 9:00–11:00, tel. 08/783-5300, www.usemb.se).

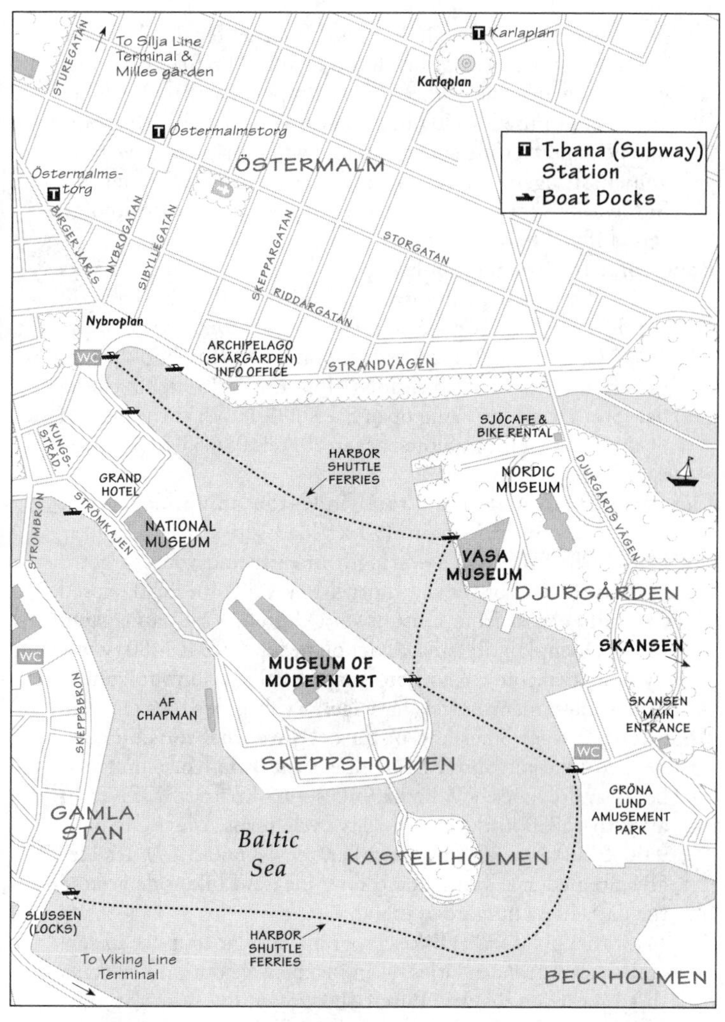

Emergency Assistance: In case of an emergency, dial 112.

Medical Help: For around-the-clock medical advice, call 08/320-100, then press 2 to get into the queue. A 24-hour pharmacy is near the train station at Klarabergsgatan 64 (tel. 08/454-8130).

Telephone Calls: For operator assistance, call 118-118. Numbers starting with 020 are toll-free. Numbers beginning with 070 and 073 are mobile phones—about triple the cost of a regular call. Kiosks sell cheap international phone cards (1 kr/min calls to the US).

Internet Access: 7-Eleven stores and **Pressbyrån** newsstands all over town host "Sidewalk Express" Internet terminals. These are the best deal going. Just buy a card (20 kr/hr), remember your password, and you can pop into participating branches anywhere in town to log on. The card is shareable (but only one person at a time can use it) and valid for three days from your first log-in (branches open daily until late). There's a Sidewalk Express nook at the airport departure lounge (good if you have time to kill and an unexpired card).

Bookstore: The **Sweden Bookshop** has English versions of books by local writers, with a great selection of books by Astrid Lindgren (including her classic, *Pippi Långstrump,* a.k.a. *Pippi Longstocking*), local guidebooks, and tiny booklets on various aspects of Swedish life (Mon–Fri 10:00–18:00, closed Sat–Sun except July–Aug open Sat 11:00–16:00, at the bottom of the Palace Hill at Slottsbacken 10, tel. 08/453-7800, www.swedenbookshop.com).

Laundry: Tvättomaten is a rare find—the only independent launderette in Stockholm (90 kr/load self-service, 190 kr/load 24-hr full-service—bring it in early and you can get it back at the end of the day, open Mon–Fri 8:30–18:30, closed Sat–Sun, across from Gustav Vasa church, Västmannagatan 61 on Odenplan, T-bana: Odenplan, tel. 08/346-480, www.tvattomaten.com). Your hotel may be able to do your laundry for you, and many hostels have laundry facilities on site.

Bike Rental: Rent bikes and boats at **Djurgårdsbrons Sjöcafe,** next to Djurgårdsbron Bridge near the *Vasa* Museum (rowboats and canoes—75 kr/hr; bikes—65 kr/first hr, 55 kr/hr after that, 250 kr/day; handy city cycle maps, May–Oct daily 9:00–21:00, closed in bad weather, tel. 08/660-5757). It's ideally situated as a springboard for a pleasant bike ride around the park-like Djurgården island.

Stockholm's **CityBikes** program, similar to those in several other European cities, is an inexpensive option for seeing this bike-friendly city. Purchase a 25-kr, one-day CityBike card at the Sweden House or at the SL Center (Stockholm Transport) office at Sergels Torg. The card allows you to grab a bike from one of the 80 CityBike racks around the city. Return the bike to any rack within three hours and pick up another one. You can do this over and over until the end of the day (available April–Oct only).

Getting Around Stockholm

By Subway and Bus: Stockholm has a fine subway (called "T-bana") and bus system, and special passes that take the bite out of the cost. It's a spread-out city, so most visitors will need public transport at some point (transit info tel. 08/600-1000 and

press * for English, www.sl.se/english). The subway is easy to figure out, but many sights are better served by bus. The main lines are listed on the map in *What's On Stockholm*. A more detailed system map is posted around town and available free from subway ticket windows and SL (Stockholm Transport) info desks in main stations. Check out the modern public art in the subway (such as at Kungsträdgården station).

A simple ticket takes you anywhere in town on either the subway or buses. There are four ticket options: a single ticket (30 kr at Pressbyrån newsstand or in-station machine, 40 kr at T-bana station ticket window), a book of eight tickets (180 kr—or 22.50 kr per ticket), a 24-hour ticket (100 kr, sold only at Pressbyrån newsstands—not at stations), and a three-day ticket (200 kr, sold only at Pressbyrån newsstands).

By Harbor Shuttle Ferry: In summer, ferries let you make a fun, practical, and scenic shortcut across the harbor to Djurgården island. Boats leave from Slussen (at the south end of Gamla Stan) every 10–20 minutes, docking near the Gröna Lund amusement park on Djurgården (May–mid-Sept only, 10-min trip, 40 kr). Another company makes the five-minute journey from Nybroplan to Djurgården, landing next to the *Vasa* Museum (3/hr, June–Aug daily 10:00–20:00, 40 kr). While buses and trams run between the same points for about half the price, this option gets you out onto the water.

By Taxi: Stockholm is a good taxi town if you get an honest cab (45-kr starting fare). I've been ripped off enough by cabs here to take only "Taxi Stockholm" cabs with the phone number (08/150-000) printed on the door. (Taxi Kurir is also reportedly honest: tel. 08/300-000.) Your hotel, restaurant, or museum can call a cab, which will generally arrive within minutes (you'll pay no extra charge—the meter starts when you hop in).

Tours in Stockholm

A company called **Stockholm Sightseeing** seems to have a lock on all city sightseeing tours, whether by bus, by boat, or on foot. Their website (www.stockholmsightseeing.com) covers the entire program, many of which are listed below. For more information on all their tours, call 08/1200-4000. Tours can be paid for in advance online, or simply as you board. The Stockholm Card provides the following discounts: 1.5-hour bus tour—50 percent discount on afternoon departures from 14:00 on; 50-minute Historic Canal boat tour—free; Royal Canal Tour—40 kr off the 140 kr price. The Stockholm Card does not cover the hop-on, hop-off bus and boat tours, Under the Bridges boat tour, or Old Town walk.

By Bus

Hop-on, Hop-off Bus Tour—Like hop-on, hop-off buses throughout Europe, Stockholm Sightseeing's topless double-decker buses make a 1.5-hour circuit of the city, connecting all the essential places (two lines intersect at three spots, total of 25 stops). You can hop off, tour a sight, and catch a later bus. The bus provides a convenient connection to sights from Skansen to City Hall, and the recorded commentary is good (260 kr/24-hr ticket for both lines, covers entry to Gröna Lund amusement park; buses run May–Sept 2/hr daily 10:00–16:00, April and Oct–mid-Dec 2/hr Fri–Sun only, none mid-Dec–March; start from Sweden House TI).

Quickie Orientation Bus Tour—Several different city bus tours leave from the Royal Opera House on Gustav Adolfs Torg. Stockholm Sightseeing's Stockholm Panorama tour provides a good overview (250 kr, 1.5 hours; daily at 10:00, 12:00, and 14:00; more frequent in summer).

By Boat

▲City Boat Tours—For a good floating look at Stockholm and a pleasant break, consider a sightseeing cruise. The handiest are the Stockholm Sightseeing boats, which leave from Strömkajen in front of the Grand Hotel. You have two choices (each with recorded commentary): The **Royal Canal Tour** is short and informative (140 kr, 50 min, departs at :30 past each hour, generally daily May–Aug 10:30–18:30 but often as late as 19:30, April and Sept 10:30–15:30, Oct–Dec 10:30–13:30, none Jan–March). The nearly two-hour **Under the Bridges Tour** goes through two locks and under 15 bridges (190 kr, May–mid-Sept daily 10:00–18:00, July–Aug until 20:00, departures on the hour). A third boat tour, the **Historical Canal Tour**, leaves from the dock at City Hall (Stadshuskajen; 140 kr, 50 min, daily June–Aug 10:30–18:30, departs at :30 past each hour). This tour circles Kungsholmen island via canals and past leafy shorelines as you listen to a history of the town and its development from the early Industrial Age to modern times. To venture farther into Stockholm's archipelago, see the next chapter.

Hop-on, Hop-off Boat Tour—Stockholm is a city surrounded by water, making this boat option enjoyable and practical. The boat makes a small loop, stopping at key spots such as Djurgården (Skansen and *Vasa* Museum), Gamla Stan (near Slussen and again near Royal Palace), and Nybroplan. Use the boat strictly as transport from Point A to Point B, or make the whole 50-minute, six-stop loop and enjoy the recorded commentary (100-kr ticket good 24 hours, includes entrance into Gröna Lund amusement park, runs June–late Aug daily 1–2/hr 10:05–16:05, late Aug–mid-Sept 2/hr Sat–Sun only, pick up map for locations of boat stops).

By Foot

Old Town Walk—Stockholm Sightseeing offers a one-hour Old Town walk (150 kr, daily July–Aug at 11:30 and 13:30, leaves from Gustav Adolfs Torg, near the Royal Opera House).

Local Guides—To hire a private guide, call 08/5082-8508 (Mon–Fri 9:00–17:00, closed Sat–Sun) or visit www.guidestockholm.com. The standard rate is about 1,350 kr for up to a three-hour tour. **Marita Bergman** is a schoolteacher and a licensed guide who enjoys taking around visitors during her breaks (1,200 kr/half-day tour, tel. 08/5909-3931, mobile 073-511-9154, maritabergman@bredband.net). **Håkan Frändén** is also good (mobile 070-531-3379, hkan.frndn@telia.com).

Self-Guided Walks

This section includes two different walks to introduce you to Stockholm, both old (Gamla Stan) and new (the modern city).

▲▲Welcome to Stockholm's Old Town (Gamla Stan)

Stockholm's historic island core is charming, photogenic, and full of antiques shops, street lanterns, painted ceilings, and surprises. Until the 1600s, all of Stockholm fit on Gamla Stan. Stockholm traded with other northern ports such as Amsterdam, Lübeck, and Tallinn. German culture influenced art, building styles, and even the language, turning Old Norse into modern Swedish. With its narrow alleys and stairways, Gamla Stan mixes poorly with cars and modern economies. Today, it's been given over to the Royal Palace and to the tourists—sometimes seemingly unaware that most of Stockholm's best attractions are elsewhere—who throng Gamla Stan's main drag, Västerlånggatan. While you could just happily wander, this quick walk gives meaning to Stockholm's Old Town.

• *Start at the base of Slottsbacken (the palace hill esplanade) leading up to the...*

Royal Palace: Check out the ❶ **statue of King Gustav III** gazing at the palace (bottom of Slottsbacken; palace described

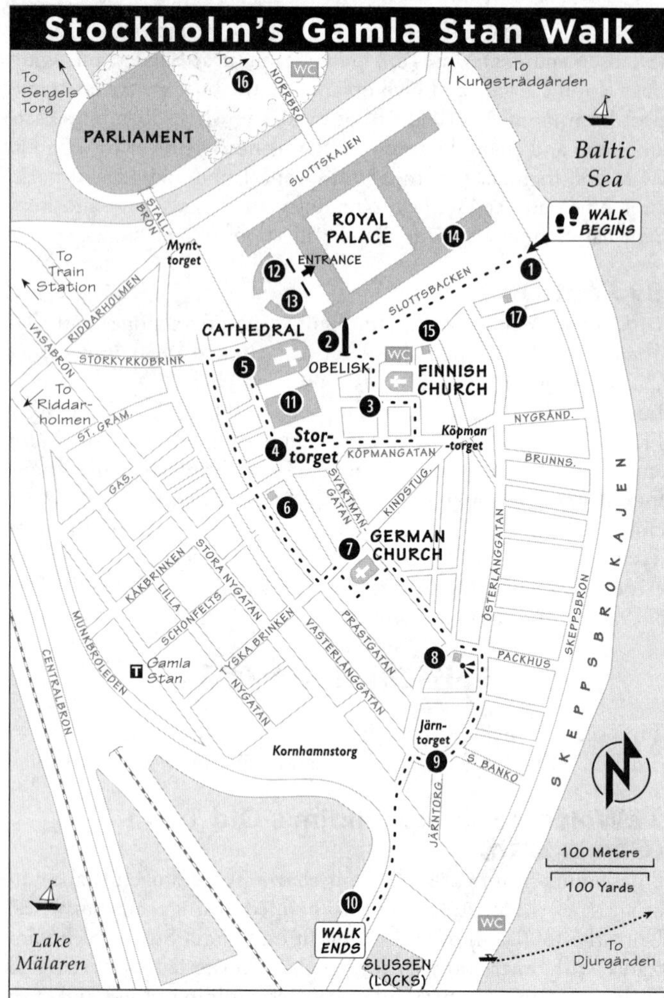

Self-Guided Walk

1. King Gustav III Statue
2. Obelisk
3. Iron Boy Statue
4. Stortorget
5. Cathedral
6. Rune Stone
7. German Church
8. Viewpoint
9. Järntorget
10. Bridge & Lock

Additional Sights

11. Nobel Museum
12. Changing of the Guard
13. Palace Info Booth
14. Royal Armory
15. Royal Coin Cabinet & Swedish Economy Museum
16. To Museum of Medieval Stockholm
17. Sweden Bookshop

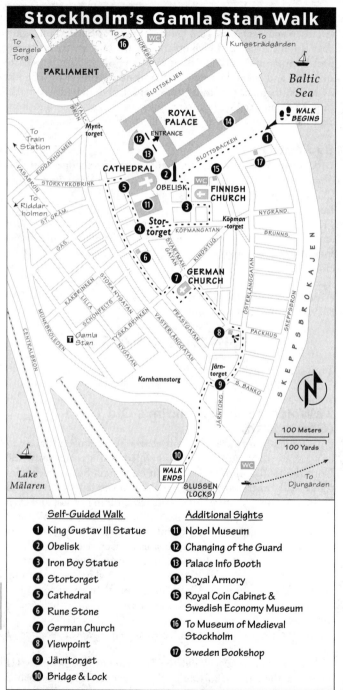

later, under "Sights in Stockholm"), which was built on the site of Stockholm's first castle. Gustav turned Stockholm from a dowdy Scandinavian port into a sophisticated European capital, modeled on buildings he'd seen in Paris, Vienna, and Berlin. Gustav loved the arts, and he founded the Royal Dramatic Theater and the Opera in Stockholm. Ironically, he was assassinated at a masquerade ball at the Royal Opera House in 1792, inspiring Verdi's opera *Un Ballo in Maschera.*

Walk up the broad, cobbled boulevard. (The recommended Sweden Bookshop, with English books, is on the left near the bottom.) Partway up the hill, stop and scan the harbor. The grand building across the water is the National Museum, which is often mistaken by illiterate tourists for the palace. In the distance beyond that is a fine row of buildings—Strandvägen. Until the 1850s, this area was home to peasant shacks, but as Stockholm was entering its grand stage, it was cleaned up and replaced by fine apartments, including some of the city's smartest addresses. Live here, and you call Tiger Woods (who married a Swede) your neighbor. The TV tower—a major attraction back in the 1970s—stands tall in the distance. Turn to the palace facade on your left (finished in 1754, replacing one that burned in 1697). The niches are filled with Swedish bigwigs (literally) from the mid-18th century.

The ❷ **obelisk** honors Stockholm's merchant class for its support in a war against Russia (1788). In front of the obelisk are tour buses (their drivers worried about parking cops) and a sand pit used for *boules.* The royal family took a liking to the French game during a Mediterranean vacation, and it's quite popular around town today. Behind the obelisk stands Storkyrkan, Stockholm's cathedral (which we'll visit later in this walk). From this angle, you see its Baroque facade, added to fit with the newer palace. Opposite the palace (orange building on left) is the Finnish church (Finska Kyrkan), which originated as the royal tennis hall. When the Renaissance hit in 1527, church services could at last be said in the peoples' languages rather than Latin. Suddenly, each merchant community needed its own church. Finns worshipped here, the Germans built their church (coming up on this walk), and the Swedes got the cathedral.

Stroll behind the Finnish church into the shady churchyard where you'll find the fist-sized ❸ ***Iron Boy,*** the tiniest public statue (out of about 600 statues) in Stockholm. Swedish grannies knit caps for him in the winter. Local legend says the statue honors the orphans who had to transfer cargo from sea ships to lake ships before Stockholm's locks were built. Some people rub his head for good luck (which the orphans didn't have). Others, likely needy when it comes to this gift, rub his head for wisdom. The artist says it's simply a self-portrait of him as a child, sitting on his bed and gazing at the moon (notice the moonbeam-projecting light on the top of a pipe).

• *Continue through the yard, cross Trädgårdsgatan, go down the tiny lane to Köpmangatan (the medieval merchants' street, now popular with antiques dealers), turn right, and head for Stortorget, the old square.*

❹ **Stortorget, Stockholm's Oldest Square:** Colorful old buildings topped with gables line this square, which was the heart of medieval Stockholm (pop. 6,000 in 1400). This was where the many tangled lanes intersected, becoming the natural center for shopping and the town well. Today Stortorget is home to tourists, concerts, occasional demonstrators, and—in winter—Christmas shoppers at an outdoor market.

The grand building on the right is the Stock Exchange. This building now houses the noble Nobel Museum (described later, under "Sights in Stockholm"). Upstairs is the Swedish Academy, which awards the Nobel Prize for literature each year. On the immediate left is the Stockholm Stadsmission (offering the cheapest and best lunch around at Grillska Huset—see listing on page 391), and at #5 is their secondhand shop, affording those who peek in a fine look at the richly decorated ceilings characteristic of Gamla Stan in the 17th century. The exotic flowers and animals implied that the people who lived or worked here were worldly. The town well is still a popular meeting point. Scan the fine old facades.

The site of the Stockholm Bloodbath of 1520, this square has a notorious history. During a Danish power grab, many of Stockholm's movers and shakers who had challenged Danish rule—Swedish aristocracy, leading merchants, and priests—were rounded up, brought here, and beheaded. Rivers of blood were said to have flowed through the streets. Legend holds that the 80 or so white stones in the fine red facade across the square symbolize the victims. (One victim's son escaped, went into hiding, and resurfaced to lead a Swedish revolt against the Danish rulers. Three years later, the Swedes elected that rebel, Gustav Vasa, as their first king. He went on to usher in a great period in Swedish history—the Swedish Renaissance.) This square long held the town's pillory.

• *At the far end of the square (under the finest gables), turn right and follow Trangsund toward the cathedral.*

❺ **Cathedral (Storkyrkan):** Just before the church, you'll see my personal phone booth (Rikstelefon) and the gate to the churchyard—guarded by statues of Caution and Hope. Enter the yellow-brick church—Stockholm's oldest, from the 13th century (30 kr, free on Sun, daily mid-May–mid-Sept 9:00–18:00, until 16:00 off-season; worthwhile included English-language flier describes the interior). Signs explain events (busy with tours and services in summer).

The interior is cobbled with centuries-old tombstones. At one time, more than a thousand people were buried under the church. The tombstone of the Swedish reformer Olaus Petri is appropriately simple and appropriately located—under the pulpit. A witness to the Stockholm Bloodbath, Petri was nearly executed himself. He went on to befriend Gustav Vasa and guide him in Lutheranizing Sweden (and turning this cathedral from Catholic to Protestant).

Opposite the pulpit, find the bronze plaque. It recalls the 1925 Swedish-led ecumenical meeting of all Christian leaders—except the pope—that encouraged the Church to speak out against the type of evil that resulted in World War I's horrific death toll.

The royal boxes (between the pulpit and the altar) date from 1684. In front (on the left), *Saint George and the Dragon* (1489) is carved of oak and elk horn. To some, this symbolizes the Swedes' overcoming the evil Danes. In a broader sense, it's an inspiration to take up the struggle against even non-Danish evil. Regardless, it must be the gnarliest dragon's head in all of Europe.

Near the exit, a painting depicts Stockholm in the early 1500s, showing a walled city filling only today's Gamla Stan. It's a 1630 copy of the 1535 original. The strange sun and sky predicted big changes in Sweden—and as a matter of fact, that's what happened. Gustav Vasa brought on huge reforms in religion and beyond. (The copies show you the same painting, minus the glare.)

In June of 2010, this church is hosting a royal wedding. (Crown Princess Victoria, heir to the throne, is marrying Daniel, her personal trainer.) Expect a very crowded and boisterous city at that time.

The plain door on the right leads to a free WC. The exit door next to the painting takes you into the kid-friendly churchyard (which was once the cemetery).

• *With your back to the church's front door, turn right and continue down Trangsund. At the next corner, go downhill on Storkyrkobrinken and take the first left on...*

Prästgatan Lane: Enjoy a quiet wander down this peaceful "Priests' Lane." (Västerlånggatan, the touristy drag, parallels this lane one block to the right—you can walk back up on it later.) As you stroll this 15th-century lane, look for hoists (merchants used these to lift goods into their attics), tie bolts (iron bars necessary to bind the timber beams of tall buildings together), small coal

or wood hatches (for fuel delivery back in the good old days), and flaming gold phoenixes under red-crown medallions (telling firefighters which houses paid insurance and could be saved in case of fire—for example, #46). Like other Scandinavian cities, Stockholm was plagued by fire until it was finally decreed that only stone, stucco, and brick construction (like you see here) would be allowed in the town center.

After two blocks (at Kåkbrinken), a cannon barrel on the corner guards a Viking-age ❻ **rune stone.** In case you can't read the old Nordic script, it says: "Torsten and Frogun erected this stone in memory of their son."

Continue farther down Prästgatan to Tyska Brinken and turn left. You will see the powerful brick steeple of the ❼ **German Church** (Tyska Kyrkan, free, open 11:00–16:00). Its carillon has played four times a day since 1666. Think of the days when German merchants worked here. Today, Germans come to Sweden not to run the economy, but to enjoy its pristine nature (which is progressively harder to find in their own crowded homeland). Sweden formally became a Lutheran country before Germany—making this the first German Lutheran church.

• *Wander through the churchyard and out the back. Exit right onto Svartmangatan and follow it to the right, ending at an iron railing overlooking Österlånggatan.*

❽ **Viewpoint:** From this perch, survey the street below to the left and right. Notice how it curves. This marks the old shoreline. In medieval times, piers stretched out like fingers into the harbor. Gradually, as land was reclaimed and developed, these piers were extended, becoming lanes leading to piers farther away. Behind you is a cute shop where elves can actually be seen making elves.

Walk right along Österlånggatan to ❾ **Järntorget**—a customs square in medieval times, and home of Sweden's first bank back in 1680 (the yellow building with the bars on the windows). A nearby Co-op Nara supermarket offers picnic fixings. From here, Västerlånggatan—the eating, shopping, and commercial pedestrian mall of Gamla Stan—leads back across the island. You'll be there in a minute, but first finish this walk by continuing out of the square (opposite where you entered) down Järntorgsgatan.

Walk out into the traffic hell and stop on the ❿ **bridge** above the canal. This area is called Slussen, named for the locks between the salt water of the Baltic Sea (to your left) and the fresh water of the huge Lake Mälaren (to your right). In fact, Stockholm exists because this is where Lake Mälaren meets the sea. Traders would sail their goods from far inland to this point, where they'd meet merchants who would ship the goods south to Europe. In the 13th century, the new Kingdom of Sweden needed revenue, and began levying duty taxes on all the iron, copper, and furs shipped through here. From the bridge, you may notice a current in the water, indicating that the weir has been lowered and water is spilling from Lake Mälaren (about two feet about sea level) into the sea. Today, the locks are nicknamed "the divorce lock" because this is where captains and first mates learn to communicate under pressure and the public eye.

Survey the view. Opposite Gamla Stan is the island of Södermalm—bohemian, youthful, artsy, and casual—with its popular view elevator. Moored on the saltwater side are the cruise ships, which bring thousands of visitors into town each day during the season. Many of these boats are bound for Finland. The old steamer *Patricia* (see its two white masts, 200 or so yards toward Södermalm) is a local favorite for raucous dining and dancing (described on page 394). The towering white syringe is the Gröna Lund amusement park's free-fall ride. The revolving *Djurgården Färjan* sign marks the ferry that zips from here directly to Gröna Lund and Djurgården. The equestrian statue is Jean-Baptiste Bernadotte, the French nobleman invited to establish the current Swedish royal dynasty 200 years ago.

You could catch bus #2, which heads back downtown (the stop is just beyond Bernadotte, next to the waterfront). But better yet, linger longer in Gamla Stan—day or night, it's a lively place to enjoy. Västerlånggatan, Gamla Stan's main commercial drag, is a festival of distractions that keeps most visitors from seeing the historic charms of Old Town—which you just did. Now you can window-shop and eat (see "Eating in Stockholm"). Or, if it's late, find some live music (see "Nightlife in Stockholm").

• *For more sightseeing, consider the other sights in Gamla Stan or at the Royal Palace (all described later, under "Sights in Stockholm"). If you continue back up Västerlånggatan (always going straight), you'll pass the Parliament building and cross the water back over onto Norrmalm (where the street becomes Drottninggatan). This street leads back into Stockholm's modern, vibrant new town.*

From here it's also a 10-minute walk to Kungsträdgården, the starting point of my Modern City self-guided walk (below). On the way there, you'll walk past the Royal Opera House and Gustav Adolfs Torg, with its imposing statue of Gustavus Adolphus. He was the king who established the Swedish empire. Considered by many the father of modern warfare for his innovative tactics, he was a Protestant hero of the Thirty Years' War.

Stockholm at a Glance

▲▲▲**Skansen** Europe's first and best open-air folk museum, with more than 150 old homes, churches, shops, and schools. **Hours:** Park—daily mid-May–mid-June 10:00–20:00, mid-June–Aug 10:00–22:00, Sept 10:00–20:00, Oct and March–mid-May 10:00–16:00, Nov–Feb 10:00–15:00; historical buildings—generally 11:00–15:00, June–Aug some until 19:00, most closed in winter. See page 375.

▲▲▲***Vasa* Museum** Ill-fated 17th-century warship dredged from the sea floor, now the showpiece of an interesting museum. **Hours:** June–Aug daily 8:30–18:00; Sept–May Thu–Tue 10:00–17:00, Wed 10:00–20:00. See page 377.

▲▲▲**Archipelago** Mostly half-day cruises to Vaxholm and many other small island destinations. **Hours:** Several options per day in summer, some including a meal on board. See the next chapter.

▲▲**Military Parade and Changing of the Guard** Punchy daily pomp starting at Nybroplan and finishing at Royal Palace outer courtyard. **Hours:** Mid-May–mid-Sept Mon–Sat at 11:45 (reaches palace at 12:15), Sun at 12:45 (palace at 13:15); April–mid-May and mid-Sept–Oct Wed and Sat at 11:45 (palace at 12:15), Sun at 12:45 (palace at 13:15); Nov–March starts at palace Wed and Sat at 12:00, Sun at 13:00. See page 369.

▲▲**Royal Armory** A fine collection of ceremonial medieval royal armor, clothing, and carriages, in the Royal Palace. **Hours:** June–Aug daily 10:00–17:00; Sept–May Tue–Sun 11:00–17:00, Thu until 20:00, closed Mon. See page 370.

▲▲**City Hall** Gilt mosaic architectural jewel of Stockholm and site of Nobel Prize banquet, with tower offering the city's best views. **Hours:** Required tours daily generally June–Aug on the hour 9:00–16:00, off-season at 10:00, 12:00, and 14:00. See page 372.

▲▲**Nordic Museum** Danish Renaissance palace design and five fascinating centuries of traditional Swedish lifestyles. **Hours:** June–Aug daily 10:00–17:00; Sept–May Mon–Fri 10:00–16:00, Wed until 20:00, Sat–Sun 11:00–17:00. See page 378.

▲▲**Drottningholm Palace** Resplendent 17th-century royal residence with a Baroque theater. **Hours:** May–Aug daily 10:00–

16:30, Sept daily 11:00-15:30, Oct-April Sat-Sun only 12:00-15:30 except closed mid-Dec-mid-Jan. See page 380.

▲**Nobel Museum** Star-studded tribute to some of the world's most accomplished scientists, artists, economists, and politicians. **Hours:** Mid-May-mid-Sept Wed-Sun 10:00-17:00, Tue 10:00-20:00; off-season Wed-Sun 11:00-17:00, Tue 11:00-20:00; closed Mon year-round. See page 368.

▲**Royal Palace Museums** Complex of Swedish royal museums, the two best of which are the State Apartments and Royal Treasury. **Hours:** June-Aug daily 10:00-17:00; early Sept Mon-Sat 10:00-16:00, Sun 12:00-15:00; late May daily 10:00-16:00; mid-Sept-Dec and mid-Fed-mid-May Tue-Sun 12:00-15:00, closed Mon; closed Jan-mid-Feb. See page 371.

▲**Royal Coin Cabinet and Swedish Economy Museum** Europe's best look at the history of money, with a sweep through the evolution of the Swedish economy to boot. **Hours:** Daily 9:00-16:00. See page 371.

▲**Kungsträdgården** Stockholm's lively central square, with life-size chess games, concerts, and perpetual action. **Hours:** Always open. See page 366.

▲**Sergels Torg** Modern square with underground mall. **Hours:** Always open. See page 367.

▲**National Museum of Fine Arts** Convenient, crowd-free gallery with work of locals Larsson and Zorn, along with Rembrandt, Rubens, and Impressionists. **Hours:** June-Aug Wed-Sun 11:00-17:00, Tue 11:00-20:00, closed Mon; Sept-May Tue and Thu 11:00-20:00, Wed and Fri-Sun 11:00-17:00, closed Mon. See page 373.

▲**Thielska Galleriet** Enchanting waterside mansion with works of local artists Larsson, Zorn, and Munch. **Hours:** Mon-Sat 12:00-16:00, Sun 13:00-16:00. See page 379.

▲**Millesgården** Dramatic cliffside museum and grounds featuring works of Sweden's greatest sculptor, Carl Milles. **Hours:** Mid-May-Sept daily 11:00-17:00; Oct-mid-May Tue-Sun 12:00-17:00, closed Mon. See page 379.

Exploring Stockholm's Modern City

On this walk, we'll use the park called Kungsträdgården as a springboard to explore the modern center of Stockholm—a commercial zone designed to put the focus not on old kings and mementos of superpower days, but on shopping.

▲**Kungsträdgården:** Centuries ago, this "King's Garden Square" was the private kitchen garden of the king, where he grew his cabbage salad. Today, this downtown people-watching center is considered Stockholm's living room, symbolizing the Swedes' freedom-loving spirit. While the English info board (near the harbor, 20 yards to the statue king's immediate right) describes the garden as a private royal domain, the nearby giant clump of elm trees reminds locals that it's the people who rule now. In the 1970s, demonstrators chained themselves to these trees to stop the building of an underground train station here. They prevailed, and today, locals enjoy the peaceful, breezy ambience of a tea house instead. Watch the life-size game of chess and enjoy a summer concert at the bandstand. There's always something going on.

Kungsträdgården—surrounded by the harborfront and tour boats, the Royal Opera House, and, on the far side, the Sweden House (TI), a welcoming Volvo showroom (next to the TI, showing off the latest in Swedish car design), and the NK department store—is *the* place to feel Stockholm's pulse (but always ask first: *"Far jag kanna din puls?"*).

Kungsträdgården also throws huge parties. Restaurant Days is the "Taste of Stockholm" festival, running for a week in early June, when restaurateurs show off and bands entertain all day. The beer flows liberally, a rare public spectacle in Sweden.

The nearby Kungsträdgården T-bana station is famous for having the best art of any station in town. The man at the turnstile is generally friendly to tourists who ask *snälla rara* (snel-lah rar-rah; pretty please) for permission to nip down the escalator to see the far-out design, proving to the gullible that Stockholm sits upon a grand, ancient civilization.

• *From the T-bana station, walk underground across the square, following signs to the Gallerian mall. (Or, if you're not in the T-bana station, walk aboveground—ask anyone to direct you to the Gallerian.)*

Gallerian Mall and Sergelgången: Among a world of shops, you'll find plenty of affordable little lunch bars, classy cafés for your *fika* (traditional Swedish coffee-and-bun break), and even a spa providing an oasis of relaxation for stressed-out shoppers. Designtorget (a fun store on the lower level, immediately under the fountain) is designed for independent Swedish designers to market and sell their clever products. Perhaps you need a banana case (75 kr).

• *Beyond this huge mall, more shops lead along Sergelgången eventually to Sergels Torg. (To get there, ask anyone for Sergels Torg.)*

Sergels Torg: This square, worth ▲, dominates the heart of modern Stockholm (between Kungsträdgården and the train station) with its stark 1960s-era functionalist architecture. The glassy tower glows at night, symbolic of Sweden's haunting northern lights. The big, boxy, and glassy building overlooking the square is Stockholm's "culture center," the **Kulturhuset**. Inside, just past the welcoming info desk, you'll find a big model of the city. There's a library, Internet café, chessboards, fine art cinema, art exhibits, a venue for new bands, and a rooftop café with foreign newspapers and a grand view (Tue–Fri 11:00–18:00, Sat–Sun 11:00–18:00, until 21:00 in winter, closed Mon, tel. 08/5083-1508, www.kulturhuset.stockholm.se).

Stand in front of the Kulturhuset (across from the fountain) at the railing above the expansive square nicknamed "Plattan" (the platter). Survey the scene. Everything around you dates from the 1960s and 1970s. This was a run-down area in the 1950s. Then, in the 1960s, it was reinvented as an urban "space of the future," envisioning a car-dominated world. In the 1980s, with no nearby residences, the desolate Plattan became the domain of junkies. Now the city is actively revitalizing it, and the Plattan is becoming a people-friendly heart of the commercial town.

Nearby are the major boutiques and department stores: Nordiska Kompaniet (NK), H&M (popular with my female staff for trendy and inexpensive Euro-fashion), and Åhléns. The thriving pedestrian street **Sergelgatan** leads past the five uniform white towers you see beyond the fountain. These office towers, so modern in the 1960s, have gone from seeming hopelessly out-of-date to being considered "retro," and are now quite popular with young professionals.

• *Walk up Sergelgatan past the towers, enjoying the public art and people-watching, to the market at Hötorget.*

Hötorget: "Hötorget" means "Hay Market," but today its stalls feed people rather than horses. The adjacent indoor market, Hötorgshallen, is fun and fragrant. It dates from 1914 when, for hygiene reasons, the city forbade selling fish and meat outdoors. Carl Milles' statue of *Orpheus Emerging from the Underworld* (with seven sad muses) stands in front of the city concert hall (which hosts the annual Nobel Prize award ceremony). The building, from 1926, is Swedish Art Deco (a.k.a. "Swedish Grace"). The lobby (open through most of summer, 40-kr tours) still evokes Stockholm's Roaring Twenties.

Popping into the Hötorget T-bana station provides a fun glimpse at local urban design. Stockholm's subway system was inaugurated in the 1950s, and many stations are modern art installations in themselves.

• *Our walk ends here. For more shopping and an enjoyable pedestrian boulevard leading back into the Old Town, cut down a block to Drottninggatan and turn left. This busy drag leads straight out of the commercial district, passes the Parliament, then becomes the main street of Gamla Stan.*

Sights in Stockholm

Gamla Stan

The best of Gamla Stan is covered in my self-guided walk, earlier. But here are a few ways to extend your time in the Old Town.

▲Nobel Museum (Nobelmuseet)—Opened in 2001 for the 100-year anniversary of the Nobel Prize, this wonderful little museum tells the story of the world's most prestigious prize. Stockholm-born Alfred Nobel was a great inventor, with more than 300 patents. His most famous invention: dynamite. Living in the late 1800s, Nobel was a man of his age. It was a time of great optimism, wild ideas, and grand projects. His dynamite enabled entire nations to blast their way into the modern age with canals, railroads, and tunnels. It made warfare much more destructive. And it also made Alfred Nobel a very wealthy man.

Wanting to leave a legacy that celebrated and supported people with great ideas, Alfred used his fortune to fund the Nobel Prize. Every year since 1901, laureates have been honored in the fields of physics, chemistry, medicine, literature, and peacemaking. Portraits of all 700-plus prizewinners hang from the ceiling—shuffling around the room like shirts at the dry cleaner's (miss your favorite, and he or she will come around again in three hours). Two video rooms run a continuous montage of quick programs (three-minute bios of various winners in one program, five-minute films celebrating various intellectual environments—from Cambridge to Parisian cafés—in the other). The Viennese-style Kafé Satir is the place to get creative with your coffee...and sample the famous Nobel ice cream. All Nobel laureates who visit the museum are asked to sign the bottom of a chair in the café. Turn yours over and see who warmed your chair. And don't miss the lockable hangers, to protect your fancy, furry winter coat (60 kr, free Tue after 17:00; open mid-May–mid-Sept Wed–Sun

10:00–17:00, Tue 10:00–20:00; off-season Wed–Sun 11:00–17:00, Tue 11:00–20:00; closed Mon year-round; on Stortorget in the center of Gamla Stan a block from the Royal Palace, tel. 08/5348-1800, www.nobelmuseum.se). The Swedish Academy, which awards the Nobel Prize for literature each year, is upstairs.

Parliament (Riksdaghuset)—For a firsthand look at Sweden's government, tour its Parliament buildings (free one-hour tours in English late June–Aug, usually Mon–Fri at 12:00, 13:00, 14:00, and 15:00, enter at Riksgatan 3a, call 08/786-4000 to confirm times). It's also possible to watch the Parliament in session.

Museum of Medieval Stockholm (Medeltidsmuseet)—This museum provides a good look at medieval Stockholm, but it's closed through early 2010 for renovation (when open, likely Tue–Fri 11:00–19:00, Sat–Sun 11:00–17:00, closed Mon; enter museum from park in front of Parliament, tel. 08/5083-1790, www.medeltidsmuseet.stockholm.se).

The **Strömparterren** park, with its café and Carl Milles statue of the *Sun Singer* greeting the day, is a pleasant place for a sightseeing break (pay WC in park, likely free WC in museum when it reopens).

Royal Palace (Kungliga Slottet)

Although the royal family beds down at Drottningholm, this complex in Gamla Stan is still the official royal residence. The palace, designed in Italian Baroque style, was completed in 1754 after a fire wiped out the previous palace.

The Changing of the Guard and the awesome, can't-miss Royal Armory are the palace's highlights. The Royal Treasury is worth a look; the chapel is nice but no big deal; the Apartments of State are not much as far as palace rooms go; and you can skip Gustav III's Museum of Antiquities and the Museum of Three Crowns. The information booth in the semicircular courtyard (at the top, where the guard changes) gives out an explanatory brochure with a map marking the different entrances (main entrance is on the west side—away from the water—but the Royal Armory has a separate entrance). They also have a list of today's guided tours. In peak season, there are up to three different English tours a day (included in the admission)—allowing you to systematically cover nearly the entire complex. Since the palace is used for state functions, it is sometimes closed to tourists.

▲▲Military Parade and Changing of the Guard—Starting at Nybroplan, Stockholm's daily military parade marches over Norrbro Bridge and up to the Royal Palace's outer courtyard, where the band plays and the guard changes (mid-May–mid-Sept Mon–Sat at 11:45—reaches palace at 12:15, Sun at 12:45—palace at 13:15; April–mid-May and mid-Sept–Oct Wed and

Sat at 11:45—palace at 12:15, Sun at 12:45—palace at 13:15; Nov–March starts at palace Wed and Sat at 12:00, Sun at 13:00). In summer, you might also catch the mounted guards (but they do not appear on a regular schedule).

The performance is fresh and spirited, because the soldiers are visiting Stockholm just like you—and it's a chance for young soldiers from all over Sweden in every branch of the service to show their stuff in the big city. Pick your place at the palace courtyard, where the band arrives at about 12:15 (13:15 on Sun). The best spot to stand is along the wall in the inner courtyard, near the palace information and ticket office. There are columns with wide pedestals for easy perching, as well as benches that people stand on to view the ceremony (arrive early). Generally, after the barking and goose-stepping formalities, the band shows off for an impressive 30-minute marching concert. Though the royal family now lives out of town at Drottningholm, the palace guards are for real. If the guard by the cannon in the semicircular courtyard looks a little lax, try wandering discreetly behind him.

▲▲Royal Armory (Livrustkammaren)—The oldest museum in Sweden is more than an armory and less than an armory. It displays impressive ceremonial royal armor (never used in battle), but there's a lot more to see. Everything is beautifully lit and displayed, and well-described in English and by the museum's evocative audioguide (50 kr; June–Aug daily 10:00–17:00; Sept–May Tue–Sun 11:00–17:00, Thu until 20:00, closed Mon; 20-kr audioguide is excellent—romantic couples can share it if they crank up the volume; entrance at bottom of Slottsbacken at base of palace, tel. 08/5195-5546, www.livrustkammaren.se).

The first room is almost a shrine for Swedish visitors. It contains the clothes Gustavus Adolphus wore, and even the horse he was riding when he was killed in the Thirty Years' War. The exquisite workmanship on the ceremonial armor in this room is a fine example of weaponry as an art form. The next room shows royal suits and gowns through the ages. The 1766 wedding dress of Queen Sofia is designed to cleverly show off its fabulously rich fabric (the dress seems even wider when compared to her 20-inch corseted waist). The royal children get a section for themselves, featuring a cradle that has rocked heirs to the throne since the 1650s; eventually it will leave the armory to rock the next royal offspring as well. It's fun to imagine little princes romping around their 600-room home with these toys. A century ago, one prince treasured his boxcar and loved playing cowboys and Indians.

The basement is a royal garage filled with lavish coaches. The highlight: a plush coronation coach made in France in about 1700 and shipped to Stockholm, ready to be assembled Ikea-style. It last rolled a king to his big day—with its eight fine horses and what was then the latest in suspension gear—in the mid-1800s.

▲Other Royal Palace Museums—The four museums below can be accessed through the main entrance and are covered by a 140-kr combo-ticket (otherwise 100 kr each, generally includes guided tour; June–Aug daily 10:00–17:00; early Sept Mon–Sat 10:00–16:00, Sun 12:00–15:00; late May daily 10:00–16:00; mid-Sept–Dec and mid-Feb–mid-May Tue–Sun 12:00–15:00, closed Mon; closed Jan–mid-Feb; tel. 08/402-6130, www.royalcourt.se). Stockholm Card-holders can go straight into each museum, bypassing the ticket office.

Royal Apartments: The stately palace exterior encloses 608 rooms (one more than Britain's Buckingham Palace) of glittering 18th-century Baroque and Rococo decor. Clearly the palace of Scandinavia's superpower, it's steeped in royal history. You'll walk the long halls through four sections: the Hall of State (with an exhibit of fancy state awards), the lavish Bernadotte Apartments (some fine Rococo interiors and portraits of the Bernadotte dynasty), the State Apartments (with rooms dating to the 1690s), and the Guest Apartments, where visiting heads of state still crash. Guided tours run daily at 12:00, 14:00, and 15:00 (45 min, no tours Sept–Oct).

Royal Treasury (Skattkammaren): Climbing down into the super-secure vault, you'll see 12 cases filled with fancy crowns, scepters, jeweled robes, and plenty of glittering gold. Nothing is explained, so get the 5-kr flier or take the guided tour (May–Sept daily at 13:00, Oct–April only Tue and Sun at 13:00).

Gustav III's Museum of Antiquities (Gustav III's Antikmuseum): In the 1700s, Gustav III traveled through Italy and brought home an impressive gallery of classical Roman statues. These are displayed exactly as they were in the 1790s. This was a huge deal for those who had never been out of Sweden (closed mid-Sept–mid-May).

Museum of Three Crowns (Museum Tre Kronor): This museum shows off bits of the palace from before a devastating 1697 fire. It's basically just more old stuff, interesting only to real history buffs (guided tours at 12:00 in summer).

▲Royal Coin Cabinet and Swedish Economy Museum—More than your typical royal coin collection, this is the best money museum I've seen in Europe. A fine exhibit tells the story of money from crude wampum to credit cards, and traces the development of the modern Swedish economy. Unfortunately, there aren't many English translations, which makes the included audioguide critical (50 kr, free on Mon, open daily 9:00–16:00, Slottsbacken 6, tel. 08/5195-5304).

Downtown Stockholm

Waterside Walk—Enjoy Stockholm's ever-expanding shoreline promenades. Tracing the downtown shoreline while dodging in-line skaters and ice-cream trolleys (rather than cars and buses), you can walk from Slussen across Gamla Stan, all the way to the good ship *Vasa* in Djurgården. Perhaps the best stretch is Strandvägen (from Nybroplan past weather-beaten old boats and fancy facades to Djurgården). As you stroll, keep in mind that there's free fishing in central Stockholm, and the harbor waters are restocked every spring with thousands of new fish. Locals tell of one lucky lad who pulled in an 80-pound salmon.

▲▲City Hall (Stadshuset)—The Stadshuset is an impressive mix of 8 million red bricks, 19 million chips of gilt mosaic, and lots of Stockholm pride. While churches dominate cities in southern Europe, in Scandinavian capitals, city halls seem to be the most impressive buildings, celebrating humanism and the ideal of people working together in community. Built in 1923, this is still a functioning city hall. The city council—101 people (mostly women) representing the 818,000 people of metropolitan Stockholm—are hobby legislators with regular day jobs. That's why they meet in the evening. One of Europe's finest public buildings and site of the annual Nobel Prize banquet, City Hall is particularly enjoyable and worthwhile for its entertaining and required 50-minute tour (70 kr, English-only tours daily generally June–Aug at the top of the hour 9:00–16:00; off-season at 10:00, 12:00, and 14:00; call to confirm, 300 yards behind station, bus #3 or #62, tel. 08/5082-9059, www.stockholm.se/cityhall). City Hall's cafeteria, which you enter from the courtyard, serves complete lunches for 75 kr (Mon–Fri 11:00–14:00, closed Sat–Sun).

▲City Hall Tower—This 348-foot-tall tower (an elevator takes you halfway up) rewards those who make the climb with a grand city view. As you huff your way up, you'll come upon models of busts and statues that adorn City Hall and a huge, 25-foot-tall statue of St. Erik. Erik, the patron saint of Stockholm, was originally intended to be hoisted by cranes up through the middle of the tower to stand at its top. But the plans changed, big Erik is forever

parked halfway up the structure, and the tower's top is open for visitors to gather and enjoy the view. At the roof terrace, you'll find smaller statues of Erik, Klara, Maria Magdalena, and Nikolaus: patron saints facing their respective parishes. Finally, you'll find yourself in the company of the tower's nine bells, with Stockholm spreading out all around you (30 kr, daily June–Aug 9:00–17:00, May and Sept 10:00–16:00, closed Oct–April). As only 30 people at a time are allowed up into the tower, there's often a very long wait. If there's a long line, I'd skip it.

▲Orientation Views—For a bird's-eye perspective on this wonderful urban mix of water, parks, concrete, and people, consider these four viewpoints: **City Hall Tower** (described above; view from tower pictured on previous page); **Kaknäs Tower** (at 500 feet, once the tallest building in Scandinavia; 35 kr, daily May–Aug 9:00–22:00, Sept–April 10:00–21:00, restaurant on 28th floor, east of downtown—bus #69 from Nybroplan or Sergels Torg, tel. 08/667-2105); or the **Katarina elevator** (circa 1930s, ride 130 feet to the top; 10 kr, daily mid-May–Aug 8:00–22:00, Sept–mid-May 10:00–18:00, near Slussen T-bana stop—walk behind Katarinavägen toward Fjallgatan for grand city and harbor views).

▲National Museum of Fine Arts—Though mediocre by European standards, this 200-year-old museum is small, central, and user-friendly (100 kr; June–Aug Wed–Sun 11:00–17:00, Tue 11:00–20:00, closed Mon; Sept–May Tue and Thu 11:00–20:00, Wed and Fri–Sun 11:00–17:00, closed Mon; Södra Blasieholmshamnen, T-bana: Kungsträdgården, tel. 08/5195-4310, www.nationalmuseum.se). If you'd like a private tour with the former museum director, rent the excellent audioguide (30 kr), which describes the top works.

Highlights include several works by Rembrandt and Rubens, a fine group of Impressionists, and a sizeable collection of Russian icons. Seek out the exquisite works by the Swedish artists Anders Zorn and Carl Larsson.

The Stockholm-born **Carl Larsson** (1853–1919) became very popular as the Swedish Norman Rockwell, chronicling the everyday family life of his own wife and brood of kids. In the large central entrance hall, his two vast, 900-square-foot murals celebrating Swedish history (above the grand staircase) are worth a close look. *The Return of the King* shows Gustav Vasa astride a white horse. After escaping the Stockholm Bloodbath and leading Sweden's revolt, he drove out the Danes and was elected Sweden's first king (1523). Now he marches his victorious troops across a drawbridge, as Stockholm's burghers bow and welcome him home. In *The Midwinter Sacrifice,* it's solstice eve, and Vikings are gathered at the pagan temple at Gamla Uppsala. Musicians blow the *lur* horns, a priest in white raises the ceremonial hammer of Thor, and another priest in red (with his back to us) holds a sacrificial knife. The Viking king arrives on his golden sled, rises from his throne, strips naked, gazes to the heavens, and prepares to sacrifice himself to the gods of winter, so that spring will return to feed his starving people.

The museum's middle floor is dedicated to **design;** one wing covers the 1500s to the 1800s, the other 1900–2000. With thoughtful English descriptions, this exhibit walks you through the evolution of modern Swedish design: gracefully engraved glass from the 1920s, works from the Stockholm Exhibition of 1930, industrial design of the 1940s, Scandinavian Design movement of the 1950s, plastic chairs from the 1960s, modern furniture from the 1980s, and the Swedish new simplicity from the 1990s.

Museum of Modern Art (Moderna Museet)—This bright, cheery gallery on Skeppsholmen island is as far out as can be, with Picasso, Braque, Dalí, Matisse, and lots of goofy Dada art (such as *Urinal*), as well as more contemporary stuff. Don't miss the beloved *Goat with Tire.* The excellent and included audioguide makes modern art meaningful to visitors who wouldn't otherwise appreciate it (80 kr, Tue 10:00–20:00, Wed–Sun 10:00–18:00, closed Mon, fine bookstore, harborview café, T-bana: Kungsträdgården plus 10-min walk, or take bus #65, tel. 08/5195-5200, www.modernamuseet.se).

▲Swedish Massage, Spa, and Sauna—To treat yourself to a Swedish spa experience—maybe with an authentic "Swedish massage"—head for the elegant circa-1900 **Central-Badet Spa.** The regular 130-kr admission (180 kr Fri–Sat after 15:00, 50 kr for use of a towel and bathrobe) includes entry to an extensive gym, "bubblepool," sauna, steam room, and an elegant Art Nouveau pool. A classic massage costs 650 kr per hour. Reservations are smart (Mon–Sat 6:00–21:00, Sun 8:00–18:00, last entry one hour before closing, closed Sun–Mon July–Aug, ages 18 and up, Drottninggatan 88, 10 min up from Sergels Torg, tel. 08/5452-1300, tel. 08/5452-1313, www.centralbadet.se). If you won't make it to Finland, enjoy a sauna here (for more info on saunas, see page 493 in the Helsinki chapter). There are two saunas—one mixed, one not. Bring your towel into the sauna—not for modesty, but for hygiene (to separate your body from the bench). The steam room is mixed; bring two towels (one for modesty and the other to sit on). The pool is more for floating than for jumping and splashing. The leafy courtyard restaurant is a relaxing place to enjoy affordable, healthy, and light meals.

Stockholm's Djurgården

Four hundred years ago, Djurgården was the king's hunting ground. Now this entire lush island is Stockholm's fun center, protected as a national park. It still has a smattering of animal life among its biking paths, picnicking local families, art galleries, and various amusements. Of the three great sights on the island, the *Vasa* and Nordic museums are neighbors, and Skansen is a 10-minute walk away (or hop on any bus—they come every couple of minutes). To get around more easily, consider renting a bike as you enter the island (see page 354).

Getting There: Take bus #47 from the train station or Sergels Torg and get off at the Nordic Museum (also for the *Vasa* Museum), or continue on to the Skansen stop. In summer, you can also take a ferry from Nybroplan or Slussen (see "Getting Around Stockholm," earlier) or a tram from Nybroplan (daily in summer, weekends only in spring and fall). Walkers can enjoy the harborside Strandvägen promenade, which leads from Nybroplan directly to the island.

▲▲▲Skansen

This is Europe's original open-air folk museum, founded in 1891. It's a huge park gathering more than 150 historic buildings (homes, churches, shops, and schoolhouses) transplanted from all corners of Sweden.

Skansen was the first in what became a Europe-wide movement to preserve traditional architecture in open-air museums. Other languages have even borrowed the Swedish term "Skansen" (which originally meant "the Fort") to mean "open-air museum." Today, tourists still explore this Swedish-culture-on-a-lazy-Susan, seeing folk crafts in action and wonderfully furnished old interiors (lively June–Aug before about 17:00, otherwise pretty dead).

In "Old Stockholm" (top of the escalator), shoemakers, potters, and glassblowers are busy doing their traditional thing (daily 10:00–17:00) in a re-created Old World Stockholm. The rest of Sweden spreads out from Old Stockholm. Northern Swedish culture and architecture is in the north (top of park map), and southern Sweden's in the south (bottom of map).

Take advantage of the free map, and consider the 50-kr museum guidebook. With the book, you'll understand each building you duck into and even learn about the Nordic animals awaiting you in the zoo. Check the live crafts schedule at the information stand by the main entrance beneath the escalator to make a smart Skansen plan. Guides throughout the park are happy to answer your questions—but only if you ask them. The old houses come alive when you take the initiative to get information.

Kids love Skansen, where they can ride a life-size wooden *Dala*-horse and stare down a hedgehog, visit Lill' Skansen (a children's zoo), and take a mini-train or pony ride.

Cost, Hours, Information: 110 kr (less in winter); park open daily mid-May–mid-June 10:00–20:00, mid-June–Aug 10:00–22:00, Sept 10:00–20:00, Oct and March–mid-May 10:00–16:00, Nov–Feb 10:00–15:00; historical buildings generally open 11:00–15:00, June–Aug some until 19:00, most closed in winter. Check their excellent website for "What's Happening at Skansen" during your visit: www.skansen.se, tel. 08/442-8000. Gröna Lund, Stockholm's amusement park, is across the street (described later).

Music: Skansen does great music in summer. There's fiddling (30-min performances June–Aug Tue–Fri at 18:15), folk-dancing (June–Aug Tue–Fri at 19:00, also Sat–Sun at 16:00), and public dancing to live bands (Mon–Sat from 20:00, call for that evening's theme—big band, modern, ballroom, folk).

Eating at Skansen: While Skansen's main restaurant, **Solliden,** serves a big *smörgåsbord* lunch in a grand blue-and-white room (285 kr, daily 12:00–16:00 in summer), and the adjacent **Ekorren** cafeteria offers less-expensive self-service lunches with a view (70–90-kr daily specials, daily 11:00–19:00), the most memorable meals are at the small folk food court on the main square, **Bollnastorget.** Here, among the duck-filled lakes, frolicking families, and peacenik local toddlers who don't bump on the bumper cars, kiosks dish up "Sami slow food" (smoked reindeer), waffles, hot dogs, and more. There are lots of picnic benches—Skansen encourages **picnicking.** (A small grocery store is tucked away across the street and a bit to the left of the main entrance.) The old-time **Stora Gungan Krog,** in Old Stockholm at the top of the escalator, is a cozy inn; their freshly baked cakes will tempt you (80–120-kr indoor or outdoor lunches—meat, fish, or veggie—with a salad-and-cracker bar, daily 11:00–20:00, until 15:00 in winter).

Aquarium: Admission to the aquarium is the only thing not covered on your Skansen ticket, but it is covered by the Stockholm Card (aquarium entry-80 kr, daily June–Aug 10:00–18:00, July until 20:00, Sept–May 10:00–16:00, tel. 08/660-1082).

▲▲▲*Vasa* Museum (Vasamuseet)

Stockholm turned a titanic flop into one of Europe's great sightseeing attractions. This glamorous but unseaworthy warship—top-heavy with an extra cannon deck—sank 20 minutes into her 1628 maiden voyage when a breeze caught the sails and blew her over. After 333 years at the bottom of Stockholm's harbor, she rose again from the deep with the help of marine archaeologists.

Rediscovered in 1956 and raised in 1961, this Edsel of the sea is today the best-preserved ship of its age anywhere—housed since 1990 in a brilliant museum. The masts perched atop the roof—best seen from a distance—show the actual height of the ship.

The *Vasa*, while not quite the biggest ship in the world, had the most firepower, with two fearsome decks of cannons. The 500

STOCKHOLM

carved wooden statues draping the ship—once painted in bright colors—are all symbolic of the king's power. The 10-foot lion on the magnificent prow is a reminder that Europe considered the Swedish King Gustavus Adolphus the "Lion from the North." With this great ship, Sweden was preparing to establish its empire and become more engaged in European power politics.

Painstakingly restored, 95 percent of the wood is original (modern bits are the brighter and smoother planks). Displays are well-described in English. Learn about the ship's rules (bread can't be older than eight years), why it sank (heavy bread?), how it's preserved (the ship, not the bread), and so on.

Cost, Hours, Location: 100 kr; June–Aug daily 8:30–18:00; Sept–May Thu–Tue 10:00–17:00, Wed 10:00–20:00; Galärvarvet, Djurgården, tel. 08/5195-4800, www.vasamuseum.com. The *Vasa* is on the waterfront immediately behind the stately brick Nordic Museum (described below), a 10-minute walk from Skansen. Or you can take bus #47 from downtown. The museum also has a good café inside. To get from the Nordic Museum to the *Vasa* Museum, face the Nordic Museum and walk around to the right (going left takes you into a big dead-end parking lot).

Sightseeing Strategy: For a thorough visit, plan on spending an hour watching the 25-minute video and taking the free 25-minute tour (in either order), then explore the boat and wander through the various exhibits. From June through August, the English-subtitled video generally runs at the top of the hour (last movie at 17:00), with English tours at :30 past each hour beginning at 9:30 (last tour departs at 16:30, fewer tours off-season, call for times). Both the video and tour are included with your admission.

▲▲Nordic Museum (Nordiska Museet)

Built to look like a Danish Renaissance palace, this museum offers a fascinating peek at 500 years of traditional Swedish lifestyles. It's arguably more informative than Skansen. Take time to let the excellent, included audioguide enliven the exhibits. Carl Milles' huge painted-wood statue of Gustav Vasa, father of modern Sweden, overlooks the main gallery.

Highlights are on the top two floors. The middle floor (Level 3) holds the *Traditions* exhibit (showing and describing each old-time celebration of the Swedish year) and a section of exquisite table settings, and fancy fashions from the 18th through the 20th centuries. The top floor (Level 4) has an extensive Sami (Lapp) collection, old furniture, and an exhibit showing Swedish living rooms over the last century; it provides an insightful look at today's Swedes, including an intimate peek at modern bedrooms (match photos of the owners with the various rooms).

Cost, Hours, Location: 70 kr; June–Aug daily 10:00–17:00; Sept–May Mon–Fri 10:00–16:00, Wed until 20:00, Sat–Sun 11:00–17:00; Djurgårdsvägen 6–16, at Djurgårdsbron, bus #47 from downtown, tel. 08/5195-6000, www.nordiskamuseet.se.

Other Djurgården Sights

Gröna Lund—Stockholm's venerable and lowbrow Tivoli-type amusement park still packs in the local families and teens on cheap dates (70 kr, May–mid-Sept daily 12:00–23:00, shorter hours off-season). It's a busy venue for local pop concerts.

▲Thielska Galleriet—If you liked the Larsson and Zorn art in the National Gallery, and/or if you're a Munch fan, this charming mansion on the water at the far end of the Djurgården park is worth the trip (60 kr, Mon–Sat 12:00–16:00, Sun 13:00–16:00, bus #69—not #69K—from downtown, tel. 08/662-5884, www.thielska-galleriet.se).

▲Biking the Garden Island—In all of Stockholm, Djurgården is the natural place to enjoy a bike ride. There's a good and reasonably priced bike-rental place just over the bridge as you enter the island (see Djurgårdsbrons Sjöcafe on page 354), and a world of park-like paths and lanes with harbor vistas to enjoy.

Outer Stockholm

▲Millesgården—The villa and garden of Carl Milles is a veritable forest of statues by Sweden's greatest sculptor. Millesgården is dramatically situated on a bluff overlooking the harbor in Stockholm's upper-class suburb of Lidingö. While the art is engaging and enjoyable, even the curators have little to say about it from an interpretation point of view—so your visit is basically without guidance. But in Milles' house, which dates from the 1920s, you can see his north-lit studio and get a sense of his creative genius.

Carl Milles spent much of his career living in Michigan. But he's buried here at his villa, where he lived and worked for 20 years, lovingly designing this sculpture garden for the public. Milles wanted his art to be displayed on pedestals...to be seen "as if silhouettes against the sky." His subjects—often Greek myths such as Pegasus or Poseidon—stand out as if using the sky as a blank paper. Yet unlike silhouettes, Milles' images against the sky can be enjoyed from many angles. And Milles liked to enliven his sculptures by incorporating fountains into his figures. *Hand of God,* perhaps his most famous work, gives insight into Milles' belief that when the artist created, he was—in a way—divinely inspired.

Cost and Hours: 90 kr, 30-kr English booklet explains the art; mid-May–Sept daily 11:00–17:00; Oct–mid-May Tue–Sun 12:00–17:00, closed Mon; tel. 08/446-7580, www.millesgarden.se.

Getting There: Catch the T-bana to Ropsten, then take bus #207 to within a five-minute walk of the museum.

▲▲Drottningholm Palace—The queen's 17th-century summer castle and current royal residence has been called "Sweden's Versailles." Touring the palace, you'll see art that makes the point that Sweden's royalty is divine and belongs with the gods. The required tour covers two floors of lavish rooms, where you'll see how Sweden's royalty did their best to live in the style of Europe's divine monarchs. While rarely absolute rulers, Sweden's royals long struggled with stubborn parliaments. Perhaps this made the propaganda value of the palace decor even more important. Portraits and busts legitimize the royal family by connecting the Swedish blue bloods with Roman emperors, medieval kings, and Europe's great royal families. From the age when a few families ruled all of Europe, you'll see portraits of France's Louis XVI and Russia's Catherine the Great—reminding all that Sweden's royalty was related to or tightly networked with the big players. The king's bedroom looks like (and was) more of a theater. In the style of the French monarchs, this is where the ceremonial tucking-in and dressing of the king would take place. The Room of War—with kings, generals, battle scenes, and bugle-like candleholders—is from the time when Sweden was a superpower (1600–1750).

Of course, today's monarchs are figureheads ruled by a constitution. The royal family makes a point to be accessible and as "normal" as royalty can be. King Carl XVI Gustaf (b. 1946)—whose main job is handing out Nobel Prizes once a year—is a car nut who talks openly about his dyslexia. He was the first Swedish king not to be crowned "by the grace of God." The popular Queen Silvia is a businessman's daughter. At their 1976 wedding festivities, she was serenaded by ABBA singing "Dancing Queen." Their daughter and heir to the throne, Crown Princess Victoria, studied political science at Yale and interned with Sweden's European Union delegation. Now that Victoria is 32, some court-watchers say it's time for her to settle down and make princes. The big news for 2010: She's marrying Daniel (her personal trainer). Victoria lives in the palace...he lives across the street.

Cost and Hours: 80 kr, May–Aug daily 10:00–16:30, Sept daily 11:00–15:30, Oct–April Sat–Sun only 12:00–15:30 except closed mid-Dec–mid-Jan; call 08/402-6280 to reserve free-with-admission palace tours in English—offered June–Aug usually at 10:00, 12:00, 14:00, and 16:00; fewer off-season, www.royalcourt.se.

Getting There: Reach the palace via a relaxing one-hour boat ride (110 kr one-way, 150 kr round-trip, 110 kr round-trip with Stockholm Card, departs from Stadhusbron across from City Hall on the hour through the day, tel. 08/1200-4000), or take the T-bana to Brommaplan, where you can catch any #300-series bus to Drottningholm. Consider approaching by water (as the royals traditionally did) and then returning by bus and T-bana (as a commoner).

Drottningholm Court Theater (Drottningholms Slottsteater): This 18th-century theater somehow survived the ages—complete with its instruments, sound-effects machines, and stage sets. It's one of two such theaters remaining in Europe (the other is in Český Krumlov, Czech Republic). Visit it on a 30-minute guided tour, offered at the top of the hour (80 kr, May–Aug 11:00–16:30, Sept 13:00–15:30, no tours off-season, tel. 08/759-0406), or check their schedule for the rare opportunity to see perfectly authentic operas (about 25 performances each summer). Tickets for this popular time-travel musical and theatrical experience cost 165–600 kr and go on sale by phone, fax, or mail each March (see www.dtm.se).

Sigtuna—This town, an old-time lakeside jumble of wooden houses and waffle shops, presents a fluffy, stereotyped version of Sweden in the olden days. You'll see a medieval lane lined with colorful tourist boutiques, cafés, a romantic park, waterfront promenade, old town hall, and rune stones. The TI can help you get oriented (tel. 08/5948-0650, http://sal.sigtuna.se/turism). If traveling by car to Uppsala (described on page 398) or Oslo (see the Oslo chapter), Sigtuna is a short detour, good for a browse and an ice-cream cone, but little more. By public transport, it's probably not worth the tedious one-hour trip out (take the *pendeltåg* suburban train from Stockholm to Märsta and then change to bus #570).

▲Uppsala—A charming and historic university town with an impressive cathedral, Uppsala is a satisfying sidetrip from Stockholm, described in detail at the end of this chapter.

▲▲▲Archipelago (Skärgården)—Some of Europe's most scenic islands (thousands of them) stretch 80 miles from Stockholm out to the open Baltic Sea. If you cruise to Finland, you'll get a good dose of this island beauty. Otherwise, consider one of many half- or full-day trips from downtown Stockholm to the archipelago. Hopping the

local ferries to visit an island or two and see the lazy comings and goings of the island vacationers makes for a great day. For all the details, see the next chapter.

Shopping in Stockholm

Sweden offers a world of shopping temptations. Nordiska Kompaniet (NK, short for "no kronor left"), Stockholm's top-end department store, is located in an elegant early 20th-century building just across from the Sweden House. If it feels like an old-time American department store, that's because its architect was inspired by grand stores he'd seen in the US (circa 1910). The Swedish design section (downstairs) and the kitchenware section are particularly impressive.

The classy Gallerian mall starts just up the street from the Sweden House and stretches seductively nearly to Sergels Torg. The Åhléns store, nearby at Sergels Torg, is less expensive than NK and has two cafeterias and a supermarket. Drottninggatan is a long pedestrian boulevard lined with shops.

Designtorget, a store dedicated to contemporary Swedish design, receives a commission for selling the unique works of local designers (Mon–Fri 10:00–19:00, Sat–Sun 11:00–17:00, underneath Sergels Torg—enter from basement level of Kulturhuset).

For more on Swedish design, pick up the *Design Guide* flier at the TI (listing smaller stores throughout town with a flair for design). The trendy and exclusive shops (including Orrefors and Kosta) line Biblioteksgatan just off Stureplan.

Traditionally, stores are open weekdays from 10:00 to 18:00, Saturdays until 15:00, and closed on Sundays. Some of the bigger stores (such as NK and Åhléns) are open later on Saturdays and on Sunday afternoons (12:00–17:00).

For a *smörgåsbord* of Scanjunk, visit the Loppmarknaden, Northern Europe's biggest flea market, at the planned suburb of Skärholmen (free entry on weekdays, 15 kr on weekends—when it's busiest, Mon–Fri 11:00–18:00, Sat 10:00–16:00, Sun 11:00–16:00, T-bana: Varberg—on line #13—is just steps from the shopping action, tel. 08/710-0060). Hötorget, the produce market, also hosts a Sunday flea market in summer (see page 395).

Systembolaget is Sweden's state-run liquor store chain. A sample of each bottle of wine or liquor sits in a display case. A card in front explains how it tastes and suggests menu pairings. Look for the item number and order at the counter. There's a branch on Gamla Stan at Lilla Nygatan 18, and another on Norrmalm at Vasagatan 21 (both Mon–Wed 10:00–18:00, Thu–Fri 10:00–19:00, Sat 10:00–15:00, closed Sun).

Nightlife in Stockholm

Bars and Music in Gamla Stan—The street called Stora Nygatan, with several lively bars, has perhaps the most accessible and reliable place for good jazz in town: Stampen.

Stampen Jazz & Rhythm n' Blues Pub has two venues: a stone-vaulted cellar below and a fun-loving saloon-like bar upstairs (check out the old instruments and antiques hanging from the ceiling). From Monday through Thursday, there's live music only in the saloon. On Friday and Saturday, bands alternate sets in both the saloon and the cellar (140-kr cover Fri–Sat only, 50-kr beers, open Mon–Sat 20:00–1:00 in the morning, even later Fri–Sat, free blues Mon–Thu, special free jam session Sat 14:00–18:00, closed Sun, Stora Nygatan 5, tel. 08/205-793, www.stampen.se). For the location, see the map on page 392.

Several other lively spots are within a couple of blocks of Stampen on Stora Nygatan, including **Wirtströms Irish Pub** (live blues bands play in crowded cellar Tue–Sat 21:00–24:00, no cover, 50-kr beers, open daily 12:00–1:00 in the morning, Stora Nygatan 13) and **O'Connells Irish Pub** (a lively expat sports bar with music downstairs, daily 12:00–1:00 in the morning, Stora Nygatan 21). Just beyond Gamla Stan, the good ship ***Patricia*** rocks with live music and well-lubricated locals most nights (no cover, often live music, described on page 394). Another pub with music is a few doors down.

Absolut Icebar Stockholm—If you just want to put on a heavy coat and gloves and drink a fancy vodka in a modern-day igloo, consider the fun, if touristy, Absolut Icebar. Everything's ice—shipped down from Sweden's far north. The bar, the glasses, even the tip jar are made of ice. For 180 kronor, you get your choice of vodka drinks and 45 minutes to enjoy the scene (additional drinks-95 kr, reservations smart during busy times, June–Aug Mon–Fri 13:00–24:00, Sept–May generally 15:00–24:00, in the Nordic Sea Hotel adjacent the main train station at Vasaplan 4, tel. 08/5056-3124, www.icebar.se). People are let in all at once every 45 minutes. That means there's a long line for drinks, and the place goes from being very crowded to almost empty as people gradually melt away. At first everyone's just snapping photos. While there are ice bars all over Europe now, this is the second one (after the Ice Hotel in Lapland). And it really is pretty cool...a steady 23°F.

Cinema—In Sweden, international movies are shown in their original language with Swedish subtitles. Swedish theaters sometimes charge more for longer films (85–110 kr, movies longer than 2 hours are usually the higher price), and tickets come with assigned seats (drop by to choose seats and buy a ticket, box offices generally open 11:00–22:00 daily). The Hötorget and Drottninggatan neighborhoods have many theaters.

Sleeping in Stockholm

Peak season for Stockholm's hotels is dictated by business travelers: weeknights outside of summer vacation time. In June 2010, you may have to compete for rooms with Swedes who've come to witness Crown Princess Victoria's wedding. Rates drop by 30–50 percent in the summer (mid-June–mid-Aug) and on Friday and Saturday nights year-round. When I list two hotel rates, the first is the peak-season rate, and the second is the summer/weekend rate. In summer, prices can be very soft. If you ask for discounts and comparison-shop, you're likely to save plenty.

While good deals are everywhere in summer and on weekends, even in peak times Stockholm has plenty of money-saving deals for the savvy visitor willing to compromise a bit. Many places keep an odd misfit room (100 kr cheaper than the others) lashed to a bedpost in the attic, but will only tell you if you ask. Several backpacker places have a range of rooms, blurring the distinction between "hotel" and "hostel." Money-conscious travelers should consider doubles in hostels and rooms in simple hotels with shared bath—a respectable option in clean and wholesome Stockholm. Using websites and online booking services (including Expedia.com) can often snare you big savings, since many hotels allocate a baseline number of rooms at deep discounts to jumpstart their bookings. Hotels will often match deals available on online booking services. With the economic jitters these days, hotels are all over the board with their pricing. You'll save money by emailing several places and asking for their best rate.

Plenty of people offer private accommodations (600–800-kr doubles). Stockholm's hostels are among Europe's best, offering good beds in simple but interesting places for about 250 kr per night. Each has helpful English-speaking staff, pleasant family rooms, and good facilities. Hosteling is cheapest when you're a member, provide your own sheets, and buy your own food for breakfast.

A program called **Stockholm à la Carte** is, for many (especially families), the best way to book a big hotel on weekends or during the summer. A Stockholm à la Carte card is thrown in for free with your hotel room. It covers public transportation, most major sights, and lots of tours—and is even better than the Stockholm Card. Kids sleep and get cards for free, and you get

Sleep Code

(7 kr = about $1, country code: 46, area code: 08)
S = Single, **D** = Double/Twin, **T** = Triple, **Q** = Quad, **b** = bathroom, **s** = shower. Unless otherwise noted, all of my listings have non-smoking rooms and elevators, accept credit cards, and include big breakfast buffets. Everyone speaks English.

To help you sort easily through these listings, I've divided the rooms into three categories, based on the price for a standard double room with bath during high season:

$$$ Higher Priced—Most rooms 1,700 kr or more.
$$ Moderately Priced—Most rooms between 800-1,700 kr.
$ Lower Priced—Most rooms 800 kr or less.

cards for your arrival and departure days, too. You can sign up for Stockholm à la Carte by phone or online (tel. 08/663-0080, www.destination-stockholm.com).

In Downtown Norrmalm, near the Train Station

$$$ Freys Hotel is a Scan-mod, four-star place, with 124 compact, smartly designed rooms on a quiet pedestrian street. While big, it works hard to be friendly and welcoming. It's well-situated, located on a dead-end street across from the central train station. Its cool, candlelit breakfast room becomes a bar in the evening, popular for its selection of Belgian microbrews (Sb-1,850/900 kr, Db-2,250/1,190 kr, Bryggargatan 12, Internet access, tel. 08/5062-1300, fax 08/5062-1313, www.freyshotels.com, freys@freyshotels.com). Check their website for summer specials.

$$$ Rica Hotel Kungsgatan, central but characterless, fills the top floors of a downsized department store with 270 rooms. If the Starship *Enterprise* had a low-end hotel, this would be it. Save 150 kr by taking a room with no windows—the same size as other rooms, extremely quiet, and well-ventilated. You'll get the best price by booking online with a travel website—calling this hotel direct will get you a more expensive rate (Db-1,400/1,200 kr, Kungsgatan 47, tel. 08/723-7220, fax 08/723-7299, www.rica.se).

$$ Queen's Hotel enjoys a great location at the quiet top end of Stockholm's main pedestrian shopping street (about a 10-minute walk from the train station or Gamla Stan). The 52 well-priced rooms feel old-fashioned but have been renovated, and the plush Old World lounge is inviting. Three types of double rooms vary only in size (Sb-1,220/1,020 kr, "small standard" Db-1,320/1,120 kr, "large standard" Db-1,520/1,220 kr, "superior" Db with pull-out sofa bed-1,620/1,320 kr, 10 percent discount for readers who

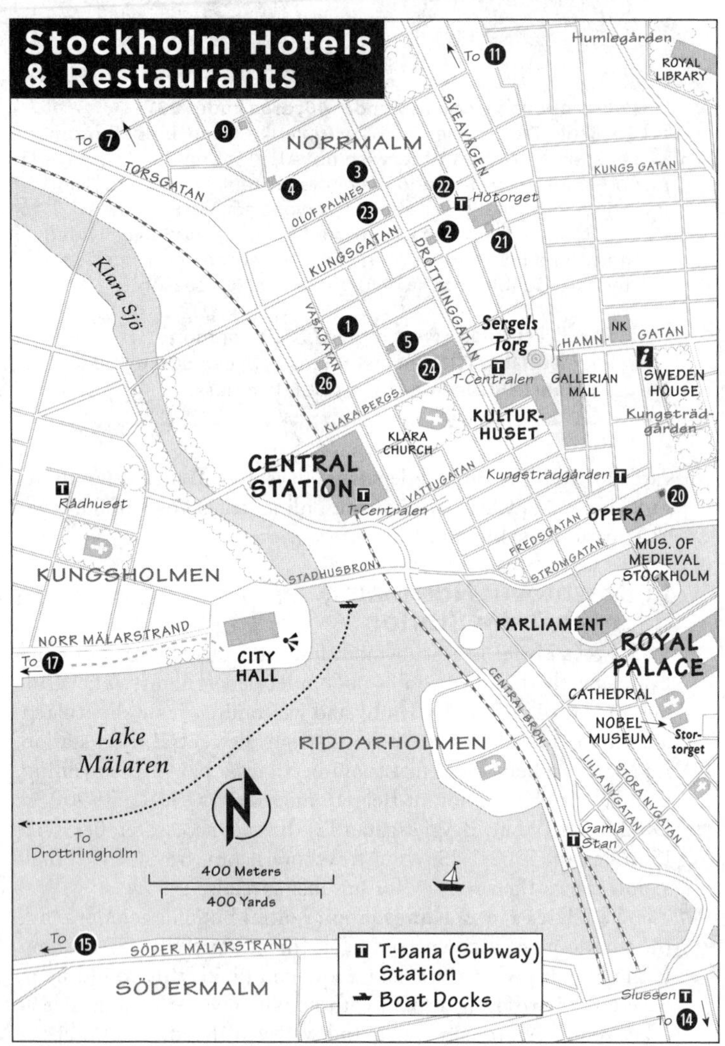

book direct—be sure to ask for it, extra bed-250 kr, elevator, free Internet access and Wi-Fi, Drottninggatan 71A, tel. 08/249-460, fax 08/217-620, www.queenshotel.se, info@queenshotel.se).

$ City Backpackers is central—a quarter-mile from the station—and open year-round. It's enthusiastically run, with 220 beds and plenty of creativity (bunk in 8-bed room-230 kr, bunk in 4- or 6-bed room-280 kr, bunk-bed D-650 kr, 40 percent more for Fri- or Sat-night stay without weeknight, sheets-50 kr, free pasta, breakfast-45 kr, laundry, free Internet access and Wi-Fi, movies, sauna, lockers, kitchen, shoes-off policy, Upplandsgatan 2A, tel.

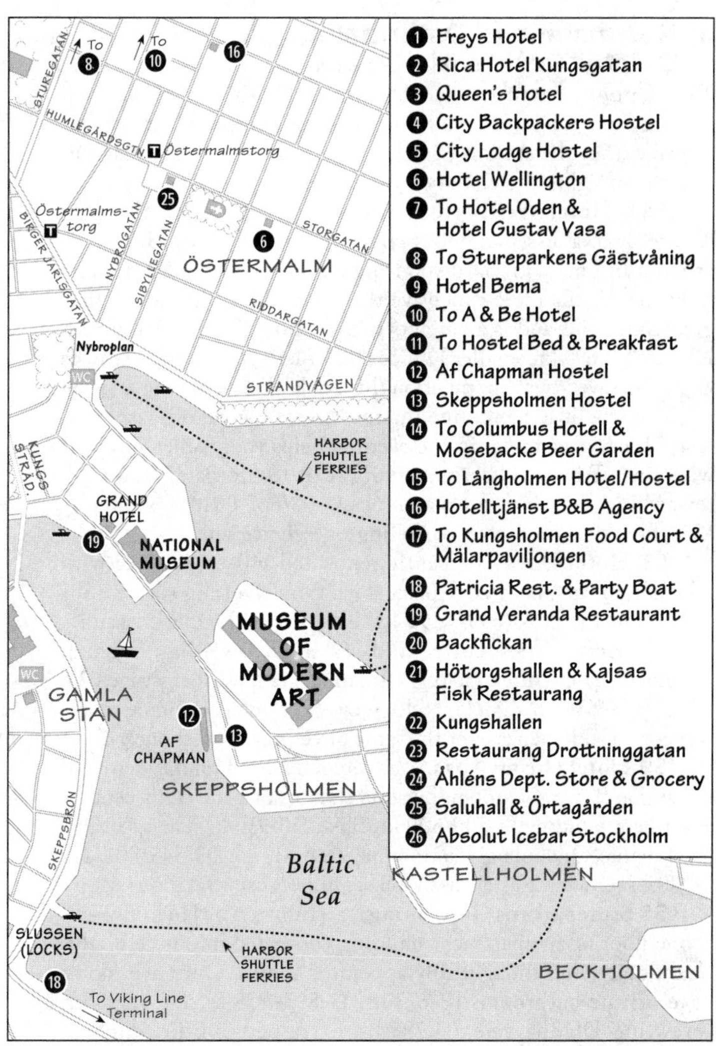

08/206-920, fax 08/100-464, www.citybackpackers.se, info@city backpackers.se).

$ City Lodge Hostel, new and well-run, is just a block in front of the central station on a quiet side street. It has a convivial lounge, kitchen, free Internet access, laundry, and no curfew. It's a good value for backpackers in Stockholm (65 beds, bunk in 18-bed dorm-220 kr, in 6-bed dorm-270 kr, in quad-315 kr, a few tiny bunk-bed doubles-640 kr, cheaper outside of summer, sheets-50 kr, 60-kr breakfast available, Klara Norra Kyrkogata 15, tel. 08/226-630, www.citylodge.se, info@citylodge.se).

In Norrmalm and Östermalm, in Quieter Residential Areas

These options are in stately, elegant neighborhoods of five- and six-story turn-of-the-century apartment buildings. All are too far to walk from the station with luggage, but still in easy reach of downtown sights and close to T-bana stops.

$$$ Hotel Wellington, two blocks off Östermalmstorg square, is in a less-handy but charming part of town. It's modern and bright, with hardwood floors, 60 rooms, and a friendly welcome. While more expensive than the others, this hotel offers great amenities and is a cut above in comfort (Sb-2,095/1,295 kr, Db-2,695/1,695 kr, smaller Db for 200 kr less, fill out their Choice Card and save 5 percent, mention this book when reserving and you might save a little more, free Internet access, sauna, old-fashioned English bar, free buffet in the evening helps your wallet and your waistline, T-bana: Östermalmstorg, exit to Storgatan and walk toward big church to Storgatan 6; tel. 08/667-0910, fax 08/667-1254, www.wellington.se, cc.wellington@choice.se).

$$ Hotel Oden, a recently renovated 140-room place with all the comforts, is three T-bana stops from the train station (Sb-1,290/890 kr, Db-1,695/1,195 kr, extra bed-150/135 kr, sauna, Internet access, free coffee and tea in the evening; T-bana: Odenplan, exit in direction of Västmannagatan, Karlbergsvägen 24; tel. 08/457-9700, fax 08/457-9710, www.hoteloden.se). Some rooms come with a kitchenette for the same price (just request one).

$$ Hotel Gustav Vasa, a half-block from Hotel Oden (and not as good), rents 42 rooms on several floors of a late–19th-century apartment building (S-700/600 kr, Sb-1,250/930 kr, Db-1,450/950 kr, T-bana: Odenplan, Västmannagatan 61, tel. 08/343-801, fax 08/307-372, www.gustavvasahotel.se, info@gustavvasahotel.se).

$$ Stureparkens Gästvåning, carefully run by Jan Lönnberg, is one floor of an apartment building converted into nine bright, clean, quiet, and thoughtfully appointed rooms. Only two rooms have private bathrooms (S-675 kr, D-895–975 kr, Db-1,395 kr, sprawling Db apartment-1,795 kr, extra bed-200 kr, kitchen; T-bana: Stadion, across from Stureparken at Sturegatan 58, take elevator to fourth floor; tel. 08/662-7230, fax 08/661-5713, www.stureparkens.nu, info@stureparkens.nu).

$$ Hotel Bema is a humble place that rents out 12 fine rooms for some of the best prices in town (S-850/650 kr, Db-950/750 kr, bigger Db-1,050/850 kr, extra person-250 kr, breakfast served in room, bus #65 from station to Upplandsgatan 13, tel. 08/232-675, www.hotelbema.se, hotell.bema@stockholm.mail.telia.com).

$$ A & Be Hotel, with 12 homey rooms, fills the first floor of a grand old building in a residential section of town (S-540 kr, Sb-840 kr, D-690 kr, Db-990 kr, breakfast-50 kr, T-bana: Stadion,

Grev Turegatan 50, tel. 08/660-2100, fax 08/660-5987, www.abe hotel.com, info@abehotel.com).

$ Bed and Breakfast is a tiny, woody, and easygoing independent hostel renting 39 cheap beds in various dorm-style rooms (bed in 10-bed rooms-270 kr, bed in triple-340 kr, sheets-50 kr, kitchen, laundry, across the street from T-bana: Rådmansgatan, just off Sveavägen at Rehnsgatan 21, tel. & fax 08/152-838, www .hostelbedandbreakfast.com).

On Gamla Stan and Skeppsholmen

These options are in the midst of sightseeing, a short bus or taxi ride from the train station. For the first two hotels, see the map on page 392. For the rest, see pages 386–387.

$$$ Rica Hotel Gamla Stan offers Old World elegance in the heart of Gamla Stan (a 5-min walk from Gamla Stan T-bana station). Its 51 small rooms are filled with chandeliers and hardwood floors (Sb-1,800/900 kr, Db-2,200/1,200 kr, 200 kr extra for larger room, Lilla Nygatan 25, tel. 08/723-7250, fax 08/723-7259, www.rica.se, info.gamlastan@rica.se).

$$$ Lady Hamilton Hotel, expensive and lavishly furnished, is shoehorned into Gamla Stan on a quiet street a block below the cathedral and Royal Palace. The centuries-old building has 34 small, plush rooms and is filled with antiques and thoughtful touches (Db-3,200/1,450 kr, Internet access, Storkyrkobrinken 5, tel. 08/5064-0100, fax 08/5064-0110, www.ladyhamiltonhotel.se, info@ladyhamiltonhotel.se).

$ *Af Chapman* Hostel, a permanently moored 100-year-old schooner, is Europe's most famous youth hostel and has provided a berth for the backpacking crowd for years. Renovated from keel to stern, the old salt offers 120 bunks in two- to six-bed rooms (290 kr, lockout daily 11:00–15:00). Reception is at Skeppsholmen Hostel (next).

$ Skeppsholmen Hostel, just ashore from the *Af Chapman*, has 160 beds in two- to six-bed rooms plus one 17-bed dorm (bunk in 17-bed dorm-240 kr, in 3- to 6-bed room-280 kr, D-650 kr, 50 kr less for hostel members, sheets-70 kr, breakfast-80 kr, laundry service, no lockout, bus #65 from train station or walk about 20 min, tel. 08/463-2266, www.stfchapman.com, chapman @stfturist.se).

On or near Södermalm

Södermalm is residential and hip, with Stockholm's best café and bar scene. You'll need to take the bus or T-bana to get here from the train station.

$$ Columbus Hotell—located in a 19th-century building that formerly housed a brewery, a jail, and a hospital—has 69 quiet rooms in the heart of Södermalm. Half of its rooms (first and second floors) have private facilities. Third-floor rooms have facilities down the hall (S-725 kr, Sb-1,250/1,000 kr, D-925 kr, Db-1,600/1,300 kr, T-1,150 kr, Tb-1,775/1,520 kr, no elevator; T-bana: Medborgarplatsen or bus #53 from train station to Tjärhovsplan, then a 5-min walk to Tjärhovsgatan 11; tel. 08/5031-1200, fax 08/5031-1201, www.columbushotell.se, info@columbus hotell.se).

$$ Långholmen Hotel/Hostel is on Långholmen, a small island off Södermalm that was transformed in the 1980s from Stockholm's main prison into a lovely park. Rooms are converted cells in the old prison building. You can choose between hostel- and hotel-standard rooms at many different price levels (hostel rooms: dorm bed-280 kr, D-670 kr, Tb-960 kr, Q-1,120 kr, 50-kr discount for hostel members, sheets-60 kr, breakfast-90 kr; hotel rooms: Db-1,890/1,490 kr, extra bed-250 kr, includes breakfast; laundry room, kitchen, cafeteria, free parking, on-site swimming, T-bana: Hornstull, walk 10 min down and cross small bridge to Långholmen island, follow hotel signs 5 min farther, tel. 08/720-8500, fax 08/720-8575, www.langholmen.com, hotel@langholmen .com).

Rooms in Private Homes

Stockholm's private rooms can be a deal in high season if you want to have an at-home experience. During hotels' weekend/summer discount periods, private rooms don't save you much over a hotel. Be sure to get the front-door security code when you call, in case there's no intercom. Contact **Hotelltjänst,** a B&B booking agency (S-600 kr, D-750 kr, cash only, no breakfast, 2-night minimum; fully furnished apartments also available: Sb-800 kr, Db-1,200 kr; Nybrogatan 44, tel. 08/104-437, fax 08/213-716, www.hotelltjanst .com, caretaker@hotelltjanst.com).

Eating in Stockholm

To save money, eat your main meal at lunch, when cafés and restaurants have 75-kr daily special plates called *dagens rätt* (generally Mon–Fri only). Most museums have handy cafés (with lots of turnover and therefore fresh food, 100-kr lunch deals, and often with fine views). Convenience stores serve gas station–style food (and often have seats). As anywhere, department stores and malls are eager to feed shoppers and can be a good, efficient option. If you want culturally appropriate fast food, stop by a local hot dog stand. Picnics are a great option—especially for dinner, when restaurant prices are highest. There are plenty of park-like, harborside spots to give your cheap picnic some class.

In Gamla Stan

Most restaurants in Gamla Stan serve the 75-kr weekday lunch special mentioned above, which comes with a main dish, small salad, bread, and free tap water. Choose from Swedish, Asian, or Italian cuisine. Several popular places are right on the main square (Stortorget) and near the cathedral. Järntorget, at the far end, is another fun tables-in-the-square scene and has a small Co-op Nara supermarket for picnic shopping. The Munkbrohallen supermarket downstairs in the Gamla Stan T-bana station is very picnic-friendly (daily 7:00–22:00). Touristy places line Västerlånggatan. You'll find more romantic places hiding on side lanes. I've listed my favorites below (for locations, see the map on page 392).

Grillska Huset is a cheap and handy cafeteria run by Stockholms Stadsmission, a charitable organization helping the poor. It's grandly situated right on the old square, with indoor and outdoor seating (tranquil garden up the stairs and out back), fine daily specials (listed in Swedish only), a hearty salad bar, and a staff committed to helping others. You can feed the hungry (that's you) and help house the homeless at the same time. The 75-kr daily special gets you a hot plate, salad, and coffee; or choose the 70-kr salad bar—both available Mon–Fri 11:00–14:00 (restaurant serves daily 9:00–18:00, Stortorget 3, tel. 08/787-8605). They also have a fine little bakery.

Vapiano Pasta Pizza Bar, a mod, high-energy Italian place, issues you an electronic card as you enter. You circulate, ordering up whatever you like as they swipe your card. It's fun to oversee the construction of your 100-kr pasta, pizza, or salad. Portions are huge and easily splittable. As you leave, your card indicates the bill. Season things by picking a leaf of basil or rosemary from the potted plant on your table. They have Pilsner Urquell on tap (daily 11:00–24:00, next to entrance of Gamla Stan T-bana station, Munkbrogatan 8, tel. 08/222-940).

O'Leary's Sports Bar is a smoky place that transports you to Ireland. While sloppy, it's good for basic pub grub and beer. And if a game is on, this is the place to be—their motto is, "Better than live" (120-kr meals, Järntorgsgatan 3, tel. 08/239-923).

Hermitage Restaurant serves tasty vegetarian food in a warm communal dining setting. Their daily special (85-kr lunch, 95-kr dinner after 15:00) buys a hot plate, salad, bread, and coffee (Mon–Fri 11:00–20:00, Sat 12:00–21:00, Sun 12:00–20:00, Stora Nygatan 11, tel. 08/411-9500).

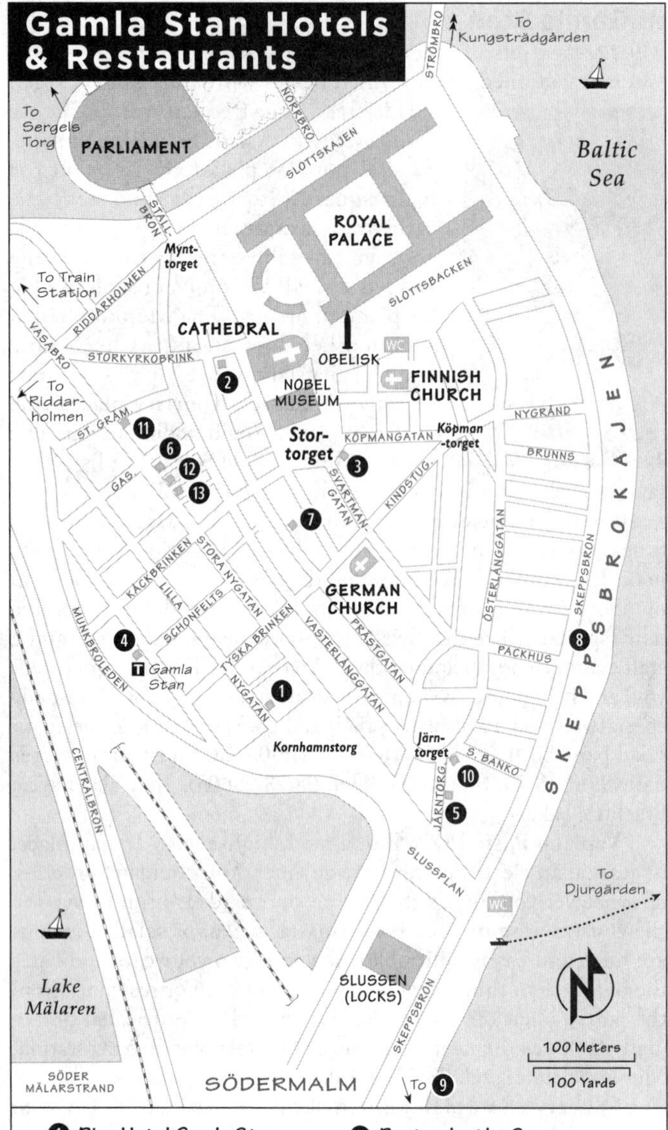

1 Rica Hotel Gamla Stan
2 Lady Hamilton Hotel
3 Grillska Huset Cafeteria
4 Vapiano Pasta Pizza Bar
5 O'Leary's Sports Bar
6 Hermitage Restaurant
7 Kryp In Restaurant
8 Pontus by the Sea
9 To Mosebacke Beer Garden; Patricia Rest. & Party Boat
10 Co-op Nara Supermarket
11 Stampen Jazz Club
12 Wirtströms Irish Pub
13 O'Connells Irish Pub

Kryp In, a small, cozy restaurant (the name means "hide away") tucked into a peaceful lane, has a stylish hardwood and candlelit interior, great sidewalk seating, and an open kitchen letting you in on Vladimir's artistry. If you dine well in Stockholm once (or twice), I'd do it here. It's gourmet without pretense. They serve delicious, modern Swedish cuisine with a 408-kr three-course dinner. From June to August, they have 120-kr weekend lunch specials. Reserve ahead for dinner (200–250-kr plates, Mon–Fri 17:00–23:00, Sat 12:30–23:00, Sun 12:30–22:00, a block off Stortorget at Prästgatan 17, tel. 08/208-841).

Harborview Dining in Gamla Stan and Östermalm

Pontus by the Sea is a classy restaurant with a long, covered, and heated veranda offering grand harbor views. Pontus is well-respected for its modern mix of French and Swedish cuisine. Half the place is a sofas-on-the-harbor cocktail lounge. Though the restaurant is pricey, their bar menu offers 140-kr plates. Call to reserve a harborside table (daily 12:00–24:00, off-season closed Sun, Tullhus 2, tel. 08/202-095).

Djurgårdsbrons Sjöcafe, beautifully situated and greedily soaking up the afternoon sun, fills a woody terrace stretching along the harbor just over the Djurgårdsbron Bridge. This is a fine place for a meal or just a drink before or after your Skansen or *Vasa* visit. They have cheap lunch plates (90 kr, Mon–Fri 11:00–13:00 only); at other times, you'll pay 130–180 kr per plate (order at the bar, daily 11:00–22:00, behind the bike-rental hut, tel. 08/661-4488). For the location, see the map on page 377.

Dinner Cruises: Several ships sail nightly from Strandvägen, offering three-course dinners during a scenic 2.5–4.5 hour cruise (570 kr regardless of which trip you choose, drinks extra, departing daily in summer 17:30–22:00, tel. 08/1200-4000, www.strommakanalbolaget.com).

In Kungsholmen: Lakefront Behind City Hall

On a balmy summer's eve, **Mälarpaviljongen** is a dreamy spot with hundreds of locals enjoying the perfect lakefront scene, as trendy glasses of rosé shine like convivial lanterns. From City Hall, walk 15 minutes along Lake Mälaren (a treat in itself) and you'll find a hundred casual outdoor tables on a floating restaurant and among the trees on shore. Line up at the cafeteria to order a drink, snack, or complete meal. If it's cool, they have heaters and blankets. The walk along the lake back into town caps the experience beautifully (56-kr beer, 125-kr cocktails, 100-kr lunch plates, 150–200-kr evening plates, open in good weather April–Sept daily 11:00–late, easy lakeside walk or T-bana to Freedomsplace plus a 5-min walk to Norr Mälarstrand 63, no reservations, tel. 08/650-8701).

Kungsholmen is a high-energy food court surrounded by six open "bars," with busy kitchens serving six different cuisines from Asian to fish. This is a trendy scene. It's a bit pricey, but with big portions, reliable quality, no tourists, and a classy local clientele (200-kr plates, nightly from 17:00, from City Hall walk along Lake Mälaren 5 min to Nörr Mälarstrand Kajplats 464, tel. 08/5052-4450, www.kungsholmen.com).

In Södermalm: Dining Sloppy with Noisy Locals and Lots of Beer

Mosebacke is a gravelly beer garden with a grand harbor view, perched high above town just past Slussen in Södermalm. Open only on warm summer evenings and priding itself on its beer rather than the cheap grub, it's a good place to mix with a relaxed young crowd (a block inland from the top of the Katarina elevator, occasional live music, Mosebacke Torg 3, tel. 08/556-09890).

***Patricia* Restaurant and Party Boat** is a fun, raucous place to enjoy a basic Swedish meal surrounded by good-time Swedes. The menu on this old steamer is a fun-loving surf-and-turf mix, with 200-kr plates and a 129-kr lobster feed on Wednesday nights. The boat has one deck packed with dinner tables, a bar on the top deck, and two dance zones below: one that's a *schlager* pop bar and dance floor, and the other that's a late-night disco. The boat really rocks with live music on weekends (music from 20:00, 120-kr cover after 22:00). Consider having dinner here beforehand to get in free (Wed–Sun from 18:00 until late, gay night on Sun, closed Mon–Tue, 200 yards past Djurgården boat dock, near Slussen at Stadsgårdskajen 152, tel. 08/743-0570, www.patricia.st).

On Norrmalm

Royal Smörgåsbord at the Grand Hotel

To stuff yourself with all the traditional Swedish specialties (a dozen kinds of herring, salmon, reindeer, meatballs, lingonberries, and shrimp, followed by a fine table of cheeses and desserts) with a super harbor view, consider splurging for Stockholm's best *smörgåsbord* at the Grand Hotel's dressy **Grand Veranda Restaurant.** While very touristy and a bit tired, this is the finest *smörgåsbord* in town. The Grand Hotel, where royal guests and Nobel Prize winners stay, faces the harbor across from the palace. Pick up their English flier for a good explanation of the proper way to enjoy this grand buffet (and read about *smörgåsbords* on page 28 of the Introduction). Reservations are necessary (445 kr, tap water is free, other drinks extra, nightly 18:00–22:00, Sat–Sun also 13:00–16:00, May–Sept also Mon–Fri 12:00–15:00, no shorts, Södra Blasieholmshamnen 8, tel. 08/679-3586).

Fika: Sweden's Coffee Break

Swedes drink more coffee per capita than just about any other country in the world. The Swedish coffee break—or *fika*—is a ritual. *Fika* is to Sweden what teatime is to Britain. The typical *fika* is a morning or afternoon break in the workday, but can happen any time, any day. It's the perfect opportunity (and excuse) for tourists to take a break as well.

Fika-fare is coffee with a snack—something sweet or savory. Your best bet is a *kanelbulle,* a Swedish cinnamon bun. These can be found nearly everywhere coffee is sold, including just about any café or *konditori* (bakery) in Stockholm. A coffee and a cinnamon bun in a café will cost you about 30 kr. (Most cafés will give you a coffee refill for free.) But at Pressbyrån, the Swedish convenience stores found all over town, you can satisfy your *fika*-fix for 20 kr by getting a coffee and bun to go. Grab a park bench or waterside perch, relax, and enjoy.

At the Royal Opera House

The Operakällaren, one of Stockholm's most exclusive restaurants, runs a little "hip pocket" restaurant called **Backfickan** on the side, specializing in traditional Swedish quality cooking at reasonable prices. It's ideal for someone eating out alone, or for anyone wanting an early dinner (they serve daily specials from 12:00 all the way up to 20:00). Sit inside—at tiny private side tables or at the big counter with the locals—or, in good weather, grab a table on the sidewalk. Choose from two different daily specials (about 150–200 kr), or pay 200–250 kr for main dishes from their regular menu (Mon–Sat 12:00–22:00, closed Sun, on the inland side of Royal Opera House, tel. 08/676-5809).

At or near Hötorget

Hötorget ("Hay Market"), a vibrant outdoor produce market just two blocks from Sergels Torg, is a fun place to picnic-shop. The outdoor market closes at 18:00, and many merchants put their unsold produce on the push list (earlier closing and more desperate merchants on Sat).

Hötorgshallen, next to Hötorget (in the basement under the modern cinema complex), is a colorful indoor food market with an old-fashioned bustle, plenty of exotic and ethnic edibles, and—in the tradition of food markets all over Europe—some great little eateries. The best is **Kajsas Fisk Restaurang,** hiding behind the fish stalls. They serve delicious fish soup to little Olivers who can hardly believe they're getting...more. For 85 kr, you get a big bowl of hearty soup, a simple salad, bread and crackers, butter, and water—plus one soup refill (100-kr daily fish specials, Mon–Fri 11:00–18:00, Sat 11:00–15:00, closed Sun, Hötorgshallen 3, tel. 08/207-262).

Kungshallen, an 800-seat indoor food court across the street from Hötorget, has 14 eateries—mostly chain restaurants and fast-food counters, including Chinese, sushi, pizza, Greek, and Mexican (Mon–Fri 9:00–23:00, Sat–Sun 12:00–23:00).

Restaurang Drottninggatan is a busy place with tables perfectly positioned for people-watching on the busy pedestrian boulevard (90-kr lunch plates daily until 15:00, hearty 150–200-kr plates, open Mon–Sat 11:00–24:00, Sun 12:00–23:00, Drottninggatan 67, tel. 08/227-522).

Near Sergels Torg

The many modern shopping malls and department stores around Sergels Torg all have appealing, if pricey, eateries catering to the needs of hungry local shoppers. **Åhléns** department store has a Hemköp supermarket in the basement (Mon–Fri 8:00–21:00, Sat–Sun 10:00–21:00) and two restaurants upstairs with 80–110-kr daily lunch specials (Mon–Fri 11:00–19:30, Sat 11:00–18:30, Sun 11:00–17:30).

In Östermalm

Saluhall, on Östermalmstorg square (near recommended Hotel Wellington), is a great old-time indoor market with plenty of fun eateries (Mon–Thu 9:30–18:00, Fri–Sat 9:30–18:30, closed Sun). Upstairs, the **Örtagården,** primarily a vegetarian restaurant, serves a 95-kr buffet weekdays until 17:00 and a larger 135-kr buffet evenings and weekends (Mon–Sun 10:30–21:00, entrance on side of market building at Nybrogatan 31, tel. 08/662-1728).

Stockholm Connections

By Bus

Unless you have a railpass, long-distance buses are cheaper than trains and preferable on some routes, such as from Stockholm to Oslo or Kalmar. Buses usually take longer, but have more predictable pricing, shorter ticket lines, and student discounts. Swebus is the largest operator (tel. 0771-21-8218, www.swebusexpress.se); Säfflebussen also has lots of routes, including to Oslo (www.saffle bussen.se). It's worth knowing about discount offers: Buy tickets at least 24 hours ahead for Swebus discounts; Säfflebussen cuts ticket prices on low-demand days and times.

From Stockholm by Bus to: Copenhagen (2/day, 9 hrs, 500 kr), **Oslo** (2/day, 8 hrs, 500 kr), **Kalmar** (3/day, fewer on weekends, 6 hrs, 350 kr).

By Train

The easiest and cheapest way to book train tickets is online at www.sj.se. Simply select your journey and pay for it with a credit card. When you arrive at the train station, print out your tickets at a self-service ticket kiosk (bring your purchase confirmation code). You can also buy tickets at a ticket window in a train station, but this comes with long lines and a 5 percent surcharge. For timetables and prices, check online, call 0771/757-575, or use one of the self-service ticket kiosks. (Tourists can't purchase tickets on the phone or at a kiosk, however; this requires a locally issued credit card.)

As with airline tickets, Swedish train ticket prices vary with demand. I've listed the base price for each destination, but ask for the *"Just nu"* ("Just now") fare, which can earn you up to a 60 percent discount if you book far enough in advance.

For railpass-holders, seat reservations are required on express (X2000) and overnight trains, and recommended on some other trains (to Oslo, for example). Second-class seat reservations to Copenhagen cost 75 kr (150 kr in first class). If you have a railpass, the only way you can make a seat reservation is by going to a ticket window in a train station (not online, by phone, or at self-service ticket kiosks).

From Stockholm by Train to: Uppsala (1–3/hr, 40 min, 60–70 kr), **Växjö** (every 2 hrs, 3.5 hrs, change in Alvesta, reservations required), **Kalmar** (8/day, 3.5 hrs, transfer in Alvesta or Linköping, reservations required, 920 kr), **Copenhagen** (almost hourly, 5.5 hrs on X2000 high-speed train, most with a transfer at Malmö Central Station, 1,210 kr, reservation required; overnight service departs at 23:08 and requires a change in Malmö at 6:42, 875 kr; all trains stop at Copenhagen airport before terminating at central station), **Oslo** (2/day direct Intercity trains, 6 hrs, 560 kr; 2/day with changes in Karlstad or Katrineholm, 7 hrs, 540 kr; plus a direct 9-hour night train that runs on weekends only).

By Boat

The boat companies run shuttle buses from the train station to coincide with each departure; check for details when you buy your ticket.

From Stockholm to: Helsinki and **Tallinn** (daily/nightly boats, 16 hrs, see Helsinki and Tallinn chapters), **Turku** (daily/nightly boats, 11 hrs).

By Plane

For information on arriving at Stockholm's airports, see "Arrival in Stockholm," earlier in this chapter.

To Helsinki and Tallinn: The boat trip to Helsinki or Tallinn takes 16 hours. Though less romantic, flying is faster, and inexpensive now that many low-fare airlines are offering flights across the Baltic. For flights from Stockholm to Helsinki, check www.blue1.com; to Tallinn, also visit www.flynordic.com and www.estonian-air.com. When comparing prices between boats and planes, remember that the boat fare includes a night's lodging.

Route Tips for Drivers

Stockholm to Oslo: It's an eight-hour drive from Stockholm to Oslo. **Årjäng,** just before the Norwegian border, is a good place for a rest stop. At the border, change money at the little TI kiosk (on right side). Pick up the Oslo map and *What's On in Oslo,* and consider buying your Oslo Card here.

Near Stockholm: Uppsala

Uppsala is a compact city with a cathedral and university that win Sweden's "oldest/largest/tallest" awards. If you're not traveling anywhere else in Sweden other than Stockholm, Uppsala makes a pleasant day trip. But if you're short on time, Uppsala is not worth sacrificing time in Stockholm or a boat trip through the archipelago. If you visit, allow the better part of a day, including the trip out and back. During summer vacations, this university town is very quiet.

Getting There: Take the train from Stockholm's central station (1–3/hr, 40 min, 60–70 kr, buy tickets at ticket windows). Since the Uppsala station has lockers and is in the same direction from Stockholm as the airport, you could combine a quick visit here with an early arrival or late departure.

Orientation to Uppsala

(area code: 018)

Tourist Information

The helpful TI, overlooking the canal through the heart of town, has free maps and the informative *What's On Uppsala* magazine (Mon–Fri 10:00–18:00, Sat 10:00–15:00, closed Sun except mid-June–Aug open Sun 11:00–15:00, Fyristorg 8, tel. 018/727-4800, www.uppsala.to).

Arrival in Uppsala

From the train station (lockers-20–30 kr), walk straight out the front door, cross the busy street, and walk two blocks. Turn right along the newly pedestrianized shopping street called Kungsängsgatan. Walk three more blocks (passing the Åhléns department store, with its handy Hemköp grocery downstairs) and you'll run into the town's main square, Stora Torget. From here, you can turn left and cross the canal. The TI is just to the right after the canal, and you can see the cathedral spires (which also mark the university zone) just behind it.

Sights in Uppsala

▲▲Uppsala Cathedral (Domkyrkan)

One of Scandinavia's largest, most historic cathedrals feels as vital as it does impressive. The building was completed in 1453; the spires and interior decorations are from the late 19th century.

The cathedral—with a fine Gothic interior, the relics of St. Erik, and the tomb of King Gustav Vasa—is well worth a visit (free, open daily 8:00–18:00). If you're interested in a guided tour in English, ask inside (mid-June–mid-Aug Mon–Sat at 11:00 and 14:00, Sun at 16:00; off-season call to arrange time, tel. 018/187-177, www.uppsaladomkyrka.se). Or, just inside the nave, look for the self-service kiosk and buy the handy 10-kr leaflet outlining an excellent self-guided tour.

Near the entrance is the tomb and memorial to scientist Carolus Linnaeus, who created the formal system for naming different species of plants and animals. Farther into the church you'll find the gorgeously carved, gold-slathered Baroque pulpit, and the transept where today's services take place. Look high above in the choir area (beyond the transept) to enjoy fine murals that gleam, thanks to a major restoration of the church in the 1970s.

At the far end of the church, don't disturb the woman peering toward the grave in the apse. This eerily lifelike statue from 2005, called ***Mary (The Return)***, captures Jesus' mother later in life, wearing a scarf and timeless garb. The chapel she's looking at once

housed a shrine to her, but for more than 300 years after the Reformation, images of Mary were downplayed in this church. In keeping with the Protestant spirit here, this new version of Mary is shown not as an exalted queen, but as an everywoman, saddened by loss of her child and seeking solace—or answers—in the church.

Follow Mary's gaze into the chapel housing the **tomb of King Gustav Vasa** and his family. Notice that in the sculpture, Gustav is shown flanked by not one, but two wives—his first wife died after suffering a fall; his second wife bore him 10 children. The chapel is ringed with murals of his illustrious life.

Back at the entrance to the church, by the gift shop, you can pay to enter the **treasury** collection. Here you'll find medieval textiles (tapestries and vestments), swords and crowns found in Gustav's grave, and the Nobel Peace Prize won by Nathan Söderblom, an early-20th-century archbishop here (30 kr, Mon–Sat 10:00–17:00, Sun 12:30–17:00). In this same narthex area, notice the debit-card machine soliciting donations: The church doing its same old work in a new way.

University Attractions and Nearby Sights

Scandinavia's first university was founded here in 1477. Two famous grads are Carolus Linnaeus (father of modern taxonomy) and astronomer Anders Celsius (who developed the temperature scale that bears his name). The following two university buildings are interesting and open to non-students.

▲▲Gustavianum—Directly across from the cathedral is the university's oldest surviving building, with a bulbous dome that doubles as a sundial (notice the gold numbers). Today it houses a well-presented museum that features an anatomical theater, a cabinet filled with miniature curiosities, and Celsius' thermometer. The collection is unaccountably engaging for the glimpse it gives into the mind-set of 17th-century Europe (40 kr, June–Aug Tue–Sun 10:00–16:00, Sept–May Tue–Sun 11:00–16:00, closed Mon year-round, tours in English Sat–Sun at 13:00, Akademigatan 3, tel. 018/471-7571, www.gustavianum.uu.se).

➲ **Self-Guided Tour:** Find the elevator (hiding near the gift shop/ticket desk) and ride it up to the fourth floor, then see the

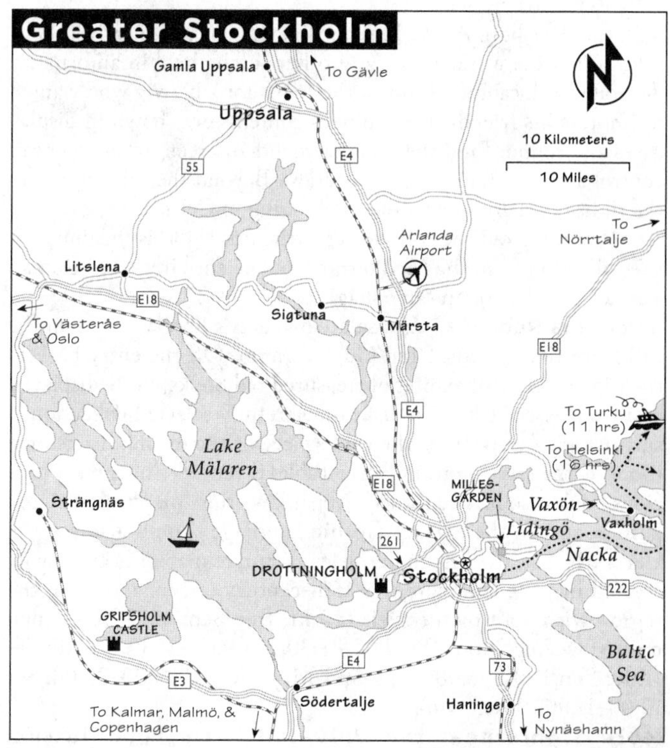

exhibits as you walk back down. Up top is a collection of artifacts discovered at Valsgärde, a site near Uppsala used for prehistoric burials for more than 700 years. Archaeologists have uncovered 15 boat graves here (dating from A.D. 600–1050—roughly one per generation), providing more insight on the Viking Age.

Next you'll find the museum's highlight, the anatomical theater (accessible from the fourth and third floors). Its only show was a human dissection. In the mid-1600s, as the enlightened ideas of the Renaissance swept far into the north of Europe, scholars began to consider dissection of the human body the ultimate scientific education. Corpses of hanged criminals were carefully sliced and diced here, under a dome in an almost temple-like atmosphere, demonstrating the lofty heights to which science had risen in society. Imagine 200 students (and others who'd paid admission) standing tall all around and leaning in to peer intently at the teacher's scalpel.

Another floor down (on the second floor) is an exhibit on the history of the university, which is far more interesting than it sounds. The Physics Chamber features a collection of instruments from the 18th and 19th centuries that were used by university teachers. But the most fascinating item is in the room across the hall: the Augsburg Art Cabinet, a dizzying array of nearly a thousand miniscule works of art and other tidbits held in an ornately decorated oak cabinet. Built in the 1620s for a bigwig who wanted to impress his friends, the cabinet's contents are shown in display cases all around. Find the interactive video screen, where you can control a virtual tour of the collection. Beyond the cabinet and to the right is a thermometer once belonging to Celsius.

Rounding out the collection (on the first floor) is the university's collection from the Mediterranean: ancient Greek and Roman artifacts and Egyptian sarcophagi.

▲Carolina Rediviva—Uppsala University's library is just up the hill from the cathedral and Gustavianum. Off the entry hall (to the right) is a small exhibit of treasured old books. Well-displayed and well-described in English, the carefully selected collection is surprisingly captivating. The centerpiece of the exhibit, in its own room, is the sixth-century Silver Bible. Sweden's single most precious book is so named for its silver-ink writing (on purple-colored parchment) in the extinct Gothic language. You'll also see the Carta Marina, the first more-or-less accurate map of Scandinavia, created in 1539. Compare this 16th-century understanding of the region with your own travels (20 kr, free Sept–mid-May; open mid-May–Aug Mon–Thu 9:00–18:30, Fri 9:00–17:30, Sat 10:00–17:00, Sun 11:00–16:00; Sept–mid-May Mon–Fri 9:00–20:00, Sat 10:00–17:00, closed Sun).

More Sights near the University—Uppland Museum (Upplandsmuseet), a regional history museum with prehistoric bits and folk-art scraps, is on the river by the waterfall, near the TI (free, Tue–Sun 12:00–17:00, closed Mon). Uphill from the university library are the **botanical gardens** and museum named after Linnaeus, and the 16th-century **Uppsala Castle,** which houses an art museum and runs slice-of-castle-life tours (required 70-kr tour, offered in English only a few weeks each summer Tue–Sun at 13:00 and 15:00, tel. 018/727-2485).

▲Gamla Uppsala

This site on the outskirts of town, which gives historians goose bumps even on a sunny day, includes nine large royal burial mounds circled by a walking path with English descriptions. Fifteen hundred years ago, when the Baltic Sea was higher and it was easy to sail all the way to Uppsala, the pagan Swedish kings had their capital here. You can wander the grounds for free, or learn more by visiting the

attractive Gamla Uppsala Museum, which gives a good overview of early Swedish history and displays items found in the mounds (50 kr; May–Aug daily 10:00–17:00; Sept daily 11:00–16:00; Oct–Nov and Jan–April Mon, Wed, and Sat–Sun 12:00–15:00, closed Mon and Tue–Fri; closed Dec; included guided tours in English available May–Aug daily at 15:30, tel. 018/239-300, www.raa.se/gamlauppsala). The venerable Gamla Uppsala church dates from the 12th century (free, daily April–Aug 9:00–18:00, Sept–March 9:00–16:00).

Eating at Gamla Uppsala: Gamla Uppsala is great for picnics, or you can recharge at the half-timbered **Odinsborg café,** which serves sandwiches, mead, and a 165-kr all-you-can-eat buffet lunch (café daily 10:00–18:00, restaurant daily 12:00–18:00—reservations required, tel. 018/323-525).

Getting There: From downtown Uppsala, go to the bus stop at Vaksalagatan 7–13 (a block and a half from Stora Torget, the main square) and take bus #2, marked *Gamla Uppsala,* to the last stop (30 kr, pay driver, 2–4/hr, 15-min trip). Allow two or three hours for your visit, including the time it takes to bus there and back.

Eating in Uppsala

Eateries abound along the river and in the business district. **Domtrappkällaren,** tucked behind the cathedral, serves up traditional Swedish meals in its characteristic interior or outside at streetside tables (95-kr lunches served Mon–Fri 11:00–14:30, then 100–150-kr dishes until 17:00, then pricier dinners—100–135-kr starters, 165–300-kr main dishes; open Mon–Fri 11:00–22:00, Sat 13:00–22:00, closed Sun, St. Eriks Gränd, go through the little tunnel behind the cathedral and look left, tel. 018/130-955).

For picnic fixings, stop by **Hemköp,** a grocery located on the ground floor of Åhléns department store (Mon–Fri 7:00–22:00, Sat–Sun 9:00–22:00, on Stora Torget). Enjoy the picnic at one of Uppsala's parks, or join the locals down on the boardwalk along the river, below St. Olof's Bridge.

STOCKHOLM'S ARCHIPELAGO

Skärgården

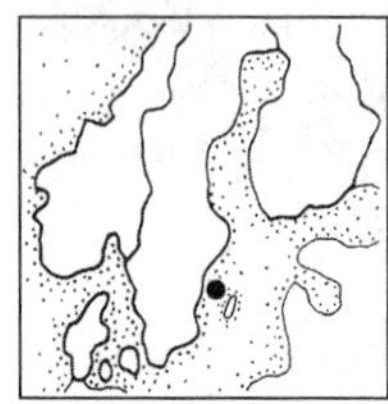

Some of Europe's most scenic islands stretch from Stockholm 80 miles out into the Baltic Sea. If you're cruising to (or from) Finland, you'll get a good look at this island beauty. If you have more time and want to immerse yourself in all that simple Swedish nature, consider spending a day or two island-hopping.

The Swedish word for "island" is simply *ö,* but the local name for this area is *Skärgården*—literally "garden of skerries," unforested rocks sticking up from the sea. That stone is granite, carved out and deposited by glaciers. The archipelago closer to Stockholm is rockier, with bigger islands and more trees. Farther out (such as at Sandhamn), the glaciers lingered longer, slowly grinding the granite into sand and creating smaller islands.

Locals claim there are more than 30,000 of these islands, and as land here is rising slowly, more pop out every year. Some 150 are inhabited year-round, and about 100 have ferry service. There's an unwritten law of public access in the archipelago. Technically you're allowed to pitch your tent anywhere for up to two nights, provided the owner of the property can't see you from his house. It's polite to ask first and essential to act responsibly.

With thousands of islands to choose from, every Swede seems to have their favorite. This chapter covers four very different island destinations that offer an overview of the archipelago. Vaxholm, the gateway to the archipelago, comes with an imposing fortress, a charming fishermen's harbor, and the easiest connections to Stockholm. Rustic Grinda feels like—and used to be—a Swedish summer camp. Sparsely populated Svartsö is another fine back-to-nature experience. And swanky Sandhamn thrills the sailboat set, with a lively yacht harbor, a scenic setting at the far edge of the archipelago, and (true to its name) sandy beaches.

The flat-out best way to experience the magic of the archipelago is simply stretching out comfortably on the rooftop deck of your ferry. The journey truly is the destination. Enjoy the charm of the lovingly painted cottages as you glide by, the delicate pairs of lounge chairs positioned to catch just the right view and sun, the steady rhythm of the ferries lacing this world together, and people savoring quality time with each other and nature.

Planning Your Time

On a Tour: For the best quick look, consider one of the many half- or full-day package boat trips from downtown Stockholm to the archipelago. **Strömma Kanalbolaget** runs several options, including the three-hour Archipelago Tour (2–4/day, 120 kr), or the all-day Thousand Island Cruise (departs daily in summer at 9:30, 975 kr includes lunch and dinner). Or, to be efficient, combine a three-hour island joyride with a meal—choose between a lunch cruise (380 kr) and a dinner cruise (various options, around 500–600 kr; for all cruises: tel. 08/1200-4000, www.stromma kanalbolaget.com).

On Your Own: For more flexibility, freedom, and a better dose of the local vacation scene, do it on your own. Any one of the islands in this chapter is easily doable as a single-day side-trip from Stockholm. And, because all boats to and from Stockholm also pass through Vaxholm, that town is easy to tack on to any other one.

For a very busy all-day itinerary that takes in the two most enjoyable island destinations (Grinda and Sandhamn), consider this plan: 8:00–Set sail from Stockholm; 9:30–Arrive in Grinda for a quick walk around the island; 10:50–Catch the boat to Sandhamn; 11:45–Arrive in Sandhamn, have lunch, and enjoy the town; 17:00–Catch boat to Stockholm (maybe have dinner on board); 19:05–Arrive back in Stockholm. Depending on your interests, you could craft a more in-depth route: For example, for a back-to-nature experience, try Stockholm–Grinda–Svartsö–Stockholm. For an urban mix of towns, consider Stockholm–Vaxholm–Sandhamn–Stockholm.

Overnighting on an island really lets you get away from it all and enjoy the island ambience. I've listed a few island accommodations, but note that there are few midrange options; most tend to be either pricey top-end or very rustic (i.e., rented cottages with minimal plumbing). Decide up front whether you want to splurge or rough it.

Don't struggle too hard with the "which island?" decision. The main thing is to get well beyond Vaxholm, where the scenery gets more striking. I'd sail an hour or two past Vaxholm, have a short stop on an island, then stop in Vaxholm on the way home. Again, the real joy is the view from your ferry.

Getting Around the Archipelago

Only a few archipelago destinations (including Vaxholm) are accessible overland, thanks to modern bridges. For other islands, you'll take a boat. Two major companies run public ferries from downtown Stockholm to the archipelago: the bigger Waxholmsbolaget and the smaller Cinderella Båtarna.

Tickets: Regular tickets are sold on board. Simply walk on, and at your convenience, stop by the desk to buy your ticket before you disembark. Waxholmsbolaget offers a deal that's worthwhile if you're traveling with a small group or doing a lot of island-hopping. You can save 25 percent by buying a 1,000-kr ticket credit for 750 kr (sold only on land; use the splittable credit to buy tickets on the boat).

Schedules: Check both companies' schedules when planning your itinerary; you might have to mix and match to make your itinerary work. A single, confusing schedule booklet mixes together times for both lines. Ferry schedules are complex even to locals, especially outside of peak season.

It's essential to carefully review and confirm your plans, ideally at the information desk in the glassy house on the embankment called Strandvägen. Attendants will help you sort through your options and plan your archipelago visit (Mon–Fri 9:00–17:00, Sat–Sun 11:00–16:00, Strandvägen Kajplats 18—that's boat landing #18, www.visitskargarden.se).

Note that the departures mentioned below are for summer (mid-June–mid-Aug); the number of boats declines off-season.

Waxholmsbolaget: Their ships depart across from Stockholm's Grand Hotel, at the stop called Stromkäjen (tel. 08/679-5830, www.waxholmsbolaget.se). Waxholmsbolaget boats run from Stockholm to: **Vaxholm** (at least hourly, 75 min, 75 kr), **Grinda** (nearly hourly, 2 hours, 90 kr), **Svartsö** (3/day, 2.5 hours, 110 kr),

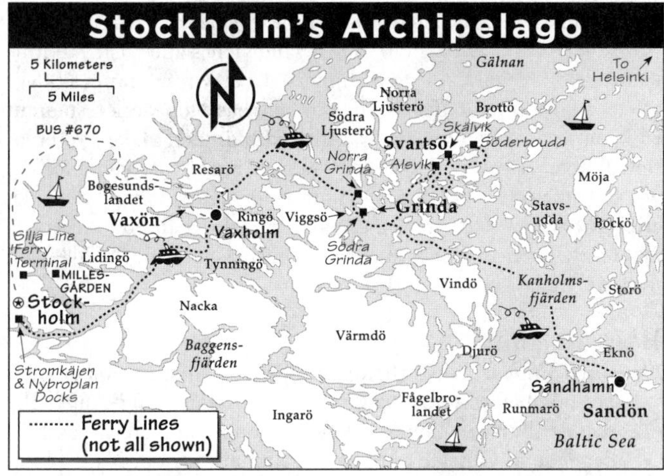

and **Sandhamn** (1/day, Sat–Sun only, 3.5 hours). These destinations are all listed in Waxholmsbolaget's challenging-to-decipher schedule for the Middle Archipelago (Mellersta Skärgården). The same company has routes and schedules for the North and South Archipelago as well.

Cinderella Båtarna: This company focuses its coverage on the most popular destinations. Their ships—generally faster, more comfortable, and a little pricier than their rival's—leave from near Stockholm's Nybroplan, along Strandvägen (tel. 08/1200-4000, www.cinderellabatarna.com). Cinderella boats sail frequently (4/day Mon–Thu, 5/day Fri–Sun) from Stockholm to **Vaxholm** (50 min, 100 kr) and **Grinda** (1.25 hours, 120 kr). After Grinda, the line splits, going either to **Sandhamn** (from Stockholm: 1/day Mon–Thu, 2/day Fri–Sun, 2.75 hours, 150 kr), or Finnhamn, with a stop en route at **Svartsö** (from Stockholm: 2/day, 1.5 hours, 145 kr). Cinderella's fares are slightly cheaper off-season.

On Board: When you board, tell the conductor which island you're going to. They don't stop at all of the smaller islands unless they know there are passengers who want to get off. Hang on to your ticket, as you'll have to show it to disembark. Some boats have luggage-storage areas (ask when you board).

You can usually access the outdoor deck; if you can't get to the front deck (where the boats load and unload), head to the back. Or you can nab a window seat inside. For the best seat, with less sun and nicer views, I'd go POSH: Port Out, Starboard Home (on the left side leaving Stockholm, on the right side coming back). As you sail, a monitor on board shows the position of your boat as it motors through the islands.

Food: You can usually buy food on board, ranging from simple fare at snack bars (50–60-kr sandwiches and basic 80–100-kr meals) to elegant sea-view dinners at fancy restaurants (100-kr starters, 200-kr main dishes). If your boat has a top-deck restaurant and you want to combine your cruise with dinner, make a reservation as soon as you board. Once you have a table, it's yours for the whole trip, so you can simply claim your seat and enjoy the ride, circling back later to eat. You can also try calling ahead to reserve a table for a specific cruise (for Waxholmsbolaget, call 08/243-090; for Cinderella, call 08/1200-4000).

Helpful Hints

Opening Times: All of the opening hours I list in this chapter are reliable only for peak season (mid-June–mid-Aug). The rest of the year, hours are flexible and completely weather-dependent. Outside of the short summer season, many places close down entirely.

Money: Bring cash. The only ATMs are in Vaxholm; farther out, you'll wish you'd stocked up on cash in Stockholm. Fortunately, most vendors do accept credit cards.

Signal for Stop: At the boat landings or jetties on small islands, you'll notice a small signal tower (called a semaphore) that's used to let a passing boat know you want to be picked up. Pull the cord to spin the white disc and make it visible to the ship. Be sure to put it back before boarding the boat. At night, you signal with light—locals just use their mobile phones.

Weather: The weather on the islands is often better than in Stockholm. For island forecasts, check Götland's (the big island far to the south) instead of Stockholm's.

Local Drink: A popular drink here is *punsch,* a sweet fruit liqueur. Stately old buildings sometimes have *punsch-verandas,* little glassed-in upstairs porches where people traditionally would imbibe and chat.

Vaxholm

The self-proclaimed "gateway to the archipelago," Vaxholm (VAX-holm) is more developed and less charming than the other islands. Connected by bridge to Stockholm, it's practically a suburb, and not the place to commune with Swedish nature. But it also has an illustrious history as the anchor of Stockholm's naval defense network, and it couldn't be easier to reach (constant buses and boats from Stockholm). While Vaxholm isn't the rustic archipelago you might be looking for, you're almost certain to

pass through here at some point on your trip. If you have some extra time, hop off the boat for a visit.

Getting There: Boats constantly shuttle between Stockholm's waterfront and Vaxholm (1–2/hr, 1.25 hours, 75–100 kr depending on boat company). **Bus** #670 runs regularly from the Tekniska Högskolan T-bana stop in northern Stockholm to the center of Vaxholm (3/hr Mon–Fri, 2/hr Sat–Sun, 45-min trip, 60 kr one-way—three zones). Unless you're on a tight budget, I'd take the boat for the scenery.

Orientation to Vaxholm

(area code: 08)

Vaxholm, with about 11,000 people, is on the island of Vaxön, connected to the mainland (and Stockholm) by a series of bridges. Everything of interest is within a five-minute walk of the boat dock.

Arrival in Vaxholm

Ferries stop at Vaxholm's south harbor (Söderhamnen). The **bus** from Stockholm begins and ends at the bus stop called Söderhamnsplan, a few steps from the boats. To get your bearings, follow my self-guided walk. There are luggage lockers in the Waxholmsbolaget building on the waterfront (10 kr). The handy electronic departure board (*Nasta Avgang* means "next departure") near the ticket office shows when boats are leaving. For more help, confirm your plans with the person at the ticket office.

Tourist Information

Vaxholm's good TI is well-stocked with brochures about Vaxholm itself, Stockholm, and the archipelago, and can help you with boat schedules (June–Aug Mon–Fri 10:00–18:00, Sat–Sun 10:00–16:00; May and Sept Mon–Fri 11:00–16:00, Sat–Sun 11:00–15:00; Oct–April Mon–Fri 10:00–15:00, Sat–Sun 10:00–14:00; in the Town Hall building on Rådhustorget, tel. 08/5413-1480, www.roslagen.se). They also have pay Internet access.

Self-Guided Walk

Welcome to Vaxholm

This 30-minute, two-part loop will take you to the most characteristic corners of Vaxholm. Begin at the boat dock—you can even start reading as you approach.

Waterfront: Dominating Vaxholm's waterfront is the big Art Nouveau Waxholms Hotell, dating from the early 20th century. Across the strait to the right is Vaxholm's stout fortress, a reminder of this town's strategic importance over the centuries.

With your back to the water, turn left and walk with the big hotel on your right-hand side. Notice the Waxholmsbolaget office building. Inside you can buy tickets, confirm boat schedules, or stow your bag in a locker. After the hamburger-and-hot-dog stand, you'll reach a roundabout. Just to your left is the stop for bus #670, connecting Vaxholm to Stockholm. Beyond that, a wooden walkway follows the seafront to the town's private boat harbor (Västerhamnen, or "west harbor"), where you can count sailboats and rent a bike.

But for now, continue straight up Vaxholm's appealing, shop-lined main street, Hamngatan. After one long block (notice the handy Coop/Konsum grocery store across the street), turn right up Rådhusgatan (following signs to *Rådhustorget*) to reach the town's main square. The TI is inside the big, yellow Town Hall building on your left. Continue kitty-corner across the square (toward the granite slope) and head downhill on a street leading to the...

Fishermen's Quarter: This Norrhamnen ("north harbor") is ringed by former fishermen's homes. Walk out to the dock and survey the charming wooden cottages. In the mid-19th century, Stockholmers considered Vaxholm's herring, called *strömming,* top-quality. Caught fresh here, the herring could be rowed into the city in just eight hours and eaten immediately, while herring caught farther out on the archipelago, which had to be preserved in salt, lost its flavor. There's only one fisherman left in Vaxholm, but he still sells his catch fresh (more on him in a minute).

As you look out to sea, you'll see a pale green building protruding on the left. This is the charming Homestead Museum, with a pleasant indoor-outdoor café. It's worth heading to this little point (even if the museum is closed, as it often is): As you face the water, go left about one block, then turn right down the gravel lane called Trädgårdsgatan (also marked for *Hembygdsgården*). At this corner, the red house on the right (at #18) belongs to that lone Vaxholm fisherman who still sells his freshly caught herring. Look for the *Strömmingslådan* ("herring shop") sign for the chance to buy what herring connoisseurs consider top-notch fish (summer only, Tue–Fri 10:00–16:00, Sat 10:00–14:00, closed Sun–Mon).

Continuing down Trädgårdsgatan lane, you'll run right into Homestead Garden (Hembygdsgården). The big house features an endearing museum showing simple, traditional fishermen lifestyles (free but donation requested, June–Aug Fri–Sun 12:00–16:00, plus Mon in July, otherwise closed). Next door is a fine café serving sweets and light meals with idyllic outdoor seating (both in front of and behind the museum—look around for your favorite perch, taking the wind direction into consideration). This is the best spot in town for coffee or lunch (see listing under "Sleeping and Eating in Vaxholm," later). From here, look across the inlet at the tiny beach (where we're heading next).

Backtrack to the fishermen's harbor, then continue straight uphill on Fiskaregatan road, and take the first left up the tiny gravel lane marked Vallgatan. This part of the walk takes you back in time, as you wander among old-fashioned wooden homes. At the end of the lane, head left; then, when you reach the water, go right along a path leading to a thriving little sandy beach. In good weather, this offers a fun chance to commune with Swedes at play. (In bad weather, it's hard to imagine anyone swimming or sunning here.)

When you're done relaxing, take the wooden stairs up to the top of the rock and Battery Park (Batteripark)—where giant artillery helped Vaxholm flex its defensive muscles in the late 19th century. As you crest the rock and enjoy the sea views, notice (on your right) the surviving semicircular tracks from those old artillery guns. With a range of 10 kilometers, the recoil from these powerful cannons could shatter glass in nearby houses. Before testing them, they'd play a bugle call to warn locals to stow away their valuables. More artifacts of these defenses are dug into the rock.

To head back to civilization, turn right before the embedded bunker (crossing more gun tracks and passing more fortifications on your left). As you leave the militarized zone, take a left at the fork, and the road will take you down to the embankment—just around the corner from where the boat docks, and our starting point. From along this stretch of embankment, you can catch a boat across the water to Vaxholm Fortress.

Sights in Vaxholm

Vaxholm Fortress (Vaxholms Kastell)—Vaxholm's only real attraction is the fortification just across the strait. While the town feels sleepy today, for centuries it was a crucial link in Sweden's nautical defense because it presided over the most convenient passage between Stockholm and the outer archipelago (and, beyond that, the Baltic Sea, Finland, and Russia). The name "Vaxholm" means "Island of the Signal Fire," emphasizing the burg's strategic importance. In 1548, King Gustav Vasa decided to pin his chances on this location, ordering the construction of a fortress here and literally filling in other waterways, effectively making this the only way into or out of Stockholm...which it remained for 450 years. A village sprang up across the waterway to supply the fortress, and Vaxholm was born. The town's defenses successfully held off at least two major invasions (Christian IV of Denmark in 1612, and Peter the Great of Russia in 1719). Vaxholm's might gave Sweden's kings the peace of mind they needed to expand their capital to outlying islands—which means that the pint-size powerhouse of Vaxholm is largely to thank for Stockholm's island-hopping cityscape.

The current, "new" fortress dates from the mid-19th century, when an older castle was torn down and replaced with this imposing granite behemoth. During the 30 years it took to complete the fortress, the tools of warfare changed. Both defensively and offensively, the new fortress was obsolete before it was even completed. The thick walls were no match for the invention of shells (rather than cannonballs), and the high hatches used for attacking tall sailing vessels were useless against the new, low-lying, monitor-style attack boats.

Today, the fortress welcomes visitors to wander its tough little island and visit its museum. A **ferry** shuttles visitors back and forth from Vaxholm (50 kr round-trip, every 15 min during museum opening hours—see below, catch the boat just around the corner and toward the fortress from where the big ferries put in). Once there, hike into the castle's inner courtyard and look to the left to find the good **Vaxholm Fortress Museum** (Vaxholms Fästnings Museum). Presented chronologically on two floors (starting upstairs), the modern exhibit traces the military history of this fortress and of Sweden generally. It uses lots of models and mannequins, along with actual weaponry and artifacts, to tell the story right up to the 21st century. There's no English posted, but

Sleep Code

(7 kr = about $1, country code: 46, area code: 08)
S = Single, **D** = Double/Twin, **T** = Triple, **Q** = Quad, **b** = bathroom, **s** = shower. Unless otherwise noted, all of my listings accept credit cards and include big breakfast buffets. Everyone speaks English.

To help you sort easily through these listings, I've divided the rooms into three categories, based on the price for a standard double room with bath during high season:

$$$ Higher Priced—Most rooms 1,500 kr or more.
$$ Moderately Priced—Most rooms between 1,000–1,500 kr.
$ Lower Priced—Most rooms 1,000 kr or less.

you can pick up the good English translations as you enter. It's as interesting as a museum about Swedish military history can be (50 kr, July–Aug daily 11:00–17:00, June daily 12:00–16:00, first and second Sat–Sun in Sept 11:00–17:00, closed off-season, tel. 08/5417-1890, www.vaxholmsfastning.se). The fortress also houses a B&B and a convention center (used by a local company for group-building exercises).

Sleeping and Eating in Vaxholm

Since Vaxholm is so close to Stockholm, there's little reason to sleep here. But in a pinch, Waxholms is the only hotel in town.

$$$ Waxholms Hotell's stately Art Nouveau facade dominates the town's waterfront. Inside are 42 pleasant rooms with classy old-fashioned furnishings (Sb-1,400/1,100 kr, Db-1,750/1,400 kr, lower prices are for weekends and July, free Wi-Fi, loud music some nights in summer—ask what's on and request a quiet room if necessary, Hamngatan 2, tel. 08/5413-0150, fax 08/5413-1376, www.waxholmshotell.se, info@waxholmshotell.se). The hotel has a grill restaurant outside and a fancy dining room inside.

Hembygdsgården ("Homestead Garden") **Café** is Vaxholm's most tempting eatery, serving "summer lunches" (salads and sandwiches) and homemade sweets, with delightful outdoor seating around the Homestead Museum in Vaxholm's characteristic fishermen's quarter. Anette's lingonberry muffins are a treat (25–65-kr light meals, 85-kr quiches, daily mid-June–Aug 11:00–18:00, May–mid-June 11:00–16:00, closed Sept–April, tel. 08/5413-1980).

Grinda

The rustic, traffic-free isle of Grinda—half retreat, half resort—combines back-to-nature archipelago remoteness with easy proximity to Stockholm. The island is a tasteful gaggle of hotel buildings idyllically situated amid Swedish nature—walking paths, beaches, trees, and slabs of glacier-carved granite sloping into the sea. Since Grinda is a nature preserve (owned by the Stockholm Archipelago Foundation), only a few families actually live here. There's no real town. But in the summer, Grinda becomes a magnet for day-tripping urbanites, which can make it quite crowded. Adding to its appeal is the nostalgia it holds for many Stockholmers, who fondly recall when this was a summer camp island. In a way, with red-and-white cottages bunny-hopping up its gentle hills and a stately old inn anchoring its center, it retains that vibe today.

Orientation to Grinda

(area code: 08)

Grinda is small and easy to manage. It's a little wider than a mile in each direction; you can walk from end to end in a half-hour. Its main settlement—the historic Wärdshus building (a busy hub of tourist activities), hotel, and related amenities—sits next to its harbor, where private yachts and sailboats put in. Public ferries use one of two docks, at opposite ends of the island: Most use Södra Grinda to the south (nearest the hostel and cottages), while a few use Norra Grinda to the north (closer to the campground). From either of these, it's about a 10- to 15-minute walk to the action. Everything on the island is owned and operated by the same company; fortunately, it does a tasteful job of managing the place to keep the island's relaxing personality intact.

Major points of interests are well-signposted in Swedish: *Södra Bryggan* (south dock), *Norra Bryggan* (north dock), *Värdshus* (hotel at the heart of the island), *Gästhamn* (guest harbor); *Affär* (general store); *stuga/stugby* (cottage/s); *Grindastigen* (nature trail); and *Tältplats* (campground).

Tourist Information

The red cottage marked *Expedition* greets arriving visitors just up the hill from the Södra Grinda ferry dock. The staff answers questions, and the cottage serves as a small shop, a place to rent kayaks or saunas, and a reception desk for the island's cottages and hostel (mid-June–mid-Aug daily 9:00–18:00; shoulder season Mon–Fri 10:00–16:00, Sat 10:00–18:00, Sun 10:00–14:00; general info tel. 08/5424-9491).

Sights in Grinda

Grinda is made to order for strolling through the woods, taking a dip, picnicking, and communing with Swedish nature. Watch the boats bob in the harbor and work on your Baltic tan. You can simply stick to the gravel trails connecting the island's buildings, or for more nature, take the Grindastigen trail, which loops to the far end of the island and back in less than an hour (signposted from near the Wärdshus).

You can also rent a kayak or rent the private little sauna hut bobbing in the harbor. There's no bike rental here—and the island is a bit too small to keep a serious biker busy—but you could bring one on the boat from Stockholm.

As you stroll, you might spot a few haggard-looking tents through the trees. The right to pitch a tent here was established by the Swedish government during World War II, to give the downtrodden a cheap place to sleep. Those permissions are still valid, inherited, bought, and sold, which means that Grinda has a thriving community of tent-dwelling locals who camp out here all summer long (April–Oct). While some may be the descendants of those original hobos, these days they choose this lifestyle and live as strange little barnacles attached to Grinda. Once each summer they have a progressive tent-crawl bender before heading to the Wärdshus to blow a week's food budget on a fancy meal.

The island just across from the Södra Grinda dock (to the right) is Viggsö, where the members of ABBA have summer cottages and wrote many of their biggest hits.

Sleeping in Grinda

You have various options, in increasing order of rustic charm: hotel, hostel, and cottages. You can reserve any of these through the Wärdshus. This hub of operations has a restaurant, bar, free Wi-Fi, and conference facilities (tel. 08/5424-9491, www.grinda.se, info@grinda.se).

Grinda is busiest in the summer, when tourists fill its hotel; in spring and fall, it mostly hosts conferences. If sleeping at the hostel or cottages, arrange arrival details (you'll probably pick up your keys at the *Expedition* shed near the dock). The hostel and cottages don't include bed linens, which you can rent for 80 kr. If you have a tent, you can pitch it on the island for 80 kr.

$$$ Grinda Hotel rents 30 rooms in four buildings just above the Wärdshus. These are modern, comfortable, and made for relaxing, intentionally lacking distractions such as TVs or phones (Sb-1,400 kr, Db-1,800 kr, larger suite-2,440 kr, 120 kr less per person if you skip breakfast, 20 percent cheaper if you stay more than 3 nights, extra bed-350 kr, if dining at the restaurant the "Wärdshus package" will save you a few kronor).

$ The 27 **cottages**—most near the Södra Grinda ferry dock—are rentable, offering a rustic retreat (kitchenettes but no running water, shared bathroom facilities outside). From mid-June to mid-August, these come with a one-week minimum and cost more (2-bed cottage-2,800 kr/week, 4-bed cottage-3,500 kr/week, 6-bed cottage-4,000 kr; at other times rentable by the night: 2-bed-700 kr, 4-bed-1,000 kr, 6-bed-1,200 kr).

$ Grinda Hostel (Vandrarheim) is the place to sleep if you wish you'd gone to Swedish summer camp as a kid. The 44 bunks are in simple two- and four-bed cottages, surrounding a pair of fire pits (250 kr/bed regardless of room size, great shared kitchen/dining hall). A small pebbly beach and a basic sauna are nearby.

Eating in Grinda

All of your options (aside from bringing your own picnic from Stockholm) are run by the hotel. Fortunately, there are choices for each price range.

Grinda Wärdshus, the inn at the center of the complex, has a good restaurant that combines rural island charm with fine food. You can choose between traditional Swedish meals and contemporary international dishes. Servings are small but thoughtfully designed to be delicious. Choose between the woody dining room and the terrace out front (495-kr three-course meal, 165–300-kr main dishes, 115–165-kr starters, late June–Aug daily 12:00–24:00; off-season Fri 17:00–23:00, Sat 12:00–23:00, Sun 12:00–18:00, closed Mon–Thu; also closed Fri Dec–early March).

Grindas Framficka ("Grinda's Front Pocket") is a pleasant bistro that serves up basic but tasty food (such as fishburgers and grilled shrimp) right along the guest harbor. Order at the counter, then choose a table to wait for your food (100–140-kr dishes, early

June–mid-Aug daily 11:00–22:00, otherwise sporadically open in good weather—especially weekends).

The **general store and café** (Lanthandel) just below the Wärdshus is the place to rustle up some picnic fixings. You'll also find coffee to go, ice cream, and 40-kr "one-time grills" for a disposable barbecue (early June–mid-Aug daily 8:00–19:30; shoulder season Sat 10:00–18:00, Sun 10:00–16:00, open sporadically Mon–Fri).

Svartsö

The remote and lesser-known isle of Svartsö (svert-show, literally "Black Island"), a short hop beyond Grinda, is the "Back Door" option of the bunch. Unlike Grinda, Svartsö is home to a real community; islanders have their own school and library. But with only 80 year-round residents, the old generation had to specialize. Each person learned a skill to fill a niche in the community—one guy was a carpenter, the next was a plumber, the next was an electrician, and so on. While the island is less trampled than the others in this chapter (just one B&B and a great restaurant), it is reasonably well-served by ferries. Svartsö feels remote and potentially even boring for those who aren't wowed by simply strolling through meadows. But it's ideal for those who want to slow down and immerse themselves in nature.

Orientation to Svartsö

The island, about five miles long and a half-mile wide, has three docks. The main one, at the southwestern tip, is called Alsvik (with the general store and restaurant). Halfway up is Skälvik (near the B&B), and at the northeastern end is Söderboudd. Most boats stop at Alsvik, but if you want to go to a different dock, you can request a stop (ask the conductor on board, or use the semaphore signal at the dock).

At the **Alsvik dock,** the great little general store, called Svartsö Lanthandel, sells anything you could need and also acts as the town TI, post office, and liquor store (mid-June–mid-Aug Mon–Fri 9:00–19:30, Sat–Sun 10:00–18:00; mid-May–mid-June

Mon–Thu 9:00–17:30, Fri 9:00–19:30, Sat–Sun 10:00–14:00; less off-season, tel. 08/54247325, run by friendly Matte Hedelin). You can rent bikes here (50 kr/hr, 125 kr/day, 175 kr/24 hours); call ahead to reserve in busy times. The little café on the dock sells drinks and light food, and rents cottages (550 kr/night, shared showers and toilets, tel. 08/5424-7110).

The island has a few paved lanes and almost no traffic. Residents own three-wheeled utility motorbikes for hauling things to and from the ferry landing. The interior consists of little more than trees. With an hour or so, you can bike across the island and back, enjoying the mellow landscape and chatting with the friendly big-city people who've found their perfect escape.

Svartsö hosts the school for this part of the archipelago. Because Swedish law guarantees the right to education, even kids living on remote islands are transported to class. A school boat trundles from island to island each morning to collect kids headed for the school on Svartsö. If the weather is bad, a hovercraft retrieves them. If it's really bad, and all of the snow days have been used up, a helicopter takes the kids to school.

Eating and Sleeping in Svartsö

If you leave the Alsvik dock to the right and walk five minutes up the hill, you'll find the excellent **Svartsö Krog** restaurant. Opened by a pair of can-do foodies who also run a top-end butcher shop at a Stockholm market hall, this place has a deep respect for the sanctity of meat. Specializing in well-constructed, ingredient-driven dishes, the restaurant brings Stockholm culinary sophistication to a castaway island. Choose one of the three eating zones (each with the same menu): outside, the upscale dining room, or in the original pub interior (an Old West-feeling tavern that the new owner has kept as-is to respect the old-timers). The menu is pricey but good (130–160-kr starters, 200–280-kr main dishes). Their specialty is "golden entrecôte," grilled steak that's been aged for eight weeks (figure a hefty 800 kr but potentially worth it for meat-lovers; June–Aug daily 11:00–24:00; May Thu 16:00–24:00, Fri–Sat 12:00–24:00, Sun 12:00–18:00, closed Mon–Wed; Sept Thu–Sun 12:00–24:00, closed Mon–Wed; Oct–April Thu–Fri 16:00–24:00, Sat 12:00–24:00, closed Sun–Wed; tel. 08/5424-7255).

$$ Svartsö Herrgårdspensionat, the only real accommodation on the island, is a B&B that oozes traditional charm mixed with modern style. Its 14 rooms are spread between the main house—a pretty yellow villa overlooking the water—and several smaller cottages. All of the rooms share toilets and showers (the showers are in an outbuilding—not in the house). Well-run by Marianne and Lena, it's rustic-chic

(D-1,200 kr, or 1,000 kr in some of the older cottages, three-course dinner-450 kr/person extra, open May–Sept, rentable sauna floating in the bay, 500 yards from the Skälvik dock—be sure to use this dock if you're staying here, tel. 08/5424-7017, www.svartsoherrgardspensionat.se, info@svartsoherrgardspensionat.se).

Sandhamn

Out on the distant fringe of the archipelago—the last stop before Finland—sits the proud village of Sandhamn (on the island of Sandön). Literally "Sand Harbor," this is where the glacier got hung up and kept on churning away, grinding stone into sand. The town has a long history as an important and posh place. In 1897, the Royal Swedish Sailing Society built its clubhouse here, putting Sandhamn on the map as the yachting center of the Baltic—Sweden's answer to Nantucket. It remains an extremely popular stop for boaters—from wealthy yachties to sailboat racers—as well as visitors simply seeking a break from the big city.

You'll find two halves to Sandhamn: In the shadow of that still-standing iconic yacht clubhouse is a ritzy resort/party zone throbbing with big-money nautical types. But just a few steps away, around the harbor, is an idyllic time-warp Old Town of colorfully painted shiplap cottages tucked between tranquil pine groves. While most tourists come here for the resort, the quieter part of Sandhamn holds the real appeal.

Orientation to Sandhamn

(area code: 08)

The island of Sandön feels stranded on the edge of the archipelago, rather than immersed in it. On its sheltered side is the town of Sandhamn. Though it's far from Stockholm, Sandhamn is very popular. During the peak of summer (mid-June through late August), it's extremely crowded. Expect to stand in line, and call ahead for restaurant reservations. But even during these times, the Old Town is relatively peaceful and pleasant to explore. If the weather's decent, shoulder season is delightful (though it can be busy on weekends).

Sandhamn's hopes of opening a TI may produce one in time for your visit, but don't count on it. There's also no ATM in Sandhamn, so bring cash (or use your credit card).

Self-Guided Tour

Welcome to Sandhamn

To get your bearings from the ferry dock, take the following tour. Begin by facing out to sea.

As you look out to the little point across from the dock, notice the big yellow building. In the 18th century, this was built as the **pilot house.** Because the archipelago is so treacherous to navigate—with its tens of thousands of islands and skerries, not to mention untold numbers of hidden underwater rocks—locals don't trust outsiders to bring their boats here. So passing ships unfamiliar with these waters were required to pick up a local captain (or "pilot") to take them safely all the way to Stockholm. The tradition continues today. The orange boats marked *pilot,* moored below the house, ferry loaner captains to oncoming ships. And, since this is the point of entry into Sweden, foreign ships can also be processed by customs here.

The little red shed just in front of the pilot house is home to a humble **town museum** that's open sporadically in the summer, featuring exhibits on Sandhamn's history and some seafaring tales. Just below that, notice the waterfront red barn with the *T* sign. The owner of this boat-repair shop erected this marker for Stockholm's T-bana just for fun.

Just above the barn, look for the yellow building with the blue letters spelling ***Sandhamns Värdshus.*** This traditional inn, built in the late 17th century, housed sailors while they waited here to set out to sea. During that time, Stockholm had few exports, so ships that brought and unloaded cargo there came to Sandhamn to load up their holds with its abundant sand as ballast. Today the inn still serves good food (see "Eating in Sandhamn," later).

Stretching to the left of the inn are the quaint storefronts of most of Sandhamn's **eateries** (those that aren't affiliated with the big hotel)—bakery, deli, and grocery store, all of them humble but just right for a simple bite or picnic shopping. Local merchants enjoy a pleasantly symbiotic relationship. Rather than try to compete with each other, they attempt to complement what the next shop sells—each one finding just the right niche. (For details, see "Eating in Sandhamn," later.)

The area stretching beyond these storefronts is Sandhamn's **Old Town**—a maze of wooden cottages that's an absolute delight to explore (and easily the best activity in town). Only 50 of Sandhamn's homes (out of around 450) are occupied by year-rounders. The rest are summer cottages of wealthy Stockholmers, or bunkhouses for seasonal workers in the tourist industry. Most locals live at the farthest-flung (and therefore least desirable) locations. Imagine the impact of 100,000 annual visitors on this little town.

Where the jetty meets the island, notice (on the right) the old-fashioned telephone box with the fancy *Rikstelefon* logo. It contains the island's lone working pay phone. Just to the right of the phone box, you can see the back of the town's bulletin board, where locals post their classified ads. To the left at the base of the dock is Sandhamns Kiosk, a newsstand selling local and international publications (as well as candy and ice cream). A bit farther to the left, the giant red building with the turret on top is the **yacht clubhouse** that put Sandhamn on the map, and still entertains the upper crust today with a hotel, several restaurants, spa, mini-golf course, outdoor pool, and more (see page 419). You'll see its proud SSS-plus-crown logo (standing for Svenska Segelsällskapet—Swedish Sailing Society) all over town. In the 1970s, the building was owned by a notorious mobster who made meth in the basement, then smuggled it out beneath the dock to sailboats moored in the harbor.

Spinning a bit farther to the left, back to where you started, survey the island across the strait (Lökholmen). Just above the trees, notice the copper dome of an observatory that was built by this island's eccentric German oil-magnate owner in the early 20th century. He also built a small castle (not quite visible from here) for his kids to play in.

For a narrated stroll to another fine viewpoint, walk into town and turn left along the water. After about 50 yards, a sign on the right points up a narrow lane to *Post*. This unassuming gravel path is actually one of Sandhamn's most important streets, with the post office, police department (which handles only paperwork—real crimes are deferred to the Stockholm PD), and doctor (who visits town every second Wednesday). While Sandhamn feels remote, it's served—like other archipelago communities—by a crack emergency-response network that can dispatch a medical boat, or in extreme cases, helicopter. With top-notch hospitals in Stockholm just a 10-minute chopper ride away, locals figure that if you have an emergency here, you might just make it to the doctor faster than if you're trying to make it through congested city streets in an ambulance. At the end of this lane, notice the giant hill of the town's namesake sand.

Continuing along the main tree-lined harborfront strip, you can't miss the signs directing yachters to the *toalett* (toilet) and *sopor* (garbage dump). Then you'll pass the Sandhamns Guiderna office, a **travel agency** where you can rent bikes, kayaks, and fishing gear. (If they've managed to open a TI in time for your visit, this is where you'll find it.) Just after that is the barn for the volunteer fire department (Brandstation). With all the wooden buildings in town, fire is a concern—one reason why Sandhamn restricts camping (and campfires).

Go beneath the skyway connecting the big red hotel to its modern annex. Then veer uphill (right) at the *Badstranden Trouville* sign, looking down at the minigolf course. After you crest the top of the hill, on the left is a big, flat expanse of rock nicknamed Dansberget ("Dancing Rock") because it once hosted community dances with a live orchestra. Walk out to enjoy fine **views** of the Baltic Sea—from here, boaters can set sail for Finland, Estonia, and St. Petersburg, Russia. Looking out to the horizon, notice the three lighthouse towers poking up from the sea, used to guide ships to this gateway to the archipelago. The finish line for big boat races stretches across this gap (from the little house on the point to your left). In summer, this already busy town gets even more jammed with visitors, thanks to the frequent sailing races that end here. The biggest annual competition is the Götlandrunt, a round-trip from here to the island of Götland. In 2009, Sandhamn was proud to be one of just 10 checkpoints on the Volvo Ocean Race, a nine-month race around the world that called

mostly at bigger cities (such as Boston, Singapore, and Rio). It was such a huge deal here that locals are aghast at the thought that anyone hasn't heard about it.

Our walk is finished. You can head back into town. Or, to hit the beach, continue another 15 minutes to Trouville beach (explained below).

Sights in Sandhamn

Beaches (Stränder)—True to its name, Sandön ("Sandy Island") has some of the archipelago's rare sandy beaches. The closest and local favorite is the no-name beach tucked in a cove just behind the Old Town (walk through the community from the main boat dock, then follow the cove around to the little sandy stretch).

The most popular—which can be quite crowded in summer—is Trouville beach, at the opposite end of the island from Sandhamn (about a 20-minute walk). Two swathes of sand are marked off by rocks stretching toward Finland. To find it, walk behind the big red hotel and take the right, uphill fork (marked with the low-profile *Badstranden Trouville* sign) to the "Dancing Rock," then proceed along the road. Take a left at the fork by the tennis courts, then walk about 10 minutes through a mysterious-feeling forest until you reach a little settlement of red cottages. Take a right at the fork (look up for the *Till Stranden* sign), and then, soon after, follow the middle fork (along the plank walks) right to the beach zone.

Sleeping in Sandhamn

Sandhamn has a pair of very expensive top-end hotels, a basic but comfortable B&B, and little else. If you're sleeping on Sandhamn, the B&B is the best choice.

$$$ Sands Hotell is a stylish splurge sitting proudly at the top of town. While oriented mostly to conferences and private parties, its 19 luxurious rooms also welcome commoners in the summer (Sb-1,900 kr, Db-2,200 kr, elevator, spa in basement, tel. 08/5715-3020, www.sandshotell.se, info@sandshotell.se).

$$$ Sandhamns Seglarhotellet rents 79 nautical-themed rooms in a modern annex behind the old yacht club building (where you'll find the reception). The rooms are fine, but the prices are sky-high (Sb/Db-2,090 kr, 200 kr more for balcony, extra bed-400 kr, free Wi-Fi, loud music from disco inside the clubhouse—

light sleepers should ask for a quieter back room, great gym and pool area in basement, tel. 08/5745-0400, www.sandhamn.com, reception@sandhamn.com).

$ Sandhamns Värdshus B&B rents five rustic but tasteful, classically Swedish rooms in an old mission house buried deep in the colorful Old Town. To melt into Sandhamn and get away from the yachties, sleep here (S-740 kr, D-990 kr, mostly twins, all rooms share WC and shower, tiny cottage with its own bathroom for same price, includes breakfast, reception is at the restaurant—see below, tel. 08/5715-3051, www.sandhamns-vardshus.se, info@sandhamns-vardshus.se). The rooms are above a reception hall that is rented out for events, but after 22:00, quiet time kicks in.

Eating in Sandhamn

In the Old Town

Sandhamn's most appealing eateries are along the Old Town side of the harbor.

Sandhamns Värdshus, right on the water, is the town's best eatery. They serve traditional Swedish food in three separate dining zones (which mostly share the same menu, but each also has its own specials): out on an inviting deck overlooking the water; upstairs in a salty dining room with views; or downstairs in a simple pub (100–150-kr starters, 100–250-kr main dishes, pub serves cheap lunch deal for 69–89 kr; Easter–Oct daily 11:00–22:30, closed 14:00–17:00 and after 21:00 in shoulder season; Nov–Easter Mon–Fri 11:00–14:00, Sat–Sun 17:00–21:00; reservations possible only in restaurant—otherwise first-come first-served, tel. 08/5715-3051).

To grab a bite or assemble a picnic, browse through these smaller eateries (listed in the order you'll reach them from the boat dock): **Westerbergs Livsmedel** grocery store has basic supplies (Mon–Fri 10:00–13:00 and 16:00–18:00, Sat 10:00–15:00, Sun 10:00–13:00). **Dykarbaren Café** serves meals with indoor and outdoor seating (95–175-kr lunches, 140–240-kr dinners, summer daily 11:00–24:00; May–mid-June and mid-Aug–Sept Wed–Sat 11:00–15:00 and 18:00–24:00, Sun 11:00–15:00, closed Mon–Tue; tel. 08/5715-3554). **Sandhamns Deli** is a bright, innovative shop where you can buy 45-kr sandwiches and salads, a wide array of meats for grilling, cheeses, cold cuts, drinks, fresh produce, and other high-quality picnic fixings (daily 10:00–19:00, later in good weather). Just around the corner (uphill from the harbor and behind the Värdsgasthus) is **Sandhamns Bageriet,** a popular bakery/café serving coffee, sweet rolls, and 25-kr sandwiches (daily in summer 8:00–17:00, "self-service café" opens at 7:00).

Among the Yachties

Sandhamns Seglarhotellet has several eateries, open to guests and non-guests. Out on the dock is the Café Seglar'n, an American-style grill with a take-out window and outdoor tables (40–80-kr dishes, 130-kr combo meals, open in summer in good weather only). Upstairs in the building's main ballroom is an eatery serving good but pricey Swedish and international food. There are two parts—the cheaper, mellow bistro (100–120-kr starters, 165–250-kr main dishes, traditional daily lunch special for 125 kr), and the fancier restaurant (115–200-kr starters, 185–275-kr main dishes). Both parts enjoy fine sea views, and they meet at the bar/dance hall zone in the middle (with loud disco music until 2:00 in the morning nearly nightly in summer). Down on the ground floor is a pub/nightclub.

SOUTHEAST SWEDEN

Växjö • Glass Country • Kalmar • Öland

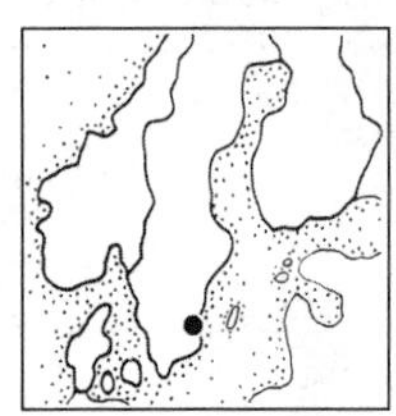

Ranking Sweden's sights, Stockholm is tops, but the southeastern province of Småland is the top runner-up. More Americans came from this densely forested area than any other part of Scandinavia, and the House of Emigrants in Växjö tells the story well. Between Växjö and Kalmar is Glass Country, a 70-mile stretch of forest sparkling with glassworks that welcome guests to tour and shop. Historic Kalmar has a rare Old World ambience and the most magnificent medieval castle in Scandinavia. From Kalmar, you can cross one of Europe's longest bridges to hike through the Stonehenge-like mysteries of the strange island of Öland.

Planning Your Time

By train, on a three-week Scandinavian trip, I'd skip this area in favor of the direct, high-speed train from Copenhagen to Stockholm, or the night train from Malmö (just over the Øresund Bridge from Copenhagen) to Stockholm. Side-trips from Stockholm to Helsinki and Tallinn merit more time than this part of Sweden.

But if you have at least three weeks in Scandinavia and a car, the sights described in this section are an interesting way to spend a couple of days. While I'm not so hot on the Swedish countryside (OK, blame my Norwegian heritage), you can't see only Stockholm and say you've seen Sweden. Växjö and Kalmar give you the best possible dose of small-town Sweden. (I find Lund and Malmö, both popular side-trips from Copenhagen, relatively dull. And I'm not old or sedate enough to find a sleepy boat trip along the much-loved Göta Canal appealing.)

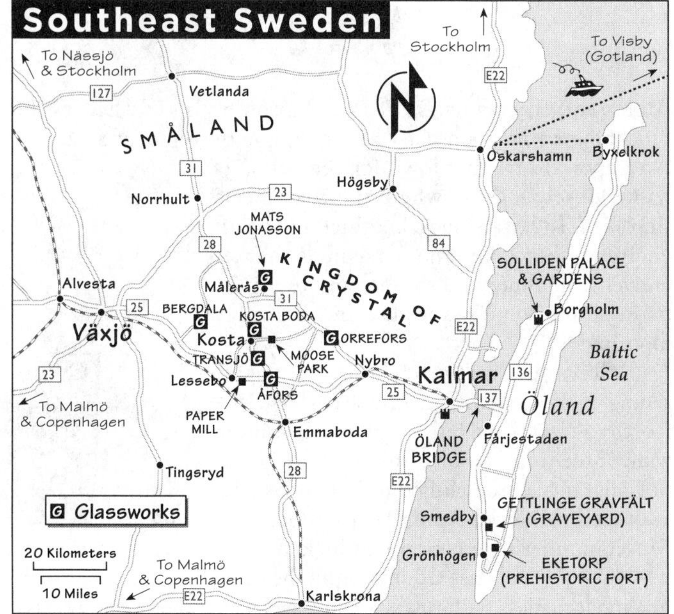

By Car: Drivers can spend three days getting from Copenhagen to Stockholm this way:

Day 1: Leave Copenhagen after breakfast, drive over the bridge to Sweden and on to Växjö, tour Växjö's House of Emigrants, drive into Glass Country, tour Kosta Boda and Transjö glassworks, and arrive in Kalmar in time for dinner.

Day 2: Spend the day in Kalmar touring the castle and Kalmar County Museum, and browsing its people-friendly streets. If you're restless, cross the bridge for a joyride on the island of Öland.

Day 3: 8:00–Begin five-hour drive north along the coast to Stockholm; 10:30–Break in Västervik; 12:00–Stop in Söderköping for picnic lunch and a walk along the Göta Canal; 13:30–Continue drive north; 16:00–Arrive in Stockholm.

Shorten your stops on Day 3 and you'll arrive in Stockholm in time to make the overnight boat to Tallinn or Helsinki. This is an especially good plan on Sunday through Wednesday in the off-season, when boat fares are cheaper. You can see Stockholm on the way back.

By Public Transit: Växjö and Kalmar are easy to visit by train. I'd skip Glass Country and Öland, but if you wouldn't, take the bus (from Växjö to Kosta Boda glassworks, and from Kalmar to Öland).

Växjö

A pleasant, sleepy town of 78,000, Växjö (locals say VEK-hwuh; Stockholmers pronounce it VEK-shuh) is in the center of Småland. An important trading town for centuries, its name loosely means "where the road meets the lake." Today an enjoyable three-mile path encircles that lake, and a farmer's market enlivens the otherwise too-big and too-quiet main square on Wednesday and Saturday mornings.

While there isn't much heavy-duty sightseeing in Växjö, it does have a trio of visit-worthy attractions (all within a 10-minute walk of the train station): The excellent House of Emigrants, chronicling the plight of Swedes who fled to North America; the Smålands Museum, offering a convenient look at the region's famous glass without a trip to Glass Country; and the cathedral, decorated with fine modern glass sculptures. Train travelers not interested in glass can skip the Smålands Museum and make Växjö a convenient three-hour stopover en route to Kalmar.

In 1996, Växjö set itself a goal to become a fossil-fuel–free city by the year 2050. Now a single biomass power plant provides nearly all the community's heat and hot water, half of its energy comes from renewable sources, and carbon dioxide emissions are down by 30 percent. Växjö earned the title "Greenest City in Europe" when it received the EU's first award for sustainable development in 2007.

Orientation to Växjö

(area code: 0470)
Växjö's town center is compact and pedestrian-friendly; the train station, main square, and two important museums are all within two blocks of each other. Blocks here are short; everything I mention is within about a 15-minute walk of everything else.

Arrival in Växjö

Växjö's modern woody train station has snack stands and lockers (35 kr). Pick up a city map at the train station information desk. The station faces the heart of town; walk a few steps straight ahead, and you'll be in the pedestrian shopping zone. Everything in town is in front of you except the two main museums, which are behind the station; to reach these, cross the tracks using the big pedestrian walkway.

Tourist Information

The **TI** is inside the town library, about a 10-minute walk from the train station (June–Aug Mon–Fri 9:30–18:00, Sat 10:00–14:00, closed Sun; Sept–May Mon–Fri 9:30–16:30, closed Sat–Sun; free Internet access, room-booking service, Västra Esplanaden 7, tel. 0470/41410, www.turism.vaxjo.se).

Internet Access: Everlast Internet café, two blocks in front of the train station, is open later and has more computers than the TI (30 kr/hr; June–mid-Aug Mon–Fri 11:00–19:00, Sat 11:00–17:00, closed Sun; mid-Aug–May Mon–Sat 10:00–20:00, Sun 13:00–20:00; Sandgärdsgatan 12, next to recommended Ali Baba restaurant).

Sights in Växjö

Behind the Train Station

You'll find the two museums on the hill just behind the train station (use the pedestrian overpass to cross the tracks). They're listed in the order you'll reach them. Beyond that is Växjö's delightful lake and surrounding park.

▲Smålands Museum/Swedish Glass Museum (Sveriges Glasmuseum)—This instructive museum celebrates the region of Småland and its glassmaking tradition. On the ground floor, the "Six Centuries of Swedish Glass" exhibit traces the history of the substance that still powers the local economy. Upstairs you'll find more on glass, along with displays on the region's prehistory, and a look at Kronoberg County (which includes Växjö) in the 19th century. Rounding out the collection are temporary exhibits. While the collection is poorly described (minimal English), this is a handy place to learn a bit about glass if you're not headed deeper into Glass Country (40 kr, Mon–Fri 10:00–17:00, Sat–Sun 11:00–17:00, Sept–May closed Mon, café with 50–70-kr light meals, Järnvägsgatan 2, tel. 0470/704-200, www.smalandsmuseum.se).

▲▲House of Emigrants (Utvandrarnas Hus)—If you have Swedish roots, this tidy museum and archive is really exciting. Even if you don't, it's an interesting stop for anyone with immigrant ancestors. While modest, the well-presented, inspiring "Dream of America" exhibit offers powerful insight into the experience of more than one million Swedes who sought refuge in North America in the late 19th and early 20th centuries.

Cost and Hours: 40 kr; May–Aug Mon–Fri 9:00–17:00, Sat–Sun 11:00–16:00; Sept–April Tue–Fri 9:00–16:00, Sat 11:00–16:00, closed Sun–Mon; just down the hill behind the glass museum, Vilhelm Mobergs Gata 4, tel. 0470/20120, www.utvandrarnashus.se.

Special Events: Minnesota Day, the second Sunday in August, is a real hoot, as thousands of Minnesotans storm Växjö; it caps a larger Emigration Festival that starts on Thursday evening.

Background: As economic woes wracked Sweden from the 1850s to the 1920s (even a potato famine hit at one point), the country was caught up in an "American Fever." Nearly 1.3 million mostly poor Swedes endured long voyages and culture shock to find prosperity and freedom in the American promised land. In that period, one in six Swedes went to live in the US. So many left the country that Swedish authorities were forced to rethink their social policies and to institute reforms.

➲ **Self-Guided Tour:** In the "Dream of America" exhibit, well-worded displays—all translated into English—explain various aspects of the immigrant experience.

A display on Ellis Island vividly recounts how 3.8 million new arrivals from around the world entered the US through Manhattan's Castle Garden processing center between 1886 and 1890. Firsthand accounts recall the entry procedure, including medical evaluations and an uncomfortable eye exam. (While the US's immigration policies are more stringent today, even in those days about 2 percent of would-be Americans were rejected.) The display's name, "Isle of Hopes, Isle of Tears," evokes the bittersweet experience of leaving a comfortable (if troubled) old home for an unfamiliar new one.

The model of a poor, potato-famine-stricken village demonstrates why so many Swedes were forced to emigrate. The Swedes formed enclaves across North America: on farms and prairies, from New York to Texas, from Maine to Seattle—and, of course, in Chicago's "Swede Town" (the world's second-biggest Swedish town in the world in 1900) and in Minnesota's Twin Cities. The life-size *Snusgatan* re-creates the main street in a Swedish neighborhood—called "Snoose Boulevard," for Swedish snuff. Other displays trace various aspects of immigrant lifestyles, including religion, the press, women's experiences, and Swedish cultural societies to preserve the traditions of the Old World in the New. Rounding out the exhibit, homage is paid to prominent Swedish-Americans, including Charles Lindbergh and the second man on the moon, Buzz Aldrin.

In the next room, a small section on the *Titanic* takes pains to point out that after Americans, Swedes were the second-biggest nationality to perish on that ill-fated vessel. On display are a few items that went to the bottom of the Atlantic with one of those Swedes.

The Moberg Room celebrates local writer Vilhelm Moberg (1898–1973), who put the Swedish immigrant experience on the map with his four-novel series *The Emigrants.* (These books—

and two Max von Sydow/Liv Ullmann films based on them, *The Emigrants* and *The New Land*—are essential pre-trip reading and viewing for Swedish-Americans.) Here you'll see a replica of Moberg's "writer's hut," his actual desk, and some original manuscripts.

Powerful as the museum is, it's become even more poignant in recent years, as Sweden—which not long ago scattered its people far and wide—has become known for taking in other countries' emigrants.

Research Your Roots: Upstairs is an excellent library and genealogical research center. You're welcome to take a peek. Swedish-American roots-seekers (10,000 a year come from the US) are welcome, but if you're serious about finding anything, it's essential to plan ahead and look up some crucial information before leaving home (just showing up and saying, "My name is Svensson and I'm from Minneapolis" will elicit only a bemused shrug from the research staff). First, visit the museum website (www.utvandrarnashus.se) and make a reservation. Then print out their research form and mail it in with $60 in cash (no checks or credit cards), and they'll get started on researching your family's history in preparation for your arrival (research-center services: 150 kr/half-day, 200 kr/day; May–Aug Mon–Fri 9:00–16:00, closed Sat–Sun; Sept–April Tue–Fri 9:00–16:00, closed Sat–Mon).

Växjö Town Park (Växjö Stadspark)—Directly downhill from the House of Emigrants, you'll reach the big lake called Växjösjön. This is a fine place to relax with a picnic or go for a stroll. The pleasant three-mile path around the lake takes you from manicured flower gardens through forested areas. The top part of the lake borders the delightful Linnéparken next to the cathedral (both described below). The TI has a good *Växjö Town Park* brochure in English that explains your options.

A 10-minute walk around the top of the lake from the House of Emigrants is the town's modern **swimming hall** *(Simhall,* 75-kr base price includes sauna, extra fee if you want to tan, use the exercise room, or rent a towel or locker; 230-kr family ticket, call for open-swim hours, tel. 0470/41204, www.medley.se/vaxjosimhall).

Cathedral (Domkyrka)

Växjö's striking orange church, with its distinctive double-needle steeple, features fine sacred art—in glass, of course (free entry, daily 9:00–17:00). Its austere, bright-white interior is enlivened by gorgeous, colorful, and highly symbolic glass sculptures. Pick up the thoughtfully written (if evangelical) 15-kr brochure, which offers a detailed self-guided tour. At the back-right corner

of the church, find the *Spring of Life* baptistery, which resembles a spring bubbling up from underground. Near the back-left corner, the *Tree of Life and Knowledge* is a fantastically detailed candelabra shaped like a tree. On one side, find Adam, Eve, and the snake; on the other, Jesus and Mary with arms outstretched. Notice the thematically parallel design—the snake opposite the dove (representing the Holy Spirit); the snake's tempting apple opposite the bunch of grapes (symbolizing the wine of the Eucharist). At the front of the church, the main altar stands before a glass-decorated triptych showing the subtle interplay between light and dark. Explore the other pieces of glass art around the church, and take in its trio of pipe organs. The church offers **concerts** on many Thursday evenings in summer (60 kr, late June–mid-Aug at 19:00).

The **Linnéparken,** a peaceful park beside the cathedral, is dedicated to the great Swedish botanist Carl von Linné (a.k.a. Carolus Linnaeus). It has an arboretum, lots of well-categorized perennials, a cactus garden, and a children's playground.

Sleeping in Växjö

As elsewhere in Scandinavia, hotels charge less on Friday and Saturday nights and from late June through early August. When I list two hotel rates, the first is the peak-season rate and the second is the summer/weekend rate.

$$$ Elite Stadshotell is a big, modern, business-class hotel with all the comforts in its 163 rooms. It's in a royal setting on the town's main square (very flexible prices, but usually Sb-1,100/550 kr, Db-1,400/900 kr, 200 kr more for plush and newly renovated "deluxe" rooms, free Wi-Fi, park on square out front—pay by day but free at night, about a block from the train station's main entrance at Kungsgatan 6, tel. 0470/13400, fax 0470/44837, www.elite.se, info.vaxjo@elite.se).

$$ Hotell Värend is friendly, comfortable, and inexpensive. It has 24 worn but workable rooms at the edge of a residential neighborhood six blocks from the front of the train station along Kungsgatan (Sb-895/595 kr, Db-995/795 kr, Tb-1,050/995 kr, non-

Sleep Code

(7 kr = about $1, country code: 46, area code: 0470)
S = Single, **D** = Double/Twin, **T** = Triple, **Q** = Quad, **b** = bathroom, **s** = shower. All of these hotels accept credit cards and include breakfast.

To help you sort easily through these listings, I've divided the rooms into three categories, based on the price for a standard double room with bath during high season:

$$$ Higher Priced—Most rooms 1,300 kr or more.
$$ Moderately Priced—Most rooms between 800–1,300 kr.
$ Lower Priced—Most rooms 800 kr or less.

smoking, elevator, free Wi-Fi, free parking, a block beyond N. Esplanaden at Kungsgatan 27, tel. 0470/776-700, mobile 076-769-0700, fax 0470/36261, www.hotellvarend.se, info@hotellvarend.se). If driving, follow *Centrum* signs into town from the freeway. At the Royal Corner Hotel, turn left; 200 yards later, at the first light, turn right onto N. Esplanaden, then left onto Kungsgatan.

$$ Hotel Esplanad, nearby on a busy street, is a bit more modest, with 25 less-expensive rooms, some with private baths on the hall (S-600/400 kr, Sb-850/550 kr, D-750/600 kr, Db-950/720 kr, free parking, N. Esplanaden #21A, tel. 0470/22580, fax 0470/26226, www.hotellesplanad.com, Anna). From the train station, walk five blocks up Klostergatan and turn left on N. Esplanaden.

$ *Hostel:* Växjö's fine **Evedal Hostel** is near a lake three miles out of town (200 kr/bed in 2- to 4-bed rooms, D-350–550 kr, 45 kr cheaper for members, breakfast-60 kr, sheets-75 kr, office open daily 8:00–10:00 and 17:00–20:00—shorter off-season, tel. 0470/63070, fax 0470/63216, www.vaxjovandrarhem.nu, vaxjo.vandrarhem@telia.com). From Växjö's train station, catch bus #7 (June–Aug hourly Mon–Fri, less Sat–Sun and off-season, 15 min). A taxi costs 200 kr.

Eating in Växjö

After-hours Växjö is not very exciting. Consider livening things up by dining out.

PM is a trendy eatery where a younger crowd stands in line to see and be seen. They have good international cuisine with Swedish flair, a mod black-and-white interior, and nice outdoor tables on the pedestrian mall (110-kr lunch special, 135-kr dinner special; otherwise 150–190-kr starters, 160–270-kr main dishes, Mon–Sat 11:30–23:00, often later Fri–Sat, closed Sun, Storgatan 24 at corner of Västergatan, tel. 0470/700-444).

Lagerlunden, the elegant, glassed-in restaurant at the recommended Elite Stadshotell, has dinner specials for 150–250-kr (Tue–Sat 18:00–24:00, closed Sun–Mon, Kungsgatan 6, tel. 0470/13400).

Ethnic Options: If you're looking to save money, or if it's a Sunday—when other restaurants are closed—visit one of downtown Växjö's dozen or so Asian restaurants and kebab-and-pizza-shops. Of these, **Ali Baba's** is a cut above, with a glitzy, Lebanese-casino vibe and a fun stalactite ceiling (50–100-kr meals, Mon–Thu 10:00–22:00, Fri–Sat 12:00–late, Sun 12:30–22:00, Sandgärdsgatan 10, tel. 0470/27900). **La Gondola,** serving Swedish, Chinese, Thai, and Greek food, is simple and engagingly multinational, and offers seating indoors and out (40–65-kr starters, 105–160-kr main dishes, Mon–Thu 11:00–22:00, Fri–Sat 12:00–23:00, Sun 12:00–22:00, Storgatan 33).

Groceries: Visit the **ICA supermarket** at the corner of Sandgärdsgatan and Klostergatan, one block from the front of the train station (Mon–Fri 8:00–20:00, Sat 8:00–17:00, Sun 11:00–17:00). **Coop/Konsum** is farther away, but bigger and open later (daily 7:00–23:00, about a 7-min walk left of the train station at Sandgärdsgatan 44).

Växjö Connections

From Växjö by Train to: Copenhagen (8/day, 2.5–3 hrs), **Stockholm** (every 2 hrs, 3.5 hrs, change in Alvesta, reservations required), **Kalmar** (12/day, 60–70 min). See the Stockholm chapter (page 347) for information on taking trains in Sweden. Växjö does not have good long-distance bus connections.

Glass Country

Filling the remote-feeling woods between Växjö and Kalmar with busy glassmaking workshops, Sweden's famous Glasriket ("Kingdom of Crystal") is worth ▲▲ for drivers. It's touristy, yes—but it also wins over skeptics. There's something to please everybody here: Shoppers thrill at the chance to pick up deeply discounted factory seconds, art-lovers enjoy seeing all of the creative uses for glass, and engineers are fascinated by the skilled glassblowers who persuade glowing globs of molten glass to become fine pieces of tableware or art.

Visiting a glassworks *(glasbruk)* has three parts: the shop; an exhibition of attractive pieces by local artists; and the hot shop, or *hytta*, where glassblowers are hard at work. At most glassworks, it's possible to walk through the hot shop—close enough to feel the heat from the globs of glass as they're being worked (come before the 15:00 quitting time). The shops and exhibitions are usually free, but sometimes charge a token admission fee. To visit the hot shop, most places technically charge admission—but since there's nobody posted at the hot-shop door at smaller glassworks, in practice you can usually just stroll through for free. Taking a guided tour of at least one hot shop—which costs extra—is a must to really understand the whole process. (For starters, read the "Glassmaking in Sweden" sidebar.)

The glassworks I describe in this chapter are a representative mix of the 15 or so that you can visit in Glass Country, ranging from big corporate factories to charming artistic workshops. On the corporate side, the Kosta company dominates; its flagship Kosta Boda complex is the biggest and most accessible of all the glassworks to tour (though its smaller subsidiaries, Åfors and Orrefors, are also tourable). But it's more satisfying to round out your look at the region with at least one smaller, independent producer as well (Transjö Glashytta is the most appealing, but I've also described Bergdala and Mats Jonasson Målerås). And, for a change of pace, you can learn about traditional papermaking (at the Lessebo mill) and the local moose population. For more tips on which glassworks to visit—and which to skip—see "Planning Your Time," later.

Information: The *Glasriket/Kingdom of Crystal* magazine (available at any TI) and the region's official website (www.glasriket.se) describe the many glassworks that welcome the public. The 95-kr **Glasriket Pass** includes free entry to exhibitions and hot shops, and discounts on tours, shopping, and *hyttsill* dinners (explained on page 442). The pass, sold at glassworks and local TIs, is worthwhile only if you're visiting several hot shops and doing some serious shopping (10 percent discount at certain shops, often with a 500-kr minimum purchase). Note that in Swedish, *glas* is glass, while *glass* is ice cream.

Planning Your Time

Though you can take a bus from Växjö to Kosta, the glassworks aren't worth the time and trouble unless you have a car. Train travelers should instead take a careful look at the glass exhibit in Växjö's Smålands Museum, and then go straight to Kalmar.

With a car, the drive from Växjö to Kalmar is a 70-mile joy—light traffic with endless forest-and-lake scenery punctuated by numerous glassworks. The driving time between Växjö and Kosta is 45 minutes; it's another 45 minutes between Kosta and Kalmar.

Looking at a map, you'll notice the glassworks are scattered around the center of the region. While it would take the better

Glassmaking in Sweden

In the mid-16th century, King Gustav Vasa decided he wanted more fine glass to decorate his palace, so he invited German glassmakers to train his subjects, and the trend took off. It's no surprise that glassmaking caught on here in Sweden: While the very rocky soil makes farming difficult, the resources needed for glass are abundant: vast forests to fire the ovens, and lakes with an endless supply of sand. By the difficult 19th century—when a sixth of Sweden's population emigrated to North America—the iron mills had closed, leaving behind unemployed workers who were highly skilled at working with materials at high temperatures. Glassmaking was their salvation, and by the early 1900s, this region had more than 100 glassworks.

While glassmaking was important throughout Sweden, it was in the area between Växjö and Kalmar (engulfed in a dense forest) that it took hold the strongest, and lasted the longest. When other materials became cheaper than glass (for example, paper cartons instead of glass bottles for milk), the glassmaking industry was hit hard, and it dried up in other parts of Sweden. But here in Glass Country, the workers refocused their efforts: They still make some everyday items, but their emphasis is on high-quality art pieces that command top kronor. An Ikea wine glass made in China costs 10 kr, while a handmade Swedish one might cost 150 kr—but for consumers interested in quality, that's a premium they're willing to pay.

The glassmaking process is fascinating—and hasn't changed much over the centuries. The glass begins as little white pellets that are about 70 percent sand (most of the sand for the clearest-color glass is imported from Belgium). Soda and potash are added to lower the melting point, and limestone and zinc are added to minimize boiling (and the resulting bubbles). Other additives determine the glass' final qualities—glassmakers use a different mix for a thin champagne flute than for a thick platter.

You'll see two different types of glass being created: everyday tableware and art pieces. The mass-produced tableware—such as wine glasses—is created by small teams of glassblowers who use an assembly-line system, supervised by a "master," who monitors quality control. Art-glass pieces, however, are never the same. The region has a passel of big-name designers, each with their own aesthetic and all considered local celebrities. Most glass artists conceptualize the design, but leave the actual grunt work to their assistants—you might see the artist hovering off to the side, directing the glassblowers.

As you watch these masters at work, keep in mind they're working with a molten medium that can melt skin. First, a worker places the glassblowing rod into the furnace (notice the foot pedals used to open and close the doors) and grabs a blob of molten glass. Glassblowers have to move quickly—before the glass hardens too much—but still be careful to avoid shattering the medium or burning their colleagues. After rolling the glass out on a heat-resistant graphite table to give it the desired shape, they blow into the end of the rod to create an open space inside. If creating a mass-produced item, they generally stick it into a mold to ensure the correct dimensions. Other appendages are added; for example, if it's a wineglass with a stem and foot, separate pieces of glass are stretched out to the appropriate shape and stuck on the bottom.

For this entire process, the glass is at about 2,100 degrees Fahrenheit. If it gets too hot, glassblowers cool it down with water or air; if the glass needs to be reheated, they use a blowtorch or poke it momentarily back into the furnace. All glass begins clear. To make colored glass, they either add powdered dye during production, or paint the finished piece, then refire it. Finally, the area where the glass was attached to the rod is cut with an industrial diamond, broken off, and ground and polished smooth. When the piece is finished, it's set in a special oven to cool gradually—over a few hours for smaller pieces, or for a day or more for large items.

The workday ends around 15:00, when the raw materials for the next day's glass are dumped into giant, custom-made clay pots and placed in the ovens. Overnight, these will gradually melt down to the molten medium the glassblowers will need by tomorrow morning at 7:00.

The last stop is quality control. Only the best pieces are deemed "first quality" *(1:A Sortering)*—you'll pay a premium for these flawless items. Some items, deemed "second quality" *(2:A Sortering),* have minor imperfections that bring the price down substantially. When shopping, pay close attention to these labels; if you don't need your glass perfect, you can save by looking for second quality. Quite a few items are simply too imperfect—these are dumped into a bin and disposed of. Sorry, budget travelers—these "factory thirds" are trashed, not sold.

part of a day to loop around and visit them all, distances are relatively short and roads are good. Still, it's smart to be selective. On a tight schedule, I'd visit Kosta and Transjö, possibly Bergdala or Åfors, and maybe the Lessebo paper mill, skipping the rest.

If you're visiting Glass Country en route from Växjö to Kalmar, consider this driving plan: Head southeast from Växjö on highway 25, following signs for *Kalmar.* If you want to visit Bergdala, turn off after Hovmantorp; to skip it, head straight to Lessebo (and its paper mill). In Lessebo, turn off to the north for Kosta and tour the big Kosta Boda glassworks there. Then, if you'd like to visit the Moose Park, detour slightly east (toward Orrefors) to reach it (just on the outskirts of Kosta). This is also the time you could detour much farther northeast to the Mats Jonasson glassworks in Målerås, if you're interested. Either way, from Kosta, you'll head south on highway 28, watching for signs to *Transjö* for the best of the smaller, artsy glassworks. The same road 28 takes you to Eriksmåla, where the Åfors workshop is also worth a visit if you're not glassed out. In Eriksmåla you can pick up highway 25 and make a beeline east to Kalmar.

Sights in Glass Country

Remember that these attractions are tied together by the driving tour described above. Don't forget the two non-glass sights (the historic paper mill and Moose Park), described after the glassworks.

Glassworks *(Glasbruks)*

These are listed in the order you'll reach them, from Växjö to Kalmar. Remember, while many of these places charge admission to watch the hot shop at work, most aren't set up to actually collect this fee at the door—so curious tourists can simply poke around and might not even have to pay (the entrance fee is waived if you have the 95-kr *Glasriket* Pass). Also note that many workshops take a lunch break sometime between 10:00 and 11:00, and stop working entirely after about 15:00 or 15:30.

▲Bergdala Studioglas—The small, independent Bergdala glassworks, in a village of the same name, has an enjoyably artsy hot shop (20 kr, Mon–Fri 7:00–15:30, also Sat–Sun late June–July). Its well-stocked shop is full of its trademark blue-rimmed tableware, and the engaging gallery upstairs shows off a different sampling of local artists every year (free; June–Aug Mon–Fri 10:00–18:00, Sat 10:00–16:00, Sun 12:00–16:00; Sept–May Mon–Fri 10:00–17:00, Sat–Sun 12:00–16:00; tel. 0478/31650, www.bergdaladesign.se).

▲▲Kosta (a.k.a. Kosta Boda)—About an hour east of Växjö, the village of Kosta boasts the oldest of the *glasbruks,* dating back to 1742. Today, the sprawling Kosta complex—the only real jolt of civilization in this otherwise remote-feeling landscape—includes a modern outlet mall, a factory store (labeled *Kosta Boda*), a fancy new art hotel...and, of course, a glassworks (www.kostaboda.se).

Glassworks and Exhibition: The highlight here is unquestionably watching the **glassworks** in action. Arguably the best hot-shop tour in the region, this allows you to look over the shoulders of glassblowers crafting both mass-produced, crank-'em-out tableware, and high art fit to be shown off in a museum. You can pay 30 kr to visit the glassworks on your own (and the exhibition, described below). But if you're coming here anyway, you owe it to yourself to call a day ahead and arrange a 45-minute English tour for just 20 kr extra—usually guided by Kristina, whose enthusiasm makes the place meaningful (tel. 0478/34529). In the surprisingly modest **exhibition,** each piece is identified with a photo and brief bio (in English) of its designer, which personalizes the art. You'll also see historical pieces. The glassworks and exhibition are open daily (usually Mon–Fri 10:00–18:00, Sat–Sun 11:00–17:00, last tour departs one hour earlier). The glassworks is much quieter—and less interesting—after about 15:30. During the four weeks in summer that the glassblowers are on vacation (early July–early Aug), there's less glassblowing and more tourists—and the complex is open daily 11:00–17:00.

Shopping: In the **Kosta Boda shop,** crystal "seconds" (with tiny bubbles or sets that don't quite match) and discontinued models are sold at good prices. This is duty-free shopping, and they'll happily mail your purchases home (Mon–Fri 10:00–18:00, Sat 10:00–17:00, Sun 11:00–17:00, open one hour later mid-June–Aug). Don't confuse this with the big outlet mall across the street.

Sleeping and Eating: I ate well at the **cafeteria** inside the outlet mall, which features 85-kr lunch specials. Nearby is the newly opened **$$$ Kosta Boda Art Hotel,** designed to impress. Everything's decorated to the hilt with (of course) artistic glass, created in the hot shop across the street. With Växjö and Kalmar so close, there's little reason to pay a premium to sleep here (rooms start at Db-2,500 kr, tel. 0478/34830, www.kostabodaarthotel.se). But if you have a few extra minutes, poke around this surreal, over-the-top, world-of-glass complex, which includes a "glass bar," a mind-bending indoor swimming pool, and a restaurant where, on most evenings, you can watch an actual glassblower at work while you dine (250-kr two-course meals in fine dining section, 150-kr one-course meals in bistro).

▲▲Transjö Glashytta—Set up in an old converted farm 10 minutes south of Kosta, this tiny glassworks does expensive but unique fine-art pieces. From the main shop, a canal-like pond (with glass art pieces suspended overhead) leads back to the hopping hot shop. Transjö—started by a pair of highly regarded glass designers—uses up-and-coming artists as apprentices; they imbue it with a youthful vigor. You can feel the art oozing out of the ovens. The tiny glassworks is funkier and less predictable than the big boys; it's most worthwhile if you catch the artists in action. In the summer (early June–mid-Sept), the shop out front is usually open daily 11:00–17:00, but unfortunately the hot shop is often closed (they don't do much glassblowing in warmer weather). Off-season, if the shop out front is closed, try following the canal back to the workshop, where you might find the glassblowers at work; they can take a break and open the shop for you on request (most pieces in shop 1,000–4,000 kr, the *elevarbete*/apprentice works are cheaper, smart to call ahead—tel. 0478/50700, www.transjohytta.com). To find it, look for *Transjö* signs just south of Kosta.

▲Åfors—The Åfors (OH-foss) glassworks is near Eriksmåla, a charming village south of Kosta and Transjö. While it's part of the Kosta corporate scene, Åfors focuses on individual art pieces rather than mass-produced tableware. This makes it refreshingly intimate, with a looser and more artistic vibe than its assembly-line cousins. You can visit the hot shop (technically 30 kr but often free, Mon–Fri 10:00–15:30, closed Sat–Sun) and stop by the shop and exhibition (free, Mon–Fri 10:00–18:00, Sat 10:00–16:00, Sun 12:00–16:00).

Mats Jonasson Målerås—In the town of Målerås northeast of Kosta, Mats Jonasson's glassworks specializes in engraving, mixed metal-and-glass sculptures, and necklaces. While it started small, the facility has grown quite big, giving the glassworks a less personal atmosphere. The "design arena" shows off works by other local glass artists (free; watch glassmaking Mon–Fri 9:00–15:00, also weekends in July–Aug; shop and

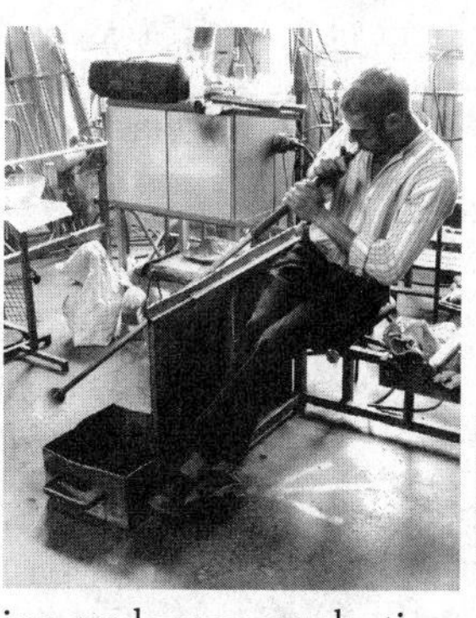

gallery open June–Aug Mon–Fri 9:00–18:00, Sat 10:00–17:00, Sun 11:00–17:00; Sept–May Mon–Fri 10:00–18:00, Sat 10:00–16:00, Sun 11:00–16:00; tel. 0481/31402, www.matsjonasson.com).

Orrefors—Once a glassworks with its own proud history, Orrefors (OH-reh-fohs) is now part of the Kosta empire and plays second fiddle to the flagship brand. While Kosta does more of the handmade pieces, Orrefors focuses more on machine-made mass production. Orrefors feels drearily industrial and sadly neglected, but might be worth visiting if you know your glass and have a special affinity for their works. The free, dazzling **museum** displays its historic art pieces chronologically (from early-20th-century pieces with Art Nouveau flair, through works from the 1940s) and includes a "crystal bar" (Mon–Fri 10:00–15:00, closed Sat–Sun, longer hours in summer). You can pay 30 kr to visit the **hot shop** and observe the work from platforms (same hours as museum). In summer, if you really want an English tour at Orrefors, you can pay 20 kr extra to arrange it with Kristina at Kosta (described earlier, tel. 0478/34529)—but the Kosta tour is better anyway. Like Kosta, Orrefors' **shop** sells nearly perfect crystal seconds at deep discounts (Mon–Fri 10:00–18:00, Sat 10:00–16:00, Sun 12:00–16:00, tel. 0481/34195, www.orrefors.se).

Non-Glass Attractions

▲Lessebo Paper Mill (Handpappersbruk)—The town of Lessebo has a 300-year-old paper mill (tucked next to a giant modern one) that's kept working for visitors to enjoy. If you've never seen handmade paper produced, this mill is worth a visit (20 kr, late June–late Aug Mon–Fri 9:15–17:00, closed Sat–Sun, off-season until 16:00 and closed for lunch 12:00–13:00, tel. 0478/47691). Cotton linters (fibers) are soaked, packed into a frame, pressed, dried, glazed, and hand-torn into the perfect size and shape. While the methods seem antiquated, this paper is still used today for special purposes: top-of-the-line stationery, impossible-to-forge embossed document paper (such as for certificates, or for important examinations), and paper for "wet painting" (for which it's considered better than machine-made paper).

You can pick up the English brochure, but there's little point in visiting unless you can join the 40-minute English **tours** with one of the papermakers who still run the place, Devis or Lisbeth (35 kr extra, late June–late Aug Mon–Fri 9:30, 10:30, 13:00, and

14:15, no tours off-season). If you're not here for a tour, it's unlikely you'll see much papermaking action at all.

By car, Lessebo is an easy stop between Växjö and Kosta. Just after the Kosta turnoff, you'll see a black-and-white *Handpappersbruk* sign.

Grönåsen's Moose Park (Älgpark)—This offbeat attraction, just outside Kosta, demonstrates the love-hate relationship Swedes feel toward their moose population. (The Swedish word *älg* can be translated both as "moose" and "elk," but these are the same Bullwinkle-type moose you'll find in the northern latitudes of North America.) A third of a million of these giant, majestic beasts live in Sweden. They're popular with hunters but unpopular with drivers, because collisions on backcountry roads have caused fatalities. At this attraction, you'll walk through the moose-happy gift shop before taking a mile-long stroll around the perimeter of a pen holding live moose. Periodic museum exhibits—life-size dioramas with stuffed moose (including one plastered to the hood of a car)—round out the attraction. You can even buy moose sausage. Sure it's a hokey roadside stop, and will hardly be a hit with animal-rights activists, but for many the park is an enjoyable place to learn about Swedish moose (40 kr, Easter–mid-Nov daily 10:00–18:00, closed off-season, just outside Kosta on the road to Orrefors, tel. 0478/50770, www.moosepark.net).

Eating in Glass Country

You'll find plenty of simple eateries designed for day-trippers. For example, the cafeteria in the outlet mall at the big Kosta complex is the perfect place for fast and cheap, Ikea-style Swedish grub (85-kr lunch specials).

If you'd like to linger over a more serious dinner, consider joining one of the special ***hyttsill* dinners** at various glass workshops. Traditionally, the hot shops' fires made them a popular place to convene after hours on frigid winter nights. People would huddle around the ovens and be entertained by wandering minstrel-type entertainers called *luffar*. The food was nothing special (*hyttsill* literally means "hot shop herring," usually served with crispy pork, potatoes, and other stick-to-your-ribs fare), but it was a nice opportunity for a convivial rural community to get together. Today modern glassworks carry on the tradition, inviting tourists on several nights through the summer. They usually have live music and glassblowers working while you dine (figure around 300 kr per person; see complete schedule and reserve at www.glasriket.se).

Kalmar

Kalmar feels formerly strategic and important. In its heyday—back when the Sweden/Denmark border was just a few miles to the south—they called Kalmar Castle the "Key to Sweden." But today Denmark is distant, and Kalmar is a bustling small city of 60,000 (with 9,000 students in its university and maritime academy). Kalmar's salty old center, classic castle, and busy waterfront give it a wistful sailor's charm.

History students may remember Kalmar as the place where the treaty establishing the 1397 Kalmar Union was signed. This "three crowns" treaty united Norway, Sweden, and Denmark against their common enemy: German Hanseatic traders. It created a huge kingdom. But the union, which was dominated by Denmark, lasted a bit more than a hundred years. When Gustav Vasa came to power in 1523, Kalmar was rescued from the Danes, the Union was dissolved...and even the European Union hasn't been able to reunify the Scandinavian Peninsula since.

Kalmar town was originally next to the castle, but after a huge fire in 1647, the town was entirely rebuilt on the nearby island of Kvarnholmen. There it was encircled by giant 17th-century earthworks and bastions, parts of which still survive.

The town center of Kvarnholmen, the charming Old Town, the castle, and nearby vacation island of Öland are all enjoyable to explore, making Kalmar Sweden's most appealing stop outside of Stockholm.

Orientation to Kalmar

(area code: 0480)

For a relatively small city, Kalmar has a complicated layout; its many small islands are connected to the mainland—and to each other—by bridges. Kalmar is easily walkable and fun by bike.

The mostly pedestrianized core of town is on the island of Kvarnholmen, walled and with a grid street plan. The Old Town district is between Kvarnholmen and Kalmar Castle, which is on a little island of its own (a 10-min walk from Kvarnholmen). The train station, TI, and ugly industrial "new harbor" are on a man-made extension just south of Kvarnholmen.

Additional islands make up Kalmar (including charming Ängö

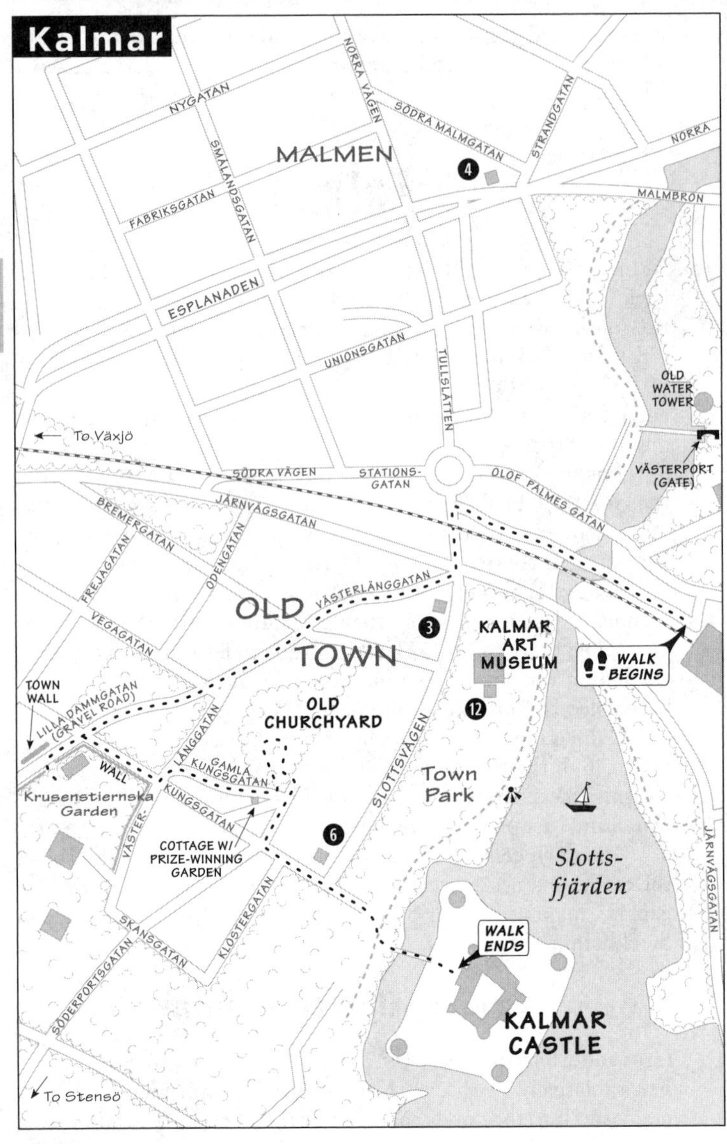

and mod Varvsholmen), but most visitors stick to Kvarnholmen, the Old Town, and the castle. If your time is limited, the castle should be your top priority.

Tourist Information

Look for the TI in the big, modern building next to the marina. The staff hands out helpful brochures and maps of town, including the

Wander Round Kalmar self-guided tour booklet (late June–mid-Aug Mon–Fri 9:00–21:00, Sat–Sun 10:00–17:00; early June and late Aug Mon–Fri 9:00–19:00, Sat–Sun 10:00–16:00; Sept–May Mon–Fri 10:00–17:00, closed Sat–Sun—except open some Sat in May and Sept; Ölandskajen 9, tel. 0480/417-700, www.kalmar.se/turism).

The TI has Internet access (60 kr/hr) and can book you a local hotel room (no booking charge) or a room in a private home (50-kr fee). Ask about biking tips (you can rent a bike at some hotels, or at the Baltic shop across the street from the TI). Kalmar, with its cheery lanes, surrounding parks, and brisk harborfront, makes for happy biking.

The TI shares a building with the Kalmar Maritime Academy, which is part of the university. It's built to look like a ship, and the bridge simulator above is used to train future sailors.

Arrival in Kalmar

Arriving at the combined train and bus station couldn't be easier (train ticket office open Mon–Fri 6:40–18:00, Sat 8:40–15:00, Sun 10:30–17:00; lockers available). As you walk out the front door, the town center (Kvarnholmen) is dead ahead. The TI is to your right (exit station to the right, turn right around the bottom of the tracks, cross the street to the harbor, and walk to its end). And Kalmar Castle and the Old Town are behind you (follow the tracks to your left until the first crosswalk, then follow the big tree-lined boulevard to the castle).

Sights in Kalmar

▲▲Kalmar Castle (Kalmar Slott)

This moated castle is one of Europe's great medieval experiences. The imposing exterior, anchored by stout watchtowers and cuddled by a lush park, houses a fine Renaissance palace interior. Built in the 12th century, the castle was enlarged and further fortified by the great King Gustav Vasa (r. 1523–1560) and lived in by two of his sons, Erik XIV and Johan III. In the 1570s, Johan III redecorated the castle in the trendy Renaissance style, giving it its present shape. Kalmar Castle remained a royal hub until 1658, when the Swedish frontier shifted south and the castle lost its strategic importance. Kalmar Castle was neglected, being used as a prison, distillery, and granary. Finally, in the mid-19th century, a newfound respect for history led to the castle's renovation.

Cost and Hours: 80 kr (tickets sold in gift shop inside, or sometimes outside the gate in summer); July daily 10:00–18:00; Aug daily 10:00–17:00; May–June and Sept daily 10:00–16:00; April and Oct Sat–Sun 11:00–15:30, closed Mon–Fri; Nov–March open only Sat–Sun 11:00–15:30 on second weekend of month; tel. 0480/451-490 or 0480/451-491, www.kalmarslott.se.

Getting There: To reach the castle from the center of town, consider taking a short detour to the Old Town and ending your stroll at the castle (route described under "In the Old Town, near the Castle," next).

Tours: If you can catch the 45-minute English tour, it's worthwhile to hear about the goofy medieval antics of Sweden's kings (included in admission price, offered daily late June–mid-Aug usually at 11:30 and 14:30, reconfirm times by phone or on website). You can buy a too-thorough, 45-kr English guidebook; or, for the highlights, follow my self-guided tour.

➲ **Self-Guided Tour:** Approaching the castle, you'll cross a wooden drawbridge. Peering into the grassy, filled-in moat, look for sunbathers, who enjoy soaking up rays while the ramparts protect them from cool winds. To play "king of the castle," you can scramble along these outer ramparts (included in castle ticket, or open and free when castle interior is closed).

In the central **courtyard** is the canopied Dolphin Well, a particularly fine work of Renaissance craftsmanship. If you haven't bought your ticket yet, buy one in the gift shop on the left. Then follow the well-marked, one-way tour route.

Near the gift shop, the models and drawings in the **Governor's Quarters** illustrate the evolution of the castle over time. Notice the bulky medieval shape of the towers, before they were capped by fancy Renaissance cupolas; and the Old Town that once huddled in the not-protective-enough shadow of the castle. In the adjoining **Prisoners' Tower**, you can peer down into the dungeon pit. The room was later converted into a kitchen (notice the big fireplace), and the pit became a handy place to dump kitchen waste. Nearby, behind the WCs, the **Women's Prison** exhibit explains a grim 19th-century chapter of the castle's history.

Then you'll climb up the **Queen's Staircase,** up steps made of Catholic gravestones. While this might have simply been an economical way to recycle building materials, some speculate that it was a symbolic move in support of King Gustav Vasa's Reformation, after the king broke with the Pope in a Henry VIII–style power struggle.

At the top of the stairs, go through the wooden door into the **Queen's Suite.** The ornate Danish bed (captured from the Danes after a battle) is the only surviving original piece of furniture in the castle. The faces decorating the bed have had their noses chopped off, as superstitious castle-dwellers believed that potentially troublesome spirits dwelled in the noses. This bed could easily be disassembled ("like an Ikea bed," as my guide put it) and moved from place to place—handy for medieval kings and queens, who were forever traveling throughout their realm. Adjoining this room is a smaller servants' quarters, called the Maidens' Chambers.

Proceed into the **Checkered Hall.** Examine the incredibly detailed inlaid wall panels, which make use of 17 different types of wood—each a slightly different hue. Notice the unmistakably Renaissance aesthetic of this room, which strives to achieve symmetry and perspective. Door handles were left off so as not to break up the harmony. (When the queen wanted to go into the next room, she'd clap her hands to alert servants to open the doors for her.)

Speaking of which, continue into the **dining room** (a.k.a. Gray Hall, for the frescoes of Samson and Delilah high on the wall). The table is set for an Easter feast (based on a detailed account by a German visitor to one particular Easter meal held here). For this holiday feast, the whole family was in town—including Gustav Vasa's two sons, Erik XIV and Johan III. The giant birds are for decoration, not for eating. Notice all the fish on the table. Since Erik's wife Katarzyna Jagiellonka was a Polish Catholic (their marriage united Sweden, Poland, and Lithuania into a grand empire), she was abstaining from meat during this holy time. Forks (which resembled the devil's pitchfork) were not used—just spoons, knives, and hands. At the adjacent table, peruse the dessert selection, with marzipan and expensive herbs and spices.

The door with the sun above it leads to the **King's Chamber.** Notice the elaborate lock on the door, installed by King Erik XIV because of constant squabbles about succession. The hunting scenes inside have been restored a bit too colorfully, but the picture of Hercules over the window is original—likely painted by Erik himself. Examine more of those elaborate inlaid panels. Peek into the little room (to the left of the fireplace, with a fine castle illustration embedded in its hidden door) to see the king's toilet. Also in here was a secret escape hatch the king could use in case of trouble. Perhaps King Erik XIV was right to be so paranoid; he eventually died under mysterious circumstances, perhaps poisoned by his brother Johan III, who succeeded him as king.

Backtrack through the dining room and continue into the **Golden Hall,** with its gorgeously carved (and painstakingly restored) gilded ceiling. The entire ceiling is suspended from the true ceiling by chains. If you visually trace the ceiling, the room seems crooked—but it's actually an optical illusion to disguise the fact that it's not perfectly square. Find the portraits of the (dysfunctional) royal family whose tales enliven this place: Gustav Vasa, one of his wives, sons Erik XIV and Johan III, and Johan's son Sigismund.

Peek into **Agda's Chamber,** the bedroom of Erik's consort. The replica furniture re-creates how it looked when the king's kept woman lived here. Later, the same room was used for a different type of captivity: as a prison cell for female inmates.

Go to the top of the King's Staircase (also made of gravestones like the Queen's Staircase, and topped by a pair of lions). The big door leads to the grand **Green Hall,** once used for banquets and now for concerts.

At the end of this hall, the **chapel** is one of Sweden's most popular wedding venues (up to four ceremonies each Saturday). As reflected by the language of the posted Bible quotations, the sexes sat separately: men, on the warmer right side, were more literate and could read Latin; women, on the cooler left side, read Swedish. The fancy pews at the front were reserved for the king and queen.

At the far end, near the altar, a door leads to a stairwell with a model ship, donated by a thankful sailor who survived a storm. In the next room is Anita, the stuffed body of the last horse who served with the Swedish military (until 1937); beyond that you might find some temporary exhibits.

The rest of the castle complex includes the vast **Burned Hall,** which—true to its name—feels stripped-down and is not as richly decorated.

In the Old Town, near the Castle

The tidy, quiet residential zone between the castle and the town center is actually more rewarding to explore than downtown Kalmar. For centuries, this *was* the town center of Kalmar. But it burned down in 1647, and sat deserted for a century. Now it's a toy village of colorfully painted wooden homes, tidy yards, and perfect picket fences. Locals still call it the Old Town (Gamla Stan), even though almost everything here is newer than the buildings on Kvarnholmen, now the heart of town.

Consider a slight detour strolling through this neighborhood on your way from the town center to the castle. I've connected the sights in this area with some self-guided commentary.

From the train station at the edge of Kvarnholmen, walk along the tracks (toward Växjö) until your first opportunity to cross over. Across the tracks is Slottsvägen, a pleasant, tree-shaded boulevard that leads to the castle. (If you want to visit the castle first, head up this drag to do it now before following this walk.) At the start of this boulevard, take the angled, cobbled street on the right (Västerlånggatan). The grand mansion you'll walk behind once belonged to the prestigious Jeansson family, who donated the parkland near the castle to the town (now the Slottshotellet, recommended under "Sleeping in Kalmar"). Enjoy the time-passed cottages as you peek over fences into private gardens. At the intersection, continue straight with the cobbles, then follow the path through the middle of the big park. As you cross the road on the other side of the park, and continue onto the gravel road, you'll pass a small surviving chunk of Kalmar's town wall on the right. Straight ahead and on the left is the entrance to the...

▲Krusenstiernska Gården—This relaxed, kid-friendly garden, with its breezy café selling traditional homemade cakes, is a treat. Poke inside to discover a manicured world of charming plantings clustered around a well (free; June–Aug Mon–Fri 11:00–18:00, Sat–Sun 12:00–17:00, except closed Sat in July; Sept Mon–Fri 11:00–16:00, closed Sat–Sun; May Mon–Fri 11:00–17:00, Sat–Sun 12:00–17:00; closed Oct–April; Stora Dammgatan 11, tel. 0480/411-552).

On most weekday afternoons, you can take a guided tour of the early-19th-century upper-middle-class **home** located in the garden. It's lovingly cluttered with old family photos, toys, and Gustavian-style furniture. A helpful English leaflet gives a room-by-room inventory (tour-25 kr; June–Aug Tue–Fri at 13:00, 14:00, and 15:00; no tours Sat–Mon).

On summer evenings, this garden is a venue for a Swedish comedy duo, Allan Svensson and Suzanne Reuter—stars of one of Sweden's most popular sitcoms of all time, the 1990s hit *Svensson, Svensson.* (Think of it as the Swedish *Honeymooners.*) Their sold-out shows here in July and early August flood the town with Swedish comedy fans, bringing new life to this otherwise sedate quarter of town.

• *Leaving the garden, follow the red fence to the right, along the top of the park. At the end of the fence (and park), jog left and squeeze between the yellow and red houses, heading up Gamla (G:a) Kungsgatan. Immerse yourself in this Swedish village world. At the fork, the yellow cottage on the right, surrounded by an almost huggable flower garden, often wins nationwide garden contests. About 20 yards farther down on the left, you'll reach the...*

Old Churchyard (Gamla Kyrkogården)—Dating from the 13th century, this field scattered with headstones is virtually all that remains of the original Old Town. Look for the monument topped by a statue of a man carrying a boy (St. Christopher, patron of traders and seafarers). Circling this slab, you'll see the floor plan of the original cathedral, an image looking down the cathedral's nave, and a rendering of the town before it was destroyed. The cathedral tower—which had partially survived the 1647 fire—was torn down in 1678 by the Swedes themselves, who wanted to ensure that their enemies (i.e., the Danes) couldn't use the tower to launch an attack on the castle.

About 50 yards farther into the yard, the stone slab on the pedestal (marked *Kalmarunionen 600 ar*) commemorates the 600th anniversary of the 1397 Kalmar Union, which united the Nordic states. On June 14, 1997, the contemporary leaders of those same nations—Sweden, Norway, Denmark, Finland, and Iceland—came here to honor that union. You can see their signatures etched in the stone.

• *Exit the churchyard the way you came in, and turn right on the paved street (along the big building). Take the first left (down Kungsgatan) and you'll wind up back on the main boulevard. The castle entrance is just across the boulevard, and on your left is the appealing, recommended Söderportcafé.*

But first, stretching to the left of the castle (across the boulevard) is Kalmar's best public space...

Town Park (Stadsparken)—This entertaining English-style garden is Kalmar's playground. While thoughtfully planned, it's also rugged, with surprises around each corner. Locals brag that their region is a "banana belt" that enjoys a milder climate than most of Sweden; some of the plants here grow nowhere else in the country. This diversity of foliage, and the many sculptures and monuments, make the park a delight to explore.

• *The big, black, mysterious-looking box in the middle of the park is the new...*

Kalmar Art Museum (Kalmar Konstmuseum)—Completed in 2008, this bold museum building caused quite a stir in Kalmar, both for its expense and for the way it faces down the fanciful medieval/Renaissance castle with a jolt of staid modernity. Its interior, with clean concrete spaces, is ideal for showing off constantly changing exhibits of modern and contemporary art. Some rooms provide fine views back on the castle. If the exhibits advertised appeal to you—or if you're an art-lover intrigued by the space—it's worth a visit (40 kr, daily 11:00–17:00, Wed until 20:00, Stadsparken, tel. 0480/426-282, www.kalmarkonstmuseum.se).

Attached to the museum—and complementing its style, though it was built some 70 years earlier—is the recommended **Byttan restaurant.** This is a good spot for a meal or a drink, with cozy indoor or castle-view outdoor seating.

• *Our walk is finished. The castle is easy to visit from here. If you have time for a long walk (or a bike or car ride), consider exploring the coastline beyond (southwest of) Kalmar Castle, lined with more parks and inviting beaches. About a mile after the castle is the charming little seafront community of* ***Stensö****, with its own pocket-size harbor, charming* *fishing cottages, and (another half-mile farther) a lightly forested island with a popular campground (www.stensocamping.se).*

In Kvarnholmen, Kalmar's Town Center

Today, downtown Kalmar is on the island of Kvarnholmen. Get your bearings with the following walk, and then—if you're interested—dig into its museums.

Kvarnholmen Self-Guided Walk—Most action centers on the lively, restaurant-and-café-lined square called **Larmtorget**, a few steps uphill from the train station. This is the most inviting square in town for outdoor dining—scout your options for dinner later tonight. The fountain depicts David standing triumphantly over the slain Goliath—a thinly veiled allusion to King Gustav Vasa, who defeated the Danes (the fountain's reliefs depict his arrival in Kalmar in 1520). The area just to the north, up Larmgatan, is a charming old quarter (with a recently restored old water tower and the historic Västerport gate) that's worth exploring.

But for now, we'll stroll straight through town on the main pedestrian shopping street, **Storgatan.** Because Kvarnholmen is a planned Renaissance town (built after the devastating 1647 fire consumed the Old Town), it's laid out on a regular grid plan. This uniformity makes it a bit less appealing than it could be, and a 1960s push to "modernize" the town stripped away whatever Old World character the place once enjoyed. Still, the lack of traffic on most of its central streets makes Kvarnholmen a delightful place to stroll. And some buildings still have stories to tell.

The first major cross-street, Kaggensgatan, leads (to the right) down to the town harbor; a block to the left, on the right-hand side (at #26), is the landmark Kullzénska Café, whose owners refused to let it be torn down to make way for "progress" (it remains a good place for a drink or light meal in a genteel setting—see "Eating in Kalmar," later).

Back on Storgatan, on the right just before the big square (after #20), look for the building marked *1667,* with the cannonballs decorating the doorway. This was the home of a war profiteer—a lucrative business in this military-minded town.

Storgatan leads to the main square, **Stortorget.** Built in the 17th century in a grand style befitting a European power, the square tries a little too hard to show off—today it feels too big and too quiet (locals prefer hanging out on the cozier Larmtorget where this walk started). The numbered spaces in the cobbles show where market stalls were located (though there's no regular market schedule today).

The **cathedral** *(domkyrkan)* dominating the square is the biggest and (some say) finest Baroque church in Sweden. Its interior, which contains a gigantic pulpit and bells from the earlier town cathedral, is nearing the end of an ambitious restoration (if it's open, step inside to check on the progress).

Facing the cathedral is the decorated facade of the **Town Hall** *(rådhuset)*. Notice the biggest windows are on the second (middle) floor, where the courts are located. During the spring (generally May and June), you can duck around the left side of the Town Hall and poke into its courtyard to see the blooming "handkerchief tree," whose flowers have hanky-sized petals.

From here, you have two options:

Beaches and Parks (East): Continue straight through Stortorget, and proceed three more blocks on Storgatan. The area beyond Östra Vallgatan (the old eastern wall of the city) has a pleasant park and small swimming beach. This area is called Kattrumpan (literally, "cat's rear end") because of the widely held and disturbing notion that Kvarnholmen looks like a cat's skin splayed out. To the left, on a little pier in the water, look for the last remaining *Klapphus* in Kalmar. In the mid-1800s, there were four of these small, wooden buildings—used for washing laundry—at the seaside. Today the *Klapphus* is still occasionally used for washing rugs and carpets; take a peek inside and see if anyone is at work. Across the water is the island neighborhood of Varvsholmen, which once housed an eyesore shipyard, but in the last decade was converted into a futuristic residential development. Just for fun, imagine if they did this with the grim industrial zone in your hometown. To the left of Varvsholmen is the sleepy residential island neighborhood of Ängö, traditionally home to sailors and fishermen, now one of Kalmar's most desirable areas.

Or, also from Stortorget, you can head for the...

Ramparts and Harbor (South): Turn right on Sjögatan (at the start of Stortorget) and head down to the little square called Lilla Torget, with some fine old wooden homes. Just beyond, the surviving ramparts (which are free to walk on top of) mark the old harbor line. It's strange to think that these sturdy ramparts became largely irrelevant so soon after they were built, when the Swedish-Danish border shifted dramatically to the south. As you pass through the walls, a giant, modern shopping mall called Baronen is ahead and to the right; beyond it, around the little guest harbor, is the maritime academy building that also houses the TI. To the left are some charming old merchant houses and the stand-alone old Customs House (Tullhuset); beyond those, the waterfront is dominated by giant red-brick buildings—steam mills once used to grind flour and strip rice. Today this complex houses a concert hall and the Kalmar County Museum, worth visiting and described next.

▲▲Kalmar County (Läns) Museum—Dedicated to telling the story of Kalmar County, this museum is worth a visit mostly for its excellent exhibit on the royal ship *Kronan,* a shipwrecked 17th-century warship that still sits on the bottom of the Baltic just off the island of Öland. Soggy bits and rusted pieces, well-described in English, give visitors a here's-the-buried-treasure thrill. It's a much more intimate look at life at sea than Stockholm's grander *Vasa* Museum—though, crucially, this exhibit lacks the boat's actual hull.

Cost, Hours, Location: 50 kr; June–Aug daily 10:00–17:00; Sept–May Mon–Fri 10:00–16:00, Sat–Sun 11:00–16:00; Skeppsbrogatan 51, tel. 0480/451-300, www.kalmarlansmuseum.se.

➲ **Self-Guided Tour:** As you enter the building, notice that from the museum's door, you can see the distant half of the long bridge leading to the island of Öland (described later).

Beyond the entry, the first floor has temporary exhibits and shows off the cannons recovered from the *Kronan* wreckage. In those days, cannons were so valuable they were prized the way a Rolls Royce would be today, so each one has its own story (described in English). In the years following the ship's sinking, these cannons were the only artifacts worth recovering.

The stairs and elevator in the center of the building let you zip right to your choice of exhibits. Floor 2 has skippable exhibits on the history of Kalmar County from the Bronze Age and more temporary exhibits.

From the first floor, I'd head right for the highlight: Floor 3, which displays salvage from the ***Kronan.*** Twice the size of Stockholm's famous *Vasa*, this warship was a floating palace and the most heavily armed vessel in the world. But it exploded and sank about three miles beyond the island of Öland in 1676. The giant illustration at the elevator shows the dramatic event: The *Kronan*'s admiral misjudged conditions and harnessed too much wind, causing the vessel to tip and its gun ports to fill with water. As the ship began to list into the water, a fallen lantern ignited explosives in the hold, and...BLAM! The ship was a goner, and its Danish and Dutch foes—who hadn't fired a shot—watched it sink into the deep. Of the 850 people on board, only about 40 were rescued. The wreck's whereabouts were forgotten until 1980, when it was rediscovered by the same oceanographer who found the *Vasa*.

Head into the exhibit, where you'll view a model of the shipwreck site (press the button for a seven-minute English explanation). You'll see a cross-section of the mighty vessel; a recovered carving of the potbellied Swedish king (one of many such carvings that decorated the ship); a street scene from Kalmar in that era, also illustrated by a good map and model; and an excellent 12-minute film about the ship (push the button for English).

The replica of the middle gun deck leads to the exhibit's most interesting section, which explains everyday life on board. The sailors who manned the ship numbered 850 (about the population of a mid-sized town of that age) and represented all walks of life, "all in the same boat." Engaging illustrations, eyewitness accounts, and actual salvage items bring the story to life. You'll see guns, musical instruments, a medicine chest, dishes, and clothing—items that emphasize the nautical lifestyles of the simple, common people who worked and perished on the ship. A treasure chest contains coins from all around the known world at the time, each one lovingly displayed and carefully identified.

The final exhibit reminds us that the *Kronan* still sits on the sea floor, awaiting funding to be raised to the surface. You'll see the diving bell that was used for very early dives to the site. Today a dedicated crew of scientists and enthusiasts—including, at times, Sweden's King Carl XVI Gustav—continue to dive to recover bits and pieces.

For extra credit, head up to Floor 4 for its exhibit on **Jenny Nyström,** an early-1900s Kalmar artist who gained fame for her cute Christmas illustrations featuring elves and pixies. You'll see some of her children's books and textbooks, as well as some less commercial, more artistic portraits (with a touch of Art Nouveau flair). Ponder Nyström's status as a proto-feminist icon, as she was one of the first female artists who supported her family by selling her paintings. Nearby are other exhibits and a tiny café serving light lunches.

Maritime History Museum (Sjöfartsmuseum)—This humble, dusty little exhibit sits a long block beyond and behind the Kalmar County Museum. It's a jumble of photos of vessels, model boats, charts, and other seafaring bric-a-brac that trace the nautical story of Kalmar up to modern times. The collection is displayed in three rooms of a former apartment, shuffled between beautiful porcelain stoves left behind by a previous owner. While it's well-explained by the 10-kr English booklet, the exhibit is really interesting only if you sail (30 kr, mid-June–mid-Sept daily 11:00–16:00, off-season open only Sun 12:00–16:00, Södra Långgatan 81, tel. 0480/15875).

Sleeping in Kalmar

(7 kr = about $1, country code: 46, area code: 0480)
The TI can nearly always find you a room in a private home (400–500 kr per double, 50-kr fee per booking, no breakfast). They can also get you special last-minute discounts on fancy hotels.

In Kalmar's Town Center (Kvarnholmen)

$$$ Calmar Stadshotell is an uninspired, 126-room business hotel filling a historic shell right on Kalmar's too-big main square, Stortorget. The standard rooms are rather faded, but you can pay 200 kr extra for a bigger, renovated "superior" room (standard Sb-1,280/895 kr, standard Db-1,495/1,050 kr, all rooms often cheaper on winter weekends; elevator, free Wi-Fi in some rooms—request when you reserve, Stortorget 14, tel. 0480/496-900, fax 0480/496-910, www.profilhotels.se, calmarstadshotell@profilhotels.se).

$$ Frimurare Hotellet fills a grand old building overlooking Kalmar's most inviting square, just steps from the train station. The place has soul and is warmly run by Marianne, her daughter Linda, and a disarmingly friendly staff. Rich public areas, broad hardwood halls, chandeliers, and pilasters give it 19th-century elegance. Guests can help themselves to coffee, tea, and cookies in the lounge anytime. The 35 rooms have been thoughtfully renovated and provide modern comfort amid period decor. Because it's squeezed between a café-packed square and a park that's popular for concerts, it can come with some noise (Sb-1,000/750 kr, Db-1,210/920 kr, these special rates promised with this book, family rooms at same price as doubles, non-smoking, elevator, pay Wi-Fi, free sauna, bike rental-50 kr/day, 50 yards in front of train station facing square at Larmtorget 2, tel. 0480/15230, fax 0480/85887, www.frimurarehotellet.com, info@frimurarehotellet.com).

Outside the Town Center

$$$ Slottshotellet ("Castle Hotel") is an enticing splurge in the atmospheric Old Town. It's the nicely upgraded but still homey former mansion of a local big shot. The 44 rooms—some in the mansion, others sprinkled throughout nearby buildings—sit across a leafy boulevard from Kalmar's Town Park, just up the street from the castle (standard Sb-1,390/1,190 kr, standard Db-1,590/1,390 kr, bigger "superior" Db-1,790/1,590 kr, free Wi-Fi, Slottsvägen 7, tel. 0480/88260, www.slottshotellet.se, info@slottshotellet.se).

$$ Hotell Hilda has eight good rooms in an updated old house, located in a modern residential zone just over the canal from the town center (Sb-695 kr, Db-995 kr, elevator, free Wi-Fi, free parking, Esplanaden 33, tel. 0480/54700, www.hotellhilda.se, info@hotellhilda.se). The ground-floor Kallskänken café, which doubles as the reception, serves good salads and sandwiches (40-kr sandwiches, 55-kr salads, Mon–Fri 8:00–18:00, Sat 8:00–14:00, closed Sun; if arriving to check in outside of these opening times, call ahead for the door code).

$$ Hotell Svanen, a 15-minute walk or short bus ride from the center in the Ängö neighborhood, is a new breed of budget hotel with a mix of nicer hotel rooms with private bath, cheaper rooms with shared bath, and hostel beds (no more than six beds per room). All guests have access to laundry and kitchen facilities, a TV room, Internet access (60 kr/hr), and a sauna. While it's a bit institutional, you can't argue with the value (hotel: S-550 kr, Sb-670–795 kr, D-730 kr, Db-840–950 kr, price depends on size, includes sheets and breakfast; hostel: dormitory bed-195 kr, D-450 kr, Db-550 kr, T-675 kr, Tb-780 kr, Q-900 kr, Qb-980 kr, sheets-55 kr, no member discount, breakfast-70 kr; reception open daily 7:30–21:00, elevator, Rappegatan 1, tel. 0480/25560, fax 0480/88293, www.hotellsvanen.se, info@hotellsvanen.se). You'll see a blue-and-white hotel sign and a hostel symbol at the edge of town on Ängöleden street, a mile from the train station. Catch bus #402 at the station to Ängöleden (2–3/hr, 5 min, 20 kr, pay driver), or take a taxi for about 70 kr. They rent canoes for exploring the small bays around Kalmar (100 kr/half-day, 170 kr/day).

$ Söderportsgården, a university dorm with 35 simple yet classy rooms above a popular music café (mentioned under "Eating in Kalmar," next), welcomes tourists from mid-June through mid-August. It's idyllically located in the Old Town, across the tree-lined boulevard from the Town Park and the entrance to Kalmar Castle (S-550 kr, D-695 kr, Db-795 kr, Tb-995 kr, Qb-1,390 kr, includes sheets and breakfast, Slottsvägen 1, tel. & fax 0480/12501, www.soderportsgarden.se).

Eating in Kalmar

Kalmar has a surprising number of good dining options for a small city. For lunch, look for the *dagens rätt* (daily special) for 70–90 kr, which gets you a main dish, salad, bread, and usually coffee or a soft drink. Many restaurants in Kalmar offer fixed-price meals at dinner.

In Kalmar's Town Center (Kvarnholmen)

All of these are in the downtown pedestrian zone.

Källaren Kronan, open only for dinner (except on Sat), is an elegant candlelit cellar restaurant with tables under stone arches. They serve old-time Swedish dishes as well as modern cuisine (85–125-kr starters, 115–225-kr main dishes, 210-kr two-course meals, 250-kr three-course meals, 150-kr three-course veggie meals, Tue–Fri 18:00–23:00, Sat 12:00–23:00, Sun 17:00–22:00, closed Mon, look for stairwell just inside southern town wall at Ölandsgatan 7, tel. 0480/411-400).

Calmar Hamnkrog is *the* place for a dressy harborview meal among the Swedish sailing set. Its mod white interior creates a cool elegance; call ahead to reserve window seating (100–150-kr starters, 230-kr main dishes, 95-kr lunch specials, 295-kr fish and seafood dinner buffet—summer only, 325-kr three-course dinners, Mon–Fri 11:30–14:00 and 18:00–22:00, Sat 18:00–22:00, closed Sun, in peak season open Sun 12:00–20:00 and longer hours on other days, just beyond the Baronen mall at Skeppsbrogatan 30, tel. 0480/411-020).

Kullzénska Café is a cozy, antique-filled eatery in a historic building. Locals adore its cakes and sandwiches (Mon–Fri 10:00–18:30, Sat 10:00–15:30, Sun 12:00–16:30, Kaggensgatan 26 at the corner of Norra Långgatan, go up the stairs).

Pizzeria Italia, right on the main Storgatan shopping street, is a handy place to get a break from Swedish food. While they serve up yummy pizzas (60–80 kr, or 160–200 kr for family-size), the best deal might be their all-you-can-eat buffets: pizzas at lunch (85 kr on Mon–Fri 11:00–15:30; 95 kr on Sat 12:00–16:00) and tacos at dinner (95 kr, Mon–Thu 16:00–20:30; both buffets include drinks). Sit inside or out front (open Mon–Thu 11:00–21:00, Fri 11:00–22:00, Sat 12:00–22:00, closed Sun, Storgatan 10, tel. 0480/87087).

Supermarket: In the pedestrian district, you'll find the **Co-op/Konsum** in the Kvasten mall, at the corner of Kaggensgatan and Storgatan (daily 8:00-22:00, if mall is closed, you can enter supermarket around the corner on Norra Långgatan).

Near the Castle

The castle lawn cries out for a picnic (buy one in the town center before your visit). Or you can grab a bite in the café inside the castle itself. Otherwise, consider one of these options.

Byttan sits in a landmark 1930s functionalist building adjoining the new art museum in the leafy Town Park, offering fine dining (or just a coffee break) with views of the castle. Choose between trendy indoor and castle-view outdoor tables. In summer only, their best deal is the all-you-can-eat buffet, offered at lunch for 95 kr (available Mon–Fri 11:30–14:30) and at dinner, called the "grill buffet," for 225 kr (from 18:00). You can order off the menu anytime (Mon–Fri 11:00–22:00, Sat 12:00–22:00, Sun 12:00–17:00, you'll pass it as you walk to the castle, tel. 0480/16360).

Söderportcafé, just across the street from the castle drawbridge, is handy for a quick, light lunch or afternoon snack.

They're well-regarded locally for their live music in the evenings (meals 100–160 kr, dinner buffet 250 kr, Mon–Fri 9:00–23:00, Sat 13:00–23:00, Sun 13:00–22:00, Slottsvägen 1).

Kalmar Connections

From Kalmar by Train to: Växjö (12/day, 60–70 min), **Copenhagen** and its airport (8/day, 3.5–4 hrs, transfer in Alvesta), **Stockholm** (8/day, 3.5 hrs, transfer in Alvesta or Linköping, reservations required).

By Bus to Stockholm: The bus to Stockholm is much cheaper but also much slower than the train (3/day, fewer on weekends, 6 hrs, 350 kr, 10 percent discount if you buy your ticket a day in advance).

Route Tips for Drivers

Kalmar to Copenhagen: See "Route Tips for Drivers" at the end of the Near Copenhagen chapter.

Kalmar to Stockholm (230 miles, 6 hrs): Leaving Kalmar, follow *E-22 Lindsdal* and *Nörrköping* signs. Sweden did a cheap widening job, paving the shoulders of the old two-lane road to get 3.8 lanes. Fortunately, traffic is polite and sparse. There's little to see, so stock the pantry, set the compass on north, and home in on Stockholm. Make two pleasant stops along the way: Västervik and the Göta Canal.

Västervik is 90 miles north of Kalmar, with an 18th-century core of wooden houses (3 miles off the highway, *Centrum* signs lead you to the harbor). Park on the waterfront near the great little smoked-fish market (Mon–Sat).

Sweden's famous **Göta Canal** consists of 190 miles of canals cutting the country in half, with 58 locks *(slussen)* working up to a summit of 300 feet. It was built 150 years ago, with more than seven million 12-hour man-days (60,000 men working about 22 years) at a low ebb in the country's self-esteem—to show her industrial might. Today it's a lazy three- or four-day tour, which shows Sweden's zest for good living.

Take just a peek at the Göta Canal over lunch, in the medieval town of **Söderköping:** Stay on E-22 past where you'd think you'd exit for the town center, then turn right at the *Kanalbåtarna/Slussen*. Look for the *Kanal P* signs leading to a handy canalside parking lot. From there, walk along the canal into the action. The TI on Söderköping's Rådhustorget (a square about a block off the canal) has good town and Stockholm maps, a walking brochure, and canal information (www.ostergotland.info). On the canal is the Kanalbutiquen, a yachters' laundry, shower, shop, and WC, with idyllic picnic grounds just above the lock. From the lock, stairs lead up to the Utsiktsplats pavilion (commanding view).

From Söderköping, E-22 takes you to Nörrköping. Follow *E-4* signs through Nörrköping, past a handy rest stop, and into Stockholm. The *Centrum* is clearly marked. (Viking's ferry terminal for Helsinki is in Södermalm; Silja's is northeast of town in Ropsten and is called Stockholm Värtan—see ferry terminal info in beginning of Helsinki chapter, page 473.)

Near Kalmar: The Island of Öland

The island of Öland—90 miles long and only 8 miles wide—is a pleasant resort known for its windmills, wildflowers, old limestone buildings, happy birdwatchers, prehistoric sights, roadside produce stands on the honor system, and Swede-filled beaches. This castaway island, with only about 25,000 permanent residents, attracts some 2.5 million visitors annually. It's a top summer vacation destination for Swedes—even the king and queen have their summer home here. Because of its relatively low rents, better weather, and easy bridge access to the mainland, Öland is also a popular bedroom community for Kalmar. If you've got a car, good weather, and some time to kill—and if the place isn't choked with summer crowds—Öland is a fine destination for a quick joyride. (For a basic map of Öland, see page 427.)

Dubbed the "Island of Sun and Wind," Öland enjoys an even warmer climate than already-mild Kalmar, and a steady sea breeze. And, because its top layer of soil was scraped off by receding glaciers, it has a completely different landscape than the pines-and-lakes feel of mainland Sweden. The island's chalky limestone, rich soil, and lush vegetation make it feel almost more Mediterranean than Baltic. Öland is one of Sweden's premier agricultural zones. Some call it "Sweden's Provence." While that's a stretch, skeptical visitors are pleasantly surprised by its colorful wildflowers (in spring) and by the bright sunshine, which works like a magnet both on holidaymakers and on artists.

Centuries ago, the entire island was the king's private hunting ground. Because local famers were not allowed to fell trees, they made their simple houses out of limestone. The island's 34 limestone churches, which were also used for defense, have few windows. Stone walls demarcate property and were used to contain grazing livestock.

When built in 1972, the **Öland Bridge** from Kalmar to the island was Europe's longest (free, 3.7 miles). The channel between Kalmar and Öland is filled with underwater rocks, making passage here extremely treacherous—but ideal for the Vikings' flat-bottomed boats. (In fact, "Kalmar" comes from the phrase "stones in water.") The little town of Färjestaden, near the island end of the bridge, was once the "ferry town" where everyone came and went; today it sits sad and neglected.

Getting There: Public transportation is tricky but workable; the island is most worthwhile if you have a car and at least three extra hours to explore. **Drivers** simply head north from Kalmar a few minutes on highway 137 to the Öland Bridge. Once across, highway 136 is the island's main north-south artery. **Buses** regularly connect Kalmar with the town of Borgholm (nearly hourly in summer, 50–60 min, 52 kr, off-season every 2 hrs) and, with less frequency, to other Öland destinations (check www.klt.se). **Bikers** who are in shape might enjoy biking to and around Öland, but note that you're not allowed to ride your bike on the bridge; instead, take the free, hourly shuttle bus that carries bikers across (catch it at the start of the bridge). It's possible to rent bikes on Öland, including in Borgholm (though hours and quantities are limited—try to call and pre-arrange, see below).

Sights on Öland

Visitors can (and do) spend days exploring this giant island's pleasures. But on a quick visit of a few hours, you'll want to narrow your focus. Your basic choices are center/north Öland (more developed and resorty, with royal sights, and easier to reach on a quick visit) or south Öland (more rugged and remote-feeling, with prehistoric sites, and demanding more time). I've outlined a few basic ideas for each area below, but these are just the beginning—there's much more to discover on Öland.

Central/North Öland

On a quick spin to the island, I'd stick with the strip of Öland just north of the bridge. As you drive north along highway 136, keep an eye out for some of Öland's characteristic, old-fashioned windmills. Occasional stone churches dot the landscape (including the one in Räpplinge—just off the main road—where the royals worship when in town).

The island's main town is **Borgholm** (BOY-holm), about a 30-minute drive north of the bridge. Borgholm itself isn't much to see, unless you enjoy watching Swedes at play. It's got a smattering of turn-of-the-century wooden villas, erected here after the royal palace was built nearby (described below). Notice that many of these have a humble shack in the garden: Locals would move into these cottages so they could rent the main villa to vacationing Stockholmers in the summer and make a killing. The traffic-free main drag, Storgatan, is lined with tacky tourist shops and ice-cream parlors (Ölandsglass, at #10, is tops). At the handy **TI,** in the old train depot a five-minute walk up from the town center, you can get maps and advice for your visit (generally Mon–Fri 9:00–17:30, in summer until 18:00 and also 10:00–16:00 on Sat and sometimes Sun, Sandgatan 25, tel. 0485/89000). This is where buses from Kalmar arrive. To rent a bike, get tips from the TI, or try Hallbergs Hojar (mobile 070-514-1937).

A pair of interesting sights sits on the hill just above Borgholm (to reach them, you can either drive or hike—get details at TI). **Borgholm Castle** (Borgholms Slott), which looks like Kalmar Castle with its top blown off, broods on the bluff above town, as if to remind visitors of the island's onetime strategic function. Its hard-fought history has left it as the empty shell you see today—impressive, but not worth the 50-kr entry fee (www.borgholms slott.se).

From near the castle, you can hike down to a more recent and appealing royal sight, the current royal summer residence, **Solliden Palace** (Sollidens Slott). It was built in 1906 in an Italian villa style, after the tastes of the Austrian-import queen, who hated Sweden. The palace interior is off-limits, but its sprawling, gorgeously landscaped garden is open to us commoners. Divided into Italian (geometrical and regimented), English (rough), and Dutch (flowers) sections, the Solliden garden complex is well worth a wander (70 kr, mid-May–mid-Sept daily 11:00–18:00, last entry at 17:00, closed in winter, on-site café open the same hours, tel. 0485/15356, www.sollidens slott.se).

The Swedish royalty is smart about not testing the patience of their subjects. The palace and garden complex is financially self-sufficient. And locals brag that when the royals come down from Stockholm, they fly commercial. If the first two rows are open when you board your Stockholm–Kalmar flight, you know it'll soon be filled by a royal backside.

South Öland

A 60-mile loop south of the bridge will give you a good dose of the island's more remote, windy rural charm. Head south on highway 136 to the part of the island that's characterized by the savannah-like Alvaret landscape, old graveyards, and mysterious prehistoric monuments.

Gettlinge Gravfält (off the road about 10 miles up from the south tip, just south of Smedby) is a wonderfully situated, boat-shaped, Iron Age graveyard littered with monoliths and overseen by a couple of creaky old windmills. It offers a commanding view of the windy and mostly treeless island.

Farther south is the **Eketorp Prehistoric Fort** (Eketorps Borg), a reconstructed fifth-century stone fort that, as Iron Age forts go, is fairly interesting. Several evocative huts and buildings are filled with what someone imagines may have been the style back then, and the huge rock fort is surrounded by strange, runty, piglike creatures, which were common in gardens 1,500 years ago. A sign reads: "For your convenience and pleasure, don't leave your children alone with the animals" (75 kr, May–Aug daily 10:00–17:00, July–mid-Aug until 18:00, free English tours daily—call for times, tel. 0485/662-000, www.eketorp.se). It's near the southern tip of the island, on the eastern side: When you approach Grönhögen on the main road from the north, look for signs on the left.

FINLAND

FINLAND

Suomi

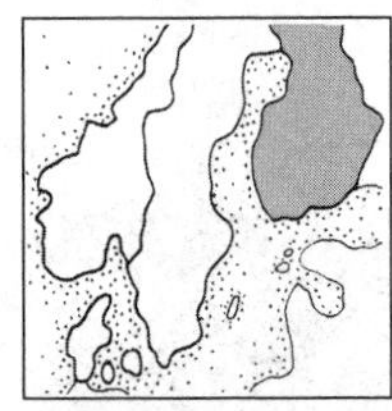

From medieval times to 1809, Finland was part of Sweden. City fires have left little standing from this period, but Finland still has a sizeable Swedish-speaking minority, bilingual street signs, and close cultural ties to Sweden.

In 1809, Sweden lost Finland to Russia. Under the next century of relatively benign Russian rule, Finland began to industrialize, and Helsinki grew into a fine and elegant city. Still, at the beginning of the 1900s, the rest of Finland was mostly dirt-poor and agricultural, and its people were eagerly emigrating to northern Minnesota. (Read Toivo Pekkanen's *My Childhood* to learn about the life of a Finnish peasant in the early 1900s.)

In 1917, Finland and the Baltic states won their independence from Russia, fought brief but vicious civil wars, and then enjoyed two decades of prosperity...until the secret Nazi–Soviet pact of August 1939 assigned them to the Soviet sphere of influence. When Russia invaded, only Finland resisted successfully, its white-camouflaged ski troops winning the Winter War against the Soviet Union in 1939–1940 and holding off the Russians in the Continuation War from 1941 to 1944.

After World War II, Finland was made to suffer for having fought against one of the Allied Powers. The Finns were forced to cede Karelia (eastern Finland) to the USSR, to accept Soviet naval bases on Finnish territory, and to pay huge reparations to the Soviet government. Still, Finland's bold, trendsetting modern design and architecture blossomed, and it built up successful timber, paper, and electronics industries. All through the Cold War, Finland teetered between the West and the Soviet Union, trying to be part of Western Europe's strong economy while treading lightly and making nice with her giant neighbor to the east. The collapse of the Soviet Union has done to Finland what a good long sauna might do to you.

When Moscow's menace vanished, so did about 20 percent of Finland's trade. After a few years of adjustment, Finland is on an upswing now. Many Finns used to move to Sweden (where they are the biggest immigrant group), looking for better jobs in

Stockholm. Some still nurse an inferiority complex, thinking of themselves as poor cousins to the Swedes. But now Finland is the most technologically advanced country in Europe. Home to the giant mobile-phone company Nokia, Finland has more mobile-phone numbers than fixed ones, and ranks fourth among European nations (15th globally) in the number of Internet users per capita. Finns are counting on their membership in the European Union and the euro zone to cement the strength of their economy.

We think of Finland as Scandinavian, but it's better to call it "Nordic." Technically, the Scandinavian countries are Denmark, Sweden, and Norway—all constitutional monarchies with closely related languages. Add Iceland, Finland, and maybe Estonia—former Danish or Swedish colonies that speak separate languages—and you have the "Nordic countries." Iceland, Finland, and Estonia are republics, not monarchies. In 1906, Finnish women were the first in Europe to vote, and today 40 percent of the Finnish parliament—as well as the Finnish president—is female.

Finland is known as a nation of few words; Finns value silence, yet are easily approachable. Tourists are not considered a headache to the locals the way they might be in places like Paris and Munich. Compared to Sweden or Denmark, Finland has not attracted many immigrants, and fewer of the service workers you'll encounter come from elsewhere.

Finnish is a difficult-to-learn Finno-Ugric language originating east of Russia's Ural Mountains; its only related European languages are Estonian (closely) and Hungarian (distantly).

Finland Almanac

Official Name: Republic of Finland.

Population: Finland is home to 5.2 million people (40 per square mile). The majority are Finnish in descent (93.4 percent). Other ethnicities include Swedish (5.6 percent), Russian, Estonian, Roma, and Sami (less than 1 percent each). The official languages are Finnish, spoken by 92 percent, and Swedish, spoken by 5.5 percent. Small minorities speak Sami and Russian. Finland is 83 percent Lutheran, 1 percent Orthodox, 1 percent other Christian, and 15 percent unaffiliated.

Latitude and Longitude: 64°N and 26°E, similar latitude to Nome, Alaska.

Area: 130,500 square miles (almost the size of Montana).

Geography: Finland is bordered by Russia to the east, Sweden and Norway to the north, the Baltic Sea to the west, and Estonia (across the Gulf of Finland) to the south. Much of Finland is flat and covered with forests, with the Lapland region extending north of the Arctic Circle. Finland is home to thousands of lakes and encompasses nearly as many islands: It has 187,800 lakes and 179,500 islands (the last time I counted).

Biggest City: Helsinki is the capital of Finland and has a population of 579,000; 1.3 million people—about one in four Finns—live in the Helsinki urban area.

Economy: Finland's Gross Domestic Product is $195 billion and its per capita GDP is $37,200. Manufacturing, timber, engineering, electronics, and telecommunications are its chief industries, with mobile phones among its top exports.

Currency: €1 (euro) = about $1.40.

Government: Finland has both a president, responsible for foreign policy, and a prime minister, who—along with the 200-member Parliament (Eduskunta)—is responsible for domestic legislation. President Tarja Halonen was reelected to a second six-year term in January 2006. Matti Vanhanen was reelected as prime minister in April 2007.

Flag: The Finnish flag is white with a blue Scandinavian cross. The blue represents the lakes of Finland and the white its winter snow.

The Average Finn: The average Finn is 42 years old, has 1.73 children, and will live to be 79.

Finland is officially bilingual, and about 1 in 20 residents speaks Swedish as a first language. You'll notice that Helsinki is called *Helsingfors* in Swedish. Helsinki's street signs list places in both Finnish and Swedish. Nearly every educated young person speaks effortless English—the language barrier is just a road turtle. But to get you started, I've included a selection of Finnish survival phrases on page 588.

The only essential word needed for a quick visit is *kiitos* (KEE-tohs)—that's "thank you," and locals love to hear it. *Hei* (hey) means "hi" and *hei hei* (hey hey) means "goodbye." *Kippis* (KIHP-pihs) is what you say before you down a shot of Finnish vodka or cloudberry liqueur *(lakka)*.

HELSINKI

The next best thing to being in Helsinki is getting there. Europe's most enjoyable cruise, from Stockholm to Helsinki, starts with dramatic archipelago scenery, a setting sun, and a royal *smörgåsbord* dinner. Dance until you drop and sauna until you drip. Budget travel rarely feels this hedonistic. Seventeen hours after you depart, it's "Hello Helsinki."

The Cruise from Stockholm to Helsinki

Two fine and fiercely competitive lines, Viking and Silja, connect the capitals of Sweden and Finland. Each line offers state-of-the-art ships with luxurious *smörgåsbord* meals, reasonable cabins, plenty of entertainment (discos, saunas, gambling), and enough duty-free shopping to sink a ship. Of the two, Viking has the reputation as the party boat. Silja is considered more elegant (but still has its share of sometimes irritating and noisy passengers).

The Pepsi and Coke of the Scandinavian cruise industry vie to outdo each other with bigger and fancier boats. The ships are big—at 56,000 tons, nearly 200 yards long, and with 2,700 beds, they're the largest (and cheapest) luxury hotels in Scandinavia. Many other shipping lines buy their boats used from Viking and Silja.

Which line is best? You could count showers and compare *smörgåsbords,* but both lines go overboard to win the loyalty of the

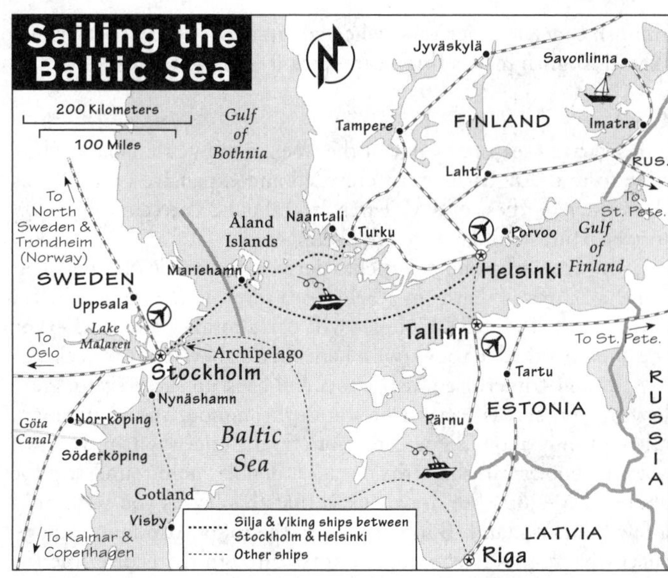

nine million duty free–crazy Swedes and Finns who make the trip each year. Viking has an older, less luxurious fleet, but caters better to low-budget travelers, selling cheap *ekonomi* cabins (shower down the hall) and allowing passengers to pay for deck passage only and sleep for free on chairs, sofas, and under the stars or stairs.

Cruise Schedules

Both Viking and Silja sail nightly from Stockholm and Helsinki year-round. In both directions, the boats leave about 17:00 and arrive the next morning around 10:00. Both companies also sail daily between Stockholm and Turku, Finland. For exact schedules, see www.vikingline.fi and www.silja.com.

Scenery: During the first few hours out of Stockholm, your ship passes through the *Skärgården* (archipelago). The third hour features the most exotic island scenery—tiny islets with cute red huts and happy people. I'd have dinner at the first sitting (shortly after departure) and be on deck for sunset. But if you don't like cold temperatures, book the second sitting because the deck gets chilly later in the cruise.

Time Change: Finland is one hour ahead of Sweden. Sailing from Stockholm to Helsinki, operate on Swedish time until you're ready to go to bed, then reset your watch. Morning schedules are

Finnish time, and vice versa when you return. The cruise-schedule flier in English makes this clear—pick it up as you board.

Cost

Fares vary by season, by day of the week, and by cabin class. Mid-June to mid-August is most crowded and expensive (with prices the same regardless of day). Fares drop about 25 percent off-season for departures Sunday through Wednesday.

In summer, a one-way ticket per person for the cheapest bed that has a private bath (in a below-sea-level, under-car-deck "C" quad) costs about €55. Couples will pay a total of about €150 for the cheapest double room (with bath) that's above the car deck.

Round-trip cruise fares (across and back on successive nights, leaving you access to your bedroom throughout the day) generally cost only about 25 percent more than a one-way trip. In peak season, couples can share the cheapest double cabin round-trip for about €220–260. The drawback is that this leaves you with only a few hours on land. But you can get the round-trip fare on non-successive nights if you book a hotel through the cruise line for every intervening night—if it fits your schedule, this is a good deal.

The fares are cheap because locals sail to shop and drink duty- and tax-free. It's a huge operation—mostly for locals. The boats are filled with about 45 percent Finns, 45 percent Swedes, and 10 percent cruisers from other countries. The average passenger spends as much on booze and duty-free items as for the boat fare. The boats now make a midnight stop in the Åland Islands—a self-governing, demilitarized province of Finland that's exempt from the European Union's Value-Added Tax (VAT)—to preserve the international nature of the trip and maintain the duty-free status.

Discounts: Travelers with railpasses that include Sweden or Finland get a 50 percent discount on deck passage on the Viking and Silja lines between Stockholm and Helsinki/Turku (doesn't use up a flexi-day); Silja extends the railpass discount to its cheapest cabin berths. Discounts can also be given for early booking, families (look for family-cabin rates), and seniors. Check the cruise lines' websites for specifics.

Age Restrictions: To take a Silja cruise, travelers under 21 unaccompanied by a parent or guardian will need a permission form (downloadable from their website) or a documented reason for their travel. Viking may deny passage or accept documentation, depending on the route. Check for age limits and regulations on the websites.

Reservations

For summer or weekend sailings, reserve well in advance. Both companies have US reservation lines: for Silja, call 800-533-3755 ext. 1

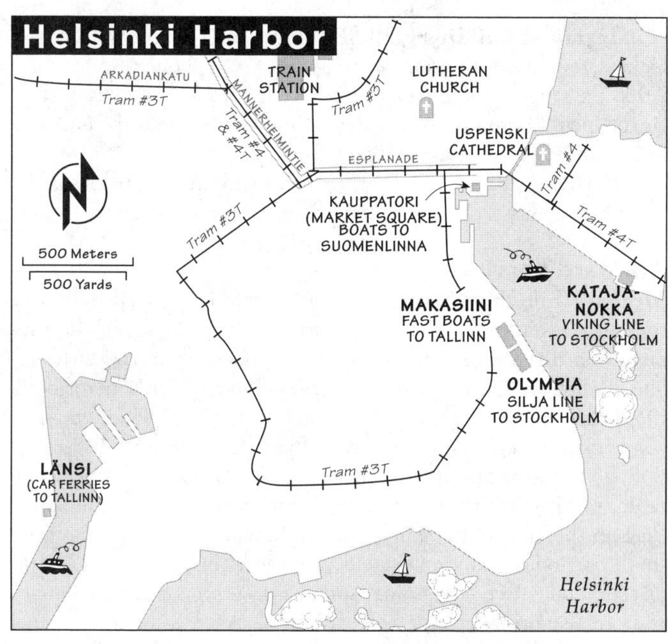

(www.seaeurope.com); for Viking, call 800-843-0602 (no online reservations).

If you're already in Scandinavia, call the cruise line direct to reserve your crossing: The Swedish reservations numbers are tel. 08/222-140 for Silja, and tel. 08/452-4000 for Viking. In Helsinki, call 09/18041 for Silja, or 09/12351 for Viking. You can pay by credit card and pick up your ticket at the terminal (arrive one hour before departure), or pick them up early at the city office (in Stockholm, Viking's is at Cityterminalen and Silja's is at Kungsgatan 2; in Helsinki, Viking's is at Mannerheimintie 14 and Silja's is at Mannerheimintie 2). Operators speak English. Any travel agent in Scandinavia can also sell you a ticket (with a small booking fee).

Terminals

Locations: In **Stockholm**, Viking Line ships moor at Stadsgården on Södermalm. To get there from Stockholm's bus station, take Viking's shuttle bus (30 kr) to the dock or public bus #53 to the Londonviadukten stop. Silja Line's harbor is northeast of the center and is called Stockholm Värtan. You can walk to the terminal from the Gärdet T-bana station (about 10 min), but it's easier to catch the Silja shuttle bus (40 kr) from the bus station.

In **Helsinki,** both lines are perfectly central, on opposite sides of the main harbor, a 10-minute walk from the center. See the Helsinki map on page 484 for details.

Terminal Buildings: These are well-organized, with cafés, lockers, tourist information desks, lounges, and phones. Remember, 2,000 passengers come and go with each boat. Customs is a snap. Boats open 90 minutes before departure, and you must be checked in 15 minutes before departure.

Parking: Both lines offer safe and handy parking in Stockholm. Ask for details when you reserve your ticket.

Onboard Services

Meals: While ships have cheap, fast cafeterias as well as classy, romantic restaurants, they are famous for their *smörgåsbord* dinners. Board the ship hungry. Dinner is self-serve in two sittings, one at about 18:00, the other a couple of hours later. Pay for both the dinner buffet (€42) and breakfast buffet (€13) when you buy your ticket (you'll save 10 percent). If you board without a reservation, go to the restaurant and make one. Make sure to reserve your table, not just your meal; window seats are highly sought after. Pick up the *How to Eat a Smörgåsbord* brochure. The key is to take small portions and pace yourself. (For more tips, see page 28.) The price includes free beer, wine, soft drinks, and coffee. Of course, you can also bring a picnic and eat it on deck.

Sauna: Each ship has a sauna, which costs about €8 extra. Silja also offers massage on board from 15:00 to 22:00, for an extra fee. Reserve sauna time or massage appointments immediately upon boarding.

Banking: Ships take euros and Swedish kronor, and just about every vendor or shop also accepts credit cards. Each boat has a handy exchange desk on board with acceptable rates. None of the boats has an ATM, but all terminals have ATMs and exchange windows.

Tourist Info on Board: Boats generally offer racks of *Stockholm* or *Helsinki This Week* magazines. Grab a copy for some practical bedtime reading.

Options

Tallinn: You can visit Tallinn as a day trip from Helsinki, or Helsinki as a day trip from Tallinn, or you can make a triangle trip: Stockholm–Helsinki–Tallinn–Stockholm, or vice versa. See the Tallinn chapter for details on the Helsinki–Tallinn and Stockholm–Tallinn crossings.

Turku: Both Viking and Silja also sail from Stockholm to Turku in Finland, a shorter crossing (11 hours, departing daily at about 7:00–9:00 and 19:30–21:00). Turku is two hours from Helsinki by bus or train. The boats are usually smaller, with less cruise-ship excitement. The cheaper fare saves you enough to pay for the train trip from Turku to Helsinki.

Helsinki

Helsinki is the only European capital with no medieval past. Although it was founded in the 16th century by the Swedes to counter Tallinn as a strategic Baltic port, the location was poor, and it never amounted to more than a village until the 18th century. In 1746, Sweden built a huge fortress on an island outside its harbor. The town of Helsinki grew up to supply the fortress. After taking over Finland in 1809, the Russians decided to move Finland's capital and university closer to St. Petersburg—from Turku to Helsinki. They hired a young German architect, Carl Ludvig Engel, to design new public buildings for Helsinki and told him to use St. Petersburg as a model. This is why the oldest parts of Helsinki (around Market Square and Senate Square) feel so Russian—stone buildings in yellow and blue pastels with white trim and columns. Hollywood used Helsinki for the films *Gorky Park* and *Dr. Zhivago,* because filming in Russia was not possible during the Cold War.

Though the city was part of the Russian Empire in the 19th century, most of its residents still spoke Swedish, which was the language of business and culture. In the mid-1800s, Finland began to industrialize. The Swedish upper class in Helsinki expanded the city, bringing in the railroad and surrounding the old Russian-inspired core with neighborhoods of four- and five-story apartment buildings, including some Art Nouveau masterpieces. Meanwhile, Finns moved from the countryside to Helsinki to take jobs as industrial laborers. The Finnish language slowly acquired equal status with Swedish, and eventually Finnish speakers became the majority in Helsinki.

Since downtown Helsinki didn't exist until the 1800s, it was more consciously designed and laid out than other European capitals. With its many architectural overleafs and fine Neoclassical and Art Nouveau buildings, Helsinki often turns guests into students of urban design and planning. In bookstores, look for the two concise guides to Helsinki architecture by Jonathan Moorhouse. Katajanokka, Kruununhaka, and Eira are good walking neighborhoods for architecture buffs.

Helsinki can be windy and cold, but it's worth the chill.

Planning Your Time

On a three-week trip through Scandinavia, Helsinki is worth at least the time between two successive nights on the cruise ship—about seven hours. To do the city justice, two days is ideal.

For a quick one-day visit, start with the two-hour orientation bus tour that meets the boat at the dock. Then take my self-guided walking tour through the compact city center from the harbor—enjoying Helsinki's ruddy harborfront market and getting goose bumps in the churches—to the National Museum of Finland. In the afternoon, dive into Finnish culture in the open-air folk museum or take a boat tour of the harbor. Enjoy a cup of coffee at the recommended Café Kappeli before sailing away.

Orientation to Helsinki

Helsinki's natural gateway is its harbor, where ships from Stockholm and Tallinn dock. At the top of the harbor is Market Square (Kauppatori), an outdoor food and souvenir bazaar. Nearby are two towering, can't-miss-them landmarks: the white Lutheran Cathedral and the brick Eastern Orthodox Uspenski Cathedral.

Helsinki's grand pedestrian boulevard, the Esplanade, begins right at Market Square, heads up past the TI, and ends after a few blocks in the central shopping district. The broad, traffic-filled Mannerheimintie, a bustling avenue that veers north through town past the train and bus stations, begins at the far end of the Esplanade. For a do-it-yourself orientation to town along this route, follow my "Hello Helsinki" self-guided walk on page 482. The "Tram #3T Tour" (see page 486) also provides a good drive-by introduction to the main sights.

Tourist Information

There are two TIs: a main TI on Market Square, and a small branch at the train station. The friendly, energetic **main TI** offers great service and is fun to graze through. It's located a half-block inland from Market Square, on the right just past the fountain, at the corner of the Esplanade and Unioninkatu (May–Sept Mon–Fri 9:00–20:00, Sat–Sun 9:00–18:00, closes two hours earlier off-season; Internet access, tel. 09/169-3757, www.visithelsinki.fi). Pick up the city map, the public-transit map, *Helsinki on Foot* (six well-described walking tours with maps, €3), the free monthly *Helsinki This Week* magazine (lists sights, hours, and events), and *City* magazine (good, opinionated restaurant listings, geared for the younger crowd, free). Ask for the brochure on the scenic #3T tram and go over your sightseeing plans.

The tiny **train-station TI,** which consists of a one-person desk inside the Helsinki Expert office, provides many of the same services and publications as the main TI and has similar hours.

Helsinki Expert: This private service sells the Helsinki Card (described next), ferry tickets, and transport passes, and also makes hotel bookings. They have one branch in the train station hall, another occupying the front desks in the main TI on Market Square, and a small sightseeing kiosk out on the Esplanade (summer only, not all services). They always know about wild bargains, like luxury-hotel clearance deals that cost only €20 more than the cheapies. There's a €5 fee for walk-in hotel reservations (email and phone reservations are free), and ferry bookings cost €8 (hours of branch at main TI: June–Aug Mon–Fri 9:00–19:00, Sat–Sun 9:00–17:00; Sept–May Mon–Fri 9:00–17:00, Sat 10:00–16:00, closed Sun; branch at train station has similar hours, tel. 09/2288-1500, fax 09/2288-1599, www.helsinkiexpert.fi).

Helsinki Card: If you're planning to do a lot of sightseeing in Helsinki, this card can be a good deal (€33/24 hours, €45/48 hours, €55/72 hours, includes free entry to over 50 museums, fortresses, and other major sights; free use of buses, trams, and the ferry to Suomenlinna; free audioguide city bus tour and discount on live-guide city bus tour; and a 72-page booklet; sold at all Helsinki Expert locations, most hotels, and both Viking and Silja ferry terminals, www.helsinkicard.com).

Arrival in Helsinki

By Boat: Helsinki has four boat terminals *(terminaali)*; for locations, see the map on page 473 and the color map in the front of this book. The Olympia and Makasiini terminals are on the west side (to the left as you face inland) of the main harbor. The Katajanokka terminal is on the east side (right) of the main harbor. Most Silja Line boats use the Olympia terminal; most Viking boats use the Katajanokka terminal. The Makasiini terminal is mostly for fast boats to Tallinn. Trams stop near all the main-harbor terminals. The Länsi terminal, in Helsinki's western harbor, is for large car ferries to Tallinn and is inconvenient to reach by public transportation (take a taxi).

By Train and Bus: The train station, an architectural landmark, is near the top of the Esplanade, a 15-minute walk from Market Square. Local buses leave from both sides of the building, trams stop out front, and the Metro runs underneath. The long-distance Kamppi bus station is two blocks away, on the other side of Mannerheimintie; the ticket windows are on the ground floor, with bus platforms below.

By Plane: To get between the airport and downtown Helsinki, take the Finnair bus (€6, downtown terminus is platform 30 at Elielinaukio on west side of train station, 3/hr, 35-min trip) or public bus #615 (€4, pay driver, not covered by Tourist Ticket transit pass, downtown terminus is platform 5 at Rautatientori on east side of train station, 2–4/hr, 45-min trip, also stops at Hakaniemi).

Or take the Yellow Line door-to-door shared van service (€22 for 1–2 people, €28 for 3–4 people, €40 for 5–6 people, €55 for a private taxi, tel. 010-00700 or toll tel. 0600-555-555, www.yellowline.fi). An ordinary taxi from the airport runs about €35.

Helpful Hints

US Embassy: It's at Itäinen Puistotie 14B (passport services available Mon–Thu 9:00–12:00, tel. 09/616-25701, http://finland.usembassy.gov).

Time: Finland and Estonia are one hour ahead of Sweden and the rest of Scandinavia.

Money: Finland's currency is the euro. ATM machines are labeled *Otto.*

Telephones: Finland doesn't have international phone cards. For cheap long distance, even locals use Skype at the Fexco Service Centre in the train station (www.fexco.se).

Finland's phone system generally uses area codes, but has some national numbers (starting with 010 or 020) that must be dialed in full when you're calling from anywhere in the country.

Pharmacy: A 24-hour pharmacy—*apteekki*—is located at Mannerheimintie 96 (tel. 020-320-200).

Internet Access: These places are handy: **National Museum of Finland** (six ignored and free terminals in its superb second-floor information center); **Mbar Café** (€5/hr, 10 terminals, Mon–Sat 9:00–24:00, Sun 12:00–22:00, in Lasipalatsi complex, Mannerheimintie 22–24, enter on Salomonkatu and go to the back); **Library 10** (12 free terminals in post office across from train station, Mon–Thu 10:00–22:00, Fri–Sun 12:00–18:00, pick up free visitors card from desk and ask for a time slot, often a wait, Elielinaukio 2G); and **City Hall** (facing Market Square on the harbor, with six free, fast terminals, Mon–Fri 9:00–19:00, Sat–Sun 11:00–17:00).

Bike Rental: Try **Greenbike** (one-speed bike-€15/12 hours, €20/24 hours; three-speed bike-€5 more; May–Sept daily 10:00–18:00, June–Aug until 20:00, Bulevardi 32, mobile 050-404-0400, www.greenbike.fi).

Best View: The **Torni Tower's Ateljee Bar** offers a free panorama view. Ride the elevator from the lobby of the venerable Torni Hotel (built in 1931) to the 14th floor, where you can browse around the perch or sit down for a drink (nightly until 24:00, Yrjonkatu 26, tel. 020-123-4604).

Getting Around Helsinki

In compact Helsinki, you won't need to use public transportation as much as in Stockholm.

By Bus and Tram: With the public-transit route map (available at the TI) and a little mental elbow grease, the buses and trams are easy, giving you Helsinki by the tail. Single tickets are good for an hour of travel (€2.50 from driver, €2 at automatic vending machines at larger stops). The Tourist Ticket (€6.80/24 hours of unlimited travel) pays for itself if you take three or more rides; longer versions are also available (€13.60/72 hours, €20.40/120 hours). The single Metro line uses the same tickets, but is not useful unless you're traveling to my recommended sauna (www.hkl.fi). Public transportation is covered by the Helsinki Card.

Tram #3T makes the rounds of most of the town's major sights in an hour. It runs every 10 minutes in a confusing but convenient figure-eight route; tram #3B follows the same route in the opposite direction. Either buy a single ticket—good for one hour—and stay on the tram for the circuit, or get the Tourist Ticket, allowing you to hop off to tour a sight, then catch a later tram. Ask for the helpful tram #3T explanatory brochure—available at TIs and often on board—and follow my self-guided tram tour (described later).

In summer, the antique red **Pub Tram** makes a 50-minute circle through the city while its passengers get looped on the beer for sale on board (€9 to ride, €5.50 beer, mid-May–Aug Tue–Sat 14:00–19:00, July until 20:00, no trams Sun–Mon, leaves at the top of each hour from in front of the Fennia building, Mikonkatu 17, across from train-station tower).

Tours in Helsinki

▲▲▲Orientation Bus Tours—These bus tours give an ideal city overview with a look at all the important buildings, from the recently remodeled Olympic Stadium to Embassy Row. A 10-minute stop at the Sibelius Monument is long enough, but 10 minutes is rushed at Temppeliaukio ("Church in the Rock"). You'll learn strange facts, such as how they took down the highest steeple in town during World War II so that the Soviet bombers flying in from Estonia couldn't see their target.

Bus Tours Departing from Boat Dock: Conveniently, the tours depart from each boat dock in the morning, soon after the boats arrive from Stockholm (generally around 10:30); tours end back at the dock they started from, though you can get off

Helsinki at a Glance

▲▲▲Temppeliaukio Church Awe-inspiring, copper-topped 1969 "Church in the Rock." **Hours:** Daily 10:00-18:00, until 20:00 most summer nights, closed to tourists Sunday morning. See page 491.

▲▲Lutheran Cathedral Green-domed, 19th-century Neoclassical masterpiece. **Hours:** June-Aug Mon-Sat 9:00-18:00, Sun 12:00-20:00, until midnight in summer many nights; Sept-May Mon-Sat 9:00-18:00, Sun 12:00-18:00. See page 489.

▲▲Uspenski Cathedral Orthodoxy's most prodigious display outside of Eastern Europe. **Hours:** May-Sept Mon-Fri 9:30-16:00, Tue until 18:00, Sat 9:30-15:00, Sun 12:00-15:00; Oct-April Tue-Fri 9:30-16:00, Sat 9:30-15:00, Sun 12:00-15:00, closed Mon. See page 490.

▲▲National Museum of Finland The scoop on Finland, featuring folk costumes, an armory, czars, and thrones; the prehistory exhibit is best. **Hours:** Tue-Wed 11:00-20:00, Thu-Sun 11:00-18:00, closed Mon. See page 492.

▲▲Seurasaari Open-Air Folk Museum Island museum with 100 historic buildings from Finland's farthest corners. **Hours:** June-Aug daily 11:00-17:00; late May and early Sept Mon-Fri 9:00-15:00, Sat-Sun 11:00-17:00, buildings closed mid-Sept-mid-May. See page 494.

▲▲Suomenlinna Fortress Helsinki's harbor island, sprinkled with picnic spots, museums, and military history. **Hours:** Daily May-Sept 10:00-18:00, Oct-April 10:00-16:00. See page 495.

▲Senate Square Consummate Neoclassical square, with Lutheran Cathedral. **Hours:** Always open. See page 490.

▲Sibelius Monument Stainless-steel sculptural tribute to Finland's greatest composer. **Hours:** Always open. See page 492.

▲Ateneum, The National Gallery of Finland Largest collection of art in Finland, including local favorites plus works by Cézanne, Chagall, Gauguin, and Van Gogh. Hours: Tue-Fri 10:00-18:00, Wed and Thu until 20:00, Sat-Sun 11:00-17:00, closed Mon. See page 492.

Kiasma Modern-art museum. **Hours:** Tue 10:00-17:00, Wed-Sun 10:00-20:30, closed Mon. See page 494.

downtown near the end of the tour. Both tours cost €25 and last just under two hours; the one leaving from the Silja dock has a live guide, while the Viking tour has an audioguide. You'll get a €3 discount if you book your tour on board or online at www.helsinkiexpert.fi. It's wise to book ahead—rather than just showing up at the bus—if you're counting on taking a tour.

Note that the Helsinki Card covers Viking's audioguide tour and gives a discount on Silja's live-guide tour. To get a Helsinki Card before the bus tour starts, buy it on board the Silja cruise ship, at either terminal (inside Silja's, outside Viking's), or online (www.helsinkicard.com or www.helsinkiexpert.fi). Show the card at the bus ticket booth to get your free or discounted tour.

If you want to take the bus tour and end up downtown for an overnight stay, stow your bag on the bus, and get off in the city center before the end of the tour (cost-effectively using the tour for transportation as well as for information).

Bus Tour Departing from the Center: A 1.5-hour audioguide bus tour leaves from Esplanade Park at the corner of Fabianinkatu and the Esplanade (€25, pay driver, free with Helsinki Card, June–Aug daily at 11:00, 12:00, 13:00, 14:00, and 15:00; off-season daily at 11:00, Sat–Sun also at 13:00, www.helsinkiexpert.fi). Reservations are recommended; your hotelier can make them for you.

Hop-on, Hop-off Bus Tour: Helsinki's Open Top Tours comes with a recorded narration and connects the main sights about every 20 minutes. Stops include the Olympia/Silja terminal, Market Square, Sibelius Monument, Temppeliaukio Church, and more (€25/24 hours, discounted to €10 with Helsinki Card, buy ticket on bus, 1.25 hrs, tel. 050/430-2050, www.stromma.se).

Harbor Tours—Several boat companies compete for your attention along Market Square, offering 90-minute, €19 cruises around the waterfront roughly hourly from 10:00 to 18:00 in summer. The narration is slow-moving—often recorded and in as many as four languages. I'd call it an expensive nap. Taking the ferry out to Suomenlinna and back gets you onto the water for much less money (€4.40, see page 497). But if the weather's good and you're looking for something one step above a snooze in the park...then all aboard.

Local Guides—Helsinki Expert can arrange a private guide (book at least three days in advance, €170/3 hours, tel. 09/2288-1222). **Christina Snellman** is a good licensed, local guide (mobile 050-527-4741, chrisder@pp.inet.fi).

Self-Guided Walk

▲▲Hello Helsinki

This walk offers a convenient spine for your Helsinki sightseeing.

❶ Market Square: Start at the obelisk in the center of the harborfront market. This is the Czarina's Stone, with its double-headed eagle of imperial Russia. It was the first public monument in Helsinki, designed by Carl Ludvig Engel and erected in 1835 to celebrate the visit by Czar Nicholas I and Czarina Alexandra. Step over the chain and climb to the top step for a clockwise spin-tour:

The big, red Viking ship and white Silja ship are each floating hotels for those making the 40-hour Stockholm–Helsinki round-trip. The brown-and-tan brick building is the old market hall. A number of harbor cruise boats vie for your business. The trees mark the beginning of Helsinki's grand promenade, the Esplanade (where we're heading). Hiding in the leaves is the venerable iron-and-glass Café Kappeli. The yellow building across from the trees is the TI. From there, a string of Neoclassical buildings face the harbor. The blue-and-white City Hall building was designed by Engel in 1833 as the town's first hotel (built to house the czar and czarina, now housing a public Internet point, WCs, and historic exhibitions). The Lutheran Cathedral is hidden from view behind this building. Next is the Swedish Embassy (flying the blue-and-yellow Swedish flag and designed to look like Stockholm's Royal Palace). Then comes the Supreme Court and, in the far corner, Finland's Presidential Palace. Standing proud, and reminding Helsinki of the Russian behemoth to its east, is the Orthodox Uspenski Cathedral.

Explore the colorful outdoor market—part souvenirs and crafts, part fruit and veggies, part fish and snacks (Mon–Fri roughly 6:30–17:00, Sat 6:30–16:00, only tourist stalls on Sun 10:00–16:00). Then, with your back to the water, walk left to the fountain, *Havis Amanda*, designed by Ville Vallgren and unveiled here in 1908. The fountain has become the symbol of Helsinki, the city known as the "Daughter of the Baltic." The voluptuous figure, modeled after the artist's Parisian mistress, was a bit too racy for the conservative town, and Vallgren had trouble getting paid. But as artists often do, Vallgren had the last laugh: For more than a hundred years now, the city budget office (next to the Sasso restaurant across the street) has seen only her backside.

A one-block detour up Unioninkatu (noteworthy shops listed in "Shopping in Helsinki," later) takes you to the Neoclassical Senate Square and Lutheran Cathedral.

To continue with this walk, backtrack to the TI. In the park across the street is the delightful...

❷ **Café Kappeli:** If you've got some time, dip into this old-fashioned, gazebo-like oasis of coffee, pastry, and relaxation (get what you like at the bar inside and sit anywhere). In the 19th century, this was a popular hangout for local intellectuals and artists. Today the café offers romantic tourists waiting for their ship a great €3-cup-of-coffee memory. The bandstand in front hosts nearly daily music and dance performances in summer.

❸ **The Esplanade:** Behind Café Kappeli stretches the Esplanade, Helsinki's top shopping boulevard, sandwiching a park in the middle (another Engel design from the 1830s). The grandiose street names Esplanadi and Bulevardi, while fitting today, must have been bombastic and almost comical in rustic little 1830s Helsinki. To help you imagine this elegant promenade in the 19th century, informative signs (in English) explain Esplanade Park's background and its many statues.

The north side (with the TI) is interesting for window-shopping, people-watching, and sun-worshipping. You'll pass several stores specializing in Finnish design. At #35, Gamla Passage leads to a courtyard hopping with bars and live music at night (see "Nightlife in Helsinki," later). Farther up on the right, at #39, is the huge Academic Bookstore (Akateeminen Kirjakauppa), designed by Alvar Aalto, with an extensive map and travel section, periodicals, English books, and Café Aalto (bookstore and café open Mon–Fri 9:00–21:00, Sat 9:00–18:00, also open Sun 12:00–18:00 in summer only).

❹ **Stockmann department store:** Finally, you'll come to the prestigious Stockmann department store—Finland's Harrods. Stockmann is the biggest, best, and oldest department store in town, with a great gourmet supermarket in the basement (see listing in "Shopping in Helsinki"). Just beyond is Helsinki's main intersection, where Esplanade and Mannerheimintie meet. (Mannerheimintie is named for the Finnish war hero who frustrated the Soviets in World War II.)

❺ **The *Three Blacksmiths* Statue:** Turn right on Mannerheimintie and at the far side of Stockmann's, you'll see the famous ***Three Blacksmiths*** (from 1932). While there's no universally accepted meaning, most say it celebrates human labor and cooperation and shows the solid character of the Finnish people. Note the rare, surviving bullet damage from World War II on the base. The most serious Russian shelling came in February 1944.

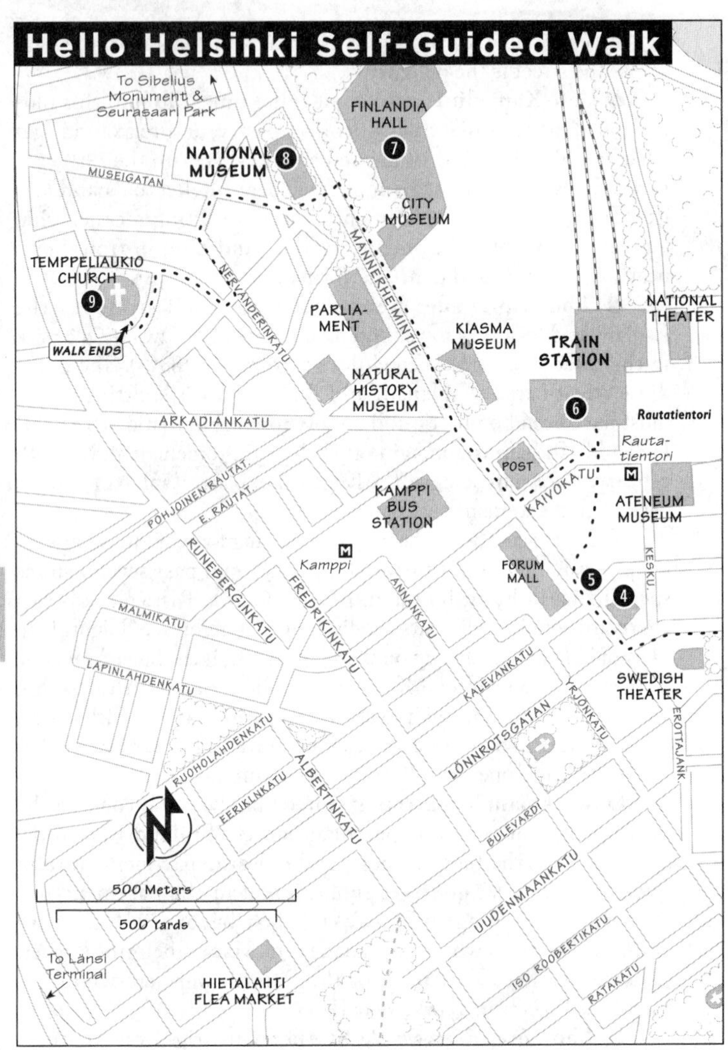

The Stockmann's entrance on Aleksanterinkatu, facing the *Three Blacksmiths,* is one of the city's most popular meeting points. Everyone in Finland knows exactly what it means when you say: "Let's meet under the Stockmann's clock." Tram #3T also makes a stop right at the clock (see "Tram #3T Tour," page 486). Across the street from the clock, the Old Student Hall is decorated with mythic Finnish heroes.

Sights Within a Short Walk of the *Three Blacksmiths*: From here, though things spread out, there are lots of interesting sights within an easy walk (refer to the map in this chapter). Two blocks

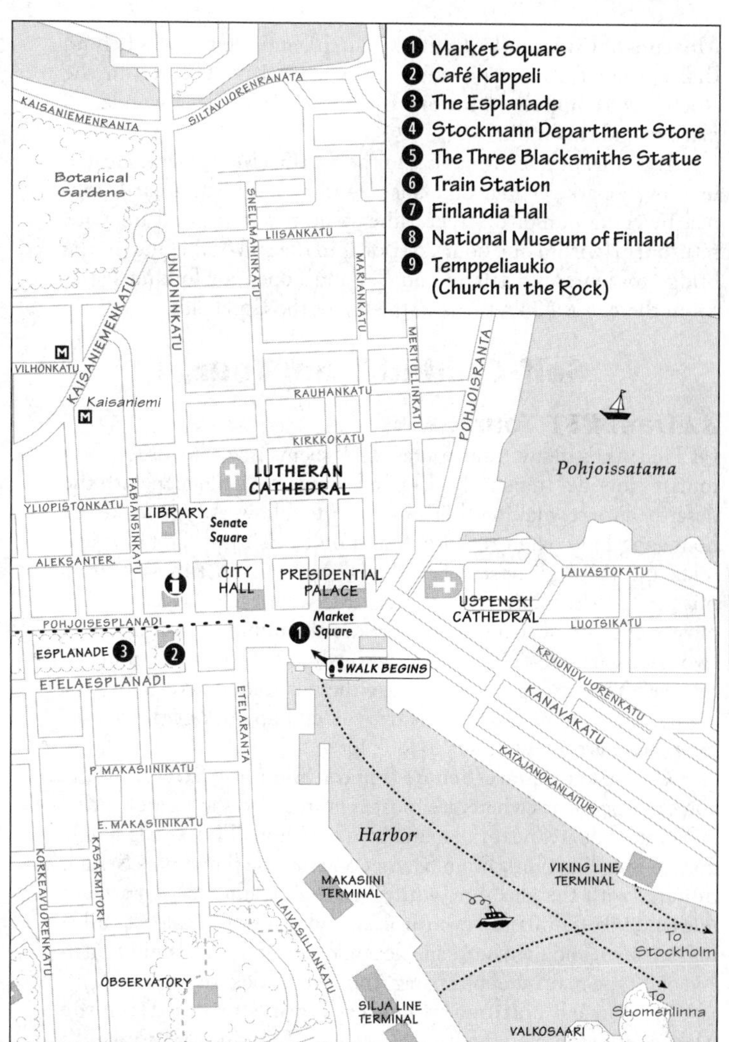

away, just past the *Three Blacksmiths,* look for a passageway to your right through a shopping arcade. Walking through it, you'll emerge in front of the harsh (but serene) architecture of the ❻ **train station** (by Eliel Saarinen, 1916). The four people on the facade symbolize peasant farmers with lamps coming into the Finnish capital. Wander around inside.

Continuing past the post office and the equestrian statue (of Field Marshal Carl Mannerheim), return to Mannerheimintie, which leads to the large, white ❼ **Finlandia Hall,** another Aalto masterpiece. Across the street is the excellent little ❽ **National**

Museum of Finland (looks like a church), and a few blocks behind that is the sit-down-and-wipe-a-tear beautiful "Church in the Rock," ❾ **Temppeliaukio.** Sit. Enjoy the music. It's a wonderful place to end this walk.

If you want to continue on to the Sibelius Monument, located in a lovely park setting, take bus #24 (direction: Seurasaari) from nearby Arkadiankatu street. The same ticket is good for your return trip (within one hour), or ride it to the end of the line for the bridge to Seurasaari Island and Finland's open-air folk museum. From there, bus #24 returns to the top of the Esplanade.

Self-Guided Tram Tour

▲▲Tram #3T Tour

Of Helsinki's many tram routes, #3T seems made-to-order for a tourist's joyride. In fact, the TI hands out a free little map with the described route, making this tour easier to follow. As you make the hour-long loop, you can hop off and on to visit the sights, or just relax and enjoy glimpses of workaday Helsinki that most visitors miss (€2.20/hr—buy from driver, free with Helsinki Card). At most stops, an electronic sign displays the minutes until the next two trams arrive (#3T goes one way, while #3B does this route in reverse). You can't get lost because the bus route makes a figure-eight, and an hour after you start, you end up back at the beginning. Here are a few things to look for:

❶ **Market Square/Senate Square/Shopping Street:** While you can hop on anywhere, it's most convenient to start—and end—at Market Square (near the fountain, across from TI, tram #3T only goes in one direction). From Market Square, you'll first pass **Senate Square** (with the gleaming white Lutheran Cathedral, a statue of Alexander II—Finland's favorite czar, and many of the oldest buildings in town) and then head up Alexander Street. It's Helsinki's Fifth Avenue-type main shopping drag (tram stop: Aleksanterinkatu).

❷ **Finnish National Theater/Train Station:** After the Mikonkatu stop, you'll pass a big square. Fronting it is Finland's granite, château-like National Theater (in Art Nouveau style). The statue in the square honors Aleksis Kivi, the father of Finnish literature, who in 1870 wrote *The Seven Brothers*, the first great novel in Finnish. The mid-19th century was a period of national awakening. By elevating the language to high culture, Kivi helped inspire his countrymen to stand strong and proud during a period of attempted "Russification." On the left is the **Ateneum,** The National Gallery of Finland. From there (on the right), you'll pass the striking train station—with its iconic countrymen stoically holding their lamps—designed by the great Finnish architect, Eliel Saarinen (1914).

Helsinki Self-Guided Tram Tour

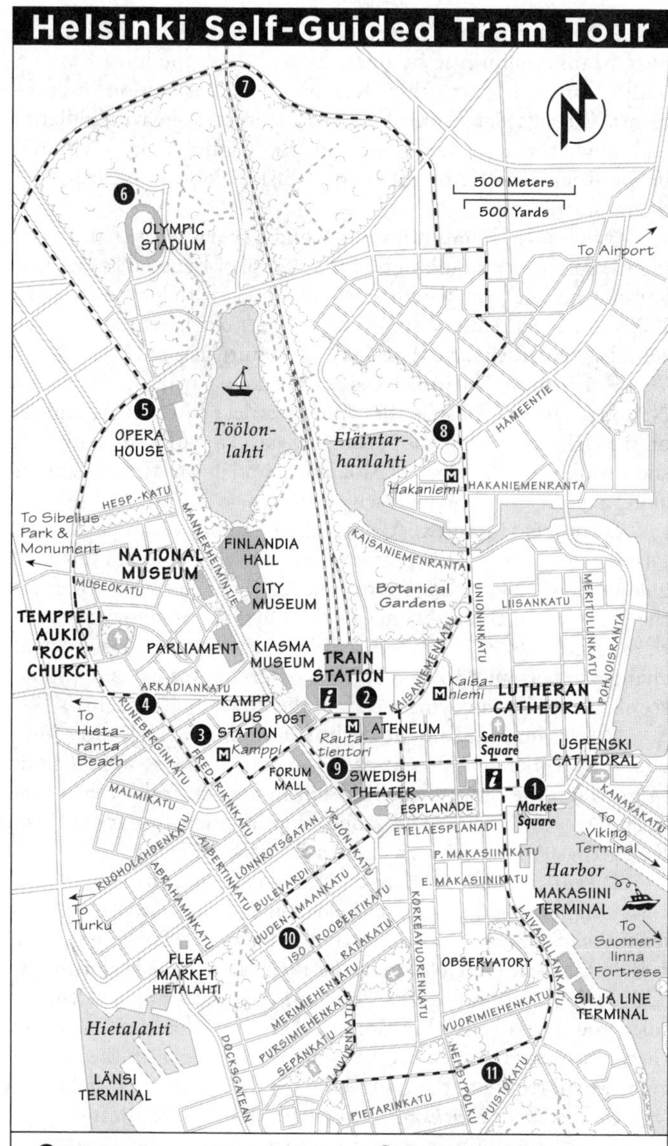

1. Market Square/Senate Square/Shopping Street
2. Finnish National Theater/Train Station
3. Shopping & Entertainment District
4. School of Economics & Trendy Apartments
5. Finnish National Opera House
6. Sports Complex
7. Classic Amusement Park (Linnanmäki)
8. Working-Class District
9. The Three Blacksmiths Statue
10. Funky & Artsy Shops
11. Embassy Row

❸ **Shopping and Entertainment District:** Crossing the busy Mannerheimintie boulevard, you'll pass the busy Kamppi mall (tram and Metro stop: Kamppi, with bus station in basement). The adjacent Tennis Palace is a cultural zone with galleries and movie theaters. The Temppeliaukio Church (a.k.a. "Church in the Rock"), while out of sight, is just a block uphill from the Sammonkatu stop.

❹ **School of Economics and Trendy Apartments:** After passing the yellow brick buildings of the School of Economics (on your left, note facade), you'll enter a neighborhood with lots of desirable 1920s-era apartments. Young couples start out here, move to the suburbs when they have their kids, and return as empty-nesters.

❺ **Finnish National Opera House:** Built in 1993, the National Opera House is the white, sterile, shower-tile building on the right (tram stop: Ooppera). The next stop (Toolon halli) is a short walk from the Sibelius Monument and its pretty park (detour along a street called Sibeliuksenkatu).

❻ **Sports Complex:** A statue honors long-distance runner, Paavo Nurmi (early 20th-century Finn who won a slew of Olympic gold medals, on left). The white building with the skinny tower (in the distance on the right) marks the Olympic Stadium, used for the summer games in 1952. About here, the tram may pause as it changes to become #3B (stay seated). After the Auroran stop, you'll see skateboarders enjoying a park of their own (on the right).

❼ **Classic Amusement Park: Linnanmäki,** Helsinki's low-end, Tivoli-like amusement park is by far the most-visited sight in town (on the right, free admission to park but rides cost €4–6, open daily until late, tram stop: Alppila, www.linnanmaki.fi). Roller-coaster nuts enjoy its classics from the 1950s.

❽ **Working-Class District:** Next you'll enter an old working-class neighborhood. Its soccer fields (on your left) are frozen into ice rinks for hockey in the winter. You'll pass the striking granite **Kallio Church** (Art Nouveau, on your right) and **Hakaniemi,** a big indoor/outdoor market (on your left). Crossing a saltwater inlet, you'll pass Helsinki's **Botanical Gardens** (on the right), and then return to the town center. Finishing one loop of the figure-eight, you'll return to the train station with its buff lamp-holders.

❾ **The *Three Blacksmiths* Statue:** After turning left on big, busy Mannerheimintie, you'll pass the most famous statue in town, the *Three Blacksmiths* (on your left), which honors hard work and cooperation. Towering above the smiths is the Stockmann department store. Then (at the Ylioppilastalo stop), the round white Swedish Theater marks the top of the town's graceful park—the Esplanade—which leads back down to the harbor (where you began this tour). From here, you'll loop through a colorful and artsy district.

⑩ **Funky and Artsy Shops:** The cemetery of the church (which dates from 1827) on the right was cleaned out to make a park. It's called the "Plague Park," recalling a circa 1700 plague that killed more than half the population. Coming up, funky small boutiques, cafés, and fun shops line the streets (stops: Fredrikinkatu, Iso Roobertinkatu, and Viiskulma). After the Art Deco brick church (on your right), the tram turns hard left (at Eiran Sairaala, the hospital) entering an Art Nouveau district. Look down streets on the right for facades and decorative turrets leading to the Baltic Sea.

⑪ **Embassy Row and Back to Market Square:** After the Neitsytpolku stop, spy the Russian Embassy (on left), still sporting its hammer and sickle; it was built to look like London's Buckingham Palace. Across the street is the Roman Catholic church, and beyond that (on the right), a street marked "no entry" leads to an embattled US Embassy. Returning to the harbor, you'll likely see the huge Silja ship that leaves at 17:00 each evening for Stockholm. The terminal was built for the 1952 Olympics, which inundated Helsinki with visitors. Across the harbor stands the Orthodox Uspenski Cathedral. Then, after passing the cute brick market hall (with several great little eateries), you'll arrive back at Market Square, where you started.

Sights in Helsinki

Near the Harbor

▲▲Lutheran Cathedral—With its prominent green dome and the 12 apostles overlooking the city and harbor, this church is Carl Ludvig Engel's masterpiece. Finished in 1852, the interior is pure architectural truth. Open a pew gate and sit, surrounded by the saints of Protestantism, to savor Neoclassical nirvana. Physically, this church is perfectly Protestant—austere and unadorned—with the emphasis on preaching (prominent pulpit) and music (huge organ). Statuary is limited to the local Reformation big shots: Martin Luther, Philipp Melanchthon (Luther's Reformation sidekick), and the leading Finnish reformer, Mikael Agricola. A follower of Luther at Wittenberg, Agricola brought the Reformation to Finland. He also translated the Bible into Finnish and is considered the father of the modern Finnish language. Agricola's Bible is to Finland what the Luther Bible is to Germany and the King James Bible is to the English-speaking world (free; June–Aug Mon–Sat 9:00–18:00, Sun 12:00–20:00,

until midnight in summer many nights; Sept–May Mon–Sat 9:00–18:00, Sun 12:00–18:00; on Senate Square). In summer, free organ concerts are held on Sundays at 20:00.

▲▲**Uspenski Cathedral**—This Orthodox cathedral was built in 1868 for the Russian military back when Finland belonged to Russia. It hovers above Market Square and faces the Lutheran Cathedral as Russian culture faces Europe. The uppermost "onion dome" represents the "sacred heart of Jesus," while the smaller ones represent the hearts of the 12 apostles. The cathedral's interior is a potentially emotional icon experience. Its rich images are a stark contrast to the sober Lutheran Cathedral. While commonly called the "Russian church," the cathedral is actually Finnish Orthodox, answering to the patriarch in Constantinople (Istanbul). Much of eastern Finland (parts of the Karelia region) is Finnish Orthodox.

The cathedral's Orthodox Mass is beautiful, with a standing congregation, candles, incense, icons in action, priests behind the iconostasis (screen), and timeless music (human voices only—no instruments). In the front left corner, find the icon featuring the Madonna and child, surrounded by rings and jewelry (under glass), given in thanks for prayers answered. Across from the icon is a white marble table with candle holes and a dish of wheat seeds, representing recent deaths. Wheat seeds symbolize that death is not the end, but just a change (free; May–Sept Mon–Fri 9:30–16:00, Tue until 18:00, Sat 9:30–15:00, Sun 12:00–15:00; Oct–April Tue–Fri 9:30–16:00, Sat 9:30–15:00, Sun 12:00–15:00, closed Mon; Kanalgatan 1, tram stop: Ritarihuone).

▲**Senate Square**—Once a town square with a church and City Hall, this square's original buildings were burned in 1808. Later, after Finland became a grand duchy of the Russian Empire, the czar sent in architect Carl Ludvig Engel (a German who had lived and worked in St. Petersburg) to give the place some Neo-class. The result: the finest Neoclassical square in Europe.

Survey Senate Square from the top of the Lutheran Cathedral steps. The Senate building (now the prime minister's office) is on your left. The small, blue, stone building with the slanted mansard roof in the far-left corner, from 1757, is one of just two pre-Russian-conquest buildings remaining in Helsinki. On the right, the line of once-grand Russian administration buildings now house the **university** (36,000 students, 60 percent women). Symbolically (and physically), the university and government buildings are connected via the cathedral, and both use it as a starting point for grand ceremonies.

The **statue** in the center of the square honors Russian Czar Alexander II. While he wasn't popular in Russia (he was assassinated), he was well-liked by the Finns. That's because he gave Finland more autonomy in 1863 and never pushed the "Russification" of Finland. The statue shows him holding the Finnish constitution, which he supported. It defined internal independence and affirmed autonomy.

The huge staircase leading up to the cathedral is a popular meeting (and tanning) spot in Helsinki. This is where students from the nearby university gather...and romances are born. Café Engel (opposite the cathedral at Aleksanterinkatu 26) is a fine place for a light lunch or cake and coffee. The café's winter lighting seems especially designed to boost the spirits of glum, daylight-deprived Northerners.

The interesting **Helsinki City Museum** is around the corner at Sofiankatu 4, with thorough descriptions in English (free, Mon–Fri 9:00–17:00, Thu until 19:00, Sat–Sun 11:00–17:00, www.helsinkicitymuseum.fi).

The **National Library,** in its fine purpose-built Neoclassical building, is immediately to the left as you face the cathedral. It's free, open to the public, and worth a look (July–Aug Mon–Fri 9:00–18:00, closed Sat–Sun; Sept–June Mon–Fri 9:00–20:00, Sat 9:00–16:00, closed Sun; www.nationallibrary.fi). In czarist times, the National Library received a copy of every book printed in the Russian Empire. With all the chaos Russia suffered throughout the 20th century, a good percentage of its Slavic texts were destroyed. But Helsinki, which enjoyed relative stability, claims to have the finest collection of Slavic books in the world.

Elsewhere in Central Helsinki

▲▲▲Temppeliaukio Church—A more modern example of great church architecture (from 1969), this "Church in the Rock" was blasted out of solid granite. It's barren of decor except for a couple of simple crosses, capped with a copper-and-skylight dome, and normally filled with live or recorded music and awestruck visitors. Grab a pew. Gawk upward at a 13-mile-long coil of copper ribbon. Look at the bull's-eye and ponder God. Forget your camera. Just sit in the middle, ignore the crowds, and be thankful for peace...under your feet is an air-raid shelter

that can accommodate 6,000 people (free, daily 10:00–18:00, until 20:00 most summer nights, closed to sightseers on Sunday morning and for special events and concerts, Lutherinkatu 3, tel. 09/2340-5920). The church is at the top of a hill in a residential neighborhood, about a 15-minute walk north of the bus station (or take tram #3T to Sammonkatu stop). You can attend the English-language Lutheran service (Sun at 14:00) or one of many concerts.

▲▲National Museum of Finland (Kansallismuseo)—This pleasant, easy-to-handle collection (covering Finland's story from A to Z, with good English descriptions) is in a grand building designed by three of Finland's greatest architects in the early 1900s. The Neoclassical furniture, folk costumes, armory, and portraits of Russia's last czars around an impressive throne are interesting, but the highlight is the "Prehistory of Finland" exhibit, Finland's largest permanent archaeological collection. Following the clear English-language descriptions, you'll learn how Stone, Bronze, and Iron Age tribes of Finland lived. The interactive top-floor workshop is worth a look for its creative teaching (€7, free on Tue 17:30–20:00, open Tue–Wed 11:00–20:00, Thu–Sun 11:00–18:00, closed Mon, peaceful second-floor info center with Internet access, Mannerheimintie 34, tel. 09/4050-9544, www.kansallismuseo.fi). The museum café, with a tranquil outdoor courtyard, has light meals and Finnish treats such as lingonberry juice and reindeer quiche. It's just a five-minute walk from Temppeliaukio Church.

▲Ateneum, The National Gallery of Finland—This museum showcases Finnish artists on the top floor (mid-18th to 20th century), hosts exhibits, and has a fine international collection including works by Cézanne, Chagall, Gauguin, and Van Gogh (€8, Tue–Fri 10:00–18:00, Wed–Thu until 20:00, Sat–Sun 11:00–17:00, closed Mon, near train station at Kaivokatu 2, tel. 09/173-361, www.ateneum.fi).

▲Sibelius Monument—Six hundred stainless-steel pipes called "Love of Music"—built on solid rock as is so much of Finland—shimmer in a park to honor Finland's greatest composer, Jean Sibelius. It's a forest of pipe-organ pipes in a forest of trees. The artist, Eila Hiltunen, was forced to add a bust of the composer's face to silence critics of her otherwise abstract work. City orientation bus tours stop here for 10 minutes—long enough. Bus #24 stops here (25 min until the next bus, or catch a quick glimpse on the left from the bus) on its way to the Seurasaari Open-Air Folk Museum. The #3T tram, which runs more frequently, stops a few blocks away.

Sauna

Finland's vaporized fountain of youth is the sauna—Scandinavia's answer to support hose and facelifts. A traditional sauna is a wood-paneled room with wooden benches and a wood-fired stove topped with rocks. The stove is heated blistering hot. Undress entirely before going in. Lay your towel on the bench, and sit or lie on it (for hygienic reasons). Ladle water from the bucket onto the rocks to make steam. Choose a higher bench for hotter temperatures.

The famous birch branches are always available for slapping. Finns claim this enhances circulation and say the chlorophyll released with the slapping opens your sinuses while emitting a refreshing birch aroma. (Follow the lead of the locals around you—tourists merrily flagellating themselves can be really annoying.) Let yourself work up a sweat, then, just before bursting, go outside to the shower for a Niagara of liquid ice. Suddenly your shower stall becomes a Cape Canaveral launch pad, as your body scatters to every corner of the universe. A moment later you're back together and can re-enter the steam room and repeat as necessary. Only rarely will you feel so good. The Finnish Sauna Society's informative website details the history of saunas and sweat baths (www.sauna.fi).

Your hostel, hotel, or the ship you came to Finland on may have a sauna. Ask them when they heat it, and whether it's semi-public (separate men's and women's hours, pay per person) or for private use (book and pay for a 45- to 60-minute time slot, and save money by bringing a group of friends, either mixed or same-sex). Public saunas are a dying breed these days, because most Finns have private saunas in their homes or cabins. But some public saunas survive in rougher, poorer neighborhoods.

For a good, traditional wood-heated sauna with a coarse and local crowd, try the **Kotiharjun Sauna.** There are no tourists and no English signs, but the guy at the desk speaks English and can help: Pay €10 plus €2 for a towel, find a locker, strip (keep the key on your wrist), and head for the steam. Cooling off is nothing fancy, just a bank of cold showers. A woman in a fish-cleaner's apron will give you a wonderful scrub with Brillo pad-like mitts (€7, only on Tue, Fri, and Sat). Regulars relax with beers on the sidewalk just outside (Tue-Fri 14:00-22:00, Sat 13:00-21:00, closed Sun-Mon, last entry 2 hours before closing; men-ground floor, women-upstairs; 200 yards from Sörnäinen Metro stop, Harjutorinkatu 1, tel. 09/753-1535, www.kotiharjunsauna.fi).

Finlandia Hall (Finlandia-Talo)—Alvar Aalto's most famous building in his native Finland means little to the non-architect without a tour (€7, many days at 13:00 in summer, 45 min, call ahead to check times; hall information shop open July–Aug Mon–Fri 9:00–16:00, Sat–Sun 11:00–13:00; Sept–June Mon–Fri 9:00–16:00, closed Sat–Sun; Mannerheimintie 13e, tel. 09/40241, www.finlandia talo.fi). To see the building from its best angle, view it from the seaside parking lot, not the street—where nearly everyone who looks at the building thinks, "So what?"

Kiasma—Finland's museum of contemporary art, designed by American architect Steven Holl, doesn't have a permanent collection, but you can ask at the TI or check online to find out what's showing (€6, free on Fri after 17:30, open Tue 10:00–17:00, Wed–Sun 10:00–20:30, closed Mon, pay €2 for audioguide or download it for free at www.kiasma.fi, Mannerheiminaukio 2, near train station).

Natural History Museum—Reopened in 2008 after being closed for renovation, this arm of the University of Helsinki has the largest collection of animal specimens in Finland (about 8 million items). Displays range from spiders to dinosaurs, all with English descriptions (€5, Tue–Fri 10:00–18:00, Sat–Sun 10:00–17:00, Pohjoinen Rautatiekatu 13).

Concerts—Concerts in Helsinki's churches, including the Lutheran Cathedral (free organ recitals on summer Sundays at 20:00) and Kallio Church (with its magnificent new organ), can be excellent. Ask at the TI, check their daily events board, and keep an eye out for posters. Many venues post listings in *Helsinki This Week* magazine.

Outer Helsinki

A weeklong car trip up through the Finnish lakes and forests to Mikkeli and Savonlinna would be relaxing, but you can actually enjoy Finland's green-trees-and-blue-water scenery without leaving Helsinki. Here are three great ways to get out and go for a walk on a sunny summer day.

▲▲Seurasaari Open-Air Folk Museum

Inspired by Stockholm's Skansen, also on a lovely island on the edge of town, this is a collection of 100 historic buildings from every corner of Finland. It's wonderfully furnished and gives rushed visitors an opportunity to sample the far reaches of Finland without leaving the capital city. The €1.20 map or the helpful €6 guidebook provide needed information if you're not taking a tour (free park entry, €6 to enter buildings; June–Aug daily 11:00–17:00; late May and early Sept Mon–Fri 9:00–15:00, Sat–Sun 11:00–17:00; closed mid-Sept–mid-May; tel. 09/4050-9660, www.seurasaari.fi). Check their website to confirm the times for English tours (free with €6 entry ticket, 60 min, mid-June–mid-Aug, generally at 15:00). Off-season, when the buildings are closed, the place is empty and not worth the trouble. To reach the museum, ride bus #24 (from the top of the Esplanade, 2/hr) to the end (note departure times for your return) and walk across the quaint footbridge. For locals, it's just a delightful park.

Eating at or near Seurasaari: Try the café in the center of the island, or you're welcome to bring a picnic. The separate **Café Villa Tomtebo,** with a sprawling front yard at the mainland end of the bridge to Seurasaari, has great homemade cakes and hosts occasional folk-dance performances in summer (June–Aug daily 11:00–17:00, closed off-season; €5 performances generally Wed at 19:00 and Sun at 17:00; for folk-dance info: tel. 09/484-511 or 09/484-234).

▲▲Suomenlinna Fortress

The island guarding Helsinki's harbor served as a strategic fortress for three countries: Finland, Sweden, and Russia. It's now a popular park with several museums and a Visitors Center located about five minutes from the boat dock. The free Suomenlinna guidebook (stocked at the Helsinki TI, ferry terminal, and the Visitors Center) covers the island thoroughly.

The fortress was built by the Swedes with French financial support in the mid-1700s to counter Russia's rise to power. (Peter the Great had built his new capital, St. Petersburg, on the Baltic and was eyeing the West.) Named Sveaborg ("Fortress of Sweden"), the fortress was Sweden's military pride and joy. With five miles of walls and hundreds of cannons, it was the second strongest fort of its kind in Europe after Gibraltar. Helsinki, a small peasant community of 1,500 people before 1750, soon became a boomtown supporting this grand "Gibraltar of the North."

The fort, built by more than 10,000 workers, was a huge investment and stimulated lots of innovation. In the 1760s, it had the world's biggest and most modern dry dock. In 1790, a decisive

Swedish naval victory was launched from Sveaborg, costing Russia 9,500 men and 60 boats. But in 1809, the Russians took the "invincible" fort without a fight—by siege—as a huge and cheap military gift.

The timeline, while complicated, is interesting:

1748—Construction began.

1788—The fort was used as a base for a Swedish war against Russia.

1808—It was surrendered by Sweden to Russia.

1809—Finland became part of the Russian Empire and the fort was used as a Russian garrison for 108 years.

1855—French and British navies bombarded the fort during the Crimean War, inflicting heavy damage.

1917—Finland declared independence.

1918—The fort was annexed by Finland and renamed Soumenlinna.

1939—The fort served as a base for the Finnish navy.

1973—The Finnish garrison moved out, the fort's administration was transferred to the Ministry of Education, and the fort was opened to the public.

Don't miss the Suomenlinna Museum within the Visitors Center, where the complete story is presented in a fascinating 25-minute "multi-vision" show. Also on the island are a toy museum and several military museums. Suomenlinna has 1,000 permanent residents, is home to Finland's Naval Academy, and is most appreciated by locals for its fine scenic strolls. The island is large—actually, it's four islands connected by bridges—and you and your imagination get free run of the fortifications and dungeon-like chambers. When it's munch-time, you'll find a half-dozen cafés and plenty of picnic opportunities.

Across from the ferry landing, the Panimo Brewery restaurant and a free modern art exhibit fill the jetty barracks (convenient WC here, tel. 09/228-5030, www.panimo.com). From here, start your stroll of the island. The garrison church, which was Orthodox until its 20th-century conversion to Lutheranism, doubled as a lighthouse.

Climb uphill to the right into Piper Park, past its elegant 19th-century café, up and over the ramparts to a surreal swimming area. Finish at the King's Gate on the far side of the island from where you can catch a boat back to town (€4, free with Helsinki Card, JT Line, 2/hr, mostly at :25 and :55).

Cost, Hours, Information: Visitors Center—free, daily May–Sept 10:00–18:00, Oct–April 10:00–16:00. Suomenlinna Museum-€5, same hours as Visitors Center. Its "multi-vision" show on the island's history runs twice hourly (last showing at

30 min before museum closes). Pick up the English translation of exhibits by the entrance. Tel. 09/684-1880, www.suomenlinna.fi. The island has several skippable smaller museums (€3–4 each, open summer only).

Tours: Consider a 60-minute English-language tour (€7, free with Helsinki Card, departs Visitors Center June–Aug daily at 11:00 and 14:00, off-season Sat–Sun only at 13:30).

Getting There: Catch a ferry to Suomenlinna from Market Square. Walk past the higher-priced excursion boats to the public HKL ferry (€4 round-trip, covered by Tourist Ticket transit pass and Helsinki Card, 15-min trip, 2–3/hr in summer—generally at :00, :20, and :40 past the hour, but pick up schedule to confirm, hourly in winter—more frequent during afternoon hours).

Peninsula Promenade

For a breezy, salty seaside walk, consider this promenade around the Kaivopuisto Park peninsula. Allow 90 minutes at a leisurely pace. From Market Square, wander past the old brick market hall and Silja Terminal (with its huge ship likely at the dock) and follow the shoreline pedestrian path. The first island you come to, Valkosaari, hosts the local yacht club—NJK—the oldest in Scandinavia, with a classy restaurant (daily 17:00–24:00). The next island, Luoto, is home to the posh Palace Kämp by the Sea restaurant (with shuttle boat service). During a typical winter, the bay freezes (18 inches is strong enough to allow cars to drive to the islands—in the past there was even a public bus route that extended to an island during the winter). The fortress island of Suomenlinna is in the distance. The hill you're circling (on the right) is home to several embassies; ahead, Ursula Café, with its fine harbor views, is good for a coffee break.

Around the corner, the next island, Uunisaari, belonged to the military until the 1980s. Its unique plant life (much studied by local students) is believed to have hitched a ride all the way to Finland from Siberia on the boots of Russian soldiers. The odd-looking pier nearby is a station for washing rugs (those are not picnic tables). Saltwater brightens the rag rugs traditionally made by local grandmas. While American men put on aprons and do the barbeque, Finnish men wash the carpets. After the scrub, the rugs are sent through big mechanical wringers and hung on nearby racks to dry in the wind. The posted map shows 11 such stations scattered around Helsinki. Buy an ice cream at the nearby stand and watch the action (best in the morning).

In the distance, beyond its massive shipyards, looms Helsinki's big new port, hosting 270 cruise ships a year. From here you can follow Neitsytpolku street back to the town center, keeping an eye out for fun Art Nouveau buildings.

Near Helsinki

Porvoo, the second-oldest town in Finland, has wooden architecture that dates from the Swedish colonial period. This coastal town can be reached from Helsinki by bus (one hour) or by excursion boat from Market Square.

Turku, the historic capital of Finland, is a two-hour bus or train ride from Helsinki. Overall, Turku is a pale shadow of Helsinki, and there is little reason to make a special trip. It does have a handicraft museum in a cluster of wooden houses (the only part of town to survive a devastating fire in the early 1800s), an old castle, a fine Gothic cathedral, and a market square. Viking and Silja boats sail from Turku to Stockholm every morning and evening, passing through the especially scenic Turku archipelago. Christianity was first brought to Finns here in the 12th century.

Naantali, a cute, commercial, well-preserved medieval town with a quaint harbor, is an easy bus ride from Turku (4/hr, 20 min).

Shopping in Helsinki

The Esplanade: The Esplanade is capped by the enormous, sprawling **Stockmann** department store, with a downstairs supermarket stocked with great Finnish picnic provisions (Mon–Fri 9:00–21:00, Sat 9:00–18:00, Sun 12:00–18:00, closed Sun in winter, Aleksanterinkatu 52B, www.stockmann.fi). The street is lined with smaller stores ideal for window-shopping. Keep an eye out for sleek Scan-design gifts. Consider the purses, scarves, clothes, and fabrics from **Marimekko,** the well-known Finnish fashion company (sold in several shops along the Esplanade including #14, www.marimekko.fi). Fans of Tove Jansson's Moomin children's stories won't want to miss the **Moomin Shop,** at #33 in the Kämp Galleria (Mon–Fri 10:00–19:00, Sat 10:00–17:00, closed Sun). Bookworms enjoy the impressive **Academic Bookstore** just before Stockmann (#39). The **Artek Store** (#18) was founded by designers Alvar and Elissa Aalto and showcases the Aalto-friendly, modern, and practical style that is standard in Finnish homes today. For less glamorous shopping needs, visit the Kamppi mall above and around the bus station. If you're into Finnish design, ask the TI for their brochure with that title.

Market Square: This harborfront square is packed not only with fishmongers and producers, but also with stands selling Finnish souvenirs and more refined crafts (roughly Mon–Fri 6:30–

17:00, Sat 6:30–16:00, only tourist stalls open on Sun 10:00–16:00). Sniff the stacks of trivets, made from cross-sections of juniper twigs—an ideal, fragrant, easy-to-pack gift for the folks back home (they smell even nicer when you set something hot on them).

Flea Market: If you brake for garage sales, Finland's biggest flea market, the outdoor **Hietalahti Market,** is worth the 15-minute walk from the harbor or a short ride on tram #6 from Mannerheimintie (June–Aug Mon–Fri 10:00–18:00, Sat 8:00–16:00, Sun 10:00–16:00; less action and closed Sun off-season). The stalls in the adjacent red-brick indoor market specialize in antiques. In the distance, notice the shipyard—once the birthplace of many of the world's luxury cruise ships.

Unioninkatu Street: This short street (connecting the market with the Lutheran Cathedral) is lined with a fun variety of popular shops. **Kiseleffin Talo,** a top-end craft market, is a collection of 20 special boutiques with excellent handicrafts, popular for small, typically Finnish gifts (Mon–Fri 10:00–18:00, Sat 10:00–16:00, Sun 11:00–16:00 in summer only—otherwise closed Sun, at Unioninkatu 27 and Aleksanterinkatu 28).

Kalevala Jewelry sells quality made-in-Finland jewelry at Unioninkatu 25. While modern in feel, it's clearly inspired by archeological finds from ancient Finn and Sami tombs. Traditional costumes in the back show how folkloric people would have sported their jewels (12 percent VAT refunds, tel. 020-761-1380, www.kalevalakoru.com).

Fishermen head next door where the **Schroder Sport Shop** shows off its famous selection of popular Finnish-made Rapala fishing lures—ideal for the fisherfolk on your gift list.

Nightlife in Helsinki

While it's easy to make friends in a bar, anything alcoholic is expensive. For the latest on hot nightspots, read the English insert of *City* magazine that lists the "best" of everything in Helsinki.

A good bet for a drink, live music (generally jazz), and lots of fun-seeking locals (young and old) is **Michelle Bar & Grill,** where three lively bars share a courtyard. The boomer-friendly scene hops almost nightly through the summer (Gamla Passage, enter at Aleksanterinkatu 46 or at #35 off the Esplanade, tel. 09/8568-5750). Wednesday, called "little Friday" here, is livelier than other weeknights.

For cheap fun, Hietaranta Beach and the park on Suomenlinna island are where the local kids hang out (and even skinny-dip) at 22:00 or 23:00. Helsinki is one of Europe's safest cities after dark.

Sleeping in Helsinki

The rack rate (highest rate) for a standard hotel double starts at about €160, but you rarely need to pay this much. You have three basic money-saving options: modest but comfortable smaller hotels; discounted big-hotel rooms in summer and on weekends; and unusually comfortable hostels and student dorms that rent plenty of twin-bedded rooms. Also remember that some of the cheapest beds in Helsinki are on the cruise ships to Stockholm.

Most large Helsinki hotels have a two-tiered pricing system: weekend discounts on Friday and Saturday nights, and higher rack rates the rest of the week. From late June to early August, you get the weekend discount every day of the week. A few hotels extend the weekend discount to Sunday nights as well. When two prices are listed, the first is for weeknights, the second for weekends and summer.

Business-class hotels play a complicated game of price discrimination with computer programs that tell them exactly how much to charge for a room based on demand. They often jumpstart things by offering a number of deeply discounted rooms to those who book long in advance on the Web. My listings will save you money when the hotel is busy, but you'll likely do better with an online booking when it's quiet.

Helsinki Expert's hotel-booking service, with branches at the TI and the train station, can reserve you a hotel bed for a €5 fee and always knows where the best deals are (see page 476).

Central Hotels

$$$ Hotel Anna is comfortable and feels like home. Its 64 rooms are efficiently run as a fundraiser for the Finnish Free Church. For more air in the rooms, ask at the desk for a key to open the windows (Sb-€120/€70, superior Sb-€130/€105, Db-€170/€105, superior Db-€185/€120, extra bed-€15, book by email and ask for a Rick Steves discount—generally 10 percent off business rate and 25 percent for summer and weekends, non-smoking rooms, elevator, 4 blocks south of the top of the Esplanade, Annankatu 1, tel. 09/616-621, fax 09/602-664, www.hotelanna.fi, info@hotelanna.fi).

$$ Hotel Arthur, a five-minute walk from the train station on a quiet street, is well-worn and run by the YMCA, with 160 forgettable industrial-strength rooms (S-€60/€45, D-€78/€60, small twin Db-€125/€92, nicer Db-€144/€112, extra bed-€20, weekend rates also valid Sun night, non-smoking rooms, Vuorikatu 19, tel. 09/173-441, fax 09/626-880, www.hotelarthur.fi, reception@hotel arthur.fi).

$$ Hotelli Finn is wonderfully central, stowed quietly on the sixth floor of an office building at the top of the Esplanade. While

Sleep Code

(€1 = about $1.40, country code: 358)
S = Single, **D** = Double/Twin, **T** = Triple, **Q** = Quad, **b** = bathroom, **s** = shower. All places listed have elevators, accept credit cards, and speak English. Unless otherwise noted, breakfast is included.

To help you sort easily through these listings, I've divided the rooms into three categories, based on the full (non-weekend) price for a standard double room with bath:

$$$ Higher Priced—Most rooms €150 or more.
$$ Moderately Priced—Most rooms between €80–150.
$ Lower Priced—Most rooms €80 or less.

its carpets are frayed and stained, its 27 simple, comfy rooms—all with toilet and sink, some with a shared shower—are a good choice when other places are charging rack rates (S-€65, Sb-€75, D-€75, Db-€90, Tb-€110, Qb-€125, small breakfast served in room-€7, Kalevankatu 3B, tel. 09/684-4360, fax 09/6844-3610, www.hotellifinn.fi, hotelli.finn@kolumbus.fi).

$ Omena Hotelli ("Apple Hotel"), with two equally handy 100-room locations in downtown Helsinki, is the newest concept in budget slumbermills. Omena's hotels are entirely automated: You book on the Web, they bill you, and you receive a room access code. The rooms, while spartan, are perfectly good, with flat-screen TVs, refrigerators, microwaves, and modern bathrooms. Because the price is for the room, and each room comes with a double bed and two petite hide-away beds, this can be a fine value for families (Qb-€60–85, breakfast-€5.80–7.60 at nearby cafés, pay Wi-Fi, Lönnrotinkatu 13 or Eerikinkatu 24, toll tel. 0600-18018, www.omena.com). Check their website for deals and details.

Expensive Hotels with Great Weekend Deals

On Friday and Saturday nights and from late June to early August, even Helsinki's more expensive hotels have great deals on doubles. Hotels set aside a certain number of rooms at great prices for those who book long in advance. Prices get even better for nonrefundable hotel rooms. These Web-based savings can save you a bundle.

$$$ Scandic Grand Marina, a huge 480-room, four-star hotel filling a big, brick warehouse building near the Viking cruise ship terminal, discounts its €232 doubles to €100 or less (Katajanokanlaituri 7, tel. 09/16661, fax 09/664-764, www.scandic-hotels.com/grandmarina, grandmarina@scandic-hotels.com).

$$$ Hotel Linna, with 48 modern rooms and elegant public spaces behind a striking Art Nouveau facade, feels like a stony

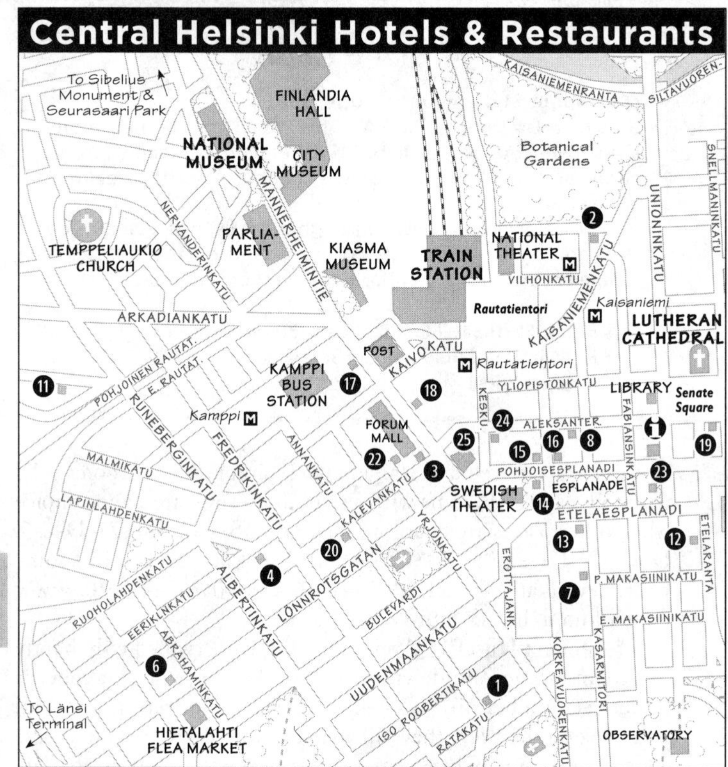

medieval château in the middle of Helsinki (Db-€210/€100 or less in summer and on weekends, Lönnrotinkatu 29, tel. 010-344-4100, fax 010-344-4101, www.palacekamp.fi, linna@palace.fi).

$$$ Hotel Rivoli Jardin is a cozy 55-room place tucked away right in the town center. Warm and personal, it has an inviting lounge and modern, comfortable rooms (Db-€245 but €80–€100 in summer and weekends, Kasarmikatu 40, tel. 09/681-500, fax 09/656-988, www.rivoli.fi, rivoli.jardin@rivoli.fi).

$$$ Hotel Glo, which has a well-designed spa-type quality, gives you an appreciation for how an extremely wealthy society manages to survive a long, dark winter. It's well-run, perfectly located, and reasonably priced in slow times (Db-€330 but often discounted to €150 or so, Kluuvikatu 4, tel. 010-3444-400, www.palacekamp.fi).

$$ Hotel Katajanokka is a former red-brick prison built in 1888. Its last prisoner checked out in 2002 and it was converted in 2007 into a four-star, business-class hotel. Its 100 rooms are very quiet—the walls are so thick that the hotel provides free Internet cables rather than Wi-Fi. While the windows no longer have bars

(thanks to the local fire code) and walls have been removed so that two or three cells make a room, you can still imagine the guards strolling up and down the corridors. It rents by the room for single, double, or triple use in three categories: Queen (just a queen-sized double bed with shower), Twin (two large twin beds in smallish room, some with showers only), and Premier (two large twin beds in bigger room with bath). The prices run around €100, €120, and €140 in summer and on weekends—and much more during busy times (free sauna and gym, Vyokatu 1 near the Viking cruise ship terminal, tel. 09/686-450, fax 09/670-290, www.bwkatajanokka.fi, sales@bwkatajanokka.fi).

Hostels

Helsinki's hostels are unusually comfortable. While they offer €3 discounts for those with hostel cards, all ages are welcome with or without a hostel membership. Eurohostel and Academica are more like budget hotels than hostels.

$ Eurohostel, a modern hostel with 255 beds, is 400 yards from the Viking ferry terminal and a 10-minute walk from

Market Square. The more expensive rooms have been recently renovated and come with TVs. It's packed with facilities, including a laundry room, a members' kitchen with unique refrigerated safety-deposit boxes for your caviar and beer, a restaurant, and plenty of good budget-travel information. While generally fully booked in advance, they release no-show beds at 18:00 (S-€40–47, D-€50–58, T-€75–85, family room with up to 4 kids under age 15-€72, shared twins or triples-€25 per person, includes sheets; breakfast-€7, free morning sauna, evening sauna-€5, private lockable closets, laundry, handy tram #4 stop around the corner, Linnankatu 9, tel. 09/622-0470, fax 09/655-044, www.eurohostel.fi, eurohostel@eurohostel.fi).

$ Academica Summer Hostel is a university dorm that's extremely well-run as a hostel from June through August. Finnish university students have it good—the 200 rooms are hotel-quality with private baths and kitchenettes, though all doubles have twin beds. Guests can have a morning sauna and use the swimming pool for free (Sb-€45, Db-€70, extra bed-€23, prices include sheets; probably only doubles will be available in 2010; tram #3T to the Kauppakorkeakoulu stop, between Mechelininkatu and Runeberginkatu at Hietaniemenkatu 14, tel. 09/1311-4334, fax 09/441-201, www.hostelacademica.fi, hostel.academica@hyy.fi).

Eating in Helsinki

Helsinki is filled with restaurants serving everything from traditional Finnish and Russian food to nouvelle cuisine in modern, bright interiors. Finland's restaurants are entirely smoke-free.

Restaurants are a good value for lunch. Finnish companies get a tax break if they distribute lunch coupons (worth €8) to their employees. It's no surprise that most downtown Helsinki restaurants offer weekday lunch specials that cost exactly the value of the coupon. Dinner reservations are smart in summer at nicer restaurants.

Dressy Splurge Dinners

Sundmans Krog Bistro is sedate and Old World but not folkloric, filling an old merchant's mansion facing the harbor. As it's the less fussy and more affordable (yet still super-romantic) little sister of an adjacent, posh, Michelin-rated restaurant, quality is assured. A rare and memorable extra is their Baltic herring buffet—featuring pickled, creamed, and grilled herring with potatoes and all the toppings—€13 as a starter, €18 as a main course. The €19 lunch special (Mon–Fri 11:00–15:00) includes the herring buffet and a daily fish dish (€20–25 entrées, €40 three-course "Helsinki" dinner, daily 11:00–22:00, Etelaranta 16, tel. 09/6128-5450).

Savoy Restaurant, where locals go for a special occasion, is expensive, formal, and drenched in Alvar Aalto design. Everything—from the chairs and lampshades to the doors—is 1937 original. The food is Continental with a Finnish touch. While the terrace offers a great eighth-floor, rooftop view, the interior is where you'll experience a classic Finnish atmosphere (€80 three-course meal, €110 five-course meal, Mon–Fri 11:30–14:30 and 18:00–23:00, closed Sat–Sun, Etelaesplanadi 14, tel. 09/6128-5300).

Venerable Esplanade Cafeterias

Highly competitive restaurants line the sunny north side of the Esplanade—offering enticing and creative lunch salads and light meals in their cafés (with fine sidewalk seating), plush sofas for cocktails in their bars, and fancy restaurant dining upstairs. Most are open daily 10:00–22:00.

Teatteri Wine & Deli is a hit with locals for its great salad bar (crispy base, you choose two meats or extras to add, €9 with bread, Caesar salad option). Their cocktail bar—trendy with office workers yet comfortable for baby-boomer tourists—has fine, parkside seating indoors and out (facing Café Esplanade at the top of Esplanade Park, Pohjoisesplanadi 2, tel. 09/6128-5000).

Café Esplanade, across from Teatteri, competes head-on with an equal €9 salad bar (add your two favorite extras to the base). The cafeteria is lined with temptations, including famous cinnamon rolls. Sit outside and enjoy the Parisian-style sidewalk setting. Their bistro in back is fast, affordable, and popular with locals for a light meal (€9 lunch specials, Pohjoisesplanadi 37, tel. 09/665-496).

Strindberg is also popular (at the corner of the Esplanade and Mikonkatu). Downstairs is an elegant cafeteria with outdoor and indoor tables great for people-watching (€6–8 sandwiches and salads). The upstairs cocktail lounge—with big sofas and bookshelves, giving it a den-like coziness—attracts the after-work office crowd. Also upstairs, the inviting restaurant has huge entrées for €15–25, with fish, meat, pasta, and vegetarian options. Consider their "classics" list. Reservations are smart—and a must for a window seat overlooking the Esplanade (Pohjoisesplanadi 33, tel. 09/681-2030).

Functional Eating

Lasipalatsi, the renovated, rejuvenated 1930s Glass Palace, houses a trendy upstairs restaurant and cheaper downstairs café across Mannerheimintie from the train station. The café (with a youthful terrace on the square out back) offers a self-service soup, salad bar, bread, and coffee for €12 at lunch, plus €5 sandwiches and €4 cakes (very long café hours, restaurant open Mon–Sat 11:00–24:00, closed Sun, across from post office at Mannerheimintie 22–24, tel. 09/612-6700).

Theme Dining: Tractors, Peasant Maidens, and Lapp Cuisine

Zetor, the self-proclaimed *traktor* restaurant, mercilessly lampoons Finnish rural culture and cuisine (while celebrating it deep down). Where else can you get "Gone with the Broth" soup with herring and reindeer? Sit next to a cow-crossing sign at a tractor-turned-into-a-table, in a "Finnish Western" atmosphere reminiscent of director Aki Kaurismäki's movies. Main dishes run €12–20 and include elk stew, Rudolph, and less exotic fare. This place, while tacky and touristy, can be fun (daily until 24:00 but no lunch Sat–Sun, 200 yards north of Stockmann department store, across street from McDonald's at Mannerheimintie 3–5, tel. 010-766-4450).

Savotta Traditional Finnish Restaurant is also tacky and touristy, with traditionally garbed maidens serving tourists Finnish plates. The decor is as if Disneyland had a corner called Finlandia—but the location is handy, the food is decent, and the ambience is memorable (facing Lutheran Cathedral at Aleksanterinkatu 22, tel. 09/7425-5588).

Lappi Restaurant is a fine place for Lapp cuisine, with an entertaining menu (they smoke their own fish) and creative decor that has you thinking you've traveled north and lashed your reindeer to the hitchin' post. The friendly staff serves tasty Sami dishes in a snug and very woody atmosphere. Dinner reservations are strongly recommended (€25–40 dinner plates, Mon–Fri 17:00–22:30, Sat 13:00–22:30, closed Sun, off Bulevardi at Annankatu 22, tel. 09/645-550).

Fun Harborfront Market Eateries and Picnics

Market Square: Helsinki's delightful and vibrant square is magnetic any time of day...but especially at lunchtime. This really is the most memorable, casual, quick-and-cheap lunch place in town. A half-dozen orange tents (erected to shield diners from bird bombs) serve fun food on paper plates until 18:00. It's not unusual for the Finnish president to stop by here with visiting dignitaries. There's a crêpe place, and at the far end—my favorites—several salmon grills (€8 for a good meal). The only real harborside dining in this part of town is picnicking. While these places provide picnic tables, you can also have your food foil-wrapped to go and grab benches right on the water down near Uspenski Cathedral.

Market Hall: Just beyond the harborside market is a cute, red-brick, indoor market hall. Today, along with produce stalls, it's a hit for its fun, inexpensive eateries. **Keitto Soups** serves filling, tasty fish soup and an €8 daily special with bread and water (splittable, daily 11:00–16:00). A sushi place is across the lane. And **Kahvipaikka Snellman** is popular for its €3 meat pies and €2.50 pastries called "apple pigs."

In **supermarkets,** buy the semi-flat bread (available dark or light) that Finns love—every slice is a heel. Finnish liquid yogurt is also a treat (sold in liter cartons). Karelian pasties, filled with rice or mashed potatoes, make a good snack. A good, big supermarket is beneath the Stockmann department store (Mon–Fri 9:00–21:00, Sat 9:00–18:00, open Sun 12:00–18:00 only in summer, Aleksanterinkatu 52b).

Helsinki Connections

From Helsinki, it's easy to get to **Turku** (hourly, 2 hrs) or **St. Petersburg, Russia,** by either bus or train. To St. Petersburg, the bus is slower and cheaper (3/day—departing at 9:00, 12:00, and 23:00; 9 hrs, about €38–40, less for students) than the train (2/day, 7 hrs, €59–103—price depends on train and accommodation class, no student discount). Travelers to Russia need a visa and should not wait until Helsinki to plan their trip (see www.russianembassy.org). For train info, visit www.vr.fi. For bus info in English, consult www.matkahuolto.fi.

By Boat from Helsinki to: Stockholm (Silja and Viking lines sail nightly; see beginning of this chapter for details), **Tallinn** (ferries and—in summer only—fast boats travel the 50 miles many times a day; see the Tallinn chapter for details). See "Arrival in Helsinki" for terminal locations.

ESTONIA

ESTONIA

Eesti

Estonians are related to the Finns and have a similar history—first Swedish domination, then Russian (1710–1918), and finally independence after World War I. In 1940, Estonians were at least as affluent and as advanced as the Finns, but they could not preserve their independence from Soviet expansion during World War II. As a result, Estonia sank into a 50-year communist twilight from which it is still emerging. In 2004, Estonia took a significant step forward when it joined the European Union. In 2011, it hopes to switch its currency from the krooni to the euro.

Estonia will always face both West, across the Baltic; and East, into the Russian hinterlands. After the Cold War, the pendulum has swung farther West. EU membership seemed like a natural step to many Estonians; they already thought of themselves as part of the Nordic world. Language, history, religion, and twice-hourly ferry departures connect Finns and Estonians. It's only 50 miles between Helsinki and Tallinn, and an overnight boat ride to Stockholm. Finns visit Tallinn to eat, drink, and shop more cheaply than at home. While some Estonians resent how Tallinn becomes a Finnish nightclub on summer weekends, most people on both sides are happy to have friendly new neighbors.

One problematic legacy of the Soviet experience is Estonia's huge Russian population. Most Estonian Russians' parents and grandparents were brought to Estonia in the 1950s and 1960s to work in now-defunct factories in Tallinn and in the northeastern cities. Twenty-five percent of Estonia's population is now ethnically Russian. Making Russians feel at home in Estonia while building a distinctly Estonian culture and identity is one of independent Estonia's biggest challenges. In

Estonia Almanac

Official Name: Eesti Vabariik—the Republic of Estonia—or simply Estonia.

Population: Estonia is home to 1.3 million people (77 per square mile). Nearly three in four are of Estonian heritage, and about one-quarter are of Russian descent, with smaller minorities of Ukrainians, Belarusians, and Finns. About 70 percent speak the official language—Estonian—and nearly 30 percent speak Russian. The majority of Estonians are unaffiliated with any religion. About 14 percent are Lutheran and 13 percent are Orthodox.

Latitude and Longitude: 59°N and 26°E, similar latitude to Juneau, Alaska.

Area: 17,500 square miles, about the size of New Hampshire and Vermont combined.

Geography: Between Latvia and Russia, Estonia borders the Baltic Sea and Gulf of Finland. It includes more than 1,500 islands and islets, and has the highest number of meteorite craters per land area in the world.

Biggest City: The capital of Estonia, Tallinn, has 400,000 people (500,000 in the metropolitan area).

Economy: Estonia's transition to a free-market system included joining the World Trade Organization and the European Union. Once a Baltic tiger, the recent economic downturn has devastated its economy. It had a Gross Domestic Product of $27.7 billion in 2008, but the economy slumped in 2009. Estonia's per-capita GDP of $21,200 is still the highest of the Baltic states. Its unemployment rate rose from 4.2 percent in mid-2008 to 13.3 percent in mid-2009. Its three major trading partners are Finland, Sweden, and Germany; its strengths are electronics and telecommunications.

Currency: 11 Estonian krooni (kr) = about $1.

Government: Estonia is a constitutional democracy, with a president elected by parliament (Toomas Hendrik Ilves, since October 2006) and a prime minister (Andrus Ansip, since April 2005). The 101-member parliament (Riigikogu) is elected by popular vote every four years.

Flag: The pre-1940 Estonian flag was restored in 1990. It has three equal horizontal bands with blue at the top, black in the middle, and white on the bottom. The blue represents Estonia's lakes and sea, and the loyalty and devotion of the country to its people. The black symbolizes the homeland's rich soil and the hardships the people have suffered. The white represents hope and happiness.

The Average Estonian: The average Estonian is 40 years old, has 1.4 children, and will live to be 72. About 58 percent of the population are women (they live longer), and when she sings the national anthem, she uses the same melody as Finland.

2007, Tallinn made international headlines when it controversially relocated a giant "Liberation Monument" depicting a WWII-era Russian soldier (as well as actual remains of Soviet soldiers) from the city center to a cemetery on the outskirts of town. This sparked protests in both Tallinn and Moscow. In retaliation, Estonia suffered a flurry of "cyber attacks," as many of its governmental, political, and business websites were crippled by an overload of traffic. Many of the attacks originated from within Russia, leading some to allege that the Kremlin was waging "cyber war."

But despite a sometimes fitful adjustment to its post-Soviet reality, Estonia is a welcoming place. Younger Estonians speak English—it's the first choice these days at school. Estonian is similar to Finnish and equally difficult. Only a million people speak Estonian worldwide. Two useful phrases to know are "*Tänan*" (TAH-nahn; "Thank you") and "*Terviseks!*" (TEHR-vee-sehks; "Cheers!"). If you'd like to learn a few more phrases, see the Estonian Survival Phrases on page 587. The farther you go beyond the touristy zones, the more you see that Russian is still Estonia's main second language. If you know some Russian, use it. It's the mother tongue of more than 40 percent of Tallinners (many of whom have no intention of learning Estonian).

TALLINN

Stepping off the boat in Tallinn, you feel that you've traveled farther culturally than you have throughout the rest of Scandinavia. Tallinn's Nordic Lutheran culture and language connect it with Stockholm and Helsinki, but two centuries of Tsarist Russian rule and 45 years in the Soviet Union have blended in a distinctly Russian flavor. Like Prague and Kraków, Tallinn has modernized at an astounding rate since the fall of the Soviet Union in 1991. Yet it has beautifully preserved the Old World ambience within its walled town center. Colorfully painted medieval houses share cobbled lanes with blocky, communist-style buildings...and everything is enlivened with Estonians thoroughly enjoying their freedom.

If you're pondering a cultural detour on your Nordic vacation, Tallinn and Helsinki are the logical choices—both are quite different from the "core" Scandinavian countries, and both are easily reached on a night cruise from Stockholm (or a quick flight from any Scandinavian capital). Tallinn is much cheaper than Helsinki, with great restaurants and good shopping. It's also more challenging. Why not give yourself a few extra days and do both as a triangular side-trip from Stockholm?

Sailing from Stockholm to Tallinn

Tallink's ships leave Stockholm at 19:00 every evening and arrive in Tallinn at 10:00 the next morning. Return trips leave Tallinn at 18:00 and arrive in Stockholm at 10:00. All times are local (Tallinn is an hour ahead of Stockholm).

Fares vary by the day and season—highest on Friday nights and from July 1 to August 15; lowest on Sunday through Wednesday

Helsinki/Tallinn Connections

Company	Ship Type	Helsinki Terminal	Helsinki Phone #
Tallink/Silja	Ferries and fast boats	Länsi	09/228-311
Linda Line	Fast boats	Makasiini	09/668-9700
Eckerö Line	Ferries	Länsi	09/228-8544
Viking	Ferries	Katajanokka	09/12351

Note: Finland's country code is 358 (drop initial zero of area code when calling Finland internationally).

nights the rest of the year. I've given high/low prices here in Swedish currency (7 kr = about $1). A one-way berth in a four-person cabin with a private bath costs 500/300 kr on the *Regina Baltica*, 600/400 kr on the *Victoria*. Round-trip prices cost only a little more: 600/400 kr on the *Regina Baltica*, 700/500 kr on the *Victoria*. The two legs of a round-trip don't have to be on successive days (unlike the Stockholm–Helsinki ferries), and the price depends on both the outbound and return days of the week. Couples can rent a cabin for themselves for roughly four times the per-person prices above.

Breakfast is 90 kr, and the *smörgåsbord* dinner is 240 kr. Reserve your meal (and even, if possible, a window table) when you buy your ticket. The boats have exchange offices with acceptable rates for your leftover cash.

Reserve by calling either the Stockholm reservations line (Swedish tel. 08/666-6001) or the Estonian booking number (Estonian tel. 640-9808). Pick up your tickets at the port on the day of departure or at their downtown office (Klarabergsgatan 31 in Stockholm). Online booking is possible only in Swedish and for entire cabins (www.tallink.se).

In Stockholm, Tallink ships leave from the Frihamnen harbor. To get from downtown Stockholm to Frihamnen harbor, take the shuttle bus from the main station (30 kr, leaves at about 15:30, check times when buying ticket), or take public bus #1 (marked *Frihamnen*) from Kungsgatan to the end of the line (30 kr, 3–6/hr, 25 min). In Tallinn, the Tallink ships dock at Terminal D (see "Arrival in Tallinn," later).

Company	Tallinn Terminal	Tallinn Phone #	Website
Tallink/Silja	Ferries: A; Fast boats: D	640-9808	www.tallink.ee, www.tallink.se
Linda Line	Linnahall	699-9333	www.lindaline.ee
Eckerö Line	B	631-8606	www.eckeroline.fi
Viking	A	666-3966	www.vikingline.fi

Note: Estonia's country code is 372 (dial number in full when calling Estonia internationally).

Speeding Between Helsinki and Tallinn

From April to October, two companies offer **fast boats** that link Helsinki and Tallinn (2/hr, 2-hour journey, first departure about 7:00, last about 21:30). You can reserve in advance by phone or online, or buy tickets from a travel agency (such as the Helsinki Expert office in the TI—see below), but it's rarely necessary. Fast-boat trips may be canceled in stormy weather (in which case you'll be put on a bigger, slower boat).

Fares run €30–50 one-way (evening departures from Helsinki and morning departures from Tallinn are cheapest). Round-trips start at about €40 if you come back with the same company. Linda Line, which uses small hydrofoils, is the fastest (only 90 min, 45-pound luggage limit), but is routinely canceled in windy weather.

Big, very slow **car ferries** also run year-round between Helsinki and Tallinn (7/day, 3.5 hours, cheaper at €20–30 one-way, 15 percent discount for round-trip, student and senior discounts) and come with great *smörgåsbord* buffets (expect €12 extra for breakfast, €25 for dinner). These boats are filled with "four-legged Finns" crazy about cheap booze and karaoke. Foot passengers prefer the Viking ferries, which depart from central Helsinki. The Tallink and Eckerö Line ferries use Helsinki's Länsi terminal (no problem for drivers, but hard to reach by public transit).

The helpful **Helsinki Expert** desk in the Helsinki TI sells tickets (€7 fee per booking) and posts a sheet clearly explaining departures and costs. The TI in Tallinn posts a list but does not sell tickets. The chart in this chapter lists the names, ship types, phone numbers, terminals, and websites for the main ferry operators. Websites have all the latest information, and most allow online booking. Tallinn and Helsinki each have several different ferry terminals; make sure you know which one your boat leaves from (for descriptions of Helsinki's terminals, see page 477; for Tallinn's, see "Arrival in Tallinn").

Tallinn

Among Nordic medieval cities, there's none nearly as well-preserved as Tallinn. Its mostly intact city wall includes 26 watchtowers, each topped by a pointy red roof. Baroque and choral music ring out from its old Lutheran churches. I'd guess Tallinn has more restaurants, cafés, and surprises per capita and square inch than any city in this book—and the fun is comparatively cheap.

Tallinn is busy cleaning up the mess left by the communist experiment. New shops, restaurants, and hotels are bursting out of old buildings. The city changes so fast, even locals can't keep up. The Old Town is getting a lot of tourist traffic now, so smart shopping is wise. You'll eat better for half the price by seeking out places that cater to locals.

As a member of the Hanseatic League, the city was a medieval stronghold of the Baltic trading world. (See Hanseatic League sidebar on page 306.) In the 19th and early 20th centuries, Tallinn industrialized and expanded beyond its walls. Architects encircled the Old Town, putting up broad streets of public buildings, low Scandinavian-style apartment buildings, and single-family wooden houses. After 1945, Soviet planners ringed the city with stands of now-crumbling concrete high-rises where many of Tallinn's Russian immigrants settled.

Tallinn's Old Town is a fascinating package of pleasing towers, ramparts, facades, *striptiis* bars, churches, shops, and people-watching. It's a rewarding detour for those who want to spice their Scandinavian travels with an ex-Soviet twist.

Planning Your Time

On a three-week tour of Scandinavia, Tallinn is certainly worth a day. Get oriented with either the official walking tour or my "Hello Tallinn" self-guided walk. Check concert schedules if you'll be around for the evening.

Day-Trippers: Whether arriving from Helsinki or Stockholm, hit the ground running by following my self-guided walk right from the ferry terminal. Enjoy the best restaurant you can afford in the Old Town for lunch. Then spend the afternoon shopping and browsing (or out at the Estonian Open-Air Museum if you enjoy folk history, or out at the Kumu Art Museum if you like art).

Remember to bring a jacket—Tallinn can be chilly even on sunny summer days. And, given that locals call their cobbled streets "a free foot massage," sturdy shoes are smart, too.

Orientation to Tallinn

(11 Estonian krooni = about $1)
Almost everything of interest to tourists is in Tallinn's walled Old Town, an easy 15-minute walk from the ferry terminals where most visitors land (see "Arrival in Tallinn," next page). The Old Town is divided into two parts (historically, two separate towns): the upper town, Toompea, and the lower town, with Town Hall Square. It's all surrounded by a remarkably intact medieval wall, and within that wall, another wall separates the two towns.

Town Hall Square (Raekoja plats) marks the heart of the medieval lower town. The TI and nearly everything of sightseeing and edible interest is nearby. Pickpockets have become a problem in the more touristy parts of the Old Town, so keep valuables carefully stowed.

Tourist Information

The hardworking, English-speaking **main TI** has maps, concert listings, and free brochures. It also sells *Tallinn in Your Pocket* and the Tallinn Card, both described below (Mon–Fri 9:00–20:00, Sat–Sun 10:00–18:00, closes earlier off-season, a block off Town Hall Square at Kullassepa 4, tel. 645-7777, www.tourism.tallinn.ee). A helpful **branch TI** is at the Viru Keskus shopping center, next to Hotel Viru just outside the Old Town walls (daily 9:00–21:00, through Viru Gate, Viru Valjak 4, tel. 610-1557).

Travelers' Tent is a creative service offered by young people for young visitors, located in a tent in the park immediately in front of the TI. The friendly staff is a great source for backpacker info, youthful tours, bike rental, and cheap accommodations, with longer hours than the TI. Their map (free, but give a donation) is packed with fun tips to enjoy Tallinn down, dirty, and on the cheap. Seriously consider their creative, cheap, and spirited tours (see "Tours in Tallinn," later).

TALLINN

Tallinn in Your Pocket is the best city guidebook on Tallinn (may be free at your hotel, otherwise 35 kr all over town, on ships, at airport newsstands, and at the TIs). It has complete restaurant, hotel, and sight listings that go far beyond what's listed in this book, plus a rare Old Town map listing all of the tiny streets (for pre-trip planning, use the online edition at www.inyourpocket.com).

Tallinn Card: This card—sold at the TIs, airport, train station, travel agencies, ferry ports, and big hotels—gives you free use of public transport and entry to more than 40 museums and major sights (185 kr/6 hours, 375 kr/24 hours, 435 kr/48 hours, 495 kr/72 hours, comes with good info booklet, www.tallinncard.ee).

From the 24-hour level up, it also covers various bus tours (including the fun bus-and-walking tour and the hop-on, hop-off tour) and bike tours; see "Tours in Tallinn" for specifics. If you're planning on taking one of the tours (250–300 kr) and visiting several sights (ranging from 40 kr to 95 kr), this card will likely save you money. Add up the cost of your intended sightseeing to confirm.

Arrival in Tallinn

By Boat: Tallinn has four terminals lettered A through D, and a fifth terminal called Linnahall (used only by the fast Linda Line boat). Terminals A, B, and C are clustered together; Terminal D is a 10-minute walk to the east (and is the farthest from the Old Town); and the Linnahall terminal is a 10-minute walk to the west (just over the large stairway). Each terminal offers baggage storage. Find out which terminal you're leaving from so that you don't miss your return boat.

If you have no luggage, walk 15 minutes to reach the center of town—just follow signs to the city center and set your sights on the spire in the distance (or follow my "Hello Tallinn" walk, below). The zone between the port and town is a sprawling, car-friendly commercial zone—the first stop for many Finns bargain-hunting for booze, cigarettes, and clothing.

If you have luggage, it's best to grab a cab (see taxi advice under "Getting Around Tallinn")—otherwise your rolling bags will take a pounding on the Old Town's cobbled streets. Good luck getting a cabbie to use the meter; the ride shouldn't cost more than 80–100 kr.

The public transportation option is bus #2, which runs from the ferry terminal and stops behind Hotel Viru, several blocks from the Old Town (2/hr, single tickets cost 13 kr from kiosks, or pay driver 20 kr, see port stop curbside, get off at Laikmaa stop).

By Plane: The airport is close to town and has a small info desk (www.tallinn-airport.ee, tel. 605-8888). A taxi to the Old

Town should cost around 100 kr (confirm price first, see taxi advice under "Getting Around Tallinn"). Public bus #2 connects the airport and stops behind Hotel Viru, a few blocks from the Old Town (departs from curb in front of arrivals area, ride it six stops to Laikmaa); from there bus #2 continues on to the ferry terminals (2/hr, single tickets cost 13 kr from kiosks, 20 kr from driver).

By Train: While Tallinn has a sleepy and cute little train station, few tourists will need to use it. The station, a 10-minute walk across the busy highway from the Old Town, is adjacent to the big, cheap Hotel Shnelli and the colorful Balti Jaam Market.

Helpful Hints

US Embassy: It's at Kentmanni 20 (tel. 668-8100, http://estonia.usembassy.gov).

Money: About 11 Estonian krooni (kr) equal $1. The kroon is permanently tied to the euro (15.65 krooni = €1). Euros aren't accepted everywhere yet, and in places where they are accepted, don't expect a good exchange rate. ATMs—the easiest way to get krooni—are everywhere, including at the ferry terminals and the airport. Plenty of exchange offices compete to change your leftover Swedish kronor and euros, but skip them if you can—banks have the best rates. A bank near the main TI is **SEB** (Mon–Fri 9:00–16:30, closed Sat–Sun, Harju 13). Credit cards are widely accepted.

Telephones: Estonian phone numbers are seven digits with no area codes. Tallinn numbers begin with 6, and mobile phones (more expensive to call) begin with 5. (From outside Estonia, you'll first dial the country code: 372.) Phone cards for public booths are sold at kiosks around town (in 50-kr and 100-kr denominations). Estonia doesn't sell international phone cards for making cheap calls abroad. Skype, which allows you to make free Internet calls using your laptop, was founded in Estonia and is relied on for international calls (www.skype.com). In case of emergency, dial 112.

Internet Access: Just outside the Old Town, several places advertise Internet access. The **Apollo Bookstore** has three terminals upstairs in a cool café (60 kr/hr; see listing on page 536). The top floor (A5) at the **Kaubamaja** department store charges a straight 35 kr per hour (daily 9:00–21:00, in far building of the Viru Keskus shopping center). **24 Metro** is on the lower level of the shopping center where the regional buses depart (25 kr/hr, daily 7:00–22:00). Many hotels offer free Internet access in their lobbies, and some have Wi-Fi. At the **Travelers' Tent**, you can briefly check your email for free, courtesy of the friendly students (in front of main TI).

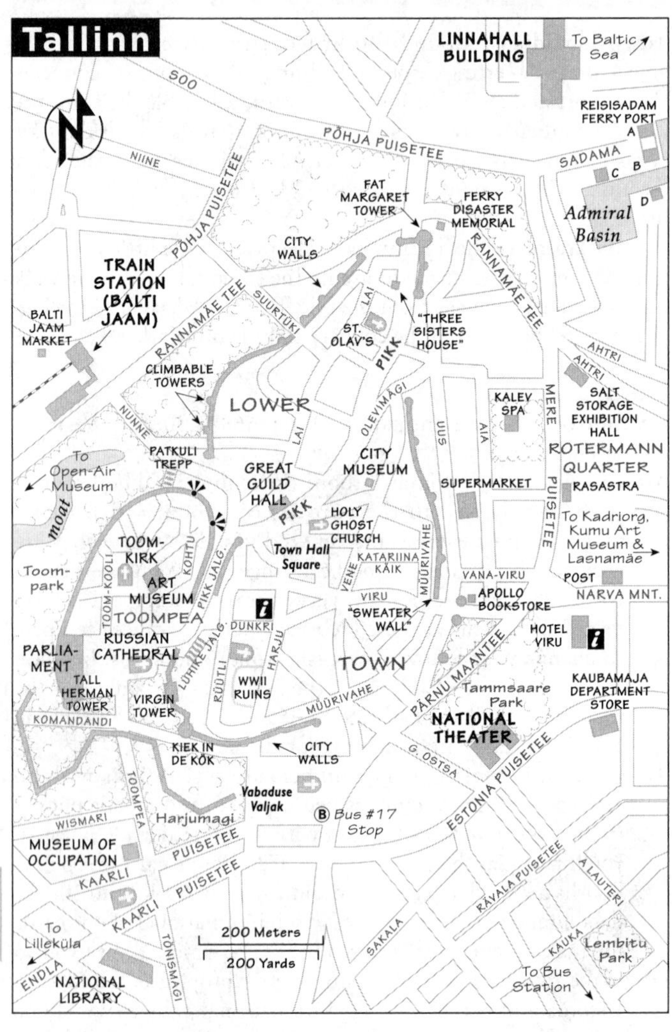

Postage: Stamps can be purchased at kiosks and many of the postcard-selling souvenir stores.

Laundry: Top Clean is in the bottom level of the Viru Keskus shopping center (full service-90 kr/load, daily 9:00–21:00, tel. 610-1405). **Pesumaja** is less expensive but farther from the center (full service-67 kr/load, drop off before noon for same-day service, Mon–Fri 8:00–20:00, Sat–Sun 11:00–19:00, Pärnu maantee 48, across from Kosmos stop of tram lines #3 or #6, or walk 10 min from Vabaduse väljak, Tallinn's Freedom Square).

Travel Agency: Mainedd Travel Agency (on Town Hall Square) is as good as any. It's handy and sells tickets to all boats for no extra fee (Mon–Fri 9:30–17:30, closed Sat–Sun, Raekoja plats 18, tel. 644-4744).

Good Guides: Mati Rumessen is a top-notch guide, especially for car tours outside of town (450 kr/hr walk, 3,500 kr/day with car, mobile 509-4661, www.tourservice.ee, mati700@hot.ee). Other fine guides are **Antonio Villacis** (generally 120 kr/person per hour, mobile 5662-9306, antonio.villacis@gmail.com) and **Miina Puusepp** (€20/hr, mobile 551-7028, miinap@hot.ee).

Video Prep: To understand the spirit of modern Estonia, you need to understand their musical fight for freedom. The 90-minute documentary movie, *The Singing Revolution*, tells the story well. See it before your trip.

Getting Around Tallinn

To explore the Old Town and surrounding areas, your feet are all you need.

Take a **bus, tram,** or **trolley** if you're sleeping outside of the Old Town, or if you're visiting Kadriorg (palace), the Kumu Art Museum, or the Estonian Open-Air Museum. If you're arriving or departing by ferry or plane, remember that bus #2 links the port and airport, with a handy stop downtown behind Hotel Viru, several blocks from the Old Town (get off at Laikmaa).

One ticket, valid for a single ride on any type of public transport, costs 13 kr from a kiosk at a bus stop or 20 kr when purchased from the driver. Frequent riders save by purchasing a packet of 10 tickets for 90 kr from a kiosk, or by buying a transit pass (55 kr/24 hours, 100 kr/72 hours, sold at newsstands, www.tak.ee). The Tallinn Card covers public transportation (described earlier in "Tourist Information").

Taxis in Tallinn are expensive and quick to rip off tourists. Any pickup in the Old Town comes with a steep minimum charge, so you'll save a bit by walking away from the tourist center and into the real world. Each of the countless companies is free to charge what they like. Take a close look at the price list printed on the rear passenger-side door. The base fare is usually 45–70 kr; the per kilometer charge is generally 10–15 kr. Anything more is considered too high. Glance inside—a photo ID license should be attached to the middle of the dashboard.

Cabbies are required to use the meter and to give you a receipt printed from the meter. If you don't get a receipt, it's safe to assume you're being ripped off and you legally don't need to pay.

If you've just arrived at the airport or the ferry port, it may be hard to avoid taking a cab. The cabbies who flag *you* down ("Taxi?"), and have run-down-looking cars or offer strip-club brochures, are likely into creative income augmentation.

Tours in Tallinn

Bus and Walking Tour—This thoroughly enjoyable, narrated 2.5-hour tour of Tallinn comes in two parts: first by bus for an overview of sights outside of the Old Town such as the Song Festival Grounds and Kadriorg (palace), then on foot to sights within the Old Town (300 kr, pay driver; covered by Tallinn Card that's valid for 24 hours or more—not by the 6-hour version; in English and Finnish; May–Sept daily departures from Terminal A, Terminal D, and major hotels in city center—for example, Hotel Viru at 10:30, 13:20, and 15:30, bus leaves harbor terminals about 30 min beforehand, tel. 610-8634).

Tallinn Alternative Tours—These student-run tours show you the real city without the political and corporation correctness of the official tourist agencies. All tours start from the Travelers' Tent, run from June through August, and are offered daily (except for the pub crawl, only on weekends). Reserve tours by calling mobile 5554-2111 or dropping by the tent (www.tallinnfreetour.com). Their **City Introductory Walking Tour** is free (daily at noon, 2 hours, English only). On the **Funky Bike Tour,** you'll bike to an old market and through residential districts; you'll learn about the Russian community, Soviet heritage, and the divide between Estonians and Russian Estonians that survives to this day (150 kr, daily at 12:00, 3 hours). The **Beautiful Bike Tour** takes you to the Song Festival Grounds, Kadriorg, and more (150 kr, daily at 16:00, 3 hours). The rowdy **Tallinn Pub Crawl** includes three drinks and a barf bag (225 kr, Thu–Sat at 21:00, 3 hours).

Hop-on, Hop-off Bus Tours—**City Sightseeing** offers a 50-minute bus tour with eight stops. Aside from a stop near Toompea Castle, the route is entirely outside the Old Town, and the frequency is low (just 4/day, so you need to coordinate your sightseeing to the rare departures). But if you want to rest your feet and listen to a fairly good recorded commentary, the tour does get you to outlying sights such as Kadriorg and the towering Russalka Monument. You can catch it at the port terminals and some major hotels (250 kr, free with Tallinn Card valid for 24 hours or more, May–Oct daily 10:30–15:30 plus summer nights at 20:45 and 22:00, no buses Nov–April, tel. 655-8328, www.citysightseeing.ee).

Bike Tour—**City Bikes** offers a two-hour, nine-mile biking tour that takes you outside the city walls to the harder-to-reach Tallinn sights: Kadriorg, Song Festival Grounds, the beach at Pirita, and more (250 kr, free with Tallinn Card valid for 24 hours or more; daily May–Sept at 11:00 and 17:00, Oct–April at 11:00; departs from their office at Uus 33 in the Old Town, mobile 511-1819, www.citybike.ee). They also rent bikes for exploring the city on your own (35 kr/1 hour, 150 kr/6 hours, 200 kr/24 hours).

Self-Guided Walk

▲▲▲Hello Tallinn

This walk explores the "two towns" of Tallinn. The city once consisted of two feuding medieval towns separated by a wall. The upper town—on the hill, called Toompea—was the seat of government ruling Estonia. The lower town was an autonomous Hanseatic trading center filled with German, Danish, and Swedish merchants who hired Estonians to do their menial labor.

Two steep, narrow streets—the "Long Leg" and the "Short Leg"—connect Toompea and the lower town. This walk winds through both towns, going up the short leg and down the long leg. If you're coming from the ferry terminal, you'll enter the town at #1 (see map on page 520). If you're coming from Town Hall Square, walk out to the Fat Margaret Tower.

❶ To Fat Margaret Tower and Start of Walk: From the ferry terminal, hike toward the tall tapering spire, go through a small park, and enter the Old Town through the archway by the squat Fat Margaret Tower. Just outside the tower on a bluff overlooking the harbor is a broken black arch, a memorial to 852 people who perished in 1994 when the *Estonia* passenger ferry sank during its Tallinn-Stockholm run. The details remain murky, and conspiracy theorists still think Sweden sank it. (The boat went down very quickly; Sweden has never allowed any divers to explore the remains, and now there's talk of entombing it in concrete, leading some to believe the incident involved some kind of nuclear material-related mischief.)

Fat Margaret Tower guarded the entry gate of the town (in medieval times, the sea came much closer to this point than it does today). The relief above the gate dates from the 16th century, during the Hanseatic times, when Sweden took Estonia from Germany. (The paltry Estonian Maritime Museum in the tower costs 50 kr and is open Wed–Sun 10:00–18:00.)

Just inside the gate, you'll feel the economic power of those early German trading days. The merchant's home, nicknamed the "Three Sisters" (on your right with your back to the sea), is a textbook example of a merchant home/warehouse/office from the 15th-century Hanseatic Golden Age. The charmingly carved door near the corner evokes the wealth of Tallinn's merchant class.

• *Head up Pikk (which means "long") street.*

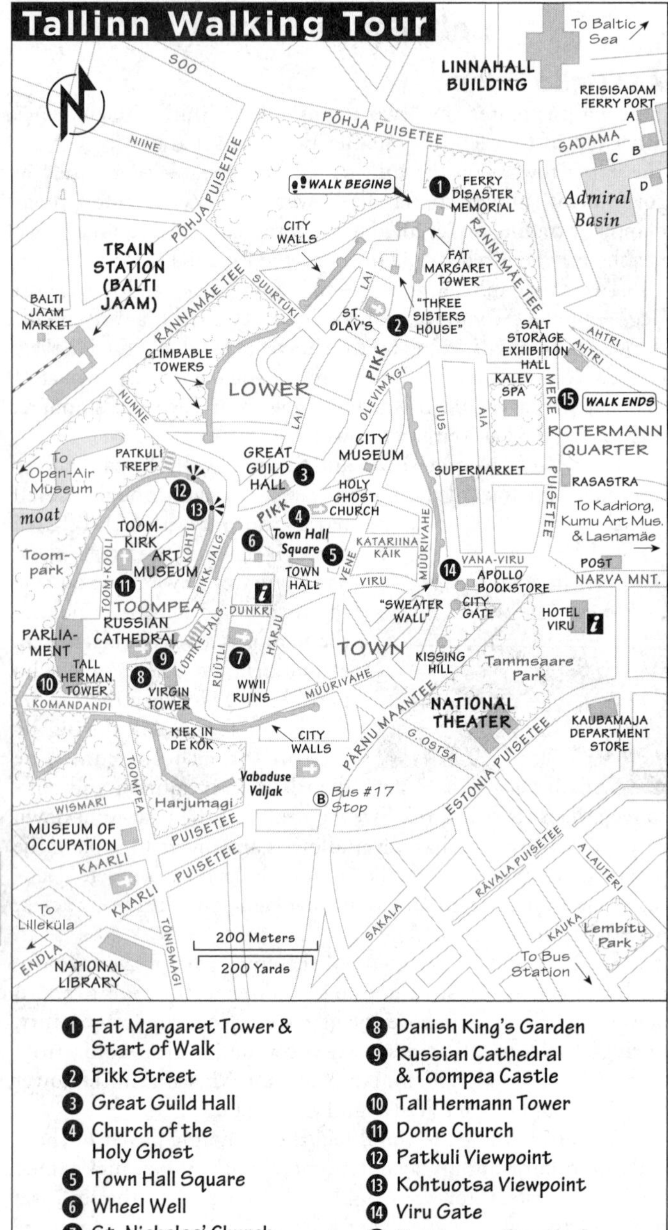

1. Fat Margaret Tower & Start of Walk
2. Pikk Street
3. Great Guild Hall
4. Church of the Holy Ghost
5. Town Hall Square
6. Wheel Well
7. St. Nicholas' Church
8. Danish King's Garden
9. Russian Cathedral & Toompea Castle
10. Tall Hermann Tower
11. Dome Church
12. Patkuli Viewpoint
13. Kohtuotsa Viewpoint
14. Viru Gate
15. Rotermann Quarter & End of Walk

❷ **Pikk Street:** This street, the medieval merchants' main drag leading from the harbor up into town, is lined with interesting buildings—many were warehouses complete with cranes on the gables. You'll pass St. Olav's Church (Oleviste Kirik, a Baptist church today), notable for what was once the tallest spire in Scandinavia. Its plain whitewashed interior is skippable, though climbing 234 stairs up the tower rewards you with a great view (church entry free, daily 10:00–18:00; tower-30 kr, open April–Oct only; www.oleviste.ee).

While tourists see only a peaceful scene today, locals strolling this street are reminded of dark times under Moscow's rule. The KGB used the tower at St. Olav's Church to block Finnish TV signals. And the ministry of police (nearby at Pikk 59) was, before 1991, the sinister local headquarters of the KGB. "Creative interrogation methods" were used here. Locals well knew that "from here started the road of suffering," as Tallinn's troublemakers were sent to Siberian gulags. The ministry building was called "the tallest building in town" (because "when you're in the basement, you can already see Siberia"). Notice the bricked-up windows at foot level.

The Navitrolla Gallerii (at #36) is much happier, filled with art by a well-known Estonian artist. His whimsical, animal-themed prints are vaguely reminiscent of *Where the Wild Things Are* (Mon–Fri 10:00–18:00, Sat–Sun 10:00–16:00, next to Hell Hunt Pub, tel. 631-3716, www.navitrolla.ee).

Farther up Pikk, the fine **Hall of the Black Heads Society** (at #26) dates from 1440. For 500 years, until Hitler invited Estonian Germans "back to their historical fatherland" in the 1930s, this was a German merchants' club.

Until the 19th century, Estonians were essentially serfs under German merchants who dominated the economy. The German big shots were part of the Great Guild, while the German little shots had to make do with the Black Heads Society. This was a union or business fraternity limited to single German men. In Hanseatic towns, when a fire or battle had to be fought, single men were deployed first, because they had no family. Single men were considered unattached to the community and therefore had no opportunity for power in the Hanseatic social structure. When a Black Head Society member married a local woman, he was considered to have a vested interest in the town's economy and well-being. He could then join the more prestigious Great Guild, and with that status, a promising future economically and politically often opened up.

Today the hall is a concert venue. Its namesake "black head" is the head of St. Mauritius, an early Christian martyr beheaded in Switzerland (A.D. 200). Reliefs decorating the building recall Tallinn's Hanseatic glory days.

Architecture fans enjoy several fanciful facades along here (including the boldly Art Nouveau #18 and the colorful, eclectic facade across the street).

❸ **Great Guild Hall:** Pikk, home to the big-shot merchants, feels Germanic because it once was. The Great Guild Hall was the epitome of wealth, with its wide (and therefore highly taxed) front.

Across the street, at #16, the famous Maiasmokk ("Sweet Tooth") coffee shop, which was the sweetest place in town during Soviet days, remains a fine spot for a cheap coffee-and-pastry break (see "Eating in Tallinn").

❹ **Church of the Holy Ghost (Pühavaimu kirik):** Sporting a great clock from 1633, the church is worth a visit. The plaque on the wall is in Estonian and Russian. Before 1991, things were designed for "inner tourism" (within the USSR). This church retains its 14th-century design. In back, the old flag of Tallinn—the same as today's red and white Danish flag—recalls the 13th-century Danish rule. (The name "Tallinn" means "City of the Danes".) The Danes sold Tallinn to the German Teutonic Knights, who lost it to the Swedes, who lost it to the Russians. Except for two decades in the early 20th century, Tallinn remained Russian until Estonia regained its independence in 1991. The windows are mostly from the 1990s (suggested 15 kr donation, Pühavaimu 2, tel. 644-1487, www.eelk.ee). The church hosts English-language Lutheran services Sundays at 15:00.

• *From the church, tiny Saiakang lane (meaning "White Bread"—bread, cakes, and pies have been sold here since medieval times) leads to...*

❺ **Town Hall Square (Raekoja plats):** A marketplace through the centuries, this is the natural springboard for Old Town explorations. The cancan of fine old buildings is a reminder that this was the center of the autonomous lower town, a merchant city of Hanseatic traders. Once this was the scene of criminals chained to pillories for public humiliation and knights showing off in chivalrous tournaments; today it's full of Scandinavians savoring the cheap beer, children singing on the bandstand, and cruise-ship groups listening to their guides. (While you'll see few Americans early and late, the old center is inundated with them throughout midday, following the numbered paddles carried high by their well-scrubbed, young, local guides.)

The 15th-century Town Hall (Raekoda) dominates the square; it's now a museum, and climbing its tower earns a commanding view (see page 531). On the opposite side of the square, across from #12 in the corner, the pharmacy (Raeapteek) dates from 1422 and claims—as do many—to be Europe's oldest. While it's still a functioning pharmacy, the decor goes back to medieval times and welcomes guests with painted ceiling beams, English descriptions, and long-expired aspirin (Mon–Fri 9:00–19:00, Sat 9:00–17:00, closed Sun). Town Hall Square is ringed by touristy restaurants and inviting cafés. The TI is a block away (behind Town Hall).

• *Facing the Town Hall, head right up Dunkri street one block to the...*

❻ **Wheel Well:** The well is named for the "high-tech" wheel, a marvel that made fetching water easier. Most of the Old Town's buildings are truly old, dating from the 15th- and 16th-century boom-time. Decrepit before the 1991 fall of the USSR, Tallinn is now more affluent and has been quickly revitalized.

• *Turn left on Rüütli street and walk two blocks to...*

❼ **St. Nicholas' (Niguliste) Church:** This 13th-century Gothic church-turned-art-museum served the German merchants and knights who lived in this neighborhood 500 years ago. The Russians bombed it in World War II: In one terrible night, on March 9, 1944, Tallinn was hit, and the area around this church—once a charming district, dense with medieval buildings—was flattened (35 kr, Wed–Sun 10:00–17:00, closed Mon–Tue; organ concerts Sat and Sun at 16:00).

• *From the church, turn right and climb the steep, cobbled, Lühike jalg ("Short Leg Lane"). It's lined with high-quality Estonian craft shops. At the gate, notice the original oak door, one of two gates through the wall separating the two cities. This passage is still the ritual meeting point of the mayor and prime minister whenever there is an important agreement between town and country. Don't go through the gate, but continue straight into the view courtyard. Then climb right toward the Russian Cathedral for a good view of the wall.*

❽ **Danish King's Garden:** Stand in the former garden of the Danish king. The imposing city wall once had 46 towers—the stout, round tower way ahead is nicknamed "Kiek in de Kök." (While fun to say, it means "Peek in the Kitchen.") It was situated so that "peek" is exactly what guards could do. (It's now a small museum with cannons; see "Sights in Tallinn," later.)

Tallinn is famous among Danes as the birthplace of their flag. According to legend, the Danes were losing a battle here. Suddenly, a white cross fell from heaven and landed in a pool of blood. The Danes were inspired and went on to win. To this day, their flag is a white cross on a red background.

• *Walk to the entrance of the onion-domed Russian Cathedral facing the pink palace.*

❾ **Russian Cathedral and Toompea Castle:** The Alexander Nevsky Cathedral was built here in 1900 over the supposed grave of a legendary Estonian hero—Kalevipoeg. While it's a beautiful building, most Estonians don't like this church. Built to face the national parliament, it was a crass attempt to flex Russian cultural muscles during a period of Estonian national revival. Step inside for a whiff of Russian Orthodoxy; about a third of Tallinn's population is ethnic Russian (church free and open daily 8:00–19:00).

Cross the street to the pink palace—an 18th-century addition that Russia built onto the Toompea Castle. Today, it's the Estonian Parliament building, flying the Estonian flag—the flag of both the first (1918–1940) and second (1991–present) Estonian republics. (Locals say they were always independent...just occupied—first by the Soviets, then by the Nazis, and then again by the USSR.) Notice the Estonian seal: three lions for three great battles in Estonian history, and oak leaves for strength and stubbornness. Ancient pagan Estonians, who believed spirits lived in oak trees, would walk through forests of oak to toughen up. (To this day, Estonian cemeteries are in forests. Keeping some of their pagan sensibilities, they believe the spirits of their departed loved ones live on in the trees.)

• *Step left across the parking lot, around the palace, and into the park to see the...*

⑩ **Tall Hermann Tower:** This tallest tower of the castle wall is a powerful symbol here. For 50 years, while Estonian flags were hidden in cellars, the Soviet flag flew from Tall Hermann. As the USSR was unraveling, the Estonians proudly and defiantly replaced the red Soviet flag here with their own black, white, and blue flag.

• *Backtrack and go uphill, passing the Russian church on your right. Climb Toom-Kooli street to the...*

⑪ **Dome Church (Toomkirik):** Estonia is ostensibly Lutheran, but few Tallinners go to church. A recent Gallup Poll showed Estonia to be the least religious country in the EU—only 14 percent of the respondents stated that religion is an important part of their daily lives. Most churches double as concert venues or museums. Enter the Dome Church (free, Tue–Sun 9:00–17:00, closed Mon, www.eelk.ee/tallinna.toom). It's a textbook example of simple Northern European Gothic, built in the 13th century during Danish rule, then rebuilt after a 1684 fire. Once the church of Tallinn's wealthy, it's littered with medieval coats of arms, each representing a rich merchant family and carved by local masters—the smaller the coat of arms, the older the family. The floor is paved with tombstones.

• *Leaving the church, turn left. Pass the slanted tree and the big, green, former noblemen's clubhouse on your right (vacated when Germans returned home in the 1930s), and go down cobbled Rahukohtu lane. Local businesses and embassies are moving their offices here and sprucing up the neighborhood. As you pass under the yellow Patkuli Vaateplats arch, notice a ramshackle bit of the 1980s surviving. Just a few years ago, the entire city looked like this. Belly up to the grand viewpoint.*

⓬ **Patkuli Viewpoint:** Survey the scene. On the far left, the Neoclassical facade of the executive branch of Estonia's government enjoys the view. Below you, a bit of the old moat remains. The *Group* sign marks Tallinn's tiny train station, and the clutter of stalls behind that is the rustic market. In the distance, ferries shuttle to and from Helsinki (just 50 miles away). Beyond the lower town's medieval wall and towers stands the green spire of St. Olav's Church, once 98 feet taller and, locals claim, the world's tallest tower in 1492. Beyond that is the 985-foot-tall TV tower (much appreciated by Estonians for the heroics involved in keeping the people's airwaves open during the harrowing days when they won independence from the USSR). During Soviet domination, Finnish TV was responsible for giving Estonians their only look at Western lifestyles. Imagine: In the 1980s, many locals had never seen a banana or pineapple—except on TV. People still talk of the day that Finland broadcast the soft-porn movie *Emmanuelle.* A historic migration of Estonians flocked from the countryside to Tallinn to get within rabbit-ear's distance of Helsinki and see all that flesh on TV.

• *Go back through the arch, turn immediately left down the narrow lane, turn right, take the first left, and pass through the trees to another viewpoint.*

⓭ **Kohtuotsa Viewpoint:** On the far left is the busy cruise port and the skinny white spire of the Church of the Holy Ghost; the spire to its right is the 16th-century Town Hall spire. On the far right is the tower of St. Nicholas' Church. Visually trace Pikk street, Tallinn's historic main drag, which winds through the Old Town, leading from Toompea down the hill (below you from right to left), through the gate tower, past the Church of the Holy Ghost (and Town Hall Square), and out to the harbor. The undesirable part of

this city of 400,000 is the clutter of Soviet-era apartment blocks in the distant horizon. The nearest skyscraper (white) is Hotel Viru, in Soviet times the biggest hotel in the Baltics, and infamous as a clunky, dingy slumbermill. Locals joke that Hotel Viru was built from a new Soviet wonder material called "micro-concrete" (60 percent concrete, 40 percent microphones). To the left of Hotel Viru is the Rotermann Quarter, an industrial plant revamped into a new commercial zone. Our walk will end there.

• *From the viewpoint, descend to the lower town. Go out and left down Kohtu, past the Finnish Embassy (on your left). Back at the Dome Church, the slanted tree points the way, left down Piiskopi ("Bishop's Street"). At the onion domes, turn left again and follow the old wall down Pikk jalg ("Long Leg Street") into the lower town. Wander back to Town Hall Square.*

⓮ Through Viru Gate, to ⓯ Rotermann Quarter and End of Walk: Cross through the square (left of the Town Hall's tower) and go downhill (passing the kitschy medieval Olde Hansa Restaurant, with its bonneted waitresses and merry men). Continue straight down Viru street toward Hotel Viru, the blocky white skyscraper in the distance. Viru street is old Tallinn's busiest and kitschiest shopping street. Just past the strange and modern wood/glass/stone mall, Müürivahe street leads left along the old wall, called the "Sweater Wall." This is a colorful and tempting gauntlet of women selling handmade knitwear (although anything with images and bright colors is likely machine-made). Beyond the sweaters, Katariina Käik, a lane with top-notch local artisan shops, leads left. Back on Viru street, the golden arches lead to the medieval arches—Viru Gate—that mark the end of old Tallinn. Outside the gates (at Viru 23), an arch leads into the Bastion Gardens, a tangle of antiques, quilt, and sweater shops that delight shoppers, and the fine Apollo bookstore (with Internet access and a fine little café upstairs). Opposite Viru 23, above the flower stalls, is a small park on a piece of old bastion known as the Kissing Hill (come up here after dark and you'll find out why).

Just beyond is Hotel Viru, the Viru Keskus shopping center (with a branch TI, Internet café, supermarket in the basement, and laundry service—see "Helpful Hints"), and the real world. For a look at today's Tallinn, browse through the Rotermann Quarter. Sprawling between Hotel Viru and the port, this 19th-century industrial zone is now a much-hyped commercial district with office parks, fancy condos, department stores, and restaurants.

Sights in Tallinn

In or near the Old Town

Tallinn has dozens of small museums, most suitable only for specialized tastes (complete listings in *Tallinn in Your Pocket*). The following sights are the ones I'd consider visiting.

Town Hall (Raekoda)—This building facing Town Hall Square is a museum with exhibits on the town's administration and history, and an interesting bit on the story of limestone (50 kr, July–Aug Mon–Sat 10:00–16:00, closed Sun and Sept–June, tel. 645-7900, www.tallinn.ee/raekoda).

Town Hall Tower—The place to see all of Tallinn, it rewards those who climb its 155 steps with a wonderful city view (40 kr, June–Aug daily 11:00–18:00, closed rest of year).

Kiek in de Kök—The "Peek in the Kitchen" tower, now a museum, mixes medieval cannons and charts left over from the Livonian wars (floors 3–5) with modern photography exhibits (floors 1, 2, and 6; 25 kr, good English descriptions, Tue–Sun 10:30–18:00, closed Mon, tel. 644-6686).

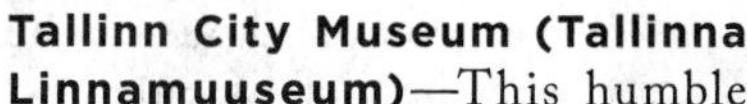

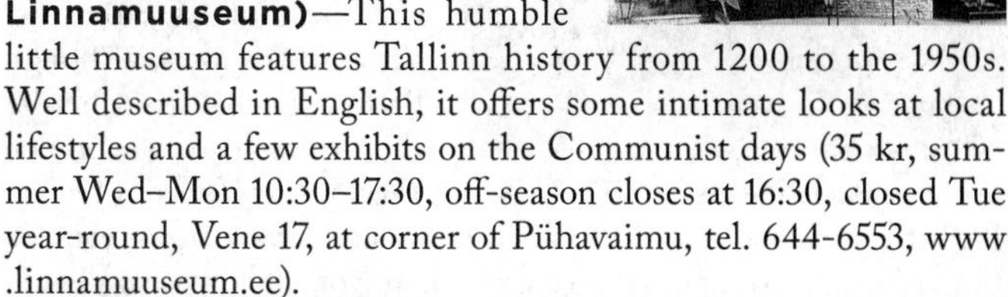

Tallinn City Museum (Tallinna Linnamuuseum)—This humble little museum features Tallinn history from 1200 to the 1950s. Well described in English, it offers some intimate looks at local lifestyles and a few exhibits on the Communist days (35 kr, summer Wed–Mon 10:30–17:30, off-season closes at 16:30, closed Tue year-round, Vene 17, at corner of Pühavaimu, tel. 644-6553, www.linnamuuseum.ee).

Estonian History Museum—Usually located in the Great Guild Hall at Pikk 17, this museum tells the story of the country in a chronological sweep, including Vikings, Crusades, foreign lords, and lots of artifacts on one easy floor. The building is closed for major renovations until 2011, but if you're determined to see the collection, you'll find its temporary home in Maarjamäe Palace, outside of town (45 kr, Pirita tee 56, take buses #1, #5, #8, or #34, tel. 641-1630, www.eam.ee).

Outer Tallinn

▲Song Festival Grounds—At this open-air theater, built in 1959 and resembling an oversized Hollywood Bowl, the Estonian nation gathers to sing. Every five years, these grounds host a huge national song festival with 25,000 singers and 100,000 spectators.

While it hosts big pop-music acts, too, it's a national monument for the compelling role it played in Estonia's fight for independence.

Since 1988, when locals sang patriotic songs here in defiance of Soviet rule, these grounds have taken on a symbolic importance to the nation. Locals vividly recall putting on folk costumes knitted by their grandmothers (some of whom later died in Siberia) and coming here with masses of Estonians to sing. Overlooking the grounds from the cheap seats is a statue of Gustav Ernesaks, who directed the Estonian National Male Choir for 50 years through the darkest times of Soviet rule. He was a power in the drive for independence, and he lived to see his country gain its freedom (the grounds are free, open long hours, bus #1, #5, #8, or #34 to Lauluväljak stop).

▲▲**Kumu Art Museum**—When this new home for the Art Museum of Estonia opened in 2006, it was big news on the local art scene: For the first time, Estonia's art was properly displayed all together. The striking building designed by Finnish architect Pekka Vapaavuori houses the very best of Estonian art through the ages, although little survives from before the 19th century and much of the collection was destroyed during World War II. From 1945 to 1991, the purchasing policies for the collection were subservient to the dominant communist ideology—many of the key works could only be added after 1991.

Estonian art evolved along with the basic European art styles against the background of the nation's history. Nineteenth-century Estonian art was Romantic, shaped by the tastes of rich German landlords who had lots of time and favored paintings of idyllic Estonian peasant women, wearing silk folk costumes in Italianesque settings. Impressionism, then Expressionism followed. Then came the artistic earthquake—the Soviet takeover and party-line art.

The permanent exhibition is shown in three parts: The third floor features classic art until World War II. The fourth floor is "Difficult Choices," an exhibit devoted to art from the last half of the 20th century (fascinating for its Soviet influence and Social Realism). And the top floor (fifth) features contemporary art (more

Estonia's Singing Revolution

When you are just a million people in a humble country lodged between Russia and Germany (and dealing with tyrants such as Stalin and Hitler), simply surviving as a nation is a challenge. Estonia was free from 1920 to 1939. Then they had a 50-year German/Russian nightmare. Estonians say, "We were so few in numbers that we had to emphasize that we exist. We had no weapons. Being together and singing together was our power." While forced to be part of the Soviet Union, Estonian culture was besieged. Moscow wouldn't allow locals to wave their flag or sing their patriotic songs. Russians were moved in, and Estonians were shipped out in an attempt to "Russify" the country. But as cracks began to appear in the USSR, the Estonians mobilized by singing.

In 1988, 300,000 Estonians—imagine...a third of the population—gathered at the Song Festival Grounds outside Tallinn to sing patriotic songs. (Singing has long been a national form of expression in this country; the first Estonian Song Festival was held in 1869, and has been held every five years since then.)

On August 23, 1989—the 50th anniversary of a notorious pact between Hitler and Stalin—the people of Latvia, Lithuania, and Estonia held hands to make "the Baltic Chain," a human chain that stretched 360 miles from Tallinn to Vilnius in Lithuania. A Tiananmen Square–type bloodbath was feared, but the country kept singing.

In February 1990, the first free parliamentary elections took place in all three Baltic states, and pro-independence candidates won majorities. In 1991, on the eve of an expected violent crackdown of the Singing Revolution, the makeshift Estonian Parliament declared independence. At that time Moscow was in disarray after hard-line Communists failed in their attempted coup of Mikhail Gorbachev. Suddenly, the USSR was gone, and Estonia was free.

Any visitor to Estonia not tuned into this stirring bit of modern history misses a beautiful opportunity to be inspired by a valiant people's struggle. Watching the documentary film *The Singing Revolution* before your visit will enrich your experience (www.singingrevolution.com).

fun than most contemporary collections). The Kumu also always has stimulating temporary exhibits. It does its best to be true to its motto: "Not a place where art is kept, but a place where art lives." The worthwhile 50-kr audioguide explains exhibits on the third and fourth floors (75 kr; May–Sept Tue–Sun 11:00–18:00, closed Mon; Oct–April Wed–Sun 11:00–18:00, closed Mon–Tue; trendy café, tram #1 or #3 to the end of the line, 200 yards behind Kadriorg, at end of Weizenbergi street, tel. 602-6000, www.ekm.ee).

▲**Kadriorg**—This seaside park and cute, pint-sized summer residence, a 10-minute tram ride from Tallinn or a 15-minute walk from Hotel Viru, was built by Peter the Great for Czarina Catherine after Russia took over Tallinn in 1710. Occupying Peter's palace, the **Foreign Art Museum** (Väliskuunsti Muuseum) has a very modest Russian and Western European collection in a pretty building with sculpted formal gardens out back (65 kr, Tue–Sun 10:00–17:00, closed Mon year-round, closed Tue Oct–April, tel. 606-6400, www.ekm.ee). The park is stately and peaceful, with a rose garden, duck-filled pond, and old tsarist guard houses harkening back to the days of Russian rule. The mansion on the far side of the gardens is the local White House (although it's pink)—home of Estonia's president. The most important sight in the park is the **Kumu Art Museum** (described earlier). The park, which runs north down to the sea, is delightful for a stroll or picnic. Trams #1 and #3 take 10 minutes to go east from the center of Tallinn to Kadriorg, the end of the line (where the tram makes a U-turn, stopping 200 yards from Kadriorg, 400 yards from the Kumu Art Museum).

▲**Estonian Open-Air Museum (Vabaõhumuuseum)**—As in every Nordic country, Estonians salvaged farm buildings, windmills, and an old church from rural areas and transported them to a park-like setting just outside of town. The goal: to both save and share their heritage. Attendants are posted in many houses and you are encouraged to engage them in conversation, but to really visualize life in the old houses, you'll need to rent the audioguide (100 kr/3 hours). The park's Kolu Tavern serves traditional dishes. You can rent a bike (40 kr/hr) for a breezy roll to quiet, faraway spaces in the park (May–Sept: 95 kr, park open daily 10:00–20:00, historic buildings close at 18:00; Oct–April: 40 kr, park open daily 10:00–17:00 but historic buildings closed; take bus #21 from train station to Rocca al Mare stop—because buses back to Tallinn run infrequently, check the departure schedule as soon as you arrive; tel. 654-9100, www.evm.ee).

Lasnamäe, Tallinn's Russian Suburb—In its attempt to bring Estonia into the Soviet fold, Moscow moved tens of thousands of Russian workers into Tallinn, using the promise of new apartments as an incentive. Today, a generation later, Tallinn is left with a huge Russian minority (nearly 40 percent of the city's population) and a huge, charmless suburb of ugly, Soviet-built apartments: Lasnamäe. The challenge for Estonia is to live with the rotten fruit of this forced Russian "plantation." They try to make the best of a tough situation, but some Russian-speaking Estonians are determined not to speak Estonian or be assimilated in the country. These people worked against the break with the USSR in 1990, and even today they stay connected with their historical motherland. The result is a split society with a simmering undercurrent of ethnic tension. Because there are people on both sides who refuse to speak the other's language, English is often used to communicate between the two groups.

One in five Tallinners live in a Brezhnev-era suburb of massive, cookie-cutter apartment blocks. About 90,000 units have been privatized, and 80 percent of the residents who live in this suburb are Russian-speaking. It's a poor and rough district with an edgy, Russian friction (not comfortable after dark). Public toilets here have blue lights so that junkies can't see their veins. For a quick look, hop bus #67 or #68 (catch on Gonsiori Street near Hotel Viru), which circle through Lasnamäe from the town center.

Lahemaa National Park—This vast, flat, forested coastal preserve is only a one-hour drive east of Tallinn. While it is a popular tour destination, the actual sights are underwhelming. I had a great guide, and it was a fascinating day out. But with an average guide, it could be a snore. Highlights include the thick forest (including cemeteries, because Estonians bury their dead in the woods), bog walks, rich berry and mushroom picking, rebuilt manor homes, and peaceful fishing villages surrounded by the evocative ruins of Soviet occupation. While the nature is pristine, the park's charms are modest. There is very little commerce, a sparse population, and a feeling that you can survive only so many horrible wars.

Shopping in Tallinn

With so many cruise-ship tourists inundating Tallinn, the Old Town is full of trinkets, but it is possible to find good-quality stuff.

The **"Sweater Wall"** is a great place to buy sweaters and woollens. Find the stalls under the wall on Müürivahe street (daily 10:00–17:00, near the corner of Viru street, described on page 530). Butter knives and juniper-wood trivets are a good value. From there, explore **Katariina Käik,** a small alley between Müürivahe and Vene streets, which has several handicraft stores and workshops selling pieces that make nice souvenirs.

Apollo Bookstore has a fine English selection (Mon–Fri 10:00–20:00, Sat 10:00–19:00, Sun 11:00–17:00, Internet access-60 kr/hr, just outside the Viru Gate at Viru 23).

The **Mere Art Market,** just outside the Old Town, is a lively little handicrafts market selling mostly clothing and cloth goods (daily May–Sept 9:00–17:00, Oct–April 10:00–16:00, north of Viru street at Mere puiestee 1).

Balti Jaam Market, Tallinn's bustling traditional market, is behind the train station and has little of touristic interest besides wonderful photo ops. That's why I like it. It's a great time-warp scene (look for the Jaama Turg gate, daily 8:00–18:00). Just outside the market at the end of the train station is a café (or *Kohvik*), an unimpressive-looking diner (open 24/7) with a bustling stainless-steel kitchen cranking out traditional dishes—the cheapest hot food in town. While you won't see or hear a word of English here, the glass case displays the various offerings and prices (35-kr meals, 20-kr soups, dirt-cheap-yet-wonderful savory pancakes, and tasty *beljas*—Estonian pierogi). Unfortunately, this market area feels dangerous after dark.

Entertainment in Tallinn

Music: The TI has a list of concerts and tickets available (generally about 120 kr). Tallinn has a dense schedule of Baroque, Renaissance, and choral music performances, especially during the annual Old Town Days, generally the first weekend in June (www.tourism.tallinn.ee). Choral singing became a symbol of the struggle for Estonian independence after the first Estonian Song

Festival in 1869 (still held every five years—next one in 2014). Even outside of festival times, you'll find performances in Tallinn's churches and concert halls (advertised on posters around town). Tickets are usually available at the door. Hortus Musicus is one of Estonia's best classical ensembles.

Estonia's three best modern choral composers and arrangers are Arvo Pärt, Veljo Tormis, and Erkki-Sven Tüür. Other Estonian groups have also put out a lot of good CDs. A good music shop is on the ground floor of the Kaubamaja department store (daily 9:00–21:00, behind Hotel Viru).

Swimming: When the **Kalev Spa** opened in 2006, it was Estonia's largest and newest spa. While it's old news now, many Finns still come here on fitness travel packages. Simply enjoying the indoor water park and its 50-meter pool is lots of fun (95 kr/90 min before 15:00, 130 kr/90 min after 15:00, daily 8:00–21:30, at the edge of the Old Town, Aia 18, tel. 649-3300, www.kalevspa.ee).

Sleeping in Tallinn

Tallinn has a good selection of hotel choices. There are some bargains, even in the Old Town, but even more if you're willing to stay a short walk or bus ride away.

Many hotels, especially the bigger ones, have cheaper deals on their websites and offer individuals only the inflated rack rates, as the bulk of their business comes from agencies.

Summer is high season (Tallinn has more tourists than business travelers), and prices almost always drop from October to April. I've listed high-season prices here. Use a taxi to get to your hotel when you arrive, and then figure out public transportation later.

In the Old Town

$$$ Baltic Hotel Imperial is a fine four-star hotel set in a lovely park-like spot under the Old Town wall. Its 32 rooms are modern and small, while the public spaces have a generally spacious, professional ambience. Though it feels like a chain (and is), when it's discounted, it's the best Old Town, top-end value I've found (Db-1,170–2,500 kr depending on demand, Nunne 14, tel. 627-4800, fax 627-4801, www.imperial.ee, imperial@baltichotelgroup.com).

$$ Meriton Old Town Hotel, extremely trendy and comfy yet wearing an Old World jacket, sits grandly for a hotel in its category at the tip of the Old Town, not far from the ferry terminals. Its 41 rooms include tight doubles with twin beds and showers (Db-1,200–1,510 kr, save by booking on their website, non-smoking, elevator, free Internet access, Lai 49, tel. 614-1300, fax 614-1311, www.meritonhotels.com, oldtown@meritonhotels.com).

Sleep Code

(11 kr = about $1, country code: 372)
S = Single, **D** = Double/Twin, **T** = Triple, **Q** = Quad, **b** = bathroom, **s** = shower. Credit cards are accepted and breakfast is included unless otherwise noted.

To help you sort easily through these listings, I've divided the rooms into three categories, based on the full price for a standard double room with bath:

$$$ Higher Priced—Most rooms 1,600 kr or more.
$$ Moderately Priced—Most rooms between 800–1,600 kr.
$ Lower Priced—Most rooms 800 kr or less.

$ Hotel Shnelli, a big, high-rise "efficiency hotel" adjacent to the sleepy little train station (in a neighborhood that's a bit seedy at night), rents 120 Ikea-mod rooms. It fronts a noisy street, so request a quiet room in the back (Db-600–900 kr, 10-min walk from Old Town, Toompuiestee 37, tel. 631-0100, fax 631-0107, www.gohotels.ee, reservations@gohotels.ee).

$ Villa Hortensia, in a ramshackle courtyard tucked away from the Vene shopping street, rents six cozy rooms with kitchenettes above a sophisticated little café. The three twin-bed rooms and one double-bed room are furnished sparsely, with beds in a sleeping loft. The "deluxe" room comes with a double bed and a small balcony. The apartment is on two floors, with a double bed upstairs and a foldout sofa bed in the living room. Creatively run by jewelry designer Jaan Pärn, this is a good choice for a home-away-from-home in the heart of the Old Town. Jaan's jewelry shop, across the courtyard, serves as the reception (Sb-600 kr, Db-800 kr, deluxe Db-1,200 kr, Estonian-chic apartment-2,000 kr—good for a family, no breakfast, no elevator, 50 yards off the corner of Vene and Viru streets at Vene 6, look for *Master's Courtyard* and *Chocolaterie* signs, mobile 504-6113, www.hoov.ee, jaan.parn@mail.ee).

$ Old House Guesthouse and Hostel is small, snug, and well-run, with two peaceful locations halfway between Town Hall Square and the ferry terminals (bunk in 6-bed dorm-300 kr, S-500 kr, D-700 kr, 5-person room-1,250 kr, see their website for deals, no lockout, shared shower and WC, kitchen facilities, free Wi-Fi, free parking, Uus 22, tel. 641-1464, fax 641-1604, www.oldhouse.ee, info@oldhouse.ee). The manager, Christian, promises a 10 percent discount for those reserving directly with this book.

$ Tallinn Backpackers is a hip, leave-your-shoes-at-the-door place renting 30 beds in four rooms to backpackers. Smoothly run

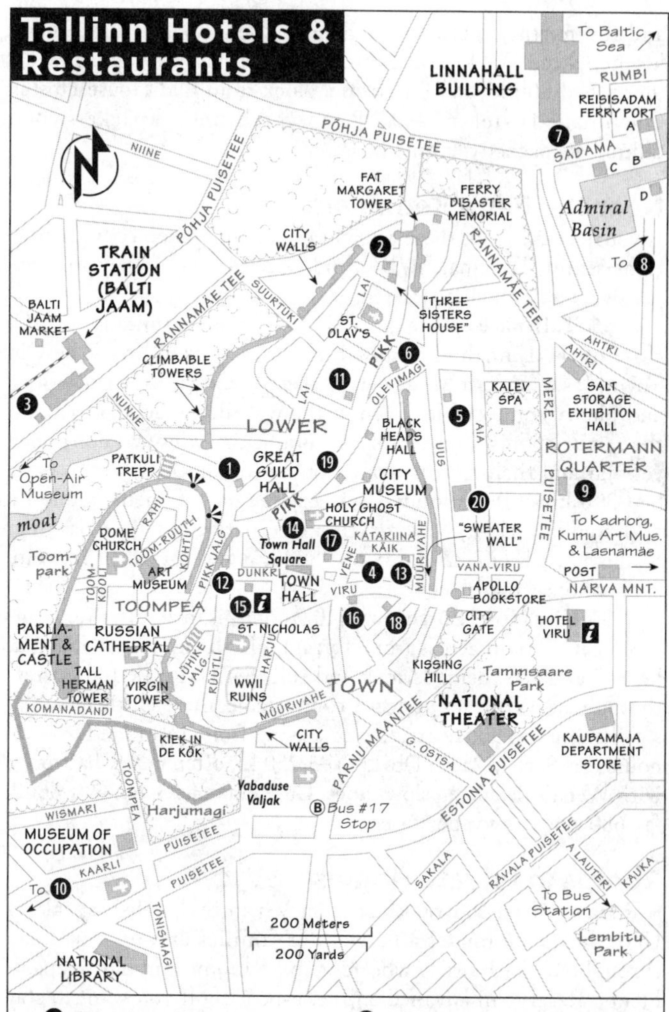

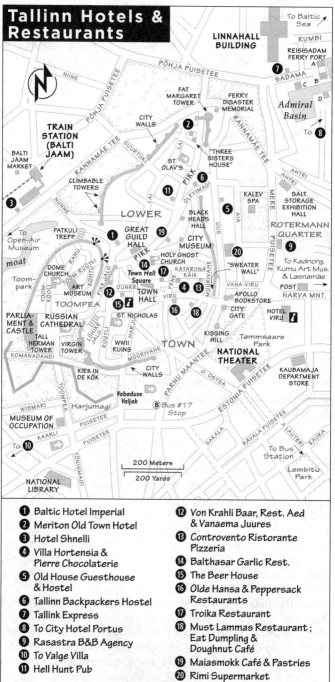

1. Baltic Hotel Imperial
2. Meriton Old Town Hotel
3. Hotel Shnelli
4. Villa Hortensia & Pierre Chocolaterie
5. Old House Guesthouse & Hostel
6. Tallinn Backpackers Hostel
7. Tallink Express
8. To City Hotel Portus
9. Rasastra B&B Agency
10. To Valge Villa
11. Hell Hunt Pub
12. Von Krahli Baar, Rest. Aed & Vanaema Juures
13. Controvento Ristorante Pizzeria
14. Balthasar Garlic Rest.
15. The Beer House
16. Olde Hansa & Peppersack Restaurants
17. Troika Restaurant
18. Must Lammas Restaurant; Eat Dumpling & Doughnut Café
19. Maiasmokk Café & Pastries
20. Rimi Supermarket

and fun for the right crowd, there's a friendly party vibe, plus a kitchen, free Wi-Fi and Internet access, laundry, and lockers (dorm bed-200 kr, in Old Town a block from Old House Hostel, Olevimagi 11, tel. 644-0298, www.tallinnbackpackers.com, tallinnbackpackers@hotmail.com).

Near the Ferry Terminals

If you're cruising in, these two places are almost too convenient—right next to Terminals A/B/C and D, respectively. They are inexpensive, but without character.

$$ Tallink Express is a few steps from Terminals A/B/C, close to the Linnahall terminal, and a short walk from the Old Town. It's a modern Motel 6-type place—cheery, excellent prices, and plenty comfortable. Each of the well-designed 163 rooms is the same. Rooms can be stuffy in summer, as windows don't open very far and there's no air-conditioning (Sb or Db-1,070 kr, extra bed-390 kr, children under 16 sleep free on sofa beds, request a non-smoking floor, elevator, free Internet access, free parking, Sadama 1, tel. 667-8700, fax 667-8800, www.hotels.tallink.com, expresshotel@tallink.ee).

$$ City Hotel Portus, with 107 rooms, is in an utterly charmless location right across from Terminal D. Its motto is "young at heart," and the theme is rock and roll, with Muzak and posters throughout. While it's perfectly comfortable, there's little reason to stay here unless you're arriving or leaving from Terminal D at odd hours (Sb-925–1,125 kr, Db-1,000–1,250 kr, often nearly half-price with Web deals during slow times, Uus-Sadama 23, tel. 680-6600, fax 680-6601, www.portus.ee).

Rooms in Private Homes

$ Rasastra Bed & Breakfast agency, run by English-speaking Urve Susi, coordinates a network of families around town (and throughout the Baltics) who rent spare rooms and entire apartments. Reserve in advance online, especially if you want to stay in the Old Town (S-325 kr, D-550 kr, T-700 kr; apartments with sitting room, bedroom, kitchen, and private bathroom average 900 kr; cheaper in the off-season, breakfast-50 kr). Arrange everything by email, drop by the office upon arrival to pay and pick up the address, and then get settled in. You might be staying alone or with a family. Expect little English and to share the family bathroom. The office, which has an array of TI booklets and maps, is at Mere puiestee 4 near Hotel Viru. It's the red-brick building—not the brown-brick building with the same address; follow the signs one flight up the stairs (daily 9:30–18:00, she'll wait until 20:00 for late arrivals, tel. & fax 661-6291, www.bedbreakfast.ee, rasastra @online.ee).

In Lilleküla, Outside the Center

Lilleküla is a quiet, green, and peaceful residential area of single-family houses, small Soviet-era apartment blocks, and barking dogs. For a clearer understanding of Estonian life, stay here. You'll save money without sacrificing comfort. The downside: It's a 15-minute, 20-kr bus ride into the center.

$$ Valge Villa ("White Villa"), a homey guest house set in a great garden run by Anne and Andres Vahtra and their family, does everything right and is worth the high-for-a-guesthouse price. Its 10 rooms are spacious and well-furnished (Sb-780 kr, Db-880 kr, small suite-990 kr, larger suite-1,170 kr, suite-apartments-1,600 kr, extra bed-300 kr, kids under 12 stay free in same room, lower prices off-season, free Internet access and Wi-Fi, bikes-225 kr/day, sauna-300 kr, laundry service-120 kr; take bus #17 to Räägu stop, or trolleybus #2, #3, or #4 to Tedre stop; Kännu 26/2, between Rästa and Räägu streets, tel. & fax 654-2302, www.white-villa.com). I'd take a taxi here to check in, and try public-transit options later.

Eating in Tallinn

Restaurants in Tallinn are cheap, plentiful, and usually good. Visiting Scandinavians gorge themselves on inexpensive food. Most places accept credit cards. Prices are often listed in euros, and euros may be accepted as payment—but you'll likely get a poor exchange rate. If you liked the service, it's customary to round things up by 5–10 percent when paying your bill.

A few years ago it was hard to find authentic local cuisine, but now it seems Estonian food is trendy—a hot and hearty Northern mixture of meat, potatoes, root vegetables, mushrooms, bread, and soup. Pea soup is a local specialty. A typical pub snack is Estonian garlic bread *(küüslauguleivad)*—deep-fried strips of dark rye bread smothered in garlic and served with a dipping sauce. Estonia's Saku beer is good, cheap, and on tap at most eateries. Try the nutty, full-bodied Tume variety.

Pubs in the Old Town

Young Estonians eat well and affordably at pubs. Soup, a main dish, and a beer will run you about $10. At lunch on weekdays, look for the *päeva praad* (dish of the day—meat, veggies, and a starch) for as little as 35–40 kr. In some pubs, you go to the bar to look at the menu, order, and pay. Then you find a table, and they'll bring your food out when it's ready.

Hell Hunt Pub ("The Gentle Wolf") attracts a mixed expat and local crowd with its tasty food. Known as the first Western-style pub to open after 1991, this place offers conviviality inside and rustic courtyard seating across the street (soups-60 kr, main dishes-80–120 kr, daily 12:00–1:00 in the morning, Pikk 39, tel. 681-8333).

Von Krahli Baar serves cheap, substantial Estonian grub—such as potato pancakes *(torud)* stuffed with mushrooms or shrimp (8 kr)—in a tiny courtyard and a dark, beer-stained interior that doubles as a center for Estonia's alternative theater scene. It started as the bar of the theater upstairs, then expanded to become a restaurant, so it has a young, avant-garde vibe. You'll feel like you're eating backstage with the stagehands (daily 12:00–23:30, Rataskaevu 10/12, a block uphill from Town Hall Square, near Wheel Well, tel. 626-9090).

Restorant Aed is an elegant, almost gourmet, health-food eatery calling itself "the embassy of pure food." While not vegetarian, it is passionate about serving modern, organic Estonian cuisine in a woody, romantic setting (tasty dinner plates-about 200 kr, Mon–Sat 12:00–22:00, Sun 12:00–18:00, Rataskaevu 8, tel. 626-9088).

Controvento Ristorante Pizzeria is a hit with the regulars for its serious Italian cuisine. While local kids like the USA diner feel of the "American Pizza" chain, this place is more stylish. Enjoy the interior, old and rustic yet classy, or sit outside on a quiet cobbled lane lined with 14th-century tombstones (pizzas and pastas-120 kr, daily 12:00–22:30, on the handicraft-filled Katariina Käik lane, which you enter at Vene 12, tel. 644-0470).

Balthasar Garlic Restaurant is pretty touristy, but it's worth considering if you like "European cuisine with a passion for garlic" served in a rustic, Old World setting. The second floor of this creaky, open-beam palace overlooks Town Hall Square. Call to reserve a window-view table (main dishes-300 kr, daily 12:00–22:30, on Town Hall Square opposite the Town Hall at Raekoja plats 11, tel. 627-6400).

The Beer House is best described as a sprawling and boisterous Tirolean Hooters. Billing itself as the "home of the living beer," this big, modern, and sloppy beer hall brews its respected beer on-site. Its waitresses serve hearty portions as if they're just aching to slap dance (main dishes-160–200 kr, Sun–Thu 10:00–24:00, Fri–Sat 10:00–2:00 in the morning, vast indoor section, cute garden out back and streetside tables out front, live music Wed–Sat from 20:00, dancers Fri–Sat, a block above Town Hall Square at Dunkri 5).

Traditional Dining in the Old Town

The Old Town is full of restaurants packed with atmosphere and traditionally dressed servers. Dine under medieval arches, in candle-lit restaurants, or at tables outside in good weather. Most offer stick-to-your-ribs Estonian fare as well as more modern options.

Vanaema Juures ("Grandma's Place"), a small cellar restaurant, serves homey, traditional Estonian meals, such as pork roast with sauerkraut and horseradish. This is your best bet for local cuisine, and dinner reservations are strongly advised. No tacky medieval stuff here—just good food in a pleasant ambience, where you expect your waitress to show up with her hair in a bun and wearing granny glasses (main dishes-125–260 kr, Mon–Sat 12:00–22:00, Sun 12:00–18:00, Rataskaevu 10–12, tel. 626-9080, Ava mothers you).

Medieval Cuisine

Two restaurants just below Town Hall Square specialize in re-creating medieval food (from the days before the arrival of the potato and tomato from the New World). They are each grotesquely touristy, complete with gift shops where you can buy your souvenir goblet. And both have street seating where you'll get all the tourists but none of the atmosphere.

Olde Hansa, filling three creaky old floors and outdoor tables with tourists, candle wax, and scurrying medieval waitresses, has gotten quite expensive (main dishes-200–275 kr, daily 11:00–24:00, music circulates nightly after 18:00, a belch below Town Hall Square at Vana turg 1, reserve in advance, tel. 627-9020). **Peppersack,** across the street, tries to compete (Vana turg 6, tel. 646-6800).

Russian and Caucasian Food

As about a third of the local population is enthusiastically Russian, there are plenty of places serving cuisine from the former Soviet Union. You choose—Russian, Georgian, or Azerbaijani.

Troika is my choice for Russian food. Right on Town Hall Square, with a folkloric-costumed waitstaff, they serve 80–100-kr *bliny* (pancakes) and *pelmeni* (dumplings), and 175–250-kr main dishes. Sit in the tavern (more casual, ground level out back), out on Town Hall Square, or down in the trippy, trendy cellar restaurant. A balalaika player usually strums and strolls after 19:00 (daily 12:00–23:00, Raekoja plats 15, tel. 627-6245).

Must Lammas is straightforward and elegant, focusing on just plain tasty Caucasian food from Georgia, Armenia, and Azerbaijan (main dishes-150–250 kr, Mon–Sat 12:00–23:00, Sun until 18:00, Sauna 2, tel. 644-2031).

More Eateries

Eat Dumpling and Doughnut Café is fresh, cheap, and cheery. This laid-back student hangout, which comes with Foosball and other games, serves the best-value lunch in town. Its menu is very simple: three varieties of dumplings, sauces, and doughnuts. You dish up what you like and pay by the weight. Ask for an education in the various dumplings and sauces and then go for the complete experience. Order and enjoy with abandon—you can't spend much money here, and you'll feel good stoking their business (daily 11:00–23:00, Sauna 2, tel. 644-0029).

Maiasmokk ("Sweet Tooth") café and pastry shop, founded in 1864, is the grande dame of Tallinn cafés—ideal for dessert or breakfast. Even through the Soviet days, this was *the* place for a good pastry or a glass of herby Tallinn schnapps ("Vana Tallinn"). Point to what you want from the selection of classic local pastries at the pastry counter, and sit down for breakfast or coffee on the other side of the shop. Everything's reasonable (Mon–Sat 8:00–20:00, Sun 10:00–18:00, Pikk 16, across from church with old clock, tel. 646-4079). They also have a marzipan shop (separate entrance).

The Pierre Chocolaterie at Vene 6 has scrumptious fresh pralines, sandwiches, coffee, and a lovely courtyard (tel. 641-8061).

Supermarkets: The **Rimi** supermarket at Aia 7 is just outside the Old Town, a few minutes from the "Sweater Wall" (daily 9:00–22:00). Another supermarket is in the basement of the Viru Keskus shopping center directly behind Hotel Viru.

Tallinn Connections

The bus is usually the best way to travel by land from Tallinn (Eurolines tel. 680-0909, www.eurolines.ee, or Ecolines tel. 614-3600, www.ecolines.net). The bus station *(autobussijaam)* is a short taxi ride away, or a few stops outside Town Hall Square on trams #2 or #4 (tram stop: Autobussijaam, Lastekodu 46).

From Tallinn to: Riga (6 buses/day, 4.5 hrs, no train option), **Vilnius** (3 buses/day, 10 hrs, transfer in Riga), **St. Petersburg** (7–8 buses/day, 7–9 hrs), **Moscow** (take the overnight train or fly). Americans and Canadians need a passport and a visa to travel to Russia (see www.russianembassy.org or www.rusembcanada.mid.ru). For the latest bus and train schedules, consult *Tallinn in Your Pocket*.

SCANDINAVIAN HISTORY

On your trip, you'll see reminders everywhere of Scandinavia's long history. Eerie graves, carved rune stones, and horned helmets bring to mind *Lord of the Rings*-style warriors of old who worshipped Thor and Odin. You'll see the ships and weapons of their descendants—the Vikings—who terrorized Europe with their fierce, pagan culture. Evocative wooden stave churches show how Christianity slowly seeped into the region.

You'll visit the harbors of these seafaring peoples and tour the stark castles of nobles who fought for control of Baltic trade. As modern nations emerged, absolute monarchs built luxurious palaces intended to rival Versailles. Today's streets and main squares are studded with statues and monuments honoring great kings and their battles, great patriots who lobbied for national independence, and great writers and musicians who enriched Scandinavian culture. Scandinavian museums are filled with paintings that capture the beauty of the landscape and celebrate its people. You'll hear bittersweet stories of the millions of 19th-century Scandinavians who left their homes for a better life in America. You'll learn about those who suffered under WWII Nazi occupation, and the heroes who organized resistance and sheltered Jewish people. And you'll experience the richness of Scandinavia today—its wealth, its liberal policies, and its global outlook.

Want to hear more of the Scandinavian story? Read on.

Hunters with Spears: Prehistory (c. 8000 B.C.–A.D. 1)

Scandinavia emerged when the glaciers receded at the end of the last ice age and Stone Age hunters moved north, chasing valuable deer, elk, and fish. These were the forebearers of the Sami—or Laplanders—of northern Scandinavia, some of whom continue to herd reindeer and live a nomadic lifestyle today. For more on the Sami, visit Oslo's National Historical Museum (page 200) or Norwegian Folk Museum (page 207), or Stockholm's Nordic Museum (page 378). The early Scandinavians began farming (c. 4000 B.C.) and eventually developed tools and weapons made of bronze (c. 1800 B.C.). We know these people mainly by their graves—either burial mounds (such as on the Island of Öland, Sweden, page 460) or the heavy stone tombs called dolmens (such as on Denmark's isle of Ærø, page 123).

Warriors with Horned Helmets: Iron Age and Romans (A.D. 1–800)

Isolated from the Continent and unconquered by the Romans, Scandinavia kept close to its prehistoric past. The 2,000-year-old Grauballe Man—whose corpse was preserved in a peat bog (and is now displayed at the Moesgård Museum just outside Århus, page 157)—was a contemporary of Julius Caesar. But in his world, people spoke not Latin but a Germanic language, wore animal-horned helmets, and used ceremonial curvy-shaped *lur* horns. They forged iron implements decorated with the gods of their pagan religion (such as the Gundestrup Cauldron displayed in Copenhagen's National Museum, page 78). They commemorated heroic deeds with large stones carved with the angular alphabet known as runes (such as the rune stones at Copenhagen's National Museum, page 78, and at Jelling, Denmark, page 148). One of their most sacred sites is at Gamla Uppsala near Stockholm (page 402), where mighty chieftains were buried along with their worldly possessions—weapons, jewels, dogs, horses, and even slaves. This distinct, pre-Christian Scandinavian culture thrived in the first centuries A.D. and continued even as the rest of Europe fell under the sway of Rome's Latin culture and, later, Christianity.

Though isolated, the Scandinavians made fleeting contact with Roman Europe, trading furs and amber (a petrified tree sap, used in jewelry) for crucial tool-making metals from the Continent. Eventually, the Scandinavians learned to extract their own bronze and iron. With better tools, they became productive farmers and shipbuilders. The population boomed due to a warmer climate and better nutrition. The Scandinavians were soon eyeing Europe and the North Atlantic as a source for new resources and for potential expansion of their clans.

Vikings with Ships (800–1000)

Scandinavia's entrance onto the European stage was swift, dramatic, and unforgettable. On January 8, A.D. 793, a fleet of Scandinavian pirates came ashore on the northeast coast of England and sacked the Lindisfarne monastery, slaughtering monks, burning buildings, and plundering sacred objects. Word spread like wildfire of brutal pirates who seemed to come from nowhere, looted and pillaged with extreme prejudice, then moved on. Their victims called them *Normanni, Dani, Rus,* or worse, but the name they gave themselves came from the inlets and fjords *(vik)* where they lived: the Vikings.

For the next 200 years, hardy Viking sailors plundered and explored the coasts of northern Europe. Vikings from Norway primarily went west to the British Isles and settled Iceland, Greenland, and beyond; Swedes ventured east to the Baltic states, navigated the Russian rivers, and reached Constantinople; and Danes headed south (to England, France, Spain, and Italy).

The Vikings attacked in fleets of sleek, narrow, open-topped ships a hundred feet long, called *drakkars.* (See them for yourself at the Viking Ship Museums in Oslo, page 208, or Roskilde, page 115.) Rigged with square sails and powered by dozens of men at the oars, they could attack at 15 miles an hour and land right on the beach, where they would pour out, brandishing their weapons.

Each Viking was decked out with a coat of mail, a small shield, and a helmet (though not one with horns, which by Viking times were merely ceremonial). Each warrior specialized in a particular kind of warfare: sword, spear, battle-axe, or bow-and-arrow. At the battle's crucial moment, the Vikings might send in their secret weapon—the so-called *berserkers.* These warriors attacked with a seemingly superhuman (and possibly drug-induced) frenzy, scaring the leotards off their enemies and giving us our English word "berserk."

Despite their reputation as ruthless pirates, the Vikings were also settlers, who established towns, married the locals, farmed the land, hunted in the forests, and traded with their neighbors. They spread Viking culture and rune stones far and wide. In Northern France, the region of "Normandy" was settled by the "North-men." Leif Eriksson, a Norwegian Viking, sailed as far as the coast of North America (c. A.D. 1000).

To the dismay of Roman Catholic bishops, while the rest of Europe became Christian, the Vikings held onto their pagan gods, many of whom were, like themselves, warriors: Odin, the king of the gods (who gave us our word for Wednesday), and Thor with his hammer, the god of war (and of Thursday). Believing in an afterlife, the Vikings buried their dead ceremonially along with their possessions. Some were interred beneath large mounds of dirt (such as the Gamla Uppsala burial mounds described on page 402). Others were laid to rest in ships that were buried underground, or in graves marked with stones placed upright in the shape of a full-size ship.

By the year 1000, Viking society was gradually changing—

Castle Architecture

A castle is a fortified residence for a medieval noble. Castles come in all shapes and sizes, but knowing a few general terms will help you understand them.

The Keep (or Donjon): A high, strong stone tower in the center of the castle complex that was the lord's home and refuge of last resort.

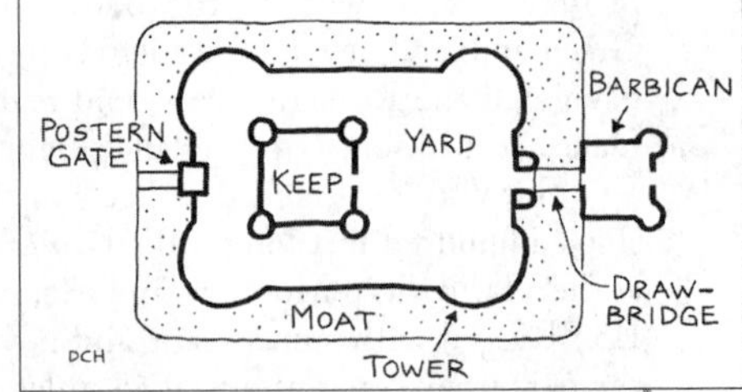

Great Hall: The largest room in the castle, serving as throne room, conference center, and dining hall.

The Yard (or Bailey or Ward): An open courtyard inside the castle walls.

Loopholes: Narrow slits in the walls (also called embrasures, arrow slits, or arrow loops) through which soldiers could shoot arrows at the enemy.

Towers: Tall structures serving as lookouts, chapels, living quarters, or the dungeon. Towers could be square or round, with either crenellated tops or conical roofs.

Turret: A small lookout tower projecting up from the top of the wall.

Moat: A ditch encircling the wall, often filled with water.

Wall Walk (or Allure): A pathway atop the wall where guards could patrol and where soldiers stood to fire at the enemy.

Parapet: Outer railing of the wall walk.

Crenellation: A gap-toothed pattern of stones atop the parapet.

Hoardings (or Gallery or Brattice): Wooden huts built onto the upper parts of the stone walls. They served as watch towers, living quarters, and fighting platforms.

Machicolation: A stone ledge jutting out from the wall, fitted with holes in the bottom. If the enemy was scaling the walls, soldiers could drop rocks or boiling oil down through the holes and onto the enemy below.

Barbican: A fortified gatehouse, sometimes a stand-alone building located outside the main walls.

Drawbridge: A bridge that could be raised or lowered, using counterweights or a chain-and-winch.

Portcullis: A heavy iron grille that could be lowered across the entrance.

Postern Gate: A small, unfortified side or rear entrance used during peacetime. In wartime, it became a "sally-port" used to launch surprise attacks, or as an escape route.

unifying, Christianizing, and assimilating into European culture. Scattered Viking tribes coalesced into kingdoms, united under the banner of Christianity. In Norway, there was King (later "Saint") Olav II (c. 1020). Among the Svea people (Sweden), King Olof Skotkonung (c. 968–1020) unified and Christianized the land. The Danes were united by King Harald Bluetooth (c. 980), who commemorated Denmark's Christian conversion on a now-famous rune stone (located in Jelling, page 148)—although in reality, Bluetooth's "conversion" was a ploy to keep the German-Catholic bishops and missionaries at bay. Under Harald's grandson, King Canute, Denmark ruled a large empire that included parts of southern England (c. 1020). One of Canute's battles there inspired the nursery song "London Bridge Is Falling Down."

By 1100, the last pagans were gathering at Gamla Uppsala to put on their ceremonial horned helmets, worship the sun, bury fallen heroes, and retell the sagas of their ancestors. Viking culture blended into the European mainstream, but we still see traces of it today—in rune stones and burial sites; in surviving tools, weapons, and jewelry; and in the dragon-prowed designs found on Christian stave churches and even on contemporary Scandinavian coins.

Christians, Bickering Nobles, and German Businessmen: The Medieval Era (1000–1400)

In the Middle Ages, three separate (if loosely united) kingdoms emerged: Denmark, Sweden, and Norway. They were Christian and feudal, with land worked by peasants who owed allegiance to a petty noble sworn to the king. Towns sprang up, including what would become the main cities: Oslo (1048), Copenhagen (1165), and Stockholm (1255). Rulers began flying flags featuring a cross, which eventually became the main motif in each country's national flag.

Christianity dominated. Some of the region's oldest churches (especially in Norway) are wooden stave, made with vertical planks and ornamented with dragons and other semi-pagan figures to ward off evil and ease the transition to Christianity (see page 169). Devout Christians laid the cornerstones for huge cathedrals, such as the skyscraping Uppsala Cathedral in 1287, Århus Cathedral in 1201, and Stockholm Cathedral in 1306.

Finland entered the Scandinavian sphere when zealous Swedes launched a series of crusades to convert their neighbors to the east. They conquered and assimilated the region (c. 1200), making it a part of their own country for the next 600 years. Even today, Swedish is spoken on Finland's southern coast.

The many castles that dot Scandinavia attest to the civil warfare between nobles. A strong central government headed by a dominant king was still centuries away.

Sea trade between the Scandinavian neighbors boomed.

Unfortunately, the lucrative trade was controlled by foreigners—enterprising German businessmen—who organized Scandinavia's ports into a free-trade zone known as the Hanseatic League (c. 1200–1400). Under German direction, Scandinavia became a powerful player in overseas commerce with the Continent. Cities such as Bergen, Norway, reaped big rewards under the Hanse (see Håkon's Hall on page 304). By 1370, these German businessmen were so rich that they wielded more actual power than any Scandinavian king. It took a queen to break them.

Dominant Danes: Wars and Reformation (1400–1600)

When Margrethe I of Denmark married the Norwegian king in 1363, Norway came under Danish control (where it would remain for the next 300 years). Denmark emerged as the region's main power. In 1397, Margrethe took on the Hanseatic League by uniting the three Scandinavian nations against the league with the Treaty of Kalmar. The German monopoly was broken, and Scandinavia gained control of its own wealth. But after Margrethe, the union faltered. For a century, Swedish nobles chafed and occasionally rebelled against Danish domination.

In 1520, Denmark invaded Sweden and—in the notorious Stockholm Bloodbath—massacred 80 rebellious Swedish nobles in the city's main square, Stortorget (see page 360). Gustav Vasa rallied the enraged Swedes and drove out Denmark's King Christian (known as Christian II in Denmark and as Christian the Tyrant in Sweden). Vasa was crowned King of Sweden on June 6, 1523 (now Sweden's flag day). He centralized the Swedish government and Protestantized the country, seizing church property to form a strong nation-state. In many ways, this was the birth of modern Sweden (and the origin of the name for Wasa flatbread).

By the 1500s, all of Scandinavia had converted to Lutheran-style Protestantism. They'd been primed by the influence of German Hanseatic traders and preachers. And their kings jumped at the chance to confiscate former church property and authority to augment their own power.

For the next century, Denmark and Sweden—the region's two powerhouses—battled for control of the Baltic's lucrative trade routes, particularly for the Øresund, the crucial strait between Denmark and Sweden that connects the Baltic with the North Sea (and is now spanned by a modern bridge—see sidebar on page 121).

Swedish Superiority: Absolute Monarchs (1600–1800)

By 1600, Denmark-Norway was still the region's superpower, but Sweden-Finland was rising fast. Denmark's one-eyed, high-living

King Christian IV was spending centuries' worth of acquired wealth building lavish castles—including Rosenborg and Frederiksborg—and putting a Renaissance face on Copenhagen and Oslo (see page 182 and the sidebar on page 51). Meanwhile, his wars with Sweden and others were slowly sapping the country, emptying its coffers, and undermining Danish superiority. Christian IV even sold the Orkney and Shetland Islands to England to raise funds.

Sweden emerged under the inspired military leadership of King Gustavus Adolphus (1594–1632). The "Lion of the North" roared southward, conquering large chunks of Russia, Poland, Germany, and Denmark during the Thirty Years' War. The vast *Vasa* ship in Stockholm, which the king commissioned in 1628, trumpeted the optimism of the era—but sank ignominiously on its maiden voyage in the middle of Stockholm harbor (see page 377).

Sweden's supreme moment came under Gustavus' great-grandson, Charles X Gustav (1622–1660). In 1657, Charles invaded Denmark through the back door—from the south. The winter was extremely cold, and the seas froze between several of Denmark's islands. In one of the most daring maneuvers in military history, Charles X Gustav led his armies across the ice between the islands—from Funen to Langeland to Lolland to Zealand—then sped toward Copenhagen. The astonished Danes surrendered, signing the humiliating Treaty of Roskilde (1658). The treaty gave Sweden a third of Danish territory, plus shared control of the Øresund Strait. Denmark would never again dominate, while Sweden became a major European power, with an imposing fleet and a Baltic empire that included Finland, Estonia, Latvia, and parts of Poland, Russia, and Germany.

In the 1660s, the kings of Denmark-Norway and Sweden-Finland—following the trend set by Louis XIV in France—declared themselves to be absolute, divinely ordained monarchs. For the next 50 years, these kings scuffled with each other (and neighboring countries) for superiority in the Baltic. By 1720, the wars had drained both countries, at the very time that France and England were on the rise. Scandinavia sank back into relative obscurity.

For the rest of the 1700s, Denmark-Norway and Sweden-Finland avoided war while trying to modernize and expand their economies. But the French Revolution (1789) and the Europe-wide wars that followed stirred up this relative peace, awakening a desire for democracy, ethnic recognition, and national independence.

Patriots, Artists, Industrialists, and Emigrants (1800s)

As Europe's monarchs ganged up on Revolutionary France under Napoleon, Scandinavia was forced to take sides. Through a series of complicated alliances, Denmark ended up backing the loser (France), while Sweden backed the winners (Britain and others). At war's end, Denmark was forced to cede Norway to Sweden in the 1814 Treaty of Kiel. Meanwhile, Sweden had just lost Finland to Russia in 1809. Thus began the nation-building process that, a century later, would result in the four independent nations we have today.

The wars also gave Sweden a new king—a French soldier who spoke not a word of Swedish, was not Scandinavian, and had not a drop of noble blood. But Jean-Baptiste Bernadotte, a career military man in Napoleon's army, was loved by Sweden's childless king, admired by Sweden's soldiers for his fighting prowess, and popular with the people for treating Swedish prisoners well during the wars. The bizarre choice of a French commoner was a surprise, but everyone said *oui-oui*, and Jean-Baptiste was crowned Sweden's King Karl Johan XIV (and Karl Johan III in Norway). During his reign (1818–1844), Bernadotte brought peace, prosperity, and fresh DNA, founding the royal dynasty that would produce the current monarchs of Sweden—and, by intermarriage, of Norway and Denmark.

The French Revolution (and Napoleon) spread the idea throughout Europe that people should embrace their ethnic roots and demand self-rule. Norwegians—having been ruled for centuries by Danes, and now Swedes—met at Eidsvoll Manor (outside Oslo—see page 216), drafted a constitution with a parliament, elected a king, and demanded independence. Though the country was still too weak to make this a political reality, the date of May 17, 1814, has become the country's Fourth of July, celebrated today with plenty of flag-waving and folk costumes by Norwegians both in and out of Norway.

Culturally (if not politically), nationalism flourished, producing artists like J. C. Dahl, who captured the beauty of the Norwegian countryside and the simple dignity of its people. (You can see his works at Oslo's National Gallery, page 193.) Playwright Henrik Ibsen realistically portrayed the complexities of a changing Norwegian society. And composer Edvard Grieg used music to convey the majesty of the landscape near his home in Bergen (Troldhaugen, page 312).

In Denmark, nationalism inspired German-speaking Danes in the provinces of Schleswig and Holstein to call for independence (1848–1851). They were finally taken by force from Denmark by Prussia (1864) and incorporated into the new state of Germany. The resulting nationwide sense of humiliation and self-critique actually spurred a cultural golden age. Philosopher Søren Kierkegaard captured the angst of an age when traditional certainties were crumbling. Storyteller Hans Christian Andersen (*The Ugly Duckling, The Emperor's New Clothes, The Little Mermaid,* and others) gained a Europe-wide reputation. And sculptor Bertel Thorvaldsen, who studied and worked in Rome, decorated Copenhagen with his realistic, Neoclassical statues (at Copenhagen's Cathedral of Our Lady, page 66; and the Thorvaldsen Museum, page 80).

Throughout the 1800s, Scandinavia was modernizing. The Industrial Revolution brought trains, factories, and larger cities. While some got rich, millions of poor farmers were forced to emigrate from Sweden and Norway to America between 1850 and 1920, due to the changing economy, overpopulation, and famine. (The House of Emigrants museum in Växjö, Sweden, tells their story—see page 429.) As in other European countries, Scandinavia saw the steady advance of democracy, parliaments, labor unions, and constitutional monarchies. The 20th century would quicken that pace.

Independence, World Wars, and the Social Welfare State (1900–Present)

In 1905—after five and a half centuries of Danish and Swedish rule—Norway finally was granted independence when it voted overwhelmingly to break from Sweden. National pride ran high, as Oslo's own Roald Amundsen became the first person to reach the South Pole (in 1911—for more, see the *Fram* Museum on page 209). In 1919, Finland—after 700 years of Swedish and Russian rule—won its independence while Russia was distracted by the Bolshevik Revolution.

The Scandinavian nations remained neutral through World War I. But when Hitler's Nazi Germany began its European conquest in World War II, it was impossible for Scandinavians—try as they might—to remain uninvolved. Sweden stayed officially neutral, but allowed Nazi troops "on leave" to march through. (Sweden's neutrality later provided a safe haven for Danish and Swedish Jews and a refuge for the Danish and Norwegian resistance movements.)

Germany invaded Denmark and Norway on April 9, 1940, with Operation Weserübung. Scattered fighting at the Danish border was quickly put down, and Denmark capitulated and officially cooperated with the Nazis until 1943, when the Germans took over the government. Danish resistance groups harried the Nazis and provided intelligence to the Allies (see the Museum of Danish Resistance, page 83). In 1943, a German diplomat informed Copenhagen's rabbi that the Jews were about to be deported. Danish citizens quickly hid and eventually evacuated all but 500 of Denmark's Jews to neutral Sweden.

Norway's army held out a few weeks longer, allowing time for King Håkon VII to flee and organize a vital resistance movement (memorialized at Oslo's Norwegian Resistance Museum, page 192). Norway spent the war chafing under a Nazi puppet government headed by Vidkun Quisling, whose surname has become synonymous with "traitor."

Denmark, Sweden, and Norway came out of the war without the horrendous damage and loss of life suffered elsewhere in Europe—in part, probably, because Hitler wanted to turn the Scandinavian countries into model states. After all, these were the people Germany was trying to emulate: tall, blonde, blue-eyed symbols of the Aryan race.

Finland's fate was more complicated. During the war, the Finns valiantly battled Russian invaders, who were Hitler's allies. But by war's end, the Soviets had switched sides. As postwar Europe was divvied up between the communist East and the democratic West, Finland was handed over to the Soviet sphere of influence. But unlike other Soviet satellites behind the Iron Curtain, Finland kept a strong measure of independence, thanks to the policy of "Finlandization." The Finns paid lip service to Soviet authority, censored their own media, acted as a buffer against military invasion from the West, rejected rebuilding money from the US (the Marshall Plan), and avoided treaties with the West. In return, Finland remained a self-ruling capitalist democracy. They imported raw materials from the Soviets, then shipped them back as manufactured products, in a mutually beneficial trade agreement.

Meanwhile, Norway, Denmark, and Sweden stood firmly with the West, joining international organizations such as NATO and the United Nations. Sweden's Dag Hammarskjöld served as the UN's Secretary General from 1953 to 1961. When the Iron Curtain fell in 1989, Finland was fully prepared to join the West as a fellow democracy.

In the decades since World War II, the Scandinavian countries have made themselves quite wealthy following a mixed capitalist-socialist model. In the late 1960s, Norway discovered oil in the North Sea, instantly transforming itself into a rich nation. Citizens across Scandinavia have come to take for granted cradle-to-grave security—health care, education, unemployment benefits, welfare, and so on—all financed with high taxes. In social policies, Scandinavia has often led the way in liberal attitudes toward sexuality, drug use, and gay rights. For more on current-day Scandinavia, see page 36.

Immigration in the late 20th century brought many citizens from non-European nations. While adding diversity, it also threatens the homogenous fabric of a society whose roots have traditionally been white, Christian, European, democratic, and blonde.

Today, Finland, Sweden, and Denmark are all members of the European Union, while Norway has stayed firmly outside (while reaping most of the economic benefits of membership). All the

Little Maria...or Metallica?

Scandinavia is viewed as one of the most liberal corners of Europe, so Americans are often surprised to learn there are government restrictions on what parents can name their children. Historically, parents in Denmark, Norway, Sweden, and Finland were required to choose their child's name from a published list of acceptable monikers. Any variations had to be approved by a government board. The intent of the rules was to prevent commoners from using royal names and to ban names considered ridiculous, inappropriate, potentially harmful to the child, or just not Scandinavian enough. One Norwegian mom even spent two days in jail in the '90s for naming her son Gesher (it means "bridge" in Hebrew). But following a recent series of court rulings, Scandinavian countries are relaxing parts of their naming laws. Denmark has allowed some Legolas and Gandolfs, and in Sweden there's a little girl named Metallica and a little boy named Q.

Scandinavian countries have maintained a measure of independence from Europe (and America), and their level of participation in international agreements and organizations varies from country to country. For example, though Denmark and Sweden are EU members, they don't use the euro (though Denmark is planning a referendum to revisit the issue in 2011). Meanwhile, Finland belongs to the EU and uses the euro.

As the Scandinavian people forge into the 21st century, they are adamant about preserving their culture, traditions, and high standard of living while competing in a global economy.

APPENDIX

Contents

Tourist Information

Tourist Offices

The Scandinavian Tourist Board's office **in the US** is a wealth of information on Norway, Denmark, Sweden, Finland, and Iceland. Before your trip, get the free general information packet and request any specifics you want (such as regional and city maps and festival schedules). Call 212/885-9700 or visit www.goscandinavia.com (info@goscandinavia.com).

Similar information on **Estonia** is available from their US tourist office (tel. 212/883-0636, www.visitestonia.com, info@visitestonia.com).

In Scandinavia, your best first stop in every town is generally the tourist information office—abbreviated **TI** in this book. Throughout Scandinavia, you'll find TIs are usually well-organized and always have an English-speaking staff. Most TIs are run by the government, which means their information isn't colored by a drive for profit. The big exception is the commercially operated

Wonderful Copenhagen.

A TI is a great place to get a city map, advice on public transportation (including bus and train schedules), walking-tour information, tips on special events, and recommendations for nightlife. Many TIs have information on the entire country or at least the region, so try to pick up maps for destinations you'll be visiting later in your trip. If you're arriving in town after the TI closes, call ahead or pick up a map in a neighboring town.

Important: Each big city publishes a *This Week in...* or *What's On...* guide (to Copenhagen, Stockholm, Oslo, Bergen, and Helsinki). These are free, found all over town, and packed with all the tedious details about each city (24-hour pharmacy, embassies, tram/bus fares, restaurants, sights with hours/admissions/phone numbers), plus a useful calendar of events and a map of the town center.

While TIs offer room-finding services, they're a good deal only if you're in search of summer and weekend deals on business hotels. The TIs can help you with small pensions and private homes, but you'll save both yourself and your host money by going direct with the listings in this book.

Communicating

Hurdling the Language Barrier

In Scandinavia, English is all you need. These days every well-educated person seems to speak English. Still, knowing the key words in the language of the country you are visiting is good style and helpful.

A few words you'll see and hear a lot (these are all in Norwegian; the Danish and Swedish versions differ slightly): *takk* (thanks), *gammel* (old), *lille* (small), *stor* (big), *slot* (palace), *fart* (trip), *centrum* (center), *gate* (street), *øl* (beer), *forbudt* (not allowed), and *udsalg*, *salg*, or *rea* (sale).

Each country has its own language. Danish, Norwegian, and Swedish are so closely related that locals can laugh at each other's TV comedies. The languages are similar to English but with a few letters we don't have (Æ, Ø, Ö, Å, Ä). These letters barely affect pronunciation, but do affect alphabetizing. If you can't find, say, Århus in a map index, look after Z. Finnish and Estonian are vastly different from the other Scandinavian languages and English; in fact, Finnish has more in common with Hungarian than with Swedish (see page 467).

Give it your best shot. The locals will appreciate your efforts.

Telephones

Smart travelers use the telephone to reserve or reconfirm rooms, get tourist information, reserve restaurants, confirm tour times, or phone home. Generally the easiest, cheapest way to call home is to use an international phone card purchased in Scandinavia. This section covers dialing instructions, phone cards, and types of phones.

How to Dial

Calling from the US to Scandinavia, or vice versa, is simple—once you break the code. The European calling chart in this chapter will walk you through it.

Dialing Domestically in Scandinavia

Denmark, Estonia, and **Norway** use a direct-dial system, which means you dial the same number whether you're calling across the country or across the street. For example, to call one of my recommended Copenhagen hotels from anywhere in Denmark (including Copenhagen), simply dial its local number (33 13 19 13).

Sweden and **Finland,** on the other hand, use area codes. This means you dial the local number when calling within a city, and add the area code if calling long distance within the same country. For example, Stockholm's area code is 08, and the number of one of my recommended Stockholm hotels is 723-7250. To call the hotel within Stockholm, just dial 723-7250. To call it from Kalmar (in southeast Sweden), dial 08/723-7250.

Don't be surprised that Scandinavian phone numbers may vary in length; for instance, a hotel can have a six-digit phone number and an eight-digit fax number.

Dialing Internationally to or from Scandinavia

If you want to make an international call, follow these steps:

1. Dial the international access code (011 if you're calling from the US or Canada, 00 if you're calling from Europe—except in Finland, which uses 999 or another 900 number depending on the phone service you're using).

2. Dial the country code of the country you're calling (see the European calling chart in this chapter).

3. Dial the area code (if applicable) and the local number, keeping in mind that calling many countries requires dropping the initial zero of the area code or local number (the European calling chart lists specifics per country).

Here are some examples:

Calling from the US to direct-dial countries (Denmark, Estonia, and Norway): To call from the US to the recommended Ibsens hotel in Copenhagen, dial 011 (the US international access code), 45 (Denmark's country code), then 33 13 19 13 (the hotel's local number).

European Calling Chart

Just smile and dial, using this key:
AC = Area Code, LN = Local Number.

European Country	Calling long distance within...	Calling from the US or Canada to...	Calling from a European country to...
Austria	AC + LN	011 + 43 + AC (without the initial zero) + LN	00 + 43 + AC (without the initial zero) + LN
Belgium	LN	011 + 32 + LN (without initial zero)	00 + 32 + LN (without initial zero)
Bosnia-Herzegovina	AC + LN	011 + 387 + AC (without initial zero) + LN	00 + 387 + AC (without initial zero) + LN
Britain	AC + LN	011 + 44 + AC (without initial zero) + LN	00 + 44 + AC (without initial zero) + LN
Croatia	AC + LN	011 + 385 + AC (without initial zero) + LN	00 + 385 + AC (without initial zero) + LN
Czech Republic	LN	011 + 420 + LN	00 + 420 + LN
Denmark	LN	011 + 45 + LN	00 + 45 + LN
Estonia	LN	011 + 372 + LN	00 + 372 + LN
Finland	AC + LN	011 + 358 + AC (without initial zero) + LN	999 (or other 900 number) + 358 + AC (without initial zero) + LN
France	LN	011 + 33 + LN (without initial zero)	00 + 33 + LN (without initial zero)
Germany	AC + LN	011 + 49 + AC (without initial zero) + LN	00 + 49 + AC (without initial zero) + LN
Gibraltar	LN	011 + 350 + LN	00 + 350 + LN
Greece	LN	011 + 30 + LN	00 + 30 + LN
Hungary	06 + AC + LN	011 + 36 + AC + LN	00 + 36 + AC + LN
Ireland	AC + LN	011 + 353 + AC (without initial zero) + LN	00 + 353 + AC (without initial zero) + LN

European Country	Calling long distance within...	Calling from the US or Canada to...	Calling from a European country to...
Italy	LN	011 + 39 + LN	00 + 39 + LN
Montenegro	AC + LN	011 + 382 + AC (without initial zero) + LN	00 + 382 + AC (without initial zero) + LN
Morocco	LN	011 + 212 + LN (without initial zero)	00 + 212 + LN (without initial zero)
Netherlands	AC + LN	011 + 31 + AC (without initial zero) + LN	00 + 31 + AC (without initial zero) + LN
Norway	LN	011 + 47 + LN	00 + 47 + LN
Poland	LN	011 + 48 + LN (without initial zero)	00 + 48 + LN (without initial zero)
Portugal	LN	011 + 351 + LN	00 + 351 + LN
Slovakia	AC + LN	011 + 421 + AC (without initial zero) + LN	00 + 421 + AC (without initial zero) + LN
Slovenia	AC + LN	011 + 386 + AC (without initial zero) + LN	00 + 386 + AC (without initial zero) + LN
Spain	LN	011 + 34 + LN	00 + 34 + LN
Sweden	AC + LN	011 + 46 + AC (without initial zero) + LN	00 + 46 + AC (without initial zero) + LN
Switzerland	LN	011 + 41 + LN (without initial zero)	00 + 41 + LN (without initial zero)
Turkey	AC (if there's no initial zero, add one) + LN	011 + 90 + AC (without initial zero) + LN	00 + 90 + AC (without initial zero) + LN

- The instructions above apply whether you're calling a land line or mobile phone.
- The international access codes (the first numbers you dial when making an international call) are 011 if you're calling from the US or Canada, or 00 if you're calling from virtually anywhere in Europe (except Finland, where it's 999 or another 900 number, depending on the phone service you're using).
- To call the US or Canada from Europe, dial 00, then 1 (the country code for the US and Canada), then the area code and number. In short, 00 + 1 + AC + LN = Hi, Mom!

From the US to area-code countries (Sweden and Finland): To call from the US to the recommended Freys Hotel in Stockholm, dial 011, 46 (Sweden's country code), 8 (Stockholm's area code minus the initial zero), then 5062-1300 (local number).

From any European country to the US: To call from Scandinavia to my office in Edmonds, Washington, I dial 00 (Europe's international access code), 1 (the US country code), 425 (Edmonds' area code), and 771-8303. Remember that Finland has different international access codes; see point #1 on page 559.

Note: You might see a + in front of a European number. When dialing the number, replace the + with the international access code of the country you're calling from (00 from anywhere in Europe except Finland, 011 from the US or Canada).

Public Phones and Hotel-Room Phones

To make calls from public phones, you'll need a prepaid phone card. There are two types: international and insertable. (If you have a live card at the end of your trip, give it to another traveler to use.)

International Phone Cards: These are the cheapest way to make international calls from Europe—with the best cards, it costs literally pennies a minute. They also work for local calls.

You can use international phone cards from any type of phone, even the one in your hotel room (but ask at the front desk if there are any fees for toll-free calls). The cards are sold all over; look for them at many post offices, newsstands, mini-marts, and exchange bureaus. Ask the clerk which of the various brands has the best rates for calls to America. Because cards are occasionally duds, avoid the high denominations. Some cards are rechargeable (you can call up the number on the card, give your credit-card number, and buy more time). Some shops also sell cardless codes, printed right on the receipt.

To use the card, scratch to reveal your code, then dial the free access number. The message tells you to enter your code. Dial the number you're calling. When using an international calling card, the area code must be dialed even if you're calling across the street. Usually the prompts are in fairly concise English, but if you hear a Scandinavian language, or worse, an interminable English sales pitch, experiment: Dial your code, followed by the pound sign (#), then the number, then pound again, and so on, until it works. Sometimes the star (*) key is used instead of the pound sign.

Remember that you don't need the actual card to use a card account, so it's shareable. You can write down the access number and code in your notebook and share it with friends.

Most merchants promise that the cards work throughout Scandinavia (cards are generally printed with local access numbers for each country), but often they don't work in neighboring countries, leaving you stuck with extra minutes that you can't use. Unfortunately, it can be difficult to find international phone cards in Finland.

Insertable Phone Cards: This type of card can only be used at public pay phones. It's handy and affordable for local and domestic calls, but more expensive for international calls. Insertable phone cards are sold at post offices, newsstands, and tobacco shops. To use the card, physically insert it into a slot in the pay phone. These cards only work in the country where you buy them (so your Swedish phone card is worthless in Denmark).

Always an Exception: Estonia doesn't sell either type of phone card. Skype is a good option for travelers with laptops (see "Calling over the Internet," later).

Hotel Room Phones: Phoning from your room can be cheap for local calls (ask for the rates at the front-desk first), but is often a rip-off for long-distance calls, unless you use an international phone card (explained above). Incoming calls are free, making this a cheap way for friends and family to stay in touch (provided they have a good long-distance plan for calls to Europe—and a list of your hotels' phone numbers).

US Calling Cards: These cards, such as the ones offered by AT&T, Verizon, or Sprint, are the worst option. You'll nearly always save a lot of money by using a locally purchased international phone card instead.

Mobile Phones

Many travelers enjoy the convenience of traveling with a mobile phone. If you need more in-depth information than we provide below, see www.ricksteves.com/phones.

Using Your Mobile Phone: Your US mobile phone works in Europe if it's GSM-enabled, tri-band or quad-band, and on a calling plan that includes international calls. For example, with a T-Mobile phone, you'll pay $1 per minute to make or receive a call, and about $0.35 apiece for text messages.

You can save money if your phone is electronically "unlocked"—then you can simply buy a **SIM card** (a fingernail-sized chip that stores the phone's information) in Europe. SIM cards, which give you a European phone number, are sold at mobile-phone stores and some newsstand kiosks for about $5–15. When you buy the card, you'll also get some prepaid calling time (€25 gives you about 30 minutes). Simply insert the SIM card in your phone (usually in a slot behind the battery), and it'll work like a European mobile phone. When buying a SIM card, always ask about fees for domestic and international calls, roaming charges, and how to check your credit balance and buy more time.

Many **smartphones**, such as the iPhone or BlackBerry, work in Europe—but beware of sky-high fees, especially for data downloading (checking email, browsing the Internet, watching videos, and so on). Ask your provider in advance how to avoid unwittingly "roaming" your way to a huge bill. Some applications allow for cheap or free smartphone calls over a Wi-Fi connection (described under "Calling over the Internet," below).

Using a European Mobile Phone: Local mobile-phone shops all over Europe sell basic phones for around $50–100. You'll also need to buy a SIM card (explained above) and prepaid credit for making calls. If you remain in the phone's home country, domestic calls are reasonable, and incoming calls are free. You'll pay more if you're "roaming" in another country. If your phone is "unlocked," you can swap out its SIM card for a new one when you travel to other countries.

Calling over the Internet

Some things that seem too good to be true...actually are true. If you're traveling with a laptop, you can make calls using VoIP (Voice over Internet Protocol). With VoIP, two computers act as the phones, and the Internet-based calls are free (or you can pay a few cents per minute to call from your computer to a telephone). The major providers are Skype (www.skype.com) and Google Talk (www.google.com/talk).

Useful Phone Numbers

Emergencies

In all the countries in this book, dial 112 for medical or other emergencies. For police, dial 112 everywhere except Finland (dial 10022) and Estonia (dial 110).

US Embassies

Embassies are located in all of the capital cities.

In Denmark: Dag Hammarskjölds Allé 24, Copenhagen, passport services available Mon–Tue and Thu–Fri 9:00–12:00, tel. 33 41 71 00, www.denmark.usembassy.gov

In Estonia: Kentmanni 20, Tallinn, tel. 668-8100, http://estonia.usembassy.gov

In Finland: Itäinen Puistotie 14B, Helsinki, passport services available Mon–Thu 9:00–12:00, tel. 09/616-25701, www.usembassy.fi

In Norway: Henrik Ibsens Gate 48, Oslo, passport services available Mon–Fri 9:00–12:00, tel. 22 44 85 50, www.norway.usembassy.gov

In Sweden: Dag Hammarskjölds Väg 31, Stockholm, passport services available Mon–Fri 9:00–11:00, tel. 08/783-5300, www.usemb.se

Travel Advisories

US Department of State: tel. 202/647-5225, www.travel.state.gov
Canadian Department of Foreign Affairs: Canadian tel. 800-267-6788, www.dfait-maeci.gc.ca
US Centers for Disease Control and Prevention: tel. 800-CDC-INFO (800-232-4636), www.cdc.gov/travel

The Internet

The Internet can be an invaluable tool for planning your trip (researching and booking hotels, checking bus and train schedules, and so on). It's also useful to go online periodically as you travel—to reconfirm your trip plans, check the weather, catch up on email, blog or post photos from your trip, or call folks back home (explained earlier in "Calling over the Internet").

Some hotels offer a computer in the lobby with Internet access for guests. Smaller places may sometimes let you sit at their desk for a few minutes just to check your email, if you ask politely. If you're traveling with a laptop, see if your hotel has Wi-Fi (wireless Internet access) or a port in your room where you can plug in a cable to get online. Most hotels offer Wi-Fi for free; others charge by the minute.

If your hotel doesn't have access, ask your hotelier to direct you to the nearest place to go online. Most of the towns where I've listed accommodations in this book also have Internet cafés. Many libraries offer free access, but they also tend to have limited opening hours, restrict your online time to 30 minutes, and may require reservations.

Mail

Get stamps at the neighborhood post office, newsstands within fancy hotels, and some mini-marts and card shops. While you can arrange for mail delivery to your hotel (allow 10 days for a letter to arrive), phoning and emailing are so easy that I've dispensed with mail stops altogether.

Transportation

Getting to Scandinavia

Copenhagen is usually the most direct and least expensive Scandinavian capital to fly into from the US (though Stockholm, Oslo, and Helsinki are easy to reach via Icelandair from the East Coast). Copenhagen is also Europe's gateway to Scandinavia from points south. There are often cheaper flights from the US into Frankfurt and Amsterdam than into Copenhagen, but it's a long, rather dull, one-day drive (with a 45-minute, $85-per-car ferry crossing at Puttgarden, Germany—www.scandlines.dk). By train, Copenhagen is an easy overnight ride from Amsterdam, Cologne, or Frankfurt. The base ticket price ($200 or more) is covered if you have the Eurail Global pass or a railpass covering the particular countries. Another option is flying into London and then hopping to Copenhagen on a low-cost, no-frills airline, such as bmi (British Midland, www.flybmi.com), easyJet (www.easyjet.com), or Ryanair (www.ryanair.com).

By Car or Public Transportation?

Cars are best for three or more traveling together (especially families with small kids), those packing heavy, and those scouring the countryside. Trains, buses, and boats are best for solo travelers, blitz tourists, and city-to-city travelers. While a car gives you more freedom—enabling you to search for hotels more easily and carrying your bags for you—trains, buses, and boats zip you effortlessly and scenically from city to city, usually dropping you in or near the center, often near a tourist office. Cars are great in the countryside, but a worthless headache in big cities like Copenhagen and Stockholm.

Public Transportation

Throughout this book, I'll suggest whether trains, buses, or boats are better for a particular destination (in the "Connections" section at the end of each chapter).

Trains

With a few exceptions, trains cover my recommended Scandinavian destinations wonderfully.

Schedules and Tickets: Pick up train schedules from stations as you go. To study ahead on the Web, check http://bahn.hafas.de/bin/query.exe/en (Germany's excellent Europe-wide timetable). The local train companies also have their own sites with fare and timetable information, and even online booking in English; see http://dsb.dk or www.rejseplanen.dk (Denmark), www.vr.fi (Finland), www.nsb.no (Norway), and www.sj.se (Sweden).

Railpasses: One of the great Nordic bargains, the Eurail Scandinavia pass is your best railpass deal for a trip limited to Scandinavia. Although Eurail Scandinavia passes are available only for second-class seats, Scandinavian second class is plenty comfortable. Some trains, including those that cover part of the popular Norway in a Nutshell route (see page 232), do not offer first class. For options and prices on pertinent Eurail passes, see the railpass chart in this chapter and www.ricksteves.com/rail.

If your trip extends south of Scandinavia, consider the flexible Eurail Selectpass, which allows you to choose three, four, or five adjoining countries connected by land or ferry (for instance, Germany–Sweden–Finland). A more expensive Eurail Global pass is a good value only for those spending more time throughout Europe. A three-week first-class Eurail Global pass costs about $950 (or about $100 less apiece for a Eurail Global Saverpass, if you travel with a companion).

Railpasses give you discounted use of many boats (such as Stockholm to Helsinki) and cover almost all trains in the region (though you'll need 50-kr reservations for long rides and express trains, plus a 140-kr supplement for Norway's Myrdal–Flåm ride—part of the Norway in a Nutshell route).

A ScanRail & Drive pass offers a flexible way to mix rail and car rental, and is handy if you plan to explore Sweden's Glass Country or the Norwegian mountains and fjords. However, if you're planning on using a car more than two days in a row, you're probably better off renting a car than getting a ScanRail & Drive pass.

Night Trains: To cover the long distances between the major destinations in this book, consider using night trains (other options may include an overnight cruise—see "Boats," below, or an inexpensive flight—see "Cheap Flights," later). Remember, each night spent traveling saves a day for sightseeing, and saves you the cost of a hotel room, which can be substantial in expensive Scandinavia. A bed in a compartment on a night train is a good value. Beyond the cost of your first- or second-class ticket or pass, you'll pay about $25 for a bed in a triple, $40 for a bed in a double, or $100 for a single.

Buses

Don't overlook long-distance buses, which are usually slower but have considerably cheaper and more predictable fares than trains. (In Denmark, however, the train system is excellent and nearly always the better option.) On certain routes, such as between Stockholm and Oslo, the bus is cheaper and only slightly slower than the train. Scandinavia's big bus carriers are Sweden's Swebus (www.swebusexpress.se), Norway's Nor-Way Bussekspress (www.nor-way.no), Denmark's public buses (www.rejseplanen.dk), and Finland's Matkahuolto (www.matkahuolto.fi).

Boats

Boats are romantic, scenic, and sometimes the most efficient—or only—way to link destinations in coastal Scandinavia. But boats can often be more expensive than other transportation options, although some routes may be covered or discounted if you have a railpass. Note that short-distance ferries may take only cash, not credit cards.

Advance reservations are recommended when using overnight boats in summer or on weekends to link Oslo to Copenhagen (www.dfdsseaways.com) or Stockholm to Helsinki (www.vikingline.fi and www.silja.com), and helpful for Stockholm to Tallinn (www.silja.com).

Several companies speed via fast boat between Helsinki and

Tallinn (see page 515). Other worthwhile routes connect Norway and Denmark (Kristiansand and Hirtshals several times daily, Stavanger and Hirtshals by overnight boat; see page 334, www.fjordline.com, and www.colorline.com). Ferries are essential for hopping between the mainland and Scandinavia's many islands, such as Ærø in central Denmark (drivers should reserve in advance for weekends and summer, www.aeroe-ferry.dk), or Stockholm's archipelago. Boats are both a necessary and spectacular way to travel through Norway's fjords or along its coast (www.fjordtours.no, www.fjord1.no, and www.hsd.no). Bergen, in Norway, is a departure point for boats to the Arctic (www.hurtigruten.com).

Renting a Car

The minimum age to rent a car varies by country and rental company (you must be 19 in Norway, 20 in Sweden and Finland, and 21 in Denmark and Estonia). Drivers under the age of 25 may incur a young-driver surcharge, and some rental companies do not rent to anyone 75 and over. If you're considered too young or old, look into leasing (explained later), which has less-stringent age restrictions.

If your driver's license has been renewed within the last year, an International Driving Permit is recommended, but not required ($15 through your local AAA, plus two passport photos, www.aaa.com); however, I've frequently rented cars in Scandinavia and traveled problem-free with just my US license.

Research car rentals before you go. It's cheapest to arrange most car rentals from the US. Call several companies, and look online to compare rates, or arrange a rental through your hometown travel agent. Two reputable companies among many are Auto Europe (www.autoeurope.com) and Europe by Car (www.ebctravel.com). For the best rental deal, rent by the week with unlimited mileage (but for long trips, consider leasing). To save money on gas, ask for a diesel car.

Expect to pay about $900 per person (based on 2 people sharing the car) for a small economy car for three weeks with unlimited mileage, including gas, parking, and insurance.

I normally rent the smallest, least-expensive model (e.g., a Ford Fiesta) with a stick-shift. For a bigger, roomier, more powerful but inexpensive car, move up to a Ford Focus or VW Polo. Minibuses are a great budget way to go for five to nine people.

Almost all rentals are manual by default, so if you need an automatic, you must request one in advance; beware that these cars are usually larger models (not as maneuverable on narrow, winding roads). An automatic transmission adds about 50 percent to the car-rental cost over a manual transmission.

Compare pickup costs (downtown can be cheaper than the airport) and explore drop-off options. Returning a car at a big-city train station can be tricky; get precise details on the car drop-off location and hours. Picking up and dropping off the car in different cities (such as Oslo and Bergen, or Copenhagen and Stockholm) can come with astronomical drop-off fees. Ask about this expense before you commit. I prefer to connect long distances by train or bus, then rent cars for a day or two where they're most useful (I've noted these places throughout this book).

Always tell your car-rental company up front exactly which countries you'll be entering. Some companies levy extra insurance fees for trips taken with certain types of cars (such as BMWs, Mercedes, and convertibles) in certain countries. More importantly, as you cross borders you may need to show the proper paperwork, such as proof of insurance (called a "green card"). Double-check with your rental agent that you have all the documentation you need before you drive off.

If you drop your car off early or keep it longer, you'll be credited or charged at a fair, prorated price. But keep your receipts in case any questions arise about your billing.

When picking up the car, check it thoroughly and make sure any damage is noted on your rental agreement. Find out how your car's lights, turn signals, wipers, and gas cap function. When you return the car, make sure the agent verifies its condition with you.

Car Insurance Options

When you rent a car, you are liable for a very high deductible, sometimes equal to the entire value of the car. Limit your financial risk in case of an accident by choosing one of these three options: Buy Collision Damage Waiver (CDW) coverage from the car-rental company, get coverage through your credit card (free, if your card automatically includes zero-deductible coverage), or buy coverage through Travel Guard.

While each rental company has its own variation, basic **CDW** costs $15–25 a day (figure roughly 25 percent extra) and reduces your liability, but does not eliminate it. When you pick up the car, you'll be offered the chance to "buy down" the basic deductible to zero (for an additional $10–30/day; this is often called "super CDW").

If you opt for credit-card coverage, there's a catch. You'll technically have to decline all coverage offered by the car-rental company, which means they can place a hold on your card (can be up to the full value of the car). In case of damage, it can be time-consuming to resolve the charges with your credit-card company. Before you decide on this option, quiz your credit-card company about how it works and ask them to explain the worst-case scenario.

Finally, you can buy CDW insurance from Travel Guard

($9/day plus a one-time $3 service fee covers you up to $35,000, $250 deductible, tel. 800-826-4919, www.travelguard.com). It's valid everywhere in Europe except the Republic of Ireland, and some Italian car-rental companies refuse to honor it. Residents of Washington State aren't eligible for this coverage.

For more fine print about car-rental insurance, see www.rick steves.com/cdw.

Leasing

For trips of two and a half weeks or more, leasing (which automatically includes zero-deductible collision and theft insurance) is the best way to go. By technically buying and then selling back the car, you save lots of money on tax and insurance. Leasing provides you a new car with unlimited mileage and a 24-hour emergency assistance program. You can lease for as little as 17 days to as long as six months. Car leases must be arranged from the US, and cars must be picked up and dropped off outside Scandinavia. One of many reliable companies offering affordable lease packages is Europe by Car (US tel. 800-223-1516, www.ebctravel.com).

Driving

Bring your driver's license. Except for the dangers posed by the scenic distractions and moose crossings, Scandinavia is a great place to drive. But never drink and drive—even one drink can get a driver into serious trouble.

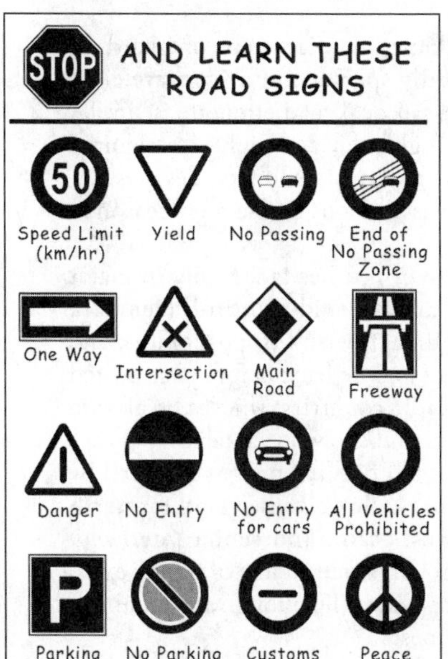

Seat belts are mandatory, and young children need a child-safety seat nearly everywhere (in Denmark-age 6 and under, Finland-age 4, Norway-age 5, and Sweden-age 7) except Estonia.

Fuel: Gas is expensive—often more than $8 per gallon. US credit and debit cards won't work at pay-at-the-pump stations, but are generally accepted (with a PIN code) at staffed stations. Diesel rental cars are common; make sure you know what type of gas your car takes before you fill up.

On the Road: Roads are good (though nerve-rackingly skinny in western Norway).

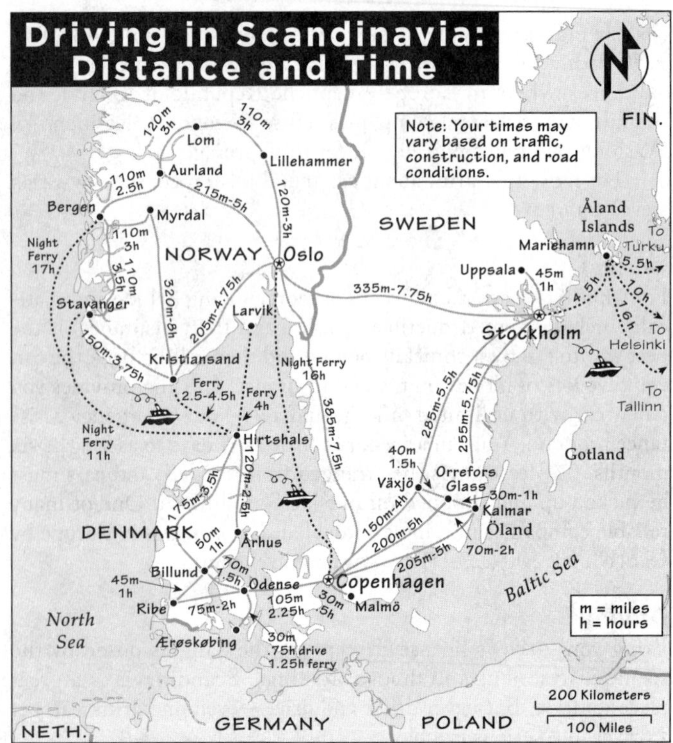

Bikes tend to whiz by close and quiet in cities, so be on guard. In the countryside, traffic is generally sparse, and drivers are civil. Signs and road maps are excellent. Local road etiquette is similar to that in the US. Use your headlights day and night; it's required in most of Scandinavia. There are plenty of good facilities, gas stations, and scenic rest stops. Snow is a serious problem off-season in the mountains.

Parking: Parking on the street is a headache only in major cities, where expensive garages are safe and plentiful. Denmark uses a parking windshield-clock disk (free at TIs, post offices, and newsstands; set it when you arrive and be back before your posted time limit is up). Even in the Nordic countries, thieves break into cars. Park carefully, use the trunk, and show no valuables.

Signage: As you navigate, you'll find town signs followed by the letters *N, S, Ø* (*Ö* in Sweden), *V,* or *C.* These stand for north *(nord),* south *(sud),* east *(øst),* west *(vest),* and center *(centrum),* respectively; understanding them will save you lots of wrong exits. Due to recent changes, some maps have the wrong road numbers. It's safest to navigate by town names.

Cheap Flights

This book covers far-flung destinations separated by vast stretches of mountains and water. While boats and trains are more romantic, cheap flights can provide an affordable and efficient way to connect the dots on a Scandinavian itinerary.

Several budget airlines have cropped up in the last few years. Most of these airlines offer flights both within Nordic Europe and to destinations all over the Continent and beyond.

SAS, the region's dominant airline, operates a low-cost Finnish subsidiary called Blue1 (hubs in Helsinki and Stockholm, www.blue1.com) and is affiliated with Oslo-based Widerøe Air (www.wideroe.no). Other options are the Swedish airline FlyNordic (hub in Stockholm, www.flynordic.com); Norwegian Airlines (hubs in Oslo and Bergen, www.norwegian.no); the Denmark-based Cimber Sterling (specializes in connecting Scandinavian capitals such as Oslo and Copenhagen with sunny destinations in southern Europe, www.cimber.com); and Tallinn-based Estonian Air (www.estonian-air.com).

A visit to www.skyscanner.net sorts the numerous options offered by the many discount airlines, enabling you to see the best schedules for your trip and come up with the best deal. Other good search engines include www.mobissimo.com and www.wegolo.com.

Be aware of the potential drawbacks of flying on the cheap: nonrefundable and nonchangeable tickets, minimal customer assistance, the typical use of airports far outside town, and pricey baggage fees. If you're traveling with lots of luggage, a cheap flight can quickly become a bad deal, due to per-piece baggage fees. To avoid unpleasant surprises, read the small print—especially baggage policies—before you book.

Resources

Resources from Rick Steves

Rick Steves' Scandinavia is one of more than 30 titles in a series of **books** on European travel, which includes country guidebooks, city and regional guidebooks, and my budget-travel skills handbook, *Rick Steves' Europe Through the Back Door.* My phrase books—for German, French, Italian, Spanish, and Portuguese—are practical and budget-oriented. My other books are *Europe 101* (a crash course

Begin Your Trip at www.ricksteves.com

At our travel website, you'll find a wealth of free information on European destinations, including fresh monthly news and helpful tips from thousands of fellow travelers. You'll also find my latest guidebook updates (www.ricksteves.com/update) and my travel blog.

Our **online Travel Store** offers travel bags and accessories specially designed by Rick Steves to help you travel smarter and lighter. These include my popular carry-on bags (roll-aboard and rucksack versions), money belts, totes, toiletries kits, adapters, other accessories, and a wide selection of guidebooks, planning maps, and DVDs.

Choosing the right **railpass** for your trip—amidst hundreds of options—can drive you nutty. We'll help you choose the best pass for your needs, plus give you a bunch of free extras.

Rick Steves' Europe Through the Back Door travel company offers **tours** with more than two dozen itineraries and about 300 departures reaching the best destinations in this book...and beyond. We offer a 14-day Best of Scandinavia tour featuring the big-city highlights of Stockholm, Copenhagen, and Oslo, as well as quieter Nordic nooks such as the Danish island of Æroskobing and a scenic cruise through the fjords; and a nine-day tour of Tallinn, Helsinki, and St. Petersburg. You'll enjoy great guides, a fun bunch of travel partners (with small groups of generally around 28), and plenty of room to spread out in a big, comfy bus. You'll find European adventures to fit every vacation length. For all the details, and to get our Tour Catalog and a free *Rick Steves Tour Experience* DVD (filmed on location during an actual tour), visit www.ricksteves.com or call the Tour Department at 425/608-4217.

on art and history, newly expanded and in full color), *Travel as a Political Act* (a travelogue sprinkled with advice for bringing home a global perspective), *European Christmas* (on traditional and modern-day celebrations), and *Postcards from Europe* (a fun memoir of my travels over 25 years). For a complete list of my books, see the inside of the last page of this book.

My **TV series**, *Rick Steves' Europe,* covers European destinations in 100 shows, with five episodes on Scandinavia. My weekly public radio show, *Travel with Rick Steves,* features interviews with travel experts from around the world, including Scandinavia. All the TV scripts and radio shows (which are easy and free to download to an iPod or other MP3 player) are at www.ricksteves.com.

If your travels take you beyond Scandinavia to Italy, France, or Great Britain, take advantage of my free, self-guided **audio tours** of the major sights in Venice, Florence, Rome, Paris, and London. Simply download them from www.ricksteves.com or iTunes (search for "Rick Steves' tours" in the iTunes Store), then transfer them to your iPod or other MP3 player.

Maps

The black-and-white maps in this book, designed by my well-traveled staff, are concise and simple. The maps are intended to help you locate recommended places and get to local TIs, where you can pick up more in-depth maps of towns or regions (free or cheap). Better maps are sold at newsstands and bookstores. Before you buy a map, look at it to be sure it has the level of detail you want.

Train travelers can use a simple rail map (such as the one that comes with your train pass). But drivers shouldn't skimp on maps—get one good overall road map for Scandinavia (either the Michelin *Scandinavia* or the Kummerly & Frey *Southern Scandinavia* 1:1,000,000 edition). The Collins Road Atlas is also good. The only detailed map worth considering is the *Southern Norway-North* (*Sør Norge-nord,* 1:325,000) by Cappelens Kart ($20 in Scandinavian bookstores).

Other Guidebooks

If you're like most travelers, this book is all you need. But if you're heading beyond my recommended destinations, $40 for extra maps and books is money well spent. For several people traveling by car, the extra weight and expense of a few books are negligible.

The following books are worthwhile, though not updated annually; check the publication date before you buy. Lonely

Planet's *Scandinavian Europe* is thorough, well-researched, and packed with good maps and hotel recommendations for low- to moderate-budget travelers. The similar *Rough Guide to Scandinavia* is hip and insightful, written by British researchers. Culture Shock's guides to Norway, Denmark, and Sweden help travelers to better understand local customs and etiquette.

Students and vagabonds will like the highly opinionated *Let's Go: Western Europe*, which includes some coverage of Scandinavia (updated by Harvard students, has thorough hostel listings). *Let's Go* is best for backpackers who have railpasses and are interested in the youth and nightlife scene.

Older travelers enjoy guides from Frommer's, even though, like the Fodor's guide, they ignore alternatives that enable travelers to save money by dirtying their fingers in the local culture.

The popular, skinny green Michelin Guides are excellent, especially if you're driving. Michelin Guides are known for their city and sightseeing maps, dry but concise and helpful information on all major sights, and good cultural and historical background. English editions are sold in Europe at gas stations and tourist shops.

The Eyewitness series—which covers Denmark, Norway, and Sweden—is popular for great, easy-to-grasp graphics and photos, 3-D cutaways of buildings, aerial-view maps of historic neighborhoods, and cultural background. But written content in Eyewitness is relatively skimpy, and the books weigh a ton. I simply borrow them for a minute from other travelers at certain sights to make sure that I'm aware of that place's highlights.

Those staying longer in Stockholm, Oslo, Bergen, or Helsinki might consider the Insight Pocket Guides to those cities. The British entertainment publication *Time Out* sells well-researched annual magazines with up-to-date coverage on Copenhagen, Oslo, Stockholm, Helsinki, and Tallinn, including the latest on hotels, restaurants, and nightlife (look for it at newsstands, www.timeout.com).

For Estonia, consider the *Bradt Guide to Estonia* (published by Globe Pequot Press).

Recommended Books and Movies

To learn about Scandinavia past and present, check out a few of these books and films.

Nonfiction

For a solid grasp of Scandinavia's past, try *A History of Scandinavia: Norway, Sweden, Denmark, Finland, and Iceland* (Derry) or *Scandinavia Since 1500* (Nordstrom). The history of the Swedish people from feudalism to democracy is recorded in *Sweden: The*

Nation's History (Scott). *The Vikings* (Else Roesdhal) offers a Scandinavian perspective on this complex Nordic society.

For insight into Hans Christian Andersen, try his autobiography, *The Fairy Tale of My Life*, and Jens Andersen's biography *Hans Christian Andersen: A New Life. Scandinavian Folk and Fairy Tales* (Boos) is a good compilation. Peter Tveskov combines historical fact with childhood memories of Denmark under German occupation during World War II in *Conquered, Not Defeated.* Norwegian biologist Thor Heyerdahl records his historic 1947 journey from Peru to Polynesia on a balsa-wood raft in *Kon-Tiki.*

Fiction

Read a collection of Hans Christian Andersen's classic fairy tales: *The Little Mermaid, The Little Match Girl, The Princess and the Pea, The Steadfast Tin Soldier,* and many more. Also beloved by children of all ages are the *Pippi Longstocking* books by Sweden's Astrid Lindgren.

Swede Selma Lagerlöf was the first woman to win the Nobel Prize for Literature (in 1909) for her fantastical children's novel, *The Wonderful Adventures of Nils.* Nobel Prize winners by Norwegians include Knut Hamsum's influential *Growth of the Soil* (w. 1920) and Sigrid Undset's epic *Kristin Lavransdatter* (w. 1928).

Music and Silence by Rose Tremain captures 17th-century Denmark through the eyes of a lute-player at court. *The Emigrants* is the first of Vilhelm Moberg's four-volume epic about Swedish immigrants settling the American frontier. The multigenerational saga *Hanna's Daughters* by Marianne Fredriksson traces a Swedish family from the 1870s through World War II. Norwegian playwright Henrik Ibsen's controversial plays explore the role of women in the 19th century (try *A Doll's House* or *Hedda Gabler*). A 19th-century Frenchwoman takes refuge in Denmark in *Babette's Feast* by Karen Blixen.

Gripping intrigue and social commentary combine in the literary thriller *Smilla's Sense of Snow* by Dane Peter Høeg. Also try *Faceless Killers*, the first of several Kurt Wallender mysteries by Swedish crime-writer Henning Mankell. *Sophie's World* by Norwegian Jostein Gaarder is a metaphysical mystery wrapped in the history of philosophy.

Films with a Nordic Accent

Watch any of Oscar-winning Swedish director Ingmar Bergman's films, especially *The Seventh Seal* (1957, a knight questions the meaning of life), *Smiles of a Summer Night* (1955, turn-of-the-century frolic), and *Fanny & Alexander* (1983, children overcome father's death).

Song of Norway (1970) is a musical based on the life of

Norwegian composer Edvard Grieg. Bergman alums Max von Sydow and Liv Ullmann star in *The Emigrants* and *The New Land* (1971, 1972) based on the Moberg novels. The bittersweet *My Life as a Dog* (1985) shows Sweden in the 1950s, while the "original foodie movie," *Babette's Feast* (1988), is set in rural 19th-century Denmark (and based on the book by Karen Blixen cited above). *Pelle the Conqueror* (1988) examines Swedish immigration to Denmark in the 19th century, and *Kristin Lavransdatter* (1995) is a much-condensed version of the epic novel. The midnight sun plays a role in the Norwegian thriller *Insomnia* (1997, later adapted by American filmmakers). A young Finnish boy is evacuated to Sweden during World War II in *Mother of Mine* (2005).

Julia Ormond plays the title role in the dramatic film adaptation of *Smilla's Sense of Snow* (1997). For lighter fare, try comedies such as *Italian for Beginners* (2000, Danish thirtysomethings learn Italian), *Together* (2000, life in a 1970s Stockholm commune), *Elling* (2001, oddballs make it on their own), and *Dalecarlians* (2005, big-city sister returns to rural hometown). The quirky *Cool & Crazy* (2001) is an uplifting documentary about a Norwegian men's choir, while *As It Is in Heaven* (2004) recounts a Swedish conductor's search for happiness.

Holidays and Festivals

This list includes many—but not all—major festivals in major cities, plus national holidays observed throughout Scandinavia. Before planning a trip around a festival, make sure you verify the dates by checking the festival's website or contacting the Scandinavian National Tourist Office (www.goscandinavia.com) or Estonia's US office (www.visitestonia.com). They can also provide specifics and a more comprehensive list of festivals.

Jan 1 New Year's Day, all countries

Late Jan Winter Jazz Festival (Jan 22–Feb 7 in 2010, www.vinterjazz.dk), Odense, Denmark

Mid-Feb "Frozen Waterfall" Winter Arts Festival (theater, music), Lillehammer, Norway

April 1 Hat Festival (spring festival), Bergen, Norway

Before Easter Easter Festival (theater, concerts), Bergen, Norway

Easter April 4 in 2010, April 24 in 2011

Late April–Early May Bergenfest Music Festival, Bergen, Norway

End of April Maritime Festival, Bergen, Norway

April 30	Walpurgis Night (bonfires, choirs), Sweden
May 1	May Day (parades, some closures), Scandinavia
Common Prayer Day	April 30 in 2010, May 20 in 2011, Denmark (businesses closed)
Ascension Day	May 13 in 2010, June 2 in 2011
May 15	St. Hallvard's Day (theater, concerts), Oslo, Norway
Mid-May	Stavanger International Jazz Festival ("MaiJazz"; May 5–9 in 2010, www.maijazz.no), Stavanger, Norway
Mid-May	Flower Festival, Copenhagen, Denmark
May 17	Constitution Day (parades, closures), Norway
Whitsunday and Whitmonday	May 23–24 in 2010, June 12–13 in 2011
Late May	International Festival (theater, music, dance), Norway
Late May	Swinging Jazz Festival, Copenhagen, Denmark
Late May	Dragon Boat Festival (Chinese boat races), Bergen, Norway, and Stockholm, Sweden
June 5	Constitution Day (businesses closed), Denmark
June 6	National Day (parades), Sweden
June 6	Archipelago Boat Day (steamboat parade), Stockholm, Sweden
Early June	Old Town Days (3 days, music), Tallinn, Estonia
Early June	Taste of Stockholm (1 week, outdoor food vendors; www.smakapastockholm.se), Stockholm, Sweden
Mid-June	Norwegian Wood Rock Music Festival (3 days, www.norwegianwood.no), Oslo, Norway
Mid-June	Medieval Festival ("Middelalderfestival"; June 19–20 in 2010, June 18–19 in 2011, www.oslomiddelalderfestival.org), Oslo, Norway
Mid-June–Mid-Aug	Fløyen Concert Festival (classical music), Bergen, Norway
Solstice	Midsummer Eve (celebrations, bonfires), Scandinavia

Late June–Aug	Hans Christian Andersen Festival, Odense, Denmark
July 4	Fourth of July festivities, Stockholm, Sweden
Early July	Copenhagen Jazz Festival (10 days, www.jazzfestival.dk), Copenhagen, Denmark
Early July	Roskilde Festival (July 1–4 in 2010, June 30–July 3 in 2011, music and theater, www.roskilde-festival.dk), Roskilde, Denmark
Mid–Late July	International Jazz Festival (www.jazzfest.dk), Århus, Denmark
Late July	Cutty Sark Tall Ship Race, Bergen, Norway
Early Aug	Water Festival (10 days), Stockholm, Sweden
Early Aug	International Chamber Music Festival (www.icmf.no), Stavanger, Norway
Mid-Aug	Emigration Festival, Växjö, Sweden
Mid-Aug	Chamber Music Festival (1 week, www.oslokammermusikkfestival.no), Oslo, Norway
Mid-Aug	Jazz Festival (www.oslojazz.no), Oslo, Norway
Late Aug	Seafood Festival, Oslo, Norway
Late Aug	International Chamber Music Festival, Bergen, Norway
Mid–Late Aug	Helsinki Festival (2 weeks, music, dance, film, theater; www.helsinkifestival.fi), Helsinki, Finland
Late Aug–Sept	Århus Festival (1 week, music, dance, theater; www.aarhusfestuge.dk), Århus, Denmark
Early Sept	Wooden Boats Festival, Stavanger, Norway
Mid-Sept	DølaJazz Festival (3 days, www.dolajazz.no), Lillehammer, Norway
Late Sept	Folk Festival, Odense, Denmark
Oct 1	Rain Festival (raincoat and umbrella parade), Bergen, Norway
Early Oct–Nov	Art Festival (jazz, dance), Bergen, Norway
Early–Mid-Oct	Contemporary Music Festival, Oslo, Norway
Early Nov	Autumn Jazz Festival, Copenhagen, Denmark

Mid-Nov–Dec 23	Christmas Fair (Tivoli Garden), Copenhagen, Denmark
Dec 6	Independence Day (candlelit windows), Finland
Dec 13	St. Lucia Day (festival of lights), Sweden
Dec 25	Christmas, Scandinavia

Conversions and Climate

Numbers and Stumblers

- Europeans write a few of their numbers differently than we do. 1 = 1, 4 = 4, 7 = 7.
- In Europe, dates appear as day/month/year, so Christmas is 25/12/11.
- Commas are decimal points and decimals commas. A dollar and a half is 1,50, and there are 5.280 feet in a mile.
- When counting with fingers, start with your thumb. If you hold up your first finger to request one item, you'll probably get two.
- What Americans call the second floor of a building is the first floor in Europe.
- On escalators and moving sidewalks, Europeans keep the left "lane" open for passing. Keep to the right.

Metric Conversions (approximate)

A kilogram is 2.2 pounds, and 1 liter is about a quart, or almost four to a gallon. A kilometer is six-tenths of a mile. I figure kilometers to miles by cutting them in half and adding back 10 percent of the original (120 km: 60 + 12 = 72 miles, 300 km: 150 + 30 = 180 miles).

1 foot = 0.3 meter	1 square yard = 0.8 square meter
1 yard = 0.9 meter	1 square mile = 2.6 square kilometers
1 mile = 1.6 kilometers	1 ounce = 28 grams
1 centimeter = 0.4 inch	1 quart = 0.95 liter
1 meter = 39.4 inches	1 kilogram = 2.2 pounds
1 kilometer = 0.62 mile	32°F = 0°C

Clothing Sizes

When shopping for clothing, use these US-to-European comparisons as general guidelines (but note that no conversion is perfect).

- Women's dresses and blouses: Add 30 (US size 10 = European size 40)
- Men's suits and jackets: Add 10 (US size 40 regular = European size 50)
- Men's shirts: Multiply by 2 and add about 8 (US size 15 collar = European size 38)

- Women's shoes: Add about 30 (US size 8 = European size 38½)
- Men's shoes: Add 32–34 (US size 9 = European size 41; US size 11 = European size 45)

Climate

First line is the average daily high temperature; second line, average daily low; third line, days without rain. For more detailed weather statistics for destinations in this book (as well as the rest of the world), check www.worldclimate.com.

	J	F	M	A	M	J	J	A	S	O	N	D
DENMARK • Copenhagen												
	37°	37°	42°	51°	60°	66°	70°	69°	64°	55°	46°	41°
	29°	28°	31°	37°	45°	51°	56°	56°	51°	44°	38°	33°
	14	15	19	18	20	18	17	16	14	14	11	12
ESTONIA • Tallinn												
	25°	25°	32°	45°	57°	66°	68°	66°	59°	50°	37°	30°
	14°	12°	19°	32°	41°	50°	54°	52°	48°	39°	30°	19°
	12	12	18	19	19	20	18	16	14	14	12	12
FINLAND • Helsinki												
	26°	25°	32°	44°	56°	66°	71°	68°	59°	47°	37°	31°
	17°	15°	20°	30°	40°	49°	55°	53°	46°	37°	30°	23°
	11	10	17	17	19	17	17	16	16	13	11	11
NORWAY • Oslo												
	28°	30°	39°	50°	61°	68°	72°	70°	60°	48°	38°	32°
	19°	19°	25°	34°	43°	50°	55°	53°	46°	38°	31°	25°
	16	16	22	19	21	17	16	17	16	17	14	14
SWEDEN • Stockholm												
	30°	30°	37°	47°	58°	67°	71°	68°	60°	49°	40°	35°
	26°	25°	29°	37°	45°	53°	57°	56°	50°	43°	37°	32°
	15	14	21	19	20	17	18	17	16	16	14	14

Temperature Conversion: Fahrenheit and Celsius

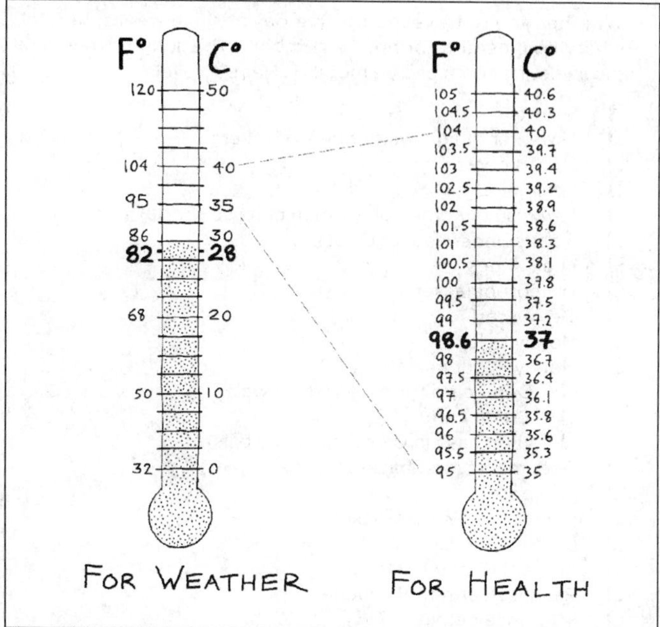

Scandinavia takes its temperature using the Celsius scale, while we opt for Fahrenheit. For a rough conversion from Celsius to Fahrenheit, double the number and add 30. For weather, remember that 28°C is 82°F—perfect. For health, 37°C is just right.

Essential Packing Checklist

Whether you're traveling for five days or five weeks, here's what you'll need to bring. Remember to pack light to enjoy the sweet freedom of true mobility. Happy travels!

- ❑ 5 shirts
- ❑ 1 sweater or lightweight fleece jacket
- ❑ 2 pairs pants
- ❑ 1 pair shorts
- ❑ 1 swimsuit (women only—men can use shorts)
- ❑ 5 pairs underwear and socks
- ❑ 1 pair shoes
- ❑ 1 rainproof jacket
- ❑ Tie or scarf
- ❑ Money belt
- ❑ Money—your mix of:
  - ❑ Debit card for ATM withdrawals
  - ❑ Credit card
  - ❑ Hard cash in US dollars ($20 bills)
- ❑ Documents (and back-up photocopies)
- ❑ Passport
- ❑ Printout of airline e-ticket
- ❑ Driver's license
- ❑ Student ID and hostel card
- ❑ Railpass/car rental voucher
- ❑ Insurance details
- ❑ Daypack
- ❑ Sealable plastic baggies
- ❑ Camera and related gear
- ❑ Empty water bottle
- ❑ Wristwatch and alarm clock
- ❑ Earplugs
- ❑ First-aid kit
- ❑ Medicine (labeled)
- ❑ Extra glasses/contacts and prescriptions
- ❑ Sunscreen and sunglasses
- ❑ Toiletries kit
- ❑ Soap
- ❑ Laundry soap
- ❑ Clothesline
- ❑ Small towel
- ❑ Sewing kit
- ❑ Travel information
- ❑ Necessary map(s)
- ❑ Address list (email and mailing addresses)
- ❑ Postcards and photos from home
- ❑ Notepad and pen
- ❑ Journal

If you plan to carry on your luggage, note that all liquids must be in three-ounce or smaller containers and fit within a single quart-size baggie. For details, see www.tsa.gov/travelers.

Hotel Reservation

To: ____________________ ____________________
hotel *email or fax*

From: ____________________ ____________________
name *email or fax*

Today's date: _____ /_____ /_____
day *month* *year*

Dear Hotel ________________________________,
Please make this reservation for me:

Name: ________________________________

Total # of people: _______ # of rooms: _______ # of nights: _______

Arriving: _____ /_____ /_____ My time of arrival (24-hr clock): _______
day *month* *year* (I will telephone if I will be late)

Departing: _____ /_____ /_____
day *month* *year*

Room(s): Single___ Double ___ Twin___ Triple___ Quad___

With: Toilet ___ Shower___ Bath___ Sink only___

Special needs: View___ Quiet___ Cheapest___ Ground Floor___

Please email or fax confirmation of my reservation, along with the type of room reserved and the price. Please also inform me of your cancellation policy. After I hear from you, I will quickly send my credit-card information as a deposit to hold the room. Thank you.

____
Name

____
Address

____
City **State** **Zip Code** **Country**

Before hoteliers can make your reservation, they want to know the information listed above. You can use this form as the basis for your email, or you can photocopy this page, fill in the information, and send it as a fax (also available online at www.ricksteves.com/reservation).

Estonian Survival Phrases

Estonian has a few unusual vowel sounds. The letter *ä* is pronounced "ah" as in "hat," but *a* without the umlaut sounds more like "aw" as in "hot." To make the sound *ö*, say "oh" and purse your lips; the letter *õ* is similar, but with the lips less pursed. Listen to locals and imitate. In the phonetics, Ī / ī sounds like the long i in "light."

Hello. *(formal)*	**Tervist.**	TEHR-veest
Hi. / Bye. *(informal)*	**Tere. / Nägemist.**	TEH-reh / NAH-geh-meest
Do you speak English?	**Kas te räägite inglise keelt?**	kahs teh RAAH-gee-the EEN-glee-seh kehlt
Yes. / No.	**Jah. / Ei.**	yah / ay
Please. / You're welcome.	**Palun.**	PAH-luhn
Thank you (very much).	**Tänan (väga).**	TAH-nahn (VAH-gaw)
Can I help you?	**Saan ma teid aidata?**	saahn mah tayd Ī-dah-tah
Excuse me.	**Vabandust.**	VAW-bahn-doost
(Very) good.	**(Väga) hea.**	(VAH-gaw) HEY-ah
Goodbye.	**Hüvasti.**	HEW-vaw-stee
one / two	**üks / kaks**	ewks / kawks
three / four	**kolm / neli**	kohlm / NAY-lee
five / six	**viis / kuus**	vees / koos
seven / eight	**seitse / kaheksa**	SAYT-seh / KAW-hehk-sah
nine / ten	**üheksa / kümme**	EW-hehk-sah / KEW-meh
hundred	**sada**	SAW-daw
thousand	**tuhat**	TOO-hawt
How much?	**Kui palju?**	quee PAWL-yoo
local currency: (Estonian) crown	**(Eesti) krooni**	(EH-stee) KROO-nee
Where is...?	**Kus asub...?**	koos ah-SOOB
..the toilet	**...tualett**	TOO-ah-leht
men	**mees**	mehs
women	**naine**	NĪ-neh
water / coffee	**vesi / kohvi**	VAY-see / KOHKH-vee
beer / wine	**õlu / vein**	OH-loo / vayn
Cheers!	**Terviseks!**	TEHR-vee-sehks
The bill, please.	**Arve, palun.**	AHR-veh PAH-luhn

APPENDIX

Finnish Survival Phrases

In Finnish, the emphasis always goes on the first syllable. Double vowels (e.g., *ää* or *ii*) sound similar to single vowels, but are held a bit longer. The letter *y* sounds like the German *ü* (purse your lips and say "oo"). In the phonetics, Ī / ī sounds like the long i in "light."

Good morning. (*formal*)	**Hyvää huomenta.**	HEW-vaah HWOH-mehn-tah
Good day. (*formal*)	**Hyvää päivää.**	HEW-vaah PĪ-vaah
Good evening. (*formal*)	**Hyvää iltaa.**	HEW-vaah EEL-taah
Hi. / Bye. (*informal*)	**Hei. / Hei, hei.**	hey / hey hey
Do you speak English?	**Puhutko englantia?**	POO-hoot-koh EN-glahn-tee-yah
Yes. / No.	**Kyllä. / Ei.**	KEWL-lah / ay
Please.	**Ole hyvä.**	OH-leh HEW-vah
Thank you (very much).	**Kiitos (paljon).**	KEE-tohs (PAHL-yohn)
You're welcome.	**Kiitos.** *Or:* **Ei kestä.**	KEE-tohs / ay KEHS-tah
Can I help you?	**Voinko auttaa?**	VOIN-koh OWT-taah
Excuse me.	**Anteeksi.**	AHN-teek-see
(Very) good.	**(Oikein) hyvä.**	(OY-kayn) HEW-vah
Goodbye.	**Näkemiin.**	NAH-keh-meen
one / two	**yksi / kaksi**	EWK-see / KAHK-see
three / four	**kolme / neljä**	KOHL-meh / NEHL-yah
five / six	**viisi / kuusi**	VEE-see / KOO-see
seven / eight	**seitsemän / kahdeksan**	SAYT-seh-mahn / KAH-dehk-sahn
nine / ten	**yhdeksän / kymmenen**	EW-dehk-sahn / KEWM-meh-nehn
hundred	**sata**	SAH-tah
thousand	**tuhat**	TOO-haht
How much?	**Paljonko?**	PAHL-yohn-koh
local currency: euro	**euro**	AY-oo-roh
Where is...?	**Missä on...?**	MEE-sah ohn
..the toilet	**..WC**	VAY-say
men	**miehet**	MEE-ay-heht
women	**naiset**	NĪ-seht
water / coffee	**vesi / kahvi**	VEH-see / KAHKH-vee
beer / wine	**olut / viini**	OH-luht / VEE-nee
Cheers!	**Kippis!**	KIHP-pihs
The bill, please.	**Saisinko laskun, kiitos.**	SĪ-seen-koh LAHS-kuhn KEE-tohs

APPENDIX

Swedish Survival Phrases

Swedish pronunciation (especially the vowel sounds) can be tricky for Americans to say, and there's quite a bit of variation across the country; listen closely to locals and imitate, or ask for help. The most difficult Swedish sound is *sj,* which sounds roughly like a guttural "*h*w" (made in your throat); however, like many sounds, this is pronounced differently in various regions—for example, Stockholmers might say it more like "shw."

Hello. (formal)	**Goddag!**	goh-DAH
Hi. / Bye. (informal)	**Hej. / Hej då.**	hey / hey doh
Do you speak English?	**Talar du engelska?**	TAH-lahr doo ENG-ehl-skah
Yes. / No.	**Ja. / Nej.**	yaw / nay
Please.	**Snälla. / Tack.***	SNEHL-lah / tack
Thank you (very much).	**Tack (så mycket).**	tack (soh MEE-keh)
You're welcome.	**Ingen orsak.**	EENG-ehn OOR-sahk
Can I help you?	**Kan jag hjälpa dig?**	kahn yaw JEHL-pah day
Excuse me.	**Ursäkta.**	OOR-sehk-tah
(Very) good.	**(Mycket) bra.**	(MEE-keh) brah
Goodbye. (formal)	**Adjö.**	ah-YEW
one / two	**en / två**	ehn / tvoh
three / four	**tre / fyra**	treh / FEE-rah
five / six	**fem / sex**	fehm / sehks
seven / eight	**sju / åtta**	*h*woo / OH-tah
nine / ten	**nio / tio**	NEE-oh / TEE-oh
hundred	**hundra**	HOON-drah
thousand	**tusen**	TEW-sehn
How much?	**Hur mycket?**	hewr MEE-keh
local currency: (Swedish) kronor	**(Svenske) kronor**	(svehn-SKEH) KROH-nor
Where is...?	**Var finns...?**	vahr feens
..the toilet	**...toaletten**	toh-ah-LEH-tehn
men	**man**	mahn
women	**kvinna**	KVEE-nah
water / coffee	**vatten / kaffe**	VAH-tehn / KAH-feh
beer / wine	**öl / vin**	url / veen
Cheers!	**Skål!**	skohl
The bill, please.	**Kan jag få notan, tack.**	kahn yaw foh NOH-tahn tack

*Swedish has various ways to say "please," depending on the context. The simplest is *snälla,* but Swedes sometimes use the word *tack* (thank you) in the way we use "please."

Norwegian Survival Phrases

Norwegian can be pronounced quite differently from region to region. These phrases and phonetics match the mainstream Oslo dialect, but you'll notice variations. Vowels can be tricky: *å* sounds like "oh," *æ* sounds like a bright "ah" (as in "apple"), and *u* sounds like the German *ü* (purse your lips and say u). Certain vowels at the ends of words (such as *d* and *t*) are sometimes barely pronounced (or not at all). In some dialects, the letters *sk* are pronounced "sh." In the phonetics, Ī / ī sounds like the long i in "light."

Hello. *(formal)*	**God dag.**	goo dahg
Hi. / Bye. *(informal)*	**Hei. / Ha det.**	hī / hah deh
Do you speak English?	**Snakker du engelsk?**	SNAHK-kehr dew ENG-ehlsk
Yes. / No.	**Ja. / Nei.**	yah / nī
Please.	**Vær så snill.**	vayr soh sneel
Thank you (very much).	**(Tusen) takk.**	(TEW-sehn) tahk
You're welcome.	**Vær så god.**	vayr soh goo
Can I help you?	**Kan jeg hjelpe deg?**	kahn yī YEHL-peh dī
Excuse me.	**Unnskyld.**	EWN-shuld
(Very) good.	**(Veldig) fint.**	(VEHL-dee) feent
Goodbye.	**Farvel.**	fahr-VEHL
one / two	**en / to**	ayn / toh
three / four	**tre / fire**	treh / FEE-reh
five / six	**fem / seks**	fehm / sehks
seven / eight	**syv / åtte**	seev / OH-teh
nine / ten	**ni / ti**	nee / tee
hundred	**hundre**	HEWN-dreh
thousand	**tusen**	TEW-sehn
How much?	**Hvor mye?**	voor MEE-yeh
local currency: (Norwegian) crown	**(Norske) kroner**	(NORSH-keh) KROH-nehr
Where is...?	**Hvor er...?**	voor ehr
..the toilet	**...toalettet**	toh-ah-LEH-teh
men	**menn** *Or:* **herrer**	mehn / HEHR-rehr
women	**damer**	DAH-mehr
water / coffee	**vann / kaffe**	vahn / KAH-feh
beer / wine	**øl / vin**	uhl / veen
Cheers!	**Skål!**	skohl
The bill, please.	**Regningen, takk.**	RĪ-ning-ehn tahk

Danish Survival Phrases

The Danes tend to say words quickly and clipped. In fact, many short vowels end in a "glottal stop"—a very brief vocal break immediately following the vowel. While I haven't tried to indicate these in the phonetics, you can listen for them in Denmark...and (try to) imitate. Three unique Danish vowels are *æ* (sounds like the *e* in "egg"), *ø* (sounds like the German *ö*—purse your lips and say "oh"), and *å* (sounds like the *o* in "bowl"). The letter *r* is not rolled—it's pronounced farther back in the throat, almost like a *w*. A *d* at the end of a word sounds almost like our *th*; for example, *mad* (food) sounds like "math." In the phonetics, Ī / ī sounds like the long i sound in "light."

Hello. *(formal)*	**Goddag.**	goh-DAY
Hi. / Bye. *(informal)*	**Hej. / Hej-hej.**	hī / hī-hī
Do you speak English?	**Taler du engelsk?**	TAY-lehr doo ENG-elsk
Yes. / No.	**Ja. / Nej.**	yeah / nī
Please. (May I?)*	**Kan jeg?**	kan yī
Please. (Can you?)*	**Kan du?**	kan doo
Please. (Would you?)*	**Vil du?**	veel doo
Thank you (very much).	**(Tusind) tak.**	(TOO-sin) tack
You're welcome.	**Selv tak.**	sehl tack
Can I help (you)?	**Kan jeg hjælpe (dig)?**	kan yī YEHL-peh (dī)
Excuse me. (to pass)	**Undskyld mig.**	OON-skewl mī
Excuse me. (Can you help me?)	**Kan du hjælpe mig?**	kan doo YEHL-peh mī
(Very) good.	**(Meget) godt.**	(MĪ-ehl) goht
Goodbye.	**Farvel.**	fah-VEHL
one / two	**en / to**	een / toh
three / four	**tre / fire**	tray / feer
five / six	**fem / seks**	fehm / sehks
seven / eight	**syv / otte**	syew / OH-deh
nine / ten	**ni / ti**	nee / tee
hundred	**hundrede**	HOON-reh
thousand	**tusind**	TOO-sin
How much?	**Hvor meget?**	vor MĪ-ehl
local currency: (Danish) crown	**(Danske) kroner**	(DAHN-skeh) KROH-nah
Where is...?	**Hvor er..?**	vor ehr
..the toilet	**..toilettet**	toh-ee-LEH-teht
men	**herrer**	HEHR-ah
women	**damer**	DAY-mah
water / coffee	**vand / kaffe**	vehn / KAH-feh
beer / wine	**øl / vin**	uhl / veen
Cheers!	**Skål!**	skohl
Can I have the bill?	**Kan jeg få regningen?**	kan yī foh RĪ-ning-ehn

*Because Danish has no single word for "please," they approximate that sentiment by asking "May I?", "Can you?", or "Would you?", depending on the context.

INDEX

D

G

H

INDEX

I

J

O

T

U

MAP INDEX

ur trip at

Free information and great gear to

▸ Plan Your Trip

Browse thousands of articles and a wealth of money-saving tips for planning your dream trip. You'll find up-to-date information on Europe's best destinations, packing smart, getting around, finding rooms, staying healthy, avoiding scams and more.

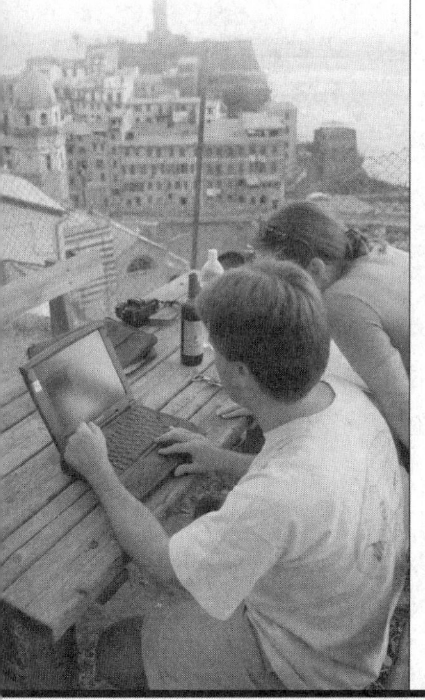

▸ Eurail Passes

Find out, step-by-step, if a rail pass makes sense for your trip—and how to avoid buying more than you need. Get a bunch of free extras!

▸ Graffiti Wall & Travelers' Helpline

Learn, ask, share—our online community of savvy travelers is a great resource for first-time travelers to Europe, as well as seasoned pros.

Rick Steves'
EUROPE
THROUGH THE
BACK DOOR
2010

Rick Steves'
BEST OF
EUROPE
2010

Rick Steves'
ITALY
2010

Rick Steves'
LONDON
2010

Credits

Researchers

To help update this book, Rick relied on...

Cameron Hewitt

Cameron writes and edits guidebooks for Rick Steves, specializing in Eastern Europe. For this book, he spent a week in Sweden sailing the Stockholm Archipelago, hobnobbing with glassblowers, and storming Kalmar Castle. When he's not traveling, Cameron lives in Seattle with his wife Shawna.

Rich Earl

Rich has been interested in Scandinavia since he was a kid listening to his *mormor*'s stories of the old country. When he's not searching for the best *kanelbulle* for his *fika*, he's exploring the rest of Europe, assisting on Rick Steves' tours, or working in the Rail and Consulting departments at Europe Through the Back Door.

Contributor

Gene Openshaw

Gene is the co-author of seven Rick Steves books. For this book, he wrote material on Europe's art, history, and contemporary culture. When not traveling, Gene enjoys composing music, recovering from his 1973 trip to Europe with Rick, and living everyday life with his daughter.

Acknowledgments

Thanks to Thor, Hanne, Geir, Hege, and Kari-Anne, our Norwegian family. Special thanks to Jane Klausen for her expertise in all things Danish. Thanks to these translators for their help with the survival phrases: Marita Bergman, Unni-Marie Kvikne, Mati Rummessen, and Christina Snellman. And in loving memory of Berit Kristiansen, whose house was my house for 20 years of Norwegian travel.

Images

Location	Photographer
Front color matter: Copenhagen-Nyhavn	Rick Steves
Introduction: Archipelago	Cameron Hewitt
Scandinavia: Viking Ships	David C. Hoerlein
Denmark: Copenhagen's Højbro Plads	Rick Steves
Copenhagen: Nyhavn	Cameron Hewitt
Near Copenhagen: Frederiksborg Castle	David C. Hoerlein
Central Denmark: Ærøskøbing	Rick Steves
Jutland: Den Gamle By	Rick Steves
Norway: Sognefjord	Rick Steves
Oslo: Vigeland Sculpture Garden	Rick Steves
Norway in a Nutshell: Aurlandsfjord	Cameron Hewitt
More on the Sognefjord: Balestrand	Cameron Hewitt
Gudbrandsdal Valley and Jotunheimen Mountains: Maihaugen Open-Air Folk Museum	Rick Steves
Bergen: Bryggen	Cameron Hewitt
South Norway: South Norway Port Town	Rick Steves
Sweden: Archipelago	Rick Steves
Stockholm: Drottningholm Palace	Rick Steves
Archipelago: Vaxholm	Cameron Hewitt
Southeast Sweden: Kalmar Castle	Rick Steves
Finland: Helsinki's Lutheran Cathedral	Cameron Hewitt
Helsinki: Helsinki Harbor	Cameron Hewitt
Estonia: Tallinn	Cameron Hewitt
Tallinn: Old Town Square	Cameron Hewitt

Rick Steves' Guidebook Series

Country Guides

Rick Steves' Best of Europe
Rick Steves' Croatia & Slovenia
Rick Steves' Eastern Europe
Rick Steves' England
Rick Steves' France
Rick Steves' Germany
Rick Steves' Great Britain
Rick Steves' Ireland
Rick Steves' Italy
Rick Steves' Portugal
Rick Steves' Scandinavia
Rick Steves' Spain
Rick Steves' Switzerland

City and Regional Guides

Rick Steves' Amsterdam, Bruges & Brussels
Rick Steves' Athens & the Peloponnese
Rick Steves' Budapest
Rick Steves' Florence & Tuscany
Rick Steves' Istanbul
Rick Steves' London
Rick Steves' Paris
Rick Steves' Prague & the Czech Republic
Rick Steves' Provence & the French Riviera
Rick Steves' Rome
Rick Steves' Venice
Rick Steves' Vienna, Salzburg & Tirol

Rick Steves' Phrase Books

French
French/Italian/German
German
Italian
Portuguese
Spanish

Other Books

Rick Steves' Europe 101: History and Art for the Traveler
Rick Steves' Europe Through the Back Door
Rick Steves' European Christmas
Rick Steves' Postcards from Europe
Rick Steves' Travel as a Political Act

Avalon Travel
a member of the Perseus Books Group
1700 Fourth Street
Berkeley, CA 94710

Printed in the USA by Worzalla. First printing January 2010.

ISBN 978-1-59880-123-1
ISSN 1084-7206

For the latest on Rick's lectures, guidebooks, tours, public radio show, and public television series, contact Europe Through the Back Door, Box 2009, Edmonds, WA 98020, 425/771-8303, fax 425/771-0833, www.ricksteves.com, rick@ricksteves.com.

Europe Through the Back Door Reviewers: Risa Laib, Cameron Hewitt, Jennifer Madison Davis, Gretchen Strauch, Sarah McCormic
ETBD Editors: Tom Griffin, Cathy Lu, Cathy McDonald
Research Assistance: Cameron Hewitt, Richard Earl
Avalon Travel Senior Editor and Series Manager: Madhu Prasher
Avalon Travel Project Editor: Kelly Lydick
Copy Editor: Judith Brown
Proofreader: Jamie Andrade
Indexer: Stephen Callahan
Production & Typesetting: McGuire Barber Design
Cover Design: Kimberly Glyder Design
Graphic Content Director: Laura VanDeventer
Maps and Graphics: David C. Hoerlein, Laura VanDeventer, Lauren Mills, Mike Morgenfeld, Chris Markiewicz, Brice Ticen, Lohnes & Wright, Albert Angulo, Kat Bennett, Hank Evans
Photography: Cameron Hewitt, Sonja Groset, Rick Steves, Ian Watson, David C. Hoerlein
Front Matter Color Photos: p. i, Copenhagen, Denmark, © Rick Steves
Cover Photo: Solvorn, Lustrafjord, Norway © Cameron Hewitt